COMPARATIVE POLITICS
Cabinets and Coalition Bargaining

COMPARATIVE POLITICS

Comparative Politics is a series for students, teachers, and researchers of political science that deals with contemporary government and politics. Global in scope, books in the series are characterised by a stress on comparative analysis and strong methodological rigour. The series is published in association with the European Consortium for Political Research. For more information visit www.essex.ac.uk/ecpr

The Comparative Politics series is edited by Professor David M. Farrell, School of Politics and International Relations, University College Dublin, Kenneth Carty, Professor of Political Science, University of British Columbia, and Professor Dirk Berg-Schlosser, Institute of Political Science, Philipps University, Marburg.

OTHER TITLES IN THIS SERIES

Linking Citizens and Parties
How Electoral Systems Matter for Political Representation

Intergovernmental Cooperation
Rational Choices in Federal System and Beyond
Nicole Bolleyer

The Dynamics of Two-Party Politics
Party Structures and the Management of Competition
Alan Ware

Cabinets and Coalition Bargaining
The Democratic Life Cycle in Western Europe
Edited by Kaare Strøm, Wolfgang C. Müller, and Torbjörn Bergman

Redistricting in Comparative Perspective
Edited by Lisa Handley and Bernard Grofman

Democratic Representation in Europe
Diversity, Change, and Convergence
Edited by Maurizio Cotta and Heinrich Best

Citizens, Democracy, and Markets Around the Pacific Rim
Congruence Theory and Political Culture
Russell J. Dalton and Doti Chull Shin

Elections, Parties, Democracy
Michael D. McDonald and Ian Budge

The Performance of Democracies
Edeltrand Roller

The European Voter
Edited by Jacques Thomassen

The Presidentialization of Politics
Edited by Thomas Paguntke and Paul Webb

Losers' Consent
*Christopher J. Anderson, André Blais, Shaun Bowler,
Todd Donovan, and Ola Listhaug*

Democratic Challenges, Democratic Choices
Russell J. Dalton

Party Politics in New Democracies
Edited by Paul Webb and Stephen White

Cabinets and Coalition Bargaining: The Democratic Life Cycle in Western Europe

Edited by
KAARE STRØM
WOLFGANG C. MÜLLER
and
TORBJÖRN BERGMAN

UNIVERSITY PRESS

OXFORD
UNIVERSITY PRESS

Great Clarendon Street, Oxford ox2 6DP

Oxford University Press is a department of the University of Oxford.
It furthers the University's objective of excellence in research, scholarship,
and education by publishing worldwide in

Oxford New York

Auckland Cape Town Dar es Salaam Hong Kong Karachi
Kuala Lumpur Madrid Melbourne Mexico City Nairobi
New Delhi Shanghai Taipei Toronto

With offices in

Argentina Austria Brazil Chile Czech Republic France Greece
Guatemala Hungary Italy Japan Poland Portugal Singapore
South Korea Switzerland Thailand Turkey Ukraine Vietnam

Oxford is a registered trade mark of Oxford University Press
in the UK and in certain other countries

Published in the United States
by Oxford University Press Inc., New York

© The several contributors 2008

The moral rights of the authors have been asserted
Database right Oxford University Press (maker)

First published 2008
First published in paperback 2010

All rights reserved. No part of this publication may be reproduced,
stored in a retrieval system, or transmitted, in any form or by any means,
without the prior permission in writing of Oxford University Press,
or as expressly permitted by law, or under terms agreed with the appropriate
reprographics rights organization. Enquiries concerning reproduction
outside the scope of the above should be sent to the Rights Department,
Oxford University Press, at the address above

You must not circulate this book in any other binding or cover
and you must impose the same condition on any acquirer

British Library Cataloguing in Publication Data
Data available

Library of Congress Cataloging in Publication Data

Cabinets and coalition bargaining : the democratic life cycle in Western Europe / edited by Kaare
Strøm, Wolfgang C. Müller and Torbjörn Bergman.
p. cm.
ISBN 978–0–19–829786–4 (acid-free paper) 1. Coalition governments—Europe, Western.
2. Europe, Western—Politics and government—20th century. I. Strøm, Kaare.
II. Müller, Wolfgang C., 1957– III. Bergman, Torbjörn.
JN94.A58C33 2008
324.094—dc22 2008009779

Typeset by SPI Publisher Services, Pondicherry, India
Printed in Great Britain
on acid-free paper by
MPG Books Group, Bodmin and King's Lynn

ISBN 978–0–19–829786–4 (Hbk.)
ISBN 978–0–19–958749–0 (Pbk.)

1 3 5 7 9 10 8 6 4 2

This volume is dedicated to the memory of Henry Valen.

Preface to the Paperback Edition

This paperback edition contains a small number of corrections in the text.

Those interested in obtaining the data for this book in electronic form should visit the *The Comparative Parliamentary Democracy Data Archive* project homepage (http://www.erdda.se).

Once again we are grateful for the enduring support and swift assistance of Oxford University Press.

April 2010
Kaare Strøm – Wolfgang C. Müller – Torbjörn Bergman
San Diego – Vienna – Stockholm

Preface and Acknowledgements

This volume completes our three-volume journey into parliamentary democracy in Western Europe. The first of these volumes, *Coalition Governments in Western Europe* (Müller and Strøm 2000, 2003), provides configurative accounts of the workings of government in thirteen European countries that all share some experience with coalition governance. The second volume, *Delegation and Accountability in Parliamentary Democracies* (Strøm, Müller, and Bergman 2003), analyses the political institutions of seventeen Western European democracies and examines their capacities to confront democratic delegation problems. In this volume, we subject the 'life cycle' of policy-making in Western European parliamentary democracies to a dynamic and cross-sectional comparative analysis. And the research we present builds on both the data and the analytical frameworks of both previous volumes.

The main sponsor of this multi-volume research effort has been the Bank of Sweden Tercentenary Foundation. The Foundation's grant to Torbjörn Bergman and the project on 'Constitutional Change and Parliamentary Democracy' (Project No. 1996-0801) enabled us to launch the whole endeavour in the first place. Over the years, the Austrian Ministry of Science, the Political Academy (Vienna), the European Consortium for Political Research, the University of Siena, the University of Kent at Canterbury, the Center for Advanced Study in the Behavioral Sciences (CASBS) at Stanford University, the University of Barcelona, and the Austrian Schumpeter Society have provided opportunities for the contributors to meet. We thank all of these institutions for giving us these valuable opportunities to pursue our joint research.

A number of individuals and institutions deserve special thanks for facilitating our research. The individuals include Maurizio Cotta, Günther Burkert Dottolo, Luca Verzichelli, Thomas Saalfeld, and Dieter Stiefel. The Center of German and European Studies at the University of California has supported the project by providing several research assistantship grants, as have the Center for the Study of Democracy at the University of California, Irvine, and the Mannheim Centre for European Social Research (MZES). We also thank the Rockefeller Foundation, which gave us the opportunity to work together intensively on the second and third books in this series at its charming and peaceful Villa Serbelloni in Bellagio.

Friends and colleagues have been tremendously helpful. In particular, the present volume would not have been possible without the painstaking work of the country experts who collected the data for the first two volumes. These data constitute the bulk of the evidence on which the present volume builds. In addition to most authors in this volume, these country specialists include Octavio

Amorim Neto, Maurizio Cotta, Carlos Flores Juberías, Indridi H. Indridason, Svanur Kristjánsson, José M. Magone, Jaakko Nousiainen, Tapio Raunio, Josep M. Reniu, Jean-Louis Thiébault, Georgios Trantas, Matti Wiberg, and Paraskevi Zagoriti.

We also gratefully acknowledge the constructive suggestions of numerous colleagues who have commented on earlier drafts of the book chapters. These include Franz Fallend, Marcelo Jenny, Dennis C. Mueller, Kenneth A. Shepsle, and Georg Vanberg. James N. Druckman deserves special thanks for reading an early draft of the manuscript in its entirety and giving us a comprehensive set of detailed and highly constructive suggestions. We hope he will agree that his suggestions have dramatically improved the manuscript, and we are endlessly grateful.

Our thanks also to Judith Bara, who initially oriented us in the comparative manifesto data. Madeleine O. Hosli helped us become familiar with the analysis of bargaining power indexes. We thank Magnus Blomgren and Ivy Orr Hamerly for excellent research assistance. And beyond their own contributions to this volume, Scott Kastner and Benjamin Nyblade have given us hugely valuable assistance on many of the data analysis tasks. We thank Emily Matthews for indexing and poof reading. We would also like to express our appreciation to Dominic Byatt and his associates at, Oxford University Press, for their enthusiasm for our project and for their patience, support, and expert execution of our volume. Last but not least, we are greatly and humbly indebted to our respective families and friends for their support and forbearance.

We have prepared an electronic file of the data on which this and the previous two volumes are based. Those interested in obtaining the data in electronic form should visit the 'Constitutional Change & Parliamentary Democracies' project homepage (http://www.pol.umu.se/ccpd/).

We dedicate this volume to Henry Valen, mentor, friend, and collaborator, who passed away in January 2007, before this volume could be completed. We greatly miss his wisdom, his dedication, and his irrepressible spirit.

Kaare Strøm
Wolfgang C. Müller
Torbjörn Bergman

Spring 2008

Contents

List of Figures	xi
List of Tables	xii
List of Contributors	xv

1. Coalition Theory and Cabinet Governance: An Introduction 1
   Wolfgang C. Müller, Torbjörn Bergman, and Kaare Strøm

2. Bargaining, Transaction Costs, and Coalition Governance 51
   Arthur Lupia and Kaare Strøm

3. The Empirical Study of Cabinet Governance 85
   Torbjörn Bergman, Elisabeth R. Gerber, Scott Kastner, and Benjamin Nyblade

4. Uncertainty and Complexity in Cabinet Formation 123
   Lieven De Winter and Patrick Dumont

5. Coalition Agreements and Cabinet Governance 159
   Wolfgang C. Müller and Kaare Strøm

6. Government Formation and Cabinet Type 201
   Paul Mitchell and Benjamin Nyblade

7. Portfolio Allocation 237
   Luca Verzichelli

8. Conflict Management in Coalition Government 269
   Rudy B. Andeweg and Arco Timmermans

9. Cabinet Termination 301
   Erik Damgaard

10. Institutions, Chance, and Choices: The Dynamics of Cabinet Survival 327
    Thomas Saalfeld

11. Coalition Membership and Electoral Performance 369
    Hanne Marthe Narud and Henry Valen

12. Conclusion: Cabinet Governance in Parliamentary Democracies 403
    *Kaare Strøm, Torbjörn Bergman, Wolfgang C. Müller,
    and Benjamin Nyblade*

Index 431

List of Figures

1.1. The coalition life cycle	10
1.2. Approaches in empirical coalition research, with examples	34
4.1. Conditions of transition and government formation	127
4.2. Prior cabinet termination and government formation (minority situations only)	132
6.1. Cabinet type by decade	208
7.1. Disproportionality index of portfolio allocation by country	245
10.1. Competing risks of discretionary cabinet terminations: early election hazards, replacement hazards, and pooled hazards	338
11.1. Cabinet electoral performance	380
11.2. Electoral performance by economic conditions	383

List of Tables

1.1. Cabinets in Western Europe, 1945–99	8
3.1. Variations in country samples in cross-national coalition studies	89
3.2. Dependent variables used in statistical analyses in this volume	93
4.1. Number of inconclusive bargaining rounds in cabinet formation	129
4.2. Cabinet formation duration	130
4.3. Inconclusive bargaining rounds and cabinet formation duration by country	130
4.4. Inconclusive bargaining rounds and cabinet formation duration by decade	131
4.5. Logistic regressions on occurrence of inconclusive bargaining rounds (minority situations only)	146
4.6. Cox proportional hazards models of cabinet formation duration (minority situations only)	149
5.1. Coalition agreements	171
5.2. The use of written coalition agreements by decade	172
5.3. Size and contents of coalition agreements by country	173
5.4. Policy programmes by country	176
5.5. Coalition discipline in legislation by country	178
5.6. Coalition discipline in other parliamentary behaviour by country	178
5.7. Coalition discipline by decade	179
5.8. Coalition discipline in legislation by regime type	179
5.9. Ex ante and ex post governance mechanisms by country	184
5.10. Ex ante and ex post mechanisms by decade	184
5.11. Logistic regressions on the existence of written coalition agreements	188
6.1. Coalition governments in Western Europe by country	206
6.2. Government type in Western Europe by country	207
6.3. Cabinet characteristics by country	210
6.4. Logistic regressions on coalition formation in minority situations	223
6.5. Multinomial logistic regressions of government type	225
7.1. Disproportionality index of portfolio allocation by country	246

7.2. OLS regressions on unweighted portfolio disproportionality index	248
7.3. Number of ministers and ministries by country	253
7.4. Change in ministers and ministry by country	254
7.5. Cross-tabulation: change in no. of parties and no. of ministers	255
7.6. OLS regressions on the number of cabinet ministers	256
7.7. 'Watchdog' junior ministers by country (coalition cabinets only)	261
7.8. Logistic regressions on watchdog junior ministers	262
8.1a. Most commonly used arenas for cabinet conflict management by country	274
8.1b. Cabinet conflict management arenas used for most serious conflicts by country	274
8.2. Conflict management arenas	278
8.3. Logistic regressions on most common conflict management arena being mixed or external (not internal)	282
8.4. Logistic regressions on arena used for the most serious conflicts being mixed or external (not internal)	284
8.5. Cabinet conflict management arenas by written coalition agreements	286
8.6. Institutionalization of arenas for cabinet conflict management	287
8.7. Arenas for cabinet conflict management across time	288
9.1. Types of termination by country	306
9.2. Types of termination by cabinet type	308
9.3. Types of termination by decade	310
9.4. Cabinet composition and predecessors by country	311
9.5. Cabinet composition and predecessors by decade	312
9.6. Multinomial logistic regressions of government termination type	317
10.1. Median cabinet duration by country	328
10.2. Median relative cabinet duration by country	331
10.3. Median cabinet duration by cabinet type	332
10.4. Cox proportional hazards models: competing risks analysis of durability	340
11.1. Electoral performance of cabinets by country	379
11.2. Electoral performance of cabinets by decade	380
11.3. Average vote change by incumbent parties and cabinets	381
11.4. Electoral performance by cabinet type	382

11.5. OLS regressions on cabinet electoral performance (government ideology and economic performance)	384
11.6. Vote change by cabinet termination	386
11.7. OLS regressions on cabinet electoral performance	389
11.8. OLS regressions on PM party's electoral performance	392
11.9. OLS regressions on finance minister's party's electoral performance	394
12.1. Core results	407

List of Contributors

Rudy B. Andeweg is professor of political science at the University of Leiden, the Netherlands.

Torbjörn Bergman is professor of political science at Södertörn University, Sweden.

Erik Damgaard is professor emeritus of political science at the University of Aarhus, Denmark.

Lieven De Winter is professor of political science at the Université Catholique de Louvain, Louvain-la-Neuve, Belgium.

Patrick Dumont is researcher at the Université du Luxembourg, Luxembourg.

Elisabeth R. Gerber is professor of political science at the University of Michigan, USA.

Scott Kastner is associate professor of political science at the University of Maryland, USA.

Arthur Lupia is Hal R. Varian collegiate professor of political science at the University of Michigan, USA.

Paul Mitchell is senior lecturer in political science at LSE, Great Britain.

Wolfgang C. Müller is professor of political science at the University of Vienna, Austria.

Hanne Marthe Narud is professor of political science at the University of Oslo, Norway.

Benjamin Nyblade is assistant professor of political science at the University of British Columbia, Vancouver, Canada.

Thomas Saalfeld is professor of political science at the University of Bamberg, Germany.

Kaare Strøm is distinguished university professor of political science at the University of California, San Diego, USA.

Arco Timmermans is research director at the Montesquieu Institute and associate professor of comparative public policy at Leiden University, the Netherlands.

Henry Valen was professor emeritus of political science at the University of Oslo, Norway.

Luca Verzichelli is professor of political science at the University of Siena, Italy.

1

Coalition Theory and Cabinet Governance: An Introduction

Wolfgang C. Müller, Torbjörn Bergman, and Kaare Strøm

INTRODUCTION

'When the idea of democracy is actively adopted by a people', Robert A. Dahl (1989: 84) claims, 'it tends to produce the best feasible political system, or at any rate the best state'. We share this belief. Democracy is indeed the most desirable political regime humankind has ever experienced. It allows citizens more personal freedom than any other type of political system, and only democracies guarantee that citizens live under laws that they have given themselves (Dahl 1998: 61). Yet, even under democracy citizens may not agree with all important political decisions, much less actually make them. Democracies do not obliterate the old distinction between those who govern and those who are governed (Sartori 1987). Like contemporary societies in general, democracies feature many divisions of labour, which also affect the making of political decisions. While citizens vote political decision-makers in and out of office, decision-making itself, with a few exceptions and some cross-national variation, is reserved for the representatives of the people. Hence, modern democracies are predominantly *representative*. This, in turn, means that popular sovereignty is exercised through *delegation* from citizens to individual politicians and collective actors, in particular political parties (Strøm, Müller, and Bergman 2003).

This is so because citizens, as a rule, do not have the requisite time, knowledge, and interest to rule their country in any literal sense. Just as they tend to delegate important tasks in their private lives to specialists (e.g. their medical treatment to physicians and the education of their children to teachers), they delegate the greater part of their public life to politicians.[1] It is politicians who deliberate, make laws, tax, spend, and make other political decisions. And the same politicians select and supervise the bureaucrats who ultimately implement their decisions.

---

[1] Or, to be more precise, such acts of delegation have happened, or are assumed to have taken place, in the past. In practice, most citizens face a set of rules of delegation that was set up without their formal participation.

In democracies, citizens delegate to politicians first and foremost through free and fair elections. If elections are not free and fair, there can be no democracy. In order to be democratic, elections must be held under conditions of political competition (freedom to form and join organizations, freedom of expression, alternative sources of information, freedom of candidacy) and there must be an independent and competent administration, as well as appropriate judicial bodies, to implement the election law (for the 'classic' argument see Dahl 1956: 84, 1971: 3, 1989: 221–2; see Reynolds and Elklit 2005 for a recent application).

Elections in mass democracies, involving millions of voters, give rise to political parties. Parties structure electoral choices by bundling issues and candidates. Without them, elections would hardly be meaningful (Cox 1987; Ware 1987). Voters can make more informed judgements about how politicians will behave once elected if these politicians are associated with a party that has built up a specific policy profile and reputation. Likewise, politicians take advantage of their party's 'brand name' to advertise themselves and solve collective action problems (Aldrich 1995; Müller 2000a).

Yet, democratic elections are only the first step in the delegation process. Under representative democracy, the people rule directly only on election day; otherwise they are ruled by the politicians to whom they have delegated the task of making authoritative decisions (Schumpeter 1942; Schattschneider 1960: ch. VIII; Sartori 1987: 28–31, 86–9). There are, however, many ways in which the citizens can delegate to politicians, and many ways in which politicians can delegate among themselves. We refer to the different configurations of political delegation and accountability structures as *political regimes*. Presidentialism and parliamentarism are the most frequent and important ones (Strøm, Müller, and Bergman 2003).

While America is the stronghold of presidentialism, Western Europe, on which the present volume is focused, is the heartland of parliamentary democracy. Parliamentarism comes in two main versions, majoritarian versus proportional (Lijphart 1995, 1999; Powell 2000). Over the course of the twentieth century, the proportional version of parliamentarism has become the most common form of democratic governance, and nowhere is it more dominant than in Western Europe. Proportional parliamentarism requires frequent and ongoing inter-party coalition bargaining, and it is therefore no surprise that this topic has become a significant concern among students of politics.

This book is a contribution to the study of government coalition bargaining in parliamentary democracies. While of course many of the most interesting features of inter-party coalition bargaining occur only in proportional systems, our study encompasses *all* parliamentary systems of Western Europe (except for a few micro-states). As we shall see, this gives us essential background and benchmarks against which we can understand and assess the proportional systems.

It would be unreasonable to claim that parliamentary coalition bargaining has been understudied. Yet, our contribution in this volume is novel in more ways than one. First and foremost, our book is predicated on the idea that coalition bargaining must be understood dynamically and as part of what we call the life cycle of coalition politics. Instead of analysing the birth, life, and death of political coalitions as separate and mutually independent events, this study has been designed to offer a more dynamic and coherent perspective. Coalition bargaining consists in a cyclical series of events, the sequence of which is sometimes given and sometimes negotiable. These events or phases are interconnected, in the sense that each set of decisions is influenced both by prior events and by the anticipation of future ones.

Second, these events and decisions do not happen only within a self-contained universe of politicians. On the contrary, as our introductory remarks make clear, democratic politicians are no more or less than the representatives of the citizens (or at least the voters), and in a well-functioning democracy, the politicians' anticipation that they will sooner or later be held to account by their masters is the most powerful constraint shaping their decisions.

Finally, since this powerful force of elections future rests on a fickle and often modestly informed citizenry acting in circumstances that cannot be fully predicted, the world of parliamentary elite bargaining is inherently uncertain and precarious. This uncertain world of democracy is beset with two important problems: on the one hand, the problem of getting the representatives of the people to act in the interest of those that they represent, and, on the other hand, the problem of preventing their mutual bargaining from becoming an endless round of cabals and musical chairs, in which no time and energy is left for actual political decisions (a state of affairs that may at least at times be undesirable). In technical terms, coalition politics features agency costs as well as transaction costs. In order to understand and assess different systems of parliamentary (or other) government, we need to pay attention to the ways in which they respond and measure up to these challenges.

Thus, the mutual interdependence of different phases of political life, the constraining effects of democratic elections, and the recognition of an uncertain world in which action is costly are the premises on which our book is based. Although they may sound commonsensical, they are not universally shared, or at least not universally articulated, in the existing literature. Our approach also leads us to ask questions that have not frequently been addressed by students of parliamentary coalition bargaining, for example concerning the bargaining process or the forms and functions of the agreements that coalition parties strike. Finally, our emphasis on the life cycle of coalition politics leads us to consider interconnections between the different phases of coalition bargaining that other scholars have downplayed or overlooked.

We therefore believe that our volume is uniquely capable of addressing deep and important questions about how and how well parliamentary democracies throughout Western Europe allocate power and make policy. It explains the very important experiences that all coalition governments share at the same time that it preserves and highlights the differences between them. Our book thus features a novel theoretical framework as well as an unprecedented data collection.

In the remainder of this chapter, we first introduce the life cycle of coalition politics and then discuss the problems of uncertainty and risk in coalition politics. Then we provide an overview of the coalitions literature, focusing first on competing theoretical explanations and later on different empirical approaches that have evolved from these analytical efforts. Given the wealth of existing research, we concentrate on the broader explanatory categories and leave much of the more specific review to the various substantive chapters that follow. Towards the end of this chapter we turn to what we see as the way forward in coalition studies and define our ambitions for the present study. We conclude by providing a brief overview of the contents of our volume.

PARLIAMENTARY GOVERNMENT AND COALITION POLITICS

Let us begin by describing the basic features of the world of multiparty coalition politics. In ideal-typical terms, presidentialism and parliamentarism can be seen as two different ways to design the democratic delegation from citizens to their political representatives. In a pure presidential system, at least its Madisonian version, the foremost concern is to *minimize the risks* of delegation. The voters select a number of different and competing agents and minimize the power of the strongest of these. Thus, each agent is reined in by a complex web of checks, balances, and accountability mechanisms. In an ideal-typical parliamentary design, on the other hand, the dominant goal is to *maximize the efficiency* of political delegation. The citizens select a single agent and maximize this agent's power. Thus, voters under parliamentarism delegate to a powerful national parliament and the institutional framework is set up to give parliament as much control as possible over the 'downstream' execution and implementation of its decisions. The key feature of this design is the mechanism that makes the chief political executive strictly accountable to the parliamentary majority. Therefore, in operational terms, parliamentary government is a system in which the prime minister and his or her cabinet are accountable to any majority of the members of parliament (in bicameral cases, its lower house) and can be voted out of office by the latter. This confidence relationship can be enforced through an ordinary or constructive vote of no confidence (see Strøm, Müller, and Bergman 2003).

Although historically, parliamentary democracy first evolved in a world of 'first-past-the-post' (FPTP) elections, the regime type does not presuppose any particular electoral system and is in fact compatible with majoritarian (in which representatives are elected by plurality or majority vote and typically in single-member districts) as well as proportional ones (in which deputies get chosen by some proportional representation [PR] formula in multi-member districts).

Under majority parliamentarism, the electoral system typically gives a bonus to the winning party. For this reason, elections often result in manufactured majorities. What was a (sometimes small) plurality in votes becomes a comfortable majority in parliamentary seats (Lijphart 1994; Siaroff 2003). And on relatively rare occasions the electoral system may grant a majority of parliamentary seats to a party that does not even have a plurality of the votes. In majoritarian parliamentarism, save the most exceptional circumstances, the winning party assumes government office and implements its programme (Blais 1991).

At first sight this may look strikingly unfair because a 'winner-take-all' system can leave large parties outside the national policy process. Yet, majoritarian parliamentarism has many virtues: it makes elections decisive, thereby empowering voters; it keeps the political process transparent; it renders the government (meaning here: the executive branch) accountable to the voters; and it produces stable government (Milnor 1969). Fairness, one can argue, is achieved (at least with regard to the main competitors), over time. That is to say, at one time the electoral system benefits the one, the next time the other party.[2] Since in Europe majority parliamentarism is the exception rather than the rule, and since it does not generate the problems and complexities to which this volume is mainly devoted, this form of parliamentarism is represented in the present volume mainly as a benchmark and a reference category.

Thus, the core concern of the present volume is parliamentarism based on PR electoral systems. While these systems frequently allow considerable deviations from perfect proportionality, they rarely manufacture majorities (see, e.g., Taagepera and Shugart 1989; Lijphart 1994). Only on rare occasions, such as in the long-time Social Democratic strongholds of Norway and Sweden, has a single party won a majority of parliamentary seats (and majorities of votes are even rarer). Otherwise, elections in proportional systems result in *minority situations*, in which no single party holds a majority of its own. Leaving aside momentarily the rare non-partisan cabinets (though see below), minority situations lead to more or less permanent and comprehensive inter-party cooperation. In this book we are concerned mostly with the most permanent and institutionalized forms of such inter-party cooperation, namely governments in which different parties commit themselves to serving together in the same cabinet and sharing the portfolios that control of the chief executive body affords them.

---

[2] This effect depends on the opposition's ability to converge and to avoid taking extreme positions. Critics argue that majoritarian parliamentarism has the built-in effect of making a party that has just been removed from office more extreme, as it will be represented primarily by MPs who hold seats that represent the party's core constituency. This may lead to long periods of one-party dominance, as in Britain after Thatcher's victory in 1979 (see Saalfeld 2003). Yet, the electoral incentives for coordination and moderation are powerful, as demonstrated by the ultimate success of the formerly fractious and radicalized British Labour Party.

The literature has defined the terms *government* and *cabinet* variously.[3] Since such definitional choices can clearly affect empirical results (cf. Damgaard 1994), they ought to be made carefully and, most importantly, in accordance with the research question. Studying cabinets 'from cradle to grave', we adopt a definition that we believe is specific enough to capture the most important variation, yet not so restrictive as to be odd or unwieldy. We thus count a new cabinet with each parliamentary election, change of party composition, or change of prime minister. Previous work (Müller and Strøm 2000) distinguishes between *cabinet* and *government*, where the former term is sensitive to the identity of the head of government and the latter not. In the present book our unit of observation is in these terms the cabinet. While our use of this operational definition is strict, we allow ourselves the luxury of using the words 'cabinet' and 'government' interchangeably.[4]

It is useful briefly to explain our terms before we delve more deeply into our subject. As will be explained in Chapter 2, a coalition is a group that includes at least two actors—in our context, at least two political parties. Note that in a broad sense, as noted in Chapter 2, a single party is in itself a coalition of individuals, groups, or organizational subunits. But while it is in many contexts reasonable to think of parties as coalitions, and while the behaviour of single-party governments can in many ways be understood within the same framework as that of multiparty ones, we shall nevertheless throughout this study make a clear conceptual distinction between, on the one hand, cabinets consisting of a single party and, on the other, those that include two or more political parties.

Thus, for our purposes, a coalition is made up out of at least two political parties, and a *government coalition* refers to the sharing of executive office by different political parties. More precisely, a coalition party is a party that has at least one designated representative that enjoys voting rights in the country's top executive policymaking body (which we generically refer to as the cabinet). We do not in this context count as a coalition the cooperation of several parties in the electoral arena, or agreements by members of several parties to vote together on specific parliamentary bills.[5] This volume is devoted to the study of *government (or cabinet) coalitions*, and shorthand references to 'coalitions' should always be interpreted accordingly.

---

[3] Thus for Dodd (1976) a government is defined exclusively by its party composition. In contrast, Mershon (2002: 201) defines a new government with each change of party composition, parliamentary election, change of prime minister, or accepted cabinet resignation. In his study of minority cabinets, Strøm (1990a) includes changes between majority and minority status that result from by-elections.

[4] As Sartori (1984) notes, using more than one term for the same concept is a waste. Yet, it is also a luxury, i.e., something that is not really needed but yet beneficial.

[5] Parliamentary voting coalitions may take the form of ad hoc voting alliances or more permanent support arrangements (cf. Bogdanor 1983a: 3–10; Strøm 1990a: ch. 4). However interesting permanent support arrangements and ad hoc voting coalitions may be (see, e.g., Sjölin 1993; Bale and Bergman 2006), they are not our concern in this volume.

Coalition governments can be distinguished from *single-party*, as well as from *non-partisan, cabinets*. In single-party cabinets one party holds all cabinet seats. In non-partisan cabinets no party has any recognized representation in the cabinet (even though some of the cabinet ministers may happen to be party members). While single-party cabinets make up a substantial share of post-war cabinets in Western Europe, non-partisan cabinets are exceptional with respect to incidence, duration, and relevance. We want in this volume to account for all types of cabinets that have serious policymaking ambitions, which excludes only non-partisan, caretaker cabinets. In contemporary Western European parliamentary democracies, the latter are quite rare and tend to occur in exceptional circumstances. We thus exclude them from most of our analysis.

Either of the two types of partisan cabinets—single-party and coalition—can be of majority or minority status. A *majority cabinet* includes political parties jointly holding a majority of seats (a minimum of 50% + one seat) in the chamber of parliament to which the cabinet is accountable. A *minority cabinet* includes parties that jointly hold no more than 50 per cent of the parliamentary seats. Where parliament is bicameral, the relevant chamber is normally the lower house (such as the House of Commons in Britain).[6]

In Western Europe, coalition cabinets are the most frequent form of government.[7] With the exceptions of the United Kingdom and Spain, all Western European countries have experienced post-war coalition governments. In most cases, this type of government has been in office for the great majority of the time that our study covers. The PR systems that have a substantial record of single-party governments often have experienced minority cabinets. Earlier studies have demonstrated that roughly a third of the post-war cabinets have fallen into this category (Strøm 1990a; Müller and Strøm 2000: 561). Minority cabinets need to build parliamentary coalitions, either in the form of permanent and comprehensive support arrangements (and hence 'disguised' government coalitions), long-term agreements in specific policy areas, or ad hoc coalitions on particular bills.

Table 1.1 provides an overview of the cabinets included in the present volume. Our data contains all cabinets in Western Europe formed between the end of the Second World War hostilities in Europe and 1 January 2000. If the current regime is of more recent origin (such as the French Fifth Republic), our sample includes all cabinets since that change of regime. The total number of cabinets in our sample is 424. As can be seen from Table 1.1, there is considerable cross-national

---

[6] In the cases of Italy, Sweden (through 1970), and Belgium (through 1995) we base our classification on the distribution of seats in the House (Italy, Belgium) or Lower Chamber (Sweden) and leave aside the Senate or Upper Chamber (Sweden), despite the fact that the cabinet is or was formally accountable to both chambers.

[7] Both government and parliamentary coalitions resemble divided government in presidential systems. Hence, more general lessons, far beyond the thematic and geographical scope of the present volume, may be drawn from the European experience with coalition governments. Yet, as Elgie (2001) reminds us, such generalizations should be approached with caution.

TABLE 1.1. *Cabinets in Western Europe, 1945–99*

Country[a]	Total	Majority cabinets		Minority cabinets		Non-partisan and other cabinets[b]
		Single-party	Coalition	Single-party	Coalition	
Austria	22	4	16	1	0	1
Belgium	33	3	26	2	2	0
Denmark	31	0	4	14	13	0
Finland	44	0	27	4	6	7
France	23	1	15	5	2	0
Germany	26	1	22	3	0	0
Greece	11	7	2	1	0	1
Iceland	26	0	21	4	1	0
Ireland	22	6	5	6	5	0
Italy	51	0	25	14	9	3
Luxembourg	16	0	16	0	0	0
The Netherlands	23	0	19	0	3	1
Norway	26	6	3	12	5	0
Portugal	14	2	6	3	0	3
Spain	10	2	0	6	0	2
Sweden	26	2	5	17	2	0
United Kingdom	20	19	0	1	0	0
Total	424	53	212	93	48	18

[a] The table includes all cabinets that conventionally are counted as the 'Post–Second World War' and democratic (thus the pre-democratic cabinets of Greece, Portugal, and Spain are excluded and one Irish cabinet dates from 1944), based on the status of cabinet at the time of formation. Countries that have experienced regime change are included only with the cabinets of the most recent regime (thus the Fourth French Republic and Greece before the military dictatorships are excluded).

[b] Other cabinets include cabinets where parliamentary support for government is unclear for other reasons, making it impossible to classify into our other categories. This includes cabinets formed prior to parliamentary elections occurring in the immediate aftermath of the Second World War and other transitional governments.

variation in the number of cabinets. While Luxembourg has been a place of cabinet stability (with only 16 cabinets since the Second World War), Finland has had more than twice as many, whereas Italy stands out with no fewer than 51 cabinets. Table 1.1 also shows that while there have been very few non-partisan cabinets, minority cabinets make up 141 cases (33%). Yet, 265 cabinets (63%) have had majority status. Finally, our 146 single-party cabinets are clearly outnumbered by the 260 coalitions. Hence, coalition cabinets are the predominant government type in post-war Western Europe. (Chapter 6 will provide more detail on cabinet membership.)

THE LIFE CYCLE OF COALITION POLITICS

Government coalitions have received a fair amount of attention from political scientists. Indeed, the coalition literature, with the first theoretical contributions published in the 1950s and 1960s and the first cross-national empirical studies in the 1970s, has become something of a self-contained field of study. Researchers have concentrated on a few topics. For obvious reasons, coalition membership was the first topic to be studied, and this question has continued to attract much attention. Over time, considerable scrutiny has also been given to the process of coalition formation and its effects on who gets in. Since the 1970s, we have had another sizeable literature dealing with the duration of coalitions once they have formed. In other words, the birth and death of coalitions have received the most attention. Coalition researchers have rarely (though increasingly) focused on what occurs between the beginning and the end of coalitions, on what we may call coalition governance.

In this volume we argue that these phases—formation, governance, and termination—are interconnected in a life cycle of coalition politics. What completes this cycle, and brings democracy back into parliamentary democracy, is elections. It is through elections that political parties receive their endowment of parliamentary seats and hence their bargaining power. And save for the occasional referendum, elections are in a representative democracy the only stage of the political process that directly involves the citizens. While history provides an enormous number of government alliances of various sorts, all of which have gone through the stages of formation, governance, and termination, the coalition politics of parliamentary democracies, as understood in this volume, is uniquely bound up with democratic elections. Nonetheless, or precisely for that reason, the electoral connection is probably the aspect of coalition politics that scholars have most seriously neglected.

We can thus distinguish four phases or stages of coalition politics: government formation, governance, government termination, and parliamentary elections. Figure 1.1 contains one conceptualization of this coalition life cycle. It is organized clockwise, beginning with the lower layer box at the top and ending with the top layer box at the same place. While most of these phases have a relatively precise meaning, governance has in recent years become a trendy catch-all term. In our context, it denotes both the practice of governing and the stage in the life cycle of governments that is devoted to policy execution and implementation. Stages such as these, of course, are not an exclusive property of coalitions. Rather, the life of any government can be described under these headings. Yet, each stage is more complex under government coalitions than under single-party majority government. What may look trivial under the latter merits close attention under the former.

The central argument of this book is that all these phases of coalition politics are interrelated. By convention, in this chapter we begin our discussion with government formation. Yet, government formation occurs against the backdrop of an election (often recently conducted) that has endowed political parties with different shares of parliamentary seats that, in turn, help determine their respective bargaining power. But it is not only past elections that impact on government

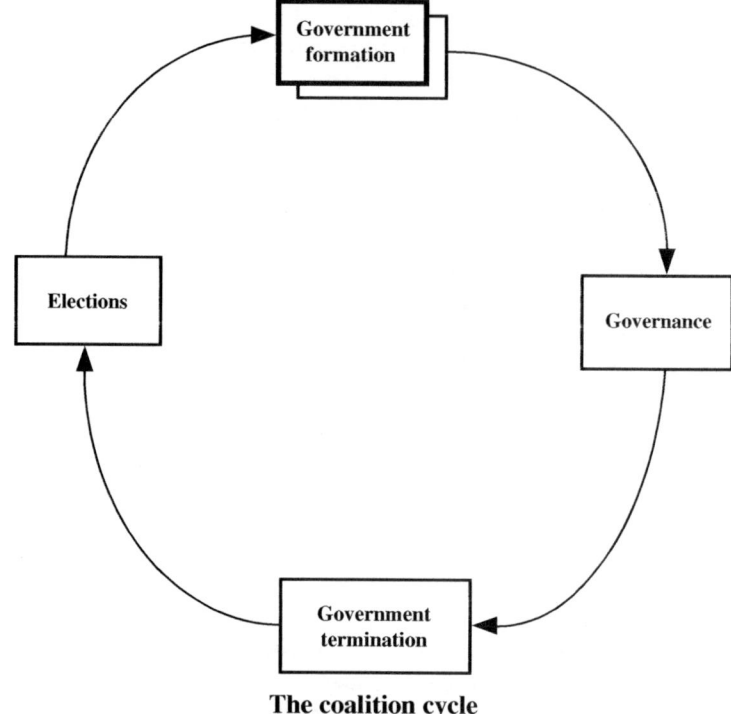

FIGURE 1.1. The coalition life cycle

formation. Government formation also takes place in the shadow of future elections, particularly the next one to come. Thus, political actors also try to anticipate and influence what will happen from the time they form their government until the time of the next election. Much of this cannot be influenced, to any meaningful degree, by these actors themselves. Acts of international terrorism (such as September 11, 2001), world economic developments, or the sudden death of domestic political leaders (who may be important allies or competitors) fall in the category of events that are largely outside the influence of party leaders engaged in coalition bargaining.

Facing the possibility that such unpredictable and fateful events may occur, coalition actors must think carefully about those parts of the agenda that they can, at least in principle, influence. Hence, before coalitions are formed the prospective participants try to anticipate what it will mean to *govern together*. Will a 'natural' alignment of preferences ease government decision-making, or will preference divergence make each cabinet decision difficult and traumatic? When after the Second World War the leaders of the Austrian People's Party and the Social

Democrats, who had quite recently fought each other in a civil war, agreed to form a 'grand coalition' government, they were aware that they had severely conflicting opinions on most of the issues that would appear on the government agenda. This, in turn, made governing together a demanding task. In contrast, when the German Christian Democrats and the Free Democrats (the CDU/CSU and FDP) joined forces to form successive cabinets in the 1980s and 1990s they knew that their disagreements were largely matters of degree and that governing together would be easier than with any other potential partner.

While it is hard to imagine a politician who, when bargaining over government formation, does not think ahead at least a few weeks, more far-sighted actors try to think ahead several years and anticipate the elections that inevitably will come at the end of the parliamentary term. One of their main concerns is to enhance their party's electoral prospects and to avoid decisions that will have adverse electoral implications. To be sure, electoral expectations can be modified through the process of governance. Even if a cabinet is not popular at the time of its formation it may eventually do well in elections if it can govern competently and pursue virtuous (or at least popular) policies. Take the Norwegian Labour government that assumed office in 1973, just after the party had suffered disastrous electoral losses. The Labour Party came to office in 1973 only because the opposition was divided. The previous year the party had lost the referendum on Norwegian membership in the European Community, experienced severe internal conflict and the departure of many younger activists, and then spent the interim in opposition. For all these reasons the government was considered weak. Yet, by the 1977 elections it had recovered much of its unity and effectiveness and ended up gaining handsomely.

The relative weights of elections past versus elections future will vary.[8] But sooner or later the next election will dominate the concerns of politicians and induce behaviour that we would not expect at other stages of the electoral cycle. The literature on political business cycles, beginning with Nordhaus (1975), argues that governments (single-party as well as coalition) time their policies to generate a positive economic environment when the next elections are due.[9] Even less foresighted government leaders, who may not have done their 'homework' well enough to manipulate the business cycle, are likely to abstain from introducing or implementing particularly unpopular policies (such as tax increases) shortly before elections. And to the extent that they have popular policies on their agenda they will be tempted to enact them immediately before rather than after elections. With coalition governments, however, things are more complicated, as what may be popular with the supporters of one coalition party may alienate those of another.

---

[8] For an empirical investigation of this connection see Mattila and Raunio (2002, 2004).
[9] For a review see Mueller (2003: ch. 19).

Thus far, we have assumed that the parliament will serve until the end of its regular term. Yet, only Norway makes this the only option. In all other countries in our sample, early dissolution is constitutionally permitted.[10] Hence, the incumbent prime minister may dissolve parliament at a convenient time rather than aim to create a convenient electoral situation on a given election day. Much of what we have said above about strategic timing with regard to economic decisions applies also to early dissolutions. Yet, there are some differences. Rational voters may perceive an early dissolution as signalling low expectations on the part of the incumbents, as governments typically 'call early elections when future performance will be poor and this decline will make the governments look worse than the voters currently think they are' (Smith 2004: 48). This, of course, raises the questions why governments ever go for early elections, as they indeed do relatively frequently (Strøm and Swindle 2002).

Smith (2004: 54–65) cites at least four reasons why going early may nevertheless be a winning strategy: First, the government may have reached the presumed peak of its popularity, so that its electoral prospects can only get worse. Second, the government may expect that its political agenda and resources will change in ways that would lead voters to take a dimmer view of its competence. Third, calling early elections is more likely to catch opposition parties on the wrong foot (i.e. unprepared for an election). Finally, voters may not be sufficiently sophisticated to decode the dissolution decision as a signal of future poor performance. To the extent that one or more of these conditions apply, going for early elections can be a rational strategy for the incumbents.

Things are more complicated with government coalitions, however, as the options include not only new elections, but also new coalitions, or new agreements with existing partners. Moreover, the outcome of the interaction between many different parties may be difficult to foresee. Future-oriented actors will, when considering early cabinet termination (i.e. before the parliamentary term expires) think at least a few steps ahead. Naturally, they will ask whether elections are likely to be held or whether a new cabinet will emerge out of the sitting parliament (see Lupia and Strøm 1995). For the case of elections, they will try to estimate not only their own electoral performance but also those of the other parties in the game. Finally, they will consider the consequences of post-election bargaining. Thus, early elections may boost the vote of a particular party (Strøm and Swindle 2002), but at the same time deprive the same party of its likely coalition partners (who may drop out of parliament or refuse to engage in further cooperation). Waiting until the very end of the parliamentary term despite a coalition partner's wish to the contrary may produce similarly detrimental effects.

---

[10] Some caveats may be in order. Even though the German Constitution (Basic Law) permits parliamentary dissolution, the circumstances are very restrictive. And in Sweden it is generally unattractive to call early elections, as a newly elected parliament serves only for the remainder of the original term. See Strøm and Swindle (2002) and Strøm, Müller, and Bergman (2003).

Uncertainty and risks

Coalition bargaining decisions are often made in a cloud of ignorance or hazy knowledge. Like the rest of us, politicians live in a world of uncertainty and risks. While uncertainty means that actors do not know which events may take place in the future, risks relate to the possibility that those events may have detrimental consequences. These sources of insecurity relate to all phases of the coalition life cycle: election, coalition formation, governance, and cabinet termination. When political actors think ahead they always do so with the knowledge that the future is hard to predict and bears many risks. Though reputation provides a proxy (Wright and Goldberg 1985), they can never be sure about the future behaviour of their partners. Their information will always be incomplete and a certain amount of uncertainty will remain until the very end of each phase of the coalition life cycle.

Politicians generally are fully aware of the fact that the future is full of uncertainties. When asked about the future prospects of the coalition in which he was serving, a leading Austrian politician, at the apex of his power, made this clear by stating, '*media vita in morte sumus*' (in the midst of life we are in death). He went on more colloquially, 'My party chairman and I know it can be over any day.'

Yet, there are important cross-national differences. Politicians in countries with stable coalition formulas and little electoral change are better placed to anticipate what will come next. (Interestingly, Austria, from which the above quote comes, has traditionally been considered as falling into that category.) Countries with a record of great electoral volatility and frequent changes in coalitions constitute environments that are even less transparent and predictable. The world of multiparty electoral politics is thus inherently uncertain and unpredictable. Hence, efforts to understand coalition politics as one big, comprehensive, and fully informed bargain made at the cabinet formation stage, are fundamentally implausible.

To provide one example, when the German Red–Green coalition formed in 1998 none of the partners anticipated that soon military intervention in a foreign country would appear on the agenda. One of the basic values of the Greens is non-violence. Legitimate as it may have been, the NATO-supported 1999 intervention in the Kosovo conflict (followed by the deployment of German troops) clearly was violent. This military engagement therefore brought the Red–Green coalition close to collapse. The crisis was resolved only when Chancellor Schröder forced a vote of confidence upon the MPs of the government parties. The need for such brinkmanship clearly had not been anticipated when the government was formed.

Austria provides another example of political uncertainty and politicians' inability to anticipate what lies ahead. One of the editors of this volume interviewed a leading Austrian Social Democrat in the summer of 1984. The interviewer was told that the existing coalition of Social Democrats and the Freedom Party (which had taken office in 1983) was working well and that a renewal of the coalition for a second term was to be expected. Yet, two years and two months later the Social Democrats (by then under the leadership of a man who had not yet been in politics in 1984) terminated the coalition with the Freedom Party (which had just been taken over by Mr Jörg Haider) and called early elections. Thus, contrary to the expectations of this well-informed elite participant, the coalition never saw a second term. Moreover, ever since 1986 the Social Democrats have rejected any coalition with the Freedom Party.

Avoiding uncertainty and containing risks

As a politician, what you do not know can certainly hurt you. It is therefore not surprising that politicians try to minimize uncertainty and risk. To be sure, addicted gamblers get part of their thrill from uncertainty about the outcomes their actions and those of others will produce. Yet, most politicians, and certainly their voters, prefer a more stable environment that allows some mid-range planning on the basis of reasonable expectations. Getting into agreements with other players can help. Hence, politicians devote much of their time and energy to negotiating deals and striking agreements. This applies to intra-party as well as to inter-party politics.

Coalition agreements may be formal or informal, and they may be concluded before a government is formed, or hammered out while holding office. Whatever form they take, such agreements are designed to reduce the uncertainty under which political actors have to conduct their business. Needless to say, party leaders cannot make agreements with each and every political player that has the capacity to affect their prospects of reaching their goals. Even when agreements can be made, not everything can be included, and the risk always exists that some partners may renege later on. In short, in the real world, political agreements in general and coalition agreements in particular always remain *incomplete contracts* and they cannot always be enforced. But even incomplete and not fully enforceable agreements matter, and the importance of such 'contracts' has been underestimated in the coalitions literature.

What specific uncertainties do political parties aim to reduce with the help of coalition agreements? In order to take office, political parties have to agree who will be their partners in government and the terms under which they will share office. At a minimum, coalition agreements need to settle the issue of portfolio allocation ('Who gets what?'). Laver and Shepsle (1990, 1996) assume that this is as far as explicit agreements need to and can go. This is because in their view portfolio allocation is the only way to make credible policy commitments. Once these cards have been dealt, the game is effectively up. To be fair, the authors assume that portfolio allocation takes place under the shadow of the future, so that parties form those coalitions that allow them to remain faithful to the policy commitments they have made vis-à-vis the voters. Otherwise, politicians believe, voters will hold them to account in the next election.

For students of coalition politics, recognizing the shadow of future elections is necessary but not sufficient. Inter-party agreements are worked out under the shadow of the past as well as the shadow of the future. The future matters because all democratic politicians are the servants of a fickle and often unforgiving master, the popular majority. The past matters because governing is hard as well as unpredictable work, and because generations of past politicians have tried to perfect their skills as well as economize on their efforts. The shadow of the past affects coalition agreements in the sense that agreements made today will reflect past experiences and efforts to learn from them. When considering potential coalition partners political parties take into account their past experiences, both positive and negative ones. In particular, parties review the records (reputations) of their potential partners: have they been faithful to previous agreements? It is similarly relevant how successful previous coalitions have been in enacting their programmes, responding to newly arising problems, and meeting the demands of the voters.

The shadow of the past may also affect the contents of the agreement. What should be in the agreement and what can safely be left out is often decided based on past experiences. Whatever problem has arisen in past government cooperation is a candidate for being included in subsequent agreements, if this is feasible. This may include issues that had been overlooked in previous negotiations and issues that had been negotiated but not agreed.

The shadow of the past is thus important because history provides clues about what is likely to happen in the future. The past can also be a politician's best guide to what measures are necessary, feasible, or cost-effective. What matters more in making the relevant decisions about government cooperation, however, is the shadow of the future. There is no one-to-one relationship between past experiences and future expectations. Even bad experiences need not repeat themselves, as actors are able to learn from these events and to think about remedies. Likewise, long-term success stories may turn into debacles under changed circumstances. So, party leaders need to ask themselves what, if anything, is different from previous situations. Examples are new leaders of potential coalition partners, relevant changes in the bargaining environment (new parties, different party strengths, changed voting behaviour, etc.), or a new policy agenda (perhaps forced upon the government by outside forces). Moreover, each party and each generation of party leaders has only a limited set of previous experiences that are directly relevant to the current situation, and some parties (e.g. those that have spent many years in opposition) may have no relevant experience at all.

As already mentioned, in order to take office political parties need to agree on their partners and the division of portfolios. In many cases coalition building also requires a restructuring of government, as the need to give coalition partners a handle on specific policy areas may require the division of existing ministries or the combination of different agencies or sections thereof into a new government department. Yet, portfolio allocation and government reorganization provide only part of the structure in which coalition governance takes place. The other part of the governance structure is the mechanisms of collective decision-making. Typically, constitutions are silent about cabinet rules (Blondel and Müller-Rommel 1997; Strøm, Müller, and Bergman 2003). Hence, each government is free to adapt the formal institutions to its own needs and can introduce informal institutions such as coalition committees of various kinds on top of them. In designing such mechanisms politicians will be guided by inter- and intra-party needs. Specifically, they need to decide who should participate in which decisions. Formal bodies such as the cabinet may at the same time be too small and too big. They may be too small if they exclude potential veto players (e.g. party heavyweights who do not hold cabinet office). Conversely, formal bodies may be too big if they include people whose consent is not critical and whose knowledge may become a risk. Some issues are simply too confidential and/or 'delicate' to run through a large body of political actors whose participation is not critical. While far-sighted and experienced politicians try to anticipate these needs when hammering out the initial contract, the coalition architecture must often be developed as the participants go along.

Another issue that at least the more comprehensive agreements will address is coalition decision rules. Formal cabinet and parliamentary decision rules will exist, but they can be amended by agreements between coalition partners. The official decision rules always constitute the default option. If no agreement can be reached or if one coalition partner is no longer willing to play according to the private coalition rules, then the official rules will be in place. Yet, political parties may be willing to participate only provided that the official rules are de facto replaced by unofficial ones. Tsebelis (2002), for instance, assumes that contrary to the official majority decision rule that applies to most cabinets (Bergman et al. 2003: 186–8), coalitions in reality decide by unanimity rules (with political parties as the constituent units). Similarly, coalition parties typically adopt rules on discipline in parliamentary voting (i.e. whether and under what conditions the members of the coalition parties are free to vote against the government's position). Although this may be less critical, the coalition agreement may also regulate other aspects of parliamentary behaviour (questions, investigation committees, elections to parliamentary offices), positions to be taken with regard to direct democratic decisions forced upon the government (if this is possible), and cooperation at other levels of government, particularly if these impact on national politics.

In working out a coalition agreement political parties typically agree on the government's policy programme. Like-minded parties with a long record of cooperation may satisfy themselves by addressing a small number of major and/or controversial issues. Yet, even under these favourable conditions we would not expect all parties to rely exclusively on common sentiments and good will. Many will explicitly address policy issues and try to nail down joint positions before beginning government cooperation. Parties with less commonly held policy positions or little experience in cooperation can be expected to conduct more comprehensive negotiations and to be more insistent on credible policy commitments before they go into government. Policy agreements will range from those that lay out only general policy principles to those describing these policies in great detail. In shaping these agreements, the coalition parties may assume that they will have exclusive agenda control, that is, that they alone will determine the issues with which they will have to deal, or they may try to anticipate issues that will be forced upon them (e.g. through the European integration process or the business cycle).

Finally, coalition architects try to anticipate the elections that inevitably will come at the end of the parliamentary term. Clearly, the electoral system and the configuration of the party system will determine to what extent *collective* coalition strategies are mandatory. If the electoral system provides a premium for victorious electoral alliances, the coalition parties have strong incentives to cooperate in the electoral arena as well. Such rewards from coordination are particularly likely if coalition parties can agree on joint candidates in single-member districts or mutual withdrawals in two-ballot systems or if, by combining their forces, they can make sure that they will overcome critical electoral thresholds (see Cox 1997).

Even in the absence of such incentives, coalition parties may anticipate and indeed agree on electoral cooperation. At a minimum they will try to protect their own electoral interests in negotiating the coalition's policies and rules of the games. Obviously, this includes the substantive policy concerns of their respective constituencies, but the timing of policy measures may be of similar importance. On the one hand, politicians generally assume that voters have short memories and that hardships inflicted upon them at the beginning of a term will not weigh heavily in subsequent elections (particularly if these hardships are sweetened by budgetary largesse later on). On the other hand, parties that do not trust their alliance to be durable may aim at an equal inter-party distribution of burdens over the government term, so that the parties would not be left with very unequal pay-offs in the event that the coalition would come to an early demise (cf. Müller 1999). Moreover, parties may try to insure themselves against the risk of being kicked out of the government by including an 'election rule' in their coalition contract, so that a breakdown of the coalition would lead to early elections rather than to the formation of a new cabinet within the existing parliament. In short, coalition agreements are influenced by the whole coalition life cycle but also influence the players in the same cycle. The shadow of the past and the shadow of the future both colour their perceptions and shape their behaviour.

Thus far our discussion has been confined to the links between the different stages of coalition politics largely within *one* cycle. We have placed the formation of a new government in the context of the elections that preceded it and the governance process, cabinet termination, and elections that will follow. Yet, individual and collective actors have longer-term memories that go back to previous cycles. Sometimes events from the distant past influence the thinking and/or rhetoric of political actors. Thus, the Austrian Social Democrats' discomforting experience with the Christian Socials in the inter-war period had a long-term impact, influencing their post-war coalition behaviour and figuring prominently in crucial decisions such as the one to abandon government participation in 1966, or to form a minority cabinet in 1970 (Müller 1999, 2008). Conversely, politicians sometimes like to think ahead more than one parliamentary term when making their decisions in the coalition game. Thus, when the CDU/CSU in 1957 won a majority of seats in the Bundestag, its leaders chose to maintain their coalition with the FDP for practical and long-term strategic reasons (Saalfeld 2000: 44–5). Important as such long-term considerations may be in individual cases, however, in the present volume we largely concentrate, for the sake of simplicity, on the links between the various stages of coalition politics that occur within a single life cycle.

THE STUDY OF COALITION POLITICS

But how should the importance of agreements, uncertainty, and risk in the coalition life cycle be studied? One way to begin is by placing these insights in the context of the existing literature of coalition politics. Thus far we have outlined the approach taken in this volume. In order to place it in context we below provide a brief sketch of the development of this literature.[11] In our review of this literature we shall focus on a number of distinct clusters of explanatory variables. We leave the more detailed review of specific coalition politics sub-fields to the respective chapters in this volume.

Our review, then, falls into three parts. First, we identify the various competing clusters of explanatory variables. Of course, not all existing explanations are 'single-cluster', but a surprising number can be associated with one of these aggregations of explanatory factors. Second, we turn our attention to the competing theoretical and methodological agendas in coalition research. Theoretically, students of coalition politics have varied in their quest for compehensiveness versus parsimony. Methodologically, we focus on the main research strategies followed by coalition researchers. The main distinction here runs between more extensive and more intensive designs. Again, more extensive reviews will follow in the subsequent chapters that deal with the various stages of the life cycle of coalition politics.

---

[11] For recent reviews of the of the state of the art in coalition research see Grofman and van Roozendaal (1997); Laver (1998); De Winter (2002); Laver (2003); Mueller (2003: 278–95); Müller (2004a); for a more technical treatment see Bandyopadhyay and Chatterjee (2006).

Clusters of competing explanations

Students of political coalitions have fashioned six different types of explanations to understand (and predict) the various outcomes of the coalition game, such as the membership of governments formed, the allocation of portfolios among government parties, cabinet duration, and, more rarely, the instruments of coalition governance. These approaches focus on the following clusters of explanatory variables: (*a*) country and period effects (spatio-temporal parameters), (*b*) structural attributes of cabinets and parliaments, (*c*) preferences, (*d*) institutions, (*e*) the bargaining environment, and (*f*) critical events, respectively. Even though the chronology is not perfect, there is also a rough temporal sequence among these clusters, corresponding to the order in which they have been listed. In our discussion, we concentrate on the major theoretical statements that highlight each of these approaches.

Country effects and other contextual factors

Of course, country studies have always been an important genre in the field of Comparative Politics. The strong claim in this tradition is that politics can be understood only configuratively.[12] And there is some credibility to the claim that democratic politics involves language, symbolism, identity, tradition, and history, and that these factors can be country specific. In part, coalition politics hence results from the unique combination of political actors and institutions that characterizes each country. This is what is behind von Beyme's dismissive comment (1985: 323) that 'the assumptions of the formalised coalition theory are largely irrelevant in Europe', which he follows by listing a number of peculiarities of several European party systems that allegedly render existing coalition theories irrelevant for these respective cases. To be sure, von Beyme moves on to specify the differences between the European countries in terms of analytical categories (such as the working of the electoral system, the number and size of parties, political polarization, crisis situations, etc.). Yet the great number of factors that impact on coalition politics and their variation is assumed to make general theories based on the translation of 'country' into analytical categories a hopeless task.

Some authors who, like ourselves, are more sympathetic to general theories of politics nevertheless seem to support von Beyme's pessimism with regard to the ability of political science to replace 'country' with analytical variables. Indeed, some of the early empirical tests of coalition theories showed remarkable country effects. Hence, in their discussion of the 'Conflict of Interest' theory, Browne, Gleiber, and Mashoba (1984: 25) conclude: 'Country explains 38 per cent of the

---

[12] This is the claim of Ragin (1987, 2000) who offers the diversity-oriented qualitative comparative analysis, also known as Ragin's comparative method, as a means to deal with the complexity of cases in comparative analyses. The purpose of this method is not to establish the relative effects of different independent variables on the dependent one, but rather to expose the configurations and hence the logical structure of the individual cases.

variance in cabinet duration which, while modest, is nearly triple the best result associated with our analysis'. Similarly, Schofield and Laver (1985) found cross-national differences to be critical to the performance of portfolio pay-off theories. And according to Franklin and Mackie (1984), size and ideology perform very differently across countries in predicting coalition formation. Estimating their regressions separately for each of three groups of countries, these authors almost doubled the explained variance.

The general conclusion from tests of formal coalition theories, as formulated by Michael Laver, is that 'the results are highly country-sensitive.... Differences *between* countries, therefore, are critical for the analysis of coalitions' (Laver 1986: 33). He thus concludes that, 'at this stage in our understanding of the coalitional process, to conduct anything other than a country-specific analysis of the phenomena involved is to do great violence to reality' (Laver 1986: 33). Similarly, Laver and Budge's eight-country test of policy-based theories reveals that 'no single model performs well enough to provide an acceptable general account of coalition formation over all the countries studied' (1992: 420).

Browne (1982: 356) concludes the survey of early coalition theories in 11 countries (Browne and Dreijmanis 1982) on a more optimistic tone:

The fact, however, that relatively simple, that is, highly restricted, models have been unable to capture in a fully satisfactory way the political realities to which they have been applied should surprise no one, and it certainly does not constitute cause for discouragement or abandoning the field. Rather, it is obvious that what is needed is to orient theoretical work more directly towards the contexts in which they are applied, basing such efforts, at least at first, on the general models now available.

Country effects thus loom large in many accounts of coalition politics. But these are hardly the only stable environmental parameters that could in principle be expected to have an effect. Although it has spawned no systematic research of which we are aware, time is an equally obvious and plausible such variable. One might expect, for example, that coalition bargaining in Europe in the economically troubled 1970s would be systematically different from the 1950s, as well as from the 1990s, both of which were periods of more sustained growth. Moreover, one might expect that conflicts that were prominent during the Cold War would be of very different importance after 1991. Even though they do not offer the most parsimonious, elegant or theoretically progressive explanations, it is thus not difficult to see the plausibility of accounts that emphasize spatio-temporal parameters.

Structural attributes

When students of coalition politics (early on) became convinced that they needed to go beyond national categories in their explanations, they soon focused on the structural attributes of cabinets and party systems. One such cluster of explanatory variables is based on the characteristics of the parliamentary bargaining environment and the attributes of the cabinets that form. 'Structural attributes' in this context refers generically to the distribution of resources among actors in a given situation or to qualities of a given cabinet. Yet, we can identify structural attributes by their *systemic* properties. When employing structural attributes as explanatory variables, we focus on the aggregate properties of the party system or the cabinet, rather than on their individual components.

Some structural attributes are numerical and related to the size of the winning coalition. Thus, cabinets that are *minimal winning* or *minimum winning* are expected to be more stable than others (Riker 1962). These are properties that are in part structural and in part preference related (see below). Beginning with Taylor and Herman (1971) and Sanders and Herman (1977), many empirical studies have lent support to these expectations. Yet, Grofman (1989) has argued that these regularities do not apply *within* most countries, and that it is hence the composition of the cross-national samples that accounts for the supportive results. Warwick's regressions (1994: ch. 4) also show that as an explanatory factor *minimal winning* status is dominated by ideological diversity.

Structural attributes may include the time that a cabinet has at its disposal until the next regular election must be called. Cabinets that are formed early in a parliamentary term may be different from cabinets that assume office close to its end. While this difference may affect many aspects of coalition governance, research has tended to focus on the risks of premature termination faced by cabinets that distinguish themselves by this criterion (Lupia and Strøm 1995; Diermeier and Stevenson 1999, 2000).

Other authors have focused on party system characteristics. According to Dodd (1976; see also Taylor and Herman 1971), the party system format influences cabinet type (as classified according to numerical criteria), and different cabinet types have different durations. Accordingly, governments in multipolar (complex) party systems are less stable than those in bipolar ones. The validity of Dodd's results has not remained unchallenged (e.g. Grofman 1989), but it is supported by other research (Schofield 1987; Laver and Schofield 1990: 156–9). The bargaining environment can influence cabinet stability through the number and size of parliamentary parties: the greater the number of potential coalitions, the greater the bargaining complexity. Hence, the more likely it is that small changes—e.g. in policy positions—lead to changes in the parties' preferences over coalition partner(s). Grofman and van Roozendaal (1997: 44) consider this one of the most powerful explanations of cabinet duration, second only to the cabinet's status as a majority or minority government.

Preferences

While structural attributes constrain actor behaviour from the 'outside', the next clusters focus on the goals of the actors themselves. The early coalition theories, beginning with John von Neumann and Oskar Morgenstern's *Theory of Games and Economic Behaviour* (1953), William Gamson's 'A Theory of Coalition

Formation' (1961), and William H. Riker's *The Theory of Political Coalitions* (1962), worked exclusively from the preferences of the actors in the coalition game. Players were considered to be largely unconstrained in their coalition behaviour. The authors just cited considered only the *office* preferences of political actors, invariably assuming their desire for membership in a winning (and hence cabinet forming) coalition.

Later generations of coalition studies have introduced policy motivations. Despite the introduction of policy preferences in earlier works (Leiserson 1966; Axelrod 1970), de Swaan (1973) is generally credited with the first pure *policy-seeking* coalition theory (Laver and Schofield 1990: 97–103). His theory was motivated by an empirical puzzle: the substantial number of non-minimal coalitions formed in nine Western European countries between 1918 and the early 1970s (de Swaan 1973: 80). De Swaan formulated a number of potential explanations (e.g. a consensus-oriented political culture and constitutional and political requirements for non-minimal coalitions) (1973: 81–7). Yet, he considered only one of them to be a 'central behavioural assumption' on which a coalition theory could build: 'Coalitions emerge from the interaction among actors, each of which strives to bring about and join a coalition that he expects to adopt a policy which is as close as possible to his own most preferred policy' (1973: 82). In other words, 'considerations of policy are foremost in the minds of the actors and ... the parliamentary game is, in fact, about the determination of major government policy' (de Swaan 1973: 88).

Empirical studies have often found substantial evidence that policy diversity matters. The greater the policy distances between cabinet parties, the lower the cabinet's stability and hence duration. The assumption, which has not yet been empirically verified, is that ideologically diverse coalitions terminate early because they can no longer agree on policy (Warwick 1994: 63). According to Warwick (1994: ch. 4) the left–right, secular–clerical, and pro- versus anti-regime dimensions are significant determinants of cabinet stability. Ideological diversity in parliament may also matter: the stronger extreme parties are, the more comprehensive coalitions among the non-extreme parties need to be. In a similar vein, moderate, or centrist, parties should be a stabilizing force: the inclusion of 'central' parties (median parties and related concepts) is expected to stabilize coalitions (cf. van Roozendaal 1997).

Other scholars have provided micro-foundations (i.e. the causal mechanisms operating at the individual level) for the claim that political parties are policy-seekers. Traditionally, the argument has been made that real-world politicians are at least as interested in policies as are voters and that they therefore sincerely care about the content of government policy (Luebbert 1986: 50). An argument that demands less of politicians is that party competition consists in the offering of alternative policy packages to the voters, and that this competition drives the behaviour of party leaders. Laver (1997: 136) argues that 'politicians do have some incentive to honour such promises when they have the opportunity to do so'. And he goes on: 'In other words, even politicians who personally have no interest whatsoever in the policy packages they promote for purely entrepreneurial reasons have an incentive to implement these, almost as if they really do care about them, when they become incumbents' (1997: 136).[13]

Laver and Schofield (1990) have alerted us to the fact that party leaders may aim at either policy or office not because of intrinsic preferences but for instrumental reasons. Intrinsically policy-seeking politicians pursue government office because being in government is the best (and sometimes only) way to affect public policy, and because such policy goals are their true concerns. Instrumental policy-seekers may behave exactly alike, except that for them these policy objectives are only the means towards an ulterior end (such as enjoying the spoils or prestige of holding government office). The latter interpretation is at the heart of the emerging consensus in coalition studies that policy is important, either because politicians genuinely care or because they are forced to do so by their voters.[14]

Yet, policy-pursuit is hardly the whole story. Another body of literature assumes *complex motivations*, that is, the coexistence of different goals such as policy and office (Budge and Laver 1986; Laver and Schofield 1990), or a combination of either or both of these goals with the parties' electoral concerns (Strøm 1990*a*, 1990*b*; Schofield 1993; Lupia and Strøm 1995; Müller and Strøm 1999). Under favourable circumstances politicians may be able to achieve their multiple goals simultaneously. Under less favourable circumstances, they may have to abandon one or more goals to achieve another. In most situations, however, politicians will pursue some mix of political 'goods'. Rather than having lexicographic preferences (i.e. giving absolute priority to one goal over all others) they will have some metric that allows them to measure potential gains (or losses) over several goals and decide for the strategy that promises them the best overall result. Searching for such optimal trade-offs is what typically happens in political bargaining.

Institutions

The first generations of coalition research basically assumed that the coalition game was acted out in an institution-free environment.[15] Only gradually during

---

[13] Note that Laver alludes to what we call the coalition life cycle as 'the continuous sequence of election, coalition formation, policy implementation, election, coalition formation, policy implementation ... that characterizes real party competition' (1997: 137).

[14] Some authors have argued that party leaders may also act on the basis of more public-spirited preferences that are difficult to fit within the prevailing categories. Thus, Ian Budge argues: 'Where the system is immediately threatened (externally or internally): all significant pro-system parties will join the government excluding anti-system parties.' (Budge 1984: 106; see also Budge and Herman 1978). While this argument may be plausible, it does not avoid the problem of collective action that seems to have motivated it. Even if the leaders of the established parties all prefer to preserve the institutions of parliamentary democracy, it is not clear why any one of them should volunteer to bear the costs of doing so. And in the absence of clear criteria by which we can identify threats to system survival, this kind of argument may lead to circular reasoning.

[15] To be more precise, these authors assume that the institutional environment is assembly government in its pure form, i.e., a voting body making decisions by the simple majority rule (50% + 1 vote).

the 1990s was the potential relevance of political institutions recognized through inductive as well as more deductive scholarship. We turn first to the more inductive work. Laver and Schofield's survey (1990: 62–6) of official rules relevant to coalitions was followed by a more comprehensive discussion of institutional (and other) constraints on the actors in the coalition game (Strøm, Budge, and Laver 1994). This survey showed that specific institutions can drastically reduce the number of feasible coalitions and cause considerable shifts of bargaining power between parties. Formation rules, parliamentary voting rules, and the shadow of the electoral institutions (the need for partners) may make the formation of some coalitions more likely than others and can lock parties into existing patterns of cooperation (Strøm, Budge and Laver 1994; Müller 2004*b*). At about the same time, Bergman (1993, 1995) introduced the distinction between positive and negative parliamentarism (while governments must have the support of a majority of MPs under the former in order to take office, in the latter it is sufficient that there is no majority opposing their inauguration) and showed that minority governments are more frequent under negative formation rules.

While most of this research was concerned with the rules that structure government formation, other work has focused on decision rules and electoral rules and hence on institutions that directly impinge on coalition governance and elections. The relevant publications include Huber's (1996) and Huber and McCarty's study (2001) of the power of the prime minister to introduce a confidence vote in parliament (and hence strong-arm co-partisans and coalition partners alike into supporting the government). Similarly, Strøm and Swindle (2002) show that differences in parliamentary dissolution rules systematically affect the incidence of early elections. Other primarily theoretical work has focused on the parliamentary voting rules. Heller (2001) demonstrates that the last amendment right of the minister in charge of the relevant portfolio can help induce the coalition parties to support government proposals. Likewise, country studies suggest the potential relevance of qualified majority requirements in coalition politics (Nousiainen 2000: 269; Müller 2000*b*: 91). These studies also suggest that coalitions need not take the form of *government* coalitions.

Bicameralism is another institutional feature that may affect coalition politics. While it is easy to see that cabinet accountability to upper chambers and a decisive role of them in decision-making should 'double' all majority considerations that enter the process of coalition formation, Druckman and Thies (2002: 769) found that 'bicameralism matters even when the upper chamber is relatively weak and generally congruent with the lower house'.

Finally, electoral institutions should obviously have an impact on coalition politics. After all, they provide political parties with very different incentives either to run alone or to stick together (see Cox 1997). While only a pure PR system provides no incentives for electoral coordination, the French type of a two-ballot system generates strong inducements for such alliances (Thiébault 2000).

To a lesser extent this is also the case for mixed-member systems such as the German one (Klingemann and Wessels 2001; Pappi and Thurner 2002), as well as for the STV system (Laver 2000). Yet, the potential gains from inter-party coordination in the electoral arena has not received much attention in coalition research.[16]

While we can easily relate specific institutions to a particular stage of the coalition life cycle, their effects are not confined to that stage. Especially if the institutions are 'strong' (i.e. have potentially large and consistent effects), political actors will anticipate their effects, which in turn may affect their behaviour at earlier stages of the coalition life cycle. Hence, the rules under which decisions are made once a government is in place may well already have influenced the formation of this government.

Studies in the non-cooperative game-theoretic tradition proceed from very specific assumptions about highly stylized institutions, such as recognition rules (Austen-Smith and Banks 1988, 1990; Baron 1991, 1993; Diermeier and Merlo 2000; Baron and Diermeier 2001). While some of these models yield elegant and powerful results, many of the models are also 'extremely complicated', to quote Norman Schofield (1993: 13). While this fact certainly does not encourage their popularization, it is more troubling that 'institutionally rich models tend to be highly sensitive to the institutional detail' of their assumptions and hence 'do not constitute good general explanations' (Austen-Smith 1996: 235). The same author goes on to question the relevance of institutions by noting that in parliamentary democracies in the post-war period very different institutional structures yielded policy outcomes that are 'very "centrally located" by virtually any measure' (Austen-Smith 1996: 235). Yet, this scepticism may be too strong even with regard to game-theoretical models based on very specific institutional assumptions.

In short, the relevance of institutions for coalition politics has been shown convincingly for specific institutions and/or cases, but as of yet no comprehensive picture of their impact on various aspects of coalition politics has emerged. Indeed, the full impact of the range of relevant institutions clearly has not yet been fully explored either in theoretical or case study work.

Bargaining environment

The explanatory clusters identified above are all very well established in the literature. By introducing the next cluster, however, we present an approach to coalition politics that is much more novel. This innovation stems from our explicit recognition of transaction costs, which are the costs that the parties to a transaction must bear. Transaction costs include search and information costs, costs from negotiating the terms of a transaction (bargaining costs), and all costs that result from supervising and enforcing the deal ex post. The literature on transaction

---

[16] See Laver (2000) for an interesting study of the coalitional aspects of the STV system.

costs in business settings argues that if these costs are likely to outweigh the expected benefits, the relevant transaction will not be made (Williamson 1985, 1996; Kreps 1990: ch. 20). It is easy to see the parallel between economic transactions and coalition deals in politics.

However, while we may intuitively recognize the role that transaction costs play in coalition politics, it is not always easy to identify and disentangle such costs empirically. Some transaction costs arise from the structural attributes, preference distributions, and political institutions that we have discussed above. Transaction costs are also likely to derive from the bargaining environment in which political parties operate. Bargaining is fundamental to coalition politics, and bargaining necessarily implies transaction costs. In this volume we have particularly sought to develop measures that capture important aspects of transaction costs that are not reflected in the more traditional clusters of variables. We group these variables together in our fifth cluster, and refer to them as our bargaining environment variables.

Such variables have been alluded to in earlier literature. For example, in a pioneering theoretical treatment of 'decision costs', Adrian and Press (1968) identified eight types of costs that relate to the making of coalitions. These include 'information costs', 'dissonance costs' (costs of conflict and disagreement within the winning coalition), and 'inertia costs' (costs involved in changing existing coalition patterns). As Adrian and Press (1968: 561) point out with regard to the latter type: 'Dissolving a coalition may involve more costs than maintaining an existing coalition that may not be minimal in size or in internal dissonance.' These considerations clearly represent what in modern parlance is called 'transaction costs'.[17] Yet, Adrian and Press's theoretical think-piece (1968) has not been very consequential for coalition research in the more than three decades that have followed. We believe that its time has come.

Similar concerns have been couched in different terms in other studies. In the empirical coalition literature, Franklin and Mackie (1983) were the first to conclude that 'past experience plays an important role' in government formation (1983: 276). Empirically, they captured this effect through the concept of inertia, defined as 'immediate past experience' (1983: 277). In their study of coalition formation, they found two-thirds of the total variance explained by size and ideology, with inertia playing a supporting role (1983: 296). Inertia, in turn, reflects the effects of past size and ideology and hence represents an indirect effect of these variables (1983: 278). Franklin and Mackie (1983: 276) also refer to the coalition governance process as the 'experience of working together' and

---

[17] While many of Adrian and Press's concerns are thus straightforwardly consistent with contemporary transaction cost economics, their conception of costs might strike today's readers as somewhat loose and awkward. For example, these authors discuss policy concessions (i.e. deviations from a party's ideal point) as 'responsibility costs' and 'persuasion costs', and the consequences of including more (or stronger) partners in the coalition as 'division-of-pay-offs costs'.

the ability to perform the tasks the parties want the government to perform. These factors can reasonably be captured within a transaction cost approach.

We can distinguish internal (or direct) from external (or indirect) transaction costs. Internal transaction costs affect the parties engaged in the coalition negotiations directly. These negotiations often demand a considerable investment of time from the individuals who conduct them (which may come on top of other duties, such as directing a government department). They may also involve considerable stress and hence increased health risks (due to a lack of sleep and excessive consumption of coffee, cigarettes, and other dangerous substances). Yet, conducting such negotiations is the very job of politicians and it is reasonable to think that they self-select partly on this basis. Thus, politicians may even enjoy some of the health hazards that they impose on themselves. Besides, many others are all too ready to bear these costs if they come with the office rewards that bring the relevant politicians to the negotiation table.

The political opportunity costs from negotiations may be more relevant. If too much time is spent in negotiations, too little remains for implementing the resulting deals and 'selling' them to the public. Some policies may come too late to be effective, simply because the world has changed while negotiations were underway. Also, time-consuming negotiations at the executive level may leave too little time for instructing and supervising the civil servants and government agencies in charge of implementation. Another aspect of long-lasting negotiations is their effect on public opinion. Andeweg, van der Tak, and Dittrich (1980: 242) have argued that bargaining under public scrutiny invites politicians to dig themselves in at their favourite positions and to 'speak more simplistically and belligerently' than at the conference table. Yet, in so doing, they tie their hands, since concessions would mean a loss of face.

The non-partisan public may well decode such behaviour as a lack of public spirit on the part of the relevant politicians and therefore turn away from their parties. This is what happened in Austria in the coalition negotiations between the Social Democrats and People's Party in 1999–2000, where polls showed that the Freedom Party gained considerable support at the expense of the parties engaged in negotiations. Finally, negotiations may send important signals even to parties that are not participating. While this effect may be desirable from the point of view of some negotiating parties, it can also produce detrimental responses by alienating potential allies or driving up their price in the event that the negotiations fail.

What is probably most critical, however, is the external transaction costs, which are the costs placed on actors who do not participate in the negotiations. As Andeweg, van der Tak, and Dittrich (1980) argue, a country has no effective government until a new cabinet is sworn in (see, however, Laver 2003: 25–6). Particularly if critical government policy is at stake, the business community may decide to wait and see what their outcome will be. Hence, business may withhold investment decisions until a new government is in place and/or until the details of important issues under negotiation (e.g. tax laws) are clear. Consequently, long-lasting negotiations may have a negative effect on the economy (see Bernhard and Leblang 2006: ch. 5). This, in turn, is likely to backfire on the negotiating parties as they may find, upon assuming office, that the economy is in a worse state than it would otherwise have been.

Following up on these suggestions in the literature, our bargaining environment variables are partly derived from the characteristics of the prior cabinet and in particular from the conditions under which it resigned. They stem also from the uncertainty and complexity that plagued the incumbent cabinet when it was first formed, as captured by the number of bargaining rounds and the formation duration that preceded its inauguration. A higher number of formation rounds and a longer process can imply an uneasy relationship (but not does necessarily have to do so, see Chapter 4). Other bargaining variables, such as a comprehensive coalition agreements and thoughtfully designed conflict resolution mechanism for coalition governance, might have the opposite effect and lessen transaction costs during the tenure of the coalition.

Critical events

Our final cluster places coalition bargaining and governance in the context of important and often unforeseen events. Critical events have so far been employed almost exclusively in duration studies and hence have had a narrower application than the other approaches. The critical events approach was introduced to the study of coalitions by a group of researchers associated with Eric C. Browne.[18] Disappointed by the limited explanatory power of structural attributes in duration studies, Browne, Gleiber, and Mashoba (1984: 26) suggested a radical change of perspective and turned to 'critical events' for analytical traction. Their approach was based on the assumption that each cabinet is equally likely to survive until the end of its term (the CIEP—Constitutional Inter-Election Period, as it was later called) but faces a 'bombardment' of critical events that have the potential to cause its termination. The relevant events are purely accidental. Browne, Frendreis, and Gleiber (1986: 633, 635) mention scandals, party splits, economic crises, wars, other international crises, conflicts over government policy, and the sudden death of the Prime Minister. According to their initial theory, the probability that critical events occur is independent of the cabinet's structural attribute and age.

In their most ambitious paper, however, Browne, Frendreis, and Gleiber (1986) found that only 4 (of 12) countries—Belgium, Finland, Israel, and Italy—conformed to their theory. The 'critical events' approach was criticized because of its lack of micro-political foundations and the vagueness of some of its core concepts (such as the term 'critical event' itself) (see the controversy in Strøm

---

[18] See Browne, Gleiber, and Mashoba (1984); Browne, Frendreis, and Gleiber (1984, 1986); and Frendreis, Gleiber, and Browne (1986).

et al. 1988). King et al. (1990; see also Alt and King 1994) later developed an integrated approach that shares with the critical events school the assumption that cabinets are subjected to a bombardment of random events, but departs from it in allowing that due to different structural attributes, cabinets are not all equally likely to terminate as a consequence of these events. This perspective is more plausible and has been supported in empirical tests, even though it did not solve the problem of micro-political foundations.

More recent scholarship has attempted to provide such foundations. Lupia and Strøm (1995) argue that critical events cause shifts in the bargaining power of the coalition parties (which is precisely what makes these events critical) and hence may trigger a new round of coalition bargaining. These shifts of bargaining power can lead to early parliamentary dissolution (as expected by Grofman and van Roozendaal 1994), a renegotiation of the existing coalition, the formation of a new coalition in the sitting parliament, or the stabilization of the incumbent coalition.[19] Laver and Shepsle (1998) have broadened this approach by considering different types of shocks (public opinion shocks, agenda shocks, policy shocks, and decision rule shocks). Tying this to their portfolio allocation theory they show that different coalitions react differently to the various types of shocks. While broadening our understanding of such events is surely a worthwhile exercise, it is useful to focus on those shocks that are most common, most clearly exogenous, and most critical to the democratic process. Public opinion shocks, as featured in Lupia and Strøm's original analysis (1995), suggest themselves in this context, as they are the only type of shock that flow directly from the delegation process between citizens and representatives.

Competing agendas

The coalition literature thus features a wide range of explanatory perspectives and variables. Moreover, the field is also divided on what is the most interesting questions concerning the coalition life cycle, as well as on the preferred design for empirical coalition studies. Below we address the two topics in order. In their now classic review of the state of the art, Laver and Schofield (1990) captured the essence of the former concern by phrasing a series of questions, the most important of which were: 'Who gets in?' and 'Will it last?' As we shall discuss below, coalition studies for a long time focused almost exclusively on these two questions (and the former more than the latter). Another one of Laver and Schofield's questions was: 'Who gets what?' It refers to their analysis of portfolio allocation. What is remarkable, however, is that the book contained no general *governance*-related question. We should be quick to add that in this respect Laver and Schofield cannot be convicted of the sin of omission. Rather, they accurately represented the state of the art at the end of the 1980s.

[19] For a test of the model see Diermeier and Stevenson (2000).

In terms of the substantive questions of the literature, not much has changed since then. Coalition research has focused on three distinct aspects of coalition politics: government formation, cabinet termination, and recently also coalition governance. The order of these topics reflects both their appearance on the research agenda and the attention given to them. Most works have dealt with one of these topics exclusively. In this volume, we shall revisit each of these substantive concerns, but also add to the overall agenda. Below we briefly describe each of these topics and point to the relevant chapters in this book.

Government formation and membership

Government formation has been at the centre stage of coalition studies since the field's inception as an area of systematic study in the 1950s. Elsewhere, we have referred to the preoccupation with the formation stage as the 'Hollywood bias'. Just as in the movies of the 1950s, the attention in early coalition studies was focused almost exclusively on the phase of courtship and wedding and the question of 'who gets whom.' The literature left out almost entirely the more mundane aspects of actually 'living together' (Müller and Strøm 2000: 13, 16–25). Thus, the life cycle of coalitions has received the same selective attention as the life cycle of movie marriages: the focus was on the beginning of this relationship, not on its day-to-day negotiations, its achievements, or its termination. Thus, the picture that emerged emphasized the happier and more glorious moments.

In the words of Laver and Schofield (1990), the bulk of the coalition literature has thus been concerned with the 'Who gets in?' (or membership) question. Early approaches defined and predicted the formation of specific cabinet types— such as minimal winning, minimum winning, and minimum connected winning governments—and hence the cabinet's party composition (Riker 1962; Leiserson 1966; Axelrod 1970; de Swaan 1973). Later works have concentrated on defining the conditions which bring about one type or the other (Crombez 1996). Alternatively, they have sought to explain a specific cabinet type, for example, surplus coalitions (Volden and Carruba 2004). Other approaches have confined themselves to predicting a cluster of parties out of which some will form the government (Schofield 1993, 1995, 1997; Schofield and Sened 2006). Yet others have ventured to explain and predict the coalition membership of individual parties with particular properties, such as the median party, the central player, or the largest party (van Deemen 1989, 1991; Laver and Schofield 1990; van Roozendaal 1990). This literature is reviewed in greater detail in Chapter 6.

A few studies have addressed the *process* of cabinet formation. Grofman (1982, 1996; see also Grofman, Straffin, and Noviello 1996) conceives of coalition formation as a sequential enterprise in which protocoalitions form and ally until an equilibrium status is reached. While Grofman and associates are still interested in predicting coalition membership by focusing on the formation process, more recently the formation process itself, more specifically its duration, has become the object of study (Diermeier and van Roozendaal 1998; Martin and Vanberg 2003). Chapter 4 takes up that research interest.

Government stability and duration

Traditionally, cabinet duration has been the second major interest in coalition research. Until recently the studies in this literature concentrated on explaining the coalitions' duration in the statistical best-fit tradition, as we introduce it below. The core research question was (and still is) the governments' probability of termination at any time (the 'hazard rate'). As already mentioned, this research assumed that the main determinants of termination were to be found either in the 'attributes' of the coalitions (coalition type) or their environment (e.g. party system characteristics), or in the nature of 'critical events' that affected these cabinets.

It was not until the mid-1990s that explicit game-theoretic models were introduced to the duration literature (Lupia and Strøm 1995; Laver and Shepsle 1998).[20] The former has done well in some empirical testing (Diermeier and Stevenson 2000), but as Laver (2003: 38) points out, more comprehensive tests of these complex models would require data-sets that are fundamentally different from everything that has so far been compiled in coalition research.

Coalition governance

Our understanding of the ongoing process of making and implementing public policy under multiparty parliamentary government builds on a broader, more amorphous, and often less self-consciously theoretical body of literature. For most countries, there are detailed journalistic accounts of great (and not so great) men and women who have formed cabinets and the fate of the governments in which they served. Within academia, there are more systematic, and ultimately perhaps more useful accounts of how cabinets form and govern together. For the sake of simplicity, we can distinguish historical from behaviouralist accounts.

The behaviouralist approach to cabinet governance was championed by Headey's study (1974) of the British case. It was made cross-national in Blondel and Müller-Rommel's project (1993), which has remained to date the most comprehensive attempt to study cabinet governance comparatively. Blondel and Müller-Rommel's volume (1993) is based first and foremost on interviews with former cabinet ministers. The unit of observation is the individual cabinet

---

[20] See Chapter 9 for a more comprehensive review of the literature.

minister. Consequently, the Blondel and Müller-Rommel volume mainly illuminates the behaviour of individual politicians. And their project could cover only those cabinets for which a sufficient number of ministers could be interviewed (basically those cabinets that served in the late 1960s, the 1970s, or the early 1980s). Blondel and Müller-Rommel cover 11 countries, 10 of them coalitional. Their project mainly identifies behavioural patterns and describes their frequency across countries. Thus, they show, for instance, that coalition cabinets are less hierarchical and at the same time more conflictual than single-party cabinets (Frognier 1993).

Both historical and behaviouralist studies have been useful sources for our country experts (see the chapters in Müller and Strøm 2000), but they constitute fundamentally different approaches from one taken in this volume. The present volume draws on a much broader range of data (including coded historical accounts, coalition documents, institutional data, behavioural data, duration data, etc.). While it is intuitively clear how the descriptive historical accounts distinguish themselves from the present study, it may be worth pointing out a few differences between our approach and the behaviouralist one, as both deal in numbers and aim at systematic general theories (rather than understanding 'unique' cases). For many reasons, which we make explicit in this chapter, we think that the most useful way to approach the study of coalitions is from the theoretical perspective that was founded by Gamson (1961) in sociology and Riker (1962) in political science, the Rational Choice research programme. The behaviouralist approach, in contrast, draws on a bundle of hypotheses that can be related to different theories or research programmes.

It was Laver and Shepsle (1990, 1996) who forcefully introduced governance questions to coalition research. In their original work, they argued that previous coalition research had treated government coalitions as 'a special type of legislative coalition' (1990: 873), as these studies were not based on 'a clear conception of what is being formed' (1990: 873). But in contrast to a legislative voting coalition, which by forming in parliament has already achieved its purpose (enacting a piece of legislation), government coalitions generate benefits for their participants only by holding office and using the resources that come with it for some time.

Laver and Shepsle make two important assumptions about the motivations of politicians. The first is that party leaders are policy-seekers. Hence, coalition parties have a most-preferred set of policies that they will seek to implement. The second assumption is that the distribution of ministerial portfolios among the cabinet parties is critical to the parties' ability to leave an imprint on government policy. Indeed, in the early version of their theory, the authors label ministers 'policy dictators in their respective jurisdictions' (1990: 888, n. 2). This means that *only* the party holding a specific portfolio can influence public policy in the respective area. Indeed, this party should be able to implement its most-preferred policy fully, though at the price that the other coalition parties implement their ideal points in the jurisdictions held by their respective ministers. Yet, even Laver and Shepsle are first and foremost interested in government formation (and stability). Coalition governance concerns enter their theory in a series of strong assumptions that allow Laver and Shepsle to explain coalition formation (and stability).

To be sure, country-specific research has for many years focused on coalition governance mechanisms.[21] Yet, comparative work is of recent origin. While Müller and Strøm (2000) provide a general overview, specialized studies have addressed the issues of coalition contracts (Timmermans 1998, 2003, 2006; Strøm and Müller 1999) and some of the means of 'policing the bargain', specifically the use of parliamentarians (Martin 2004; Martin and Vanberg 2004) and junior ministers (Thies 2001). It is fair to say that this research has barely scratched the surface of the issue of coalition governance.

Research strategy

Coalition scholars have adopted research strategies that can conveniently be mapped onto two dimensions: one having to do with their theoretical aims and the other with their empirical research design. Theoretically, coalition studies can be distinguished by their explanatory strategy, more specifically by the number of explanatory variables employed (few vs. many) and the analytical structure of the explanation (tight vs. loose). Thus, we can distinguish between parsimonious and complete theoretical specifications. Parsimonious approaches typically employ a few variables only, but are based on a clearly articulated theory, often with strong micro-foundations. The main thrust of parsimonious explanations is to test the explanatory power of particular well-specified propositions. Such propositions are considered promising if the empirical tests demonstrate that the expected relationship obtains and is statistically significant. Complete approaches, in contrast, seek to extract and test a number of plausible and potentially complementary hypotheses. The main objective of such approaches is to maximize the statistical model's explanatory power. A model is considered good if it correctly predicts (or, rather, 'postdicts') a substantial proportion of the cases under investigation and, particularly, if it performs better than alternative models. The logic behind the model is the 'best fit' one, that is, the enterprise is driven by the attempt to find the combination of independent variables which best predicts the dependent variable. Complete approaches therefore tend to do better in empirical tests than parsimonious approaches, but often at the price of leaving us with an unspecified causal mechanism, or an inelegant understanding of different explanatory factors.

---

[21] See, e.g., Rudzio (2003: 290–305) and Müller (2006), who summarize the literatures on Germany and Austria, respectively.

	Complete theoretical approaches	Parsimonious theoretical approaches
Intensive empirical designs	Andeweg, De Winter and Dumont (2010) Müller and Strøm (1999)	Laver and Shepsle (1994) Thies (2001) Timmermans (2003, 2006)
Extensive empirical designs	Browne (1970) Martin and Stevenson (2001) Taylor and Laver (1973) Warwick (1994)	De Swaan (1973) Laver and Budge (1992) Laver and Shepsle (1996) Strøm (1990a)

FIGURE 1.2. Approaches in empirical coalition research, with examples

On our second dimension coalition studies fall into small-n (intensive) versus large-n (extensive) designs (see Figure 1.2). Work in the intensive design logic is typically concerned with single cases (e.g. the formation of a specific coalition) or a small number of observations. Country studies have long been the backbone of that research tradition (Groennings, Kelley, and Leiserson 1970: Part I; Browne and Dreijmanis 1982; Bogdanor 1983b; Pridham 1986; Müller and Strøm 2000; Kropp, Schüttemeyer, and Sturm 2002). Other studies employ the 'most similar cases' research design and examine specific aspects of coalition politics in focused comparisons (e.g. Strøm 1986; Jungar 2000; Timmermans 2003, 2006). More recently they have become augmented by a body of studies that focus on individual episodes of coalition politics, often using archival material and interviews with actors (Müller and Strøm 1999; De Winter, Andeweg, and Dumont 2008). This tradition of research aims at a configurative understanding of coalition politics. The underlying assumption is that context, events, and the sequence of events are crucial and can only be fully understood through in-depth studies. These studies are case-driven, that is, they first and foremost constitute attempts to understand the specific patterns of coalition politics in a particular country or the outcome of a particular episode. This, in turn, may help us discover the relevance of previously neglected variables (Lijphart 1971). Such accounts can also take the form of analytical narratives, which by employing game-theoretic models marry the narrative account with 'parsimony, refinement, and (in the sense used by mathematicians) elegance' (Bates et al. 1998: 11).

Extensive design studies can best be exemplified by the large-n cross-national studies that have been the centre of modern coalition research since the 1970s (Browne 1970; de Swaan 1973; Taylor and Laver 1973; Dodd 1976). The logic of such studies is to maximize the number of observations so as to control for as many factors as possible and reach the greatest possible statistical confidence in the results. The ideal hence is to include all coalitions ever formed regardless of year and their geographic setting as long as the conditions are roughly comparable. Of course, the number of stable parliamentary democracies is still relatively small. Hence, the data limitations are quite obvious. Some scholars have tried to increase their N by using annual data (Volden and Carrubba 2004), while others have sought to avoid that problem by focusing on subnational coalitions (Mellors and Pijnenburg 1989; Downs 1998; Bäck 2003a, 2003b). Figure 1.2 summarizes these comparisons by bringing both dimensions together and referring to some prominent works in each tradition.

THE WAY FORWARD

Without a doubt, coalition studies constitute a strong field in the study of comparative politics. The field counts a large number of publications in top journals and books published by the most prestigious publishers. Even more critically, we find a gratifying and continuous cumulation of knowledge, in the sense that today's research can build on previous efforts rather than having to start anew (Sjöblom 1977). Cumulation indicates real progress and generally typifies a mature discipline. Unfortunately, it is still unusual in many fields of political science. Hence, coalition studies stand out.

Nevertheless we can identify three serious shortcomings or imbalances in emphasis. The first one is substantive: what happens between coalition formation and termination is still poorly understood. Although coalition governance questions have been addressed recently in a small number of publications, the territory remains largely uncharted. The second problem is an imbalance between theory and data. On the one hand, we have seen sophisticated developments in formal theory that are way ahead of empirical work. On the other hand, we see empirical work that provides relevant information but fails to capture the main concerns in the theoretical debate.[22] Finally, coalition studies have not yet effectively responded to the early criticism that they lack dynamics (see, e.g., Laver 1974, 1986). Typically, the various aspects of coalition politics—formation, governance, and termination—are not understood in a common context. In other words, the coalition life cycle is broken up into its components and these are examined in mutual isolation.

So, what is the way forward in coalition studies? We think that it can be summarized under three headings: 'better theory', 'better data', and 'better methods'. In the present volume, we hope to make advances in all three directions.

---

[22] For such a claim, see Michael Laver's review of Blondel and Müller-Rommel (1993) in the *American Political Science Review*, 89: 506–7.

Better theory

Given the impressive theoretical advances that have been made in coalition studies, the need for 'better theory' may not seem self-evident. Yet, the field continues to be divided between studies that rely on ad hoc theorizing and put a premium on empirical data analysis and those that are thoroughly theoretical, but do not employ real-world data. To be sure, the gap between these two traditions is narrowing. This is thanks to studies such as those of Laver and Shepsle (1996) and Diermeier, Eraslan, and Merlo (2002, 2003), who start from full-blown theoretical models. Yet, even the most empirically rich studies of this kind have focused on a few issues of coalition politics only and often use real-world coalition data more for purposes of illustration than empirical testing.

This volume has several theoretical agendas. Our approach is more comprehensive than any other coalition study in as much as it incorporates all phases of the coalition life cycle. The theoretical advantage of so doing is that we can more easily appreciate the roles of the shadow of the past, as well as that of the future, in coalition politics. Furthermore, we assume that bargaining is both critical and difficult.[23] And in the same spirit our study diverges from the common assumptions in existing coalition research that the players in this game have complete and perfect information (e.g. Austen-Smith and Banks 1988; Baron 1991, 1993).[24] As we have argued above, our conception of the coalition life cycle leads us to find such assumptions fundamentally flawed for the study of democratic coalition politics. In these theoretical commitments, the present volume is motivated by two strands of microeconomic theory: transaction cost economics and bargaining theory. Because politicians face uncertainty, complexity, and risk, we direct attention to such concepts as walk-away values and opportunistic behaviour as well as to the various sources of transaction costs. These points are elaborated in Chapter 2 by Arthur Lupia and Kaare Strøm.

In that chapter, Lupia and Strøm do not attempt to present a model that explains all facets of coalition bargaining, but rather a general conception of coalition bargaining. When our contributors apply the logic and conceptual infrastructure of Chapter 2 to the separate stages of the life cycle, they do so in a way that is sensitive to—and builds on—the pre-existing literature on each topic. This also means that they are free to apply the lessons of Chapter 2 to their particular topic in the way that they best see fit. By so doing, they push the knowledge on each individual topic further. We, the editors, are convinced that our joint efforts also

---

[23] Of course, we are not the first students of coalitions to take bargaining seriously. Indeed, such considerations entered even the first generation of coalition theory, when Michael Leiserson (1966) introduced his 'bargaining proposition'. More recently, Diermeier and van Roozendaal (1998) have applied the insights of economic bargaining theory to the empirical analysis of coalition formation processes in Western Europe. But such scholarship still represents the exception, rather than the rule, in coalition studies.

[24] See, e.g., Diermeier and van Roozendaal (1998) or case studies of bargaining failures in which incomplete information figures prominently (Strøm 1994; Müller 1999, 2008).

provide a general contribution to the coalition bargaining and cabinet formation literatures.

Better data

Cross-national studies of coalition politics, and particularly those committed to an extensive research design, have tended to recycle the same, or very similar, data on the post–Second World War parliamentary democracies. We seek to improve on this state of affairs in several ways. For one thing, it is clear that we can make some improvements simply by considering a greater number of cases and especially data not previously collected. Obviously, each new generation of coalition studies has the chance to include *more observations* simply by adding data for the years that have passed since the previous one. In our case, we are able to include in our analysis the entire decade of the 1990s, which has not been well represented in previous studies. We also improve on the data in existing coalition studies by bringing in coalitional systems (such as Iceland and Portugal) that are often not included in such projects. Finally, we add an important dimension to our research by systematically comparing such coalitional systems, whenever it is appropriate, with countries (such as Greece, Spain, and the United Kingdom) in which cabinet coalitions are not common. We believe the shortage of such comparisons in the existing literature may have at least two undesirable effects. First, it tends to conceal what is common to all coalitional systems, when compared to more majoritarian parliamentary systems. Second, it may lead to systematic selection bias in the study of parliamentary cabinets.

We also improve on existing studies by adding a broad range of institutional and historical data on parliaments, cabinets, and other central institutions of parliamentary democracies. In so doing, we have benefited from previous research outside the field of coalition studies narrowly defined. For example, both historical and behaviouralist studies of cabinet governance have been useful sources of information and insight (see the chapters in Müller and Strøm 2000).

A third way to improve the data is by improving its *quality* in terms of *validity* and *reliability*. While there may not be such serious problems with regard to some 'standard' coalitions variables (such as the cabinet's party composition or date of formation), such issues are certainly real with regard to many other variables. To spell this out, it is necessary to distinguish between three different types of data commonly used in coalition research. First, the coalition literature has relied extensively on some standard secondary sources, such as Keesing's Record of World Events (before 1987: Keesing's Contemporary Archives). We shall refer to this source of information as type 1 data. Second, the coalition literature and closely associated literatures have generated their own data by sending out questionnaires to scholars in the field who are considered experts on particular countries (Laver and Hunt 1992; Druckman and Warwick 2005; Benoit and Laver 2006; Warwick 2006) (type 2 data). Finally, some coalition studies have drawn on data collected by country experts but then centrally processed and analysed, such as the electoral manifestos of political parties (Laver and Budge 1992) (type 3 data).

Each of these approaches has its advantages, as well as disadvantages. Type 1 data have the advantages of economy and of being compiled at a time close to the events (and hence are not so susceptible to interpretation in the light of subsequent developments). Yet, the second of these advantages is also a disadvantage, since much of the information may be produced hastily and without a full knowledge of the events in question. It may therefore be rather superficial. Moreover, the criteria employed in interpretation are often unclear and the quality of reporting remains uneven over time and between countries. Rightly, most research that has drawn on such data has confined itself to some simple standard variables.

Questionnaires sent to academic colleagues (type 2 data) may at first sight have the advantage of building on the wisdom of the discipline. Yet, for many countries most surveys have had to rely on a very small, sometimes tiny, number of experts. And those few respondents tend to be busy people who spend no more than a few minutes (at least this is what they are promised in the typical cover letter) of their precious research time on questions about which most of them have never thought carefully. Chased by reminders, many of them nevertheless fill in the questionnaire. The answers of those few who know more than the rest or think carefully about the questions are treated in the same way as those from their more ignorant or irresponsible colleagues.

The appropriateness of expert surveys varies according to the type of data that one wishes to collect. The politics of any country contains many facts that constitute common knowledge among its regular observers. Contemporarily these facts constitute trivial information, often not considered worth reporting in the media (because they have no news value) or in academic works (because they appear to be irrelevant). If for some reason these facts become important, it is relatively easy to collect contemporary data just by asking an appropriate sample of political observers. Going back only a few years, however, may be difficult. Another type of data is less trivial and harder to find. Perhaps it can be found somewhere in the literature, but in a language not accessible to the researcher. Still another category is information that practitioners and a few academics have come across in their research but not reported (perhaps due to confidentiality). Finally, there is information available to no one outside an inner circle of politicians.

Obviously, the survey method is less appropriate the closer we move from our first to the last type of information. And the real danger is not declining response rates, but declining quality of answers. Overly polite respondents (who send in their best guestimates) and respondents that have been mobbed into completing their questionnaires by several insistent or imploring reminders from valued colleagues will never produce reliable data.

Another potential problem in some such research, for example on political parties, is bias. Just like everybody else, academics are likely to be more sympathetic and knowledgeable about some parties than others. Thus, among European political scientists, there will be many more that are familiar with Social Democratic parties than with Christian Democrats. And most scholars who write about right-wing populist parties have probably never attended a meeting of such a party or had a serious conversation with any of its officers. While most political scientists work hard to overcome such biases in their own work, at least by not making claims about things they do not know and by trying to avoid biased research designs and one-sided interpretations, these constraints are likely to be less effective when they are filling in somebody else's questionnaire.[25]

Type 3 data have the advantage of combining country expertise (employed in the field work) and cross-national comparability. Obviously, the quality of the data depends on the care that has gone into its collection and management. Equally important is the fit between the data and the research purpose. Data that may be perfect for one purpose may not well serve a seemingly related one.[26] As more Comparative Politics data-sets become available, this is likely to become an increasing concern. The danger has certainly increased that many scholars will employ *some* existing data (as long as it bears *any* relationship to their theoretical concerns) rather than collect the really appropriate information.

In this volume, we do not use type 1 data. Occasionally, we draw on type 2 data. We use a range of type 3 data collected by other researchers. One example lies in our measures of party preferences. The early policy preference-based studies (de Swaan 1973; Dodd 1976) had to satisfy themselves with ordinal placements of parties derived from the descriptive literature of parties and party systems. Now we can draw on research locating each party in several policy dimensions for each election year (Budge et al. 2001), data that 'Finally!' allows the 'Comparative over-time mapping of party policy movement', to paraphrase Budge and Klingemann (2001).[27]

First and foremost, however, we draw on our own type 3 data. In contrast to other efforts in that tradition, we do not draw on a single source of data (such as party manifestos) but on a wide range of different ones. In collecting these data we have drawn heavily on the expertise and collaboration of country specialists. These colleagues are not just 'country experts', but also scholars in

---

[25] To the best of our knowledge, Laver and Hunt (1992: 122–32) are the only authors in this literature who have ever tried to test for respondent bias. The problem may well be more pervasive than their study suggests.

[26] This is the essence of Michael Laver and John Garry's criticism (2000) of the Manifesto Research Group project.

[27] Recent years have witnessed significant and ongoing efforts to improve on existing measures of party policy preferences. Huber and Gable (2000) have suggested a new method to calculate the Left–Right placements of parties from manifesto data, while Michael Laver and associates (Laver and Garry 2000; Laver, Benoit, and Garry 2003) have developed a computer-based technique that aims at revolutionizing the measurement of party preferences.

the field of coalition studies.[28] It is worth pointing out that our country experts have published most of the data employed in this volume under their own names (see chapters in Müller and Strøm 2000; Indridasson 2005) and hence—unlike survey respondents—have tied their professional reputations to the quality of the data. In order to ensure a high and consistent quality of data, we have kept up intense communication within the project over its lifetime by continuous face-to-face interaction (in conferences and meetings of subgroups) and the virtually (no pun intended) daily use of contemporary means of communication. While it would be unrealistic to expect that we have managed to get around the problem of inter-coder reliability entirely, the crucial question is whether we would have done better by resorting to any other method of data collection. After close to a decade of hard and painstaking work, we firmly believe that no other method would have allowed us to collect the data first presented in Müller and Strøm (2000) and now employed in this volume.

Chapter 3 and the subsequent empirical chapters will provide a detailed overview of the variables employed in this volume. Suffice it to say at the moment that we improve on existing coalition studies by bringing in data on the formation *process* (in particular on its time and bargaining rounds), the structure of coalition governance, the size and content of coalition agreements, the assignment of junior ministers, and the causes of cabinet termination. Finally, thanks to our efforts in a different project (Strøm, Müller, and Bergman 2003), we also have at our disposal the best institutional data ever employed in coalition research.

Better methods

The development of coalition studies has been paralleled by the general improvement of statistical techniques and their availability in standard computer packages. So, each successive generation of coalition studies can draw on a greater variety of increasingly appropriate tools. While the first studies using inference statistics had to satisfy themselves with OLS regression analysis, we can now avail ourselves of a rich tool kit of statistical methods that allows us to examine non-linear data, time series data, and event data (see Chapter 3). This type of progress is certainly not confined to our study. Yet, the present volume applies a range of appropriate statistical methods to an unusually broad and diverse spectrum of research questions and data. Chapter 3 maps out this range of methods and explains our

---

[28] One frequent criticism of collections of country studies is that the 'independent variable' with the greatest impact on the results is the author/country expert (Peters 1998: 53, referring to Christopher Hood). We generally agree that much research in comparative politics, in particular many projects which are one-off conference volumes or where the contributors have never met, fall into that category or are dangerously close to it. Interestingly, the various volumes consisting of studies of coalition politics in single countries have never resulted in systematic comparative research in the quantitative tradition. Yet, there are ways to get around this problem, as we explain below.

choice of specific techniques and specifications. In short, our ambition is to make better use of improvements that have been made in various parts of the discipline.

PREVIEW OF THE VOLUME

This volume is organized in accordance with the coalition life cycle we identified at the outset. Before confronting the various stages, however, we present a more thorough introduction to our theoretical framework. This is the task of Chapter 2 by Arthur Lupia and Kaare Strøm. It is followed by an account of the database of this volume and the methods applied (Chapter 3 by Torbjörn Bergman, Elisabeth R. Gerber, Scott Kastner, and Benjamin Nyblade).

The empirical chapters follow in two main sections. The first one is devoted to cabinet formation and related problems of coalition governance. It begins with an analysis of the coalition bargaining process (Chapter 4). In this chapter Lieven De Winter and Patrick Dumont focus on the duration and number of bargaining rounds. Chapter 5, by Wolfgang C. Müller and Kaare Strøm, is devoted to coalition agreements. The chapter provides an overview of the real world of coalition agreements and tries to explain the existence and types of such 'contracts'. Chapter 6, by Paul Mitchell and Benjamin Nyblade, provides an overview of the relative frequency of various government types—single party versus coalition, majority versus minority, and various types of coalition—and seeks to explain their occurrence. In Chapter 7 Luca Verzichelli addresses the issue of portfolio allocation. Taking into account the quality of offices, he takes a fresh look at the proportionality of portfolio allocation and its consequences for coalition governance.

The second main section is devoted to the tensions that governance implies and the consequences that flow from them. We begin with processes of conflict management within existing coalitions. Chapter 8, by Rudy B. Andeweg and Arco Timmermans, examines conflict resolution mechanisms. The authors map out the universe of such political devices and try to explain under which circumstances coalitions will favour one conflict resolution mechanism over the others. Even though conflicts can often be resolved, cabinet termination is always a possibility if the conflicts are serious enough. Therefore, in Chapter 9 Erik Damgaard looks directly at the events that bring down governments. Again, the chapter provides both a descriptive account and an attempt to explain the relative frequency of different terminal events. In Chapter 10 Thomas Saalfeld addresses the classic question of government duration. In the final empirical chapter Hanne Marthe Narud and Henry Valen investigate the relationship between coalition membership and electoral performance. Chapter 12 sums up the main lessons of the volume.

REFERENCES

Adrian, Charles R. and Press, Charles (1968). 'Decision Costs in Coalition Formation', *American Political Science Review*, 62: 556–63.

Aldrich, John H. (1995). *Why Parties? The Origin and Transformation of Party Politics in America*. Chicago, IL: University of Chicago Press.

Alt, James and King, Gary (1994). 'Transfer of Governmental Power', *Comparative Political Studies*, 27: 190–210.

Andeweg, Rudy B., De Winter, Lieven, and Dumont, Patrick (eds.) (2010, forthcoming). *Puzzles of Government Formation*. London: Routledge.

Andeweg, R(udy) B., van der Tak, Th(eo), and Dittrich, K(arl) (1980). 'Government Formation in The Netherlands', in Richard T. Griffiths (ed.), *The Economy and Politics of The Netherlands*. The Hague: Martinus Nijhoff.

Austen-Smith, David (1996). 'Refinements of the Heart', in Norman Schofield (ed.), *Collective Decision-Making: Social Choice and Political Economy*. Boston, MA: Kluwer.

——and Banks, Jeffrey (1988). 'Elections, Coalitions and Legislative Outcomes', *American Political Science Review*, 82: 405–22.

———— (1990). 'Stable Governments and the Allocation of Policy Portfolios', *American Political Science Review*, 84: 891–906.

Axelrod, Robert (1970). *Conflict of Interest*. Chicago, IL: Markham.

Bäck, Hanna (2003a). *Explaining Coalitions. Evidence and Lessons from Studying Coalition Formation in Swedish Local Government*. Uppsala: Uppsla Universitet.

—— (2003b). 'Explaining and Predicting Coalition Outcomes: Conclusions from Studying Data on Local Coalitions', *European Journal of Political Research*, 42: 441–72.

Bale, Tim and Bergman, Torbjörn (2006). 'Captives No Longer, But Servants Still? Contract Parliamentarism and the New Minority Governance in Sweden and New Zealand', *Government and Opposition*, 41: 422–49.

Bandyopadhyay, Siddhartha and Chatterjee, Kalyan (2006). 'Coalition Theory and Its Applications: A Survey', *Economic Journal*, 116: F136–55.

Baron, David P. (1991). 'A Spacial Bargaining Theory of Government Formation in a Parliamentary System', *American Political Science Review*, 83: 1181–206.

—— (1993). 'Government Formation and Endogenous Parties', *American Political Science Review*, 88: 33–47.

——and Diermeier, Daniel (2001). 'Elections, Governments, and Parliaments in Proportional Representation Systems', *Quarterly Journal of Economics*, 116: 933–67.

Bates, Robert H., Greif, Avner, Levi, Margaret, Rosenthal, Jean-Laurent, and Weingast, Barry R. (1998). *Analytical Narratives*. Princeton, NJ: Princeton University Press.

Benoit, Kenneth and Laver, Michael (2006). *Party Policy in Modern Democracies*. London: Routledge.

Bergman, Torbjörn (1993). 'Formation Rules and Minority Governments', *European Journal of Political Research*, 23: 55–66.

—— (1995). *Constitutional Rules and Party Goals in Coalition Formation*. Umeå: Umeå University.

——Müller, Wolfgang C., Strøm, Kaare, and Blomgren, Magnus (2003). 'Democratic Delegation and Accountability: Cross-National Patterns', in Kaare Strøm, Wolfgang C. Müller, and Torbjörn Bergman (eds.), *Delegation and Accountability in Parliamentary Democracies*. Oxford: Oxford University Press.

Bernhard, William and Leblang, David (2006). *Democratic Processes and Financial Markets. Pricing Politics*. Cambridge: Cambridge University Press.

Blais, André (1991). 'The Debate over Electoral Systems', *International Political Science Review*, 12: 239–60.

Blondel, Jean and Müller-Rommel, Ferdinand (eds.) (1993). *Governing Together*. London: Macmillan.

——— (eds.) (1997). *Cabinets in Western Europe*. London: Macmillan.

Bogdanor, Vernon (1983a). 'Introduction', in Vernon Bogdanor (ed.), *Coalition Government in Western Europe*. London: Heineman.

—— (ed.) (1983b). *Coalition Government in Western Europe*. London: Heineman.

Browne, Eric C. (1970). *Coalition Theories: A Logical and Empirical Critique*. Beverly Hills: Sage.

—— (1982). 'Introduction', in Eric C. Browne and John Dreijmanis (eds.), *Government Coalitions in Western Democracies*. New York, NY: Longman.

—— and Dreijmanis, John (eds.) (1982). *Government Coalitions in Western Democracies*. New York, NY: Longman.

—— Frendreis, John P., and Gleiber, Dennis W. (1984). 'An "Events" Approach to the Problem of Political Stability', *Comparative Political Studies*, 17: 167–97.

——————— (1986). 'The Process of Cabinet Dissolution: An Exponential Model of Duration and Stability in Western Democracies', *American Journal of Political Science*, 30: 628–50.

—— Gleibes, Dennis W., and Mashoby, Casolyn S. (1984). 'Evoluating Conflict of Interest Theory: Western European Cabinet Coalitions 1945–80', *British Journal of Political Science*, 14: 1–32.

Budge, Ian (1984). 'Parties and Democratic Government: A Framework for Comparative Explanation', *West European Politics*, 7(1): 95–118.

—— and Herman, Valentine (1978). 'Coalitions and Government Formation: An Empirically Relevant Theory', *British Journal of Political Science*, 8: 459–77.

—— and Keman, Hans (1990). *Parties and Democracy: Coalition Formation and Government Functioning in Twenty States*. Oxford: Oxford University Press.

—— and Klingemann, Hans-Dieter (2001). 'Finally! Comparative Over-Time Mapping of Party Policy Movement', in Ian Budge, et al. (eds.), *Mapping Policy Preferences. Estimates for Parties, Electors, and Governments 1945–1998*. Oxford: Oxford University Press.

—— and Laver, Michael (1986). 'Office Seeking and Policy Pursuit in Coalition Theory', *Legislative Studies Quarterly*, 11: 485–506.

———— Volkens, Andrea, Bara, Judith, and Tannenbaum, Eric (2001). *Mapping Policy Preferences. Estimates for Parties, Electors, and Governments 1945–1998*. Oxford: Oxford University Press.

Cox, Gary W. (1987). *The Efficient Secret*. Cambridge: Cambridge University Press.

—— (1997). *Making Votes Count*, Cambridge: Cambridge University Press.

Crombez, Christophe (1996). 'Minority Governments, Minimal Winning Coalitions and Surplus Majorities in Parliamentary Systems', *European Journal of Political Research*, 29: 1–29.

Dahl, Robert A. (1956). *A Preface to Democratic Theory*. Chicago, IL: University of Chicago Press.

—— (1971). *Polyarchy*. New Haven, CT: Yale University Press.

Dahl, Robert A. (1989). *Democracy and Its Critics*. New Haven, CT: Yale University Press.
—— (1998). *On Democracy*. New Haven, CT: Yale University Press.
Damgaard, Erik (1994). 'Termination of Danish Government Coalitions: Theoretical and Empirical Aspects', *Scandinavian Political Studies*, 17: 193–211.
de Swaan, Abram (1973). *Coalition Theories and Cabinet Formations*. Amsterdam: Elsevier.
De Winter, Lieven (2002). 'Political Parties and Government Formation, Portfolios and Policy Definition', in Kurt Richard Luther and Ferdinand Müller-Rommel (eds.), *Political Parties in the New Europe*. Oxford: Oxford University Press.
Diermeier, Daniel and Merlo, Antonio (2000). 'Government Turnover in Parliamentary Democracies', *Journal of Economic Theory*, 94: 46–97.
—— and van Roozendaal, Peter (1998). 'The Duration of Government Formation in Western Multi-Party Democracies', *British Journal of Political Science*, 28: 609–26.
—— and Stevenson, Randolph T. (1999). 'Cabinet Survival and Competing Risks', *American Journal of Political Science*, 43: 1051–68.
———— (2000). 'Cabinet Terminations and Critical Events', *American Political Science Review*, 94: 627–40.
—— Eraslan, Hulya, and Merlo, Antonio (2002). 'Coalition Government and Comparative Constitutional Design', *European Economic Review*, 46: 893–907.
———— (2003). 'A Structural Model of Government Formation', *Econometrica*, 71: 27–70.
Dodd, Lawrence C. (1976). *Coalitions in Parliamentary Government*. Princeton, NJ: Princeton University Press.
Downs, William M. (1998). *Coalition Government, Subnational Style*. Columbus, OH: Ohio State University Press.
Druckman, James N. and Thies, Michael F. (2002). 'The Importance of Concurrence: The Impact of Bicameralism on Government Formation and Duration', *American Journal of Political Science*, 46: 760–71.
—— and Warwick, Paul V. (2005). 'The Missing Piece: Measuring Portfolio Salience in Western European Parliamentary Democracies', *European Journal of Political Research*, 44: 17–42.
Elgie, Robert (ed.) (2001). *Divided Government in Comparative Perspective*. Oxford: Oxford University Press.
Franklin, Mark N. and Mackie, Thomas T. (1983). 'Familiarity and Inertia in the Formation of Governing Coalitions in Parliamentary Democracies', *British Journal of Political Science*, 13: 275–98.
———— (1984). 'Reassessing the Importance of Size and Ideology for the Formation of Government Coalitions in Parliamentary Democracies', *American Journal of Political Science*, 28: 671–92.
Frendreis, John P., Gleiber, Dennis W., and Browne, Eric C. (1986). 'The Study of Cabinet Dissolutions in Parliamentary Democracies', *Legislative Studies Quarterly*, 11: 619–28.
Frognier, André (1993). 'The Single-Party/Coalition Distinction and Cabinet Decision-Making', in Jean Blondal and Ferdinand Müller-Rommel (eds.), *Governing Together*. Houndmills: Macmillan.
Gamson, William A. (1961). 'A Theory of Coalition Formation', *American Sociological Review*, 26: 373–82.

Groennings, Sven, Kelley, E. W., and Leiserson, Michael (eds.) (1970). *The Study of Coalition Behavior*. New York, NY: Holt, Rinehart and Winston.

Grofman, Bernard (1982). 'A Dynamic Model of Protocoalition Formation in Ideological *N*-Space', *Behavioral Science*, 27: 77–90.

—— (1989). 'The Comparative Analysis of Coalition Formation and Duration: Distinguishing Between-Country and Within-Country Effects', *British Journal of Political Science*, 19: 291–302.

—— (1996). 'Extending a Dynamic Model of Protocoalition Formation', in Norman Schofield (ed.), *Collective Decision-Making: Social Choice and Political Economy*. Boston, MA: Kluwer.

—— and van Roozendaal, Peter (1994). 'Toward a Theoretical Explanation of Premature Cabinet Termination', *European Journal of Political Research*, 26: 155–70.

———— (1997). 'Review Article: Modelling Cabinet Durability and Termination', *British Journal of Political Science*, 27: 419–51.

—— Straffin, Philip, and Noviello, Nicholas (1996). 'The Sequential Dynamics of Cabinet Formation, Stochastic Error, and a Test of Competing Models', in Norman Schofield (ed.), *Collective Decision-Making: Social Choice and Political Economy*. Boston, MA: Kluwer.

Headey, Bruce (1974). *British Cabinet Ministers*. London: Allen & Unwin.

Heller, William B. (2001). 'Making Policy Stick: Why the Government Gets What It Wants in Multiparty Parliaments', *American Journal of Political Science*, 45: 780–98.

Huber, John D. (1996). 'The Vote of Confidence in Parliamentary Democracies', *American Political Science Review*, 90: 269–82.

—— and Gable, Matthew J. (2000). 'Putting Parties in Their Place: Inferring Party Left–Right Ideological Positions from Party Manifesto Data', *American Journal of Political Science*, 44: 94–103.

—— and McCarty, Nolan (2001). 'Cabinet Decision Rules and Political Uncertainty in Parliamentary Bargaining', *American Political Science Review*, 95: 345–60.

Indridason, Indridi H. (2005). 'A Theory of Coalitions and Clientelism: Coalition Politics in Iceland, 1945–2000', *European Journal of Political Research*, 44: 439–64.

Jungar, Ann-Cathrine (2000). *Surplus Majority Government. A Comparative Study of Italy and Finland*. Uppsala: Uppsla Universitet.

King, Gary, Alt, James, Burns, Nancy, and Laver, Michael (1990). 'A Unified Model of Cabinet Dissolution in Parliamentary Democracies', *American Journal of Political Science*, 34: 846–71.

Klingemann, Hans-Dieter and Wessels, Bernhard (2001). 'The Political Consequences of Germany's Mixed-Member System: Personalisation at the Grass Roots?', in Matthew Soberg Shugart and Martin P. Wattenberg (eds.), *Mixed-Member Electoral Systems*. Oxford: Oxford University Press.

Kreps, David M. (1990). *A Course in Microeconomic Theory*. New York, NY: Harvester Wheatsheaf.

Kropp, Sabine, Schüttemeyer, Suzanne S., and Sturm, Roland (eds.) (2002). *Koalitionen in Western- und Osteuropa*. Opladen: Leske+Budrich.

Laver, Michael (1974). 'Dynamic Factors in Government Coalition Formation', *European Journal of Political Research*, 2: 259–70.

Laver, Michael (1986). 'Between Theoretical Elegance and Political Reality: Deductive Models and Cabinet Coalitions in Europe', in Geoffrey Pridham (ed.), *Coalition Behaviour in Theory and Practice*. Cambridge: Cambridge University Press.

——(1997). *Private Desires, Political Action*. London: Sage.

——(1998). 'Models of Government Formation', *Annual Review of Political Science*, 1: 1–25.

——(2000). 'STV and the Politics of Coalition', in Shaun Bowler and Bernard Grofman (eds.), *Elections in Australia, Ireland, and Malta under the Single Transferable Vote*. Ann Arbor, MI: University of Michigan Press.

——(2003). 'Government Termination', *Annual Review of Political Science*, 6: 23–40.

——and Budge, Ian (eds.) (1992). *Party Policy and Coalition Government*. London: Macmillan.

——and Garry, John (2000). 'Estimating Policy Positions from Political Texts', *American Journal of Political Science*, 44: 619–34.

——and Hunt, Ben W. (1992). *Policy and Party Competition*. New York, NY: Routledge.

——and Schofield, Norman (1990). *Multiparty Government*. Oxford: Oxford University Press.

——and Shepsle, Kenneth A. (1990). 'Coalitions and Cabinet Government', *American Political Science Review*, 84: 873–90.

————(eds.) (1994). *Cabinet Ministers and Parliamentary Government*. Cambridge: Cambridge University Press.

————(1996). *Making and Breaking Governments: Cabinets and Legislatures in Parliamentary Democracies*. Cambridge: Cambridge University Press.

————(1998). 'Events, Equilibria, and Government Survival', *American Journal of Political Science*, 42: 28–54.

——Benoit, Kenneth, and Garry, John (2003). 'Extracting Policy Positions from Political Texts Using Words as Data', *American Political Science Review*, 97: 311–31.

Leiserson, Michael (1966). *Coalitions in Politics: A Theoretical and Empirical Study*. Ph.D. dissertation: Yale University.

Lijphart, Arend (1971). 'Comparative Politics and the Comparative Method', *American Political Science Review*, 65: 682–93.

——(1994). *Electoral Systems and Party Systems*. Oxford: Oxford University Press.

——(1995). 'The Virtues of Parliamentarism: But Which Kind of Parliamentarism?' in H. E. Chehabi and Alfred Stepan (eds.), *Politics, Society, and Democracy: Comparative Studies*. Boulder, CO: Westview Press.

——(1999). *Patterns of Democracy*. New Haven, CN: Yale University Press.

Luebbert, Gregory M. (1986). *Comparative Democracy. Policymaking and Governing Coalitions in Europe and Israel*. New York, NY: Columbia University Press.

Lupia, Arthur and Strøm, Kaare (1995). 'Coalition Termination and the Strategic Timing of Parliamentary Elections', *American Political Science Review*, 89: 648–65.

Martin, Lanny W. (2004). 'The Government Agenda in Parliamentary Democracies', *American Journal of Political Science*, 48: 445–61.

——and Stevenson, Randolph T. (2001). 'Government Formation in Parliamentary Democracies', *American Journal of Political Science*, 45: 33–50.

——and Vanberg, Georg (2003). 'Wasting Time? The Impact of Ideology and Size on Delay in Coalition Formation', *British Journal of Political Science*, 33: 323–44.

—— and Vanberg, Georg (2004). 'Policing the Bargain: Coalition Government and Parliamentary Scrutiny', *American Journal of Political Science*, 48: 13–27.

Mattila, Mikko and Raunio, Tapio (2002). 'Government Formation in the Nordic Countries: The Electoral Connection', *Scandinavian Political Studies*, 25: 259–80.

—— —— (2004). 'Does Winning Pay? Electoral Success and Government Formation in 15 West European Countries', *European Journal of Political Research*, 43: 263–85.

Mellors, Colin and Pijnenburg, Bert (eds.) (1989). *Political Parties and Coalitions in European Local Government*. London: Routledge.

Mershon, Carol (2002). *The Costs of Coalition*. Stanford, CA: Stanford University Press.

Milnor, A. J. (1969). *Elections and Political Stability*. Boston, MA: Little, Brown.

Mueller, Dennis C. (2003). *Public Choice III*. Cambridge: Cambridge University Press.

Müller, Wolfgang C. (1999). 'Decision for Opposition: The Austrian Socialist Party's Abandonment of Government Participation in 1966', in Wolfgang C. Müller and Kaare Strøm (eds.), *Policy, Office, or Votes?* Cambridge: Cambridge University Press.

—— (2000*a*). 'Political Parties in Parliamentary Democracies: Making Delegation and Accountability Work', *European Journal of Political Research*, 37: 309–33.

—— (2000*b*). 'Austria: Tight Coalitions and Stable Government', in Wolfgang C. Müller and Kaare Strøm (eds.), *Coalition Governments in Western Europe*. Oxford: Oxford University Press.

—— (2004*a*). 'Koalitionstheorien', in Ludger Helms and Uwe Jun (eds.), *Politische Theorie und Regierungslehre*. Frankfurt am Main: Campus.

—— (2004*b*). 'Die Relevanz von Institutionen für Koalitionstreue: theoretische Überlegungen und Beobachtungen zur Bundesrepublik Deutschland', in Philip Manow and Steffen Ganghof (eds.), *Theoretische Perspektiven auf das deutsche Regierungssystem*. Frankfurt am Main: Campus.

—— (2006). 'Regierung und Kabinettsystem', in Herbert Dachs et al. (eds.), *Politik in Österreich: Das Handbuch*. Vienna: Manz.

—— (2008, forthcoming). 'Successful Failure: Ill-Conceived Pre-Commitments and Welcome Bargaining Failure Paving the Way to Minority Government in Austria', in Lieven De Winter, Rudy B. Andeweg, and Patrick Dumont (eds.), *Puzzles of Government Formation*. London: Routledge.

Müller, Wolfgang C. and Strøm, Kaare (eds.) (1999). *Policy, Office, or Votes? How Political Parties in Western Europe Make Hard Decisions*. Cambridge: Cambridge University Press.

—— —— (eds.) (2000). *Coalition Governments in Western Europe*. Oxford: Oxford University Press.

Nordhaus, William A. (1975). 'The Political Business Cycle', *Review of Economic Studies*, 42: 169–90.

Nousiainen, Jaakko (2000). 'Finland: The Consolidation of Parliamentary Governance', in Wolfgang C. Müller and Kaare Strøm (eds.), *Coalition Governments in Western Europe*. Oxford: Oxford University Press.

Pappi, Franz Urban and Thurner, Paul W. (2002). 'Electoral Behavior in a Two-Vote-System: Incentives for Ticket Splitting in German Bundestag Elections', *European Journal of Political Research*, 41: 207–32.

Peters, B. Guy (1998). *Comparative Politics: Theory and Methods*. New York, NY: New York University Press.

Powell, G. Bingham (2000). *Elections as Instruments of Democracy. Majoritarian and Proportional Visions*. New Haven, CT: Yale University Press.
Pridham, Geoffrey (ed.) (1986). *Coalition Behaviour in Theory and Practice: An Inductive Model for Western Europe*. Cambridge: Cambridge University Press.
Ragin, Charles C. (1987). *The Comparative Method*. Berkeley, CA: University of California Press.
—— (2000). *Fuzzy-Set Social Science*. Chicago, IL: University of Chicago Press.
Reynolds, Andrew and Elklit, Jørgen (2005). 'A Framework for the Systematic Study of Election Quality', *Democratization*, 12: 147–62.
Riker, William H. (1962). *The Theory of Political Coalitions*. New Haven, CN: Yale University Press.
Rudzio, Wolfgang (2003). *Das politische System der Bundesrepublik Deutschland*. Opladen: Leske + Budrich.
Saalfeld, Thomas (2000). 'Germany: Stable Parties, Chancellor Democracy, and the Art of Informal Settlement', in Wolfgang C. Müller and Kaare Strøm (eds.), *Coalition Governments in Western Europe*. Oxford: Oxford University Press.
—— (2003). 'The United Kingdom: Still a Single "Chain of Command"? The Hollowing Out of the "Westminister Model"', in Kaare Strøm, Wolfgang C. Müller, and Torbjörn Bergman (eds.), *Delegation and Accountability in Parliamentary Democracies*. Oxford: Oxford University Press.
Sanders, David and Herman, Valentine (1977). 'The Survival and Stability of Governments in Western Democracies', *Acta Politica*, 3: 346–77.
Sartori, Giovanni (1984). 'Guidelines for Conceptual Analysis', in Giovani Sartori (ed.), *Social Science Concepts: A Systematic Analysis*. Beverly Hills, CA: Sage.
—— (1987). *The Theory of Democracy Revisited*, two volumes. Chatham, NJ: Chatham House.
Schattschneider, E. E. (1960). *The Semisovereign People*. New York, NY: Holt, Rinehart and Winston.
Schofield, Norman (1987). 'Stability of Coalition Governments in Western Europe: 1945–1986', *European Journal of Political Economy*, 3: 555–91.
—— (1993). 'Political Competition in Multiparty Coalition Governments', *European Journal of Political Research*, 23: 1–33.
—— (1995). 'Coalition Politics: A Formal Model and Empirical Analysis', *Journal of Theoretical Politics*, 7: 245–81.
—— (1997). 'Multiparty Electoral Politics', in Dennis C. Mueller (ed.), *Perspectives on Public Choice*. Cambridge: Cambridge University Press.
—— and Laver, Michael J. (1985). 'Bargaining Theory and Portfolio Payoffs in European Coalition Governments 1945–83', *British Journal of Political Science*, 15: 143–64.
—— and Sened, Itai (2006). *Multiparty Democracy: Elections and Legislative Politics*. Cambridge: Cambridge University Press.
Schumpeter, Joseph A. (1942). *Capitalism, Socialism and Democracy*. New York, NY: Harper & Brothers.
Siaroff, Alan (2003). 'Spurious Majorities, Electoral Systems and Electoral System Change', *Commonwealth & Comparative Politics*, 41: 143–60.
Sjölin, Mats (1993). *Coalition Politics and Parliamentary Power*. Lund: Lund University Press.

Sjöblom, Gunnar (1977). 'The Cumulation Problem in Political Science: An Essay on Research Strategies', *European Journal of Political Science*, 5: 1–32.
Smith, Alastair (2004). *Election Timing*. Cambridge: Cambridge University Press.
Strøm, Kaare (1986). 'Deferred Gratification and Minority Governments in Scandinavia', *Legislative Studies Quarterly*, 11: 583–605.
—— (1990a). *Minority Government and Majority Rule*. Cambridge: Cambridge University Press.
—— (1990b). 'A Behavioral Theory of Competitive Political Parties', *American Journal of Political Science*, 34: 565–98.
—— (1994). 'The Presthus Debacle: Intraparty Politics and Bargaining Failure in Norway', *American Political Science Review*, 88: 112–27.
—— and Müller, Wolfgang C. (1999). 'The Keys to Togetherness: Coalition Agreements in Parliamentary Democracies', *Journal of Legislative Studies*, 5 (3/4): 255–82.
—— and Swindle, Stephen M. (2002). 'Strategic Parliamentary Dissolution', *American Political Science Review*, 96: 575–91.
—— Budge, Ian, and Laver, Michael J. (1994). 'Constraints on Cabinet Formation in Parliamentary Democracies', *American Journal of Political Science*, 38: 303–35.
—— Müller, Wolfgang C., and Bergman, Torbjörn (eds.) (2003). *Delegation and Accountability in Parliamentary Democracies*. Oxford: Oxford University Press.
—— Browne, Eric C., Frendreis, John P., and Gleiber, Dennis W. (1988). 'Contending Models of Cabinet Stability: A Controversy', *American Political Science Review*, 82: 923–41.
Taagepera, Rein and Shugart, Matthew S. (1989). *Seats and Votes*. Cambridge: Cambridge University Press.
Taylor, Michael and Herman, Valentine M. (1971). 'Party Systems and Government Stability', *American Political Science Review*, 65: 28–37.
Taylor, Michael and Laver, Michael (1973). 'Government Coalitions in Western Europe', *European Journal of Political Research*, 1: 205–48.
Thiébault, Jean-Louis (2000). 'France: Forming and Maintaining Government Coalitions in the Fifth Republic', in Wolfgang C. Müller and Kaare Strøm (eds.), *Coalition Governments in Western Europe*. Oxford: Oxford University Press.
Thies, Michael F. (2001). 'Keeping Tabs on Partners: The Logic of Delegation in Coalition Governments', *American Journal of Political Science*, 45: 580–98.
Timmermans, Arco (1998). 'Conflicts, Agreements, and Coalition Governance', *Acta Politica*, 33: 409–32.
—— (2003). *High Politics in the Low Countries: An Empirical Study of Coalition Agreements in Belgium and the Netherlands*. Aldershot: Ashgate.
—— (2006). 'Standing Apart and Sitting Together: Enforcing Coalition Agreements in Multiparty Systems', *European Journal of Political Research*, 45: 263–83.
Tsebelis, George (2002). *Veto Players. How Institutions Work*. New York, NY: Russel Sage Foundation and Princeton, NJ: Princeton University Press.
van Deemen, A. M. A. (1989). 'Dominant Players and Minimum Size Coalitions', *European Journal of Political Research*, 17: 313–32.
—— (1991). 'Coalition Formation in Centralized Policy Games', *Journal of Theoretical Politics*, 3: 139–61.
van Roozendaal, Peter (1990). 'Center Parties and Coalition Cabinet Formation: A Game Theoretic Approach', *European Journal of Political Research*, 18: 324–48.

van Roozendaal, Peter (1997). 'Government Survival in Western Multi-Party Democracies', *European Journal of Political Research*, 32: 71–92.
von Beyme, Klaus (1985). *Political Parties in Western Democracies*. London: Gower.
von Neumann, John and Morgenstern, Oskar (1953). *Theory of Games and Economic Behavior*. Princeton, NJ: Princeton University Press.
Volden, Craig and Carrubba, Clifford J. (2004). 'The Formation of Oversized Coalitions in Parliamentary Democracies', *American Journal of Political Science*, 43: 521–37.
Ware, Alan (1987). *Citizens, Parties and the State*. Cambridge: Polity Press.
Warwick, Paul V. (1994). *Government Survival in Parliamentary Democracies*. Cambridge: Cambridge University Press.
——(1996). 'Coalition Government Membership in West European Parliamentary Democracies', *British Journal of Political Science*, 26: 471–99.
——(2000). 'Policy Horizons in West European Parliamentary Systems', *European Journal of Political Research*, 38: 37–61.
——(2006). *Policy Horizons and Parliamentary Government*. Houndmills: Palgrave-Macmillan.
Williamson, Oliver E. (1985). *Markets and Hierarchies*. New York, NY: Free Press.
——(1996). *The Mechanisms of Governance*. Oxford: Oxford University Press.
Wright, John R. and Goldberg, Arthur S. (1985). 'Risk and Uncertainty as Factors in the Durability of Political Coalitions', *American Political Science Review*, 79: 704–18.

2

Bargaining, Transaction Costs, and Coalition Governance

Arthur Lupia and Kaare Strøm[1]

INTRODUCTION

Representative democracies face two fundamental challenges, delegation and coalescence. Delegation is necessary because most citizens have neither the capacity nor the time to make many important political decisions on their own. To facilitate large-scale governance, delegation must occur. Citizens must find and select representatives whom they can trust to make public policy in accordance with particular principles. Elected representatives, in turn, must delegate to leaders of political parties or bureaucratic agencies to further the pursuit of policy goals. Heads of executive agencies have to delegate to their subordinates. While delegation makes large-scale representative democracy possible, it is not without risk. Problems of delegation need to be overcome. For with the power of the elective or appointive office also come opportunities to act against the public interest.

The second challenge is coalition-building. Coalescence is necessary because representative democracies typically produce a multitude of political actors and because democratic rules often require that decisions be supported by a simple or qualified majority of the representatives in a national legislature. In a democracy, no one person can legislate or make power without the support of others. To facilitate large-scale governance, coalitions must be built. To pass laws or implement public policy, at least some of the agents that are empowered to act on citizens' behalf must find a way to work with others who are also empowered.

All representative democracies of necessity face both of these challenges, and the ways in which they solve or confront them in the long run has a decisive influence on the feasibility and quality of democratic governance. If the problem of delegation is not solved, then we may end up with a 'democratic deficit' in

---

[1] We thank Torbjörn Bergman, James N. Druckman, Jesse Menning, Wolfgang C. Müller, Gisela Sin, and participants at Coalition Governance conferences in Vienna, Siena, and Canterbury for helpful suggestions. The authors acknowledge the support of the Center for Advanced Study in the Behavioural Sciences (CASBS).

which political representatives do not enjoy the trust of their constituents. The political order may be illegitimate in the eyes of many citizens, and therefore fragile. If coalescence does not occur, then the same representatives may not be able to make authoritative decisions. The result may be gridlock or 'immobilism'. In either case, the prospects for democratic rule are gloomy.

The challenges of delegation and coalition are not wholly distinct. In fact, they intersect in the coalition life cycle described in Chapter 1. It is the electoral setting that integrates these demands. While most democratically elected politicians work in coalitions with others on a daily basis, many such actions occur in the shadow of elections. Many politicians act knowing that the electorate that once delegated power to them will have an opportunity to take it away in the future. When coalescing, politicians must keep in mind their delegation relationship with the voters. When delegating, in turn, citizens and elected representatives are generally aware that the needs and desires of relevant political coalitions will affect the consequences of delegating to particular people.

In a previous study (Strøm, Müller, and Bergman 2003) we have explored at length the challenges of delegation in contemporary Western European democracies. Although in this book we shall frequently refer to and build on the lessons of that previous effort, our purpose here is different. Here, we turn our attention to questions of coalescence.

The previous chapter accounts for the ways in which coalition formation, maintenance, and termination in parliamentary democracies have been understood. In this chapter, we shall delve more deeply into the questions of what such political coalitions are, why they exist, and how they operate. The answers that we shall provide to these questions will inform the analysis that will be presented in the various empirical chapters in this volume.

To begin at the beginning, a coalition is a team of individuals or groups that unites for joint action. In many countries, teams of political parties coalesce for the purpose of running a government. Together, these coalition members convert a wide range of social demands into a manageable set of state-sanctioned activities. While working for a common cause, coalition members may disagree about important matters. Some disagreements come from members' attempts to please distinct constituencies (e.g. members who represent urbanites want different policies than members who represent rural regions). Conflicts can also arise from self-interest when multiple members crave a particular seat of power (e.g. that of the prime minister). How coalition members cultivate their common interests and manage internal conflicts affects the fate and effectiveness of the governments they run. Throughout this book, we study these decisions in order to better understand coalition governance around the world.

In this chapter, we offer a theoretical framework. It yields clarifying generalizations about coalition behaviour in political contexts. While this framework can be applied to governance dynamics in many nations, we focus on Western Europe's parliamentary democracies.

Generalizing about coalition politics is no trivial matter. Every country challenges those who govern it with a unique mix of historical precedents, democratic principles, political institutions, social conventions, and popular demands. It is natural, therefore, to expect that accounts that clarify one country's coalition politics will seem bizarre when applied elsewhere.

Consider, for example, the coalition politics of Italy, which since 1945 has averaged approximately one new cabinet every 13 months. This frequency of cabinet turnover is the highest in Western Europe. It is indeed more than twice the average for the region (Müller and Strøm 2000: 561). At the same time, Italian politics was uniquely stable in that for more than a third of a century (1945–81) a single political party (the Christian Democrats) dominated every government and accounted for every single person that passed through the revolving door that the Italian prime ministership often resembled. If a theoretical framework can explain important aspects of coalition governance in this unusual circumstance, can we use it to better explain coalition governance in other countries? Throughout this book, we answer 'Yes'.

Our approach builds on the premise that parliaments are deliberately organized to recognize and reinforce a central role for political parties (Müller 2000).[2] Hence, we examine coalition governance by focusing on how political parties juggle the interests of constituents and coalition partners when making critical decisions (e.g. coalition formation, policymaking, ministerial replacements, and the timing of elections). This is not to say that what happens inside parties is not important for understanding cabinet politics. Several chapters will in fact show that intra-party politics can systematically affect inter-party bargaining. Our approach is rather built on a pragmatic recognition that a full account of intra-party politics would be far beyond our capabilities in this project, and that as analysts we benefit from the fact that, for better or worse, parties have a strong incentive to maintain cohesion within their ranks.

Our framework has six components. Five of these come from established approaches to the study of coalition governance. While these components are often used one-at-a-time, we produce additional insights by integrating them into a unified framework. The sixth component, our framework's backbone, provides the means for integration. Components (1) through (5) are as follows:

(1) *Exogenous contextual factors, while important, are not the whole story.* A venerable tradition in the social sciences emphasizes the uniqueness of the

---

[2] The behaviour of political parties can, in principle, be understood as an interaction between party members, officers, and activists (see, e.g. Strøm 1994). Yet, any systematic and tractable version of such an account is beyond the grasp of current social science. Thankfully, most political parties are sufficiently institutionalized and hierarchical that many of their behaviours in the legislative setting can be understood as if they were those of a person. So, throughout this book, we assume that we can treat parties, or more specifically their parliamentary leaderships, as if they were unitary actors (see Laver and Schofield 1990; for a more elaborate exposition, see Müller and Strøm 1999: ch. 1).

contexts in which collective decisions are made. These accounts tend to highlight factors associated with the particular community in which events take place. Such accounts may seek causality in aspects of a country's culture and history. It is often argued, and no doubt true, that political decisions reflect peculiar characteristics of a national or other systemic context that are not easily captured in the form of discrete and parsimoniously defined variables. Applied to the Italian propensity for cabinet turnover cited above, such accounts might privilege particularly Italian conditions such as its culture of distrust (Banfield 1958).

A second type of account in this broad tradition stresses the historical precedents of social events. The argument is that each community is profoundly and pervasively influenced by its own past, in ways that can be neither modelled parsimoniously nor ignored. Moreover, each new historical event adds to a society's uniqueness and further constrains all future decisions. This is the argument of path dependency. A strong version of this argument would imply that political decisions are so heavily conditioned by past choices that there can be no meaningful comparisons across political settings with different histories (see Thelen and Steinmo 1992 for a review). If path dependence is indeed a fruitful perspective, then one must seek the explanation of, for example, what happened in Italy in 1950 in the events of previous years in the same country, such as its late unification or the legacy of fascism.

Contextual arguments may also stress the importance of shared, rather than separate, experiences. According to this logic, political events are determined by contemporaneous events, even if these occur in mutually remote locations. This view presumes that politicians in different countries live interdependent lives, in which they may be subject to a 'mood' of the times or simultaneously influenced by shared experience of traumatic periods such as the Great Depression or the Second World War. The mood of the times may be diffused through the common icons or symbols of a period. If such common experiences are indeed decisive, then coalition decisions of the 1950s, for example, can only be understood in that historical context, and not within those of the 1980s or 1990s. Whether one stresses cultural uniqueness, path dependency, or a shared history, however, the implication for scientific work is that once an analyst controls for context, there is little left to explain.

Yet, accounts that stress the uniqueness of time and space cannot both hold for the same phenomena. If path dependency is strictly the key to party behaviour, then similarities across countries cannot also be due to common and contemporary experiences. Despite profoundly different historical paths, many European societies, including such unlikely cases as the Netherlands and Switzerland, have in recent years witnessed the growth of populist right-wing parties. On the other hand, the pervasive 'mood' of European secularization has been reflected in party systems in surprisingly varied ways. Why, for example, did Christian Democrats in the 1990s collapse in Italy, weaken in the Netherlands, but experience exhilarating new highs in highly secular Sweden?

Approaches that stress either path dependency or other contextual factors thus seem inconsistent with the observed trajectories of political representation in contemporary democracies. Invocations of time and place clearly cannot fully substitute for more fine-grained scholarly analysis. Our own conviction is to be somewhat more ambitious on behalf of political theory. In this and subsequent chapters, we show that while temporal and country-specific effects can be important, they do not provide the whole story.

(2) *Resource distribution among political actors, while important, is not the whole story.* Some observers see political life as a contest between large and powerful political forces (e.g. Miliband 1990) in which resources ultimately decide the winners. As Stein Rokkan (1966: 105) succinctly put it, 'Votes count, but resources decide.' Such perspectives are often coupled, though they need not be, with structural understandings of political contestations. In the context of parliamentary politics, proponents of such views may contend that bigger is always better. Hence, the most important asset that a political party can bring to the political bargaining table is the size of its parliamentary delegation, complemented, perhaps, by currencies such as money. In the Italian case cited above, this approach could portray cabinet turnover as the consequence of a stand-off between two powerful forces in Italian politics: the Christian Democrats and the Communists.

While politics is often dominated by the strong and the resourceful, such domination is neither inevitable nor is it sufficient to explain many past events. In the early 1980s, for example, Italian politics did indeed seem dominated by the parties of Christian Democracy and Communism, respectively. Yet, in 1981 the Christian Democrats had to give over the prime ministership to the much smaller and less imposing Republican Party (PRI), and within about 10 years both of the once so dominant parties were effectively dead and gone.

(3) *Politicians' preferences, while important, are not the whole story.* The two perspectives we have identified above account for many of the classic studies of coalition politics. If the emphasis on country-specific and historical factors dominated the discipline up to the 1960s, the behavioural revolution brought resource questions to the fore. Riker's seminal coalition theory (1962) shifted scholarly attention to the motivations and strategic interactions of political parties. Subsequent scholars have contended that contextual factors and resources alone are insufficient explanations of coalition politics.

Some argue for a direct link between politicians' policy preferences and coalition decisions—a link that cultural factors, resources, and institutions do not affect. One manifestation of this idea is that if two parties share common policy agendas (or have policy ideal points that are close to one another), then they will have a stronger, more effective, and longer-lasting coalition than will coalitions with less common agendas (De Swaan 1973; Warwick 1994). Applied to the Italian case cited above, the argument might be that the large differences in policy preferences between Christian Democrats, Communists, and Neo-fascists make coalition bargaining difficult—and that such interests would clash under any institution, political resource distribution, or flag.

But politics sometimes makes for strange bedfellows. Countries such as Finland and the Netherlands have in recent years experienced the formation of 'purple' or 'rainbow' coalitions of ideologically very diverse parties. Even more so, studies of subnational coalitions have shown a surprising incidence of partnerships that fly in the face of those that exist at the national level and that seem to defy explanation in terms of common policy preferences (Downs 1999; Bäck 2003). In this and the chapters that follow, we argue that while preference-based hypotheses sometimes have great explanatory power, there are also contexts in which they explain very little or yield mistaken conclusions.

(4) *Institutions, while important, are not the whole story.* Another view is that institutions drive coalition politics. A strong version of the institutionalist position holds that particular institutions (such as a proportional electoral system, a constructive vote of no confidence, a powerful legislative committee structure, or an investiture requirement) have consistent effects on coalition politics, regardless of national setting, resource distribution, or the personalities involved. In the Italian example, this view could imply not only that electoral and legislative rules generate the high frequency of coalitional change but also that if you changed the nationality of the participants, while leaving the institutions constant, the outcome would be the same. Institutionalist ideas are implicit in many writings on coalition government, including the 'structural attributes' literature on cabinet duration and the literature on bargaining constraints (see, e.g., Powell 1982; Laver and Schofield 1990; Strøm, Budge, and Laver 1994; Lijphart 1999).

Institutions surely affect coalition politics, and it is important to understand their effects. We concur with scholars such as Luebbert (1986: 29–44) that institutions privilege certain behaviours. We also agree that institutions can shape the expectations and preferences of political actors. But if institutions are the sole factor in explaining coalition decision-making, then the implication for empirical work is that once an analyst controls for institutional differences, there is little left to explain. To put it starkly, if only Iraq were to adopt the institutions of New Zealand, the politics of the two countries would be interchangeable. To our regret, we suspect that reality is more complex. Throughout this book, we clarify how institutional effects depend on, and are affected by, other factors.

(5) *Critical events, while important, are not the whole story.* Finally, there are also those that stress the importance of critical events in shaping modern elite-level politics. The Great Depression brought to power many political parties with radical policy agendas and indeed brought down democracy in a number of countries. The oil crisis of the 1970s resulted in severe losses for governing parties, whoever they happened to be, all over the Western world. The collapse

of the Soviet Union and its European empire in the late 1980s and early 1990s embarrassed and severely weakened communist parties all over Western Europe. Critical events may also take more modest forms and be confined to specific countries. Thus, coalition politics may be substantially affected by national events such as political scandals, bankruptcies, natural disasters, crimes, the sexual escapades of politicians, or even the fortunes of cherished national athletes (e.g. the national football team).

Since the early 1980s, students of coalitions have tried to take the importance of political events seriously, and some have gone so far as to argue that the importance of such unpredictable factors obliterates any effort to account for coalition politics in deterministic ways (see Browne, Frendreis, and Gleiber 1986). But while critical events can certainly play a major role in coalition politics, they do not seem to preclude any attempt to account for coalition bargaining in systematic terms. Indeed, we shall argue that we can best capture the significance of critical events within a larger theoretical framework.

Bargaining requirements provide an organizing framework

Each of the five perspectives names a determinant of coalition behaviour. The primary theme of this book is that when factors such as these are examined together, within a unified framework, they can teach us even more. Our framework's final component provides a means of unification. This component begins with the fact that all members of potential governing coalitions—regardless of country, resources, institutions, or preferences—face a common prize and a common problem. The prize is the opportunities for gain, honour, and policy advantage that control of the national government affords. The problem of the same contestants is that to reap the benefits of governing, they must satisfy two requirements simultaneously:

1. **Form and maintain agreements with other parties**.
2. **Please voters**.

This is seldom easy. It is made difficult when a party's electoral constituents and coalition partners want different things. It is even more difficult when a party's political goals—such as enacting a wide-ranging policy agenda—necessitate that both requirements are met for an extended period.[3] Yet, challenging as it may

---

[3] This is why credibility can be such a difficult problem in democratic politics. The problem is not just that it takes time to forge and implement political agreements. For such agreements to be effective, it is often also necessary for other political elites and ordinary citizens to act in compliance, which they may not do unless they believe that the agreements, or the coalitions that sustain them, will endure. Consider, for example, tax schemes intended to promote investment or any policy that requires costs paid now in exchange for future benefits. If potential investors perceive a coalition government as unwilling or unable to repay such debts in the future, they may be less likely to contribute or make

be, parties must respond to both demands. Parties that fail to cultivate voter support are replaced in parliament by parties that succeed, while parties that fail to maintain coalition agreements are replaced in cabinets by parties that can. For these reasons, coalition members have an incentive to engage in coalition bargaining thinking not just about their present desires, but also about *the shadow of the future* (i.e. the likely reactions of voters and political opponents).

This representation of coalition politics is the backbone of our framework. At every stage of a coalition's life cycle, *coalition decisions are the result of bargaining, in which every bargaining outcome is the result not only of past bargains that affect history, institutions, and members' resources but also of the fact that bargaining occurs in the shadow of citizen opinions and under the constant threat posed by political rivals who want to replace those in office.*

Our bargaining-based framework will clarify how each of the components listed above influences coalition decisions. It can be applied at every stage of a coalition's life cycle, it answers important questions about when one component (i.e. country-specific attributes) dominates another (i.e. institutional), and it clarifies how uncertainty affects all components. Various applications of this framework throughout this book will also reveal the limitations inherent in attempts to simplify the analysis of coalition governance by turning a blind eye to the necessity of bargaining, to the anticipated response of the electorate, or to the shadow cast by threats to the incumbent coalition. While removing such factors can simplify analyses, the practice can yield erroneous conclusions.

This chapter continues as follows. In the second section, we introduce our theoretical framework. In the third section, we offer an example of the framework's usefulness—we use it to correct errors in widely held beliefs about the timing and nature of a coalition's decision to terminate. The fourth section summarizes our findings.

BARGAINING: THE ENGINE OF COALITION GOVERNANCE

Coalition decisions are the product of agreements between coalition members—each of whom, if they want to remain on the governing team, must satisfy the two requirements of coalition participation. Bargaining is the means by which such agreements are usually reached. With these facts in mind, we present a framework whose purpose is to clarify fundamental aspects of coalition bargaining. We introduce it first in the context of answering simple questions about coalition governance. As this chapter proceeds, we use it to engage increasingly complex situations. Throughout, we denote key concepts in **bold**.

sacrifices in the present. Indeed, economic downturns may make it extremely expensive to live up to commitments made in rosier times. Coalitions seen as unlikely to keep promises in such times will have a harder time making their policies work.

Our main premises are as follows:

- Bargaining is the means by which parties attempt to satisfy the first requirement of coalition participation—to form and maintain agreements with other coalition partners.
- Who gets what in coalition bargaining depends on what political parties can offer to one another. Which offers parties will make and accept depends on country-specific factors, institutions, party preferences, voter support, the complexity of the agreements being sought, and party leaders' beliefs about an uncertain future.
- Voter support—the second requirement for coalition participation—in turn depends on the qualities of the agreements that parties strike.
- At any stage in a coalition's life cycle (e.g. formation, policymaking, conflict management, termination) the outcome of the bargaining process depends on the past as well as the present. The past determines the resources that different players have available to them. Past bargains also affect the history and institutions under which bargaining occurs. The future affects the participants' expectations about the kinds of bargains they should accept. While most scholars have treated the different stages of bargaining as distinct, our approach implies that bargaining dynamics and outcomes at every stage of the process are inextricably linked to one another.

Let us now define the key terms of our approach. **Bargaining** is a process by which actors engage in communication for the purpose of finding a mutually beneficial agreement. Bargaining is required to reach such agreements, if

1. there exist individual benefits that can only be achieved through collective action,
2. there are multiple ways of distributing the benefits associated with such actions, and
3. no actor can simply impose a collective arrangement upon everyone else.

By **individual benefits** we mean that potential partners can accomplish more as a coalition than they can otherwise (i.e. party 1 acting alone can produce social output X, party 2 acting alone can produce social output Y, the parties acting together can produce social output Z and there is a way to distribute the benefits of Z between the parties such that each party is better off than if it had produced X or Y alone). Policy decisions, legislation, military operations, enforcement of laws, and property rights help coalition members satisfy their goals, but often require coalescence. Consider, for example, cases in which lawmaking requires a legislative majority and no single party has such support. Working alone, no single party can pass a law. Working together, however, a coalition of parties can. As we shall see, this is indeed the typical situation in European parliamentary democracies.

A challenge to every coalition is that there are usually *multiple ways to distribute the individual benefits associated with coalescence.* If public problems allowed only one solution, then coalition politics would be simple (and not very interesting). The only question would be whether or not to employ the solution—a relatively simple bargaining problem. But such simplicity is rare. More often, there are many ways to distribute social resources, many different policy platforms that a majority of MPs can support, and more politicians desirous of high office than offices available. If the different means of achieving a collective goal vary in the costs and benefits they imply for individual coalition members, then these members can have different preferences about what the coalition should do. Bargaining is the means by which such conflicts are managed.

Contracts are the usual currency of bargaining. Contracts are agreements, oral or written, in which participants commit to certain actions in return for specified benefits. A contract's purpose is to clarify terms of agreement, to delineate punishments for non-compliance and rewards for compliance, and to reduce risk. To draft a contract that serves all these purposes is rarely easy, especially when the agreement is meant to cover a broad range of future events that can only be partially anticipated. Generally, the more important the contract, the more difficult it is to craft one that is mutually agreeable to all parties. The costs of reaching such agreements are known as **transaction costs,** which Kreps (1990: 743) defines as follows:

When undertaking a transaction, parties to the transaction must incur several sorts of costs... [Some] costs are incurred before the transaction takes place. If the transaction is to be governed by a written contract, the contract must be drafted. Whether governed by a contract or simply by verbal commitments, the terms of the transaction must be negotiated. [Other] costs are incurred in consummating and safeguarding the deal that was originally struck.

Indeed, those who participate in coalition bargaining must spend time and effort obtaining an agreement that they and their constituents find acceptable. The amount of these expenditures depends on the complexity of the agreement being sought. As potential partners encounter an increasing number of issues to resolve—such as which policy stances the coalition will take and which parties will obtain particular leadership positions—more time and effort may be needed to weave each resolution into a general agreement. Similarly, when potential partners are seeking an agreement that they want to last for several months or years, they may find it worthwhile to spend time and effort setting up ways to enforce the contract's terms. Because such expenditures are an essential part of contracting, transaction costs are an important factor in understanding the role of bargaining in coalition politics.

What can we learn about coalition governance from a framework based on the premises listed above? Our initial answer to this question comes in the context of explaining why parties coalesce at all. Once we establish that parties have strong incentives to form and maintain lasting coalitions, we then turn our attention to the key decisions that enduring coalitions must make.

Why coalesce?

A single political party may gain sufficient support among the voters that it can govern alone, and in most (though not all) such cases it will. Much more commonly, however, elections in parliamentary democracies yield a result in which no single party is so privileged (i.e. a minority situation, see Strøm 1990). This result is especially common under Proportional Representation. In most such circumstances, the resulting government is a self-recognized and enduring coalition of political parties. Why does this happen?

It is not obvious that parties should prefer formal and enduring patterns of cooperation. Commitment to a coalition agreement can constrain individual parties in important ways (e.g. through the loss of voter support associated with legislative compromises that the party would not have sought on its own). Given that the world is unpredictable, why should not political parties prefer to just drop in and out of free-floating majorities? Indeed, the advantage of not coalescing is freedom—parties need not be burdened by their coalition partners' demands and could indeed change partners from issue to issue. Thus, they might avoid the most costly demands of any coalition partner and would be free to remain more responsive to their own constituents at any time.

Prevailing against such freedom, however, is a host of problems and inefficiencies. Among the most serious are the following:

- *Increased transaction costs.* Free-floating majorities force participants to negotiate every decision anew. The time and energy needed to proceed in this manner can exhaust a party's resources and reduce its abilities to accomplish broad or multiple goals. An important part of the rationale for stable coalitions is that they economize on transaction costs.
- *Less policy continuity and impact.* Without a formal coalition, why should the majority that forms on a Tuesday morning enforce the laws made by Monday evening's legislature? Such instability would greatly reduce the value of any decision that a governing coalition would be able to make. After all, what is the value of governing if you have no idea whether your decisions would stand long enough even to be implemented? In a situation of free-floating majorities, the impact of any government decision could be radically reduced, so that the public or private gain from controlling the levers of government might simply vanish.
- *Less policy credibility and outside support for government programmes.* As just mentioned, a polity governed strictly by free-floating majorities might be one in which public policy would have little long-term stability or credibility. This might adversely affect citizens in many ways. Imagine, for example, what buying a house or investing in stocks would be like if a nation's basic notion of property rights were subject to frequent and unpredictable change. The costs of such arrangements to anyone with a long-term interest in a society would be

tremendous. Indeed, for people attempting to base social, political, or economic plans on government policies, free-floating majorities can spell disaster.

Policy credibility is not a concern simply for those who 'consume' government decisions. For most government policies to be effective, people outside of government must cooperate. Citizens must abide by the laws, businesses must adhere to the terms of their contracts, and countries must act within the terms of existing treaties. If tomorrow's government cannot credibly uphold agreements that its leaders sign today, anyone who deals with that government has less incentive to trust or cooperate with it. Unstable governments might encounter such problems of cooperation very close to their own ranks. Even if a free-floating majority were in power long enough to name its cabinet ministers, there is little reason to expect others in government to abide by their ministerial directives. Indeed, we should expect bureaucrats who dislike today's legislative directives to disregard them if they believe that tomorrow's governing coalition will simply change the law (see, e.g., Huber 1998; Huber and Lupia 2001). In other words, government on land is like the government on the high seas—the prospect of leadership instability makes mutiny more attractive.

- *Less reliable voter support.* In democratic countries, parties are in a position to bargain for a place in government *only if* citizens delegate policymaking authority to them through elections. The **electoral connection**—the threat that eventually voters will judge coalition members—governs member behaviour. This connection means that parties cannot simply bargain as they please. Voters give power to parties and they can take it back. Therefore, if voters prefer a government whose actions are at least somewhat predictable, then politicians who can credibly commit themselves to something other than a transitory coalition stand to gain. Stable coalitions can tie parties to specific policies, which gives voters a more credible policy-oriented rationale for differentiating between candidates for office. Members of stable coalitions can also more easily establish 'policy brand names' that reduce citizens' uncertainty about the policy consequences of voting for a particular candidate (Cox and McCubbins 1993). Indeed, stable coalitions make it easier for voters to hold government officials accountable for their actions than would free-floating majorities.

In sum, formalized, stable coalescence is a survival strategy—it provides parties with the ability to influence government decisions, earn the trust of non-governmental actors, and maintain good long-term relations with voters while paying relatively low transaction costs. To the extent that such relations and cost savings are more important than the policy freedom that free-floating coalitions could allow, stable coalitions will prevail, and indeed in West European parliamentary democracies they do.

Having established why parties choose to coalesce, we now turn to the question of who gets what in coalition bargaining. We begin with a simple scenario in which parties are *certain about the future*. This simplification allows us to clarify important aspects of coalition bargaining. We then move to more realistic settings where parties bargain in the shadow of an uncertain future.

Walk-away values affect who gets what

In the simplest economic bargaining models, everybody knows everything. When applied to coalition governance, such models imply that every party leader knows everything about the situation at hand—such as the preferences, options, and constraints of every other party leader—both at the time of negotiation and forever into the future. In such a world, negotiators anticipate all consequences of their actions and bargainers can engage in **complete contracting**. Complete contracts allow coalitions to specify in detail what each partner will do in any circumstance. Of course, members of governing coalitions seldom know so much. However, examining some properties of complete contracting is an efficient way to uncover key insights about coalition governance. Consider, for example, the question of who gets what when coalition members disagree.

In bargaining models, the answer to the question 'Who gets what?' hinges on the credibility of a bargainer's negotiating positions. We call this factor his **walk-away value**. A walk-away value is what a negotiator, such as a party leader, can gain without a new agreement; that is, what he or she secures by walking away from the bargaining table.[4] Economists also use the term 'reservation wage' to describe this concept (see, e.g., McMillan 1992).

In a bargaining session, walk-away values function as implicit threats against other parties. The more easily a party can walk away from the bargaining table and still end up with an acceptable pay-off, the more concerned the other parties have to be about satisfying that party's demands—*if* they want that party in the coalition. Put another way, those who have little to lose from disagreement often have much to gain from negotiation. In a market economy, walk-away values are usually determined by the monetary values of other economic opportunities. For example, a worker who can earn high wages from many employers has a higher walk-away value than a similarly situated worker with no outside opportunities.

The source of walk-away values in parliamentary contexts often lies elsewhere. In democracies, **public support is the lynchpin of a political party's power**. Parties that lack public support have little to offer to other prospective coalition

---

[4] By walk-away value, we mean something related to, but different from, famous bargaining power indices such as those of Shapley-Shubik (1954) and Banzhaf (1968). Our concept is, however, directly comparable to those two only if we restrict our analysis to the case of zero transaction costs. In other words, the bargaining power indices account for the number of alternative coalitions each bargainer can join, but under the assumption that such moves do not require costly contracting. Since these indices are widely available, they will be used in some of the chapters that follow. When they are used in conjunction with this chapter's theoretical framework, they should be interpreted with this footnote's caveat in mind.

partners. **But while public support is necessary for a party to have a positive walk-away value in coalition negotiations, it is not sufficient**. For a party to have a positive walk-away value, it must be able to benefit from its assets (including its public support) without tying itself to any specific coalition agreement. For example, when one party has enough seats to govern on its own, only it has a positive walk-away value (i.e. only it can govern without the help of others). When no party has resources (i.e. seats) sufficient to govern alone, walk-away values are determined by which party combinations are capable of governing (i.e. which teams of parties can control a number of seats sufficient to control parliamentary decisions). Parties that can be members of more than one governing coalition can have an edge. For example, party X, a member of the incumbent governing coalition, gets bargaining leverage when other incumbent coalition members believe that failure to defer to it on a particular issue will cause it to join or construct a different majority. Indeed, if a party can maintain a credible exit threat throughout a coalition's term (i.e. if by defecting it can bring down a government and produce a situation from which it benefits), then we expect it to have great political influence. The religious bloc in the Israeli Knesset has often had such power—it can, and has, coalesced with each of the two major parties (Labour and Likud) and it regularly gets its way on social policy—though the bloc never holds anywhere near a majority of seats.

Coalition decisions depend on walk-away values. Understanding this fact clarifies many aspects of coalition behaviour—including the errors inherent in the common belief that resources, such as number of seats held, transfer directly into bargaining power. Many people believe that the larger a party is, the more powerful it is in coalition negotiations. This belief is true only in cases where walk-away values and size are positively and strongly correlated. In such cases, we expect allegiance to 'parity norms'—agreements where a coalition member's share of portfolios corresponds to its size relative to other coalition members. When walk-away value and size are less correlated, we expect parity norms to be abandoned.

To see how size and walk-away value can have very little relation to one another, consider a simple example. Three parties have seats in a 101-member parliament. The parliament uses majority rule to make all of its decisions. Party A has 50 seats, party B has 48 seats, and party C has 3 seats. No party has a majority. For policy reasons, all parties prefer certain coalitions to others. Suppose that all parties know these preferences and all other important aspects of the bargaining situation. Suppose further that any realized gains from coalescence are divisible among coalition members, that all parties prefer a larger share of power in a coalition to a smaller share, and that any party is free to negotiate with any other party. To simplify the example, we describe the case where any coalition including C produces individual benefits for both coalition members, whereas a coalition including both A and B produces no such benefits. Party C may be a centrist party whose members are not repulsed by the policy desires of other parties and vice versa, while A and B have disagreements so fundamental that there is nothing that they that could agree to do together.

The result of bargaining in this case (following Lupia and Strøm 1995) is as follows:

- C has the fewest seats, but is the only one with a positive walk-away value—it is the only party that can threaten potential suitors that it will seek to be part of another value-generating coalition.
- Although A and B are much larger than C, they have no positive walk-away values when negotiating with C.
- The only sustainable outcome is a contract giving party C benefits disproportionate to its small size.

In this simple example, size and bargaining power are not positively correlated. C, by far the smallest party, is the most powerful. The lesson here is that walk-away values trump size. Put another way, **size is not always power**. This example is also interesting because it resembles West Germany in the 1970s and 1980s—when the Social Democrats and the Christian Democrats were like parties A and B, and the Free Democrats were like party C. Though smaller than the other two parties, the Free Democrats (FDP) wielded great bargaining power. Our framework implies that the FDP should then have secured a disproportionate share of cabinet portfolios, and indeed they did.

Walk-away values, however, do not affect coalition bargaining outcomes in isolation. Politics often feature a variety of rules about who gets to bargain over what, and we broadly refer to such rules as institutions. **Institutions, which are the product of previous bargaining, affect walk-away values in the present**. Institutions such as size or composition rules, formateur/investiture rules (Huber and McCarty 2001), recognition rules (Bawn 1993), the independence of the judiciary/civil service, cabinet operating procedures, and internal party rules affect coalition bargaining by constraining the options of party leaders (Strøm, Budge, and Laver 1994). For a few years in the 1990s, for example, Israel's Basic Law transferred the first opportunity to form a coalition from the largest party in parliament to a separately elected Prime Minister. This change affected party walk-away values and was sufficient to affect whether its defence policies would be left or right of centre (i.e. whether Labour or Likud would be in the coalition). In Belgium, unique institutions have an analogous effect on party walk-away values. There, the constitution requires linguistic parity in the cabinet and thus constrains coalitions to contain both Flemish and Walloon parties. This constraint affects the set of coalition agreements from which parties can credibly walk away. In sum, when institutional constraints affect parties' walk-away values, then they can affect who gets what in coalition bargaining.

Understanding the role of bargaining and, by implication, walk-away values, casts the actions of coalitions in a new light. Under majority rule, size need not be power in coalition governance. Unless a party earns more than one-half of the seats in parliament, its bargaining power depends on walk-away values. The same logic implies that *any* **institutional, resource-based, preference-based, or country-specific factor affects coalition agreements only if it affects a potential coalition partner's walk-away value**. In some nations, for example, cultural taboos make certain coalition agreements untenable to voters and can make parties' relative walk-away values different from what they would otherwise be.

Another common belief about coalitions is that if parties share common preferences, then they will necessarily coalesce. Focusing on the necessity of bargaining ultimately reveals such conjectures to be false. For example, **if the transaction costs of reaching agreement with a particular partner are too high, then parties may cast agreements with that partner aside—opting instead for an agreement entailing lower transaction costs** *with a partner whose preferences are less common*. Indeed, even between parties with otherwise common interests, if there are too many items to negotiate or too many contingencies that might arise, then we cannot simply assume that they will coalesce. As Fudenberg and Tirole (1991: 397) explain:

> A bargaining situation involves players who must reach an agreement in order to realize gains from trade. The standard example is the problem of sharing a pie. No player can have any pie until they all agree about the shares each will receive. Negotiating about the shares is costly, and the pie may decay or disappear if the negotiations go on for very long.

Such concerns certainly ring true in parliamentary democracies. Bargaining can take considerable time. In the Netherlands, coalition formation negotiations often last at least three months and in 1977 lasted for the better part of a year! In the meantime, decisions on major political issues are suspended, the government is reduced to caretaker status, and parties do not enjoy the perquisites of office. In such cases, there is no doubt that the 'pie' decays as the parliamentary term passes and the next election approaches.

Uncertainty and Discount Rates Make Patience a Virtue in Bargaining

High transaction costs are sufficient to derail an otherwise successful bargaining session. Uncertainty is another factor with the same potential. An important source of uncertainty in coalition politics is *the two requirements of coalition politics* (the need to form and maintain agreements with other parties while simultaneously cultivating voter support). The first of these requirements introduces uncertainty when party leaders lack information about each other's strategies. The second requirement introduces uncertainty if voters are fickle or if their preferences are difficult to gauge.

We turn our attention now to coalition governance dynamics in cases where such uncertainty is present. Coalition members may, for instance, lack information about what other parties want or what sacrifices they are willing to make in exchange for coalition membership. In such cases, parties may try to strengthen their bargaining position by overstating their walk-away values (e.g. to insist that you will settle for nothing less than ministries X, Y, and Z, when, in fact, you would be satisfied with two of the three). Therefore, **a key to bargaining under uncertainty is separating fact from fiction when assessing other parties' walk-away values**.

A complete account of what people believe about the walk-away values of others would involve a fair amount of psychology. However, bargaining models built from the premises described above produce important insights about these cognitions with less effort (see, e.g., the review in Laffont and Tirole 1993). They show that **credible commitment** is the key to bargaining under uncertainty.

While any party can claim a high walk-away value, such claims are more credible if commitments back them. If, for example, a party leader can credibly commit to resigning his post if a particular objective is not achieved, then his coalition partners may have a greater incentive to give in (especially if they dislike his potential replacement). Thus, actors who can credibly commit can increase other players' perceptions of their walk-away values and benefit in negotiation.

How do actors credibly commit? Some make public promises that are costly to contradict (Lupia and McCubbins 1998). In 1979, for example, the Irish Labour Party adopted the Killarney Compromise, which removed the party leader's power to take the party into a coalition with another party (in this case, Fine Gael). From that time on, Labour's entry into a government coalition required ratification by a Special Conference. This commitment subsequently strengthened Labour's hand in bargaining (Marsh and Mitchell 1999).

In addition to lacking information about what other partners want now, parties may also lack information about the future. Uncertainty about the future makes discount rates a critical aspect of coalition bargaining. A **discount rate** measures an actor's valuation with respect to time—how much the enjoyment of a certain benefit today is worth relative to the enjoyment of future benefits. All else constant, the more uncertainty an actor has about the future, the higher is his discount rate (i.e. the more he prefers benefits now to promises of future benefits). Discount rates also depend on other factors, such as how much parties care about the issues facing the government at any time.

Many studies clarify how discount rates affect bargaining (see, e.g., Kreps 1990). Their main lesson is that **patience is power**. For example, if one person can afford to wait longer than another for a particular good, then the more patient person can credibly commit to give up less in the present to receive the good. Put simply, greater patience implies higher walk-away values.

To show how discount rates affect coalition bargaining, we return to the three-party example given above. Here, however, we suppose that a formateur rule gives party A the first opportunity to form a government, followed by party B. Also suppose that party A's constituents are impatient, so that party A regards the benefits of agreements reached in a second or later period of bargaining as far less valuable than agreements reached in the first round. If the constituents of parties B and C are more patient, then party A has much to lose if it fails to make a successful offer in the initial round. In such a case, party A's walk-away value is small relative to that of more patient parties.

One type of instance in which discount rates come into play is when parties delegate authority to 'term-limited' party leaders. Consider Ireland following the 1989 election. Then, long-time Fianna Fáil leader Charles Haughey, in the twilight of his career, broke his party's no-coalition rule so that he could form a coalition government with the Progressive Democrats (PD). This was remarkable not just because it conflicted with Fianna Fáil's long-standing contempt for coalitions, but also because there was considerable bad blood between the leaders of the two parties. Analysts have suggested, however, that if Haughey had failed to take this action, he might have lost his last opportunity to become prime minister. Indeed, he might even have been deposed as leader of his party (Laver and Arkins 1990; Marsh and Mitchell 1999). Haughey had a high discount rate, which likely propelled him to negotiate an unconventional agreement.

A critical implication of the fact that discount rates affect coalition bargaining is that **deadlines matter**. This is particularly important when a deadline affects parties differently. Consider, for example, Norway's 1987 Presthus debacle. The Parliament was about to take its summer recess. With no further meeting time scheduled, there would be no opportunity for the non-socialist parties to topple Gro Harlem Brundtland's Labour minority government before local and regional elections in September. Rolf Presthus was the leader of a Conservative party that had strongly committed itself to toppling the government. He felt compelled to defeat Brundtland's government, even if it meant large policy concessions to prospective coalition partners and the risk of failure. As it turned out, Presthus' attempt failed, and he paid a heavy political and personal price. The timing of his self-defeating behaviour suggests that he was driven by a high discount rate, by his need to show results before the election (Strøm 1994).

Indeed, those with low discount rates (i.e. parties that can afford to wait) can find it advantageous to use time strategically. Such parties may know that if they wait another week to come to an agreement, a desperate partner (perhaps one whose time as formateur is about to end) will offer them a much better deal. Therefore, **we should be cautious about the conventional wisdom that the time it takes a coalition to negotiate tells us something about the quality of governance**. As Gregory M. Luebbert observed, 'it is wrong to assume that, because interparty negotiations take a long time, much is being negotiated among the parties' (Luebbert 1986: 52). If people have differing preferences over time and use time strategically, the length of negotiations may reveal nothing about the policy differences between the partners or the likely success of the final agreement. Time need not imply craftsmanship in bargaining. Instead, bargaining models show that long negotiations can be a sign that at least one coalition partner is willing to be patient in order to get a more favourable contract (see, e.g.,

Fudenberg and Levine 1998 on the role of patience). The same logic reveals no relationship between length of bargaining and the success of the agreement.

Uncertainty and transaction costs induce restrictive arrangements

We address additional questions about how uncertainty affects coalition politics by focusing on transaction costs. A key tenet of transaction cost economics is that bargainers account for opportunism when making and maintaining coalitional arrangements. **Opportunism** arises when coalition members can use uncertainty to benefit at other members' expense. Attention to opportunism is particularly important in agreements under which one party receives benefits before another. In such cases, the party that gets its pay-off early may be tempted not to uphold its end of the bargain later on. If coalition members anticipate such reactions and have no way to guard against them, then otherwise valuable agreements may not be reached.

When uncertainty and opportunism are paired as described above, one likely result is increased transaction costs. Williamson's research (1975) on this topic is focal. Before his work, numerous claims about the performance of markets and negotiations were made as if transaction costs in such situations were negligible or could be ignored. It was believed that if potential gains from trade existed, negotiations would lead to their realization (present-day versions of such arguments include the conclusion that parties with similar policy interests will necessarily coalesce and the conclusion that such coalitions will necessarily be more effective or longer lasting than others). Williamson's transaction cost economics approach shows such beliefs to be false—uncertainty and opportunism can prevent such outcomes. This work redirected analysts' attention to how people structure their arrangements when they are faced with an uncertain future (see, e.g., Williamson 1975; Epstein and O'Halloran 1999).

While controversial in economics at the outset—many economists preferred to explain bargaining outcomes strictly through analyses of the relative resources of participants—the importance of transaction costs is now widely accepted. Indeed, as Williamson (1993: 105) notes:

The logic of transaction cost economics...has been applied to a wide range of phenomena—including vertical integration, vertical market restrictions, franchising, labour market regulation, the organization of work, corporate finance and corporate governance, regulation and deregulation, family firms, multinational firms, and the economics of trust, among others. Furthermore...transaction costs economics has been subject to numerous empirical tests—most of which are corroborative.

For our purpose—explaining coalition governance—an important lesson from Williamson is that bargainers have incentives to adapt to transaction costs by structuring agreements in particular ways. For example, when uncertainty and the threat of opportunism generate large transaction costs, coalition members have an incentive to seek **restrictive arrangements** (i.e. contracts that provide at least some coalition members with minimal flexibility). While restrictive arrangements may limit coalition members' future discretion, they can keep coalitions together in contexts of mistrust. In short, the threat of opportunism may force coalitions to choose between viability and flexibility.

Transaction cost economics also directs our attention to the unusual role of **specialization** in coalition politics. The complexity of modern governance can provide parties and individuals with an incentive to specialize. For parliaments as a whole, specialization can provide broad benefits (e.g. certain members become so knowledgeable about a complicated subject that they can simplify the topic for all other members). While specialization can be valuable for those with expertise, greater expertise need not imply an advantage in bargaining. In fact, the prospect of opportunism by other members can lead to a negative relationship between expertise and walk-away values. In Germany, for example, the FDP has been a member of several governing coalitions—some dominated by the left and others by the right. Switching sides for the FDP has been far from costless—it has often required leadership change within the party and has caused substantial turnover among party activists. While the FDP's pivotal position secured it a role in government, its previous commitments made its political expertise difficult to transfer, thus increasing the costs it faced for joining subsequent governments (Poguntke 1999).[5]

Attention to how transaction costs affect bargaining also directs us to the fact that coalescence, by reducing uncertainty and curtailing opportunism, can produce **convergent expectations** about government's future actions among coalition partners. In complex situations, the value of convergent expectations cannot be underestimated. Coalition members who share beliefs about the consequences of their collective actions can act with greater confidence. As a result, they are better able to adopt a long-term perspective, and their decisions are more likely to be credible. As many important policies require government to maintain support for an extended period (as is often the case, for example, with economic reforms that involve painful transition periods), convergent expectations can give everyone involved a greater confidence that they will realize long-term benefits from short-term sacrifices.

Convergent expectations generate broader benefits as well. To see how, consider that many government objectives can be achieved only if bureaucrats or private citizens cooperate (i.e. the efficiency and legitimacy of a change in the tax code are helped if citizens do not defy the changes). For such policies to work, outside interests (including private citizens) must opt to 'invest' in the government's plan of action. If outside interests do not share convergent expectations with

---

[5] This kind of problem is known as one of asset specificity. Asset specificity is the degree to which an asset's value depends on the continuation of a specific relationship. A politician's assets are specific when he invests time and prestige in pursuits that are difficult to transfer to other coalitions or portfolios. Asset specificity and walk-away values can be negatively correlated— particularly when a coalition is capable of terminating a member after it receives the value of that members' specialization.

the government, they may be reluctant to participate in activities that benefit the country. With coalition-instilled convergent expectations, it becomes less risky for private citizens to invest in publicly beneficial actions. Therefore, coalition agreements that counter uncertainty and opportunism can generate broad collective benefits.[6]

ELECTORAL CONNECTIONS, THE SHADOW OF THE FUTURE AND TERMINATION

We now apply the framework to a specific, and important, stage in a coalition's life cycle—the decision to replace the government or dissolve parliament. In most parliamentary democracies, such decisions can be made on any given day. As Lupia and Strøm (1995: 648) describe it, governments in parliamentary democracies live precariously:

Typically, they can fall on any given day, and sometimes with little or no warning. The circumstances surrounding coalition termination vary greatly, occasionally producing great drama. Some politicians are forced from their cabinet offices in a daze, never knowing what hit them. Others choose their date of departure and leave with smirks on their faces.

In most parliamentary systems, election dates are not entirely fixed by the constitution, but are subject to decisions by politicians themselves. In countries where coalition governments are the norm, the timing of elections is often the product of the kind of bargaining dynamics described above. In what follows, we apply our framework to explain why, when, and how coalition governments choose to end their reigns. The application is a formal model of coalition decision-making (Lupia and Strøm 1995) in which termination decisions are made via bargaining and where parties can factor voter reactions, transaction costs, and the shadow of the future into their negotiations. After a brief description of the model itself, we focus on conveying its main substantive insights. Lupia and Strøm (1995) contains a complete description of the model.

The model

In most parliamentary democracies, simple legislative majorities have dismissal power (the power to recall the cabinet at any time). Many parliamentary democracies also have dissolution powers (the power to dissolve parliament and force

---

[6] This point also reinforces our earlier claims about the drawbacks of floating majorities. The promise of a stable coalition reduces the risk to any member of specializing because stable coalitions are better able to offer long-term rewards. If coalition partners are better able to specialize, the number of areas in which the government has expertise will grow. Such investments in expertise permit the government to adapt to a wider range of unforeseen contingencies, which, in turn, allows it to govern more effectively.

early elections). Here, we examine the case in which both powers exist. We use the model to explain when and why parliamentarians use these powers. We find that coalition terminations are not, as they are often portrayed, automatic responses to external events. Instead, the causes and consequences of coalition terminations are negotiated and predictable responses to political circumstances.

We clarify the causes and consequences of coalition termination by modelling coalition bargaining, in a parliament with dismissal and dissolution powers, as a game between three unitary parties. We develop a three-party model because doing so provides the simplest formal framework for examining the bargaining dynamics of coalition government.

We call the three parties the 'first' party, the 'second' party, and the 'out' party. Each party's name indicates its relationship to the initial governing coalition. We describe the case in which the first and second parties are members of the initial governing coalition, the out party is not, and any two parties can form a new majority coalition. The only substantive distinction between the first and second parties, upon which none of our results depend, is that the first party reacts to the event before the second. We do not assume that a party's name necessarily indicates its relative size. Thus, neither the first nor the second party need be the largest.

Each party's objective is to maximize the value it derives from its role in parliament. We make three basic assumptions about these objectives. First, *parties care about controlling seats in parliament.* Each party prefers more seats to fewer seats, all else constant. Second, *parties value power within a governing coalition.* Each party prefers to hold any particular portfolio than not to do so, all else constant. We make no assumptions about the relative value of different appointments or about whether cabinet and other portfolios are valued for policy or patronage reasons. If we think of what a governing coalition does as dividing a valuable pie, then this assumption is akin to stating that each party prefers larger pieces of pie to smaller ones. Third, *parties can value some potential coalition partners more than others.* In other words, if we think of one of the things that a governing coalition does as making (and then dividing) a valuable pie, then we can conceive of parties preferring some flavours of pie to others. The benefits that a party receives by participating in a given coalition derive from the similarity in policy preferences and/or the complementarity of office preferences among coalition members. So, for instance, a coalition containing parties with similar policy agendas is likely to generate greater benefits for its members, all else constant, than would a coalition of parties with conflicting policy agendas. Equivalently, a coalition of parties with different preferences over cabinet appointments can have greater value to its members than one in which all parties covet the same portfolios.[7]

---

[7] In effect, we assume that parties are goal-oriented without making a general (and controversial) assumption about the extent to which they are interested in patronage, policy outcomes, or the prestige of holding office. Stated another way, we assume that the parties share convergent beliefs about the value of the gains from trade that can be created by each possible coalescence.

Having just described the benefits that parties derive from governing, we now describe an event that may lead the parties to cast these benefits aside. This event (represented by a poll that credibly signals public opinion *or* a set of shared past experiences that informs electoral expectations) provides all parties with information about what would happen to them if they were to call an election. What this event reveals is $b_i \in \Re$, the expected utility of new elections to party i (b_i is a measure of party i's post-election well-being).

For example, suppose that the first party cares only about its ability to form a single-party majority government in period 2, while the second party cares only about the number of period 2 seats it will control. We would then characterize the value of b_1 as increasing only in the first party's belief about the subjective probability that it will be able to form a single-party majority government in period 2, given new elections. Similarly, we would characterize the value of b_2 as increasing only in the second party's expectation of the number of seats that it will control in period 2 given new elections.

While elections can provide benefits, calling them can also impose several types of costs, such as the forfeiture of the policymaking opportunities or rent-collection opportunities made possible by holding valuable offices, as well as those costs involved in election-related intra-party negotiation, campaigning, and electioneering. For each party, we assume that $E_i \geq 0$ represents party i's election-related transaction and opportunity costs (i.e. the cost of achieving the benefits, b_i, revealed by the event). We do not assume that these costs are the same for all parties. Together, our assumptions about the event and election-related transaction costs imply that party i expects a utility of $b_i - E_i$ from new elections.

New elections, however, are not the parties' only possible response to the event. They can also make new offers to each other (i.e. reshuffle portfolios within a government or institute a new government without calling new elections). The consequence of an accepted offer will be either a redistribution of power among members of the initial governing coalition or the formation of a new governing coalition.

We assume that making offers may involve a transaction cost. We represent such a cost by assuming that an offering party must pay $K_i \in \Re$. Our motivation for K_i is the party-specific costs of formulating an offer to redistribute power. These costs include the effort required to obtain the approval of party members and constituents. Like electoral costs, these negotiation costs may be different for different parties.

If no party is willing to make an offer that another is willing to accept, then there may be a vote of confidence. The requirements for such a vote to occur are (a) that no offer is made and accepted and (b) that a parliamentary majority wants such a vote. If the vote is held, and parties controlling a majority of seats vote 'no', then parliament is dissolved, new elections are held, the game ends, and party i's period 2 utility is $b_i - E_i$. If no elections are held, and no new coalition contracts offered and accepted, then the incumbent government survives intact.

Results

In the model, dissolutions require a set of parties that collectively have a parliamentary majority and, individually, each prefer new elections to continuing parliament as it is. Moreover, each party that has the ability to be part of such a majority must also prefer the anticipated consequences of new elections to the most favourable and acceptable offer for a replacement cabinet that any other party can make (Lupia and Strøm 1995: Theorem 1).

This result, which comes from conceiving of coalition decisions as the product of bargaining, amends widely held beliefs about election timing. Grofman and van Roozendaal (1994: 158), for example, argue that 'anticipation of future electoral gains may cause a certain party or a group of parties to seek to bring down the cabinet at a moment when their anticipated electoral success will be greatest', and hypothesize that 'Parties terminate cabinets when they expect electoral gains'. Accounting for the role of bargaining in coalition politics reveals this hypothesis as only partially correct. Indeed, **a party with favourable electoral prospects will also consider the option of extracting advantages through non-electoral means** (e.g. bargaining with parties that have less favourable electoral prospects). A replacement cabinet, rather than new elections, is particularly likely if key members of the existing coalition have a strong desire to avoid elections. Therefore, good **electoral prospects for any particular party are not sufficient to cause a parliamentary dissolution**.

The same logic (Lupia and Strøm 1995: Corollary 1) shows that dissolution is most likely when there exist parties in the coalition that (a) expect large benefits from an election, (b) face small election-related transaction costs, (c) face large transaction costs for negotiating non-electoral transfers of power, (d) derive little value from the seats they currently control, and (e) derive little value from the other coalitions they could enter.

The corollary is important as it suggests an interactive effect between time elapsed since the last election and whether a specific event (such as a war) will end a government or parliament. To see this effect, first note that most parliamentary democracies have constitutionally mandated limits on the maximum length of a parliament's term—the 'constitutional inter-election period' (King et al. 1990). Before the time since the last election reaches this limit, calling new elections is merely an option. When this limit is reached, elections must be held.

If calling early elections means that parties sacrifice policymaking opportunities and benefit-collection opportunities, then—all else constant—the benefits parties can expect from maintaining the current agreement should decrease as the parliamentary term approaches its limit. That is, all else constant, the value of sustaining the current coalition should be relatively high early in a parliament's term, should decrease continually over that term, and should reach its minimum when parties have no other choice but to hold an election. Parties must forfeit currently held assets when an election is held. To the extent that a party derives value from being part of a coalition or parliament, the fact that such assets may be lost through an election means that, all else constant, **a coalition's value to its members should decay as parliament ages—converging to zero when there is no choice but to hold an election.** Hence (following the corollary), an event that does not cause dissolution early in a parliament's term could do so later.

In general, **focusing on coalition decision-making as a process of bargaining that occurs in the shadow of public opinion reveals that the extent to which an event is 'critical' depends on the bargaining environment.** For instance, if the transaction costs of having an early election are high, then dissolution requires a large event. Thus, if these costs decrease over time, then dissolution requires smaller events as a parliament ages.

Such conclusions run counter to the assumption of a constant hazard rate—a measure of the relationship between a government's likelihood of failure and its age—in early models of cabinet stability (Cioffi-Revilla 1984; Browne, Frendreis, and Gleiber 1986). Warwick and Easton (1992) and Kaashoek (1993) have questioned this assumption in the past, showing little empirical support. Moreover, Warwick (1992) finds impressive cross-national evidence that the hazard rate for executive coalitions increases over time. This is consistent with what our model predicts (i.e. the corollary stated above). Indeed, since the original publication of our result, scholars have used our model as the basis for more effective empirical analyses of coalition termination (e.g. Diermeier and Stevenson 1999; Gordon 2002).

Similar logic affects several widely held claims about coalitions. For example, formal theories of coalition formation in a three-party legislature predict that the governing coalition will comprise the largest and smallest legislative parties (e.g. Austen-Smith and Banks 1988; Baron 1991). Our approach reveals that these predictions are not robust to the introduction of parties that look forward to the next coalition termination or election when they bargain. To see why, notice that a necessary condition for the 'largest–smallest' prediction is that the party to whom an acceptable offer is made must control either the smallest or the largest number of seats. Now consider the general case in which the largest party is in the position to make an offer. All else constant, the offering party should prefer to coalesce with the more valuable coalition partner (assuming that there is a difference). If all else is not constant, however, then the offering party must consider the trade-off between the value of a coalition partner and the share of portfolios and other benefits that it can retain. If the larger potential coalition partner has a lower walk-away value than the smaller one (e.g. if the former is a virtual pariah) and is willing to make a better deal, then the offering party could choose to coalesce with the larger of the two remaining parties.

In sum, if an offer is made, it will be made to the party whose walk-away value is lowest. Such behaviour **does not require the largest and smallest parties to coalesce.** Instead, **an offer is made to the weakest party**, where the weakest party is the one that faces the most damaging combination of (*a*) bad electoral prospects, (*b*) high election-related transaction costs, (*c*) high bargaining costs or discount rates, (*d*) low-value coalition alternatives, and (*e*) highly valued seats or coalition-related power (that must be forfeited as a result of coalition termination or parliamentary dissolution).

Reconsidering coalition politics

Let us now briefly return to the various clusters of explanatory factors that we discussed at the beginning of this chapter. We believe that although none of these clusters is by itself sufficient to account for all the interesting variation in coalition politics, each of them contributes to understanding such matters. Moreover, each of these clusters can be captured through, or lodged within the Lupia and Strøm model.

Our model includes parameters that reflect many of the traditional concerns in the coalitions literature, including preferences, institutions, transaction costs, and critical events. These factors collectively make up the 'engine' that drives our results. Our model does not include particular terms for the contextual effects of time and place, but it is easy enough to see how such effects could be captured. Country effects, for example, could have to do with culturally induced and sustained particularities of preference. In some countries, for example, politicians may be more concerned about holding executive office than elsewhere, perhaps due to historical memories of how such offices have been used (or abused).

At the same time that our model is comprehensive, however, there are clearly also ways in which it is highly stylized and in which future research may want to consider alternative or additional specifications. This is clearly true with respect to our treatment of critical events, structural attributes, and political institutions. In all cases, we have kept our account very simple.

In our original 1995 model, we portrayed the occurrence of a potentially critical event thus: 'an event (represented by a poll that credibly signals public opinion or a set of shared past experiences that informs electoral expectations) provides all parties with information about what would happen to them if an election were to be held.' Laver and Shepsle (1998) have broadened this approach by considering additional types of shocks, such as sudden and unanticipated changes in party policy, in the policy agenda (meaning the relative importance to specific parties of different policy dimensions), or in government decision rules. Within their portfolio allocation approach, they show that different coalitions react differently to the various types of shocks.

While broadening our understanding of critical events is surely a worthwhile exercise, we believe that it is still most fruitful to focus on those shocks that are most common, most clearly exogenous, and most critical to the democratic process. Our understanding of democratic policymaking suggests that sudden, important changes in government decision rules (decision rule shocks) are not very common and rarely exogenous. And as regards changes in party ideal points and the relative weights of different policy dimensions (policy shocks and agenda shocks, respectively), Laver and Shepsle (1998: 36) themselves admit that 'party ideal points represent the tastes of parties, which Laver and Shepsle take in all other parts of their argument to be primitives, not strategic variables.' In other words, party policy positions are clearly under the control of party leaders themselves and must be understood as such if we are to have any analytical traction. Yet, like the present authors, Laver and Shepsle see party leaders as agents of their respective constituencies of voters and argue that changes in the preferences of these constituents may put pressure on party policy positions. While there is clearly some truth in this claim, we would prefer to locate the source of critical events in changes in the voters' opinions, rather than in the politicians' responses to these changes. To avoid circular or fuzzy arguments, we prefer to retain the conception of critical events as exogenous (beyond the immediate control of party leaders themselves), a conception that was very much part and parcel of the early critical events literature. Public opinion shocks, as featured in Lupia and Strøm's original analysis (1995), suggest themselves in this context. This is the only type of critical event that flows directly from the delegation process between citizens and representatives and is not just a description of the behaviour of party leaders themselves.

Structurally, our model considers only two-party majority governments in a three-party world. Needless to say, most parliamentary democracies are considerably more complex, with coalition governments of frequently up to 5 parties, and parliaments that may well contain more than 10. Although there has so far been no formal attempt to model such structural complexity within our analytical framework, our intuition suggests that the greater the structural complexity, the more important the role of transaction costs and information uncertainty.

The institutional framework captured by the Lupia and Strøm model is also very simple. We assume, for example, that parties bargain freely without the intervention of a head of state (president) and that parliamentary dissolution is always feasible if they should fail to reach a sustainable solution. Reality is obviously more complex. Most European parliamentary democracies today have presidential heads of state, and most of these presidents are at least formally empowered to affect coalition bargaining (see Amorim Neto and Strøm 2006). And although Norway is the only parliamentary democracy in which parliamentary dissolution can never occur, many constitutions put more or less stringent restrictions on the use of this procedure (see Strøm and Swindle 2002). We welcome theoretical efforts to model this more complex institutional environment, which we expect will reinforce the arguments made in this chapter. Again, the upshot of considering such institutional variation is likely to be that transaction costs and information uncertainties gain increasing salience.

Our theoretical framework, particularly as it appears in the Lupia and Strøm model, implies that empirical work that includes credible measures of each of these factors will provide more reliable and robust estimates of what parties do at each stage of a coalition's life cycle than will empirical work that includes only a subset of these factors. However, our message is not simply that more variables are better. Instead, it is that more variables are better if the rationale for including these variables is related to essential coalitional bargaining dynamics.

For the authors of this book, the theoretical framework developed in this chapter provides such a rationale. It highlights the importance of asking the question about when and whether contextual, resource-related, preference-related, or institutional variables have the ability to affect the walk-away values of the parties being studied. If such factors can affect bargaining dynamics, then the framework provides basic instructions for how to include them in empirical work. For variables representing factors that cannot affect walk-away values, more is not better. More generally, we believe that significant advances can be made in the study of government coalitions if we properly understand bargaining dynamics and the sources from which bargaining power springs, such as uncertainty and transaction costs and their implications for walk-away values.

While we believe that a framework that captures all of these factors, and specifically transaction costs, is a suitable way to understand coalition politics, it is not, however, the only possible way forward. Some scholars suggest that we would be better off ignoring transaction costs altogether. Consider, for example, the conclusion offered by Diermeier and Merlo (2000: 57):

[L]ike Lupia and Strøm (1995) we find that in equilibrium governments may terminate in early elections and replacements. However, once we allow for efficient bargaining [zero transaction costs] and reshuffles, the Lupia and Strøm framework can no longer generate early terminations. If a government commands a majority of seats—the only case considered by Lupia and Strøm—reshuffles can always be used to capture any changes in the bargaining environment within the current coalition. Once efficient bargaining is not possible, however, as in the case of bargaining between the minority government and the parties in its supporting coalition, governments may fall.

Their claim is logically sound. However, in working with all of the other contributors to this book and bearing witness to the incredible range of data about coalition governance that they have assembled, we have yet to encounter a real-world governmental setting where we have felt assured that transaction costs are zero (or where the preconditions for what Diermeier and Merlo call efficient bargaining come close to being met). Therefore, we take the difference between our results (in Lupia and Strøm 1995) and Diermeier and Merlo's claim as evidence of the importance of transaction costs in explanations of coalition dynamics. Diermeier and Merlo prove that assuming away such costs leads to very different predictions about coalition dynamics. The virtue of their approach lies in its parsimony. Yet, we believe there is a substantial price to be paid in verisimilitude, and that as a consequence, such a 'neoclassical' approach will be unable to capture many of the 'messier' but no less critical aspects of coalition politics.

The later chapters of this book reveal substantial evidence of positive transaction costs (e.g. failed or long bargaining rounds) in virtually every stage of a coalition's life cycle. While we endorse Diermeier and Merlo's attempt to study government formation dynamics in a systematic manner, we follow scholars such as Williamson in contending that as scholarly attention to the role of bargaining in coalition governance grows, so does the importance of integrating carefully considered theoretical and empirical treatments of transaction costs.

CONCLUSION

In this chapter, we offer and apply a framework for understanding coalition governance. Its main premise is that at every stage of a coalition's life cycle, coalition decisions are the result of bargaining, where every bargaining outcome is the result not only of past bargains that affect history, institutions, and members' resources but also of the fact that bargaining occurs in the shadow of citizen opinions and under the constant threat posed by political rivals who want to replace them. *This framework illuminates how factors such as walk-away values, institutions, discount rates, and deadlines affect what coalitions do. It also clarifies how uncertainty and opportunism affect the content of coalition agreements. Its main lesson is that if you want to understand coalition governance, it is important to realize that bargaining occurs at every stage of a coalition's life cycle and that the outcome of bargaining at any particular stage depends on the results of previous bargains (which give parties the resources they have at any particular time) and the prospect of future bargains (which affects walk-away values and the credibility of current agreements).*

The institutions that typify parliamentary democracies make coalition bargaining a constant and critical feature of most such systems. In that environment, coalitions regularly have to pass two tests. They have to please the voters and they have to sustain agreement. A coalition's ability to accomplish anything requires that it come to an agreement, maintain that agreement, and have it approved by the citizenry. Some policies, such as those required for economic and social development, require longer government commitments if they are to be successful. Transaction cost economics reminds us that in order to accomplish such objectives politicians must be able to overcome problems caused by opportunism and uncertainty over long periods. Coalitions must be able to write agreements that protect these policies—giving coalition partners incentives to choose to stick with the agreement rather than defect. In other words, coalitions that recognize the centrality of bargaining, electoral connections, and the shadow of the future are far more likely to succeed politically than parties that focus exclusively on any of the four factors named above. Bargaining in the shadow of the future is the key to governance at every stage in a coalition's life cycle.

One important implication of these conclusions is that coalitions that expect to survive over longer periods can accept more risk and expect higher returns from long-run policy commitments. They can expect higher returns even if a particular policy agenda can lead to bad outcomes in the short run because they are more likely to survive until the return of better days. Coalitions that expect to survive will therefore have a greater legislative range—an ability to undertake agendas that more vulnerable coalitions cannot touch.

This framework is a basis for the empirical work that will be applied in subsequent chapters. Their hypotheses describe important decisions such as coalition formation, policymaking, and coalition termination. Throughout, the analyses in these chapters correct the errors in beliefs such as 'size is power', 'length of bargaining implies effectiveness of contract', and 'external shocks cause coalition terminations' and replace them with findings that are more consistent with bargaining dynamics.

While coalition governments vary in ways that often seem inscrutable, it is imperative for the student of coalition politics to make their dynamics as transparent as possible. The point of this chapter is to provide a framework for increasing that transparency. While paying attention to bargaining dynamics is not the only way to explain coalition governance, it can be very effective. It is also a road that has been surprisingly little travelled, as many previous studies of the topic ignore bargaining entirely. Since party coalitions dominate parliamentary democracies, which in turn rule about one-third of the world's population, the potential pay-off makes research efforts like the ones that follow in this book extremely worthwhile.

REFERENCES

Amorim Neto, Octavio and Strøm, Kaare (2006). 'Breaking the Parliamentary Chain of Delegation: Presidents and Non-partisan Cabinet Members in European Democracies', *British Journal of Political Science*, 36: 619–43.

Austen-Smith, David and Banks, Jeffrey (1988). 'Elections, Coalitions and Legislative Outcomes', *American Political Science Review*, 82: 405–22.

Bäck, Hanna (2003). *Explaining Coalitions. Evidence and Lessons from Studying Coalition Formation in Swedish Local Government*. Uppsala: Uppsala Universitet.

Banfield, Edward C. (1958). *The Moral Basis of a Backward Society*. Chicago: Free Press.

Banzhaf, John F., III (1968). '*One Man, 3,312 Votes: A Mathematical Analysis of the Electoral College*', *Villanova Law Review*, 13: 304–46.

Baron, David P. (1991). 'A Spatial Bargaining Theory of Government Formation in Parliamentary Systems', *American Political Science Review*, 85: 137–64.

Bawn, Kathleen (1993). 'The Logic of Institutional Preferences: German Electoral Law as a Social Choice Outcome', *American Journal of Political Science*, 37: 965–89.

Browne, Eric C., Frendreis, John P., and Gleiber, Dennis W. (1986). 'The Process of Cabinet Dissolution: An Exponential Model of Duration and Stability in Western Democracies', *American Journal of Political Science*, 30: 628–50.

Cioffi-Revilla, Claudio (1984). 'The Political Reliability of Italian Governments', *American Political Science Review*, 78: 318–37.

Cox, Gary W. and McCubbins, Mathew D. (1993). *Legislative Leviathan*. Cambridge: Cambridge University Press.

De Swaan, Abram (1973). *Coalition Theories and Cabinet Formations*. Amsterdam: Elsevier.

Diermeier, Daniel and Merlo, Antonio (2000). 'Government Turnover in Parliamentary Democracies', *Journal of Economic Theory*, 94: 46–79.

—— and Stevenson, Randolph P. (1999). 'Cabinet Survival and Competing Risks', *American Journal of Political Science*, 43(4): 1051–68.

Downs, William (1999). *Coalition Government, Subnational Style*. Columbus, OH: Ohio State University Press.

Epstein, David and O'Halloran, Sharyn (1999). *Delegating Powers: A Transaction Cost Politics Approach to Policy Making Under Separate Powers*. New York, NY: Cambridge University Press.

Fudenberg, Drew and Levine, David K. (1998). *The Theory of Learning in Games*. Cambridge, MA: MIT Press.

—— and Tirole, Jean (1991). *Game Theory*. Cambridge, MA: MIT Press.

Gordon, Sanford C. (2002). 'Stochastic Dependence in Competing Risks', *American Journal of Political Science*, 46: 200–17.

Grofman, Bernard and van Roozendaal, Peter (1994). 'Toward a Theoretical Explanation of Premature Cabinet Termination: With Application to Post-War Cabinets in the Netherlands', *European Journal of Political Research*, 26: 155–70.

Huber, John D. (1998). 'How Does Cabinet Instability Affect Political Performance: Credible Commitment, Information, and Health Care Cost Containment in Parliamentary Politics', *American Political Science Review*, 92: 577–92.

—— and Lupia, Arthur (2001). 'Cabinet Instability and Delegation in Parliamentary Democracies', *American Journal of Political Science*, 45: 18–32.

—— and McCarty, Nolan (2001). 'Cabinet Decision Rules and Political Uncertainty in Parliamentary Bargaining', *American Political Science Review*, 95: 345–60.

Kaashoek, Remco (1993). 'The Process of Coalition Termination in European Democracies'. Paper presented at the Joint Sessions of Workshops of the European Consortium for Political Research, Leiden.

King, Gary, Alt, James E., Laver, Michael J., and Burns, Nancy E. (1990). 'A Unified Model of Cabinet Dissolution in Parliamentary Democracies', *American Journal of Political Science*, 34: 846–71.

Kreps, David M. (1990). *A Course in Microeconomic Theory*. Princeton, NJ: Princeton University Press.

Laffont, Jean-Jacques and Tirole, Jean (1993). *A Theory of Incentives in Procurement and Regulation*. Cambridge, MA: MIT Press.

Laver, Michael J. and Arkins, Audrey (1990). 'Coalition and Fianna Fáil', in Michael Gallagher and Richard Sinnott (eds.), *How Ireland Voted 1999*. Galway: Galway University Press and PSAI Press.

Laver, Michael J. and Schofield, Norman (1990). *Multiparty Government: The Politics of Coalition in Europe.* Oxford: Oxford University Press.

—— and Shepsle, Kenneth A. (1998). 'Events, Equilibria, and Government Survival', *American Journal of Political Science*, 42: 28–54.

Lijphart, Arend (1999). *Patterns of Democracy: Government Forms and Performance in Thirty-Six Countries.* New Haven, CT: Yale University Press.

Luebbert, Gregory M. (1986). *Comparitive Democracy: Policy Making and Governing Coalitions in Europe and Israel,* New York, N9: Columbia University Press.

Lupia, Arthur and Strøm, Kaare (1995). 'Coalition Termination and the Strategic Timing of Parliamentary Elections', *American Political Science Review*, 89: 648–65.

—— and McCubbins, Mathew D. (1998). *The Democratic Dilemma: Can Citizens Learn What They Need to Know?* Cambridge: Cambridge University Press.

Marsh, Michael and Mitchell, Paul (1999). 'Office, Votes, and Then Policy: Hard Choices for Political Parties in the Republic of Ireland', in Wolfgang C. Müller and Kaare Strøm (eds.), *Policy, Office, or Votes? How Political Parties in Western Europe Make Hard Decisions.* Cambridge: Cambridge University Press.

McMillan, John (1992). *Games, Strategies, and Managers: How Managers Can Use Game Theory to Make Better Business Decisions.* New York, NY: Oxford University Press.

Miliband, Ralph. 1990. *Divided Societies: Class Conflict in Contemporary Capitalism.* Oxford: Oxford University Press.

Müller, Wolfgang C. (2000). 'Political Parties in Parliamentary Democracies: Making Delegation and Accountability Work', *European Journal of Political Research*, 37: 309–33.

—— and Strøm, Kaare (eds.) (1999). *Policy, Office, or Votes? How Political Parties in Western Europe Make Hard Decisions.* Cambridge: Cambridge University Press.

—— —— (2000). 'Conclusion: Coalition Governance in Western Europe', in Wolfgang C. Müller and Kaare Strøm (eds.), *Coalition Governments in Western Europe.* Oxford: Oxford University Press.

Poguntke, Thomas (1999). 'The Winner Takes All: The FDP in 1982–1983: Maximizing Cotes, Office, and Policy?' in Wolfgang C. Müller and Kaare Strøm (eds.), *Policy, Office, or Votes. How Political Parties in Western Europe Make Hard Decisions.* Cambridge: Cambridge University Press.

Powell, G. Bingham, Jr. (1982). *Contemporary Democracies.* Cambridge, MA: Harvard University Press.

Riker, William H. (1962). *The Theory of Political Coalitions.* New Haven, CT: Yale University Press.

Rokkan, Stein (1966). 'Norway: Numerical Democracy and Corporate Pluralism', in Robert A. Dahl (ed.), *Political Oppositions in Western Democracies.* New Haven, CT: Yale University Press.

Shapley, Lloyd S. and Shubik, Martin (1954). 'A Method for Evaluating the Distribution of Power in a Committee System', *American Political Science Review*, 48: 787–92.

Strøm, Kaare (1990). 'A Behavioral Theory of Competitive Political Parties', *American Journal of Political Science*, 34: 565–98.

—— (1994). 'The Presthus Debacle: Intraparty Politics and Bargaining Failure in Norway'. *American Political Science Review*, 88: 112–27.

—— and Swindle, Stephen M. (2002). 'Strategic Parliamentary Dissolution', *American Political Science Review*, 96: 575–91.

—— Budge, Ian and Laver, Michael J. (1994). 'Constraints on Cabinet Formation in Parliamentary Democracies', *American Journal of Political Science*, 38: 303–35.

—— Muller, Wolfgang C., and Bergman, Torbjörn (eds.) (2003). *Delegation and Accountability in Parliamentary Democracies*, Oxford: Oxford University Press.

Thelen, Kathleen and Steinmo, Sven (1992). 'Historical Institutionalism in Comparative Politics', in Sven Steinmo, Kathleen Thelen, and Frank Longstreth (eds.), *Structuring Politics: Historical Institutionalism in Comparative Politics*. Cambridge: Cambridge University Press.

Warwick, Paul V. (1992). 'Rising Hazards: An Underlying Dynamic of Parliamentary Government', *American Journal of Political Science*, 36: 857–76.

—— (1994). *Government Survival in Parliamentary Democracies*. Cambridge: Cambridge University Press.

—— and Easton, Stephen (1992). 'The Cabinet Stability Controversy: New Perspectives on a Classic Problem', *American Journal of Political Science*, 36: 122–46.

Williamson, Oliver E. (1975). *Markets and Hierarchies: Analysis and Antitrust Implications*. New York, NY: Free Press.

—— (1993). 'Contested Exchange versus the Governance of Contested Relations', *Journal of Economic Perspectives*, 7: 103–8.

3

The Empirical Study of Cabinet Governance

Torbjörn Bergman, Elisabeth R. Gerber, Scott Kastner, and Benjamin Nyblade[1]

INTRODUCTION

To understand why and how political actors form, govern, and terminate cabinets we must consider the choices made by these actors under uncertainty and complexity as well as under the shadow of the past and the promise of the future. We are thus interested in both retrospective and anticipatory logics, and in how this is played out in the real world. Drawing on the first two chapters of this book, in the following eight chapters the contributors analyse specific phases of the governmental process, including the bargaining process, coalition contracts, cabinet composition, portfolio allocation, conflict management, termination, duration, and electoral performance.

These stages in a cabinet's life are interrelated. Conceptually, this interrelatedness implies a complex set of relationships between actions and outcomes, laden with multiple levels of feedback and reciprocal causality. These dynamics of cabinet governance are difficult to capture—both in analytical models and in empirical research (e.g. Laver 1974; Laver and Schofield 1990; Diermeier 2006). We nevertheless try to provide insight into each phase (or stage or set of decisions) and consider how other phases relate to them.

By necessity, we must place chapters in some order, even when the stages that we analyse do not necessarily have a precise chronological order. The logic that places the chapters on formation and coalition contracts before government type is fairly straightforward: political parties typically negotiate among each other before a new cabinet is formed, and that takes time. Coalition partners also must come to agreement with each other and work out some form of contract (either formal or informal), before the government is actually formed.

---

[1] The authors of this chapter gratefully acknowledge the help of Thomas Saalfeld, both for his advice on the chapter and for the original drafting of the section on event-history (duration) analysis (Appendix C). We have also greatly benefited from comments by Patrick Dumont.

The precise orders of the next steps in the coalition cycle are also a matter of deliberate choice on our part. We place portfolio allocation and conflict management mechanisms after the chapter on government membership. We do not believe that real-life politicians keep these phases strictly sequential. Rather, bargaining over these types of arrangements are intertwined elements of the negotiations that take place early in the coalitional life cycle. Nevertheless, it is possible to identify some sequential patterns even at the formation stage. For example, portfolios are rarely distributed and conflict management mechanisms are by necessity uncertain until the partisan make-up of the new government has been decided. Thus our chapters on the distribution of cabinet portfolios and conflict management mechanisms follow the chapter on the type of cabinet formed.

When the coming chapters search for the independent variables that most influence the dependent variables at each stage of the life cycle, our contributors review the available literature and test commonly used variables and new variables created specifically for this volume. In the next section, we present our joint approach in more detail. In the subsequent sections, we discuss our data: our sample, our independent variables, and our dependent variables. We also discuss the basic methodological choices we have made in conducting the statistical analyses. More details on the variables and the code book are presented in Appendix A, Appendix B reports on additional sources used for the macroeconomic data, while Appendix C provides more technical detail on the statistical methods we employ.

OUR APPROACH

The literature on the logic of comparative politics is huge. From John Stuart Mill's *A System of Logic* (and its method of agreement vs. the method of difference) (1843), Przeworski and Teune's 'most similar' and 'most different' systems designs (1970), and other modern 'classics' such as Lijphart (1971), Sartori (1970), and many others, the field of comparative politics has acquired both a shared analytical understanding and enduring controversies about case selection and concepts. There are also various approaches to data collection.

When Peter Mair (1998) assessed the state of the discipline in comparative politics, he suggested that

> despite the evident increase in statistical and methodological sophistication of comparative political research in recent years, and despite the very obvious theoretical ambition, the actual data which are employed remain remarkably crude... And since it is precisely this lack of solid comparative data which is encouraging the virtual fetishization of whatever indicators might be available, regardless of their potential fallibility, it must surely remain a priority for comparative research to stimulate the collection of systematically comparable data....
>
> (Mair 1998: 327–8)

As a remedy, Mair (1998: 331) favours 'the bringing together of more case sensitive, context-sensitive groups of studies which, through team effort, and through collaborative group effort, can genuinely advance comparative understanding....'

As should already be evident from the introductory chapters of this book, we agree. Precise theorizing and rigourous modelling can be undone by sloppy empirical work. In addition to contributing to a better understanding of the coalitional life cycle and the interconnections between its various stages, we strive to put rational choice inspired research on coalitional politics in parliamentary democracies on a better empirical and operational footing by creating and using the most valid cross-national indicators possible.

As Chapter 1 explains, and Mair (1998) advocates, we have applied a 'structured collaboration' approach in order to build a better data-set. For one thing, most of our data have been generated by genuine country experts, specialists on parliamentary democracy and coalition politics in their country. The contributors to *Coalition Governments in Western Europe* (Müller and Strøm 2000) collected and presented the information we have used on cabinet governance. The companion volume *Delegation and Accountability in Parliamentary Democracies* (Strøm, Müller, and Bergman 2003) presents data on institutions and constitutional rules in Western European parliamentary democracies. In both volumes, based on criteria generated at regular meetings of the research group, country experts present systematic information based on the national literature, parliamentary rules of procedures, intra-party documents, official government records, and archival material. In these meetings, the experts interacted repeatedly for the purpose of discussing, defining, and implementing cross-national operational indicators that are applicable across our sample of 17 countries. This process of interaction with and among the country experts has been the hallmark of this project, and it is our basic insurance against large measurement errors.

While we believe that we have the best available data on coalitions and political institutions in Western Europe, determining the best way to analyse this data has been a substantial challenge. In this chapter, we address some very difficult issues of variable selection and statistical estimation. As each of the subsequent chapters draws from a single data-set and uses a similar approach to statistical analysis, we believe it is most efficient to address many of these issues in this chapter instead of in the separate empirical chapters. Thus, the remainder of this chapter focuses on explaining this volume's data, dependent variables, independent variables, and choice of statistical models.

The approach taken in all of the chapters in this volume is a cross-national goodness-of-fit approach. Each chapter seeks not to explain how or why a particular cabinet formed or terminated in some country, but rather what factors produce common and generalizable trends across countries and over time. We challenge scholars of comparative politics who argue that each country must be understood in isolation, that a factor such as institutional design alone determines outcomes, or that actor preferences are all that matter. Instead, we hold that much is to be learned by understanding how the combination of institutions and preferences produces regularities in political phenomena. The analyses rely on data from the 17 countries in our data-set (our sample is discussed in more detail in the next section) to uncover these relationships.

In our statistical analyses, we consider the importance of blocks (or clusters) of variables that frequently have been studied in isolation in previous work. As other studies that the contributors to this book have conducted jointly make painstakingly clear, country studies and 'thick' empirical description have and should have a place in research on coalitions and other topics in comparative politics. But the various research strategies can and should be used in combination, and should be viewed as complementary rather than competing (King, Keohane, and Verba 1994). Since our primary concern in this study is to identify and explore trends across the 17 countries in our sample, we have chosen a quantitative approach that allows us to more efficiently consider the long history of post-war cabinet government in all these countries. We supplement the quantitative analyses with illustrative examples and illuminating cases. We believe that, building upon developments in the field and our previous data collection efforts and analyses, this comprehensive empirical approach provides us with a unique opportunity to contribute to our understanding of coalition government.

Our decision to pursue such a course involves significant trade-offs. For example, if we instead had chosen to focus on identifying historic cases in which 'give-and-take' relationships between actors have been central, we might have produced an alternative set of insights relevant to the project's goal of 'bringing bargaining into coalition analysis'. On the other hand, our analyses may provide a basis for further analytical modelling and for further empirical research that move beyond the framework developed here. One avenue is to use this style of work to identify critical cases that may improve our empirical understanding of coalition politics more generally (De Winter, Andeweg, and Dumont 2008) or as a basis to engage in process tracing (Bäck and Dumont 2007). This is a useful next step; indeed, Andeweg and Timmermans use such an approach in chapter 8 to explore the new research agenda on conflict resolution mechanisms. Our hope is that others will see this book as an inspiration to conduct in-depth case studies, as a stimulus for further development and testing of game-theoretical research, and for continuing improvements to cross-national quantitative analyses of cabinet governance.

OUR SAMPLE

All of the chapters in this volume take the cabinet as their basic unit of analysis.[2] In general, we use the data and definitions of a cabinet from our previous

---

[2] We count a change of cabinet with the occurrence of any one of the following conditions: 1. Any change in the set of parties holding cabinet membership. We count as members of the cabinet only those parties that have designated representatives with cabinet voting rights. External support

The Empirical Study of Cabinet Governance

TABLE 3.1. *Variations in country samples in cross-national coalition studies*

Country	This volume (2008)	Martin and Stevenson (2001)	Warwick (1994)	Budge and Keman (1990)	Franklin and Mackie (1984)
Australia				X	
Austria	X	X	X	X	X
Belgium	X	X	X	X	X
Canada		X		X	
Denmark	X	X	X	X	X
Finland	X		X	X	X
France IV			X	X	
France V	X			X	
Germany (West before reunification)	X	X	X	X	X
Greece	X				
Iceland	X	X	X		
Ireland	X	X	X	X	X
Israel		X		X	X
Italy	X	X	X	X	X
Japan				X	
Luxembourg	X	X	X	X	X
The Netherlands	X	X	X	X	X
New Zealand				X	
Norway	X	X	X	X	X
Portugal	X		X		
Spain	X		X		
Sweden	X	X	X	X	X
United Kingdom	X	X	X	X	

Note: Our data end on 1 January 1999. The other literature cited above use data-sets that end in the 1980s.

collaborative work (Müller and Strøm 2000, second edition 2003), though the data-set is expanded from that volume to include data from Greece, Iceland, Spain, and the United Kingdom. Our sample thus includes 424 cabinets from 1945–99 in 17 Western European countries. As Table 3.1 shows, our 17 countries closely match other samples that have been used in cross-national research from Franklin and Mackie (1984) to Martin and Stevenson (2001). What is perhaps unique to our sample is that it covers the universe of parliamentary democracies in Western

parties, i.e., parties that support the cabinet in parliament without holding cabinet portfolios, are not included. 2. Any change in the identity of the prime minister. By prime minister, we mean the head of the cabinet, whatever title that office might have (e.g. federal chancellor and president of the council of state). 3. Any general election, whether mandated by the end of the *constitutional interelection period* (CIEP) (see King et al. 1990), or precipitated by an early (or extra) election. 'Date in' is the date that the PM/cabinet was inaugurated by the head of state (in Sweden the date of the investiture vote in the Riksdag) or, if that is not applicable, the date of the general election. 'Date out' is the date of the general election (or, when applicable, the date of presidential elections if it is required or customary for governments to resign at the time of presidential elections), or the date of the formal resignation, whichever comes first (Müller and Strøm 2000: 11–17).

Europe. While there is still great variation among the countries that are commonly or sometimes included in related analyses, we exclude only countries from other continents (e.g. Australia, Canada, Israel, and Japan). Moreover, we are able to include countries from Western Europe that have rarely been included elsewhere, such as Greece, Iceland, Luxembourg, Portugal, and Spain. By including political systems that are regularly governed by coalitions in which two or more parties usually share cabinet portfolios (Continental Europe), countries where such coalitions are more infrequent (Scandinavia) and countries where coalitions are rare events at best (such as Greece, Spain, and the UK), we are able to inform not only the literature on coalitional systems but also the literature on cabinet governance in parliamentary democracies in general.

OUR DEPENDENT VARIABLES

Our empirical work is very much in the tradition of previous work on coalition bargaining in parliamentary democracies. We too analyse separate stages (or phases) of the coalition cycle such as the formation and the termination of coalitions. But we do not assume that such phases are best studied in isolation from one another. Instead, we believe that what happened at previous stages and what actors anticipate about future stages can have an important impact on bargaining today. Thus, we identify eight distinct steps in the life cycle of coalitions that we believe are useful to keep analytically separate, but recognize in our analyses that these stages influence each other. Each chapter effectively defines one or more distinct dependent variables that represent important aspects of bargaining across the entire life of a cabinet.

Unlike many analyses of coalition governance that begin with a new government taking office, this volume begins, in Chapter 4, with an analysis of the cabinet formation (bargaining) process. In that chapter, De Winter and Dumont seek to explain cross-national variation in the duration of the formation process. They ask, for example: Why does government formation takes but a few days or weeks in some cases while in others it can take months and sometimes the better part of a year? And why do inconclusive bargaining rounds (bargaining among actors who do not create a new cabinet) occur in some cases whereas in others those who first begin bargaining do end up forming a new cabinet? Chapter 4 includes event history analyses which isolate the conditions that promote long formation processes and logit analyses which identify what situations lead to inconclusive bargaining rounds. More detail on the specific statistical analysis used for each chapter will be given below and in the relevant chapters.

As potential coalition partners bargain, they often consider creating a formal coalition agreement that outlines the results of their negotiations over policies, positions, and procedures. Political parties have become much more likely to write explicit contracts over time. In Chapter 5, Müller and Strøm explore the reasoning behind and importance of these coalition agreements, focusing on their role as *ex ante* mechanisms intended to solve transaction problems of uncertainty and opportunism. This chapter both analyses the factors that lead to formal coalition agreements and considers their relationship to other potential mechanisms for solving these transaction problems.

In Chapter 6, Mitchell and Nyblade return to the classical question of what type of government forms: one-party or multiparty, minority or majority. In analysing these fundamental questions, this chapter focuses on the impact of two sets of variables, one set focusing on the distribution of bargaining power among political parties, the other on the nature of the bargaining environment.

The distribution of cabinet portfolios (and other office benefits) among parties and individuals can be a sensitive and delicate matter. When party size and walk-away values strongly correlate, we should expect the proportionality (or parity) norm to be enforced. Deviations in proportionality should occur in cases in which the size and walk-away values differ significantly. In Chapter 7, Verzichelli considers the implications of this for violations of the proportionality norm of ministerial portfolio allocation, building on the literature on 'Gamson's law'— the idea that each political party forming a coalition gets roughly the same share of cabinet portfolios as the share of parliamentary votes that it brings to the bargaining table (Gamson 1961). In this chapter, Verzichelli also explores what factors might lead parties to change the number of portfolios over which bargaining occurs, and the determinants of whether parties allocate 'watchdog' junior ministers from parties other than that of the senior minister. This latter analysis provides a consideration of one potential *ex post* mechanism used to resolve the transaction problems inherent in coalition government.

As outlined in Chapter 2, we expect future-oriented party leaders to realize that conflicts and disagreement will occur throughout the tenure of a coalition. At the very outset, in addition to designing a coalition contract and allocating portfolios, they therefore design various conflict management mechanisms. Some of these will be very informal and perhaps implicit, such as a norm that larger problems are in the end dealt with by the party leaders of the parties represented in the cabinet. Other cabinets might set up fairly elaborate intra-cabinet mechanisms, mechanisms that lie outside the cabinet (such as meetings of party elites), or institutions that combine internal and external features (e.g. including both cabinet members and party elites outside the cabinet). In Chapter 8, Andeweg and Timmermans first analyse whether these conflict resolution arrangements, regardless of formality, are internal to the cabinet or include external actors. In the second part of that chapter, via two case studies, they explore how such arrangements can develop and work in specific contexts. They also distinguish between the regular arenas, that is, those used most commonly by coalition partners, and those that are used for the most serious conflicts. This provides a novel picture of how the governance arrangements work when put under stress.

The subsequent two chapters analyse how well the coalition partners manage to sustain their coalition. In Chapter 9, Damgaard looks into the question of what factors influence the manner in which a cabinet terminates. The dependent variables are types of termination, which can be subdivided into technical and discretionary. Technical terminations are those that are necessitated by the constitution, such as the maximum length of the parliament and the requirement to hold elections, even when the incumbent cabinet is stable and popular, or are caused by reasons beyond the immediate control of the politicians themselves, such as (presumably) the death of the prime minister (PM). The discretionary category is further subdivided into whether the termination is related to conflict within the governing party or parties or is voluntary—either a voluntary early election or voluntary cabinet enlargement.

In Chapter 10, Saalfeld focuses on the determinants of cabinet duration, which has often been taken as an indicator of political stability. Cabinet duration is a well-studied topic—perhaps the most studied after cabinet formation—and is also a topic that has been characterized by strong methodological developments over the past several decades. Developing from basic bivariate comparisons, the field is now dominated by analyses of hazard rates using event history (duration) models. Saalfeld's chapter contributes to this already quite sophisticated literature by considering more explicitly the impact of transaction costs and the bargaining environment, in addition to some of the more traditional structural and preference-based factors more commonly considered.

The final empirical chapter, Chapter 11, by Narud and Valen, considers the factors that influence governments' electoral performance. Cabinets (in aggregate) and cabinet parties (individually) tend to be punished by the electorate, that is, they lose votes in the next election. But there is clear variation in the extent to which voters punish certain types of cabinets, and under what circumstances they are likely to do so. This variation is both a reason why the topic of electoral performance is so interesting to scholars and, presumably, is why politicians that join a government can harbour very different expectations of vote gains in the next election. Narud and Valen not only consider the factors that influence overall cabinet performance but also analyse the performance of the parties of the prime minister and the finance minister.

OUR INDEPENDENT VARIABLES

The dependent variables used in each chapter's statistical analyses are summarized in Table 3.2. Each of these dependent variables is analysed using a common framework for determining various types of independent variables, which we explain in more detail below.

The Empirical Study of Cabinet Governance

TABLE 3.2. *Dependent variables used in statistical analyses in this volume*

Ch	Variable	Type	Method of analysis
4	Cabinet bargaining duration	Duration	Cox prop. hazard
	Inconclusive bargaining round	Dichotomous	Logit
5	Coalition agreement	Dichotomous	Logit
6	Coalition government	Dichotomous	Logit
	Cabinet status	Categorical	Multinomial logit
7	Cabinet disproportionality	Continuous	OLS
	No. of cabinet ministers	Continuous	OLS
	Watchdog junior ministers	Dichotomous	Logit
8	Conflict management arena (most serious, most common)	Dichotomous	Logit
9	Termination type	Categorical	Multinomial logit
10	Cabinet duration	Duration	Cox prop. hazard
11	Cabinet electoral performance	Continuous	OLS
	PM, Finance Minister party electoral performance	Continuous	OLS

Scholars have looked to several different types of variables to better understand and explain cabinet governance. Some scholars have emphasized variables focusing on the policy preferences of actors, others on resources or institutions, while others have focused on contextual factors. As emphasized in Chapter 2, we think there is considerable merit in drawing on all these types of variables to better understand cabinet governance. These variables can be better drawn together by placing them in a framework that focuses on the challenges parliamentary parties face in bargaining in a world of imperfect information, commitment and delegation problems, transaction costs, and uncertainty about the future.

Analytical concepts such as walk-away values, opportunism, uncertainty, complexity, and discount rates of individual parties are difficult to operationalize, although, particularly in regards to uncertainty and complexity, there is some precedent and examples in the literature that attempt to capture these concepts. We draw on these advances. Below and in the empirical chapters that follow, our statistical analyses focus on attempting to better understand coalition governance by grouping variables in blocks. We present the results of each of these blocks separately, and then present joint models that include variables from all of the blocks.

For each dependent variable on which we conduct multivariate analyses, we start our statistical investigation with a 'time and space' block, using decade and country dummies as appropriate, followed by structural variables, preference variables, institutional variables, bargaining environment variables, and critical events variables. The appropriate independent variables to use in each block will vary according to the stage in the cycle of cabinet governance and the specific dependent variable, but below we present the overall structure of these clusters and discuss the variables included.

Cluster 1: Spatial and temporal parameters

Our analyses are based on a pooled data-set containing information about the post-war cabinets of 17 Western European countries. In pooling the data from these cabinets, we are making the judgement that the dynamics underlying cabinet governance are driven by the same fundamental factors across these countries. However, as scholars of comparative politics well know, the cases you choose can influence the results you get, and one of the most important findings in the first published multivariate analysis of political coalitions (Franklin and Mackie 1984) was that the results are sensitive to the sample of countries included in the analysis. Indeed, our analyses in subsequent chapters show that the between-country variation can sometimes be extreme. Cross-national relationships between particular variables can be different from the relationship that exists between the same variables in some specific country (Grofman 1989). We therefore take both time and space seriously by reporting the variation in our dependent variable across countries and over time descriptively, and by considering the effectiveness of time and space in explaining our dependent variables statistically.

Our first model in each of the multivariate statistical analyses includes decade dummies (binary variables), which help us consider the statistical significance of any trend over time in the dependent variable. When statistically appropriate, we also include country dummy variables in this first model. It is worth noting that our observations (424 cabinets) do not form time-consistent intervals, so given the great variation in the duration of cabinets in our data-set, with some lasting only a few weeks and others lasting up to five years, it is not clear what stronger time controls would be appropriate beyond our consideration of major trends over time. As both decade and country dummy variables are mutually exhaustive, one variable from each set is chosen to be the excluded (baseline) category in our multivariate analyses. In our multivariate analyses, Germany is the excluded country, while the 1950s are the excluded decade.[3] This means that the coefficients of the other country and decade dummies must be interpreted relative to the 1950s and to Germany.

Considering a block of space and time variables allows us to consider the extent to which there are significant trends over time, and the extent to which country peculiarities 'explain' the variation in our dependent variable. However, it is important to note that we do not include country dummies in this cluster in logistic regression models. When there is no variation in the dependent variable within any one country, logit models drop that country from the analysis. Because of this, the number of observations can vary greatly, making comparison of the predictive power of our models across blocks essentially meaningless. Instead, for

---

[3] We selected Germany as our comparison category because it a major and well-known country and it is not 'unusual' in the sense of being completely dominated by some particular type of cabinet. Similarly, the 1950s do not generally stand out as a deviant decade marked by highly unusual events.

models relying on logistic regression, we report on country effects in a note to the tables. We report the overall percentage of observations correctly predicted based on country mode (in effect assuming that a particular country always generates the same value on a particular variable), which we then compare to the prediction rate of each of our other models.

To provide a brief example, in Chapter 6 Mitchell and Nyblade conduct a logit analysis of whether or not bargaining leads to a coalition forming in minority situations. Four countries are perfectly predicted: in Luxembourg and the Netherlands coalitions always form, whereas in Spain and the UK they never do. These countries are automatically dropped if country dummies are included in the analysis, thus significantly altering the sample size compared to other models. So rather than including the country dummies in the first model, we include only decade dummies, but also report in the text and in a note at the bottom of the table that a country dummy model predicts coalitions in every country except Norway, Spain, Sweden, and Britain (the four countries in which fewer than half of all cabinets have been coalitions) and that such country dummies alone correctly predict 268 of 340 cases (79%). We report the percentage correctly predicted for each model (in addition to the frequently used McFadden's pseudo-R^2), thus providing another method of interpreting the explanatory power of our statistical models relative to country-level effects.

Cluster 2: Structural attributes

Our second block of variables focus on structural attributes of the political system. Structural attributes come primarily in three types: features of the political system, of the parliamentary party system, and of the cabinet itself. We are not simply interested in exogenously determined structures, but in endogenously determined structures as well. Many of the structures are themselves the direct result of bargained outcomes in prior stages of the cabinet governance cycle, or are at least strongly influenced by earlier experiences of cabinet governance.

Some of these structural variables reflect the 'size of the pie' either temporally or in other ways. For example, we frequently test the influence of the maximum possible duration of government (in days) and whether a government immediately follows an election on various aspects of cabinet governance. Similarly, the number of ministries and the number of cabinet members are also structural variables that may influence the resources available for division by governing parties (see Chapter 7).

A second set of variables pertain to the resource distribution in the parliamentary party system. These are the classic variables based on the size and number of parties. We rely primarily on three key variables to capture the size and number of parties: the absolute number of parliamentary parties, the effective number of parliamentary parties, and the fragmentation of the parliamentary parties' bargaining power.[4] Essentially, all three measures count the number of parties, but they weight the parties differently. The absolute number of parties gives each party equal weight, regardless of size. The effective number of parliamentary parties gives each party weight according to their seat share in parliament, as per the method first advocated in political science by Laakso and Taagepera (1979). Our measure of bargaining power fragmentation gives parties weights based on their bargaining power. As discussed in Strøm, Müller, and Bergman (2003: 667), we base our calculation on the normalized Banzhaf index because it has preferable properties, relative to its major alternative, the Shapley–Shubik index.[5]

The bargaining power of a party derives from the number of seats it holds in parliament (relative to the number of seats held by other parties) and how often the inclusion of the party turns proto-coalitions into winning coalitions. The greater the proportion of winning (majority) coalitions to which the party is crucial in forming in a given parliament, the greater the bargaining power of that party. The bargaining power scores assigned to each party are normalized such that they always sum to 1. For example, if one party holds a majority of the seats, its bargaining power score is 1, and the bargaining power value assigned to all other parties in that parliament is 0, because the party is necessary for every majority government. If there are three parties in parliament, any two of which can form a majority coalition, bargaining power is equal: each party is given a bargaining power score of one-third.

Our measure of bargaining power fragmentation is calculated similarly to the effective number of parliamentary parties, but uses bargaining weights rather than seat shares as the weight given to each party. Thus, if there is a majority party, the measure has a score of 1, if there are three parties with equal bargaining power, our bargaining fragmentation measure has a score of 3. Dumont and Caulier (2005) suggest calling this measure the 'Effective Number of Relevant Parties' as this method captures Sartori's concept of 'relevant' parties.

In our data-set, the 'effective number of parties' and 'bargaining power fragmentation' are quite highly correlated ($r=.84$). In many analyses, if these variables

---

[4] Several chapters also specifically consider the importance of the seat share or bargaining power (based on the Banzhaf index) of the largest party in parliament.

[5] We are grateful to Madeleine O. Hosli for generating the first set of indexes for this project. The scores have later been checked and updated with the help of the 'Powerslave' online calculator that is available on the web page of Antti Pajala, the University of Turku (http://powerslave.val.utu.fi/). Because of the frequent occurrence of electoral alliances and a high number of independents or small 'other parties' in Italy (both chambers) and the upper chamber in Belgium, the electoral list alliance AD in Portugal in the early 1980s, and the existence of 'over hang' seats (*Überhangmandate*) and the merger of parties during German unification, calculating seat share is not always straightforward. In these countries and cases, we avoid making heroic assumptions about placing individual MPs in particular party groups. Nor do we count all independents, who can be of many different ideological persuasions, as one group. This sometimes means that in these countries and cases not all individual MPs have been included in the calculations, but the differences that occur (e.g. in the bargain power fragmentation score) are minor and we prefer this strategy to artificially assigning MPs to party groups.

are included simultaneously, the standard errors for each coefficient become inflated and none are statistically significant, despite the fact that any single variable used to capture the underlying distribution of parliamentary seats could be highly significant and have great explanatory power. Rather than lead people to incorrectly infer that these variables are irrelevant, we choose whichever measure is superior for theoretical or empirical reasons specific to each dependent variable. For most of our chapters, we have found that bargaining power fragmentation usually is the preferred measure rather than the more commonly used effective number of parliamentary parties, a finding that we believe is based on the former variable's ability to more directly capture the bargaining situation in parliament (also consistent with Dumont and Caulier 2005). However, there are a few cases where we chose to use the effective number of parties to be more consistent with the existing literature.

A third and final set of structural variables is based on the government that actually formed. This set includes variables measuring the size and number of cabinet parties, whether the largest parliamentary party is in the cabinet and the fragmentation of bargaining power among cabinet parties. Many variables also capture the type of cabinet: whether it is non-partisan, has a parliamentary majority or minority, is a coalition, is a minimal winning coalition or surplus coalition, etc. While some of these structural variables should not be used, for example, to predict the length of the formation process (which is prior to the formation of the cabinet), these can at later stages in the cabinet life cycle turn out to be important predictors of other facets of cabinet governance.

Cluster 3: Preferences

The variables in the third cluster capture policy preferences. These variables normally pertain to some combination of the ideal points of parties in policy space, usually on the left–right dimension. One set of variables considers the nature of the policy preferences in the parliamentary party system. Variables include the range of left–right preferences, the number of issue dimensions, and the ideological cohesiveness of the opposition.

Another set of variables is based on the preferences of those in government: whether the government is connected and/or minimal connected winning, whether the government includes parties that are median on one (i.e. left–right dimension) or two major issue dimensions (i.e. left–right one and the main alternative dimension, which may differ from country to country), the range of preferences in the government, and whether the government is predominantly leftist or rightist. The preference data is based primarily on two different sources: expert placements on a first (left–right) and, when applicable, a second dimension in each country, and party manifesto data.[6]

---

[6] Two additional variables, coding whether the cabinet was made up of a majority of conservative or socialist parties (used in Chapters 10 and 11 in interaction with economic variables), are based

With respect to the expert placements, parties in each country are arranged on a left–right scale (first policy dimension), such that party 1 in each country is the party situated farthest to the left on the country's ideological spectrum. For most countries, this party alignment is from the expert survey presented in Laver and Hunt (1992). For political parties not included in that survey, country experts have placed the parties on a left–right scale using the most reliable and authoritative sources available.[7] Since the expert placements are invariant over time, this left–right ordering of parties is constant within particular countries throughout the duration of the data-set. The left–right scale is used in conjunction with seats data to determine the median legislative party for each cabinet in both the lower chamber and, if applicable, the upper chamber. The scale is also used to generate a dummy variable indicating whether the cabinet parties are connected ideologically on the left–right scale or on a second policy dimension, as determined by our country experts, and also a variable for whether there is a single party that controls the median on the first two major issue dimensions. Our country experts on Denmark and France determined that there was no single consistent second policy dimension, so for these countries we have simply assumed that there is only a single issue dimension, and coded variables relating to a second issue dimension to mirror the first.

Finally, a series of variables code a left–right ideological score for each party in each cabinet using platform data from the Party Manifesto Research Group (Budge et al. 2001). These data also allow us to consider changes in party positions over time. The manifesto data code the proportion of party manifestos devoted to various policy issues; they are transformed into a scale on a single ideological dimension using the method detailed by Laver and Budge (1992: 15–30). Briefly, each party's coding reflects the proportion of its manifesto devoted to right policy references (e.g. 'enterprise' or 'law and order') minus the proportion devoted to left policy references (e.g. 'regulation of capitalism' or 'social service expansion: positive'). The party scores range from −100 (far left) to 100 (far right). This same manifesto data is also used to calculate an 'effective number of issue dimensions' (often labelled 'issue dimensionality') based on a fairly simple method which calculates the similarity of the various issues coded in the

---

on a separate series of variables that code the family, or type, of each party in each country. All party family codings have been determined by our country experts. Parties are given 1 of 12 classifications: communist; left-socialist; social democratic; green; agrarian; regional, separatist, or ethno-nationalist; liberal; Christian; conservative; right-wing; extreme right-wing; or special interest or other parties. Parties are allowed to change families over time, thus allowing us to test the 'snap-shot' placement of expert surveys against a more detailed account that allows for variation in party alignment over time. For example, communist parties in both Italy and Sweden became left-socialist in the early 1990s.

[7] This is particularly relevant for countries not included in *Coalition Governments in Western Europe* (Müller and Strøm 2000). Countries new to the current volume are Greece, Iceland, Spain, and the United Kingdom.

manifestos and then weights the various issues by their similarity and importance, as explained in Nyblade (2004).

The manifesto data have come in for some criticism. We agree with parts of this critique, such as Pelizzo (2003), who points out that the Manifesto Group approach has generated some peculiar results for some parties at some times in some places. The manifesto left–right scale has been criticized for being (*a*) based on the UK party system and (*b*) assumed to be applicable to all countries and all periods. This is of course a heroic (and sometimes flawed) assumption, but also provides us (and the scholarly community at large) with one common 'yardstick' for all our countries. We can reasonably argue that this yardstick, which is not drawn endogenously from the party system (except perhaps in the UK), is at least independent from the measurement itself.

For an overwhelming majority of parties in an overwhelming majority of cases, the measurement errors are relatively small, and most party positions (at least for ordinal alignments) are fairly well captured in the manifesto data. In any case, it is the best data available to us. Thus, although clearly the manifesto data should be used with care, we still advocate its use (see Gabel and Huber 2000; Budge et al. 2001 for further justification). And since we use not only manifesto data but also data based on expert judgements, we are in a position to cross-validate our results.

Many of the measures we place in the preferences cluster are based not simply on the preferences of parties, but on the interaction of the parties' preferences and their size. This is the approach strongly advocated by Laver and Shepsle (1996), among others. Laver and Shepsle (1996) derive the existence of 'strong' and 'very strong' parties in coalition bargaining based on formal models. While none of our chapter authors chose to draw on Laver and Shepsle's precise definitions of terms, we have used a measure that captures whether or not a party holds the dimension-by-dimension median (coded 1 when such a party does not exist, thus we call the variable 'No Core Party'). We also consider other variables that capture the relationship between structural and preference variables as well. For example, we have a variable that considers the seat share of extremist parties. And in addition to the ideological range of any given parliament, we also calculate a preference polarization measure, which is weighted by the bargaining power of the parties.[8] This indicator allows us to estimate the impact of ideological positions while attributing importance to the distance between parties that have more bargaining power. When estimating ideological diversity in the party system, parties that are pivotal (not necessarily because they are large but because they are essential for most winning coalitions) will count more than parties that have few coalition options. This also allows for comparison with other commonly used indicators of preference divergence in parliaments such as the manifesto range

---

[8] We use the same calculation for polarization as Warwick (1998: 342), except that our weighting of policy distances is based on parties' bargaining power rather than their seat share. See also Dodd (1976: 105).

and the parliamentary seat share of extremist (communist or extreme right-wing) parties.[9]

Cluster 4: Institutions

Our fourth cluster of variables focuses on institutions and institutional rules. These variables primarily fall into three types: electoral, parliamentary, and executive institutions. Almost all of the institutional data used in the analyses in this volume are described extensively in Strøm, Müller, and Bergman (2003). When it is not, we describe the variable below or in the chapter text. For each cabinet, these variables describe the national political institutions in place during the year of cabinet formation.

The electoral systems data include a variable that codes the electoral formula in use at the beginning of each cabinet (proportional, first past the post, the single transferable vote system, and so on), as well as electoral rules such as intra-party preference voting, district magnitude, and list PR.

Among the variables that measure parliamentary institutions, we include a set of variables concerning parliamentary dissolution powers, the status of a second chamber, and the various powers of the parliament vis-à-vis the government and government ministers. Several variables describe each country's inauguration rules, including the role of the head of state in appointments, the role of parliament, and the presence or absence of mandatory screening procedures by the parliament of the new cabinet's policy programme before or shortly after it assumes power. The quorum requirements, support requirements, and voting procedures of inaugurations by act of parliament are all coded as well. Variables relating to dissolution rules include the roles of the head of state, prime minister, cabinet and parliament, as well as the presence or absence of an automatic constitutional provision for dissolution. Two variables, for example, code the prime minister's role in the dissolution process. The first is simply a dummy variable indicating whether the PM has any role in parliamentary dissolution. If so, the second variable codes the extent of his powers relative to other constitutional actors, which can range from merely a symbolic role to having both the authority to dissolve on his own initiative as well as exclusive constitutional power to dissolve parliament before the constitutionally mandated election period is over. The variables that code the rules of confidence and no-confidence indicate the object of such votes (the PM/cabinet or individual ministers), rules of proposal, time constraints, and voting rules. The data-set also includes a dummy variable indicating the presence or absence of a positive investiture requirement. Two countries (Portugal and Sweden) have investiture votes that are negatively formulated. Here, unless more than half of all Members of Parliament vote against the cabinet, it is inaugurated

---

[9] Other measures that are used in some chapters incorporate both preference and structural factors. These include whether a cabinet is a minimal connected winning cabinet, the bargaining power of the median party, and the ideological distance of the largest party in parliament to the median party.

(Bergman 1993). Our definition means that when we test for the influence of an investiture requirement, we do so for the countries that have a positive investiture requirement. The distinction is not always made, but is an important one as a 'negative' and 'positive' parliamentarism implies quite different definitions of what constitutes a 'winning' coalition (Bergman et al. 2003: 148–52).

Executive institution variables measure the functioning of the executive: cabinet decision rules, powers of the prime minister, powers of the head of state (semi-presidentialism). We include several variables to capture the prime minister's powers, including appointment and dismissal powers, agenda power at cabinet meetings, rights to determine the jurisdiction of ministries, steering or coordination rights vis-à-vis other cabinet ministers, whether an administrative structure exists under the prime minister's control, and whether ministers' parliamentary accountability is via the prime minister only. An additional variable aggregates these separate powers into a single scale of the prime minister's authority, which ranges from 0 (holding none of the powers described above) to 7 (holding all of them). Details are available in Bergman et al. (2003: 183–94).

Institutional variables primarily vary between rather than within countries, so as with the structural attributes and preference variables, the institutional variables must be treated with care in multivariate statistical analyses. Including a large number of institutional variables may create some perverse interactions or effectively turn certain variables into country proxies. For example, one might be particularly interested in certain types of bicameral rules, such as 'strong' bicameralism in which a cabinet must be explicitly tolerated by both houses of parliament. However, in our sample such a variable would effectively be a country dummy for Belgium and Italy, meaning it would also capture other shared and comparatively unique features of Belgian and Italian politics, such as for example the presence of highly fragmented party systems with tendencies towards clientelistic politics. Thus when we consider the impact of bicameralism, we use a more general bicameralism variable (see also Druckman and Thies 2002: 769). In general, we avoid using institutional variables that isolate just a few countries in our sample, unless we have strong theoretical reasons for doing so—as in the case of using a variable for semi-presidentialism (which primarily reflects the French and Finnish experiences) in several chapters.

Cluster 5: Bargaining environment

Each of the chapters in this volume shares a common theoretical perspective in arguing that cabinet governance can be better understood through consideration of the challenges of bargaining in a complex world with imperfect information, commitment and delegation problems, transaction costs, and uncertainty about the future. Some of the effects of variables in the structural, preference, and institutional clusters discussed above may capture important aspects of the transaction costs that are involved. In this volume, we have particularly sought to develop measures that capture important aspects of transaction costs that are not captured in the more traditional types of variables. We group these variables together in our fifth cluster, and refer to them as our bargaining environment variables.

This cluster thus plays a crucial rule in the inter-related approach we take to understanding the various stages of cabinet governance. As the outcomes of one stage influence the bargaining environment of subsequent stages, it is important to consider the influence of earlier stages of the cycle on latter stages. One group of variables focuses on characteristics of the previous cabinet that may provide information about the bargaining environment the current cabinet faces. For example, if the prior cabinet was terminated due to conflict or an economic crisis, it may be a sign that the current cabinet is less valuable to its members. Similarly, if the current cabinet consists of the same parties or PM, there may be less uncertainty about the bargaining environment and potentially actors may have longer time horizons.

The other major group of variables we consider in the bargaining environment cluster consists of the results of earlier stages in the coalition cycle that cabinet parties determine to help manage the challenges of bargaining and delegation in an uncertain world. Thus the length of time required in forming a cabinet, and whether or not there were inconclusive bargaining rounds in government formation, both analysed in Chapter 4 as dependent variables, may indicate greater uncertainty or inability of parties to credibly commit to each other and are used as independent variables in later chapters. Coalition agreements, and the degree to which policy agreements are comprehensive, which are analysed as dependent variables in Chapter 5, also later become independent variables, as do the conflict management mechanisms analysed in Chapter 8. Another variable of this type is the extent to which parties in government agree that coalition discipline in legislation is required.

Cluster 6: Critical events

Our final cluster of variables also includes variables that influence the bargaining environment, but unlike our bargaining environment cluster, in this case we consider variables or events in the environment that do not arise from the various phases of cabinet governance. Thus this cluster brings together exogenous events or factors that the literature has long recognized as playing an important role in understanding cabinet governance: important 'shocks' in the political environment, truly exogenous events that lead to cabinet termination, electoral volatility, and economic performance. One such exogenous variable is the death of a prime minister. We have also collected country-specific information on popular opinion shocks, international or national security events, and economic events (such as a crisis). These variables were reported in Müller and Strøm (2000). Economic performance variables, including inflation, unemployment, and growth, have been gathered for this analysis as appropriate to the stage in the cycle. We use either economic measures at the beginning (e.g. in formation analyses), the end (e.g. in electoral performance analyses), or the entire period (e.g. in cabinet duration analyses). Appendix B reports the sources we have used for these economic variables.

Full and Final models

After introducing the variables we examine in our statistical analyses and assessing their impact in separate models for each block, we present two final models for each chapter. In a penultimate (full) model we include all variables significant in the individual blocks, those that are close to significant (generally those that have p value of less than .20), and other variables as appropriate given the expectations reported in each chapter. The full model analyses consistently show the importance of incorporating variables from all blocks in analyses of cabinet governance. We then estimate a final model based on the results of the full model, excluding those variables that are not robust and significant. Occasionally a variable may be significant in the full (penultimate) model, but not be robust enough to sustain its impact and be carried over into the final model.[10]

We believe that introducing models of the variables in separate blocks, and then incorporating variables from all blocks into two final models improves both the presentation and the transparency of our statistical analyses, allowing us to see how variables that may be significant in individual blocks are not robust to considering other types of variables. Note that in most of our analyses at least one variable from each block is significant and robust in the final model, suggesting that it is in fact important that scholars consider each of the types of independent variables we have discussed when analysing any stage of cabinet governance, though we leave this point for further discussion in the concluding chapter of this volume.

STATISTICAL ANALYSIS OF CROSS-NATIONAL DATA: OUR WAY

We use statistical analysis to draw inferences about a population by analysing data from a sample collected from the population. As we noted above, however, the 'sample' used in the analyses in this volume is uniquely comprehensive: it

---

[10] Another estimation choice we have made is that we generally do not test for multiplicative interactions between variables unless we have very good theoretical reasons to do so on the basis of an established literature on the particular subject matter. We do acknowledge that such interactions may exist, and that future work should explore these interactions in more detail. For our present purposes, however, estimation of such interactions effects is beyond the scope of our study and we avoid doing so except in Chapter 11, where the authors, drawing on a sizeable existing literature, test whether the effect of economic variables on the electoral performance of government may be contingent on its partisan composition using interactions.

consists of data from the entire universe of Western European cabinets in the post-war period. From one point of view, it is therefore not immediately clear what we are trying to draw inferences about, since the sample is coterminous with the population. Following the logic described in Shively (1998) and commonly used by quantitative political scientists, we believe that the notion of statistical inference still applies to our work in the following sense. Although we have data from all cabinets that actually occurred in the countries and the time period under examination, we recognize that there was an element of randomness present in each of the cabinets we examine. In other words, the dynamics of any particular cabinet might have turned out differently if some chance, random events (as opposed to predictable, systematic factors) had been different. In the spirit of developing generalizable explanatory theory, we are thus interested in drawing inferences about the population of potential cabinets that might have occurred in the past and that may occur in the future, recognizing the inherent randomness of social phenomena.

One purpose of the multivariate analysis is to estimate the effect of an independent (causal) variable on the dependent variable (i.e. the variable to be explained), controlling for the effects of other independent or control variables. Another purpose is to evaluate the confidence with which we can suggest that a relationship between variables exists. The specific estimation technique used in each chapter depends on how the dependent variable is measured. However, in our analyses we provide a common metric concerning statistical significance and provide means to substantively interpret the magnitude of the impact of significant variables.

Estimating statistical significance is important because it tells us how confident we ought to be in our estimates, given the size of our sample. A regression estimate that has a very high level of significance should weigh more heavily in our understanding of the dynamics of cabinet government because of our greater confidence that the relationship is significantly different from 0. In all our tables, we report statistical significance using one or two asterisks. We use one asterisk when we have a 90 per cent level of confidence, that is, when the probability of observing the relationship we find in the data when none really exists is less than .10. We use two asterisks to indicate a 95 per cent level of confidence. Even when we have strong directional predictions concerning a specific independent variable we use two-tailed tests of statistical significance, so in fact we are under-reporting our level of confidence concerning variables in which we have directional predictions.[11]

Employing standard statistical principles, the chapters use OLS (ordinary least squares) regression analysis when the dependent variable is measured continuously (e.g. percentage of seats lost or gained and number of cabinet

---

[11] All statistical analyses were run using Stata 9.2.

ministers).[12] Chapters with other types of dependent variables use logistic regression or duration (or event-history) analysis. We go into further detail on techniques and estimation in Appendix C. These details are admittedly not necessary for the reader who is familiar with the techniques currently used in the field or who is not interested in such technical matters. These readers may instead want to read the empirical chapters directly. For the rest, who, like ourselves, are interested also in some of the more nitty-gritty details of our approach, or who simply want to understand the basic justifications for our choices regarding statistical models, Appendix C provides details on the techniques we use. The appendix starts with a discussion of OLS regression analysis and then moves on to the technically more complicated logit (binary and multinomial) and event-history analyses.

CONCLUSION

In sum, our 'structured collaboration' research strategy emphasizes the reduction of measurement error in variables that all too often are sloppily and hastily assembled. This provides us with a data-set that is uniquely suited for the purpose of our goodness-of-fit approach to model specification and analysis. And while some best fit statistical analyses perhaps amount to not much more than fishing trips that try to land strong statistical relationships, we work hard to avoid such adventures. For one thing, the subsequent empirical chapters build directly on the previous literature on each topic, and we explicitly seek to test many of the same variables that have been used in previous analyses on our new and improved data. In addition, when we include new variables, we focus on including those for which our common theoretical perspective provides a reasonable expectation that there is a relationship worth testing.

In the following eight chapters, we examine how the variables in six clusters of variables influence various stages of the coalition cycle, and attempt to give particular emphasis to the importance of inter-connections between the stages. For example, while Chapter 4 begins by focusing on the bargaining process of government formation, subsequent chapters incorporate information about the specific bargaining process, wihch is found to have an impact on the type of government formed (in Chapter 6) and the durability of the government (in Chapter 10). Similarly, the creation of formal coalition agreements (the focus of Chapter 5) is found to have an impact on the presence of 'watchdog' junior ministers (Chapter 7) and the choice of conflict management arenas (Chapter 8). While we leave this topic for further discussion in the concluding chapter of this

[12] We used OLS in analyses of continuous bounded variables such as percentages when we felt the range of variation of the actual values was such that the boundedness of the variables did not bias our OLS estimates.

volume, we feel confident that the collaborative approach taken in this volume—in the joint theoretical perspective, the collection of data, and the analysis of the various stages of cabinet governance—leads to important new insights.

REFERENCES

Aldrich, John H. and Nelson, Forrest D. (1984). *Linear Probability, Logit, and Probit Models*. Sage University Paper series on Quantitative Applications in the Social Sciences, No. 07-045. Newbury Park, CA: Sage University Paper Series.

Allison, Paul D. (1984). *Event History Analysis*. Sage University Paper series on Quantitative Applications in the Social Sciences, No. 07-046. Newbury Park, CA: Sage University Paper Series.

Bäck, Hanna and Dumont, Patrick (2007). 'Combining Large-n and Small-n Strategies: The The Way Forward in Coalition Research', *West European Politics*, 30: 467–501.

Bergman, Torbjörn (1993). 'Formation Rules and Minority Governments', *European Journal of Political Research*, 23: 55–66.

——Müller, Wolfgang C., Strøm, Kaare, and Blomgren, Magnus (2003). 'Democratic Delegation and Accountability: Cross-national Patterns', in Kaare Strøm, Wolfgang C. Müller, and Torbjörn Bergman (eds.), *Delegation and Accountability in Parliamentary Democracies*. Oxford: Oxford University Press.

Box-Steffensmeier, Janet M. and Jones, Bradford. S. (1997). 'Time Is of the Essence: Event History Models in Political Science', *American Journal of Political Science*, 41: 1414–61.

Blossfeld, Hans-Peter and Rohwer, Götz (1995). *Techniques in Event History Modeling. New Approaches to Causal Analysis*. Mahwah, NJ: Lawrence Erlbaum.

Budge, Ian (2001). 'Validating Party Placement', *British Journal of Political Science*, 31: 210–23.

——and Keman, Hans (1990). *Parties and Democracy: Coalition Formation and Government Functioning in Twenty States*. Oxford: Oxford University Press.

——Klingemann, Hans-Dieter, Volkens, Andrea, Bara, Judith, and Tannenbaum, Eric (2001). *Mapping Policy Preferences. Estimates for Parties, Electors, and Governments 1945–1998*. Oxford: Oxford University Press.

Crombez, Christophe (1996). 'Minority Governments, Minimal Winning Coalitions and Surplus Majorities in Parliamentary Systems', *European Journal of Political Research*, 29: 1–29.

De Winter, Lieven, Andeweg, Rudy B., and Dumont, Patrick (eds.) (2008, forthcoming). *Puzzles of Government Formation*. London: Routledge.

Diermeier, Daniel (2006). 'Coalition Government', in Barry R. Weingast and Donald Wittman (eds.), *The Oxford Handbook of Political Economy*, Oxford: Oxford University Press.

Dodd, Lawrence C. (1976). *Coalitions in Parliamentary Government*. Princeton, NJ: Princeton University Press.

Dumont, Patrick and Caulier, Jean-François (2005). 'The "Effective Number of Relevant Parties": How Voting Power Improves Laakso-Taagepera's Index', ms.

Druckman, James N. and Thies, Michael F. (2002). 'The Importance of Concurrence: The Impact of Bicameralism on Government Formation and Duration', *American Journal of Political Science*, 46: 760–71.

Franklin, Mark N. and Mackie, Thomas T. (1984). 'Reassessing the Importance of Size and Ideology for the Formation of Governing Coalitions in Parliamentary Democracies', *American Journal of Political Science*, 28: 671–92.

Gamson, William A. (1961). 'A Theory of Coalition Formation', *American Sociological Review*, 26: 373–82.

Gabel, Matthew J. and Huber, John D. (2000). 'Putting Parties in Their Place: Inferring Party Left-Right Ideological positions From Party Manifesto Data', *American Journal of Political Science*, 44: 94–103.

Grofman, Bernard (1989). 'The Comparative Analysis of Coalition Formation and Duration: Distinguishing Between-Country and Within-Country Effects', *British Journal of Political Science*, 19: 291–302.

Gujarati, Damodar N. (2002). *Basic Econometrics*, 4th edn. New York, NY: McGraw-Hill.

International Monetary Fund (1979–98). *International Financial Statistics*. Washington, DC: International Monetary Fund.

King, Gary, Alt, James E., Burns, Nancy E., and Laver, Michael J. (1990). 'A Unified Model of Cabinet Dissolution in Parliamentary Democracies', *American Journal of Political Science*, 34: 846–71.

——Keohane, Robert, and Verba, Sidney (1994). *Designing Social Inquiry: Scientific Inference in Qualitative Research*. Princeton, NJ: Princeton University Press.

Laakso, Markku and Taagepera, Rein (1979). 'Effective Number of Parties: A Measure with Applications to Western Europe', *Comparative Political Studies*, 12: 3–27.

Laver, Michael (1974). 'Dynamic Factors in Government Coalition Formation', *European Journal of Political Research*, 2: 259–70.

Laver, Michael and Hunt, Ben W. (1992). *Policy and Party Competition*. New York, NY: Routledge.

Laver, Michael J. and Budge, Ian (1992). *Party Policy and Government Coalitions*. New York, NY: St. Martins' Press.

Laver, Michael and Shepsle, Kenneth A. (1996). *Making and Breaking Governments: Cabinets and Legislatures in Parliamentary Democracies*. Cambridge: Cambridge University Press.

Laver, Michael and Schofield, Norman (1990). *Multiparty Government*. Oxford: Oxford University Press.

Lijphart, Arend (1971). 'Comparative Politics and the Comparative Method', *American Political Science Review*, 65: 682–93.

Mair, Peter (1998). 'Comparative Politics: An Overview', in Robert E. Gooding and Hans-Dieter Klingemann (eds.), *A New Handbook of Political Science*. Oxford: Oxford University Press.

Martin, Lanny W. and Stevenson, Randolph T. (2001). 'Government Formation in Parliamentary Democracies', *American Journal of Political Science*, 45: 33–50.

Mill, J. S. (1843). *A System of Logic Ratiocinative and Inductive: Being a Connected View of the Principles of Evidence and the Methods of Scientific Investigation*. London: Longmans, Green and Co. Ltd.

Mitchell, Brian R. (1998). *International Historical Statistics: Europe, 1750–1993*. London: Macmillan Reference.

Müller, Wolfgang C. and Strøm, Kaare (eds.) (2000, 2nd edn. 2003). *Coalition Governments in Western Europe*. Oxford: Oxford University Press.

Nyblade, Benjamin (2004). *The Dynamics of Dominance: Party Government Duration and Change in Parliamentary Democracies*. San Diego: Ph.D. thesis, Department of Political Science, University of California, San Diego.

Organization for Economic Cooperation and Development (Dec. 1978). *OECD Economic Outlook*. Paris: OECD.

—— (June 1988). *OECD Economic Outlook*. Paris: OECD.

—— (1998). *OECD Economic Outlook*. Paris: OECD.

—— (1966). *National Accounts Statistics: 1957–1966*. Paris: OECD.

Pelizzo, Ricardo (2003). 'Party Positions or Party Direction? An Analysis of Party Manifesto Data'. *West European Politics*, 26: 67–89.

Przeworski, Adam and Teune, Henry (1970). *The Logic of Comparative Social Enquiry*. New York, NY: Wiley-Interscience.

Sartori, Giovanni (1970). 'Concept Misformation in Comparative Politics', *American Political Science Review*, 64: 1033–53.

Shively, W. Phillips (1998). *The Craft of Political Research*, 4th edn. Upper Saddle River, NJ: Prentice-Hall.

Strøm, Kaare, Müller, Wolfgang C., and Bergman, Torbjörn (eds.) (2003, 2nd edn. 2006). *Delegation and Accountability in Parliamentary Democracies*. Oxford: Oxford University Press.

United Nations (May 1998). *UN Monthly Bulletin of Statistics*. New York, NY: UN Statistical Office.

Warwick, Paul V. (1994). *Government Survival in Parliamentary Democracies*. Cambridge: Cambridge University Press.

—— (1998). 'Policy Distance and Parliamentary Government', *Legislative Studies Quarterly*, 23: 319–45.

APPENDIX A: CODE BOOK

The Comparative Parliamentary Democracy Data Archive data-set consists of cabinet-level data for 17 Western European democracies for post–Second World War cabinets through 1 January 1999. All together, a total of 424 coalitions, single-party and non-partisan cabinets are included. Data for Greece, Portugal, and Spain exists only after their democratizations in the 1970s, while data on France are limited to the Fifth Republic beginning in 1959. For the purposes of our data-set, it can be said that the world 'froze' on 1 January 1999. The last observation in each country is coded on the basis on the information that was available on that day.

The main sources for this data are as follows:

a. The paperback edition of *Coalition Governments in Western Europe* (2003) edited by Wolfgang C. Müller and Kaare Strøm. Oxford: Oxford University Press.
b. In addition to the 13 countries included in the *Coalition Governments in Western Europe* book, data for Iceland, Spain, Greece, and the United Kingdom have been collected by the Comparative Parliamentary Democracy project—further details are available on the project home page www.pol.umu.se/ccpd
c. The paperback edition of *Delegation and Accountability in Parliamentary Democracies* (2006), edited by Kaare Strøm, Wolfgang C. Müller, and Torbjörn Bergman. Oxford: Oxford University Press.
d. Drawing on the assistance by Magnus Blomgren, Scott Kastner, Benjamin Nyblade, and Ivy Hamerly Orr, the project directors have over time coded and estimated remaining variables—an immense job. Further details on the project are again available on the project home page www.pol.umu.se/ccpd

Note on Proper Acknowledgement

Publications using the corresponding data should acknowledge in writing that it is from the Comparative Parliamentary Democracy Archive www.pol.umu.se/ccpd and that it has been assembled for the purpose of the volume on *Cabinets and Coalition Bargaining: The Democratic Life Cycle in Western Europe,* edited by Kaare Strøm, Wolfgang C. Müller, and Torbjörn Bergman. Oxford: Oxford University Press, 2008.

BLOCK 0: *Cabinet identification*

Variable	Name	Coding
v001x	Country	01 = Austria, 02 = Belgium, 03 = Denmark, 04 = Finland, 05 = France, 06 = Germany, 07 = Greece, 08 = Iceland, 09 = Ireland, 10 = Italy, 11 = Luxembourg, 12 = Netherlands, 13 = Norway, 14 = Portugal, 15 = Spain, 16 = Sweden, 17 = United Kingdom
v002x	Cabinet code	First digits = country code, second digits = cabinet number code
v003x	Cabinet	
v004x	Date in	
v005x	Date out	

BLOCK 1: *Space–time*

Variable	Name	Coding	# (of 424)	Notes
v001y	Austria	1 = Austria	22	
v002y	Belgium	1 = Belgium	33	
v003y	Denmark	1 = Denmark	31	
v004y	Finland	1 = Finland	44	
v005y	France	1 = France	23	
v006y	Germany	1 = Germany	26	
v007y	Greece	1 = Greece	11	
v008y	Iceland	1 = Iceland	26	
v009y	Ireland	1 = Ireland	22	Country dummies
v010y	Italy	1 = Italy	51	
v011y	Luxembourg	1 = Luxembourg	16	
v012y	Netherlands	1 = Netherlands	23	
v013y	Norway	1 = Norway	26	
v014y	Portugal	1 = Portugal	14	
v015y	Spain	1 = Spain	10	
v016y	Sweden	1 = Sweden	26	
v017y	UK	1 = Britain	20	
v030y	Start Decade	One Digit #	424	
v030y2	End Decade	One Digit #	424	17 cabinets are 0s (end after closing date of the data-set)
v031y	1940s	1 = 1940s	38	
v032y	1950s	1 = 1950s	80	
v033y	1960s	1 = 1950s	68	Decade dummies: Decade in
v034y	1970s	1 = 1950s	90	which cabinet starts
v035y	1980s	1 = 1950s	86	
v036y	1990s	1 = 1950s	62	
v031y2	1940s	1 = 1940s	26	
v032y2	1950s	1 = 1950s	79	
v033y2	1960s	1 = 1960s	68	Decade dummies: Decade in
v034y2	1970s	1 = 1970s	87	which cabinet ends
v035y2	1980s	1 = 1980s	85	
v036y2	1990s	1 = 1990s	62	

The Empirical Study of Cabinet Governance

BLOCK 2: *Structural attributes*

Variable	Name	Coding	n
v040y	Post-election cabinet	1 = Yes, 0 = No	424
v041y	Max. possible cab. duration	# (unit = days)	418
v042y	Absolute no. parl. parties	# (unit = parties)	419
v043y	Effective no. parl. parties	# (unit = parties)	415
v044y	Bargaining power fragmentation	# (unit = Frag. index)	415
v044y2	Cabinet bargaining power frag.	# (unit = Frag. index)	406
v045y	Largest party seat share	# (range 0 to 1)	415
v046y	Bargaining power of largest party	# (unit = Banzhaf index)	415
v047y	Minority situation in parliament	1 = Minority Situation	415
v048y	Non-partisan cabinet	1 = Yes, 0 = No	424
v049y	Coalition cabinet	1 = Yes, 0 = No	406
v050y	Cabinet seat share	# (unit = % points)	415
v051y	Number of cabinet parties	# (unit = parties)	424
v051y2	Change in cabinet parties	1 = Inc, 0 = No Ch, −1 = Dec.	407
v052y	Max. bargaining power pty. in cab.	1 = Yes, 0 = No	415
v053y	Single party majority cabinet	1 = Yes, 0 = No	415
v054y	Single party minority cabinet	1 = Yes, 0 = No	415
v055y	Minority coalition	1 = Yes, 0 = No	415
v056y	Majority cabinet	1 = Yes, 0 = No	415
v057y	Minimal winning coalition	1 = Yes, 0 = No	415
v058y	Surplus majority cabinet	1 = Yes, 0 = No	415
v058y2	Government type	1 = Minority, 2 = MWC, 3 = Surplus	353
v059y	Number of ministries	# (unit = ministries)	423
v059y2	Change in number of ministries	1 = Inc, 0 = No Ch, −1 = Dec.	405
v060y	Number of cabinet members	# (unit = people)	423
v060y2	Change in number of ministers	1 = Inc, 0 = No Ch, −1 = Dec.	405
v061y	Disproportionality index	# (unit = disproportionality index)	260
v062y	Weighted disproportionality index	# (unit = disproportionality index)	260
V063y	Watchdog junior ministers	1 = Yes, 0 = No	264

BLOCK 3: *Preferences*

Variable	Name	Coding	n	Notes
v080y	Extremist party seat share	# (seat share in %)	415	
v081y	Parliamentary preference range	# (points)	411	
v082y	Polarization (BP weighted)	# (manifesto points)	413	Polarization is based on the following equation: $$\sqrt{\sum_{i=1}^{n} b_i (x_i - \bar{x})^2}$$
v083y	Effective # of issue dimens	# (# dims)	411	
v084y	No core party	1 = No DDM, 0 = DDM	415	
v085y	Median party bargaining power	# (unit = Banzhaf Index)	414	
v086y	Largest party distance to median	# (manifesto points)	397	
v088y	Cabinet preference range	# (manifesto points)	402	
v089y	Median party (1st dim.) in cab.	1 = Yes, 0 = No	415	
v090y	Median party (2nd dim.) in cab.	1 = Yes, 0 = No	415	Experts coded Denm, Fran, Gree as having 1 dim. For these countries, this variable is coded with the 2nd dim. equalling the 1st dim.
v091y	Connected cab.	1 = Yes, 0 = No	415	
v091y2	Minimal winning connected cab.	1 = Yes, 0 = No	415	
v092y	Conservative cab.	1 = Yes, 0 = No	415	Coded 1 if cabinet majority is from conservative bloc
v093y	Socialist cab.	1 = Yes, 0 = No	415	Coded 1 if cabinet majority is from socialist bloc

BLOCK 4: *Institutions*

Variable	Name	Coding	n	Notes
v120y	List PR	1 = Yes, 0 = No	424	0 = France (except 1 cabinet), Iceland (p), Ireland, Italy (p), UK. (p) is used when the institutional dummy (1) applies for some cabinets but not others. Hence, (p) stands for 'partially'.
v121y	Lower chamber only decides leg.	1 = Yes, 0 = No	424	0 = Belgium, Denmark, Italy, Netherlands, Spain, Sweden (p)
v122y	Supermajority for const. amend.	1 = Yes, 0 = No	424	0 = Denmark, France, Iceland, Ireland, Italy, Sweden, UK
v123y	Strong second chamber	1 = Yes, 0 = No	424	1 = Belgium (–95), Italy, Sweden (–70)
v124y	Weak second chamber	1 = Yes, 0 = No	424	1 = Aust., Belg. (95–), Fran., Germ., Irel., Neth., Spain, UK
V124y2	Bicameralism	1 = Yes, 0 = No	424	1 = Aust., Belg., Denm. (p), Fran., Germ., Ire., Italy, Neth., Spain (p), Swed. (p), UK
v125y	Opposition influence	Range: 2–7.13	424	Coded as Laver–Hunt (92), except Iceland = 4
v126y	Positive parliamentarism	1 = Yes, 0 = No	424	1 = Belgium, Germany, Greece, Ireland, Italy, Luxembourg, Spain
v127y	*Ex ante* gvt. programme screen	1 = Yes, 0 = No	424	1 = Belgium, Greece, Luxembourg, Netherlands, Spain
v128y	Abs. majority no-confidence	1 = Yes, 0 = No	424	1 = Fran., Germ., Gree., Icel., Port., Spain, Swed. (70–)
v129y	Constructive no-confidence	1 = Yes, 0 = No	424	1 = Germany, Spain, Belgium 1995–
v130y	Cabinet rule: Unanimity	1 = Yes, 0 = No	424	1 = Austria, Italy, Portugal
v131y	Cabinet rule: PM consensus	1 = Yes, 0 = No	424	1 = Belgium, Denmark, Spain, Sweden, UK
v132y	Cabinet co-decides leg.	1 = Yes, 0 = No	424	1 = Denmark, Netherlands, Sweden (–70)
v133y	PM cabinet powers	Range: 1 to 7	424	1 point each of 7 PM cabinet powers
v134y	PM dissolution powers	1 = Yes, 0 = No	424	1 = Belgium, Denmark, Luxembourg, Spain
v135y	PM cab. appt. power	1 = Yes, 0 = No	424	0 = Belgium, Finland, Italy, Netherlands
v136y	HoS discretionary cab. appt. role	1 = Yes, 0 = No	424	1 = Finland, France
v137y	Semi-presidentialism	1 = Yes, 0 = No	424	1 = Finland, France, Portugal (–82)
V138y	Junior minister institution	1 = Yes, 0 = No	424	0 = Denmark, Finland, Iceland
V139y	Size of lower chamber	# of seats	415	
v140y	Continuation rule	1 = Yes, 0 = No	424	1 = Denm., Fran., Gree., Icel., Irel., Luxe., Neth., Norw., Swe.

BLOCK 5: *Bargaining Environment*

Variable	Name	Coding	n	Notes
v160y	Prior cab.: Reg. el. termination	1 = Yes, 0 = No	405	Is about whether or not the previous cabinet terminated after a regular election.
v160y1	Prior cab.: Technical termination	1 = Yes, 0 = No	405	
v161y	Prior cab.: Other tech. termination	1 = Yes, 0 = No	405	
v161y1	Prior cab.: Other constitutional term	1 = Yes, 0 = No	405	
v161y2	Prior cab.: Death of PM term	1 = Yes, 0 = No	405	
v162y	Prior cab.: Intraparty conflict term	1 = Yes, 0 = No	405	
v163y	Prior cab.: Early election term	1 = Yes, 0 = No	405	
v164y	Prior cab.: Conflict termination	1 = Yes, 0 = No	405	
v165y	Prior cab.: Behavioural termination	1 = Yes, 0 = No	407	
v166y	Same PM & cabinet	1 = Yes, 0 = No	407	
V166y2	Same parties in cabinet	1 = Yes, 0 = No	407	
V166y3	Same PM	1 = Yes, 0 = No	407	
v167y	Cabinet bargaining duration	# (days)	418	
v167y2	Cabinet bargaining duration	# (days)	418	Adds 1 to v167y (for duration analysis)
v168y	Inconclusive bargaining round	1 = Yes, 0 = No	421	
v168y2	# of inconclusive bargaining rnds.	#	421	
v169y	Coalition agreement	1 = Yes, 0 = No	262	
v169y2	Coalition agreement	0=None, 1=Pre, 2=Post, 3=IF, 4=Pre & Post	262	
v169y9	Size of agreement (approx. words)	# (words)	142	
v169y10	General procedural rules (in %)	# (%)	142	
v169y11	Policy specific procedural rule (in %)	# (%)	142	
v169y12	Distribution of offices (in %)	# (%)	142	
v169y13	Distribution of competences (in %)	# (%)	142	
v169y14	Policies (in %)	# (%)	142	
v170y	Comprehensive policy agreement	1 = Yes, 0 = No	262	
v170y2	Policy agreement	0 = No, 1 = Basic, 2 = Comprehensive	262	
v170y3	Policy agreement	0 = No, 1 = Few Issues, 2 = Many Issues, 3 = Comprehensive	255	

Variable	Description	Coding	Notes	N
v171y	Coalition discipline in legislation	1 = Yes always. 2 = Yes, except explicitly exempted. 3 = No, except explicit policies. 4 = No		262
v171y4	Coalition discipline in legislation	As v171y except 3 = 3 or 4		262
v171yt	Coalition discipline in other parliamentary behaviour	As v171y		262
v172y	Comprehensive policy agreement (alt.)	1 = Yes, 0 = No	v169y, except single party cab = 1, not missing	408
v173y	Coalition agreement (alt.)	1 = Yes, 0 = No	v170y, except single party cab = 1, not missing	408
v174y	Coalition discipline in legislation (alt.)	As v171y	v171y, except single party cab = 1, not missing	408
V174y1	Coalition discipline in legislation dummy	1 = Yes, 0 = No	1 if v171y = 1 or single party cab, 0 for all others	424
v175y	Most common CRA: Mixed	1 = Yes, 0 = No	CRA = Conflict resolution arena	249
v176y	Most common CRA: External	1 = Yes, 0 = No		249
v176y2	Most common CRA	0 = Internal, 1 = Mixed, 2 = External		249
v176y3	Most common CRA	1 = Not internal		249
v176yt	Most common conflict resolution arena	IC, CaC, CoC, Parl, Pca, PS or O	176y3l also exists (lag) IC = Inner cabinet, CaC = Cabinet comm, CoC = Coal comm, Parl = Parl leaders, Pca = Combination of cabinet members & parliamentarians, PS = Party summit, O = Other	257
v177y	Serious CRA: Mixed	1 = Yes, 0 = No		249
v178y	Serious CRA: External	1 = Yes, 0 = No		249
v178y2	Serious CRA	As v176y2		235
v178y3	Serious CRA: Not internal	1 = Not internal		235
v178yt	Conflict resolution arena for most serious conflicts	As v176yt	v178y3l also exists (lag)	257
v179y	Relative cab. duration	%		401
v179y2	Absolute cab. duration	# (Unit = Days)		405
v180y	Early election (no conflict)	1 = Yes, 0 = No		407

BLOCK 6: *Critical events*

Variable	Name	Coding	n	Notes
v200y	Terminal event lag: Security	1 = Yes, 0 = No	405	
v201y	Terminal event lag: Economic	1 = Yes, 0 = No	405	
v202y	Terminal event lag: Personal	1 = Yes, 0 = No	405	
v203y	Terminal event lag (any)	1 = Yes, 0 = No	405	
V203y2	Critical event lag	1 = Yes, 0 = No	405	
v204y	Electoral volatility	# (0–60.8)	386	
v204y2	Cabinet electoral volatility	# (0–29.3)	381	
v205y	Inflation (cab. beginning)	# (−3 to 98)	419	
v206y	Unemployment (cab. beginning)	# (0 to 22.2)	383	
v207y	Growth (cab. beginning)	# (−58.8 to 68.8)	410	
v208y	Unemployment (end)	# (.1 to 22.2)	379	
v209y	Inflation (end)	# (−3 to 98)	405	
v210y	Growth (end)	# (−7.1 to 19)	395	
v211y	Conservative cab. × Inflation	# (−1.2 to 44.2)	398	
v212y	Socialist cab. × Unemployment	# (0 to 22)	374	
v213y	Terminal events: Opinion shock	1 = Yes, 0 = No	405	
v214y	Terminal events: Security	1 = Yes, 0 = No	405	
v215y	Terminal events: Economic	1 = Yes, 0 = No	405	
v216y	Terminal events: Personal	1 = Yes, 0 = No	405	
v216y2	Critical event	1 = Yes, 0 = No	405	
v216y3	Terminal event: Any	1 = Yes, 0 = No	405	
v217y	Government termination cause	0 = Tech Term 1 = Conflict Term 2 = Vol Early El	388	

v217y2	Government termination: Regular election	1 = Yes, 0 = No	405	
v217y3	Government termination: Other technical	1 = Yes, 0 = No	405	
v217y4	Government termination: Early election	1 = Yes, 0 = No	405	
v217y5	Government termination: Voluntary early election	1 = Yes, 0 = No	405	v217y5l also exists (lag)
v217y6	Government termination: Discretionary no election	1 = Yes, 0 = No	405	
v217y7	Government termination: Technical	1 = Yes, 0 = No	405	
v217y23	Government termination: Cabinet defeat in parliament	1 = Yes, 0 = No	405	
v217y24	Government termination: Inter-party policy	1 = Yes, 0 = No	265	Coalitions only
v217y25	Government termination: Inter-party personal	1 = Yes, 0 = No	265	Coalitions only
v217y27	Government termination: Intra-party conflict	1 = Yes, 0 = No	405	
v217y31	Government termination: Other constitutional reason	1 = Yes, 0 = No	406	
v217y32	Government termination: Death of PM	1 = Yes, 0 = No	406	
v218y	Cabinet termination: Voluntary enlargment	1 = Yes, 0 = No	424	v218yl also exists (lag)
v219y	Cabinete el performance	# (%)	385	
v219y2	Cabinet el performance	# (%)	385	Electoral performance controlling for seat share
v219y3	Previous cab.: All parties lost votes	1 = Yes, 0 = No	407	
v219y4	Previous cab.: Mixed electoral fortunes	1 = Yes, 0 = No	407	
v219y5	Previous cab.: All parties gained votes	1 = Yes, 0 = No	407	
v220y	Finance minister's party electoral performace	# (percentage points)	229	Coalitions only
v221y	Prime minister's party electoral performace	# (percentage points)	234	Coalitions only

APPENDIX B: ADDITIONAL DATA SOURCES

In addition to our previous books and the other sources referred to in the chapter text, the data-set also includes a number of macroeconomic variables including the inflation rate, the unemployment rate, and the percentage change in gross domestic product (GDP) from the previous year, for both the year of cabinet formation, and the year of cabinet dissolution. Most of this data comes from the database assembled by Paul Warwick for his study of cabinet survival: for a complete overview of his sources, see Warwick (1994: 77–8). Additional data were used for recent years, and for Greece and the French Fifth Republic, using Warwick's sources (1994) whenever possible.[13] For inflation figures, recent values were taken from the International Monetary Fund's (IMF) *International Financial Statistics Yearbook* (1998). Early data on France were added using the 1979 version of the same source. Recent unemployment figures were taken from the United Nations *Monthly Bulletin of Statistics* (May 1998) for all countries except France, Spain, and the Netherlands. For these countries, data were taken from the Organization for Economic Cooperation and Development (OECD) *Economic Outlook* (1998). For percentage change in GDP, OECD data were used: recent years were added using the *Economic Outlook* (1998). Earlier years were added for France using the OECD *National Accounts Statistics* 1957–66, and the OECD *Economic Outlook* (December 1978 and June 1988). Finally, additional values for all three variables were added for the early post-Second World War years in most countries using Mitchell's *International Historical Statistics* (1998).

APPENDIX C: STATISTICAL TECHNIQUE AND ESTIMATION: OLS, LOGIT, AND EVENT-HISTORY (DURATION) ANALYSIS

Regression analysis

Two of our chapters, Chapter 7 and Chapter 11, use, among other statistical techniques, the basic multivariate linear regression model (OLS). Most readers will perhaps be familiar with this model, but a brief review might still be useful. We subsequently move on to the more complicated techniques.

OLS assumes that a simple linear relationship exists between independent and dependent variables, such that a change in an independent variable has the same effect on the dependent variable, regardless of the value of the dependent variable. So, for example, a regression coefficient of 0.4 tells us that a unit increase in the value of a particular independent variable is associated with a 0.4 increase in the

---

[13] Warwick restricts his data on France to the Fourth Republic. Our cabinets are from the Fifth Republic.

value of the dependent variable, on average, controlling for the effects of the other independent variables.[14]

When the main dependent variable of interest is measured discretely (e.g. a cabinet does or does not adopt a pre-election agreement, does or does not use internal procedures to deal with serious conflicts, does or does not terminate before the constitutional deadline), OLS regression estimates may be misleading on at least two grounds. First, OLS assumes linear relationships between the independent variables and the dependent variable, which in this case would be the probability of an event occurring. However, for most probabilistic relationships, a more realistic relationship is curvilinear. In such a relationship, small changes in the independent variable in some ranges (i.e. around p = .5) produce large changes in the probabilities. In other ranges (i.e. closer to p = 0 and p = 1), small changes in the independent variables produce only small changes in the probabilities. Second, with discrete measurements OLS can produce predicted probabilities that lie outside the range between 0 and 1, which is a logical impossibility.[15] Therefore, these chapters employ logistic regression analyses (or logit), which has been standard in the empirical political science literature.

Logit analysis

Logistic regression or logit analysis transforms the basic linear regression into a method of estimation that evaluates the impact of the various independent variables on the probability of a dichotomous variable being 0 or 1. The resultant transformation is non-linear and the probabilities are bounded between 0 and 1.[16] Note, however, that once we make this transformation, the interpretation of the estimated coefficients is now a bit more complex. A logit coefficient of 0.4 tells us that a unit increase in the value of the independent variable is associated with a 0.4 increase in the log of the odds of an event occurring, again controlling for the effects of the other independent variables. To produce a more natural interpretation, the chapters that use logit also compute the change in probability associated with changes in the values of the independent variables of interest for the final model for each dependent variable. To compute these probabilities, we hold all of the other independent variables in the model at their mean (for continuous

[14] We assume that most readers are familiar with basic regression analysis. For those who require a more extensive review, we recommend Gujarati (2002) or other basic econometrics texts.

[15] In addition, OLS estimates will be heteroscedastic, and the standard errors not normally distributed.

[16] Logit involves re-stating the basic regression equation in the following way. We begin with the equation $P(Y_i = 1) = \beta_0 + \beta_1 X_{1i} + \beta_2 X_{2i} + \ldots \beta_k X_{ki}$ or simply $P_i = Z$, where P_i is the probability that $Y_i = 1$ (i.e. that the event occurs in country i), and Z is the sum of all of the independent variables times their coefficients. As written, this equation is called a 'linear probability model', and is essentially what is estimated when we use OLS with a discrete dependent variable. Logit involves transforming P_i to $\ln(P_i/(1 - P_i))$, and estimating $\ln(P_i/(1 - P_i)) = Z$ using maximum likelihood estimation. For a full mathematical derivation of the logit model, see Aldrich and Nelson (1984).

variables) or median (for discrete variables) value and compute the change in the probability that $Y = 1$ when the independent variable of interest changes by one unit (or when a one unit change is inappropriate, we use a one standard deviation change, as noted in each table).[17] We compute these probabilities by simply plugging in values for $\hat{\beta}$ from the estimated model into the familiar formula: $\hat{P}_i = e^{\Sigma X \hat{\beta}}/(1 + e^{\Sigma X \hat{\beta}})$.[18]

When the dependent variable of interest is measured in more than two discrete categories (e.g. different types of terminal event), the chapters generally employ multinomial logistic regression rather than its main alternative: an 'ordered' logit or probit (as in Crombez 1996). Contrary to ordered logit, the multinominal specification does not assume that values of the dependent variable can be ordered in any straightforward way (such as magnitude, for example, from less to more).[19] Multinomial logit is a straightforward extension of the basic binary logit model described above. The main difference is that while binary logit compares the probability that the dependent variable takes on the value of 1 to the probability that it takes on the value of 0, the multinomial logit compares the probabilities that the dependent variable takes on each non-0 value to the probability that it takes on the value of 0. Multinomial logit thus produces several sets of coefficient estimates (equal to the number of categories on the dependent variable minus 1) for the independent variables. Each set of coefficients estimates the effect of each X on the probability that Y takes on a given value as opposed to a zero.

In effect, multinomial logit is equivalent to estimating several binary logits, one for each value of the dependent variable (except 0). It is preferable to estimating separate binary logits, however, because it uses the information from all of the observations and not just the subset that take on particular values on the dependent variable. As such, the estimates in the multinomial logit are more precise. Again for the final models, we compute the probabilities associated with a unit change (or in cases where a unit change is inappropriate, a one standard deviation change) in each independent variable, holding the other independent variables at their mean or median values.

For both binomial and multinomial logits, we report an estimate of the explained variance, McFadden's pseudo-R^2,[20] which corresponds to the R^2 (percentage of variance explained) reported for regular OLS regressions. We also

---

[17] Because the change in probability is non-linear (i.e. it is greatest when prob $(Y = 1)$ is close to .5), its value depends on the values of all of the independent variables. Thus, to isolate the effect of a unit change in one independent variable on this probability, it is necessary to specify the values of all of the other independent variables.

[18] Note that this formula is simply the antilog of the logit transformation described above.

[19] We do not use conditional logit in this work, as has become more common in the literature following Martin and Stevenson (2001), although we believe that future work along this line may be valuable, particularly in the literature on cabinet formation.

[20] McFadden's pseudo-R^2 is calculated by taking the ratio of the log-likelihood of a full model to the log likelihood of an intercept only model and subtracting it from 1.

supplement this statistic with a calculation of the percentage of cases correctly predicted, which is more readily interpretable and may be more appropriate to consider when examining predictive power across models when there are changes in the sample (particularly due to perfect prediction) or excluded cases.

Event-history analysis

When the dependent variable of interest is an event count (e.g. length of the cabinet formation process or how long a cabinet survives), the chapters employ duration (event-history) analyses. Duration analyses are similar to logit analyses in that they assume a nonlinear relationship between the independent and dependent variables. Specifically, duration models estimate a hazard rate, $h(t)$, which is the (unobserved) rate at which an event occurs. In the duration analyses in this volume, the authors employ the Cox proportional hazards model, which assumes that observations from different groups (e.g. countries) may have different baseline hazard rates, but the coefficients that relate changes in the independent variables to changes in the hazard rate are constant across countries.[21] This model is given as $ht = h_0(t)e^{\Sigma \beta_k X_{ik}}$. In tables reporting the results of these models we report hazard ratios, which is the factor by which we multiply the baseline hazard rate resulting from a unit change in each independent variable. A coefficient significantly greater than 1 represents an increase in the hazard rate (a decrease in durability), whereas a coefficient below 1 represents a decrease in the hazard rate (an increase in durability).

One of the main advantages of event-history analysis is the operationalization of the dependent variable. The traditional measure of the length of the bargaining process or cabinet stability is the duration in days. This inevitably leads to the problem that it is difficult to determine whether differences in duration between cabinet A, formed immediately after an election, and cabinet B, formed in the final year of the CIEP (the *constitutional interelection period*), are related to the lower maximum potential 'life expectancy' of cabinet B, or any of the causal factors we are interested in. One possible solution to this problem is calculating relative cabinet durations (i.e. the actual durations in days as a percentage of the maximum possible duration). This strategy is useful for descriptive purposes. However, it is a bit problematic for causal analyses. Using values for relative cabinet duration in a traditional regression analysis assumes that the chances of termination are equal in each phase of a cabinet's life. In other words, when dividing the actual duration by the maximum possible duration, we assume that each day in the maximum possible remaining period has the same weight. We know, however, that the survival chances of a cabinet may be duration dependent, that is, they may vary systematically over time. A relative duration of 100 per cent for a cabinet formed one year before the end of the CIEP may have

---

[21] See Allison (1984) for a more extensive development of the proportional hazards model.

a substantively different meaning from a relative duration of 100 per cent for a cabinet formed immediately after an election. Event-history analysis is able to deal with this problem by disaggregating the event history of a cabinet, estimating the probability of cabinet termination per cabinet-day, cabinet-month, or cabinet-year, whatever the temporal unit of measurement may be.

Disaggregating the event histories of cabinets in this way has further advantages. Both absolute and relative durations are temporal aggregates. When they are employed as dependent variables, it is difficult to utilize the information provided by time-varying covariates. For example, it would be difficult to estimate the effect of an external shock such as a sharp rise in inflation or unemployment. It has been found (Warwick 1994:111–13) that the impact of such economic shocks is likely to be duration dependent, that is, they may be more likely to contribute to cabinet terminations in the later stages of a cabinet (for a description of different duration dependent effects, see Blossfeld and Rohwer 1995:15). A further advantage is that the disaggregating technique used by event-history analysis goes some way towards tackling the problem of weighting. In classical regression-based analyses, countries with a relatively large number of relatively short-lived cabinets often have a stronger weight than countries with fewer and longer-lasting cabinets. This may have contributed to a disproportionate influence in the literature of certain explanatory variables typical of countries with relatively unstable cabinets. The use of cabinet-days as the unit for a particular record eliminates this problem without having to resort to weighting.

Event-history models also allow us to include censored cases in the analysis, which are cases where an event has not happened by the end of the observation period (e.g. surviving cabinets at the end of our observation period, December 1999). Crucially, different censoring regimes also allow us to analyse separately different kinds of termination (e.g. the 'competing' risks of cabinet replacements or early elections) without excluding other forms, which can be censored but kept in the analysis (see Box-Steffensmeier and Jones 1997: 1415–17). From the perspective of this volume's general approach, event-history analysis is a highly appropriate tool of analysis, not least because it can help capture in a more sophisticated manner the role of time in bargaining models.

4

Uncertainty and Complexity in Cabinet Formation

Lieven De Winter and Patrick Dumont

INTRODUCTION

Bargaining is a foundational process of democracy. It pervades every phase of the life cycle of parliamentary politics. In this life cycle, cabinet formation sets the stage for policymaking, which occasionally in turn leads governments to resign, which may be followed by elections, which in turn give rise to the formation of a successor government, and so forth. Then the cycle begins all over again. Any one of these moments in the cycle could serve as a starting point for an examination of coalition politics. Yet, there is one phase of the parliamentary 'life cycle' in which inter-party, and often intra-party, bargaining is truly the focal point of political interest, and that is the process of cabinet (government) formation. It is here that bargaining between and within parties is most visible, most intense, and perhaps most decisive. This formative phase of the parliamentary life cycle will indeed be the starting point of our journey in this volume.

We have good reason to begin with the formation process. The formation process has often been seen as a predictor of trouble at later stages in the cycle. The number of attempts that occur before a government is finally formed and the time that it takes to form governments have both been used as indicators of bargaining complexity (Strøm 1985: 747; King et al. 1990: 858–9; Laver and Schofield 1990: 134; Grofman and van Roozendaal 1994: 158–60; Warwick 1994: 37; van Roozendaal 1997: 82). As indicators of the difficulty of forming a government, these variables regularly serve as one of the main predictors of the subsequent performance of the government, especially its stability (Strøm 1985: 749; King et al. 1990: 859; Warwick 1994: 39). Some advocates of the Westminster system consider the long formation duration period as one of the main disadvantages of PR systems (Pinto-Dushinsky 1998), as these weeks or months of cabinet formation are time that is lost, time that cannot be devoted to major policy decisions. Others, such as Luebbert (1986), deny that there is a *necessary* connection between the length of the formation process and the substance of the process, but still see the formation process as important for what happens down the line in the life of a coalition (see Chapter 2).

Bargaining rounds and formation duration are not only important as explanatory variables but also interesting in their own right, as important and focal events in parliamentary decision-making. When political parties in parliamentary systems bargain over cabinet positions and government policy, they sometimes find agreeing easy. The process can at other times be convoluted and ridden by conflict. Therefore, we also want to explain the variation in bargaining rounds and formation duration. These are topics that have hitherto received less attention than they deserve (Bäck and Dumont 2008; De Winter and Dumont 2006: 184).

We begin our empirical inquiry by discussing the process of cabinet turnover and the criteria by which we can identify formation attempts. We then provide a schematic overview of the standard formation process in West European parliamentary democracies, before we describe two critical aspects of the formation process: the number of bargaining rounds and formation duration. We show that there are important cross-national variations as well as temporal trends. In the section that follows, we explain why we expect two variables, information uncertainty and bargaining complexity, to be especially important keys to cabinet formation processes. Next we present the empirical evidence on cabinet formation by the explanatory clusters that are common to the analysis in this volume: time and space, structural attributes, preferences, institutions, bargaining environment, and critical events (see Chapter 3). We end this chapter by answering two questions: What clusters, and what variables in these clusters, provide the best statistical explanation for these phenomena? And in what ways and to what extent may these variables reflect the effects of uncertainty or bargaining complexity?

THE FORMATION PROCESS

What is a cabinet formation? By the definition of this project, it is the process that leads from the termination of one cabinet to the installation of its successor (see Chapter 3). Every instance of cabinet turnover is thus associated with a formation process. Recall that we count a new cabinet whenever there is a general election, a new PM, or any change in the partisan composition of the cabinet. These counting rules leave us with a fairly unambiguous set of cabinet formations. The potential downside is that these formations are at the same time heterogeneous.

A closer inspection of real-life coalition bargaining inevitably reveals that cabinets are formed under greatly varying circumstances. A few examples may help illustrate this variation. First, some 'new' cabinets are identical or almost identical to their respective predecessors, so that it is likely that little or no real bargaining occurred. This may be the case, particularly in the case of single-party cabinets, when we count a new cabinet only because the PM is replaced. In such cases the outgoing PM may have well prepared his departure by designating a successor (dauphin), and little or no real bargaining takes place. Even coalition governments may work under informal rules to the effect that the prime minister's party may freely nominate a successor for this post if for unforeseen reasons a change is required, either because the incumbent PM dies, is taken ill, is promoted to higher office (the presidency or some international office), or even in case of a scandal. Thus, a prime minister is sometimes selected by no more than a handful of the leaders of one coalition party. Opportunities for inter-party bargaining may be scarce or nil.

Actual bargaining (see also Chapter 5) may be minimal even when the cabinet's party composition changes, for instance, when a coalition loses a surplus party of minor importance. In such circumstances, it can be much easier to go on without replacing the defecting party than to build a new coalition from scratch (Warwick 1996: 474). There are even situations in which the PM as well as the party composition changes, but little bargaining occurs (at least initially). One such example is when political parties decide to form a proto-coalition in the form of an explicit pre-electoral alliance, and when this proto-coalition effectively wins the elections and replaces the incumbent government (Strøm and Leipart 1993; Golder 2006).[1] Even when elections significantly shift the balance of power between the members of the proto-coalition, their pre-electoral pact may well constrain their bargaining. This is not only because the principle of *pacta sunt servanda* is important in political culture and public opinion, but also because of electoral accountability or reputational effects on future negotiations between the same parties. Another constraint on bargaining opportunities may occur when an outgoing coalition without a common manifesto but with an openly stated preference to continue the coalition formula wins a majority of seats and none of the coalition parties suffers traumatic losses. Difficult bargaining may still occur, but such circumstances favour a renewal of the outgoing coalition because there is a focal bargaining solution that minimizes transaction costs (Willemé 1996). In all these examples, there will tend to be few bargaining rounds and the formation process may be very short. Still, even under such circumstances, opportunities for bargaining exist, so we prefer to leave the actual duration and complexity of the bargaining process as an empirical question, as at times there may indeed be extensive bargaining even when the outward appearances do not suggest that it should happen.

After the demise of an incumbent government, parties do not bargain *ex nihilo* in a history-blind vacuum. On the contrary, their choice of partners is affected by a large number of short- or long-term experiences of cooperation and competition.

---

[1] Although the presence or absence of a pre-electoral alliance can have a clear impact on formation duration and attempts, we have not used it as a condition filter in the transition schema in Figure 4.1 or in our statistical analyses. This is because of the low number of cases ($n = 22$). This, in turn, is an effect of our strict cross-national counting rule which only acknowledges pre-electoral coalitions that have made a formal joint statement to the public expressing their intent to form a coalition after the election. Golder (2006) uses a less restrictive counting rule and finds many more such alliances.

126   *Lieven De Winter and Patrick Dumont*

Several authors (Laver 1974; Brams 1975; Chertkoff 1975; Franklin and Mackie 1983; Warwick 1996) have pointed to the impact of party familiarity (i.e. the experience of having governed together in the past) on subsequent coalition formations. From this perspective, each bargaining episode does not represent a totally new start but can be influenced by previous events. Others (Willemé 1996; Baron and Diermeier 2001) have also pointed to the impact of the dissolution of the previous coalition on the likelihood of conflict in the next. Messy divorces in the past may leave parties disinclined to rekindle such relationships. Election losses might also diminish the interest of some parties in joining the next cabinet.[2]

Thus, the conditions of cabinet transition can vary greatly. As the examples above show, the formation of multiparty coalitions is sometimes quite straightforward. At other times, coalition bargaining is much more challenging for the actors involved, for example, when the negotiating party leaders face radical changes in the bargaining parameters or high levels of conflict among the relevant parties.

In Figure 4.1, we illustrate the standard government formation process in the context of the coalitional life cycle.[3] The centre-right-hand side of Figure 4.1 illustrates how bargaining is conditioned by the regime type (including the role of the Head of State), by the electoral system, and by the presence of a formateur (see below) versus free-style bargaining between the political parties. Bargaining will also be conditioned by institutions such as investiture votes and mandatory screening procedures. Other factors that can be expected to matter, but which for presentational reasons are not included in the figure, include the preference divergence among the negotiating parties and events in the bargaining environment (such as an economic downturn or an international crisis). Figure 4.1 also serves the purpose of directing attention to the figure's left-hand side: the conditions under which the previous cabinet resigned and their effects on the subsequent bargaining.

Chapter 9 is devoted to cabinet termination, and we refer to this chapter for a detailed analysis of how and why cabinets terminate. Suffice it to say for present purposes that the previous cabinet may have terminated for *technical* reasons, which are circumstances beyond the direct control of its participants, or for discretionary reasons (see below). Among technical terminations, we can distinguish between (*a*) those caused by the death, illness, or voluntary resignation of the PM, (*b*) those due to other constitutional circumstances (such as a presidential election or a constitutional amendment), and (*c*) those occasioned by regular elections. The first two types of technical terminations constitute conditions under which bargaining should be relatively simple and of limited scope. As in the examples

---

[2] Yet, losing half of its seats in the Dutch 1998 elections did not prevent Democrats '66 from continuing its participation in the cabinet that followed.

[3] Laver and Schofield (1990: 63) have proposed a similar conceptualization, but ours is particularly designed to capture the period from the election/resignation until the new government takes office.

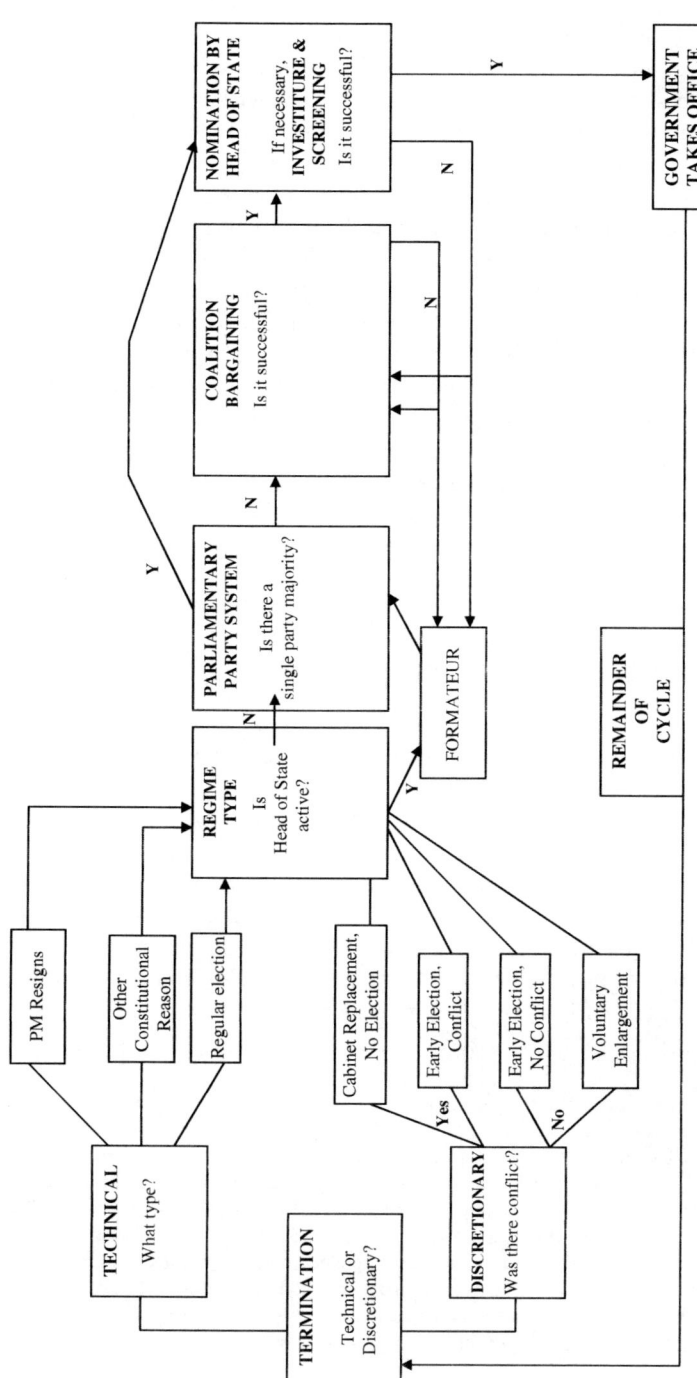

FIGURE 4.1. Conditions of transition and government formation

Notes: Adapted from Dumont (2000) and De Winter and Dumont (2001).

provided above, in the case of a 'technical' change of a PM, it may suffice to find a successor from within the PM party. Compared with these two sets of circumstances, regular elections may generate greater bargaining challenges, as elections can dramatically alter the bargaining power of the relevant parties. Electoral losses on the parts of some incumbent parties may render the previous coalition unviable, and for a minority governing party even shifts in the electoral fortunes of its support parties may be critical (Lewin 1999: 185).

Discretionary terminations are caused more directly by the actions of the cabinet parties or the parliamentary opposition. Again, there are several subtypes of discretionary resignations. The first is resignation due to conflict (which may bring about elections or a simple change of government). Such conflict may include a parliamentary defeat, an inter-party conflict within the incumbent government over policy or personnel, or an intra-party controversy. A discretionary termination may also take the form of an early election not associated with any conflict on the part of the governing parties. The final category of discretionary terminations, voluntary coalition enlargement, occurs when an existing government freely chooses to bring in one or more additional parties.

THE EMPIRICAL RECORD

In the remainder of this chapter, we shall analyse two important features of the cabinet formation process: (*a*) why there is often more than one bargaining round and (*b*) the total duration of this process in days. We identify a new bargaining round whenever there is any change in the set of parties participating in the negotiations, or there is a change in the identity of the informateur, formateur, or intended prime minister. The duration of bargaining is counted from the day that the previous government tenders its resignation, or, in the cases of general elections, the date of the election, whichever comes first. We count the formation process as concluded when the new government is sworn in or officially takes office (see Chapter 3 for further details).[4]

---

[4] There are country-specific idiosyncrasies in bargaining procedures that can affect the duration of formation. For example, Greece has procedural rules aimed at reducing the bargaining time and the number of bargaining rounds. The President first gives an exploratory formation mandate to the leader of the largest party, for a maximum of three days. If this party leader fails, then the mandate is passed on to the leader of the second largest party, and so on. If all exploratory mandates fail, the President then calls a meeting of all party leaders in order to form a coalition cabinet. Should this attempt also fail, the Chief Justice of one of the three Supreme Courts is appointed to form an interim government charged with preparing a general election within 40 days. Conversely, under the Swedish constitution of 1975, if the cabinet resigns, parliament must after a general election assemble, choose a Speaker, and hold a vote on a new government, a process that lasts over two weeks in all. Thus, even

TABLE 4.1. *Number of inconclusive bargaining rounds in cabinet formation*

Number of inconclusive rounds	N	%
0	293	69.6
1	62	14.7
2	29	6.9
3	20	4.8
4	7	1.7
5	4	1.0
6	5	1.2
7	1	0.2
Total	421	100

Notes: Average number of inconclusive bargaining rounds: 0.63 and standard deviation: 1.2.

Table 4.1 shows empirically how many bargaining rounds it takes to form a cabinet. Note that most cabinets form on the first attempt, with no inconclusive bargaining rounds. About two-thirds of all cabinet resignations are followed by a cabinet formed on the first attempt. But the one-third of all negotiations that go to a second round are important, not least because of how the literature associates these cabinets with instability and/or bargaining problems. It is also an empirical result that challenges some predictions in the theoretical literature on coalition bargaining. For example, in his complete-information model, Baron (1991) argues that the party allowed to make the first offer should always be successful in forming a government. Empirically, this is far from always the case.[5]

As Table 4.2 demonstrates, an average formation process takes about three weeks. More than half of formation processes are complete within the first two weeks, whereas two-thirds are completed within three weeks after the election or the resignation of the previous cabinet. The formation periods among the one-third of all cabinets that require more than three weeks to form vary considerably. In sum, the record demonstrates that most negotiations are relatively quick and that cabinets usually form between parties that do not need more than one bargaining round. But a sizeable minority of all cabinets are the result of many bargaining rounds and/or lengthy formation processes.

if bargaining complexity is low and actual negotiations swift, procedural time constraints may at times artificially extend the bargaining period.

[5] In order not to artificially inflate the numbers in systems where many cabinets form, or deflate the number of rounds in countries that became democratic in the 1970s (Greece, Portugal, and Spain), the information in Table 4.2 is weighted by the total number of cabinet formations that occurred in each country.

TABLE 4.2. *Cabinet formation duration*

Formation duration	N	%
Zero days	72	17.2
First week	95	22.5
Second week	55	13.2
Third week	46	11.0
Fourth week	22	5.3
Fifth week	35	8.4
Sixth week	15	3.8
Seventh week	23	5.5
Eighth week	9	2.2
More than eight weeks	46	11.0
Total	418	100

Notes: Average duration 23 days and standard deviation: 29.3.

As shown in Table 4.3, inconclusive bargaining rounds and lengthy formation processes are more frequent in some countries than in others. At the top of the list of countries with a high number of formation rounds, we find (in alphabetical order) Belgium, Finland, Greece, Iceland, and the Netherlands. In the Netherlands, the absolute frontrunner, there have been on average almost two inconclusive bargaining rounds prior to the final and successful one. At the other end of the spectrum, France, Germany, Norway, Portugal, and Spain have the fewest inconclusive bargaining rounds, with Spain having no such rounds at all. As for

TABLE 4.3. *Inconclusive bargaining rounds and cabinet formation duration by country*

Country	Inconclusive rounds	Formation duration
Austria	0.23	37.0
Belgium	1.30	37.8
Denmark	0.48	8.3
Finland	1.27	26.9
France	0.13	2.2
Germany	0.12	20.2
Greece	0.91	6.5
Iceland	1.58	32.8
Ireland	0.14	15.7
Italy	0.49	29.1
Luxembourg	0.44	24.1
The Netherlands	1.95	70.6
Norway	0.12	4.2
Portugal	0.07	22.5
Spain	0	28.4
Sweden	0.19	5.4
United Kingdom	0.10	6.5

TABLE 4.4. *Inconclusive bargaining rounds and cabinet formation duration by decade*

Decade	Inconclusive rounds	Formation duration
1940s	0.87	20.4
1950s	0.76	18.6
1960s	0.57	20.3
1970s	0.77	30.9
1980s	0.63	24.6
1990s	0.18	20.3

the length of the formation process, Belgium, Iceland, Italy, the Netherlands, and Spain (in alphabetical order) place among the top five, again with the Netherlands in first place. Note that the average formation process is almost twice as long in the Netherlands as in the country that follows next (Belgium).[6] The countries with the shortest average formation processes are France, Greece, Norway, Sweden, and the UK.

While country effects in themselves do not provide much information about the reasons behind the variance in bargaining processes, the overall pattern is that some countries, such as Belgium, Finland, Iceland, the Netherlands, and Portugal, have both more bargaining rounds and longer formation processes than other countries, such as Denmark, France, Norway, Sweden, and the UK. There are also a smaller number of countries, including Austria, Germany, and Greece, that have a more mixed record (few rounds but long processes or vice versa).

Table 4.4 reports on how the two dependent variables have changed over time. With regard to inconclusive rounds, there does not seem to be a (straight) linear relationship, but rather a curvilinear one. The post-Second World War peaks occurred in the 1950s and 1970s, whereas there was a drastic decline in the 1990s. The average duration of the formation period is less cyclical but even here we find a peak in the 1970s and a recent decline (back to the levels of the 1960s).

Finally, Figure 4.2 reports descriptive statistics on bargaining rounds and formation duration by the type of resignation of the previous cabinet. We first look at discretionary terminations. When the prior cabinet resigned for reasons associated with conflict (parliamentary defeat or inter- or intra-party conflict among the cabinet parties), there have been more rounds and longer formation processes than in the aftermath of non-conflictual resignations. This is perhaps unsurprising, but more interesting is the lack of a distinctive difference between early elections when conflict was present and early elections when no conflict was

---

[6] Since the Netherlands is an outlier with formation processes that are much longer than those of the other 16 countries, in the final models below we test for whether or not there is a 'Dutch' effect in our results.

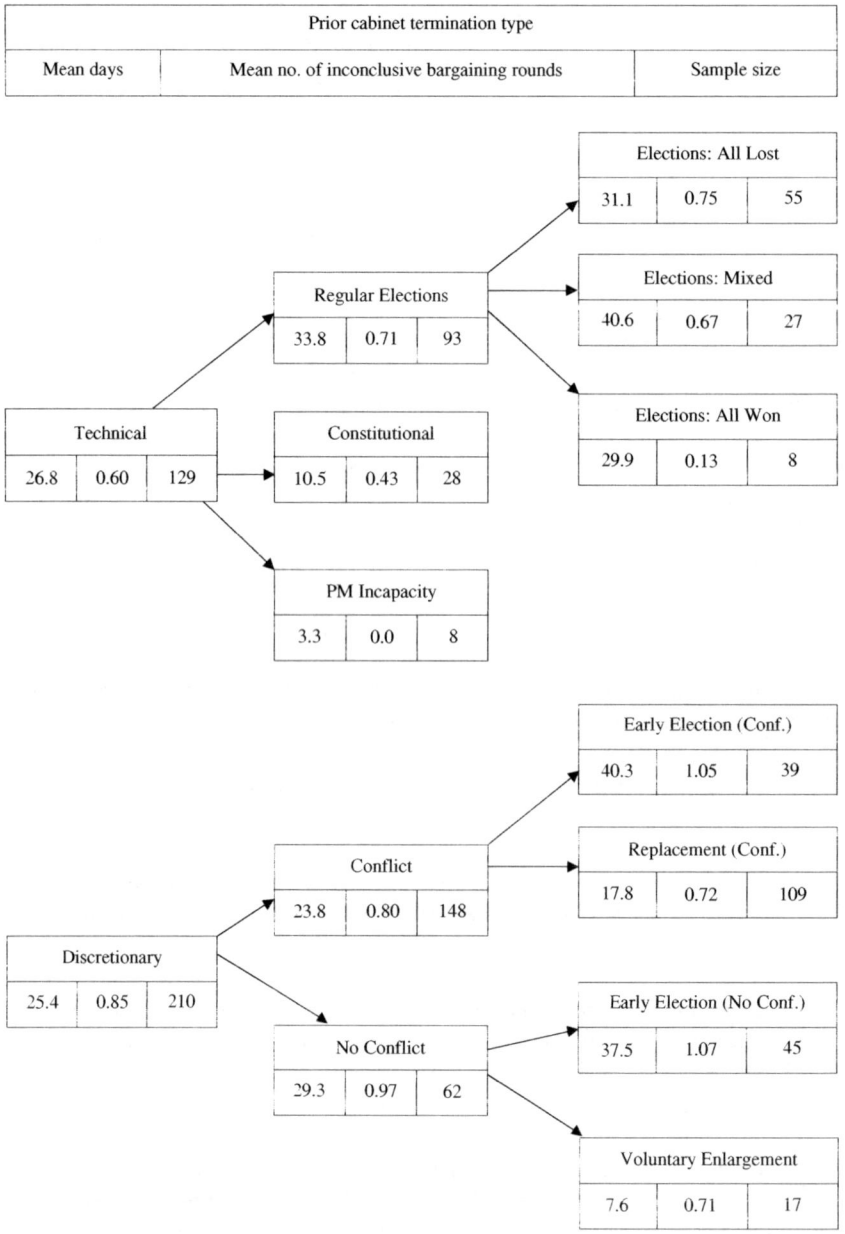

FIGURE 4.2. Prior cabinet termination and government formation (minority situations only)

present. On average, early elections have in either case been followed by more than five weeks of bargaining and one incomplete bargaining round. The averages for our entire sample are about three weeks and about two-thirds of a bargaining round. There are only a few (17) voluntary enlargements. These have been preceded by few bargaining rounds and short negotiations (at least when one counts the period from official resignation).[7]

In the case of technical terminations, the formation process tends to be slightly shorter and involve fewer rounds after regularly scheduled elections than after early elections. When we look at how the incumbent parties did in the regular elections preceding the formation of the new cabinet, we also find some interesting differences. If all the incumbent cabinet parties had suffered losses, the average new cabinet has taken roughly one month to form, and there has been an average of 0.75 inconclusive bargaining rounds. If all incumbent parties instead had increased their vote shares, the formation of a new cabinet has taken nearly as long, but with an inconclusive bargaining round in only 1 of 8 cases. After regular elections, if the incoming cabinet parties' electoral performance has been mixed (some had won while others had lost), the average duration of the formation process has been extended by about one week relative to the cases in which all the incumbent cabinet parties either lost or gained in the previous election. The number of bargaining rounds, on the other hand, does not differ much compared to incumbents who all lost.

UNCERTAINTY AND COMPLEXITY

This empirical record spurs questions about what it is that produces inconclusive bargaining rounds and long coalition negotiations. Chapter 2 tells us that there is reason to think that information uncertainty and bargaining complexity should matter. Information uncertainty means that players may be ill informed. Therefore, they may make mistakes. It also implies that there may be conditions under which players are willing to incur costs to improve their information, to learn about their options or their potential partners or competitors. Bargaining complexity means that the players are faced with a high number of options. It also means that there may be times when the players face a multitude of

---

[7] As further demonstrated in Chapter 9, there is a debate in the literature about when cabinets begin and end. This debate has implications for the definition of the formation duration period. As cabinets following immediately upon a general election base their negotiations on the seat distribution of the new parliament, the election date is a natural starting point for coalition bargaining. But for cabinets that form in the inter-election period, and in the case of voluntary enlargements, the parliamentary seat distribution is already known and it may be more difficult to establish the date when the coalition bargaining actually begins. For the purposes of this project, we consider the time between elections or the resignation of the previous cabinet, whatever comes first.

constraints. Moreover, bargaining complexity may exacerbate problems of information uncertainty: players are particularly likely to be ill informed when they confront an overwhelming and confusing array of options. Under such circumstances, it may be difficult to predict their behaviour. Here is why and how we think these considerations impinge on the formation process (De Winter and Dumont 2001).

Information uncertainty

At the time of cabinet formation, the bargaining situation may be affected by *incomplete information* about the preferences and strategies of other players. Even if government formation can be fruitfully understood as a relatively high-stakes game played by a small number of well-informed and experienced party leaders (Strøm 1990b: 588), these negotiators usually do not possess complete information. And '[t]he more limited their information, the less likely risk-averse party leaders are to gamble on new coalition partners or on moves whose electoral implications are hard to foresee. Thus in situations of highly imperfect or incomplete information, we may see fewer policy concessions and fewer unorthodox alliances than we might otherwise expect' (Strøm and Müller 1999a: 26). As we shall see, several factors can account for this information uncertainty.[8]

1. *Incomplete information on preferences and strategies*: Information can be incomplete because preferences are not transparent. Strøm (1994: 113) argues that the principal reason that coalition bargaining fails or is protracted may be that the players suffer from incomplete information and uncertainty, especially with regard to the preferences, options, pay-offs, objectives, and feasible strategies of other players. Moreover, Diermeier and van Roozendaal (1998: 610) stress that information is often unequally distributed among parties. Thus, some parties (e.g. new parties or parties with inexperienced leaders) may be more susceptible than others to the problems that derive from such uncertainty.

To counteract information opacity, parties may seek knowledge through involvement in negotiations with other players, such as parliamentary groups or neo-corporatist actors, or by forcing negotiators to clarify their policy commitments. Another strategy is to use specific procedures (e.g. inner-cabinet negotiations), policy-specific (and often restrictive) agreements, or other institutional devices to cope with unexpected and unforeseeable contextual events. This search

---

[8] Our argument is in line with 'fair division' theories (Brams and Taylor 1996; Brams 2006), which suggest that as the number and importance of stakes increase, the calculus of trade-offs between stakes (e.g. office gains in exchange for policy concessions) becomes more difficult. If parties bargain over only one stake (e.g. ministerial office), they can more easily calculate whether everybody gets a fair deal, for instance, by applying a proportionality rule. Multiple stakes least complicate bargaining when parties differ in their valuations of the various stakes (Warwick 1996; Strøm and Müller 1999a: 9–10). When all stakes are salient to all parties, the trade-offs become much more complicated (Strøm and Müller 1999a: 13).

for institutional remedies against incomplete information may require more bargaining, and therefore a longer formation. Thus, such protections come at a price in transaction costs. If these costs become excessive, parties may instead decide to succumb to the inherent uncertainty of the future, forego elaboration of any deals concerning situations years ahead, and consign themselves to ad hoc conflict resolution. In that case, formation may take less time and be less complicated.

2. *Instability of preferences and perceptions of strategies*: Even if the players' preferences are fairly well known at the outset, information about the bargaining situation may be incomplete because preferences (on policy, composition, and portfolios) may not be stable throughout the formation process. Actors may begin their bargaining with a given set of perceptions and preferences (as assumed by rational-choice theories), but these may change over time. In this learning process, preferences may be shaped by the new information acquired or by persuasion.

Instability in the bargaining position of a party may also be induced by *electoral volatility* (King et al. 1990: 857; Strøm 1990: 47; Strøm and Müller 1999*b*). In periods of high electoral stability, a party can easily be persuaded to enter a coalition, as most of its voters will continue to vote for it, irrespective of the party's coalition behaviour and policy performance. All else equal, the less party leaders have to worry about possible repercussions in future elections, the more willing they will be to reach an (coalition) agreement. In periods of high electoral competitiveness, however, the bargaining situation can be complicated by the fact that the ratio of office rewards to electoral costs may be lower or more uncertain. Thus, parties may tend to focus on vote-seeking strategies, which in turn may lead to more bargaining rounds and longer periods of negotiation. We would therefore expect electoral volatility to exacerbate uncertainty and bargaining complications.

Bargaining complexity

Bargaining complexity is the second major factor that we expect to account for differences in cabinet formation processes. But as central as this concept is to the study of coalition politics, bargaining complexity is rarely rigorously or parsimoniously defined. Even the authors who use formation duration and attempts as indicators of bargaining complexity often provide only basic conceptual definitions. Warwick (1994: 46) defines complexity as the number of obstacles to successful coalition formation but does not expand on what these obstacles may be. Laver and Schofield (1990: 162) provide a more operational definition by suggesting that complexity equals the number of alternative governing coalitions that appear viable at any given time. The greater this number, the more complex and unstable (and precarious) the coalitions that tend to form.

In spite of the lack of a generally accepted and clear-cut conceptual definition, there is broad agreement that complexity can matter in many ways in coalition bargaining. A number of authors have presented models in which coalition termination or renegotiations are conceptualized as results of the strategic choices of coalition parties whose leaders calculate the anticipated costs and benefits of changes from the status quo (Grofman and van Roozendaal 1994; Warwick 1994; Lupia and Strøm 1995; Narud 1996). As parties and their leaders can be conceived as vote maximizers (Lupia and Strøm 1995: 656), and as voters more often than not punish them for government participation (Narud and Valen in Chapter 11), the pay-offs from government office can be expected to decrease as the end of the constitutional term approaches.

In general, changes in coalition constraints and opportunities will be larger immediately after an election than in mid-term situations, and therefore cabinet formation will be more difficult. The balance of power between parties may have changed if new coalitional pre-commitments have been made during the campaign. A heated campaign may have alienated potential coalition parties that were on better terms beforehand. The electoral gains or losses of particular parties can have made some overconfident, while others may seek to regain self-confidence through an opposition cure. On the other hand, mid-term coalition breakdowns may generate among incumbent coalition partners strong feelings about excluding the 'breaker' in the new bargaining game—and if numerically possible—just continue as much as possible with what is left of the old team. This yields complexity, but not necessarily a lack of information. Bargaining complexity may also be affected by the ambition level of the relevant party leaders. Müller and Strøm (Chapter 5) argue that the longer potential duration of the cabinet, the more it is worthwhile to draft a comprehensive agreement, while with little time left, only more modest policy programmes can be implemented. The capacity to shape policy is thus smaller in mid-term formations, and therefore complexity may be lower and formation should be faster.

In line with Laver and Schofield (1990), many authors see the number of parties potentially or actually involved in the bargaining situation as the crucial cabinet-specific determinant of bargaining complexity (Leiserson 1968: 775; Warwick 1994: 47; Strøm and Müller 1999a: 25). As the number of parliamentary parties grows, the opportunities for government-seeking parties to find or build more attractive coalitions become more numerous. In Lupia and Strøm's terms, there may be a larger number of parties with significant walk-away power (see Chapter 2).[9] Therefore a broader range of coalition formulas will tend to be tested out, which may increase the number of bargaining rounds and formation duration. The number of parties involved in a bargaining attempt also determines the number of different (policy and portfolio) preferences that must be taken into account, the number of potential strategies, and to some extent the dimensionality of the potential coalition. Hence, the number of players can be expected to influence the complexity of the bargaining situation.

---

[9] Van Roozendaal (1997: 74) identifies the ability to make 'credible exit threats' as existing 'when a party has clear and viable alternatives to the present government, recognized by all other parties'.

It is nevertheless worth stressing the difference between the fragmentation of the subset of parties actually involved in bargaining attempts (specific to the bargaining situation) and the overall party system fragmentation (a more systemic factor discussed below). If many parties routinely exclude themselves or are excluded from coalition bargaining, their presence may add very little complexity to the situation. For instance, in some highly fragmented party systems, coalitions can be formed by the two largest parties, by one large party and a couple of smaller parties, or by even a 'monster coalition' of all small and medium parties against the system's major party. Overall measures of party system fragmentation do not take into consideration these different coalition logics. Therefore, Warwick (1994: 35, 47) introduces the notion of 'effective number of cabinet parties' (or 'effective government size') and convincingly argues that it is the bargaining environment within the government (or, perhaps even more precisely, the government's potential support coalition) that matters, not the larger parliamentary environment. Yet, that argument overlooks the fact that there can be multiple bargaining rounds with alternative coalition partners before a government is formed (Golder 2010). Focusing only on the parties in the cabinet that eventually formed is not appropriate since it may cause us to underestimate the complexity of the original bargaining situation. Therefore, in the multivariate analysis below, we analyse only such attributes that can be ascribed to the parliament and the political system throughout the bargaining period (and not any characteristics of the cabinet that emerges at the end of the formation process).

Uncertainty and complexity in the empirical formation literature

Diermeier and van Roozendaal (1998) were probably the first to rigorously examine the cross-national record of cabinet formation duration. Their study is based on a bargaining model of incomplete information, which suggests that formateurs (party leaders) may use strategic bids and a prolonged formation process to obtain necessary information about 'important bargaining parameters such as the preferences of the pivotal actors' (Diermeier and van Roozendaal 1998: 610). The larger the information asymmetries, the longer they expect coalition bargaining to last. Diermeier and van Roozendaal further argue that formateurs face relatively greater uncertainty if they bargain immediately after a general election or following a cabinet that resigned due to parliamentary defeat. They find empirical support for their argument that these conditions tend to be associated with longer negotiations. They also find some evidence that the 'identifiability' of coalition alternatives (see Strøm 1985, 1990) lessens uncertainty by providing readily available information about the coalition alternatives most likely to materialize. This latter finding, however, disappears when the authors control for fixed country effects. But, in general, Diermeier and van Roozendaal find the empirical results to be supportive of their model of coalition bargaining as a game of asymmetric information.

Martin and Vanberg (2003) ask themselves whether the results that Diermeier and van Roozendaal (1998) find are really due to information uncertainty, or whether it is the fact that bargaining is more complex that explains the variation in formation duration. For instance, is it not complexity (more actors and demands to consider) rather than uncertainty (lack of information about what the relevant actors want) that increases when more parties are bargaining? When they replicate Diermeier and van Roozendaal's analysis (1998) and control for the ideological diversity of the coalition that formed and the number of parties it contained, Martin and Vanberg (2003) find that the significant results for *previous defeat* disappear. The effect of post-election bargaining is still significant. But Martin and Vanberg (2003) also find that the effects of variables such as the *number of parties* and the *ideological range* of the government speak in favour of a focus on bargaining complexity rather than on uncertainty.

Investigating the partly contradictory findings of Diermeier and van Roozendaal (1998) versus Martin and Vanberg (2003), Golder (2010) suggests that factors that increase bargaining complexity (the number of parties and ideological polarization) have a noticeable effect when there is already uncertainty among the political actors. Uncertainty will always cause delays, but complexity seems to matter the most when uncertainty is sufficiently high.

We too believe that uncertainty—lack of information—matters. We note that the importance of bargaining complexity presupposes uncertainty (incomplete information). When they do not fully know each other's motives and preferences, party leaders may prolong the bargaining process through delay tactics or by making offers that they are not sure will be accepted. The more complex the bargaining situation, the more likely such behaviour may be. Yet, it is often difficult to distinguish empirically between the effects of complexity relative to those of uncertainty. Both complexity and uncertainty yield similar expectations. This can diminish the usefulness of the analytical distinction in our particular context. Nevertheless, below we investigate the relative importance of both uncertainty and complexity by assigning empirical indicators to these concepts and estimating their impact. We have more variables that are designed to capture complexity than we have measures of uncertainty, so the analysis below centres largely on the former. But we expect both factors to be important.

FROM CONCEPTS TO OPERATIONAL DEFINITIONS

From the conceptual discussion to our empirical investigation, we proceed in the following way. We expect that cabinets that form immediately after an election to have more bargaining rounds and longer formation processes than cabinets that form in the inter-election period. This expectation can be derived from the argument that under the latter circumstances formateurs face less uncertainty about the preferences of other actors. We further expect that increased bargaining complexity may flow from particular structural attributes (reflected in such variables as the seat distribution in the parliament), as well as from preference divergence among the coalitionable political parties. We would intuitively expect that a number of institutional rules might affect the bargaining process by constraining the cabinet options, or privileging some of them, or reducing or increasing information uncertainty. Even though such effects seem eminently plausible, it is worth noting that the existing scholarship has given generally weak support for the idea that institutions, such as investiture rules, have much impact on the coalition bargaining process (Diermeier and van Roozendaal 1998; Golder 2010).

In our estimates of the effects of different clusters of variables on formation duration and the number of bargaining rounds, we analyse both inconclusive bargaining (which, we should recall, need not be *failed*) rounds and formation duration. The two dependent variables call for different statistical techniques. For our analysis of inconclusive bargaining rounds, we use logistic regression (logit) models in which we assign the value 1 to any of the 128 cabinets that experienced one or more inconclusive bargaining round and 0 to the remaining cabinets. And like Diermeier and van Roozendaal (1998), Martin and Vanberg (2003), and Golder (2010), we use event history analysis for the analysis of formation duration. We estimate a series of Cox proportional hazard models using the clusters of variables that have been identified in Chapter 3 (and refer to that chapter for further detail). As in the empirical chapters that follow, we include a substantial number of independent variables in six distinct clusters. In this section, we discuss only the theoretically most interesting ones.

In any analysis of coalition bargaining, the initial distribution of bargaining power has to be a central concern. We see the importance of this concern most clearly when we consider the situation in which one party has a legislative majority (a majority situation) and under simple majority thus monopolizes all bargaining power. The literature on coalition bargaining regularly recognizes the importance of this factor by including a dummy variable for the presence of a majority party. In contrast, we believe that a single-party majority essentially (but not completely) obliterates the impact of other variables.[10] If one includes

---

[10] In our sample of 424 cabinets, 13 contain a party that held a majority of the parliamentary seats but still went into coalition with one or more other parties. Of these 13 cases, all except the last French one occurred in the late 1940s/1950s. They include two Austrian cases in which the ÖVP had a parliamentary majority: the early grand coalitions of Figl I and Figl II. There are four cases in France. The first three represent a Gaullist parliamentary majority in coalition with other centre-right parties (Couve de Murville, Chaban Delmas, and Messmer I), whereas the last one is a Socialist majority in coalition with the Communist Party (Mauroy II in 1981). There are also four German cabinets: Adenauer II–V (1953–60), during which the Christian Democrats had a majority in the lower chamber, but were in coalition with the DP and occasionally the FDP and smaller parties. And, finally, there are

majority situations in the analyses, it would make sense, rather than just including a dummy variable for majority situations, to interact certain independent variables with this dummy to see whether or not these variables matter only under minority situations. But since we in this project generally choose not to include interaction terms when we do not have very clear and well-established expectations about them (see Chapter 3), and given the small number of majority situations in our sample, we instead exclude all majority party situations from the multivariate analysis below, which leaves us with 349 minority situations.

To capture the impact of *uncertainty*, in line with Diermeier and van Roozendaal (1998), we test whether or not it matters if a cabinet formation follows immediately upon a general election. As explained above, electoral volatility is another variable that can be expected to reflect the level of uncertainty fairly directly. We measure volatility in terms of the proportion of seats in parliament that the parties won and lost in the most recent general election.

As for the variables that represent bargaining *complexity*, we first return to the most commonly used and most effective predictors of coalition politics: ideology and size. Ideological bargaining complexity is partly determined by the number of relevant policy dimensions of the party system (Lijphart 1984; Taagepera and Grofman 1985; Grofman 1989; Taagepera and Shugart 1989; Laver and Schofield 1990). Formal coalition theory indicates that party system multidimensionality tends to destabilize coalitions (De Vries 1999). As the number of relevant policy dimensions grows, the number of convex coalitions (equivalent to 'connected' ones in unidimensional systems) goes up, rendering a higher number of coalitions feasible or even equally likely (equiprobable) (Pajala 2002).[11] Hence, bargaining in multidimensional party systems will be more hazardous due to the higher risks of coalition partners walking away, during the formation or afterwards. Empirically, we distinguish between three degrees of dimensionality: unidimensional, two-dimensional, or multidimensional systems in which the party holding the median legislator on the first dimension also holds the median legislator on the second [or in Schofield's terms (1993), when there is a stable core policy position], and finally two- or multidimensional systems in which the median party on the first cleavage dimension differs from the median party on the second dimension (and in which there is hence no core).

We can think of ideological cohesion as one component of bargaining complexity that may affect coalition bargaining. One could argue that policy compromises may be more easily reached in systems with one or several large parties generally considered unfit for government (*regierungsunfähig*), as the 'coalitionable'

---

three Italian cases: De Gasperi V through VII (1948–51), which brought in the PRI, sometimes the PSDI and the PLI, despite a DC majority in the lower chamber (the Chamber of Deputies).

[11] For instance, in assemblies consisting of 6 parties, the proportion of coalitions connected on a single policy dimension is 33% (counting single-party cabinets as connected), whereas the share of all potential coalitions that would be convex in a three-dimensional setting is 92% (Pajala 2002: 56).

(*koalitionsfähige*) parties are then more likely to be situated in or relatively close to the centre of the policy space. Warwick (1994: 14), however, argues the opposite: the presence of large anti-system parties induces collaboration between parties that are ideologically more diverse than those that would choose to coalesce in non-polarized party systems. At any rate, in party systems in which uncoalitionable parties control a substantial share of the parliamentary seats, and in which the set of feasible coalitions is therefore considerably reduced, the coalition bargaining game should be less complex (*ceteris paribus*, in comparison with a party system in which all parties are coalitionable). This factor should reduce bargaining complexity and hence the likelihood of inconclusive formation rounds. In our empirical analysis, we capture the relative presence of non-coalitionable parties by the combined seat share held by communist and extreme right-wing parties (as defined by country experts).

Diermeier and van Roozendaal (1998) find some evidence that the *ex ante* identifiability of coalitional alternatives matter, though in their analysis this result is not robust. Yet, that lack of robustness may be because this variable is notoriously hard to operationalize. We employ the parliamentary preference range along the left–right dimension as a reasonable proxy. The more preference divergence along this axis, the more identifiable the alternatives should be. Our empirical measures are based on Party Manifesto data (see Chapter 3).

Bargaining complexity is also a function of party fragmentation in the parliament, as the number of parliamentary parties has a direct impact on the number of potential coalitions.[12] We thus include the number of parliamentary parties as one measure of complexity. Since the effective number of parties and bargaining power fragmentation are highly collinear, in our empirical test we include only the *absolute* number of parties and bargaining power fragmentation.

Bargaining outcomes can also be shaped by institutional rules that structure the bargaining environment in which potential partners interact (Mayntz and Scharpf 1995; Scharpf 1997: 1). Strøm, Budge, and Laver (1994: 327) illustrate empirically that even seemingly innocuous constraints may dramatically redistribute bargaining power among the parties.[13] Among the theoretically most relevant

---

[12] The number of solutions (potential cabinet compositions) increases exponentially with the number of parties (number of solutions = $(2)^{n\,parties} - 1$). In partisan terms, the 'empty' coalition can actually be analogous to a non-partisan cabinet.

[13] There is a substantial body of scholarship that supports these claims. A number of authors have pointed to the impact of formation procedural rules on the outcomes of bargaining (Austen-Smith and Banks 1988; Baron 1991, 1993; Diermeier and van Roozendaal 1998). The most prominent one is perhaps the 'formateur rules', defining which party can take the initiative in making coalition offers. We should be careful not simply to refer to the Prime Minister's party in the coalition that eventually forms as the *formateur* (see e.g. Ansolabehere et al. 2005). Two distinctions are necessary. First, Laver and Schofield (1990) distinguish between free-style bargaining situations and those in which the Head of State plays an active role by appointing a *formateur* or an *informateur*. Second, because there may have been several formateurs and bargaining rounds before the cabinet is formed, Bäck and Dumont (2008) make a crucial distinction between the first formateur party and the PM party.

constraints that can account for such effects are quantitative decision rules (investiture, special majority, and bicameralism) and procedural rules regarding formation leadership (below operationalized in terms of the continuation rule). An investiture requirement is frequently featured in analyses of coalition politics (Strøm 1990; Bergman 1993). As Chapter 3 pointed out, we define the investiture requirement in terms of positive parliamentiarism.[14]

Another institutional provision that may affect bargaining power is the continuation rule, that is, the constitutional convention that the incumbent government can remain in office after elections until it is proven that it no longer enjoys the trust of the parliamentary majority. The continuation rule can decrease complexity by privileging the incumbent PM. But the operationalization of this variable has been inappropriate, probably because it is difficult for researchers without a great deal of country-specific expertise to distinguish between enforceable rules and customary behaviour. Diermeier and van Roozendaal (1998) claim that Denmark, Norway, and Sweden have such rules, which is correct. Golder (2010) notes that the UK has one, too. A more systematic study by Lars Davidsson (2004) suggests that no fewer than nine countries (Denmark, France, Greece, Iceland, Ireland, Luxembourg, the Netherlands, Norway, and Sweden) have an enforceable constitutional continuation rule.[15] The UK is not one of these, though there is a (less enforceable) norm supporting such behaviour.

Other relevant institutional parameters include supermajority requirements for particular kinds of decisions, such as constitutional amendments. When constitutional reform is on the political agenda of some of the potential coalition parties, and supermajorities are therefore necessary, the coalition parties will have to decide whether they want to pay the costs (in terms of offices and policy concessions) of including additional parties. Such special surplus rules are to some extent 'soft' constraints, in the sense that no cabinet can be legally forced to reform the constitution, but they might still have considerable impact on actor calculations.

Yet, in our view, the literature still lacks a common cross-national distinction between formateurs in the clearly institutionalized formateur systems of countries such as Belgium, the Netherlands, and Greece (which has a constitutional rule that designates the leader of the largest party as the person who gets to make the first offer) and those in free-style bargaining systems.

[14] Bergman (1995) uses a broader definition according to which positive parliamentarism also includes countries in which a 'majority coalition' is the expected outcome of coalition bargaining. This is particularly relevant in Iceland and the Netherlands. However, here we focus exclusively on the institutional requirement that a new cabinet must win a majority vote in the parliament.

[15] Davidsson (2004) analyses continuation rules with the help of the parliamentary services in the respective countries and not for the purpose of coalition research per se. While such parliamentary services are generally well informed, they are less well placed to ensure the cross-national consistency that our project has achieved through our 'structured collaboration' approach. Therefore, we do have concerns about the cross-national reliability of this variable. Yet, since the variable has been used in the existing literature, we include it here.

Bicameralism is another important institution that has been shown to affect cabinet duration (Druckman and Thies 2002). Here we test its effects on bargaining rounds as well as on formation duration. In cases of strong bicameralism, when the two chambers are likely to differ in partisan composition but have similar competencies, the impact should be considerable (Lijphart 1984; see also Chapter 3). However, because strong bicameralism exists only in a few countries, in our sample this variable would basically amount to a dummy variable for Belgian and Italian cabinets. Hence, we do not include it in our models (see Chapter 3). Instead, we include a marker for bicameralism in general (see also Druckman and Thies 2002: 769). Even in symmetrical and congruent bicameralism, the proportion of seats of parties often slightly differs between chambers, which could complicate coalition bargaining in cases of closely divided legislatures (as has happened on several occasions in Italy). The expected effect of bicameralism is similar to that of a special threshold: as it decreases the number of viable combinations, it should facilitate bargaining over membership but could at the same time complicate bargaining over other matters (such as policy formulation).

Inter-party negotiations may also be affected by the relevant players' anticipation during the formation process of the powers of the future prime minister. The higher the powers of the PM with regard to cabinet governance, the greater incentives of the prospective PM (who is generally the formateur) to succeed and to make the formation stage short, since he or she knows that delicate policy problems not debated at this stage may be decided more unilaterally (by the PM) when the government is in power. The opposite effect, of course, would apply to the parties that do not expect to hold the prime ministership: they have incentives to hold out for all that they can get during the initial phase of coalition bargaining.

Finally, apart from electoral volatility, we may expect formation processes to be affected by critical events such as high employment figures or other bad economic news, or by national security events which may render government participation less attractive because of electoral risks. In such hard times, parties may decide to form larger coalitions than they otherwise would (Indridason 2006). Hence, it may take additional time and bargaining rounds to come to an agreement that will attract sufficiently broad support.

THE MULTIVARIATE EVIDENCE

To sort out what is behind these observations and to weigh uncertainty versus complexity, we now turn to the multivariate analysis—first concerning inconclusive bargaining rounds. In this chapter, as in the following empirical chapters, we present a series of model specifications, representing each of the clusters of explanatory variables, a full model of the most successful predictors from each cluster, and a final model containing only those variables whose effects prove robust and remain significant in a full specification that includes all the different clusters. We include in the full model those variables that are significant (or close to significant) in each cluster estimate. In addition, we can also bring over variables that fail to meet the significance criteria if they are of particular theoretical interest (as is the case with post-election cabinets below). This might be because there are clear expectations that their significance depends on variables from other blocks being included, or because the literature on the topic claims that this variable is particularly important. In the final model, we include only those variables that have proven to be significant in the presence of variables from other clusters. Sometimes, the effect of a variable that is significant in the full model is not robust in the presence of the other variables in the final model. In such cases, our final models exclude that variable. Thus, only those variables that are significant and robust show up in the final model (see Chapter 3 for more details).

Inconclusive bargaining rounds

We first examine the record on inconclusive bargaining rounds. As noted above, the models presented in Table 4.5 (pp. 146 and 147) are logistic regressions in which the dependent variables are coded 1 whenever one or more inconclusive bargaining rounds occurred, and 0 otherwise. The goodness of fit of these models can be assessed in several ways. One is the percentage of observations correctly predicted. A useful benchmark in this context is the score that one would obtain simply by always predicting the modal (more common) outcome, which in this case is the value 0, the absence of any inconclusive bargaining rounds. Thus, if one predicts that in all *minority situations* (no majority party in parliament) there will be no inconclusive bargaining rounds, one would be correct 64 per cent of the time. A slightly more sophisticated version of this benchmark (and a more exacting standard) would be to predict the modal outcome for that particular country. Thus, if one predicts that in cases in which there is no majority party, Belgium, Finland, Greece, the Netherlands, and the UK would have at least one inconclusive bargaining round but that no other country would have any such attempt (in other words, the modal outcome for each particular country), one would be correct 72 per cent of the time.[16]

In Table 4.5, in the first column and cluster, note that the 1940s, 1980s, and 1990s are significantly different from the 1950s (the control category). The 1940s results need perhaps not concern us here, but the 'cluster' test reveals the same pattern as did the descriptive table. The number of inconclusive bargaining rounds

---

[16] When inconclusive bargaining rounds occur in Iceland, there are frequently several of them. This is reflected in the fact that Iceland averages more than one inconclusive bargaining round per government formation, yet in 14 of 26 government formation opportunities there have been no inconclusive rounds.

decreased in the 1980s and 1990s. The 1980s variable is significant in the time-cluster, but not in the full model. It does reappear as significant, however, in the final model where it is included because we already know from the descriptive statistics that there is an important time trend in the data. The 1990s variable, in contrast, is unequivocally significant in any way in which it is used. Thus, the decline in bargaining rounds in the last decade of the previous century is well documented. But what is behind this empirical record?

To explain this, we first turn to attributes of the parliament and the political system. Diermeier and van Roozendaal (1998) find post-election negotiations to be systematically longer than other bargaining periods. Table 4.5 reveals that post-election bargaining is also more likely to include inconclusive bargaining rounds. Yet, this result is not absolutely robust. The coefficient for this variable is consistently in the expected direction, but does not always meet conventional standards of statistical significance. In the context of other attribute variables, such as maximum possible duration, the difference between the immediate post-election cabinets and other cabinets does not materialize. Yet in our full model, and controlling for other clusters of variables, post-election status reappears as significant and stays that way in the final model.

The complexity of the party system clearly also matters with respect to inconclusive bargaining rounds. What we can add here is to highlight the importance of the choice of operational definition. We find that bargaining power fragmentation does better than the absolute number of parties. A party system in which more parties have the ability to make and break coalitions increases the likelihood that there is more than one bargaining round.

Looking next at policy dimensionality, it turns out that Martin and Vanberg (2003) were correct when they stressed the importance of preference divergence. In the 'preference' cluster, most available measures are significant, but when the variables are controlled against variables from other clusters, it turns out that these variables are not robust. Instead, a variable that is not significant in its own cluster, a higher number of issue dimensions, is the most robust one. With increased complexity, that is, if a party system goes from being unidimensional to two or more dimensions, there are more formation rounds.

The literature on bargaining rounds and formation attempts has largely unsuccessfully tried to capture the importance of institutions. Our analysis shows that for formation rounds, there is one exception: our new measure of the institutional powers of the PM, which outperforms all other institutional variables. Greater PM power has the effect of decreasing the number of formation attempts. Given that the PM party will have considerable leverage once the coalition forms, an anticipatory logic may apply. Party leaders who believe that their party is going to get the prime ministership will be more inclined to accept concessions or postpone delicate questions in the expectation that they will have decisive power in the future, which decreases bargaining complexity at the formation stage.

TABLE 4.5. *Logistic regressions on occurrence of inconclusive bargaining rounds (minority situations only)*

Independent variables	Model 1	Model 2	Model 3	Model 4	Model 5	Model 6	Model 7	Model 8	Impact[a]
Time									
1940s	0.93 (0.49)*						1.39 (0.76)*	1.36 (0.56)**	0.31 (0.11)
1960s	−0.40 (0.38)								
1970s	−0.03 (0.35)								
1980s	−0.72 (0.37)**						−0.37 (0.41)	−0.65 (0.34)*	−0.15 (0.07)
1990s	−1.53 (0.46)**						−1.23 (0.59)**	−1.69 (0.47)**	−0.32 (0.07)
Structure									
Post-election cabinet		0.42 (0.32)					1.04 (0.39)**	0.55 (0.29)	0.13 (0.07)
Maximum cabinet duration		0.00 (0.01)					0.04 (0.10)		
Absolute no. parl. parties		−0.04 (0.05)							
Bargaining power fragmentation		0.60 (0.12)**					0.45 (0.18)**	0.52 (0.13)**	0.13 (0.03)
Preferences									
Extremist party seat share			0.02 (0.01)**				−0.01 (0.02)		
Parliamentary pref. range			−0.02 (0.01)**				−0.03 (0.01)**		
Polarization (BP weighted)			0.05 (0.03)**				0.07 (0.04)*		
Issue dimensionality			0.78 (0.48)				0.69 (0.70)	1.03 (0.53)*	0.06 (0.03)[a]
No core party			0.78 (0.25)**				−0.32 (0.41)		
Institutions									
Supermajority const. amend.				0.02 (0.34)					
Bicameralism				−0.09 (0.35)					
Positive parliamentarism				0.18 (0.49)			0.42 (0.57)		
Ex ante gvt. programme screen				0.54 (0.61)			−0.26 (0.52)		
Cabinet co-decides leg.				0.60 (0.50)			0.36 (0.52)		
PM cabinet powers				−0.37 (0.08)**			−0.29 (0.12)**	−0.20 (0.08)**	−0.05 (0.02)
PM dissolution power				0.22 (0.48)			0.66 (0.66)		
Semi-presidentialism				0.54 (0.42)					
Continuation rule				0.06 (0.38)					

Bargaining						
Prior cab.: Reg. el. termination				−0.43 (0.30)	−0.78 (0.42)*	
Prior cab.: Other tech. termination				−1.33 (0.49)**	−1.30 (0.71)*	−1.25 (0.55)** −0.26 (0.09)
Prior cab.: Intra-party conflict term				−0.89 (0.39)**	−0.82 (0.51)	
Prior cab.: Early election term				0.48 (0.41)		
Prior cab.: Early election no conflict				−0.50 (0.48)		
Critical events						
Terminal event lag: Security					0.85 (0.68)	1.94 (0.83)** 1.25 (0.70)* 0.29 (0.14)
Terminal event lag: Economic					−0.16 (0.55)	
Terminal event lag: Personal					−1.21 (0.65)*	−0.80 (0.89)
Electoral volatility					0.00 (0.02)	
Inflation					0.01 (0.01)	
Unemployment					−0.08 (0.03)**	−0.08 (0.06)
Constant	−0.24 (0.26)	−2.40 (0.55)**	−3.64 (1.37)**	0.15 (0.48)	−0.27 (0.20)	−0.29 (0.29)	−2.99 (2.13) −4.81 (1.54)**
Number of observations	349	348	348	349	339	298	306 339
Pseudo-R^2	.06	.08	.07	.10	.03	.04	.24 .21
% Correctly predicted	.67	.70	.66	.71	.64	.67	.78 .73

Notes: $^{*}p < 0.10$; $^{**}p < 0.05$.

[a] Impact is the marginal effect of a unit change in the independent variable on the probability of the outcome occurring, calculated based on Model 8, with the following exception: the impact of Issue Dimensionality is for a 0.25 change (1 standard deviation).

Note also that cabinet formations that take place after a PM dies or resigns for personal (not political) reasons, or because it is customary to resign when a new Head of State is inaugurated (other technical termination), have fewer formation rounds. In such cases, it is likely that no inconclusive bargaining round will follow. We also find that if the previous cabinet resigned over national security concerns, there are more bargaining rounds. One explanation may be that such circumstance can force parties to consider the possibility of coalescing with what they normally would consider to be 'strange bedfellows', which in turn may cause complications.

In the full model, it appears that in systems where the parties have clearly divergent positions on the left–right axis (parliamentary preference range) and the PM enjoys strong institutional powers, few, if any, inconclusive bargaining rounds are likely to occur. However, the effect of the parliamentary preference range is not robust and is therefore not included in the final specification in Table 4.5. As the final model shows, chances are that there will be more than one round of formation bargaining when negotiations occur immediately after elections, in party systems characterized by high fragmentation and multidimensionality, and in times of national security concerns.

The final column of Table 4.5 reports the substantive impact of the significant variables in the final model. These results suggest that an inconclusive bargaining round in coalition bargaining immediately following election is increased by 13 percentage points, controlling for the effect of other variables, and that an increase in bargaining power fragmentation by one unit (moving, for example, from three equal-sized parties to four such parties) also increases the likelihood of an inconclusive bargaining round occurring by 13 percentage points.

Formation duration

We then turn to the analysis of formation duration, as presented in Table 4.6. Note that there are many similarities but also some differences compared with the analysis of bargaining rounds. In Table 4.6, we recognize the spike in duration in the 1970s from our descriptive analysis above.[17] Relative to the control category (Germany), Austria, Belgium, and the Netherlands have much longer formation duration, whereas France, Norway, Sweden, and the UK have much shorter formation processes. As for structural attributes, the literature on the topic again finds support. Post-election timing is a strong predictor of a longer formation period, as suggested by Diermeier and van Roozendaal (1998). The fragmentation of bargaining power in the parliamentary party system has the same effect. The more fragmented the bargaining environment, the longer the bargaining period.

---

[17] In the duration analysis in Table 4.6, we do not include unemployment or inflation in the 'critical events' bloc, since including these variables would cause us to lose a considerable number of observations. We have tested for any effect that unemployment or inflation might have, and the results (not reported here) are insignificant.

TABLE 4.6. *Cox proportional hazards models of cabinet formation duration (minority situations only)*

Independent variables	Model 1	Model 2	Model 3	Model 4	Model 5	Model 6	Model 7	Model 8
Time and space								
1940s	0.96 (0.23)							
1960s	0.77 (0.15)							
1970s	0.46 (0.09)**							
1980s	0.62 (0.12)**							
1990s	0.72 (0.15)							
Austria	0.35 (0.12)**							
Belgium	0.47 (0.14)**							
Denmark	2.57 (0.76)**							
Finland	0.67 (0.18)							
France	5.69 (1.94)**							
Greece	2.23 (1.25)							
Iceland	0.47 (0.15)**							
Ireland	1.21 (0.41)							
Italy	0.71 (0.19)							
Luxembourg	0.78 (0.27)							
The Netherlands	0.22 (0.07)**							
Norway	4.36 (1.43)**							
Portugal	1.18 (0.48)							
Spain	0.83 (0.39)							
Sweden	3.48 (1.09)**							
United Kingdom	6.30 (6.54)*							
Structure								
Post-election cabinet		0.48 (0.07)**					0.79 (0.13)	0.72 (0.10)**
Maximum cabinet duration		0.99 (0.01)*					1.01 (0.17)	
Absolute no. parl. parties		0.95 (0.02)**					1.22 (0.27)	
Bargaining power fragmentation		0.82 (0.05)**					0.48 (0.20)*	0.42 (0.07)**
							0.99 (0.01)	0.99 (0.01)*
							0.93 (0.03)**	0.95 (0.02)**
							0.87 (0.06)**	0.86 (0.05)**

(*cont.*)

TABLE 4.6 (Continued)

Independent variables	Model 1	Model 2	Model 3	Model 4	Model 5	Model 6	Model 7	Model 8
Preferences								
Extremist party seat share			0.98 (0.01)**				0.97 (0.01)**	0.97 (0.01)**
Parliamentary pref. range			1.01 (0.01)**				1.01 (0.01)**	1.01 (0.01)**
Polarization (BP weighted)			0.98 (0.01)*				0.98 (0.01)*	0.98 (0.01)*
Issue dimensionality			1.25 (0.30)					
No core party			0.47 (0.06)**				0.58 (0.10)**	0.59 (0.08)**
Institutions								
Supermajority const. amend.				0.68 (0.11)**			0.69 (0.13)**	0.58 (0.08)**
Bicameralism				0.88 (0.14)				
Positive parliamentarism				0.96 (0.19)			1.21 (0.23)	
Ex ante gvt. programme screen				0.70 (0.19)				
Cabinet co-decides leg.				0.90 (0.22)				
PM cabinet powers				1.15 (0.04)**			1.00 (0.05)	
PM dissolution power				1.62 (0.38)**			1.60 (0.29)**	1.72 (0.26)**
Semi-presidentialism				1.99 (0.37)**			2.39 (0.60)**	2.30 (0.44)**
Continuation rule				1.33 (0.22)*			1.18 (0.23)	
Bargaining								
Prior cab.: Reg. el. termination					0.56 (0.08)**		0.83 (0.34)	
Prior cab.: Other tech. termination					1.71 (0.34)**		1.14 (0.26)	
Prior cab.: Intra-party conflict term					1.31 (0.24)			
Prior cab.: Early election term					0.37 (0.08)**		0.76 (0.32)	
Prior cab.: Early election no conflict					1.47 (0.35)		1.16 (0.27)	
Critical events								
Terminal event lag: Security						1.07 (0.34)		
Terminal event lag: Economic						1.89 (0.45)**	1.58 (0.40)*	
Terminal event lag: Personal						1.96 (0.46)**	1.05 (0.27)	
Electoral volatility						1.01 (0.01)	1.01 (0.01)	
Number of observations	349	348	348	349	339	327	327	347
Log likelihood	−1,623.8	−1,658.1	−1,670.6	−1,673.91	−1,621.7	−1,570.7	−1,489.7	−1,606.1

Notes: *p < 0.10; **p < 0.05.

The absolute number of parties has its own independent effect, and the same goes for the maximum potential tenure of the cabinet (until the next election). Both variables are positively associated with the length of the formation process.

The range of party positions in the parliament decreases the formation period, and this time the variable is robust and included in the final model. Note also that if extremist parties have a large share of the parliamentary seats, bargaining becomes more complex (and/or uncertain), which prolongs the formation process (even though it does not cause a higher number of bargaining rounds). The combined importance of size and ideological positions (weighted by polarization) stands out as significant and increases the formation duration period. Apparently, as preference divergence between pivotal players increases, so does bargaining complexity. Similarly, if no party controls the median legislator on both of the two most important dimensions, such that there is by definition no 'core party', this too increases formation duration. Thus, long bargaining periods are very much a story of ideological diversity, especially when politics is multidimensional.

Several institutions have a systematic bearing on formation duration. Among the institutional variables, our index of PM cabinet powers does not affect the length of the bargaining process as significantly as it does the number of bargaining rounds. But another PM power, the constitutionally mandated right to dissolve parliament, decreases the formation period significantly and robustly. It is possible that the incumbency advantage that matters for the incoming PM is that he or she will be able to time the early election so that it will be held in a favourable political climate (Strøm and Swindle 2002).

In formation duration, two other institutional features are important as well. One, semi-presidentialism (the intervention of presidents in the formation process, especially in Finland and France), helps decrease the formation period. The other variable has the opposite effect. Requirements that amendments to the constitution must be passed by a supermajority (normally two-thirds) prolong formation periods. And since such a requirement for constitutional amendments often signals the presence of qualified majority rules for other matters as well (as in Austria), the implication may be that in such environments negotiators need to make sure that the cabinet can meet higher hurdles than those that apply in more majoritarian systems. This higher hurdle can presumably account for the longer formation processes.

While there are thus several significant institutional determinants of formation duration, it is also worth noting that several institutional variables fail to show any significant impact. Thus, although a continuation rule tends to reduce bargaining time, the effect is generally insignificant. Somewhat contrary to expectations, positive parliamentarism does not prolong the period of negotiations.[18] Screening

---

[18] This result is not totally unexpected. Diermeier and van Roozendaal (1998) and Golder (2010) also find that positive parliamentarism has no significant direct impact on the length of the formation process. This is contrary to Bergman's thesis (1993). Golder (2010) suggests (following Strøm 1990:

requirements are associated with longer negotiations, as one might expect, but the effect is not significant. And bicameralism does not have much of a discernible impact.

Overall, though, it is clear that the duration of the formation period is affected by various institutional conditions, as well as by the configuration of preferences and the structural attributes of the cabinet and the parliament. Our two remaining clusters of variables exhibit less robust effects. In model 5, we see clear and intuitive effects of the conditions under which the previous cabinet resigned. As expected, negotiations following regularly scheduled elections or early elections associated with conflict are systematically longer than those following technical terminations or non-conflictual early elections. All these effects retain their directional effects in our full model (model 7), but all these effects are also attenuated to the extent that they lose their statistical significance.

In our critical events cluster, we find that when the previous cabinet was terminated for reasons having to do with personal or economic events, the subsequent formation period has been systematically shortened. But both of these effects are again much weaker when we control for all the other variables in model 7 and neither makes it into our final, reduced model. Note also that while national security events matter for the number of formation rounds, no such effect can be discerned in formation duration.

Recall from the descriptive statistics at the beginning of this chapter that we have one outlier country, the Netherlands, that has had significantly more bargaining rounds and longer formation periods than any of the other countries in our sample. Before we can conclude our empirical analysis, we need to consider to what extent this country may be driving our results. We have therefore examined such potential country-specific effects for both bargaining rounds and formation duration. In the final model for bargaining rounds, removing the Netherlands from the analysis has the effect of rendering the 'post-election formation' variable insignificant, but has no significant impact on the other parameter estimates. As for duration, with one exception, a similar test indicates that the results (including the estimate for post-election status) are robust. The exception is parliamentary polarization (weighted by bargaining power), which is no longer significant when the Netherlands is excluded. All the remaining variables that have significant effects in the 17-country sample remain significant and exhibit the same sign in the 16-country sample (not reported in table form).

Both these findings suggest that Dutch exceptionalism is at times important, but that the main results of our analysis do not depend on that country. For what it is worth, Dutch exceptionalism may have something to do with the particularities of the seat distribution in combination with the ideological alignment of the political parties. One place to look for a more specific explanation is with the

25) that this institutional requirement might have a clear impact on formation duration only when a minority government is already a viable option [on such interaction effects, see also the discussion in Bäck and Dumont (2008)].

strategic position of the large and centrist Christian Democratic Party (Keman 1994). The party may have a strategic position that provides it with a high walk-away value and a low discount rate. These features may in turn explain its unusual ability to wait for policy and portfolio concessions from coalition partners. But the details of this can of course only be confirmed (or refuted) by in-depth studies of coalition bargaining involving that particular party.

CONCLUSION

The bargaining process that leads from the termination of one cabinet to the formation of the next has until now been a subject of scant systematic study. In this chapter, we have made a concerted effort to remedy that situation, focusing on two aspects of the bargaining process: the number of bargaining rounds and the duration of negotiations. We have found that the formation process is much influenced by country-specific path dependency and that the effect of between-country variation is strong. We also find that both inconclusive bargaining rounds and lengthy formation processes occurred much less frequently in the 1990s than they did in the 1970s.

We have identified two main explanations of these features of the bargaining process: information uncertainty and bargaining complexity. For formation duration, we find some evidence in favour of uncertainty being important (but not for the volatility variable), but we find little robust evidence that uncertainty has a systematic effect on bargaining rounds. Variables associated with bargaining complexity, such as preference distribution and bargaining fragmentation, have a more direct impact.

Concretely, we want to highlight four of our findings. First, the impact of the outlier country, the Netherlands, needs to be carefully considered. The inclusion or exclusion of the Netherlands in our sample can influence the results for some of the variables in our analysis (though the great majority of our significant results are robust to the exclusion of the Dutch case). Second, no single cluster can account for any disproportionate share of the variation in our two dependent variables. Two blocks, however, matter more than others: preferences and structural attributes. If we want to understand the forces that drive cabinet formation processes, we are therefore well advised to focus on the bargaining situation and the preferences and bargaining powers of the main protagonists. Somewhat surprisingly, critical events and the circumstances under which the previous cabinet terminated matter less. In brief, these results may indicate that parties involved in coalition bargaining are more forward-looking than backward-looking.

Third, we note that the causes of inconclusive bargaining rounds are not exactly the same as the causes of long formation periods. While preferences and structural attributes are critical explanations of both incomplete bargaining rounds and long formation duration, there are also differences. Institutions have a greater impact on the latter. Semi-presidentialism is important for formation duration, and so is a supermajority requirement for constitutional amendments. The former shortens formation duration while the latter prolongs it. Fourth, and perhaps our most important empirical finding, is the importance of the strategic powers of the prime minister, both with regard to bargaining rounds and formation duration. If the PM has an advantageous strategic position, there tend to be fewer formation rounds (PM cabinet powers) and shorter formation processes (PM dissolution rights).

It thus appears that our bargaining perspective is correct in bringing together an emphasis on bargaining conditions with one focused on strategic action. In the spirit of process tracing, this also suggests that qualitative studies focusing on the strategic advantage of some parties and prime ministers can shed more light on how the formation process is shaped by such strategic advantages.

In general, further comparative coalition research would be most effective if it could trigger a better understanding of micro-behavioural decisions actors take in specific dynamic bargaining settings and in interaction with their larger institutional environment. While our framework and the empirical application of this framework do capture a good deal of the variation in coalition bargaining, we still explain only a small part of the real-world variation in such behaviour. In other words, coalition research could benefit from more researchers abandoning for a while their computer screens, hitting the road, and getting their tape recorders running. The ultimate aim of such an inductive approach should not be to write a *roman fleuve* of 'formation dramatics', but to feed information gathered by thick descriptions back into theory formulation (Andeweg, De Winter and Dumont 2010). Empirical scholarship inspired by rational-choice models would in the long run also benefit from such an interchange.

One thing that future empirical work cannot do by itself, however, is to close the debate on the relative importance of uncertainty and complexity. For one thing, the distinction is very difficult to operationalize empirically. In addition, the effects may be very difficult to disentangle. Judging from available research and our own findings, it seems that both matter simultaneously and significantly. But they need not matter equally much at every stage of the coalition cycle. In the formation process, complexity matters more than uncertainty.

REFERENCES

Andeweg, Rudy B., De Winter, Lieven, and Dumont, Patrick (eds.) (2010, forthcoming). *Puzzles of Government Formation*. London: Routledge.

Ansolabehere, Stephen, Snyder, Jr., James M., Strauss, Aaron B., and Ting, Michael M. (2005). 'Voting Weights and Formateur Advantages in the Formation of Coalition Governments', *American Journal of Political Science*, 49: 550–63.

Austen-Smith, David, and Banks, Jeffrey S. (1988). 'Elections, Coalitions and Legislative Outcomes'. *American Political Science Review*, 82: 405–22.

Bäck, Hanna and Dumont, Patrick (2008). 'Making the First Move: A Two-Stage Analysis of the Role of Formateurs in Parliamentary Government Formation', *Public Choice*, 135: 353–73.

Baron, David (1991). 'A Spatial Bargaining Theory of Government Formation in a Parliamentary System', *American Political Science Review*, 83: 1181–206.

—— (1993). 'Government Formation and Endogenous Parties', *American Political Science Review*, 88: 33–47.

—— and Diermeier, Daniel (2001). 'Elections, Governments, and Parliaments in Proportional Representation Systems', *Quarterly Journal of Economics*, 116: 933–67.

Bergman, Torbjörn (1993). 'Formation Rules and Minority Governments', *European Journal of Political Research*, 23: 55–66.

—— (1995). *Constitutional Rules and Party Goals in Coalition Formation: An Analysis of Winning Minority Governments in Sweden*. Umeå: Ph.D. thesis, Department of Political Science, Umeå University.

Brams, Steven J. (1975). 'Bandwagons in Coalition Formation', *American Behavioral Scientist*, 18: 472–97.

—— (2006). 'Fair Division', in Barry R. Weingast and Donald Wittman (eds.), *Oxford Handbook of Political Economy*. Oxford: Oxford University Press.

—— and Taylor, Alan D. (1996). *Fair Division: From Cake-Cutting to Dispute Resolution*. Cambridge: Cambridge University Press.

Chertkoff, Jerome M. (1975). 'Socio-psychological Views on Sequential Effects in Coalition Formation', *American Behavioural Scientist*, 18: 451–71.

Davidsson, Lars (2004). *Kammare, kommuner och kabinett—tre konstitutionella studier*. Stockholm: SNS Förlag.

De Vries, Miranda (1999). 'Governing with Your Closest Neighbour: An Assessment of Spatial Coalition Formation Theories', Ph.D. dissertation, University of Nijmegen.

De Winter, Lieven and Dumont, Patrick (2001, manuscript). 'Bargaining Complexity, Formation Duration and Bargaining Rounds: A Comparative Analysis', Draft chapter for Kaare Strøm, Wolfgang C. Müller, and Torbjörn Bergman (eds.), *Cabinets and Coalition Bargaining: the Democratic Life Cycle in Western Europe*.

—— —— (2006). 'Parties into Government: Still Many Puzzles', in Richard S. Katz and William Crotty (eds.), *Handbook of Party Politics*. London: Sage, pp. 175–88.

Diermeier, Daniel and van Roozendaal, Peter (1998). 'The Duration of Cabinet Formation Processes in Western Multi-Party Democracies', *British Journal of Political Science*, 28: 609–26.

Dumont, Patrick (2000). 'Pour une théorie intégrée des processus de formation de gouvernements : étude extensive et intensive du phénomène en Europe de l'Ouest', Ph.D. dissertation, Université catholique de Louvain.

Druckman, James N. and Thies, Michael F. (2002). 'The Importance of Concurrence: The Impact of Bicameralism on Government Formation and Duration', *American Journal of Political Science*, 46: 760–71.

Franklin, Mark N. and Mackie, Thomas T. (1983). 'Familiarity and Inertia in the Formation of Governing Coalitions in Parliamentary Democracies', *British Journal of Political Science*, 13: 275–98.

Golder, Sona N. (2006). *The Logic of Pre-Electoral Coalition Formation*. Columbus, OH: Ohio State University Press.

——(2010). 'Bargaining Delays in the Government Formation Process', *Comparative Political Studies*, 43: 3–32.

Grofman, Bernhard (1989). 'The Comparative Analysis of Coalition Formation and Duration Distinguishing Between-Country and Within-Country Effects', *British Journal of Political Science*, 19: 291–302.

—— and van Roozendaal, Peter (1994). 'Toward a Theoretical Explanation of Premature Cabinet Termination', *European Journal of Political Research*, 26: 155–70.

Indridason, Indridi (2008). 'Does Terrorism Influence Domestic Politics? Coalition Formation and Terrorist Incidents', *Journal of Peace Research*, 45: 241–59.

Keman, Hans (1994). 'The Search for the Centre: Pivot Parties in West European Party Systems', *West European Politics*, 17(4): 124–48.

King, Gary, Alt, James, Burns, Nancy, and Laver, Michael (1990). 'A Unified Model of Cabinet Dissolution in Parliamentary Democracies', *American Journal of Political Science*, 34: 846–71.

Laver, Michael (1974). 'Dynamic Factors in Government Coalition Formation', *European Journal of Political Research*, 2: 259–70.

—— and Schofield, Norman (1990). *Multiparty Government. The Politics of Coalition in Europe*. Oxford: Oxford University Press.

Leiserson, Michael (1968). 'Factions and Coalitions in One-Party Japan: An Interpretation of Coalition Bargaining and Electoral Competition', *American Political Science Review*, 62: 770–87.

Lewin, Leif (1999). 'When Should a Minority Government Resign?', in Erik Beukel, Kurt Klaudi Klausen, and Poul Erik Mouritsen (eds.), *Elites, Parties and Democracy—Festschrift for Professor Mogens N. Pedersen*. Odense: Odense University Press.

Lijphart, Arend (1984). *Democracies*. New Haven, CT: Yale University Press.

Luebbert, Gregory M. (1986). *Comparative Democracy: Policymaking and Governing Coalitions in Europe and Israel*. New York, NY: Columbia University Press.

Lupia, Arthur and Strøm, Kaare (1995). 'Coalition Termination and the Strategic Timing of Parliamentary Elections', *American Political Science Review*, 89: 648–65.

Martin, Lanny W. and Vanberg, Georg (2003). 'Wasting Time? The Impact of Ideology and Size on Delay in Coalition Formation', *British Journal of Political Science*, 33: 323–44.

Mayntz, Renate and Scharpf Fritz W. (eds.) (1995). *Steuerung und Selbstorganisation Sektoren*. Frankfurt am Main: Campus.

Narud, Hanne Marthe (1996). 'Party Policies and Government Accountability. A Comparison between the Netherlands and Norway', *Party Politics*, 2: 479–507.

Pajala, Antti (2002). *Expected Power and Success in Coalitions and Space*. Turku: Turun Yliopisto.

Pinto-Dushinsky, Michael (1998). 'Send the Rascals Packing: Defects of Proportional Representation and the Virtues of the Westminster Model', *Times Literary Supplement*, 25 September.

Scharpf, Fritz W. (1997). *Games Real Actors Play*. Boulder, CO: Westview Press.

Schofield, Norman (1993). 'Political Competition in Multiparty Coalition Governments', *European Journal of Political Research*, 23: 1–33.

Strøm, Kaare (1985). 'Party Goals and Government Performance in Parliamentary Democracies', *American Political Science Review*, 79: 738–54.

—— (1990). *Minority Government and Majority Rule*. Cambridge: Cambridge University Press.

—— (1994). 'The Presthus Debacle: Intraparty Politics and Bargaining Failure in Norway', *American Political Science Review*, 88: 112–27.

—— and Leipart, Jørn Y. (1993). 'Policy, Institutions, and Coalition Avoidance: Norwegian Governments 1945–1990', *American Political Science Review*, 87: 870–87.

—— and Müller, Wolfgang C. (1999*a*). 'Political Parties and Hard Choices', in Wolfgang C. Müller and Kaare Strøm (eds.), *Policy, Office or Votes? How Parties in Western Europe Make Hard Decisions*. Cambridge: Cambridge University Press.

—— —— (1999*b*). 'The Keys to Togetherness: Coalition Agreements in Parliamentary Democracies', *Journal of Legislative Studies*, 5: 255–82.

—— and Swindle, Stephen M. (2002). 'The Strategic Use of Parliamentary Dissolution Powers', *American Political Science Review*, 96: 565–98.

—— Budge, Ian, and Laver, Michael (1994). 'Constraints on Cabinet Formation in Parliamentary Democracies', *American Journal of Political Science*, 38: 303–35.

Taagepera, Rein and Grofman, Bernhard (1985). 'Rethinking Duverger's Law: Predicting the Effective Number of Parties in Plurality and PR Systems—Parties Minus Issues Equals One', *European Journal of Political Research*, 13: 341–52.

—— and Shugart, Matthew S. (1989). *Seats and Votes. The Effects and Determinants of Electoral Systems*. New Haven, CT: Yale University Press.

van Roozendaal, Peter (1997). 'Government Survival in Western Multi-Party Democracies', *European Journal of Political Research*, 32: 71–92.

Warwick, Paul V. (1994). *Government Survival in Parliamentary Democracies*. Cambridge: Cambridge University Press.

—— (1996). 'Coalition Government Membership in West European Parliamentary Democracies', *British Journal of Political Science*, 26: 471–99.

Willemé, Peter (1996) 'Een eenvoudig model van de vorming van Belgische federale regeringscoalities (1958–1991)', *Res Publica*, 38: 95–111.

5

Coalition Agreements and Cabinet Governance

Wolfgang C. Müller and Kaare Strøm

INTRODUCTION

All cabinet coalitions are based on some initial agreement between the partners. At a minimum, they have to agree on which parties will participate in the government and on the division of cabinet offices. Otherwise, no government could assume office. In most cases, the coalition partners will make an agreement that goes beyond the division of high office spoils. They may define the government's policy agenda, from at a minimum identifying its top priorities (e.g. budgetary restraint) to detailing a policy programme that seeks to anticipate all major legislation and government decisions of the parliamentary term. They may agree on some set of rules under which they will cooperate in government. They may even decide how they will interact in other institutions or at other levels of government. But these coalition agreements vary greatly in their contents, formality, and comprehensiveness. In this chapter, we discuss the precise nature of such agreements and identify the causes of variation.

Coalition agreements do not emerge spontaneously; they result from bargaining that can be intense, protracted, and hard-nosed. The resulting agreements are the 'contracts' that define the set of political offices to be filled, the perquisites and favours to be distributed, the mechanisms of governance, and the public policies to be conducted. The purposes of coalition agreements are typically to contain conflict within the coalition and to coordinate government policy. Yet, however good the parties' intentions, there is no guarantee that their coalition agreements will be effective. Coalition agreements are the script, not the play. They tell us what was agreed at the beginning of the coalition cycle, not how the coalition partners actually behaved later in the game. Therefore, if our interest is in actual coalition governance, then we cannot read the script as the performance.

Studies of actual coalition agreements nevertheless show them to be highly relevant guides to coalition governance and policy. De Winter, Timmermans, and Dumont (2000: 322), for example, refer to the agreement as the coalition's equivalent of the bible. According to the best available evidence, the rules that have been adopted are generally observed, and the agreed-upon policies are implemented (see the country chapters in Müller and Strøm 2000). Timmermans (2003) provides the most systematic account of the effects of coalition agreements in the Netherlands and Belgium, covering 98 controversial issues from five cabinets. He finds that the compromises hammered out in coalition negotiations and fixed in coalition agreements were implemented in slightly more than half of the cases. In turn, half of these were implemented smoothly (i.e. without further intra-coalition conflict). Thus, agreements cannot help coalition parties solve all their problems. But they will often have *some* positive effect on inter-party cooperation, and the question for coalition parties is whether this effect justifies the time and effort invested.

What drives inter-party bargaining over coalition agreements? The short answer, we argue, is calculated self-interest, in several senses. First, we expect the relevant players (in our case, political party leaders) to bargain whenever they can all make themselves better off through an agreement, and when it is not immediately obvious how to do so (which is to say, when there are multiple feasible and mutually advantageous options). We also expect that the greater the need for coalition agreements, the more common and elaborate such agreements will be. Broadly speaking, this need for agreements is driven by three factors: the preference diversity among the parties to the agreement, the uncertainty they have about their future interactions, and the risk of opportunistic behaviour that they face. Yet, the need for a coalition agreement must be balanced against its value and costs. All else equal, the more valuable the coalition, the more likely an agreement will be, and the more costly it is to forge an agreement, the less likely it is that this will be done.

In this chapter, we shall expand on this argument and use it as a guide to the coalition agreements found in our sample of Western European democracies. We shall examine the incidence and contents of coalition agreements found in our sample, focusing particularly on the policy contents of coalition agreements and the discipline to which they commit the parties that sign them. Finally, we shall examine more comprehensively the conditions under which written coalition agreements are adopted.

MODELS OF COALITION GOVERNANCE

Coalition agreements are one aspect of the governance structure of multiparty coalitions in parliamentary democracies. Despite many country-specific descriptive accounts, such governance structures have received very little comparative and analytical attention. Yet, the recent neo-institutional literature contains two contrasting stylized accounts of coalition decision-making. One of these models suggests that coalition agreements can serve no useful function because centralized coalition governance is futile. The other model suggests that coalition agreements may be superfluous because each governing party retains veto powers regardless. We shall argue that while each of these arguments may contain a kernel of truth, neither provides a persuasive overall account of coalition politics.

Ministerial government and the futility of coalition agreements

In their seminal book *Making and Breaking Governments*, Michael Laver and Kenneth Shepsle (1996) highlight the critical powers of agenda control vested in the executive branch. In the authors' own words, 'the agenda and implementation power that the cabinet exercises vis-à-vis the parliament is in turn exercised vis-à-vis the cabinet by individual ministers and their civil servants' (Laver and Shepsle 1996: 281). These powers privilege the cabinet vis-à-vis parliament, but they also pervade the organization of the executive branch itself. According to Laver and Shepsle, parliamentary democracies coordinate policy decisions by granting jurisdictionally specific 'property rights' (ministerial discretion) through the assignment of cabinet portfolios. Each portfolio, generally representing a government department, is allocated to one and only one party, and there is no mechanism by which any other party can prevent the party holding the portfolio in question from implementing its ideal point within that jurisdiction. The set of government portfolios is assumed to be exogenously fixed. We can think of this set of assumptions as a model of *ministerial government* (Strøm 1994).

Laver and Shepsle's account of coalition government is a rigorous deductive theory and as such has many merits. Yet, it is not an entirely plausible account of the delegation of authority that takes place in parliamentary systems.[1] The authors in essence argue that delegation from the prime minister or the coalition leaders to individual cabinet ministers cannot work, since these ministers can never be induced to pursue a policy different from their own most-preferred one (their ideal point). Yet Laver and Shepsle implicitly assume that delegation *from* cabinet ministers works, in the sense that their agents (junior ministers and civil servants) can be induced to act in the minister's interest. Yet, as principals, coalition leaders possess much stronger accountability mechanisms vis-à-vis individual cabinet line ministers than do those ministers vis-à-vis their respective civil servants. The parliamentary majority can instruct its ministers and, if necessary, remove them from office for non-performance. Civil servants, on the other hand, typically have protected tenure. Since they are also typically professionals with lifelong careers, information asymmetries should be at least as severe between ministers and civil servants as between coalition leaders and ministers. Hence, all else equal, we expect more agency problems in the delegation from cabinet ministers to their

[1] For the most comprehensive critique of Laver and Shepsle (1996) see Dunleavy with Bastow (2001). See also Strøm (1998), as well as Warwick (1999*a*) and the subsequent exchange with Laver and Shepsle (1999*a*, 1999*b*; Warwick 1999*b*).

subordinates than in the delegation from coalition leaders to cabinet ministers (Strøm 1998). If so, then Laver and Shepsle's model is simply implausible. If individual cabinet members can get their respective civil servants to toe the line, then surely there must be (similar?) ways for coalition leaders to control their respective cabinet ministers. If, on the other hand, cabinet members cannot effectively control their civil servants, then the model of ministerial government simply cannot have much explanatory power.

More generally, the critical challenge to Laver and Shepsle is to explain why ministerial government (departmentalism) would arise as a mechanism of cabinet governance. If cabinet portfolios entail such dramatic powers of agenda control, then when and why would politicians choose the kind of institutions Laver and Shepsle describe? Under their assumptions, government stability results from the parties' inability to agree on any mutually beneficial alternatives to the status quo. This inability is in turn due to the absence of feasible portfolio allocations that would allow the parties to enforce such agreements. But if ministerial government regularly forces party leaders to settle for inefficient (suboptimal) policy compromises, then why would the same party leaders choose this decision-making structure? In brief, if ministerial government prevents opportunities for mutual gain, then why create or sustain this institution?

Actual parliamentary democracies contain many institutions that restrict the policy discretion of individual ministers. Policy coordination on major issues takes the form of collective cabinet decision-making, which may require unanimous cabinet assent or other forms of broad agreement. Alternatively, the coalition agreement may be enforced through shared competencies of various sorts. For example, several ministers from different parties may be assigned to the same department, junior ministers from one party may be placed in ministries controlled by another, or the coalition may adopt accord clauses to the effect that laws cannot be implemented unless a pre-specified set of ministers agree on joint action (Müller and Strøm 2000). Finally, particular cabinet ministers are often given responsibilities that deliberately cross-cut other ministerial jurisdictions. For example, coalition cabinets often feature detailed and strong budgetary oversight by the Minister of Finance. The prime ministership is an even more obvious portfolio entrusted with such tasks of enforcing policy coherence (Larsson 1993; Müller, Philipp, and Gerlich 1993).

The real world thus provides a variety of examples of governance structures in which authority is not decentralized to the extent that ministerial government implies. And there are many examples of cabinet members implementing policy they do not especially favour. Speaking on conditions of anonymity, an Austrian cabinet minister charged with the implementation of important concessions that his party had made in coalition negotiations, put it thus:

The coalition agreement is duty, in addition there is enough leeway for optional policies. As far as the duties are concerned, there are things which one does like less. In these cases one tries to delay and prevent, for instance ___ [first policy], which I considered nonsense. However, the coalition partner pressed, and pressed, and pressed. I prevented the implementation of this policy until ___, but then the pressure of the coalition partner, the main opposition party, and the media became too great.... The ___ [second policy] was an unloved thing, too. I saw no demand for that and postponed it until the last year of the government's term—and then I implemented it.

Veto players and the redundancy of coalition agreements

There is an alternative account of coalition decision-making that instead emphasizes the centralization of cabinet authority. In Tsebelis' account (1995, 2002) of coalition politics, each coalition party is a veto player that can maintain the status quo against the demands of its coalition partner(s). Jean Tirole (1999: 768) refers to this as 'veto collegiality', in the sense that 'one party has authority, except that the other party has the right to impose the status quo if he does not like the other party's choice.' Tsebelis (2002: 96) argues that in the cabinet, any coalition party is a veto player regardless of the distribution of cabinet portfolios. The simple fact of membership in the executive coalition translates into veto powers. Tsebelis (2002: 106–9) argues that this veto power is exercised through the authority structures of the cabinet, or through other binding agreements between the leaders of the coalition parties. We can refer to this as a model of *cabinet government* (Strøm 1994).

Like that of Laver and Shepsle (1996), Tsebelis' model is not entirely plausible, analytically or empirically. There are many reasons why individual coalition parties often cannot veto policy proposals they do not favour. One is that they may simply have negotiated away such veto powers during the process of coalition bargaining. Indeed, it is difficult to see why coalition parties would bother to negotiate complex decision-making rules unless they resulted in a procedure less restrictive than mutual veto provisions.

Even on issues on which the coalition parties have made no prior commitment substantively or procedurally, it is not clear that any single coalition party could block a decision with which it disagrees. It could only effectively do so if it is pivotal, in other words, if the decision in question depends critically on its votes or bargaining power. But in a surplus majority coalition, by definition at least one party is not pivotal. And even minimal winning coalitions may be able to ignore dissidents in their own ranks if they can instead gain the requisite votes from members of the opposition.

Finally, even if a coalition party could technically defeat a bill favoured by its partners by voting against it in parliament or resigning from the cabinet, its threat to do so is only credible if the party's gain from defeating the bill outweighs any losses it would suffer as a consequence of exercising its veto or leaving the cabinet. If by defying its coalition partners the party would stand to lose (in terms of influence in other policy areas or office benefits) more than it would gain, then the other parties would rationally ignore its threat and effectively 'call its bluff'. And if in turn the dissenting party correctly anticipates such hardball politics (which is not entirely unknown in coalition governments), it will presumably decide to swallow its objections (see Strøm 2003: 74–7).

Empirically, consider the 1966 'popular front' Finnish government that included the Centre Party, the Social Democrats, and the Communists, plus a Social Democrats splinter party (Strøm and Müller 1999: 259–61). In this historically important coalition, the individual parties clearly did not have mutual veto powers. And despite one of the longest bargaining processes in Finnish post-war history, the coalition agreement did not specify the government's agenda in any great detail. Indeed, the coalition parties only reached substantive agreement on a few selected policies. The coalition agreement obligated the parties to voting discipline on these policies only. Nor did the rules imply mutual veto powers on other issues.

Actual party behaviour conformed to these rules. The Communist Party, for example, was not able to prevent decisions it did not favour. There were severe conflicts between the Communists and the other two parties, which were resolved in March 1968, when two Communist ministers were dismissed and replaced by reform Communists. Even the Centre Party, Finland's second largest party at the time and the party of the median legislator, was regularly defeated. Markku Laakso's study (1972) of 150 roll-call votes from the first year of this coalition's life shows that the Centre Party was outvoted by its leftist coalition partners on one of six bills. Thus, neither the Centre Party nor the Communists, both substantial parties, was effectively a veto player in the 1966–8 Finnish government coalition.

WHY COALITIONS AGREEMENTS?

Coalition agreements are indications that political parties often find it difficult to cooperate in the executive branch and that neither ministerial government nor cabinet government is an adequate description of the process of coalition policymaking in parliamentary democracies. If coalition parties could simply exercise their veto powers without them, there would be no need for coalition agreements. Or if coalition agreements could be of no use in constraining cabinet members and their subordinates, there would be no reason to have them. As we have indicated above, however, neither of these statements accurately describes the world of multiparty politics across parliamentary democracies.

Coalition agreements exist, and they are designed to cement deals that might otherwise come unstuck. Indeed, one of the main functions of coalition agreements is for each of the coalition parties to relinquish any veto power over policies to which the coalition specifically commits itself. As long as the coalition parties faithfully observe the agreement, their mutual veto power has then ceased to exist. The coalition accord may in addition contain procedural clauses by which the parties agree to solve other, unspecified issues. These procedures may well remove any implicit veto power the individual parties might otherwise have.

But coalition parties do not always craft formal agreements, and we shall see that even when they do, their agreements vary considerably in contents and comprehensiveness. The questions we want to address in this section are when coalition agreements are most likely to be made, and when they will tend to be most formalized and committal.

Before we can address this question, however, we need to consider the audiences and functions for which coalition agreements are intended. In short, such agreements are primarily designed to govern the relationship *between* governing parties but may also be intended for use *within* each party. We can thus distinguish between their internal and external audiences. The former are the respective parties' voters and rank-and-file members. In this context, coalition agreements are pre-commitments, by which the negotiating parties 'bind themselves to the mast' in such a way that when they go through unpleasant situations, party leaders have a mechanism by which they can resist temptation or intraparty pressure to renege on their commitments (Elster 1984: 36–47). Such pre-commitments reflect the fact that it is often easier to get party regulars to approve concessions to coalition partners when these are included in a package deal that includes government office, other perquisites, and policies favoured by the rank and file. Typically, in coalition agreements party leaders will therefore shed bright light on their achievements and ask the party to ratify a whole package of deals.

The external function of coalition agreements is to tie together the leaders of the different coalition parties, ease communication between them, and contain interparty conflict or facilitate its resolution. Coalition agreements typically impose some form of discipline in parliamentary votes, as well as in other parliamentary and governmental activities. It is more difficult to maintain such discipline in a multiparty coalition than in a single-party cabinet. Individual parties have well-established internal rules and governance structures, and their reliance on a common electoral label reinforces the mutual interdependence of their elected representatives. All co-partisans have a strong collective interest in their party's electoral fate. These facilitating conditions do not exist to the same extent *between* coalition parties, and hence coalition governance institutions typically have to be negotiated along with the policies and the perquisites of the coalition. The external function of coalition agreements is therefore typically the more critical one.

Preference divergence

The difficulties of governing together arise from three conditions. The most basic one is simply that the leaders of the different parties have different and often conflicting preferences over the rewards they reap from controlling the executive branch. These rewards include policy influence, office benefits (spoils), and future electoral advantage (Strøm 1990b; Müller and Strøm 1999). All of these goods are likely to be scarce, so that not all demands can be satisfied simultaneously (Müller and Strøm 1999).

At least in the short run, the division of government offices and other benefits is often a constant-sum game (though see Chapter 7). Ministerial portfolios are typically unique and indivisible. The prime ministership, for example, can be awarded to only one party, to the exclusion of all others.[2] Electoral advantage, to the extent that party leaders care foremost about *vote shares*, is even more strictly constant-sum. Ultimately, one party's gain has to be someone else's loss. In some cases, all incumbent parties may be able to gain at the expenses of the opposition, but much more commonly, coalition parties compete against each other for votes (Rose and Mackie 1983). And, finally, while the parties that make up a coalition may have more or less compatible policy preferences, it is hardly ever the case that all of their policy preferences can be realized simultaneously.

Thus, political parties, or more specifically their leaders, are likely to have different preferences over a broad range of issues, driven at least in part by their desire for policy benefits, office benefits, and electoral advantage (Strøm 1990b). Even so, there are typically multiple solutions that are at least good enough to meet every negotiating party's *reservation level*, the value of the political benefits it could enjoy without any agreement. Under such circumstances, bargaining may occur and coalitions form.

Not every situation that allows coalitions to form may require a formal coalition agreement. In some cases, the preferences of the parties may be sufficiently well aligned that there is no need to negotiate a formal agreement. Alternatively, party leaders may behave cooperatively even without such an agreement if they anticipate either repeat interactions in the same arena or other interactions with the same players in different arenas (see, e.g., Shepsle 1996: 229–31; Stiglitz 2000: 1449, 1459–60; also Axelrod 1984; Frank 1988; Kreps 1990). Thus, national coalition leaders may anticipate that they will face the same partners in subnational coalitions (cf. Jun 1994; Downs 1998: 193–202), or they may take into consideration positive spillover effects from collaboration elsewhere, for example in a corporatist arena.

Yet, such easy cases are more likely to be exception rather than the rule. Parties that enter a coalition government cannot always hope that the shadow of future interactions will be sufficiently long, or their preferences sufficiently well aligned,

---

[2] In rare cases, coalition parties may agree to split the office of prime minister between them, e.g. so that one party controls the office for one-half of the parliamentary term and another party for the remainder. Israel and Latvia have experienced such agreements, but they are rare or non-existent in our sample. At any rate, such agreements do not alter the fundamental fact that high offices are finite and scarce.

to induce voluntary cooperation. The greater the preference diversity between the parties, the more fragile their coalition is likely to be. And the greater the fragility of the coalition, the greater the need for a coalition agreement. Thus:

Proposition 1: The greater the preference diversity among the coalition parties, the more formalized their coalition agreement is likely to be.

Uncertainty

Another reason that cooperation is difficult is that elected politicians face considerable uncertainty over the set of decisions that they will have to make and the circumstances under which they will do so. Most interesting social interactions feature uncertainty, and coalition politics is no exception. Party leaders involved in coalition bargaining in parliamentary democracies face at least three important kinds of uncertainty: concerning policy instruments, the policy agenda, and the voters, respectively.

One source of uncertainty is that politicians do not fully understand the relationships between the policy instruments at their disposal and the political outcomes they seek (see Krehbiel 1991). This is, of course, reflected in the fact that governments delegate a great deal of power to agents, such as cabinet ministers and their subordinates, with highly specialized tasks. A second source of uncertainty lies in the political environment, and the political agenda, that party leaders may confront over the course of a parliamentary term. When the German coalition of Social Democrats and Greens formed in 1998, for example, these parties could not foresee the NATO intervention in Kosovo the next year, which nearly led to the coalition's breakdown. Nor could they anticipate the even more challenging issue of military intervention in Afghanistan in 2001. The third and final source of uncertainty is that even if they were intimately familiar with their policy instruments and could perfectly predict the political agenda, politicians could not know in advance how voters would respond to their decisions.

All of these forms of uncertainty make cooperation risky and therefore drive parties to formalize their cooperation. As North (1990: 57) puts it: 'No institutions are necessary in a world of complete information. With incomplete information, however, cooperative solutions will break down unless institutions are created that provide sufficient information for individuals [or coalition parties] to police deviations.' Institutions assuring cooperation need to provide (a) 'a communications mechanism that provides the information necessary to know when punishment is required' and (b) 'incentives for those individuals to carry out punishment when called on to do so' (North 1990: 57). Thus:

Proposition 2: The greater the uncertainty among the coalition parties, the more formalized their coalition agreement is likely to be.

Opportunism

Yet, uncertainty in itself is not the only stumbling block in coalition politics. Often, uncertainty gives rise to the further problem of opportunism. Politicians may fear that aspects of their political environment may be manipulated to their own disadvantage. They cannot always rest assured that whatever agreements they reach will be respected. The risk of opportunism arises when coalition partners can use uncertainty to derive private gain at the expense of others. Opportunistic parties may take advantage of unforeseen circumstances to extract policy concessions or other benefits. Non-simultaneous exchange and non-contemporaneous benefit flows create particularly tricky problems in coalition bargaining (Weingast and Marshall 1988). If the pay-offs to all partners are evenly distributed over the coalition's anticipated duration, then most likely each will have a constant incentive to keep the coalition going. If, on the other hand, the pay-offs are unevenly distributed over time, then a party that early on receives a large benefit (e.g. a major piece of legislation or key long-term government appointments) has little incentive to fulfil its part of the deal later. Thus, the sequence in which the parties secure their gains may destabilize coalitions.

Opportunism stems also from the problem of *verification*—ascertaining whether all parties in fact honour their commitments. The division of government into increasingly specialized agencies makes this an important challenge. It is most obvious in administrative matters, that is, decisions made by individual ministers (or in their name by civil servants). Although these decisions are often not in the public domain, they can nevertheless be very consequential. Legislative matters, in contrast, go through the 'clearing houses' of cabinet and parliament, where coalition partners can scrutinize the bill. What is less clear, however, is whether they will be able to grasp all its policy implications. To the extent that policy expertise is monopolized by the ministry that has prepared the bill and that one party has exclusive control over that ministry, it can be difficult for other parties to understand the fine grain of government policy.

It is important to note that the agreements that underlie cabinet coalitions generally cannot be enforced by courts of law. Thus, even if one partner recognizes that another partner is not faithful to their deal, the former may have no means outside the political arena to make the latter behave. Generally, coalition deals are private agreements between political parties that cannot bind constitutional agents, such as cabinet ministers and MPs (Müller 2000*a*). Hence, coalition deals need to be enforced by *political* means, and these means must be negotiated by the coalition parties themselves. This is a major reason that parties turn to formalized means of cooperation in the political arena. Thus:

Proposition 3: The greater the risk of opportunistic behaviour among the coalition parties, the more formalized their coalition agreement is likely to be.

The value and costs of coalition agreements

Thus, preference divergence, uncertainty, and the threat of opportunism make it attractive for coalition parties to design enforcement mechanisms and embody them in a coalition agreement. But in deciding whether to adopt a formal coalition agreement, and if so, how comprehensive and committal such an agreement should be, parties will also consider the value of the coalition and the costs of forging an agreement. The more benefits parties expect to flow from the coalition they are about to form, the more likely they are to decide to draw up an agreement about it. The expected value of an emerging coalition is likely to correlate with its structural attributes and expected duration. A majority coalition will in most circumstances be more valuable than a minority coalition, since the former is less likely to be short-lived or ineffective. And a coalition formed at the beginning of a parliamentary term is likely to be more valuable than one formed late in the term, when elections will soon have to be held. At any rate:

Proposition 4: The more valuable the coalition, the more formalized the coalition agreement is likely to be.

Finally, coalition agreements have to be cost-effective. There are transaction costs involved in writing up any coalition agreement. There may also be audience costs in the sense that some of the commitments and compromises contained in coalition agreements may offend activists and purists within the respective parties. Or there may be costs deriving from the reputational effects of deals and concessions made in the coalition agreements. All such costs render formal coalition agreements less attractive. Thus:

Proposition 5: The greater the transaction and audience costs of forging a coalition agreement, the less formalized such a coalition agreement is likely to be.

THE EMPIRICAL RECORD

Let us now turn to the empirical record of coalition agreements. As we have argued, coalition agreements are mechanisms by which coalition parties seek to attain policy objectives and protect themselves against the consequences of preference divergence, uncertainty, and opportunism. Such agreements are typically negotiated between teams of party leaders and formally approved by party bodies, ranging from the party executive to a party congress summoned for that purpose.

Most, but by no means all, cabinet coalitions are based on a single, written agreement. Coalition agreements can be informal (a gentlemen's agreement) or formal (a contract-like written document). The absence of a formal, public agreement does not necessarily mean that the coalition parties have assumed that all the contentious issues will simply sort themselves out in due course. Instead, the parties may have a private agreement that they do not release to the public. Or they may have some kind of informal understanding, based perhaps on verbal communication.

Often, parties devise more than one coalition document. In some cases, allied parties present a joint pre-electoral declaration to signal their readiness to join forces in government and to lay down a common agenda. Such pre-electoral declarations may get amended or accompanied by further agreements after the votes are in. The initial (pre- or post-electoral) document may also be supplemented by more specialized agreements or 'side letters' drawn up during the government's tenure for the purpose of cementing deals that are made along the way. These documents typically do not get the same publicity as the initial coalition agreements. Even when they are not secret it is almost impossible to collect them systematically.

Therefore, in our empirical analysis we focus exclusively on the most comprehensive and authoritative initial document. We define the coalition agreements that interest us as the *most binding, written* statements to which the parties of a coalition commit themselves, that is, the most authoritative document that constrains party behaviour. Where both a pre-electoral and a post-electoral document exist, we include both but treat them as one (hence no coalition can have more than one agreement).

Regardless of their form, we should stress that coalition agreements thus represent the initial understandings the coalition parties have concerning their mode of governance. Thus, these documents do not necessarily reflect their actual behaviour, but rather the norms agreed to by the coalition partners *ex ante*, as reconstructed by our country experts on the basis of the best available evidence.

Let us now briefly examine some simple descriptive statistics. Our overall data include more than 400 cabinets in 17 countries. In this chapter, however, our sample will be restricted to the 262 coalition (multiparty) cabinets in the 15 countries in which such cabinets have formed (that is to say, excluding Britain and Spain). As Table 5.1 demonstrates, almost two-thirds of these coalition cabinets have been based on a coalition agreement. There are nonetheless great cross-national differences. In Finland, Luxembourg, Norway, Portugal, and Sweden, as well as in Austria since 1949, all government coalitions have adopted written agreements. In contrast, coalition agreements are the exception rather than the rule in Italy, where we know of only one cabinet that has been able (or forced) to rely on such an agreement. In the remaining countries, the proportion of written agreements ranges from about 80% (Iceland and Ireland) down to 45% (Germany).

Two-thirds of the coalition agreements (67%) have been concluded immediately after elections. A good fifth (21%) have resulted from a deal that had been struck within an electoral period, probably in conjunction with a change of the government's party composition. Thirteen coalition agreements (7.6%), mainly in France and Portugal, have been purely pre-electoral; in these cases parties had agreed on a common platform, campaigned as a potential government coalition,

Coalition Agreements and Cabinet Governance

TABLE 5.1. *Coalition agreements*

Country	No coalition agreement	Pre-electoral coalition agreement	Post-electoral coalition agreement	Inter-electoral coalition agreement	Pre- and post-electoral coalition agreement	Total
Austria	3	0	14	0	0	17
Belgium	8	0	13	7	0	28
Denmark	9	0	6	2	0	17
Finland	0	0	14	18	1	33
France	9	6	0	0	2	17
Germany	12	0	8	2	0	22
Greece	1	1	0	0	0	2
Iceland	4	0	18	0	0	22
Ireland	2	1	6	1	0	10
Italy	33	0	0	1	0	34
Luxembourg	0	0	15	1	0	16
The Netherlands	12	0	10	1	0	23
Norway	0	0	2	0	6	8
Portugal	0	4	1	1	0	6
Sweden	0	1	4	2	0	7
Total	93	13	111	36	9	262

Note: Entries represent raw numbers of coalition cabinets.

and eventually assumed office. Nine cabinets, six of them Norwegian, have had both pre- and post-electoral agreements.

Of the 169 written coalition agreements, 141 (83.4%) were originally intended for publication. Coalition agreements have always been in the public domain in Finland, France, Iceland, Ireland, Norway, Portugal, and Sweden.[3] In the Netherlands (91%), Belgium (90%), Austria (86%), Denmark (75%), and Germany (70%), most coalition agreements have been public. In contrast, coalition agreements in Luxembourg and the single agreement in Greece have been kept private.[4]

There is a clear trend over time towards greater use of coalition agreements (Table 5.2). While in the 1940s no more than a third of all coalition cabinets

---

[3] Note, however, that some of these agreements could by their very nature not be private documents because they were pre-electoral coalition manifestos (France, Portugal) or alternatives to the government's budget proposed in parliament (Norway).

[4] Anecdotal evidence suggests several reasons that coalition agreements are kept wholly or partially private. First, they may violate the constitution or contain potentially embarrassing clauses (e.g., on the division of rents such as public sector jobs). Second, detailed procedural clauses signal distrust that may make the government look weak and divided. Third, a coalition agreement that is rich in policy detail may provide a potentially embarrassing yardstick against which government performance could subsequently be measured. If the government later fails in some of its professed endeavours, opposition parties may then easily turn such shortcomings against it. Finally, if the agreement contains a lot of 'fine print', the coalition parties may fear that they will have trouble keeping public debate focused on their main message to the voters.

TABLE 5.2. *The use of written coalition agreements by decade*

	1940s	1950s	1960s	1970s	1980s	1990s
Coalition cabinets	24	47	42	48	58	42
Coalition cabinets based on a coalition agreement	8	28	26	30	43	34
Per cent	33	60	62	63	74	81

Note: Entries represent coalition cabinets that have assumed office in the decade in question.

were based on written agreements, by the 1990s this was true of no fewer than 81%. Typically, formal coalition agreements have been introduced after some years of experience with coalition politics. Relevant cases are Austria (where this happened as early as 1949, after a mere four years of coalition politics), Belgium (1958), the Netherlands (1963), Germany (where the first formal coalition agreement dates from the early 1960s, but where such agreements have become a permanent feature of coalition politics only since 1980), and France (the early 1980s).

Size

Our country experts have collected and analysed the available coalition agreements. In examining these documents, which have never before been subject to a systematic scholarly investigation of this scope, our experts have focused on the size, contents, and implications of these documents. The simplest measure by which coalition agreements differentiate themselves is size. In accordance with Huber, Shipan, and Pfahler (2001: 336–8), we take the number of words as a rough indicator of the agreements' comprehensiveness. All else equal, the longer the agreement, the more of the coalition's policies it covers and the more detailed the coverage.

The shortest coalition agreement is just over 200 words long (Finland), while the longest one contains more than 43,000 words (Belgium). The average size of coalition agreements is below 3,000 words in three countries: France, Sweden, and Finland. In contrast, in Norway, Portugal, Belgium, and the Netherlands the average agreement contains more than 10,000 words.

Table 5.3 also shows substantial within-country variation. There may be a tendency for long agreements to emerge in complex bargaining situations, of which Belgium is a prime example. The length of Dutch and Portuguese agreements, however, suggests that lengthy agreements may be struck even in less complex bargaining environments. Conversely, Denmark illustrates that even complex bargaining environments may give birth to short agreements. In this case, however, we need to keep in mind that three Danish coalitions with particularly short agreements have been minority cabinets. Since such coalitions need to negotiate the support of additional parties in parliament, it may be less valuable for them to specify their internal agreements in great detail in advance.

TABLE 5.3. *Size and contents of coalition agreements by country*

Country	Size (in words)		General procedural rules (in %)		Specific procedural rules (in %)		Distribution of offices (in %)		Distribution of competencies (in %)		Policies (in %)	
	Range	Mean	Range	Mean	Range	Mean	Range	Mean	Range	Mean	Range	Mean
Austria (14)	700–23,300	6,593	1–50	18.6	0–44	14.1	1–30	10.8	0–25	8.1	0–98	48.2
Belgium (16)	3,150–43,550	14,166	0–5	1.3	0–14	5.0	0–3	0.5	0–3	0.6	83–99	92.8
Denmark (5)	910–5,613	3,619	0	0	6–30	12.4	0	0	0	0	70–94	87.4
Finland (33)	204–4,541	1,163	0–1	0	0	0	0	0	0	0	99–100	100.0
France (5)	870–3,390	1,976	0–5	1.0	0	0	0	0	0	0	95–100	99.0
Germany (10)	513–16,536	5,934	0–28	7.4	0–4	1.2	0–1	0.1	0	0	68–100	91.4
Ireland (6)	1,248–23,500	10,161	0	0	0	0	0	0	0	0	100	100.0
Italy (1)	—	3,680	—	38.1	—	23	—	0	—	7.5	—	31.3
The Netherlands (11)	3,100–36,000	14,223	0–16	2.9	0–29	4.1	0–3	0.3	0–9	2.4	52–98	90.4
Norway (8)	2,919–31,138	12,435	0	0	0–4	0.5	0	0	0	0	97–100	99.5
Portugal (3)	2,461–34,300	13,746	0–39	16.5	0–14	4.9	0–5	1.5	0	0	60–100	77.1
Sweden (7)	1,100–5,200	2,443	0	0	0–8	2.6	0	0	0	0	92–100	97.4

Note: Numbers in parentheses indicate the number of cabinets on which this table is based.

Contents

There are three general issue areas contained in coalition agreements: (*a*) policy, (*b*) office allocation, and (*c*) procedure. Most coalition agreements have substantial and explicit policy content. Yet, there are significant cross-national differences in the attention given to policy versus procedural concerns. In the majority of countries, 90 per cent or more of the contents of coalition agreements have been policy related. At the other extreme, more than half of the average Austrian or Italian coalition agreement has been devoted to non-policy matters. In-between these extremes, the policy content has been 80–90 per cent in Denmark, and more than 70 per cent in Portugal.

The second most frequent concern in coalition agreements in Western Europe has been to lay down the intra-coalitional rules of the game. Coalition agreements, formal or informal, impose various degrees of coalition discipline in parliamentary votes, as well as in other parliamentary activities. There is only one country—Ireland—where general and/or specific decision-making procedures have not made their way into coalition agreements. On the Western European average, 6.4 per cent of the space in coalition agreements has been devoted to this purpose. Yet, the countries in our sample differ substantially, from 61 per cent of the single Italian agreement, to less than 0.5 per cent in Norway.

In contrast, only in a minority of countries do formal coalition agreements deal with inter-party distributions of offices and competencies. Austria is in the lead, devoting on average almost one-fifth of the references in the coalition agreements to such purposes. The paucity of portfolio commitments in coalition agreements elsewhere should not, however, be taken as an indication that these are minor considerations. More likely, the coalition parties see formal and public portfolio deals as unnecessary and perhaps embarrassing. Thus, an intra-coalitional understanding concerning the distribution of sub-cabinet spoils is probably much more frequent than the coalition agreements suggest.

Comprehensiveness

Coalition agreements differ in completeness as well as in their centralization of authority. Some coalitions are based on a comprehensive policy programme, in which the participants commit themselves to a broad range of policy initiatives. Like other negotiators, coalition parties may devise a highly specific 'contract' that spells out exhaustively and in great detail each party's rights and obligations under any foreseeable contingency. As we have argued above, preference divergence, uncertainty, and the threat of opportunism motivate politicians to design enforcement mechanisms and embody them in coalition agreements. The more pressing these problems are perceived to be, the more attractive a comprehensive coalition agreement is likely to look.

Yet, there may well be countervailing factors. A comprehensive programme means that the degrees of freedom in subsequent coalition policymaking are reduced, as much of the cabinet's policy agenda is fixed at the outset (Peterson and De Ridder 1986). And the very conditions that drive the need for coalition agreements also make it difficult to devise comprehensive agreements. Complete contracts are most common when a great deal is at stake and the contingencies are well known. In coalition politics, however, the parties typically find it impossible to anticipate all the contingencies (e.g. potential foreign policy crises or economic shocks) that they may encounter. And some of them may be so unlikely that figuring out what to do simply is not worth the trouble. If the cost of 'taking into account an improbable contingency outweighs the benefits of writing a specific clause in the contract', or if courts or other third parties are considered unable to verify whether the contract has been observed, there is little incentive to cover the relevant aspects in the contract (Salanié 1997: 175). Hence, a complete coalition contract, one that would specify the action to be taken in every foreseeable contingency, is simply not feasible. As Persson, Roland, and Tabellini (1997) and Laffont (2000: 4) have pointed out, political constitutions are always *incomplete* contracts. This point applies with even greater force to coalition agreements. Whatever their size, specificity, or formality, they can never cover all contingencies that may arise during a cabinet's 'lifetime'.[5]

Likewise, coalition agreements cannot fully solve the problems of verification and enforcement. Even the most sophisticated verification mechanisms cannot ensure full information revelation, and even the best thoughtout political enforcement mechanisms can never guarantee complete implementation. For many reasons, coalition agreements will never definitively resolve all intra-coalition conflicts. The coalition negotiators may not have thought sufficiently carefully about the subject nature of their conflict, they may underestimate resistance to their agreement, or the nature of the subject itself may change, to name just a few causes of such imperfections. Coalition negotiators may not even try to resolve the most controversial issues. Rather, they may satisfy themselves with making some initial progress, so that these issues will not 'explode in their hands' and immediately bring down the coalition. Exactly how far they go in attempting to anticipate and settle coalition conflict is, of course, a matter of empirical record, to which we now turn.

Table 5.4 reports on the policy comprehensiveness of coalition agreements, which has been analysed with the help of a four-category ordinal coding scheme, from a comprehensive programme, to a policy programme with occasional exceptions, a programme in which commitment exists only on a few selected issues, and

---

[5] Following Stiglitz (2000: 1444, 1470), we consider 'imperfections of knowledge' as the most important source of incomplete contracts. With perfect information 'all *important* contingencies (...) would have been taken care of in the original contract' (Stiglitz 2000: 1444).

TABLE 5.4. *Policy programmes by country*

	No policy agreement	Agreement on a few selected policies only	Agreement on a variety of issues	Agreement on a comprehensive policy programme	N
Austria	1	9	2	5	17
Belgium	1	7	5	15	28
Denmark	0	0	0	17	17
Finland	0	14	6	13	33
France	12	0	5	0	17
Germany	0	9	8	5	22
Greece	0	2	0	0	2
Iceland	0	4	4	10	18
Ireland	2	1	7	0	10
Italy	0	22	12	0	34
Luxembourg	0	0	0	16	16
The Netherlands	1	8	3	8	20
Norway	0	2	1	5	8
Portugal	0	0	0	6	6
Sweden	0	0	3	4	7
Total	17	78	56	104	255

Note: Entries represent numbers of coalition cabinets.

finally no common policy agreement. In three countries, Denmark, Luxembourg, and Portugal, all coalition agreements have conformed to the highest level of comprehensiveness. Note that although Danish agreements, for example, tend to be short, they are thus also comprehensive, in the sense that they cover a broad range of issues (though presumably not in great detail). In France, at the other extreme, two-thirds of all coalitions have had no commonly agreed policy programme at all. Austria, Belgium, Ireland, and the Netherlands each feature at least one coalition that falls into the latter category. Austria, Belgium, Iceland, and the Netherlands exhibit the greatest within-country variation in policy comprehensiveness. While Belgium has fluctuated between more and less comprehensive agreements, the trend elsewhere has been towards greater comprehensiveness.

Coalition discipline

The question remains what happens with regard to those (often highly significant) details, issues, and perhaps policy areas that are not contained in the coalition's programme. Are the cabinet ministers free to decide what bills to introduce and are the coalition parties, if necessary, allowed to look for partners outside the coalition for support? Coalitions differ in the extent to which the parties commit themselves to *coalition discipline in lawmaking*, which in our definition includes the budgetary process. Some coalitions prescribe tight voting discipline, whereas others permit various exceptions or do not commit their members to any particular legislative discipline at all. The same differentiation applies to *discipline in other parliamentary behaviour* (e.g. behaviour in committees of investigation, or when questioning ministers). We characterize discipline through the use of a four-category ordinal coding scheme, in which we distinguish between 'always discipline', 'discipline on all policies except those explicitly exempted', 'no discipline, except on those policies explicitly specified', and 'no discipline'.

Restrictive procedural provisions, such as requiring the approval of centralized governance institutions for any policy initiatives or ruling out voting alliances that cut across the coalition, can indeed function both as a substitute for substantive agreement and as a means to enforce an initial policy deal. While we can understand policy comprehensiveness as *positive* coordination, such procedural rules essentially constitute *negative* coordination.[6] To some extent they can substitute for positive coordination. Hence, we should not necessarily expect that in coalition agreements policy comprehensiveness and commitments to parliamentary voting discipline will be perfectly aligned. If these are mutually substitutable means of coordination, their incidence might instead be negatively correlated.

Tables 5.5 and 5.6 report cross-national differences in coalition discipline. With respect to legislation as well as to other parliamentary behaviour, the countries that exhibit particularly high levels of coalition discipline in legislation are Denmark, Austria, Germany, and Ireland. Norway has tight coalition discipline with respect to legislation but allows more exceptions on other parliamentary votes, whereas Sweden permits exceptions even on a few legislative matters. Finland and Greece are middling countries that exhibit more variation between governments, whereas all the Benelux countries fall at the low end of the spectrum in terms of discipline.

The relevant coalitions in the high-discipline countries vary, of course, from mainly non-socialist ones in Denmark and Norway, to the centrist German ones and the grand coalitions of Austria. But interestingly, the same kinds of broad coalitions that feature strong expectations of discipline in Austria operate under much less restrictive assumptions in other consociational countries such as Belgium and the Netherlands. Although these coalitions tend to be similar in their partisan make-up, these commonalities apparently do not extend to the forms that intra-coalitional coordination is expected to take.

Table 5.7 shows the temporal development of coalition discipline in legislation and other parliamentary behaviour. In legislation it always has been high, though there is a slight trend towards more coalition discipline in recent decades. Thus, coalitions that do not oblige their members to high levels of legislative

---

[6] The Austrian grand coalitions from the late 1940s to the early 1960s were based almost exclusively on procedural rules rather than on comprehensive policy programmes. High levels of commitment to legislative unity, coupled with a strong election rule, sufficed to produce a series of 'tight' coalitions (Müller 2000b).

TABLE 5.5. *Coalition discipline in legislation by country*

Country	Coalition discipline in legislation				Number of coalition cabinets (N)
	Always	On all policies except those explicitly exempted	Only on those policies explicitly specified	No	
Austria	88	12	0	0	17
Belgium	7	93	0	0	28
Denmark	100	0	0	0	17
Finland	0	48	52	0	33
France	0	88	0	12	17
Germany	95	5	0	0	22
Greece	0	0	100	0	2
Iceland	0	100	0	0	22
Ireland	80	20	0	0	10
Italy	0	100	0	0	34
Luxembourg	0	100	0	0	16
The Netherlands	0	100	0	0	23
Norway	100	0	0	0	8
Portugal	0	83	17	0	6
Sweden	0	100	0	0	7
Total (N)	71	169	20	2	262

Note: Entries represent percentages of coalition cabinets.

TABLE 5.6. *Coalition discipline in other parliamentary behaviour by country*

Country	Coalition discipline in other parliamentary behaviour				Number of coalition cabinets (N)
	Always	On all policies except those explicitly exempted	Only on those policies explicitly specified	No	
Austria	100	0	0	0	17
Belgium	0	0	0	100	28
Denmark	100	0	0	0	17
Finland	0	48	52	0	33
France	0	88	0	12	17
Germany	95	5	0	0	22
Greece	0	50	50	0	2
Iceland	0	100	0	0	22
Ireland	100	0	0	0	10
Italy	0	0	100	0	34
Luxembourg	0	0	0	100	16
The Netherlands	0	0	0	100	23
Norway	0	100	0	0	8
Portugal	0	0	100	0	6
Sweden	0	100	0	0	7
Total (N)	62	73	58	69	262

Note: Entries represent percentages of coalition cabinets.

TABLE 5.7. *Coalition discipline by decade*

	1940s	1950s	1960s	1970s	1980s	1990s
Legislation						
Always (%)	24	23	36	10	22	43
On all policies except those explicitly exempted (%)	68	51	52	88	74	57
Only on those policies explicitly specified (%)	8	23	10	2	3	0
No discipline (%)	0	2	2	0	0	0
Other parliamentary behaviour						
Always (%)	12	23	29	10	24	40
On all matters except those explicitly exempted (%)	24	15	29	42	28	29
Only on those matters explicitly specified (%)	24	34	17	19	24	14
No discipline (%)	40	28	26	29	24	17
No. of coalition cabinets (N)	25	47	42	48	58	42

Note: Entries represent percentages of coalition cabinets that have assumed office in the decade in question.

discipline practically ceased to exist in the 1970s. Moreover, the 1990s account for the highest-ever share of coalitions that make no exceptions with respect to their expectations of legislative discipline. If anything, the trend towards greater discipline is even more obvious with regard to other parliamentary behaviour. While in the 1940s and 1950s only a minority of coalitions required such discipline from their members, it has become the dominant pattern since then. Again, the 1990s stand out as the decade of particularly high coalition discipline.

Table 5.8 shows how pure parliamentary and semi-presidential systems distinguish themselves with regard to the legislative discipline imposed on the coalition partners. Clearly, semi-presidential systems are less demanding. While universal legislative discipline is the hallmark of one-third of the parliamentary cabinets in our sample, not a single cabinet from semi-presidential systems falls into that category. And while in both types of regime about two-thirds of the cabinets require coalition discipline for the vast majority of legislative votes, coalition discipline is restricted to specific policies or even not pre-negotiated in a third of semi-presidential cabinets.

TABLE 5.8. *Coalition discipline in legislation by regime type*

	Always	All policies except exempted	None or only specific policies	All
Parliamentary	68 (33%)	137 (66%)	2 (1%)	207
Semi-presidential	0 (0%)	35 (64%)	20 (36%)	55
All regimes	68 (26%)	172 (66%)	22 (8%)	262

CENTRALIZED VERSUS DECENTRALIZED CABINET AUTHORITY

The architecture of Western European cabinet governance mechanisms varies along a number of dimensions (see, e.g., the country chapters in Müller and Strøm 2000). One of these dimensions has to do with the allocation of authority within the governing coalition. Political institutions allocate authority in different ways. The literature on contracts assumes that such issues are resolved through a specification of residual rights of control, that is, by identifying the party that has the right to make final decisions on matters not specified in the contingencies covered by the contract. On the basis of the allocation of residual rights, we can distinguish between centralized governance structures, in which such authority is vested in the principal, and decentralized arrangements, in which the agent has this power (Aghion and Tirole 1997).

In the context of government coalitions, centralized authority means that residual rights of control are placed in the hands of a team of coalition leaders, in which each party would presumably be represented. This team of coalition leaders would decide jointly, or, at least, maintain effective mutual veto powers on critical decisions. In contrast, decentralized authority would mean that such rights are held by whatever party controls a particular government agency, for example a cabinet portfolio, or even a smaller subset of government offices. As we have seen, the analytical literature on parliamentary institutions contains one prominent theory (Laver and Shepsle) that stresses the decentralization of cabinet authority and one (Tsebelis) that emphasizes its centralization.

Since neither of these models is entirely plausible for all cabinet coalitions, we need to identify the conditions under which each is most likely to be realistic. The best way to do so is by identifying the mechanisms by which parties can commit themselves to centralized authority, and examining the effectiveness of these mechanisms. If coalition partners are not content to decentralize authority entirely to individual 'line ministers', they must devise institutions by which central coalition decisions can be enforced. But if and when such mechanisms are unworkable, then only decentralized authority (though not necessarily in the form of ministerial government) is feasible.

One mechanism of centralized authority is to appoint junior ministers to serve under a minister from a different party. Such junior ministers can help reduce information asymmetries between the party in charge of the respective portfolio and the party nominating the junior minister. In effect, junior ministers, though formally the subordinates of their respective cabinet members, can serve as external checks on their superiors (see Müller and Strøm 2000; Thies 2001; Manow and Zorn 2004; and Verzichelli in Chapter 7 in this volume).

Yet, 'watchdog' junior ministers are not the only enforcement mechanism under centralized authority. In some countries, such as Denmark, Finland, and Sweden, even senior ministers sometimes share portfolios and thus function as mutual checks. Partisan bureaucrats are another alternative. If civil servants themselves have strong party loyalties, they may act as partisan 'spies' when their ministry is headed by a minister from a different party.

Finally, enforcement can take place in the parliamentary arena. Martin and Vanberg (2004) show that the greater the ideological divergence between coalition partners in a specific policy area, the more parliamentary scrutiny the relevant bills receive. Hence, parliamentary committees not only allow for the scrutiny of executive proposals by the legislature, or of government initiatives by the opposition, but also provide opportunity for one government party to keep tabs on the others (see also Kim and Loewenberg 2005).

To be sure, each mechanism has its own implications for coalition governance. Partisan bureaucrats have little formal authority. While they can provide information to their co-partisans and silently try to promote their partisan goals, they cannot formally contest the decisions of their politically appointed superiors. In contrast, junior ministers can have enough clout to raise and perhaps settle partisan issues with their respective ministers. Because of the hierarchical nature of the formal relationship between ministers and junior ministers, however, it remains in the discretion of the former to decide whether a settlement is possible at the departmental level. If not, the junior minister can officially inform his or her respective party leaders and thus lessen the informational asymmetries between these leaders and the senior ministers. (On the other hand, junior ministers may be susceptible to capture, if their respective senior minister manages to use them as 'ambassadors' to their respective parties, in order to 'sell' the senior minister's policies to the coalition partner.) Finally, parliamentary committees may have less specific information than junior ministers, but more formal authority and autonomy from the senior cabinet member. Indeed, ministers and parties typically need to win their approval in order to change the status quo.

These control mechanisms can be combined. The skilful management of a coalition party thus involves the collection of information from many sources about 'alien' government departments and the timely communication with coalition partners about controversial issues. Skilful coalition management, in turn, means that such issues get settled without much conflict and publicity—or delay. In the interest of time and administrative efficiency, coalition leaders will typically choose to delegate broadly to individual cabinet members and perhaps even directly to their subordinates. But such delegation will rarely go so far as to abandon all central coalition authority.

In the interest of sustaining central cabinet authority, suitable verification and enforcement mechanisms are important, but in a world of incomplete contracts and repeated interactions reputation is crucial (see Chen 2000; Stiglitz 2000: 1449, 1460; Aghion, Dewatripont, and Rey 2002). Parties have incentives to preserve their reputation so as to be credible in future negotiations. Moreover, party leaders will care about their cabinet members remaining faithful to the coalition agreement even when the latter are tempted to exploit their private information at the expense of their coalition partners. Party leaders may keep such behaviour in check because they have to keep in mind the big picture and preserve their party's (and their own) reputation. It is when great gains can be made quickly that reputation is most likely to break down as a mechanism of control. The prospect of gaining the prime ministership may be one such temptation that can occasionally lead coalition parties into opportunistic behaviour.

Thus, centralized cabinet governance is challenging, but coalition parties nonetheless have a range of mechanisms that they can employ. In real-world parliamentary democracies, both decentralized and centralized modes of cabinet governance exist. This is in fact reflected in the dual doctrines of individual and collective ministerial responsibility. Individual responsibility reflects decentralized authority, whereas collective responsibility rests on an assumption of centralized authority. And in parliamentary democracies these doctrines tend to coexist.

Among systems that feature some extent of central authority, we can analytically differentiate between ex ante and ex post facto modes of coalition governance. These are contrasting and stylized models based on the timing of negotiations over coalition policy. An *ex ante* mode of coalition governance means frontloading the requisite bargaining to the initial coalition negotiations by fixing the policy programme in great detail and resolving as many (potential) conflicts as possible at the outset. One critical choice in the initial negotiations is how detailed and comprehensive the policy agreement will be. The more specific policy issues the coalition parties negotiate before coming to power, the more costly (in time and other inputs) we expect their negotiations to be.

The ex ante mode of coalition governance means comprehensive initial policy agreements. These provide a master plan for the coalition and a yardstick for all its members and partners. Individual cabinet ministers and their subordinates are committed to a coalition agreement drawn up before they take office. Full ex ante coordination would require complete contracts. As we have argued above, such complete agreements are not feasible. Yet, the real world gives plenty of examples of extensive and committal coalition agreements that seek to resolve a broad range of policy issues before the governing parties take office.

One alternative is to agree on a set of mechanisms for deciding policy issues, rather than on the policies themselves. While it is no doubt possible to expend a great deal of energy creating and sustaining such governance institutions, it should in principle be possible to agree on such a regime in a way that is less costly up front, particularly if the parties choose a simple and institutionally entrenched decentralized regime such as Laver and Shepsle's model of ministerial government.

An *ex post* mode of coalition governance means settling relatively few policy issues up front, but devising more complex and elaborate mechanisms for solving policy conflicts as they might arise. Authority is not vested in a detailed policy agreement, but could, for example, remain in the hands of a group of coalition leaders who maintain veto power over cabinet decisions and review the policy of individual government departments. Junior ministers are among the most important mechanisms by which coalition leaders can gain the requisite information they need in their respective policy areas. We therefore operationalize ex post governance as the existence of junior ministers recruited from a party different from that of the senior cabinet member holding the portfolio in question (see above and Chapter 7, which examines such appointments in greater detail). A coalition governance mode based exclusively on ex post mechanisms might be no less centralized than one governed by ex ante devices. However, authority would not be vested in a detailed policy agreement. Rather, it would remain in the hands of a group of coalition leaders, who would critically rely on information from trustees at the front line of policymaking.

Since all governance is costly, we expect ex ante and ex post governance to be at least partial substitutes for one another. If the coalition parties have constructed an effective ex ante agreement, they should have less need of ex post conflict resolution and will presumably be less willing to bear the cost of such an arrangement. Yet, there is no need to see these two governance modes as mutually exclusive. A coalition can employ both ex ante and ex post modes, and skilful design of its architecture would combine these two to strengthen the coordination effect that each of them can produce.

Thus, we are left with four modes of coalition governance. In the first place, we distinguish between decentralized and centralized authority. Within the latter category, we in turn differentiate between an ex ante governance mode, an ex post governance mode, and a combination of ex ante and ex post mechanisms.

Table 5.9 shows how our 15 coalitional countries can be classified in the four coalition governance modes identified above. Four countries (Denmark, Greece, Italy, and Portugal) are 'pure cases', as all coalition cabinets fall into one and the same category. All other countries have cabinets in two or three categories, but none has employed all four. Overall, this pattern suggests that our typology does more than summarize country characteristics. To the extent that there is some regularity, we see a cluster of the Nordic countries (plus Luxembourg) relying more strongly on ex ante mechanisms, and a continental cluster relying more heavily on ex post devices.

Table 5.10 shows the evolution of different governance mechanisms over time. This table suggests a clear trend. The option of going without a coalition governance mechanism (and therefore presumably relying on decentralized authority) has fallen out of grace rapidly since the 1950s. On the other hand, ex ante mechanisms have increased monotonically in raw numbers as well as proportionally. The use of ex post mechanisms exclusively has been common throughout the post-war period, but such agreements have declined in numbers and share since the 1970s. But the most striking trend over time is the increase in cabinets employing both ex ante and ex post governance mechanisms. While there was only a single cabinet in

TABLE 5.9. *Ex ante and ex post governance mechanisms by country*

	No mechanisms	*Ex ante* mechanisms only	*Ex post* mechanisms only	*Ex ante* and *ex post* mechanisms	N
Austria	0	2	12	3	17
Belgium	6	0	7	15	28
Denmark	0	17	0	0	17
Finland	20	13	0	0	33
France	2	0	15	0	17
Germany	10	0	7	5	22
Greece	2	0	0	0	2
Iceland	12	10	0	0	22
Ireland	1	0	9	0	10
Italy	0	0	34	0	34
Luxembourg	0	16	0	0	16
The Netherlands	2	0	13	8	23
Norway	2	3	1	2	8
Portugal	0	0	0	6	6
Sweden	0	4	3	0	7
Total	57	65	101	39	262

Notes: Ex ante mechanism is a comprehensive policy agreement. Ex post mechanism is watchdog junior ministers. Entries represent numbers of coalition cabinets.

TABLE 5.10. *Ex ante and ex post mechanisms by decade*

	No mechanisms	*Ex ante* mechanisms only	*Ex post* mechanisms only	*Ex ante* and *ex post* mechanisms	N
1940s	12	3	10	0	25
1950s	22	8	17	0	47
1960s	13	8	20	1	42
1970s	6	12	22	8	48
1980s	3	17	19	19	58
1990s	1	17	13	11	42
Total	57	65	101	39	262

this category prior to the 1970s, there have been no fewer than 30 since 1980. All this suggests that parties and politicians learn from their own experience and those of others and try to find coalition governance mechanisms that are both effective and efficient.

Explaining modes of coalition governance

This inspection of the use of coalition governance mechanisms suggests a heavy dose of path dependency. This is no great surprise—there are several reasons why the choice of coalition governance mechanisms in a given context is not completely independent from previous patterns. Like all political institutions, coalition governance mechanisms are human inventions. They must first be made before they can be adopted. Although in general the writing of contracts has a long history, the special nature of the political realm makes the transfer of these experiences anything but a trivial task. Setting up coalition governance mechanisms is therefore costly. Specifically, it entails transaction costs.

Yet once a 'model' coalition agreement has been crafted that has withstood the test of real life application, the costs of writing future coalition contracts may be drastically reduced. A new coalition may simply copy clauses from previous coalition agreements, or the parties may find it sufficient to make only minor changes. This, of course, is more likely with regard to general format or procedural clauses than to the policy content, as the specific policy problems of one coalition may be very different from those of its predecessor. Yet, even with regard to policy content, existing contracts provide some guidance, as they can serve as checklists and provide some insight into the required level of detail. To the extent that the authors of coalition agreements take their cues from previous agreements, we would expect agreements to become longer over time as their authors feel obliged to address most issue domains contained in the previous document and then add some new ones derived from the present agenda. Provided that coalition agreements fulfil at least some of their purposes, we would expect them to continue with this practice. Moreover, once coalition agreements have become a regular feature of coalition politics, coalition architects encounter the expectation that their efforts result not only in a successful coalition but also in such an agreement.

Our data certainly confirm such path dependencies in the choice of coalition governance mechanisms. With regard to the existence of coalition agreements we find perfect path dependency in more than half of our countries, meaning that practically all governments after a specific point in time have been based on such agreements. This is true for Austria, Finland, France, Ireland, Luxembourg, the Netherlands, Norway, Portugal, and Sweden. Politicians in some countries have been slightly more experimental. Germany, Iceland, and Belgium eventually developed stable patterns of written coalition agreements, but in each case there was a period of fluctuation between formal and less formal (more decentralized?) accords before the pattern finally emerged. Denmark, which has seen few coalition agreements, exhibits a much more random pattern, which is not so easily ascribed to a pattern of path dependence. There is a similar, though less clear, pattern of path dependence in the adoption of ex post governance mechanisms, here represented by the appointment of 'watchdog' junior ministers (see also Verzichelli's analysis in Chapter 7).[7]

---

[7] Note, however, that our measure here is less robust, as a single watchdog junior minister is sufficient to classify the cabinet in question as having this type of governance mechanism. Clearly, though, the difference between having and not having watchdog junior ministers is less categorical than the distinction between having a written coalition agreement and having none.

Path dependence may be a politician's best friend, but it is not necessarily for ever. In some situations, established patterns of coalition governance are abandoned or considerably modified. This may happen when new actors come to the coalition game or when politicians have negative experiences with particular coalition arrangements. But it may also happen because the costs of the established practices become too high for the circumstances, even after the discounting that results from repetition. The Netherlands offers an intriguing illustration. Above we have counted it as a case fully conforming to the path dependency model. From 1963 to the present, all Dutch cabinets have been based on formal coalition agreements. Yet, four different cabinets since this time deviate from this national pattern. Interestingly, three of them, the cabinets Zijlstra (1966), Biesheuvel II (1972), van Agt III (1982), were caretaker cabinets, which were appointed to serve only a very short time until elections could be held that had already been scheduled.[8] Thus, when the benefits of familiar institutions have fallen below certain thresholds, Dutch politicians have shown no loyalty to these established patterns.

EXPLAINING COALITION AGREEMENTS

When do coalition parties choose formal coalition agreements, and why? In the remainder of this chapter, we shall address this question more systematically and rigorously, focusing specifically on the adoption of written coalition agreements. Coalition parties presumably choose such institutions on the basis of cost-benefit analysis. All else equal, the greater the potential risks of coalition participation, the greater the costs they will incur in constructing governance institutions.

As noted above, the problems involved in forging coalitions stem from such factors as (a) preference divergence, (b) information uncertainty, and (c) the risk of opportunism. We expect these factors to influence the form and contents of coalition agreements, as well as the specific institutions they set up. Specifically, we expect the incidence of formalized coalition agreements to covary positively with each of these three factors. We also expect that such agreements will be more likely the more valuable the coalition is to its members. Finally, transaction costs are an integral part of coalition bargaining, and they will affect the choice of coalition agreements. Thus, all else equal, the higher the costs of negotiating and implementing specific enforcement mechanisms, the less likely it is that coalition parties will choose them. Hence, we expect to see more complete agreements,

---

[8] The remaining Dutch exception was a very special case: what had been an agreement-based three-party cabinet was voluntarily enlarged to a five-party cabinet in which the three original cabinet parties still considered their initial agreement binding upon themselves (but not upon the two new cabinet parties) (see Timmermans and Andeweg 2000).

and more elaborate institutions for their enforcement, the lower the relevant transaction costs.

The value of the coalition, preference divergence, information uncertainty, opportunism, and transaction costs will in turn be driven at least in part by a variety of conditions that we capture through six clusters of explanatory variables:

1. the effects of time and space,
2. structural attributes of cabinets and party systems,
3. the preferences of the players, that is the relevant political parties, as represented by their leaders,
4. political institutions,
5. features of the bargaining situation, and finally
6. exogenous 'critical' events.

Below we explore the effects of each of these clusters. In Table 5.11 we present eight models that aim to explain the existence of written coalition agreements. These models are logistic regressions in which 1 indicates that a coalition was based on such an agreement and 0 otherwise. A positive score on the dependent variable thus denotes the existence of a coalition agreement. We shall seek to explain such agreements on the basis of six clusters of explanatory variables, as discussed above. These six blocks of variables are introduced separately in Models 1–6. In Model 7 we present all variables that have been statistically significant or near-significant in the previous models. Finally, Model 8 is a more parsimonious version that contains only those variables that have proved to be statistically significant in the previous model.

Model 1: Time

The first explanatory cluster is simply time. There is ample reason to believe that time matters in coalition bargaining. As Narud and Valen (Chapter 11) show, the electoral environment in Europe has become more difficult over time, and the 1980s and 1990s were a particularly difficult time for governing parties. This, in turn, may have increased the likelihood of opportunistic behaviour. Hence, *ceteris paribus*, we expect that over time we find more attempts to hammer out coalition agreements that aim at protecting coalition parties against such behaviour. At the same time, the costs of negotiating and implementing a coalition agreement may have decreased over time as parties learn from their own experiences and those of others. Writing the second or third coalition agreement should be easier than the first one. When such agreements are made public, even the parties that have not been partners to these deals can benefit. Thus, increasing demand and decreasing transaction costs both suggest that coalition agreements would become more frequent and detailed over time.

In Model 1 we introduce dummies for the fixed effects of decades. The 1950s is the excluded category and hence the yardstick for the other periods. The results

TABLE 5.11 *Logistic regressions on the existence of written coalition agreements*

Independent variables	Model 1	Model 2	Model 3	Model 4	Model 5	Model 6	Model 7	Model 8	Impact[a]
Time									
1940s	−1.08(0.53)**							−2.06(0.75)**	−0.46(0.16)
1960s	0.10(0.44)								
1970s	0.07(0.42)								
1980s	0.67(0.42)								
1990s	1.06(0.49)**						2.24(0.72)**	2.24(0.69)**	0.18(0.05)
Structure									
Post election cabinet		0.57(0.44)							
Max. possible cab. duration		0.00(0.00)							
Absolute no. Parl. parties		−0.36(0.09)**					−0.48(0.13)**	−0.49(0.12)**	−0.08(0.02)
Largest party seat share		−17.93(2.89)**					−5.83(3.88)	−6.43(3.55)*	−0.13(0.07)[a]
Cabinet seat share		0.03(0.02)*					0.01(0.02)		
Number of cabinet parties		−0.21(0.23)							
Minimal winning coalition		0.65(0.49)							
Surplus majority cabinet		−0.60(0.65)							
Preferences									
Extremist party seat share			−0.06(0.01)**				−0.06(0.03)**	−0.05(0.03)**	−0.01(0.005)
Polarization (BP weighted)			0.05(0.02)**				0.00(0.03)		
No core party			1.49(0.33)**				1.34(0.58)**	1.54(0.54)**	0.34(0.12)
Cabinet preference range			−0.01(0.01)						
Median party (1st dim.) in cab.			1.21(0.42)**				1.42(0.60)**	1.56(0.53)**	0.35(0.12)
Connected cab.			0.13(0.34)						
Institutions									
Bicameralism				−1.08(0.36)**			−1.69(0.59)**	−1.66(0.47)**	−0.16(0.05)
Positive parliamentarism				−1.23(0.43)**			0.06(0.75)		
Ex ante government programme screen				2.12(0.50)**			1.43(0.79)*	1.44(0.54)**	0.15(0.06)
PM powers				0.09(0.08)			−0.22(0.19)	−0.26(0.15)*	−0.04(0.02)
Semi-presidentialism				0.65(0.44)			1.66(0.84)**	1.35(0.60)**	0.14(0.06)

Bargaining								
Prior cab.: Conflict termination					−0.80(0.27)**			0.00(0.40)
Cabinet bargaining duration					0.00(0.01)			0.01(0.01)
Inconclusive bargaining round					0.59(0.32)*			0.36(0.50)
Critical events								
Terminal event lag (any)						−0.03(0.38)		
Electoral volatility						−0.03(0.02)		
Constant	0.39(0.30)	9.17(1.86)**	−1.38(0.55)**	1.02(0.37)**	0.78(0.23)**	1.01(0.23)**	5.39(2.79)*	6.30(2.17)**
Number of observations	262	260	257	262	255	242	255	259
Pseudo R^2	.05	.27	.18	.18	.04	.01	.45	.43
% Correctly predicted	.68	.77	.75	.74	.66	.67	.83	.80

Notes: *p < 0.10; **p < 0.05.

[a] Impact is the marginal effect of a unit change in the independent variable on the probability of the outcome occurring, calculated based on Model 8, with the following exceptions: the impact of Largest party seat share is for a 0.10 change (1 Standard Deviation).

are generally not strong, but in the expected direction. As it turns out, the 1950s distinguish themselves clearly from the 1940s and the1990s. Coalition agreements were significantly less frequent in the 1940s and more frequent in the 1990s. This cluster explains 5 per cent of the variance and its effects hold up in the final model (indeed they are stronger), when we control for the relevant variables from the other clusters.

Model 2: Structural attributes

The structural attributes of the bargaining environment and the set of negotiating parties are also plausible explanations of coalition agreements. Structural attributes render some coalitions more valuable than others. Therefore, majority cabinets and those formed early in the parliamentary term may be more likely to have formal coalition agreements. Other considerations may reinforce such tendencies. The uncertainty facing the coalition parties presumably rises with their time horizon. Therefore the longer *maximum government duration* (normally, the remaining time in the constitutional inter-election period), the more restrictive we expect the coalition agreement to be. The same applies if government formation immediately *follows elections*. (Note that these two variables are not particularly highly correlated.)

Concerns with opportunism may be most acute in the more precarious coalitions, such as *minimal winning* ones, in which each party's contribution is pivotal to the coalition's success (and survival). Hence, we expect more complete arrangements in such situations. By implication, we assume the opposite for *surplus* governments, which contain parties that are not critical for winning parliamentary votes. The same logic should apply when we consider the *cabinet seat share*: the smaller it is, the more restrictive we expect the coalition arrangements to be.

Then there are structures of the parliamentary environment that presumably correlate with the risks of opportunism as well as with the transaction costs of writing agreements. Thus, the *number of parliamentary parties* is a proxy for the complexity and uncertainty of the bargaining environment. The greater this uncertainty facing the coalition parties, the more restrictive their agreements should be. At the same time, however, the transaction costs of writing agreements may rise with the same variable, whose net effect is therefore difficult to predict. The same is true of the *size of the largest party*, as well as with the *number of cabinet parties*.

In fact, although this cluster turns out to have substantial explanatory power, few of these variables are individually significant and few of our specific expectations supported. Collectively, the structural attributes included in Model 2 explain 27 per cent of the variance in agreements (Pseudo $R^2 = 0.27$). This is the strongest result among our clusters and considerably stronger than the result for the decade fixed effects. Two variables contribute significantly to the explanation of the existence of written coalition agreements: the absolute number of parliamentary parties and the seat share of the largest party. Both effects are negative. Thus, formal coalition agreements become less likely the more parties are represented in parliament and the stronger the largest of them is. The third size-related variable is the *cabinet's share of seats in parliament*, but this effect washes out once the other blocks of variables are introduced in Model 7.

Model 3: Preferences

Of all our variables, policy preferences are probably the explanatory cluster that students of politics would find most intuitively plausible. The more parties care and disagree about policy, the more likely they are to want centralized mechanisms of policy commitment. In order to measure the preferences of actors in the coalition game coalition we employ four variables: the policy range of the cabinet as measured by party manifestos (*cabinet preference range*), the representation of the *median party in the cabinet*, the *share of extremist parties* in parliamentary seats, and the weighted *polarization of parliament* as measured by manifesto data.[9] We also include in our model the coalition's policy *connectedness* on the first policy dimension and the presence or absence of a *core party* in the cabinet.

We expect the risk of opportunism to increase with the number of feasible cabinet alternatives. Hence, the incentives for coalition agreements should correlate negatively with the party system preference range, polarization, and the presence of a core party. At the same time, the likelihood of coalition agreements should increase with the diversity of preferences and presumably with the absence of policy connectedness. The presence of the *median party* in a coalition is a proxy for unequal bargaining power, as this party may enjoy a large bargaining advantage (Laver and Schofield 1990; van Roozendaal 1990, 1993). Unequal bargaining power is likely to increase the risk of opportunism and hence should promote more complete coalition agreements.

Collectively, the six variables in this cluster explain 18 per cent of the variance, and four of them are individually significant in Model 3. The absence of a core party, policy connectedness, the representation of the median party in the cabinet, and parliamentary polarization all make a written coalition agreement more likely. Except for the polarization estimate, all these effects are upheld or even strengthened in the full and final models.

The results for connectedness and the absence of a core party are inconsistent with our expectations. The first two results, on the other hand, do conform. The *median legislator party* thus has a positive effect on the existence of written coalition agreements. Given the large bargaining advantage of the party with the median legislator, this result confirms our theoretical expectations that unequal

---

[9] The polarization of parliament is calculated as the square root of the sum of the weight of each party (the Banzhaf bargaining power) multiplied by the squared distances from the mean of all party positions.

bargaining power is positively related to the existence of coalition agreements. In contrast, the stronger anti-system parties are, the less likely are written coalition agreements. This result is again consistent with our expectations. The stronger extremist parties are, the fewer alternative coalitions are available.

Model 4: Institutions

Political institutions may influence coalition agreements directly by structuring the bargaining process or indirectly by affecting the likelihood of government opportunism. *Positive parliamentarism* and *ex ante programme screening* are two features of the institutional environment that directly affect the government formation process. The requirements that incoming cabinets need to be approved by majority vote in parliament (*positive parliamentarism*) and that their policy programme be screened by parliament at the time of formation (*ex ante programme screening*) should both make complete coalition agreements more likely, as they force incoming coalitions to formalize their deals at the outset and thus frontload some of their bargaining costs. Bicameralism might be expected to have the same effect, especially in systems with strong upper chambers.

Among the other important institutions to consider are the powers of the prime minister and the head of state. In a system with strong powers vested in the prime minister, we expect the other coalition parties to want to rein in this *primus inter pares* through explicit and binding agreements. We expect the risks of opportunism to be positively correlated with the powers of the prime minister relative to the rest of the cabinet. Hence, where such rights exist, we expect more restrictive coalition agreements. Finally, in a *semi-presidential* system the head of state typically enjoys more authority than in purely parliamentary systems and may therefore exercise considerable influence on all stages of the coalition life cycle. Yet it is not obvious how this institutional feature affects coalition bargaining. On the one hand, coalition parties have incentives to guard themselves against opportunistic behaviour on the part of a powerful president and whatever party he or she represents. On the other hand, the president is typically not a party to coalition agreements and may be sufficiently difficult to constrain that the value of *any* coalition agreement may be reduced.

Model 4 thus contains a total of five institutional variables. Together, they explain 18 per cent of the variance, and every one of them is significant in some specification of the model. *Ex ante programme screening*, the requirement that the incoming government must present its policy programme to parliament, has a statistically significant positive effect on coalition agreements, which is in line with our theoretical expectations. *Bicameralism* has a strong negative influence on coalition agreements, which is more surprising. Positive parliamentarism has a similarly negative effect in the initial cluster model, which, however, washes out in the broader specifications. *Semi-presidentialism*, which is restrictively defined as including France, Finland, and Portugal until the constitutional reform of 1982, has a positive effect on written coalition agreements, which becomes significant in the joint models. However, in a full model including the other blocks of variables, the effects of semi-presidentialism are much stronger. Finally, the authority of *the Prime Minister*, as measured by his formal powers, has only a weak and inconsistent effect on the existence of written coalition agreements.

Model 5: Bargaining environment

As we have frequently noted, coalition bargaining is coloured by the shadow of the past as well as the anticipation of the future. In block 5, we captured the most relevant aspects of prior governance that may affect the parties' inclinations to adopt formal coalition agreements. These include the circumstances under which the previous cabinet was terminated as well as the characteristics of the bargaining process that has culminated in the formation of a new one. Considering first the previous termination, we consider a *conflict termination* to signal an environment in which parties may wish to write protective agreements in the face of potential uncertainties or opportunism.

Consider next the bargaining process itself. In the coalitions literature, the time required for government formation (*cabinet bargaining duration*) has been treated as a proxy both for the difficulty of forming a government (and hence the precariousness of the cabinet) and for the care with which the government has been negotiated (Diermeier and van Roozendahl 1998). We therefore expect extensive and restrictive agreements when more time has gone into their negotiations, even though it should be noted that our measure (the *total* time between the termination of the previous cabinet or the elections and the inauguration of the new cabinet) is not always a good proxy for bargaining effort, as much time may be spent in inconclusive formation attempts. We therefore include a second indicator, *inconclusive bargaining round*, which tells us whether there was at least one inconclusive bargaining round before the cabinet took office.

As it turns out, these three variables exercise only negligible influence on coalition agreements. They collectively have only marginal explanatory power (Pseudo $R^2 = 0.04$). Although two of them have statistically significant effects when entered alone, none retains its significance when we introduce the other variables in Models 7 and 8.

Model 6: Critical events

The critical events literature has not actively tried to link such dramatic occurrences to the perceptions of risk and uncertainty in the cabinet's environment, but there is no reason not to make such a connection. Critical events are indeed often happenings that signal a situation of uncertainty or a risk of opportunism. We can think of two genuinely political events that may influence the parties' willingness to make more restrictive agreements: electoral volatility and events associated with the fate of the previous cabinet. Presumably the uncertainty facing the coalition parties rises with the volatility of the electorate. And if previous coalition experiences have been beset with traumatic events, it may induce the coalition parties to search for solutions through coalition agreements. Yet in our Model 6, critical events, captured by volatility rates and a lagged measure of the terminal events associated with the previous cabinet, can explain almost none of the variance in coalition agreements, and neither of the variables employed is statistically significant.

Models 7 and 8: Complete models

The main motivation for Models 1 through 6 is to show how much of the variance in coalition agreements various clusters of explanatory variables can explain in isolation. Yet, eventually we would like to see how much variance can be explained when these blocks of variables are entered jointly. This is the purpose of Model 7, which includes all variables that have proved statistically significant in the previous analyses plus those that came close to that mark. In brief, Model 7 suggests a picture very consistent with the previous models. Most variables remain statistically significant, and all the significant ones retain their respective signs.

The final column of Table 5.11 reports the substantive impact of each of the significant variables from the final model, controlling for the impact of the other variables. It suggests that the presence of the median party in government increases the likelihood of a written coalition agreement by 35 percentage points, and the absence of single party at the dimensions by dimension median (core party) increases the likelihood by a similar amount. Rules requiring ex ante government programme screening increase the likelihood of an agreement by 15 percentage points while positive parliamentarism decreases it by 16 percentage points.

Finally, we are interested in the predictive power of these models. To what extent do they correctly predict the existence of written coalition agreements in post-war Western Europe? A baseline model, based strictly on the modal category, would be correct in 65% of the cases. A country fixed effects model predicts the existence of coalition agreements in 79% of the cases, though it leaves us with no clue as to why some countries feature written agreements and others not. Model 7 improves predictive accuracy marginally to 83%, but it is a theoretically much better grounded model. The joint model also substantially improves on the total explanatory power of any of the partial ones (Models 1 through 6).

CONCLUSION

In this chapter we have addressed a previously largely neglected aspect of coalition politics, namely coalition governance and especially coalition agreements. The literature has given much more attention to the formation and dissolution of coalitions than to the actual process of governing. The most important ambition of this chapter has been to go some distance towards redressing that imbalance, by in various ways enhancing our understanding of coalition governance.

We have focused on the critical everyday politics of coalitions: governance in office, examining in particular the agreements and enforcement mechanisms that underpin such everyday coalition politics. Coalition agreements and the institutions that uphold them exhibit a great deal of variation, running all the way from very incomplete 'understandings' to very detailed documents setting up an intricate set of rules and a laborious set of mechanisms by which they can be implemented.

Among the reasons that such agreements are hammered out are the preference differences between coalition parties and the uncertainties that lead them to fear opportunism on the part of their coalition partners. On the other hand, coalition agreements can be extensive and complicated, and yet it is often difficult to ensure that they will be enforced. In other words, they are beset with various transaction costs. The dilemma that faces politicians in coalition negotiations is how to negotiate between the risks that face them in coalition situations and the costs of hammering out agreements designed to reduce these risks.

We have especially explored and sought to explain the variation in formal coalition agreements. As elsewhere within our larger project, we have systematically sought to explain the variance in coalition agreements by examining six clusters of explanatory variables, as well as their joint effects. We find that coalition governance mechanisms vary significantly across countries, and that many polities exhibit consistent national trends. In some countries (such as Italy) agreements tend to be informal; elsewhere (such as Finland) they tend to be formal but short; whereas in yet other countries (such as Belgium) agreements are often both formal and lengthy. In most cases, coalition agreements are predominantly or exclusively policy documents, but in some countries (such as Austria and Denmark), they often contain detailed procedural commitments. At the same time, institutions often have systematic and significant effects that cut across these national patterns. For example, semi-presidential regimes systematically dispose politicians towards formal coalition agreements but modest commitments to legislative discipline.

The variation in coalition governance also sorts itself into larger cross-national patterns. For example, our sample of European parliamentary democracies tend to sort themselves into those (in large part Northern European states) that rely primarily on ex ante mechanisms of coalition governance, such as extensive policy agreements, whereas others (such as France, Italy, and most of the consociational democracies) more typically make use of such ex post controls as 'watchdog' junior ministers. But at the same time, we find significant and striking trends over time towards more formal use of at least one of these forms of governance (or increasingly, both).

These findings indicate that much of coalition politics is driven by path dependency, but also that transaction costs matter in very obvious ways. Path dependency implies that once a certain set of governance institutions have evolved in a particular country, these institutions tend to get replicated in subsequent coalitions. But path dependency may in turn be driven by transaction costs, since the virtue of relying on established forms of governance may be precisely to economize on the costs of inventing new institutions to help politicians cement their cooperation. It is also intriguing to see evidence that in situations in which politicians know that their cooperation will be short-lived (such as in caretaker cabinets), they frequently deviate from established institutional solutions in favour of simpler and less costly ones. Again, these observations powerfully suggest the importance of transaction costs in the politics of coalition management.

The study of coalition politics has primarily been concerned with, on the one hand, the formation of coalition governments and, on the other, hand, their termination. Yet the reality of coalition politics is fundamentally about what happens in between these events. Our analysis in this chapter has begun to explore aspects of coalition governance that have never before been systematically investigated. Yet, in this brief analysis we have only been able to scratch the surface of this intriguing aspect of coalition politics. Much research thus remains to be done, but there is every reason to expect that such efforts will yield rich rewards for our understanding of coalition politics.

REFERENCES

Aghion, Philippe and Tirole, Jean (1997). 'Formal and Real Authority in Organizations', *Journal of Political Economy*, 105: 1–29.
——Dewatripont, Mathias, and Rey, Patrick (2002). 'On Partial Contracting', *European Economic Review*, 46: 745–53.
Axelrod, Robert (1984). *The Evolution of Cooperation*. New York, NY: Basic Books.
Chen, Yongmin (2000). 'Promise, Trust, and Contracts', *Journal of Law, Economics, and Organization*, 16: 209–32.
DeWinter, Lieven, Timmermans, Arco, and Dumont, Patrick (2000). 'Belgium: On Government Agreements, Evangelists, Followers and Heretics', in Wolfgang C. Müller and Kaare Strøm (eds.), *Coalition Governments in Western Europe*. Oxford: Oxford University Press.
Diermeier, Daniel and van Roozendaal, Peter (1998). 'The Duration of Government Formation in Western Multi-Party Democracies', *British Journal of Political Science*, 28: 609–26.

Downs, William M. (1998). *Coalition Government, Subnational Style*. Columbus, OH: Ohio State University Press.
Dunleavy, Patrick with Bastow, Simon (2001). 'Modelling Coalitions that Cannot Coalesce: A Critique of the Laver-Shepsle Approach', *West European Politics*, 24: 1–26.
Elster, Jon (1984). *Ulysses and the Sirenes*. Cambridge: Cambridge University Press.
Frank, Robert H. (1988). *Passions Within Reason. The Strategic Roles of the Emotions*. New York, NY: W. W. Norton.
Huber, John D. Shipan, Charles R., and Pfahler, Madelaine (2001). 'Legislatures and Statutory Control of Bureaucracy', *American Journal of Political Science*, 45: 330–45.
Jun, Uwe (1994). *Koalitionsbildung in den deutschen Bundesländern*. Opladen: Leske + Budrich.
Kim, Dong-Hun and Loewenberg, Gerhard (2005). 'The Role of Parliamentary Committees in Coalition Governments. Keeping Tabs on Coalition Partners in the German Bundestag', *Comparative Political Studies*, 38: 1104–29.
Krehbiel, Keith (1991). *Information and Legislative Organization*. Ann Arbor, MI: University of Michigan Press.
Kreps, David M. (1990). 'Corporate Culture and Economic Theory', in James E. Alt and Kenneth A. Shepsle (eds.), *Perspectives on Positive Political Economy*. Cambridge: Cambridge University Press.
Laffont, Jean-Jacques (2000). *Incentives and Political Economy*. Oxford: Oxford University Press.
Larsson, Torbjörn (1993). 'The Role and Position of Ministers of Finance', in Jean Blondel and Ferdinand Müller-Rommel (eds.), *Governing Together*. New York, NY: St. Martin's Press.
Laver, Michael and Schofield, Norman (1990). *Multiparty Government: The Politics of Coalition in Europe*. Oxford: Oxford University Press.
—— (1996). *Making and Breaking Governments: Cabinets and Legislatures in Parliamentary Democracies*. Cambridge: Cambridge University Press.
—— (1999a). 'Understanding Government Survival: Empirical Exploration or Analytical Models?' *British Journal of Political Science*, 29: 395–401.
—— (1999b). 'Government Formation and Survival: A Rejoinder to Warwick's Reply', *British Journal of Political Science*, 29: 412–15.
Laakso, Markku (1972). 'Riker's "Size Principle" and Its Application to Finnish Roll-Call Data', *Scandinavian Political Studies* (Old Series), 7: 197–218.
Manow, Philip and Zorn, Hendrik (2004). 'Office versus Policy Motives in Portfolio Allocation. The Case of Junior Ministers', Max Planck Institute for the Study of Societies, *MPIfG Discussion Chapter* 04/9.
Martin, Lanny W. and Vanberg, Georg (2004). 'Policing the Bargain: Coalition Government and Parliamentary Scrutiny', *American Journal of Political Science*, 48: 13–27.
Müller, Wolfgang C. (2000a). 'Political Parties in Parliamentary Democracies: Making Delegation and Accountability Work', *European Journal of Political Research*, 37: 309–33.
—— (2000b). 'Austria: Tight Coalitions and Stable Government', in Wolfgang C. Müller and Kaare Strøm (eds.), *Coalition Governments in Western Europe*. Oxford: Oxford University Press.

Müller, Wolfgang C. and Strøm, Kaare (eds.) (1999). *Policy, Office, or Votes? How Political Parties in Western Europe Make Hard Decisions*. Cambridge: Cambridge University Press.

——— (eds.) (2000). *Coalition Governments in Western Europe*. Oxford: Oxford University Press.

——— Philipp, Wilfried, and Gerlich, Peter (1993). 'Prime Ministers and Cabinet Decision-Making Processes', in Jean Blondel and Ferdinand Müller-Rommel (eds.), *Governing Together*. New York, NY: St. Martin's Press.

North, Douglass C. (1990). *Institutions, Institutional Change and Economic Performance*. Cambridge: Cambridge University Press.

Persson, Torsten, Roland, Gerard, and Tabellini, Guido (1997). 'Separation of Powers and Political Accountability', *Quarterly Journal of Economics*, 112: 1163–202.

Peterson, Robert L. and De Ridder, Martine M. (1986). 'Government Formation as a Policy-Making Arena', *Legislative Studies Quarterly*, 11: 565–81.

Rose, Richard and Mackie, Thomas T. (1983). 'Incumbency in Government: Asset or Liability?' in Hans Daalder and Peter Mair (eds.), *West European Party Systems: Continuity and Change*. London: Sage Publications.

Salanié, Bernard (1997). *The Economics of Contracts*. Cambridge, MA: MIT Press.

Shepsle, Kenneth A. (1996). 'Political Deals in Institutional Settings', in Robert E. Goodin (ed.), *The Theory of Institutional Design*. Cambridge: Cambridge University Press.

Strøm, Kaare (1989). 'Inter-Party Competition in Advanced Democracies', *Journal of Theoretical Politics*, 1: 277–300.

——— (1992). 'Democracy as Political Competition', *American Behavioural Scientist*, 35: 375–96.

——— (1994). 'Norway', in Michael Laver and Kenneth A. Shepsle (eds.), *Cabinet Ministers*. Cambridge: Cambridge University Press.

——— (2003). 'Parliamentary Democracy and Delegation', in Kaare Strøm, Wolfgang C. Müller, and Torbjorn Bergman (eds.), *Delegation and Accountability in Parliamentary Democracies*. Oxford: Oxford University Press.

——— and Müller, Wolfgang C. (1999). 'The Keys to Togetherness: Coalition Agreements in Parliamentary Democracies', *Journal of Legislative Studies*, 5 (3/4): 255–82.

Stiglitz, Joseph E. (2000). 'The Contribution of the Economics of Information to Twentieth Century Economics', *Quarterly Journal of Economics*, 115: 1441–78.

Thies, Michael F. (2001). 'Keeping Tabs on Partners: The Logic of Delegation in Coalition Governments', *American Journal of Political Science*, 45: 580–98.

Timmermans, Arco (2003). *High Politics in the Low Countries: An Empirical Study of Coalition Agreements in Belgium and the Netherlands*. Aldershot: Ashgate.

Tirole, Jean (1999). 'Incomplete Contracts: Where Do We Stand?' *Econometrica*, 67: 741–81.

Tsebelis, George (1995). 'Decisionmaking in Political Systems: Veto Players in Presidentialism, Parliamentarism, Multicameralism, and Multipartyism', *British Journal of Political Science*, 25: 289–325.

Tsebelis, George (2002). *Veto Players. How Political Institutions Work*. New York, NY: Russel Sage Foundation and Princeton, NJ: Princeton University Press.

van Roozendaal, Peter (1990). 'Center Parties and Coalition Cabinet Formation: A Game Theoretic Approach', *European Journal of Political Research*, 18: 324–48.

—— (1993). 'Cabinets in the Netherlands (1918–1990): The Importance of "Dominant" and "Central" Parties', *European Journal of Political Research*, 23: 35–54.

Warwick, Paul V. (1999*a*). 'Ministerial Autonomy or Ministerial Accommodation? Contested Bases of Government Survival in Parliamentary Democracies', *British Journal of Political Science*, 29: 369–94.

—— (1999*b*). 'Getting the Assumptions Right: A Reply to Laver and Shepsle', *British Journal of Political Science*, 29: 402–12.

Weingast, Barry R. and Marshall, William (1988). 'The Industrial Organization of Congress', *Journal of Political Economy*, 91: 765–800.

6

Government Formation and Cabinet Type

Paul Mitchell and Benjamin Nyblade[1]

INTRODUCTION

While political scientists over the last few decades have studied many features of coalition politics, the most sustained focus has been given to government formation. In most parliamentary democracies, government formation is not a trivial matter. Only in the few countries where plurality electoral systems (almost) invariably manufacture a majority for a single party is government formation a somewhat less interesting arena.[2] Most elections in Western Europe result in legislatures in which no single party controls a majority of seats, typically leading to periods of coalition negotiations,[3] which may involve multiple inconclusive bargaining rounds, as was discussed in the prior chapter by De Winter and Dumont. However, whether coalition bargaining takes less than a week, or several months, ultimately a government is formed, and the focus of this chapter is on explaining 'the type' of that government.

Much of the existing literature on government formation has focused on the question of 'Who gets in?' (see Laver and Schofield 1990), in the sense of which parties get into government, and what 'type of government' is formed, in the sense of whether it is single party or coalition, undersized, oversized, or minimal winning. After reviewing the literature on government formation, we suggest that two basic propositions underlie our understanding of government formation. The

---

[1] This chapter is made possible by the collaborative efforts of the large cross-national research team assembled by Wolfgang C. Müller, Kaare Strøm, and Torbjörn Bergman. We thank all team members for their help and advice. In addition, we thank the editors and James Druckman for detailed and thoughtful comments on earlier drafts.

[2] Single-party majority outcomes are of course not necessarily less interesting bargaining situations in at least two respects. First, some of these 'winning' single parties choose to form surplus majority governments. Second, even when they govern alone, the intra-party coalition politics of single-party cabinets is a fascinating topic, awaiting better data than currently available.

[3] Of course, inter-election government collapses also lead to new coalition bargaining rounds. In our data-set, 44% of government formations do not directly follow an election.

first proposition, traced primarily to the seminal work of Riker (1962), focuses on the nature of the government formation bargaining game. As Riker suggests, the more that the bargaining situation approximates a fixed pay-off, complete information bargaining game, the more likely a minimal winning coalition is. The second proposition focuses on the bargaining leverage of individual parties. When bargaining power is concentrated in the hands of a single party, a coalition is less likely to form. And the more dispersed bargaining power is among multiple parties, the larger the coalition.

After developing these two propositions in more detail, we use the new data-set collected for this volume to address two fundamental empirical questions. First, what affects whether a single-party or coalition government forms? Second, what affects whether a minority government, minimal winning coalition, or surplus coalition forms? We draw our explanatory variables from six blocks of variables: time and space parameters, structural attributes, preferences, institutions, the bargaining environment, and critical events. We find strong empirical support for prior results concerning the influence of party seat share and policy preferences, but also that variables relating to political institutions, the bargaining environment and even exogenous critical events have significant explanatory power. We discuss more specific findings in the conclusion.

The rest of this chapter is developed in five parts. The first section briefly reviews the existing literature on coalition formation and government type. The second section takes an overview of the empirical record of the type of governments that actually formed in the 17 West European states examined in this book. The third section presents our underlying theoretical framework, its major propositions and the blocks of variables that we use to explain government formation. The fourth section reports our statistical analyses, and the fifth section concludes.

PRIOR RESEARCH

Systematic analysis of coalition governments was driven by political scientists' increased interest in game theory in the 1960s and 1970s. The approaches that dominated early game theoretical accounts of cabinet formation are, respectively, the minimal winning or 'size' proposition developed by Riker (1962), and the policy distance or 'ideology' approach presented a few years later, either as a refinement or as a competing explanation, by Axelrod (1970) and De Swaan (1973). Subsequent empirical tests have compared 'size' and 'ideology' both individually and in various combinations.

The classic size proposition is associated most with Riker, who predicts: 'In n-person, zero-sum games, where side payments are permitted, where players are rational, and they have perfect information, only minimal winning coalitions occur' (Riker 1962: 32). Early theories tend to vary according to the manner in which they elaborate a definition of the size principle. In addition to the broadest definition outlined above ('minimal winning' or MW, which simply predicts no 'unnecessary' members), several other applications of the size principle have attempted to make more precise predictions by restricting the size of the solution set.[4]

Of course, while all coalitions in a solution set are formally equal even the most casual observer of real government formations knows that some coalitions are decidedly more equal than others (with apologies to Orwell). Any country specialist worth his or her salt knows that some coalitions are simply more likely to form than others. Thus, early theorists sought to cut the number of predictions by using policy compatibility as essentially 'another type of bargaining proposition' (Laver and Schofield 1990: 97). Axelrod's 'minimal connected winning' coalition (MCW) proposition has been one of the most influential in the literature (and requires only an ordinal distribution of parties on one dimension). A coalition is connected in the sense that the parties forming it are ideologically adjacent. Such a coalition is said to be 'closed' in that there are no 'gaps'.[5] De Swaan was the first to give policy a more central role. He assumed that policy coherence is the attribute actors attempt to maximize. Utility requires producing agreement on preferred policies and maintaining coalition harmony over time. This results in players wishing to be members of winning coalitions with a minimum ideological diversity ('closed minimal range' theory).[6] The general behavioural assumption in these theories is that a lower conflict of interest creates a more desirable coalition, and hence the fixed-sum assumption made by Riker and others is generally inapplicable.

Early empirical tests of size and ideology theories examined both separately and in various combinations produced fairly contradictory results. What can be said with some certainty is that no single theory was highly successful in predicting actual coalition formations. Several of the early tests suggested that theories adding an ideological element were more promising than size theories alone. For example, both De Swaan (1973) and Taylor and Laver (1973) found that Axelrod's minimal connected winning proposition achieved better results

---

[4] They do so by predicting that the smallest minimal winning coalition will form. Riker (1962) and Gamson (1961) defined 'smallest' in terms of the number of seats controlled (the 'minimum seats'—MS—proposition), whereas Leiserson (1966) interprets smallness in terms of the number of parties. Hence, he derives a minimum parties (MP) prediction, based on the logic that smaller groups of parties will find it easier to reach agreement (the 'bargaining proposition').

[5] Note that while related, minimal winning and MCWC theories are distinct. A given coalition can be minimal winning but not an MCWC, MCWC but not minimal winning, or both. In Laver and Schofield's data (1990: 101), there were 9 cases of MCWC coalitions that were not MW and 24 that were minimal winning but not MCW. Fifty-four cases were both MCW and MW.

[6] De Swaan states his central behavioural assumption as follows: 'An actor strives to bring about a winning coalition in which he is included and which he expects to adopt a policy that is as close as possible, on a scale of policies, to his own most preferred policy' (1973: 88).

than any size theory alone. Even here though, Taylor and Laver found that MCW predictions perform much better in some countries than in others (1973: 226).

Franklin and Mackie (1984) were the first to construct a multivariate test in order to reassess the relative importance of size and ideology, and claimed to have reconciled the early research findings. They found that the wide discrepancy in previous studies was explained by methodological decisions, such that the results of Browne (1973) and De Swaan (1973) can be reconciled with those of Taylor and Laver (1973) 'by simple adjustments of universe and weighting strategy' (Franklin and Mackie 1984: 681). One of their most important findings was the existence of strong 'country effects'. Patterns of coalition formation seemed to vary much more across countries than within them, suggesting that the choice of countries strongly influences the outcome of any study of coalition formation.

During the 1980s and 1990s, however, while much scholarship continued to focus on predicting specifically 'who gets in', there was also increasing interest in understanding, both theoretically and empirically, the type of government formed, based on different policy and office-based motivational assumptions as to what really drives coalition behaviour. Early coalition theories, for example, generally considered minority governments to be an aberration even though empirically they constitute perhaps as many as 40 per cent of the governments formed in post-war Western Europe (e.g. Herman and Pope 1973; Taylor and Laver 1973). Strøm (1984, 1990a), however, sought to understand minority governments as a systematic and rational outcome of coalition bargaining, and suggested that minority governments were likely outcomes of coalition bargaining in situations in which the electoral consequences of government membership are significant and the policy influence of the opposition high. Laver and Schofield (1990) additionally suggested that minority governments may be 'policy viable' when they include the median party and face a bilateral opposition (see also Strøm 1990a: 78–83). The dominant explanations for surplus governments—which also tended to be treated as 'deviant' by most of the literature—focused on two basic arguments: the prediction of minimum connected winning coalitions by Axelrod, and the suggestion by Riker that in cases of incomplete and/or imperfect information, actors would form coalitions larger than minimal winning.

Since the early 1990s, there have been efforts to expand unidimensional spatial models into multiple dimensions (notably Schofield 1993). Both Sened (1996) and Crombez (1996) present models that predict the likelihood of minority governments, minimum-winning coalitions or surplus governments based on the ideal points and weights of parties. The most elaborate of the models of coalition formation is the portfolio allocation approach developed by Laver and Shepsle (1990, 1996). Laver and Shepsle's volume (1996) develops the concept of 'merely strong' and 'very strong' parties in coalition formation. Empirical testing of the various models (Warwick 1996, 1999a, 1999b; Martin and Stevenson 2001) has provided mixed support for these models' predictions, as well as an epistemological dispute as to the nature of 'what is being tested' (Laver and Shepsle 1999*a*, 1999*b*; Warwick 1999*a*, 1999*b*).

Martin and Stevenson (2001) use a different methodology in a comprehensive test of a number of significant hypotheses. They suggest that

> The central shortcoming of [prior approaches such as Franklin and Mackie's] is that in a regression framework...each potential coalition in a formation opportunity enters the estimation as a separate case. Thus, including countries such as Italy or Denmark, with a large number of parties at any given time, means that thousands of cases enter the estimation and completely swamp out relationships in other countries (2001: 38).

These authors use McFadden's conditional logit model that uses a statistically identical estimation procedure to the better-known multinomial logistic regression model. They thereby evaluate potential coalitions as discrete alternatives that the dependent variable can take. Each potential coalition is associated with a set of size, ideology, and institutional variables that serve as the independent variables. This is a superior method for analysing partisan composition of government formation, and subsequent work in analysing coalition formation has generally adopted this methodology (e.g. Bäck 2003; Bäck and Dumont 2007; Warwick 2005). However, in analysing the type of government formed, the literature has continued to use standard logistic regression and multinomial logistic regression (e.g. Kalandrakis 2002), noting that these methods remain suitable to analysing the type of government formed.

While the bulk of the coalition formation literature has focused on variables that essentially relate to the size and policy preferences of parties, it is worth noting that other factors also have been suggested. Robertson (1986), for example, considers the potential for economic shocks to play a role in government formation. Budge and Keman (1990) suggest that threats to democracy can cause a grand coalition (of all pro-system parties) to form, and Strøm, Budge, and Laver (1994) extensively review potential institutional constraints on coalition formation. As seen in the empirical section below, one of the major contributions of this chapter is to expand on the range and types of variables that can be examined thanks to our much richer data-set. But before turning to our statistical analyses we first present a descriptive overview of the patterns and types of governments that have actually formed in Western Europe in the post-1945 era.

THE EMPIRICAL RECORD

William Riker's *The Theory of Political Coalitions* makes a strong theoretical argument for the formation of 'minimal winning coalitions' (MWC) in politics. However, this prediction has received only limited empirical support, so that each

TABLE 6.1. *Coalition governments in Western Europe by country*

Country	Cabinets	One party majority		One party minority		Coalitions	
		n	%	n	%	n	%
Austria	21	4	19.0	1	4.8	16	76.2
Belgium	33	3	9.1	2	6.1	28	84.9
Denmark	31	0	—	14	45.2	17	54.8
Finland	37	0	—	4	10.8	33	89.2
France	23	1	4.3	5	21.7	17	73.9
Germany	26	1	3.8	3	11.5	22	84.6
Greece	10	7	70.0	1	10.0	2	20.0
Iceland	26	0	—	4	15.4	22	84.6
Ireland	22	6	27.3	6	27.3	10	45.5
Italy	48	0	—	14	29.2	34	70.8
Luxembourg	16	0	—	0	—	16	100.0
The Netherlands	22	0	—	0	—	22	100.0
Norway	26	6	23.1	12	46.2	8	30.8
Portugal	11	2	18.2	3	21.4	6	42.9
Spain	8	2	25.0	6	75.0	0	—
Sweden	26	2	7.7	17	65.4	7	26.9
United Kingdom	20	19	95.0	1	5.0	0	—
Overall	406	53	13.1	93	22.9	260	64.0

Note: This table excludes 18 cabinets from the data-set, including non-partisan cabinets or other cabinets that cannot readily be classified by type.

of the components of MWCs—'minimal-winning', 'winning', and 'coalition'— have not necessarily held in practice. The empirical record shows that in minority bargaining situations, not only are the governments that form not necessarily 'minimal winning' (many have 'surplus' members), not necessarily 'winning' (many are minority government), and they are sometimes not even coalitions at all. Table 6.1 reports the frequency of single-party majority governments, single-party minority governments, and coalition governments in the post-war period in Western Europe.

In the 17 West European countries in our data-set, single-party minority cabinets (23%) have in fact been significantly more common than single-party majority cabinets (comprising 13% of cabinets). Coalition governments account for 64 per cent of all governments. The variation among countries is extreme. Spain and the UK have no instances of coalition government (with the latter only having one minority situation in the post-war years), while every government in the Netherlands and Luxembourg has included multiple parties. However, most countries have experience with both single party and coalition government. Explaining when a coalition forms, in the absence of a majority party, is the first question we address in our statistical analyses later in this chapter.

The second major focus in this chapter is the type of government formed: minority, minimal winning, or surplus majority. While Riker predicted MWC,

TABLE 6.2. *Government type in Western Europe by country*

Country	Total	One party majority		MWC		Surplus majority		Minority	
		n	%	n	%	n	%	n	%
Austria	21	4	19.0	14	66.7	2	9.5	1	4.8
Belgium	33	3	9.1	14	42.4	12	36.4	4	12.1
Denmark	31	0	—	4	12.9	0	—	27	87.1
Finland	37	0	—	7	18.9	20	54.1	10	27.0
France	23	1	4.3	7	30.4	8	34.8	7	30.4
Germany	26	1	3.8	17	65.4	5	19.2	3	11.5
Greece	10	7	70.0	1	10.0	1	10.0	1	10.0
Iceland	26	0	—	17	65.4	4	15.4	5	19.2
Ireland	22	6	27.3	5	22.7	0	—	11	50.0
Italy	48	0	—	4	8.2	21	42.9	23	47.9
Luxembourg	16	0	—	15	93.8	1	6.3	0	—
The Netherlands	22	0	—	9	40.9	10	45.5	3	13.6
Norway	26	6	23.1	3	11.5	0	—	17	65.4
Portugal	11	2	18.2	3	27.3	3	27.3	3	27.3
Spain	8	2	25.0	0	—	0	—	6	75.0
Sweden	26	2	7.7	5	19.2	0	—	19	73.1
United Kingdom	20	19	95.0	0	—	0	—	1	5.0
Overall	406	53	13.1	125	30.5	87	21.7	141	34.7

scholars of parliamentary democracies have long noted that MWCs in government formation have not been the norm in most countries. Strøm (1990*a*: 59) calculated the frequency of minority governments in 15 democracies as 35 per cent. Laver and Schofield found that 33.5 per cent of governments (in 12 countries) had only minority support and a further 25 per cent were surplus majority coalitions. As shown in Table 6.2, our data are consistent with these prior findings on the relative frequency of cabinet types. Minimal-winning coalitions account for 30.5 per cent of governments formed in our sample, marginally lower than Laver and Schofield's figure. Single-party majority cabinets account for 13 per cent. Minority cabinets constitute the single largest category with 35 per cent, while a further 22 per cent are surplus majority governments. Thus, unequivocally, non-minimal winning cabinets are the typical outcome of the government formation process in Western Europe.

There has been some oscillation in the frequency of cabinet types by decade, especially in the cases of MWC and surplus majority cabinets (see Figure 6.1). As can be seen, the number of MWC has varied quite substantially by decade, ranging from 23 per cent in the 1940s to 40 per cent in the 1990s. Nevertheless, there is no obvious linear trend towards MWC outcomes. Indeed, if we divide the data into only two periods (1945–69 and 1970–99) the period averages are very similar (29.3% and 30.6%, respectively). With the singular exception of the 1950s, the proportion of one-party majority governments has remained fairly constant at around 11.5 per cent. Between the same periods (1945–69 and 1970–99),

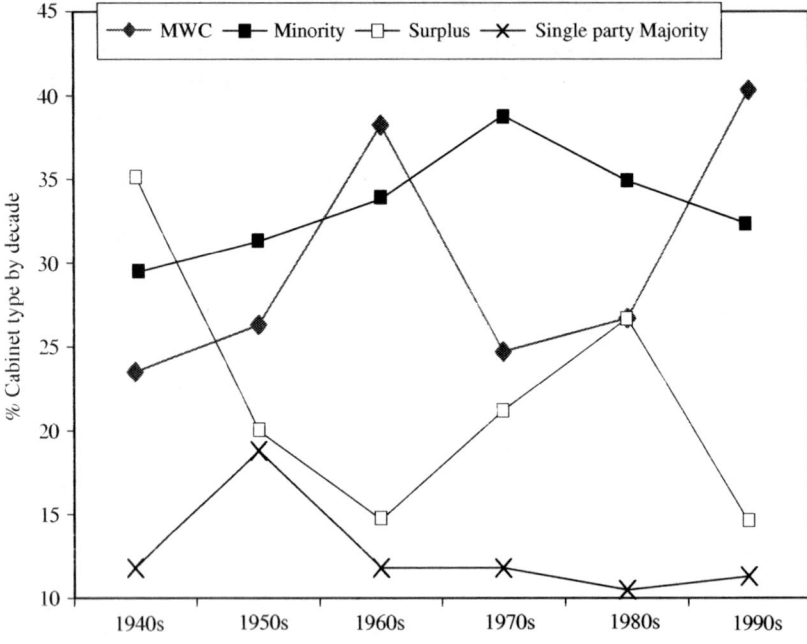

FIGURE 6.1. Cabinet type by decade

surplus majority governments have declined slightly in frequency (from 23.3% to 20.8%). Indeed, the only cabinet type showing a moderate change are minority governments that have tended to increase (from 31.5% to 35.3% in the same periods). Our statistical analyses later in this chapter also demonstrate that the differences between the decades are not significant.

Whereas there is modest oscillation by decade, the empirical variation across countries is, to say the least, much more dramatic, as shown in Table 6.2. To take just a few examples, in four countries (Austria, Germany, Iceland, and Luxembourg) more than 60 per cent of cabinets were MWC, whereas in Finland, Denmark, and Italy, MWC cabinets are very rare. These latter three countries are among those in which minority governments are frequent. Norway, Sweden, Ireland, and Spain, the other countries with large numbers of minority governments and relatively few MCW cases, are countries with high frequencies of single-party governments (both majority and minority).

What explains this large variation in government type both between and within countries? To the extent that early coalition theories like Riker 'fail' to explain the variance in actual outcomes of parliamentary government formation, it is because they are primarily office-seeking theories that cannot surrender the majority-winning post. However, minority governments are 'more or less impossible to explain on the basis of office-seeking assumptions' (Laver and Schofield 1990: 73).

A number of studies have shown that minority and surplus majority governments can be more adequately explained by taking policy and vote-seeking motivations more seriously (Laver and Schofield 1990; Strøm 1990*a*). Strøm focuses on oppositional influence and electoral decisiveness with minority governments being most likely when the values of both factors are high (and the value of being in government relative to being in opposition is comparatively low). Given that incumbents tend to suffer at the next election (at least in all European parliamentary democracies), oppositions can hope to gain from elections, or at least recover from a prior period in government (see Chapter 11 in this volume by Narud and Valen). This expectation combined with the opportunity in some legislatures for considerable policy influence provides a rationale for abstaining from office in the short term. Strøm concludes that 'electoral decisiveness is a far stronger predictor than oppositional influence' (1990: 81).

Laver and Schofield offered a complementary but more directly policy-based explanation of minority governments. Essentially, they argue that an executive coalition 'is winning as long as it is not losing' (1990: 88) and that in practice many minority governments may be feasible because of the policy divisions among opposition parties in the legislature. If these opposition parties are substantially motivated by policy, then their 'majority' of votes may remain theoretical since they cannot combine and agree on a replacement government.

Certainly when considering only the single left–right dimension it is clear that control of the median legislator is a very good predictor of government membership. Our data confirm this expectation: 78 per cent of governments included the median party on the left–right dimension (the only scale common to all countries in this data-set). In many countries, the party controlling the median legislator is virtually guaranteed inclusion in the winning coalition (see Table 6.3). Finland, Belgium, Iceland, and Denmark are the only countries in which the median party has quite often (or very often in the cases of Iceland and Denmark) been outside the government. In Norway, the small Christian People's Party (KRF) has controlled the median legislator since 1981 but has sometimes been excluded from power by single-party governments formed either by the Conservative Party (1981) or more typically by Labour (1986, 1990, 1993). In Denmark, the only country in which the median party appears to be in fewer than half of governments, median status has oscillated between the Radical Liberals (RL) and the Centre Democrats. On seven occasions, the Radical Liberals have been excluded despite being the median party (either by single-party Social Democratic governments or by Conservative-Liberal coalitions). Part of the explanation might be that while most median parties in Western Europe are fairly large, in Denmark the only parties that have ever held the median position are fairly small. In the case of Ireland, the explanation is straightforward: since the

TABLE 6.3. *Cabinet characteristics by country*

Country	Cabinets	MCWC		Connected		One party		Med-Leg1		Med-Leg2	
		N	%	N	%	n	%	n	%	n	%
Austria	21	12	57.1	14	66.7	5	23.8	18	85.7	8	38.1
Belgium	33	3	9.1	3	9.1	5	15.2	19	57.6	15	45.5
Denmark	31	4	12.9	15	48.4	14	45.2	13	41.9	N/A	—
Finland	44	3	6.8	11	25.0	4	9.1	30	68.2	24	54.5
France	23	7	30.4	17	73.9	6	26.1	21	91.3	N/A	—
Germany	26	15	57.7	18	69.2	4	15.4	24	92.3	22	84.6
Greece	11	0	—	1	9.1	8	72.7	9	81.8	N/A	—
Iceland	26	7	26.9	8	30.8	4	15.4	14	53.8	21	80.8
Ireland	22	1	4.5	1	4.5	12	54.5	16	72.7	15	68.2
Italy	49	2	4.1	24	49.0	14	28.6	48	98.0	43	87.8
Luxembourg	16	10	62.5	11	68.7	0	—	15	93.7	7	43.7
The Netherlands	22	3	13.6	8	36.4	0	—	20	90.9	14	63.6
Norway	26	3	11.5	8	30.8	18	69.2	19	73.1	17	65.4
Portugal	11	5	45.5	5	45.5	5	45.5	9	81.8	8	72.7
Spain	8	0	—	0	—	8	100	7	87.5	7	87.5
Sweden	26	5	19.2	6	23.1	19	73.1	22	84.6	21	80.8
United Kingdom	20	0	—	0	—	20	100	20	100	20	100
Total or average	415	80	19.3	150	36.1	146	35.4	324	78.1	242	69.1

largest party has always controlled the median legislator and (at least until 1989) always governed alone, the other parties had to combine against it irrespective of policy differences if they were ever to eject it from power. It is precisely these 'opportunistic' governments that did not contain the median legislator.[7] The existence of multiple issue dimensions is also potentially quite important in Ireland and elsewhere. Table 6.3 suggests that control of the second most salient policy dimension is a considerable aid in making it to the cabinet table: 69 per cent of parties located in the median position on this dimension have been included.

Predictions that the median party on the primary policy dimension will enter government do not directly help us understand whether the government formed will be a minority, minimal winning coalition, or surplus coalition, the focus of the remainder of this chapter. However, the relevance of the distribution of policy preferences among parties has played a crucial role in explanations of government formation as noted above, and we discuss this further in the next section, in which we outline in more detail two basic propositions concerning government formation.

---

[7] This result assumes that Fianna Fail and Fine Gael have not ever switched positions on the left–right dimension, which is a debatable proposition but not one that we shall pursue further in this context.

EXPLAINING COALITION FORMATION AND GOVERNMENT TYPE

Much of the existing literature, including the chapter by Lupia and Strøm in this volume, seeks to understand government formation as a bargaining game. We believe that certain basic bargaining principles indeed illuminate how a wide range of variables may influence government formation. Before examining the six categories of variables that are used throughout this volume, we suggest two basic propositions. These propositions suggest the fundamental logic of government formation as a bargaining game, and can help draw together much of the existing literature. The first proposition relates to the nature of the bargaining situation, while the second concerns the distribution of bargaining power among political actors.

Our first proposition is based on Riker's size principle, which has formed the starting point of much of the literature on political coalitions. In applying the principle, Riker succinctly suggests that 'In social situations similar to n-person, zero-sum games, with side-payments, participants create coalitions just as large as they believe will ensure winning and no larger' (Riker 1962: 47). Proposition 1 is a direct application of this suggestion.

Proposition 1 (Bargaining Situation). The more similar the coalition bargaining situation is to an n-person, fixed-sum game with side-payments and a simple majority decision rule, the more likely a minimal winning coalition will form.

Coalition formation is not always as simple as the basic games used to analyse it, and the degree to which coalition formation approximates Riker's basic game clearly varies. While the number of factors that may differ is large, three can be briefly highlighted: the decision rule, information, and the pay-offs.

Governments may need to garner more than a simple majority in one chamber in order to 'win' in coalition bargaining. For example, in some countries a government is accountable to two chambers, so that a simple majority in one chamber may not be sufficient to ensure winning in the second chamber. Similarly, in a semi-presidential or presidential system, governments may not only be accountable to parliament or the legislature but also be dismissed by the president. Governments may also be interested in pursuing actions that may require more support than a simple majority in parliament allows. For example, a government may wish to enact constitutional amendments in countries where amendments require supermajorities.

However, clear institutional determinants of the decision rule are unlikely to be able to explain all the variation in coalition type both across and within nations. Perhaps more important is recognizing that Riker's basic coalition model rests on assumptions of complete and perfect information. Government formation situations are more likely to approach this rather stringent requirement when there are few parties and when those parties' behaviour is predictable and their preferences well known.

The real world government formations analysed in this chapter emerged from bargaining encounters in which the parties typically had much less than complete and perfect information, about their rivals' true preferences, what the next election may bring, and a range of other matters. The parties can attempt to reduce uncertainty if they can make credible commitments. However, when the ability to credibly commit to the coalition formed is absent or the commitment mechanisms are imperfect, parties may have incentives to 'blackmail' the other parties in the coalition, threatening to bring down the government in order to extract concessions. In order to avoid this threat, a coalition may seek to add surplus actors as a kind of 'insurance'. This then leads smaller parties that used to have blackmail potential to face a collective action problem in arranging defection (see Carrubba and Volden 2000, 2004). In general, as Riker (1962: 88–9) suggests: 'The greater the degree of imperfection or incompleteness of information, the larger will be the coalitions that coalition-makers seek to form and the more frequently will winning coalitions actually formed be greater than minimum size.'

Finally, the zero or fixed-sum assumption in coalition bargaining, in which coalition members always receive a positive pay-off in comparison to non-members, is also an important assumption that must be questioned in certain situations. Empirically, it is well established that parties sometimes turn down the opportunity to be a government member (e.g. the Agrarians in Sweden in 1957, the Christian People's Party in Norway in 1981, and the Labour Party in Ireland on a number of occasions). As is noted in Chapter 11, government membership in European parliamentary democracies is generally more of an electoral liability than an asset. Small parties that are particularly vulnerable in the electorate may have to think carefully about whether being a minor cog in a government coalition will be worth the likely electoral cost.

In general, we should expect that the more 'valuable' government is, the more likely MWCs will form. This is the primary force driving Riker's size principle. In the dynamic version of the coalition game, the pressure to form MWCs comes from two different directions. Undersized coalitions will have incentives to add members because the majority of parliament that is excluded from government would have both the means and incentive to upset the minority government. On the other hand, members of oversized coalitions will find that the benefits of government membership are being distributed too thinly and choose to eject surplus members of the coalition. Both these pressures rely on the assumption that the value of office in government membership is the primary driving force in coalition bargaining. In general, the more valuable government is, the more likely we should expect this to be the case.

So what could make office more or less valuable? We examine this in more detail when discussing the specific blocks of variables, but it is important to recognize that fundamentally the value of office should be considered relative to the prospect of being in opposition (see Strøm 1990a: 42). Strøm (1984, 1990a) considers two primary factors when explaining minority governments: electoral consequences and oppositional influence. Government may be more valuable the greater the 'perks' associated with it, but perhaps more importantly, the value of government may depend on the degree to which it improves electoral performance and moves policy outcomes closer to the preferences of its members (Müller and Strøm 1999).

To summarize the specific predictions that we can make, we suggest three simple corollaries to our first proposition, based on the three considerations (decisions rules, information, and pay-offs) we have just discussed:

Corollary 1 (Decision Rule): The higher the proportion of parliamentary support necessary to win, the more likely a coalition will form, and the larger the coalition.

Corollary 2 (Information): The greater the uncertainty parties have about each other's preferences or the credibility of their commitments, the more likely a surplus coalition will form.

Corollary 3 (Fixed Sum): The lower the value of government relative to being in the opposition, the more likely a minority government will form.

The size principle gets us only so far. A second basic proposition exists that, like Riker's size principle, has played a major part in the existing literature on coalition formation:

Proposition 2 (Bargaining Power). The more widely dispersed the bargaining power of parliamentary parties, the more likely a (larger) coalition is to form.

Studies of government formation tend to ignore majority situations as uninteresting—models of government formation generally assume that every majority party would form a government by itself, while empirical studies (including this chapter) generally exclude government formation situations when a majority party exists. While majority situations are generally ignored, fundamentally they anchor one end of our second proposition. Majority situations are the most obvious situation in which the bargaining power of parties in parliament is disproportionately concentrated.

However, even in non-majority situations, certain parties may have disproportionate bargaining power. A large, centrally located party with many potential coalition partners may be dominant and in a position to form governments on its own. In such cases, the costs of not coalescing can often be minimized.

In non-majority situations, the greater the walk-away value of the dominant player in coalition bargaining, the more likely government is to be smaller—that is to say, the concentration of bargaining power makes minority government more likely relative to MWC and even more so relative to surplus coalition governments. This fundamental proposition underlies the logic of almost all of the policy/size arguments about coalition type noted above, and is most directly suggested by Crombez (1996) and Laver and Shepsle (1996). Logrolling or blackmail approaches to surplus government (Riker 1962, Sartori 1976, Carrubba and Volden 2000, Volden and Carrubba 2004) can also be seen in this light because the lack of information and inability to credibly commit that underlies these theories help decrease the bargaining power of the dominant actor, by increasing its need to coalesce.

As non-dominant parties improve their bargaining power—for example, by becoming useful in order to prevent 'blackmail', in order to make a connected coalition, to improve a government's position in another chamber or with another political institution, or meet a different 'winning' target such as supermajority—larger coalitions become more likely. We mention these examples only briefly here to highlight the general thrust of our propositions, because we consider specific predictions in more detail below.

Explanatory variables

Below we group our explanatory variables according to the major approaches to understanding the type of cabinet formed in parliamentary democracies: structural attributes, preferences, institutions, the bargaining environment, and critical events. We discuss each of these types of variables in turn below, consider how they represent applications of our two basic principles, and in the subsequent section assess their empirical ability to explain the type of government formed.

Structural attributes

The literature on coalition formation traditionally has focused on one primary structural attribute that has a major impact on coalition bargaining: party seat shares in parliament. Parties that are large enough to help secure a parliamentary majority for the passage of bills have particular value as government members. Importantly, it is not simply a party's seat share, but rather how the distribution of those seats creates certain coalition possibilities while ruling others out that makes parliamentary seats a valuable resource.[8] The existing literature generally has used absolute seat share as the primary measure of party resources. In the analyses below, however, we improve upon this by using more direct measures of party-specific bargaining power.

How does the distribution of seats affect government formation? Perhaps the simplest prediction based on the distribution of seats, one that is generally assumed rather than carefully examined, is that when a single party garners a majority of seats, it will form a single-party majority government. While this is generally the case, of course, of the 63 cabinets in the data-set formed when a single party has a majority of seats, in fact 13 (21%) were coalition cabinets (by

---

[8] Laver and Shepsle (1996) refer to the connection between seat shares and coalition possibilities as the 'decisive structure' of the government formation process.

definition surplus coalitions). Thus, even the most basic prediction premised on party resources is far from perfect empirically.[9]

Beyond this basic prediction, there are several others that can be made based solely on the distribution of seats in parliament. The existing literature suggests that the size of the largest party should matter even when that party does not command a majority in parliament. The prediction is relatively simple (cf. Kalandrakis 2002; see also Laver and Shepsle 2000): the larger the seat share of the largest party, the more likely a minority government is to form.

The closer a party is to a majority (the 'nearly-winning' hypothesis), the fewer the number of additional seats necessary for implementing legislation. Thus the cost of forming legislative coalitions in fact may decline, making either formalized or ad hoc legislative coalitions combined with minority governments a more viable solution. In addition to the seat share of the largest party, the distribution of seat shares should also be relevant. Even controlling for the largest party seat share, the availability of a relatively large number of potential parliamentary allies with whom the party could work out legislative compromises should also improve the viability of minority governments.

Both these predictions focus on the viability of minority governments. However, the number and size of parties may affect the likelihood of different types of coalitions forming as well. For example, as the number of parties increases, the likelihood of an MWC should decline. This in fact may be explained by two factors. First, a baseline model that suggests that all coalitions are equally likely to form would suggest this as well: the greater the absolute number of parties in parliament, the lower the percentage of all potential coalitions that are minimum winning.[10] More generally, the greater the number of parties, the greater the level of uncertainty—thus the pressures towards MWCs that Riker identifies are weakened.

There are several other structural attributes that concern the bargaining situation, rather than the distribution of bargaining power. For example, forming a government near the beginning of the constitutional inter-election period may be more valuable than doing so later in the term, since coalitions entering office may have more time to implement policy and enjoy the perks of office. This suggests that we should also consider the maximum potential duration of government in this block of variables.

---

[9] The vast bulk of these deviant cases are identified by Budge and Keman (1990) as involving war or other 'threats to democracy'. Perhaps not surprisingly, in these cases the incentives for parties to coalesce in a formal executive coalition (discussed in Chapter 2 by Lupia and Strøm) are particularly strong, and might outweigh Riker's 'disequilibrium principle' which suggests that oversized coalitions should shed excess members.

[10] For example, in a three-party parliament without a majority party 3 of 7 possible governments are minimal winning. A five-party parliament with 63 possible governments will still likely only have a handful of minimally winning coalitions (the precise number depends on the distribution of seat shares).

In our statistical analysis, we include five variables of the two types discussed above. Three variables capture attributes of the size and number of parties: the seat share of the largest party in parliament, the bargaining power of the largest party in parliament, and the absolute number of parties in parliament.[11] The bargaining power of the largest party in government is measured in terms of the percentage of all potential winning coalitions that it would be part of. Both the seat share and the bargaining power of the largest party help capture one important aspect of the walk-away value of the largest party, and as such we expect that higher values will lead to a decreased likelihood of coalitions and to greater likelihood of minority governments.[12] The absolute number of parties in parliament may capture multiple effects. A greater number of parties may suggest overall bargaining uncertainty, which we expect to increase the size of the coalition. However, a greater number of parties also lowers the baseline proportion of MWCs to all potential coalitions, which should decrease the probability of MWCs.

We also consider two variables that capture another effect of the timing of the government in the life cycle of a parliament: a dummy variable indicating whether or not the government immediately follows an election and a variable that indicates the government's maximum possible duration. There are two related expectations here: uncertainty concerning voters' preferences is expected to be the lowest at this time (immediately following an election), and the value parties place on being in government should be high, as they have more potential time to govern until the next election. Both these factors should make MWCs more likely relative to non-coalitions, minority, or surplus governments.

Preferences: The policy positions of parties

Of course, existing explanations of government formation have not confined themselves to structural attributes alone. Both theoretical and empirical research into coalition formation have come to emphasize the importance of the policy preferences of parties, and how these preferences affect the type of government that is formed. Since the work of Axelrod (1970) and de Swaan (1973), most theories of coalition formation in parliamentary democracies have coupled understanding the importance of both the size and policy preferences of parties. A large literature, including work such as Warwick (1996), Crombez (1996), and Laver

---

[11] It is not uncommon to include the effective number of parliamentary parties in this sort of analysis, and we have included this variable in analyses not reported here. However, the ENP is not significant in any of our results, largely because its effect is captured in the absolute number of parties and the bargaining power of the largest party.

[12] While the similarity of the largest party seat share and the largest party bargaining power might raise concerns of multi-collinearity (they correlate at .80), our results demonstrate that the explanatory power of the largest party's bargaining power is robust to the inclusion of seat share, whereas the effect of seat share is not similarly robust.

and Shepsle (1996), have emphasized the importance of a combination of size and preferences. For example, Axelrod (1970) emphasized the importance of 'connectedness', suggesting that minimum *connected* winning coalitions (MCWCs) should form. Minimum connected winning coalitions may be either MWCs or surplus coalitions, as Axelrod suggested that small unnecessary parties may be included if their policy position is located in between larger parties that are already involved in the coalition.

In fact, Axelrod's prediction of 'connectedness' is consistent with a large majority of governments formed in Western Europe. The vast majority of European cabinets are either ideologically connected or single-party cabinets (71.5% combined, see Table 6.3), in which case the issue does not arise. Among the countries that usually have coalitions, only Belgium, Finland, and the Netherlands do *not* have a majority of ideologically connected cabinets. While some might attribute this to high issue dimensionality, there is no consistent evidence that this is the primary causal variable: Belgium is much more obviously multidimensional than Finland. Instead of dimensionality, the lack of ideologically connected cabinets in these countries appears to be explained by two related factors. First, these are either complex or at least fragmented party systems with the largest effective number of parties in our data-set (the Netherlands 4.7, Belgium 5.0, and Finland 5.1). Second, they contain large numbers of very small parties that are located between the main political tendencies and are often excluded. In Belgium, most cabinets are either between both of the Christian Democratic parties and both of the Liberal parties, or alternatively between the Christian Democrats and both of the Social Democratic parties. Many centre-right cabinets are unconnected (at least with respect to the first ideological dimension) because the VU (Volksunie) is often excluded. Centre-left governments are always unconnected (on the first dimension) because of the exclusion of several parties that are usually not in cabinet (Rassemblement Walloon is rarely included; and the Green parties did not enter government until 1999). Of course Belgium's complex dimensionality means that some of these governments may be connected on other dimensions. The logic is similar in the other two countries. In the Netherlands, the 1989 centre-left government was unconnected because of D'66's exclusion, whereas this more typically occurs on the centre-right, due to the omission of a wide range of small parties (CP, GPV, RPF, and SGP). Finally, in Finland, the exclusion of the GR (Green's), FRP (small farmer's party), and CHR (Christian League) renders many cabinets unconnected in this one-dimensional party system.

Like the prediction that the median party will be included in government, connectedness does not directly give a prediction as to the type of government that will be formed. The connectedness prediction would suggest that when an MWC cannot be formed by connected parties, a surplus government is more likely. However, other scholars have expanded on Axelrod by using a combination of party size and preferences to predict government formation.

Laver and Shepsle (1996) build models of coalition formation based on seat shares and party preferences over multiple dimensions, which (in our terms) emphasize how the distribution of policy preferences can affect the walk-away values of the parties, and briefly discuss how this can affect the type of coalition that can be formed (pp. 261–9). Crombez (1996) develops a model focusing on the type of coalition formed, and his results are quite similar: minority governments are more likely the greater the size and ideological centrality of the largest party in parliament. As size and ideological centrality decrease, minimal winning and eventually surplus coalitions become more likely. Warwick (1998), following a somewhat similar logic, suggests that as the ideological polarization of parliament increases, the more likely minority governments are to form, due to the expected lower utility of ideologically diverse governments.

We consider two types of preference variables. The first set of variables measures the distribution of ideological preferences (as in Warwick 1998). We expect that the wider the variation of ideological preferences, the more likely a minority government (as the diversity in policy preferences among government members would make such a government less valuable to its members). The second set of variables is designed to capture the basic contention that the bargaining power of the median party is crucial (as in Crombez 1996; Laver and Shepsle 1996).

Four variables are included to capture the overall diversity of preferences of parties in parliament: the seat share of anti-system parties, effective issue dimensionality (Nyblade 2004), the left-right range of parliamentary preferences (manifesto scores), and left-right polarization (manifesto scores weighted by bargaining power). We include three additional variables to capture the importance of the median position. The first such variable is the bargaining power of the median party, the second is a dummy variable indicating whether there is a party centrally located in policy space ('No Core Party'),[13] and the third captures the distance of the largest party from the median party (cf. Crombez 1996).

Institutions: Shaping government formation

While most research to date has focused on the importance of size and preference variables, a small but growing literature has turned to the effects of institutional rules on coalition formation. Institutions influence coalition bargaining in a number of ways. They do so most directly when they act as constraints (sometimes hard, sometimes soft) on potential coalition formation (see Strøm, Budge, and Laver 1994). Institutions can strongly affect, for example, what constitutes a 'winning' coalition. In countries with bicameral legislatures situations may arise in which an MWC formed in one chamber has insufficient support (for its policy

---

[13] As noted in Chapter 3, this variable more technically captures whether a party is at the dimension-by-dimension median (DDM) and does not actually rely on the more complicated calculations necessary to determine the existence and size of the core (cf. Laver and Shepsle 1996).

agenda or even to survive confidence votes) in the other, necessitating the addition of 'surplus' parties (see Druckman, Martin, and Thies 2005). One of the most frequently noted institutions that affects what constitutes 'winning' is an investiture vote. By forcing a 'Yeah' or 'Nay' by parties in parliament on each government at its very inception, the investiture vote decreases the appeal of ad hoc legislative coalitions. Thus, it may be less feasible to form a viable minority government, which would make majority coalitions more likely (see Bergman 1995).

Other institutional rules may affect the relative value of holding executive office. Following Strøm (1990b) and Müller and Strøm (1999), this effect may primarily be considered in terms of policy and electoral considerations. If parties can successfully influence policy decisions from outside government, then there may be less value in entering government (Strøm 1984). A natural corollary is that if some parties are likely to be relatively less successful at influencing policy from inside the executive branch, government participation should also be less valuable to such parties. For example, the more the institutional decision rules advantage the party of the prime minister relative to other coalition parties, the less appealing it should be to be a junior coalition partner. Conversely, the higher the pay-offs of being in government for all coalition parties, and the more assured the prerogatives and perquisites of all cabinet ministers, the less likely minority governments should be compared to larger government coalitions.

We include three dummy variables in our analyses that might affect what makes a government 'winning': positive parliamentarism (in which an investiture vote is required), the presence of a second chamber and the presence of a semi-presidential system. We also consider three variables that help capture institutional variation in the value of government: a dummy variable for whether a constructive vote of no confidence is required (which could make government more valuable, since it is less likely to fall), an index of the powers of the prime minister over the cabinet and executive (which could make the ability of junior coalition member's to influence policy weaker, and thus government less valuable), and Laver and Hunt's expert survey score (1992) of the degree of opposition influence for each of our countries, which is the converse side of the 'policy influence differential' (Strøm 1990a: 42). While this last measure does not directly measure specific institutions, the correlation with strictly institutional indices is clear (e.g. Forestiere 2002), so we include it in this block.[14]

Bargaining environment

One of our most novel contributions in this chapter (and this book) is that we also consider variables designed to measure crucial aspects of the coalition bargaining

[14] Additionally, Laver and Hunt do not include one country in our data-set, Iceland, in their survey. By comparing the institutional features of the Icelandic parliament to those of other countries, we impute an oppositional influence score of 4 (similar to Sweden, for example). However, our results are robust to the exclusion of Iceland, and to alternative imputations.

process itself and evaluate how they might help predict the type of coalition formed. Thus we seek to incorporate variables that capture aspects of the bargaining environment not perfectly explained by structural attributes, preferences, or institutional variables. In part, we expect these variables to be partly endogenous to the prior variables, but to a certain extent they may help elucidate an important factor that is imperfectly captured in our other variables: situationally specific uncertainty and the value parties place on government membership. We suggest, for example, that inconclusive bargaining rounds indicate a lower value of government participation, while longer coalition formation processes often suggest greater uncertainty, weakness of commitment mechanisms, and potentially differences among parties in time horizons (thus changing the bargaining power of parties).

We include three variables that help capture these aspects of the bargaining environment: a dummy variable indicating whether the prior government was terminated prematurely because of discretionary party behaviour (such as conflict between parties), a second dummy reporting whether there was an inconclusive bargaining round during government formation, and a variable measuring the duration of government formation. Positive values on the first two variables suggest that the value parties place on being in government is relatively low, since both of them involve parties voluntarily terminating or rejecting governments they are (or could be) a part of. Time to formation, on the other hand, captures uncertainty and inability of parties to credibly commit. Thus we expect the first two variables to decrease the likelihood of coalition formation and MWCs or surplus government, while time to formation should increase the likelihood of coalition formation, particularly surplus coalitions.

Critical events

The critical events approach has primarily been applied to understanding government duration rather than government formation, but it is entirely possible that various exogenous 'critical events' may strongly influence coalition formation as well. Parties in government tend to be punished more at the polls than do parties in opposition (Rose and Mackie 1983; Mattila and Raunio 2004; Narud and Valen, this volume), and thus when electoral volatility is high, we expect the value parties place on being in government to be lower than normal. In particular, smaller parties vulnerable at elections might be particularly sensitive to the possibility that entering government might entail greater costs in vote loss than gains in prestige and policy influence. Similarly, critical events that bring down a government should generally indicate that the value of government is comparatively low (at a minimum for one of the parties in the prior government).

For example, during wartime or times of crisis or great uncertainty, grand coalitions are often formed, although as we consider such times to be quite rare in our data-set, we do not include any variable to systematically capture this effect.[15] However, we consider two other variables that capture how exogenous events may affect government formation: the first is whether or not a critical event caused the termination of the immediately prior government. The second variable captures electoral volatility, although not the standard overall electoral volatility measure used in most other chapters in this volume, but instead the average electoral volatility specifically for the cabinet parties in the prior election (see Strøm 1984, 1990a, on the effect of electoral factors on minority government formation). Both of these 'critical event' variables are used to attempt to capture exogenous factors that may influence how parties value government membership—in this case, we expect that when electoral volatility is high and critical events caused the termination of the prior government, the value placed on government membership is low, so we should see a decreased likelihood of coalition formation, and increasing the likelihood of minority governments relative to MWCs and surplus governments.

The next section presents quantitative analyses that examine how these factors can help explain whether a coalition is formed and the type of government formed in parliamentary democracies in Western Europe. We discuss the variables chosen, the statistical methods, and the results in more detail below.

Statistical analyses

In this section, we conduct two sets of statistical analyses concerning government formation in parliamentary democracies when there is no majority party.[16] The first set of analyses uses logistic regression to evaluate the factors that influence whether or not a coalition is formed, the second uses multinomial logistic regression to evaluate the type of government formed (minority, MWC, or surplus).[17]

We use multinomial logistic regression analysis rather than an ordered logit or probit (as in Crombez 1996), because our theoretical expectations (which are empirically confirmed) suggest that certain variables may not fit the ordered model—that is, there may be variables that decrease the probability of MWCs relatively to minority and surplus cabinets, while other variables increase the viability of minority cabinets relative to MWCs and surplus cabinets. This makes any statistical assumption that the types can be ranked in any consistent order (e.g. MWCs falling in between minority and surplus coalitions) problematic.

---

[15] We do this in part because we do not wish to risk circular reasoning in coding such a variable. This chapter also excludes economic variables that are used in the critical events block in some other chapters. We have considered and discarded them for this chapter, as they prove to be insignificant and entail a substantial reduction in our number of observations.

[16] Excluding majority situations potentially could create selection bias, however analysis by Kalandrakis (2002) suggests that this is not a major problem.

[17] In addition to majority situations, we exclude non-partisan 'caretaker' governments from our analyses. These governments are very rare (9 in our data-set, of which 7 are from Finland), so that our methods would not be appropriate for analysing their causes.

Multinominal logits also allow greater nuance in the results compared with the more common analyses of minority or surplus governments that collapse two of the three government type categories and perform logit or probit analyses (as in Kalandrakis 2002; Carubba and Volden 2004).

The results for our logistic regression on the likelihood of coalition government are reported in Table 6.4, and the multinomial regression results are reported in Table 6.5. We use a common set of independent variables for both standard and multinomial logits, arranged into the blocks discussed above and in Chapter 3 of this volume. We run each block of independent variables separately and then full models that include the significant variables from each block. We discuss the specific variables for each model below, recapping briefly the theoretical predictions for each specific variable and then discussing the results for both the logit analysis of coalition formation and the multinomial logit analysis of government type.

Model 1: Time and space variables

As is standard for this volume, our first block includes decade dummy variables and evaluates whether any of the trends over time, noted earlier in our discussion of Figure 6.1, are significant. However, the results for both coalition formation and government type suggest that the differences among decades in coalition formation and government type are not statistically significant.

However, while time trends give relatively little leverage on coalition formation, cross-national variation is substantially greater. Whereas a baseline model that predicts coalition formation in every minority situation is correct 70 per cent of the time, the decade dummies marginally improve this to 73 per cent, while a country dummy model would change this baseline prediction for Norway, Sweden, Spain, and Great Britain, improving predictive accuracy to almost 80 per cent, albeit in a rather atheoretical fashion. For the prediction of government type, a multinomial logit with only a constant would be correct only 42 per cent of the time (cases of minority cabinets). Decade dummies would improve this to 44 per cent, while atheoretical country dummies would improve the baseline model substantially, to roughly 65 per cent. As we will see, however, our theoretically derived variables outperform these atheoretical predictions.

Model 2: Structural attributes

We consider five structural attribute variables in this block, three of which capture the size and number of parties: largest party seat share, largest party bargaining power, and absolute number of parties. The results for these three variables are largely as expected. Both the seat share and bargaining power of the largest party have a negative impact on the probability of coalition formation, though only the

TABLE 6.4. *Logistic regressions on coalition formation in minority situations*

Independent variables	Model 1	Model 2	Model 3	Model 4	Model 5	Model 6	Model 7	Model 8	Impact[a]
Time									
1940s	−0.14 (0.52)								
1960s	−0.15 (0.42)								
1970s	−0.27 (0.39)								
1980s	0.15 (0.41)								
1990s	0.25 (0.45)								
Structure									
Largest party seat share		−1.55 (3.12)							
Largest party barg. power		−7.14 (1.41)**						−5.05 (1.94)**	−5.87 (1.80)** −0.13 (0.04)[a]
Abs. no. of parties		0.00 (0.06)							
Follows election		−0.04 (0.37)							
Max. potential duration		−0.01 (0.00)							
Preferences									
Anti-system seat share			0.01 (0.01)						
Parliamentary pref. range			−0.01 (0.01)*						
Polarization (BP wtd.)			0.05 (0.03)				−0.01 (0.01)		
Issue dimensionality			1.02 (0.57)*				0.05 (0.04)		
No core party			1.08 (0.29)**				0.61 (0.79)		
Median party barg. power			−2.48 (0.76)**				0.19 (0.43)		
Largest party dist. to med.			−0.01 (0.01)				−3.16 (1.35)**	−3.12 (1.19)** −0.08 (0.04)[a]
Institutions									
Positive parliamentarism				0.85 (0.35)**			0.95 (0.50)*	0.77 (0.45)*	0.06 (0.04)
Semi-presidentialism				0.68 (0.41)*			0.95 (0.67)	0.94 (0.56)*	0.07 (0.04)
Bicameralism				−0.28 (0.32)					
Constructive no-confidence				−0.60 (0.58)					
PM powers				−0.20 (0.08)**			−0.08 (0.14)		
Opposition influence				−0.38 (0.11)**			−0.19 (0.17)	−0.20 (0.12)*	−0.02 (0.01)

(*cont.*)

TABLE 6.4. (Continued)

Independent variables	Model 1	Model 2	Model 3	Model 4	Model 5	Model 6	Model 7	Model 8	Impact[a]
Bargaining									
Behavioural termination					−0.35 (0.27)		−0.38 (0.38)		
Inconclusive bargaining					−0.65 (0.30)**		−1.99 (0.44)**	−1.91 (0.42)**	−0.36 (0.09)
Cabinet bargaining duration					0.03 (0.01)**		0.03 (0.01)**	0.03 (0.01)**	0.07 (0.03)[a]
Critical Events									
Cab. electoral volatility						−0.07 (0.04)*	−0.14 (0.06)**	−0.15 (0.05)**	−0.02 (0.01)
Critical event lag						−1.36 (0.36)**	−0.97 (0.48)**	−1.15 (0.44)**	−0.18 (0.09)
Constant	1.01 (0.30)**	5.12 (1.26)**	−1.56 (1.68)	3.35 (0.74)**	0.74 (0.23)**	1.33 (0.17)**	4.16 (2.88)	5.96 (1.03)**	
Number of observations	340	339	328	340	331	312	311	311	
Pseudo-R^2	.01	.18	.14	.07	.08	.05	.36	.35	
% Correctly predicted	.73	.80	.80	.73	.73	.74	.86	.85	

Notes: *p < 0.10; **p < 0.05.

[a] Impact is the marginal effect of a unit change in the independent variable on the probability of the outcome occurring, calculated based on Model 8, with the following exceptions: the impact of Largest party bargaining power is for a 0.15 change, the impact of Median party bargaining power is for a 0.20 change, and the impact of Cabinet bargaining power is a 30 day change (1 standard deviation changes).

TABLE 6.5. *Multinomial logistic regressions of government type*

a. MWC vs. Minority

Independent variables	Model 1	Model 2	Model 3	Model 4	Model 5	Model 6	Model 7	Model 8	Impact[a]
Time									
1940s	−0.05 (0.56)								
1960s	0.30 (0.41)								
1970s	−0.28 (0.41)								
1980s	−0.09 (0.41)								
1990s	0.44 (0.42)								
Structure									
Largest party seat share		3.82 (2.99)					0.18 (4.59)		
Largest party barg. power		−8.91 (1.59)**					−4.97 (2.16)**	−5.29 (1.82)**	−0.17 (0.06)[a]
Abs. no. of parties		−0.20 (0.07)**					−0.07 (0.10)		
Follows election		0.26 (0.38)					0.26 (0.40)		
Max. potential duration		0.00 (0.01)							
Preferences									
Anti-system seat share			−0.07 (0.02)**				−0.05 (0.03)*		
Parliamentary pref. range			−0.04 (0.01)**				−0.02 (0.01)*		
Polarization (BP wtd.)			0.10 (0.04)**				0.06 (0.04)	0.02 (0.02)	0.03 (0.05)[a]
Issue dimensionality			1.73 (0.60)**				1.07 (0.82)		
No core party			0.98 (0.29)**				0.63 (0.49)	1.07 (0.44)**	0.28 (0.09)
Median party barg. power			−1.08 (0.79)				−1.47 (1.46)	−1.48 (1.30)	−0.06 (0.06)[a]
Largest party dist. to med.			−0.01 (0.01)						
Institutions									
Positive parliamentarism				0.26 (0.36)			0.77 (0.57)	0.26 (0.47)	−0.04 (0.11)
Semi-presidentialism				−0.43 (0.41)			0.58 (0.78)	−0.35 (0.51)	−0.19 (0.10)
Bicameralism				−0.38 (0.32)					
Constructive no-confidence				−0.22 (0.57)					
PM powers				−0.04 (0.08)			0.17 (0.16)	0.32 (0.13)**	0.09 (0.03)
Opposition influence				−0.69 (0.12)**			−0.24 (0.20)	−0.44 (0.16)**	−0.10 (0.04)

(cont.)

TABLE 6.5. *(Continued)*

b. Surplus vs. Minority

Independent variables	Model 1	Model 2	Model 3	Model 4	Model 5	Model 6	Model 7	Model 8	Impact[a]
Bargaining									
Behavioural termination					−0.96(0.27)**		−1.20(0.40)**	−1.39(0.36)**	−0.29(0.07)
Inconclusive bargaining					−0.56(0.30)*		−1.09(0.43)**	−0.98(0.41)**	−0.21(0.09)
Cabinet bargaining duration					0.03(0.01)**		0.02(0.01)**	0.02(0.01)**	0.13(0.05)[a]
Critical events									
Cab. electoral volatility						0.02(0.04)	−0.10(0.05)**	−0.10(0.05)*	−0.02(0.01)
Critical event lag						−1.25(0.43)**	−0.93(0.57)*		
Constant	−0.17(0.30)	3.08(1.22)**	−4.33(1.74)**	3.52(0.78)**	0.09(0.23)	−0.01(0.17)	1.07(3.71)	3.56(1.50)**	
Time									
1940s	0.81(0.59)								
1960s	−0.14(0.56)								
1970s	0.25(0.48)								
1980s	0.61(0.47)								
1990s	0.00(0.56)								
Structure									
Largest party seat share		−4.50(3.85)					−1.18(6.77)		
Largest party barg. power		−6.54(2.26)**					−5.05(3.70)	−6.24(2.93)**	−0.03(0.02)[a]
Abs. no. of parties		0.10(0.06)					0.12(0.12)		
Follows election		−0.65(0.44)					−0.55(0.52)		
Max. potential duration		0.00(0.01)							
Preferences									
Anti-system seat share			0.05(0.01)**				0.04(0.03)		
Parliamentary pref. range			−0.01(0.01)				−0.02(0.02)		
Polarization (BP wtd.)			0.02(0.04)				0.00(0.05)	−0.06(0.03)*	−0.05(0.04)[a]

	Model 1	Model 2	Model 3	Model 4	Model 5	Model 6	Model 7	Marginal effect
Issue dimensionality		0.62 (0.68)				−0.73 (1.12)		
No core party		1.20 (0.34)**				−1.34 (0.71)*	−1.39 (0.65)**	−0.20 (0.10)
Median party barg. power		−2.55 (1.02)**				−4.52 (2.13)**	−3.60 (1.81)**	−0.02 (0.02)[a]
Largest party dist. to med.		0.00 (0.01)						
Institutions								
Positive parliamentarism			1.36 (0.43)**			1.32 (0.73)*	1.78 (0.57)**	0.17 (0.07)
Semi-presidentialism			1.72 (0.46)**			2.00 (0.97)**	1.99 (0.66)**	0.27 (0.11)
Bicameralism			0.37 (0.42)					
Constructive no-confidence			−1.25 (1.17)					
PM powers			−0.45 (0.10)**			−0.31 (0.20)	−0.48 (0.17)**	−0.03 (0.01)
Opposition influence			−0.40 (0.12)**			−0.65 (0.26)**	−0.43 (0.19)**	−0.01 (0.01)
Bargaining								
Behavioural termination				−0.43 (0.32)		−1.07 (0.47)**	−0.77 (0.44)*	0.01 (0.02)
Inconclusive bargaining				−0.24 (0.35)		−1.44 (0.51)**	−1.40 (0.48)**	−0.03 (0.02)
Cabinet bargaining duration				0.04 (0.01)**		0.03 (0.01)**	0.03 (0.01)**	0.04 (0.02)[a]
Critical events								
Cab. electoral volatility					−0.34 (0.11)**	−0.21 (0.11)**	−0.23 (0.11)**	−0.01 (0.01)
Critical event lag					−1.58 (0.64)*	−0.47 (0.82)		
Constant	−0.92 (0.37)**	2.87 (1.24)**	−2.50 (1.95)	1.60 (0.82)*	−0.04 (0.21)	10.1 (4.97)**	7.80 (1.96)**	
Number of observations	340	339	328	340	312	311	311	
Pseudo-R^2	.02	.20	.17	.16	.05	.38	.34	
% Correctly predicted	.44	.61	.60	.57	.46	.70	.68	

Notes: *$p < 0.10$; **$p < 0.05$.

[a] Impact is the marginal effect of a unit change in the independent variable on the probability of an outcome occurring, calculated based on Model 8, with the following exceptions: the impact of Largest party bargaining power is for a 0.15 change, the impact of Polarization (BP weighted) is for a 10 point change. Median party bargaining power is for a 0.20 change, and the impact of Cabinet bargaining duration is a 30 day change (all 1 standard deviation changes).

latter effect is statistically significant (see Table 6.4). The absolute number of parties has no impact on whether a coalition is formed. Largest party bargaining power also increases the likelihood of minority governments relative to both MWCs and surplus governments, but the effect of seat share (controlling for bargaining power) is not significant (see Tables 6.5a and 6.5b). The absolute number of parties decreases the likelihood of MWCs relative to minority governments, but has no effect on the incidence of surplus coalition formation.

We also consider two structural variables concerning the timing of government formation: a dummy variable to capture whether the government is the first following an election, and a variable capturing the maximum potential duration of government (in days). We expect that the 'follows election' variable to capture lower uncertainty concerning voter preferences, while the latter captures the greater value attached to governments that have a longer potential duration. We expect both to increase the likelihood of coalition formation and, more specifically, MWCs. However, neither variable is significant.

Model 3: Preferences

We consider two types of preference-related measures: those that capture preference diversity and those related to the power of the median party. In predicting coalition formation, the range of parliamentary preferences and issue dimensionality are marginally significant, the former decreasing the likelihood of coalition formation, the latter increasing it. The measures capturing the importance of the median party are more significant. The absence of a party at the dimension-by-dimension median significantly increases the likelihood of a coalition formation, while the bargaining power of the party at the left-right median significantly decreases the likelihood of coalition formation (Table 6.4).

The results for government type (Tables 6.5a and 6.5b) are somewhat different from those for coalition government for the preference diversity measures, and many of the results significant in the block are not robust in models that include variables from other blocks. In the block, anti-system party seat share increases the likelihood of a surplus coalition, while decreasing the likelihood of an MWC forming. This result is not robust in subsequent models, and we suspect it is largely an artefact of a few outliers (particularly Italian ones). Greater issue dimensionality increases the likelihood of an MWC forming (relative to a minority cabinet), but again the result is not robust. Also only in the block, a greater range of preferences of parliamentary parties decreases the probability of an MWC forming, while the index of bargaining power weighted by polarization increases the likelihood of an MWC.

The bargaining power of the median party and the absence of a core party produce more significant and robust results. Consistently across our models, the greater the bargaining power of the median party, the less likely surplus coalitions are relative to minority cabinets. In all our models, the absence of a party at the core makes MWCs more likely relative to minority governments, but the effect of the absence of a core on the likelihood of surplus coalitions changes across the models. In model 3, the absence of a party at the core makes surplus coalitions more likely than minority governments, but in models 7 and 8, the absence of a party at the core makes a surplus coalition less likely than a minority government. This reversal seems to be largely a result of including the largest party bargaining power variable, suggesting that the effect of the presence or absence of a large central party on the type of government formed may be contingent on bargaining power fragmentation.

Model 4: Institutions

The results for the institutional block are generally consistent with our expectations, though the effects of many variables are not strong or statistically significant, and the institutional variables explain less of the difference between MWCs and minority governments than they do of other aspects of government formation in which we are interested. Prime minister cabinet powers and opposition influence decrease the likelihood of a coalition, though the former result is not robust in the final model. Positive parliamentarism (in which an investiture vote is required) increases the likelihood of a coalition, as does semi-presidentialism. As expected, however, when we consider the effects on the type of government formed, our results are largely driven by the impact of institutions on the likelihood of surplus coalitions. Semi-presidentialism and the requirement of an investiture vote both make oversized governments more likely than minority cabinets, while opposition influence and prime minister powers make minority governments more likely than surplus administrations (Table 6.5b). In Table 6.5a, only opposition influence similarly increases the likelihood of minority relative to MWC governments.[18]

Model 5: Bargaining variables

Model 5 introduces three variables that attempt to capture aspects of the bargaining environment in a more nuanced manner than has been done in prior analyses. Two of the three bargaining variables we consider (inconclusive bargaining round, time to government formation) are significant in explaining whether or not a coalition is formed, both in the predicted direction. Inconclusive bargaining rounds decrease the likelihood of coalitions and increase the likelihood of minority governments, as would be consistent with an interpretation of this variable indicating a lower value being placed on office holding. Furthermore, an interesting finding from the multinomial logits is that these bargaining environment variables better explain minority government formation (relative to MWCs and

---

[18] An interesting result is that PM powers in the final model of Table 6.5a decreases the likelihood of a minority government relative to an MWC. One possible explanation is that strong PM cabinet powers are an additional indication of weak opposition influence.

surplus coalitions) than help explain the formation of surplus coalitions (relative to MWCs or minority cabinets). Only time to formation is significant in explaining surplus governments, which is consistent with our argument that longer duration represents informational uncertainties and difficulty in credibly committing to potential coalition partners.

Model 6: Critical events

The two critical event variables that we expect to decrease the expected value of government (cabinet party electoral volatility and critical event lag) have the expected effect: both variables decrease the likelihood of coalition formation and increase the probability of minority governments relative to surplus governments. However, while the terminal event lag decreases the likelihood of an MWC relative to a minority government, electoral volatility has no effect on the probability of an MWC versus minority government. The findings in this block as well as in model 5 suggest that variables that influence the value parties place on government participation may strongly influence whether or not a coalition forms and the type of cabinet that takes office.

Models 7 and 8: Complete models

Naturally, we do not simply wish to consider each of our sets of explanatory variables in isolation—the purpose of our multivariate analysis is to directly compare the predictive power of competing explanations in the same model. Our final two models include the significant variables from the previous blocks: model 7 includes all significant (or close to significant) variables, while model 8 simplifies model 7 by removing those variables that are not robust or no longer close to standard levels of statistical significance. After presenting these two final models, we discuss the impact of individual variables and the overall explanatory powers of our multivariate analyses before concluding.

Model 7 of Table 6.4 is our most complete model to test which variables predict coalition formation. It includes only one structural variable (the largest party bargaining power), but most variables from models 2 to 6. Most of the variables that were significant in the initial blocks remain significant in model 7. The exceptions are primarily from the preferences and institutions blocks, including parliamentary preference range, issue dimensionality, no core party and opposition influence, which are dropped in a more parsimonious and final model 8.

More variables are brought over into the final two models in the analysis of the type of government formation in Table 6.5 than in the analysis of coalition formation in Table 6.4. Not surprisingly, a larger number of variables do not stand up to the 'competition' of being in the full model, as again all the structural variables except the largest party bargaining power, most of the preference variables (except polarization, no core party, and median party bargaining power) and the critical event lag are not robust enough to be included in the final model.

The final columns in our statistical tables report the marginal impact of changing a single variable on the probability of a coalition being formed (Table 6.4), the likelihood of an MWC forming (Table 6.5a), and the likelihood of a surplus coalition being formed (Table 6.5b). To highlight a few of the more interesting findings, it is worth noting that one or more inconclusive bargaining rounds decrease the likelihood of coalition formation by 36 percentage points, a result primarily attributable to decreasing the likelihood of an MWC forming by 21 percentage points. Increasing the bargaining power of the largest party in parliament by 1 standard deviation (0.15 points using the Banzhaf index) decreases the likelihood of a coalition by 13 per cent and that of an MWC by 17 per cent. Increasing the bargaining power of the median party in parliament by 1 standard deviation (0.20 points on the Banzhaf index) decreases the likelihood of a surplus coalition by 20 per cent, while positive parliamentarism increases it by 17 percentage points and semi-presidentialism by 27 percentage points.

Overall, our more theoretically driven models represent a substantial improvement from baseline predictions at the full sample or the country level, predicting whether or not a coalition forms correctly nearly 85 per cent of the time in models 7 and 8. Somewhat more than half of the increase in explanatory power comes from the structural and preference variables, particularly the bargaining power of the largest and median parties. Although the effect of the institutional, bargaining, and critical event variables is smaller, it increases predictive accuracy from roughly 80 to 85 per cent.

The predictive power of our models for government type is, not surprisingly, somewhat weaker than that for coalition formation, as shown by the percentage of observations correctly predicted. Our independent variables again outperform atheoretical country-based predictions, with our full model (model 7), correctly predicting the type of government in 70 per cent of our cases. Again, somewhat more than half of our improvement in predictive accuracy can be attributed to structural and preference variables, but more than two-fifths of the explanatory power in the final model is due to institutional, bargaining, and critical event variables. We address the implications of this, and several of the implications concerning specific variables, in the conclusion below.

CONCLUSION

Two propositions form the basic underpinnings of our understanding of coalition formation in parliamentary democracies. The first, concerning the general bargaining situation, suggests that when coalition bargaining is similar to that of a classical fixed pay-off, complete information bargaining game, a minimum winning coalition is more likely to form. The second, concerning the distribution of bargaining power, suggests that the greater the bargaining power of a single party, the less likely a coalition is to form, whereas when bargaining power is more dispersed, larger coalitions are more likely.

Our results generally confirm both propositions. The first proposition implies several corollaries, and we find support for all three. When government formation can only be achieved by overcoming a higher 'winning' threshold, coalitions are more likely than single-party government, and when coalitions do form they are more likely to be surplus-majority coalitions. Specifically, an investiture vote makes a coalition government significantly more likely, and semi-presidentialism, which makes the government accountable to other actors, also increases the likelihood of a surplus coalition. In support of our second corollary, it is important to note that bargaining duration (a measure of uncertainty and/or the challenge of credible commitment) increases the likelihood of a coalition relative to a single-party government, and that it also increases the probability of both MWCs and surplus coalitions (relative to minority governments).

The third corollary gets the most consistent support in our analyses: the less valuable government is, the more likely a minority government (consistent with Strøm 1990a). Both opposition influence and electoral volatility significantly reduce the likelihood of a coalition government, particularly increasing the likelihood of minority governments. Cabinet electoral volatility and the previous government being terminated because of an exogenous critical event also make MWCs less likely compared to minority governments.

The support for our second proposition is even stronger than for the first. In our analyses, the variables most robust to changes in our model specifications are those that pertain to the bargaining power of the largest and median parties. If the largest party is close to a parliamentary majority, has many potential coalition options (while its rivals have few), and particularly when it is located at the median, the party can dominate government formation, and it frequently will avoid coalitions and form a government on its own. This result, though not a direct test of the predictions of Laver and Shepsle (1996) concerning strong and very strong parties, is clearly consistent with that work. By contrast, our results do not consistently support the models and empirical tests of Crombez (1996) or Warwick (1998) concerning the distance of the largest party from the median and the polarization of parliament, respectively. This may be due to the use of different measures of party ideal points, or perhaps to the fact that we have controlled for a large number of explanatory variables not employed by earlier scholars.

The literature on government formation is extensive and has shown substantial development over the past few decades, making it one of the areas in political science in which progress is most readily apparent (cf. Strøm and Nyblade 2007). However, there remains substantial work to be done. This chapter has emphasized that even when scholars focus on a range of explanatory variables that are generally held in contrast to each other (party size, ideology, institutions, and bargaining environment), it is both possible and useful to bring them all under a unified theoretical perspective.

Much remains to be done in this regard, both theoretically and empirically. Theoretically, there remains further room for more sophisticated modelling of the interactions between the various types of explanatory variables used to understand coalition formation. Furthermore, although in this volume, we begin to explore the relationship between the government formation stage of the parliamentary life cycle and other stages, we recognize that the field is only in the relatively early stages of developing sophisticated theories and empirical tests of the relationships between cabinet formation and other aspects of cabinet governance.

More concretely, our chapter suggests a number of potential fruitful lines for future research. For example, we have found that inconclusive bargaining rounds and bargaining duration have an important impact on the type of government formed. More rigorous testing of this relationship, perhaps using a two-stage statistical model in which the determinants of inconclusive bargaining rounds are analysed in the first round (building on the work of De Winter and Dumont in Chapter 4), would improve our understanding of these effects. Similarly, while we have found that relying on bargaining power indices gives us greater predictive power than more traditional seat-share-based measures (such as the effective number of parties), there is no doubt more that can be done to improve the match between our theoretical understanding of coalition formation and our empirical measures of those concepts. The study of cabinet formation should thus remain a fruitful area for a great deal of future research.

REFERENCES

Axelrod, Robert (1970). *Conflict of Interest*. Chicago, IL: Markham.
Bäck, Hanna (2003). *Explaining Coalitions. Evidence and Lessons From Studying Coalition Formation in Swedish Local Government*. Uppsala: Uppsala Universitet.
—— and Dumont, Patrick (2007). 'Combining Large-n and Small-n Strategies: The Way Forward in Coalition Research', *West European Politics*, 30 (3): 467–501.
Bergman, Torbjörn (1993). 'Formation Rules and Minority Governments', *European Journal of Political Research*, 23: 55–66.
Browne, Eric C. (1973). *Coalition Theories: A Logical and Empirical Critique*. Beverly Hills, CA: Sage.
Budge, Ian and Keman, Hans (1990). *Parties and Democracy: Coalition Formation and Government Functioning in Twenty States*. Oxford: Oxford University Press.
Carrubba, Clifford J. and Volden, Crag (2000). 'Coalitional Politics and Logrolling in Legislative Institutions', *American Journal of Political Science*, 44: 261–77.
Crombez, Christophe (1996). 'Minority Governments, Minimal Winning Coalitions and Surplus Majorities in Parliamentary Systems', *European Journal of Political Research*, 29: 1–29.

De Swaan, Abram (1973). *Coalition Theories and Cabinet Formations.* Amsterdam: Elsevier.

Druckman, James N., Martin, Lanny W., and Thies, Michael F. (2005). 'Influence Without Confidence: Upper Chambers and Government Formation', *Legislative Studies Quarterly*, 30: 529–48.

Forestiere, Carolyn (2002). 'The Second Game: The Opposition in Parliamentary Democracies', paper presented at the 2002 Annual Meetings of the American Political Science Association.

Franklin, Mark N. and Mackie, Thomas T. (1984). 'Reassessing the Importance of Size and Ideology for the Formation of Government Coalitions in Parliamentary Democracies', *American Journal of Political Science*, 28: 671–92.

Gamson, William A. (1961). 'A Theory of Coalition Formation', *American Sociological Review*, 26: 373–82.

Herman, Valentine and Pope, John (1973). 'Minority Governments in Western Democracies', *British Journal of Political Science*, 3: 191–212.

Kalandrakis, Tasos (2002). 'Minority Governments: Ideology and Office', manuscript, Yale University.

Laver, Michael and Hunt, Ben W. (1992). *Policy and Party Competition.* New York, NY: Routledge.

—— and Schofield, Norman (1990). *Multiparty Government.* Oxford: Oxford University Press.

—— and Shepsle, Kenneth A. (1990). 'Coalitions and Cabinet Government', *American Political Science Review*, 84: 873–90.

—— —— (1996). *Making and Breaking Governments: Cabinets and Legislatures in Parliamentary Democracies.* Cambridge: Cambridge University Press.

—— —— (1999a). 'Understanding Government Survival: Empirical Exploration or Analytical Models?', *British Journal of Political Science*, 29: 395–401.

—— —— (1999b). 'Government Formation and Survival: A Rejoinder to Warwick's Reply', *British Journal of Political Science*, 29: 412–15.

—— —— (2000). 'Ministrables and Government Formation', *Journal of Theoretical Politics*, 12: 113–24.

Leiserson, Michael (1966). 'Coalitions in Politics: A Theoretical and Empirical Study', Ph.D. dissertation, Yale University.

Martin, Lanny W. and Stevenson, Randolph T. (2001). 'Government Formation in Parliamentary Democracies', *American Journal of Political Science*, 45: 33–50.

Mattila, Mikko and Raunio, Tapio (2004). 'Does Winning Pay? Electoral Success and Government Formation in 15 West European Countries', *European Journal of Political Research*, 43: 263–85.

Müller, Wolfgang C. and Strøm, Kaare (eds.) (1999). *Policy, Office, or Votes? How Political Parties in Western Europe Make Hard Decisions.* Cambridge: Cambridge University Press.

Nyblade, Benjamin (2004). 'The "Effective" Number of Issue Dimensions: A Measure With Application to West Europe', paper presented at the Annual Meetings of the Midwest Political Science Association.

Riker, William H. (1962). *The Theory of Political Coalitions.* New Haven, CT: Yale University Press.

Robertson, David (1986). *A Theory of Political Competition.* London: Wiley.

Rose, Richard and Mackie, Thomas T. (1983). 'Incumbency in Government: Asset or Liability?', in Hans Daalder and Peter Mair (eds.), *Western European Party Systems: Continuity & Change*. London: Sage.

Sartori, Giovanni (1976). *Parties and Party Systems: A Framework for Analysis*. Cambridge: Cambridge University Press.

Schofield, Norman (1993). 'Political Competition in Multiparty Coalition Governments', *European Journal of Political Research*, 23: 1–33.

Sened, Itai (1996). 'A Model of Coalition Formation: Theory and Evidence', *Journal of Politics*, 58: 350–72.

Strøm, Kaare (1984). 'Minority Governments in Parliamentary Democracies: The Rationality of Nonwinning Cabinet Solutions', *Comparative Political Studies*, 17: 199–227.

—— (1990a). *Minority Government and Majority Rule*. Cambridge: Cambridge University Press.

—— (1990b). 'A Behavioral Theory of Competitive Political Parties', *American Journal of Political Science*, 34: 565–98.

—— and Nyblade, Benjamin (2007). 'Coalition Theory and Government Formation', in Carles Boix and Susan Stokes (eds.), *Oxford Handbook of Comparative Politics*. Oxford: Oxford University Press.

—— Budge, Ian, and Laver, Michael J. (1994). 'Constraints on Cabinet Formation in Parliamentary Democracies', *American Journal of Political Science*, 38: 303–35.

Taylor, Michael and Laver, Michael (1973). 'Government Coalitions in Western Europe', *European Journal of Political Research*, 1: 205–48.

Volden, Craig and Carrubba, Clifford J. 'The Formation of Oversize Coalitions in Parliamentary Democracies', *American Journal of Political Science*, 48: 521–37.

Warwick, Paul V. (1996). 'Coalition Government Membership in West European Parliamentary Democracies', *British Journal of Political Science*, 26: 471–99.

—— (1998). 'Policy Distance and Parliamentary Government', *Legislative Studies Quarterly*, 23: 319–45.

—— (1999a). 'Ministerial Autonomy or Ministerial Accommodation? Contested Bases of Government Survival in Parliamentary Democracies', *British Journal of Political Science*, 29: 369–94.

—— (1999b). 'Getting the Assumptions Right: A Reply to Laver and Shepsle', *British Journal of Political Science*, 29: 402–12.

Warwick, Paul (2005). 'When For Apart Becomes Too Far Apart: Evidence for a Threshold Effect in Coalition Formation', *British Journal of Political Science*, 35: 383–401.

7

Portfolio Allocation

Luca Verzichelli

INTRODUCTION: THE PROBLEM OF 'WHO GETS WHAT?'

One of the first things parties entering a government coalition do is to decide how they will share the ministerial offices among themselves. Without reaching agreement on this issue, no coalition can take office. Although cabinet portfolios are only the tip of the iceberg of allocation decisions that coalition parties have to make, they are probably the most important ones. And it is easy to understand why portfolio allocation is important. Cabinet ministers are among the most important policymakers in parliamentary democracies, and ministerial offices are one of the most important pay-offs available to political parties. Political parties care about the ministries at their disposal and so do individual politicians. Although the number of such posts may vary between countries and over time, ministerial offices are position goods and rank among the most exclusive ones. The more cabinet seats a party has at its disposal, the more policy influence it can have, and the more party leaders can see their career ambitions fulfilled. It is hard to imagine a politician who does not value cabinet office. Ministerial office is typically the apex of a political career, and it is an appointment that often affords the holder considerable policy influence. Moreover, ministerial portfolios are the key to many lower-level appointments in the public sector.

Coalition theorists have long recognized the lure of ministerial office. Pure 'office-driven' theories of political coalitions assume that the thirst for ministerial office is sufficient to explain the coalitional behaviour of parties. Parties, it is posited, prefer government participation to opposition and aim at the coalition that guarantees them the greatest share of government offices. There are many reasons that party leaders seek ministerial office. One is the personal perquisites, status, or wealth that such appointments may bring them. Yet, office may be valued not only because of its intrinsic qualities but because it is a necessary prerequisite for exercising policy influence (Budge and Laver 1986; Laver and Schofield 1990: 55–8). While most coalition theories see this condition satisfied with government membership, Laver and Shepsle (1990, 1996) have tied opportunities for policy influence more closely to the specific jurisdictions of ministerial departments.

If policy influence depends strongly or wholly on holding a specific cabinet portfolio, then the allocation of government departments among the coalition parties is a critical process. And we would expect policy-seeking parties to form and maintain coalitions that provide them with the government departments most closely associated with their policy concerns. Thus, parties may care about their *qualitative,* as well as quantitative, allocation of cabinet positions.

A comprehensive investigation of qualitative as well as quantitative aspects of portfolio allocation is beyond the scope of this chapter. Yet, we shall give an overview of portfolio allocation in the 17 countries in our sample and address three specific questions about cabinet portfolios. First, we examine the 'proportionality norm' in portfolio allocation, which has been the most prominent feature of the portfolio allocation literature, and ask what accounts for this pattern, or for deviations from it. Specifically, we explain deviations from the well-established result that cabinet seats are allocated to coalition parties in proportion to the seats these respective parties contribute to the coalition's parliamentary support base.

Our second question concerns the size of the 'pie' to be shared by the coalition parties. Typically, studies of portfolio allocation proceed from the assumption that the total number of cabinet portfolios is fixed. In this chapter, we show that this is not true, and that changes in the number of cabinet portfolios from one cabinet to the next are common. We then go on to identify the determinants of such variation.

Finally, our third focus is on politicians and offices that just fail to be included in the cabinet, but that may nevertheless be critically important for coalition policy-making. While ministerial posts are the most important currency in government formation, they are not the only one. The third focus of this chapter is thus on the distribution of junior ministers. In so doing we concentrate on those junior ministers, the so-called 'watchdogs', that are located in ministries headed by a senior minister from some other party (see Müller and Strøm 2000: 24; Thies 2001). Before addressing these questions empirically, however, we briefly review the literature on portfolio allocation, focusing on its most striking and famous result.

THE PROPORTIONALITY NORM

Much of the literature on portfolio allocation is dominated by a single, powerful empirical regularity: the existence of a 'natural' proportionality in the division of government offices among coalition partners. This regularity was first briefly observed by Gamson (1961: 376) and later fully fleshed out in a seminal article by Browne and Franklin (1973) (who dubbed it the 'parity norm'). While Gamson (1961) predicted that each coalition party would receive a share of the payoffs proportional to the amount of resources that it contributes to a coalition,

Browne and Franklin (1973: 457) reformulated this proposition in operational terms: 'The percentage share of ministries received by a party participating in a governing coalition and the percentage share of that party's coalition seats will be proportional on a one-to-one basis.'

Browne and Franklin tested this proportionality proposition against data from 13 European democracies for the 1945–69 period (63 parties, 114 coalitions). They found that 85 per cent of the variation in portfolio pay-offs could be explained by differences in the share of legislative seats among the government parties (1973: 460). As Browne and Franklin (1973: 460) pointed out: 'Seldom in the social sciences does one find a simple bivariate relationship which is both theoretically meaningful and also able to explain such a high proportion of variance.' Several other studies have confirmed the *proportionality norm* (Bueno de Mesquita 1979; Browne and Frendreis 1980; Schofield and Laver 1985; Budge and Keman 1990). Laver and Schofield (1990: 193) called it 'one of the most striking non-trivial empirical relationship in political science'. De Winter (2001: 190) refers to the proportionality of portfolio allocation as an 'iron law'. For Warwick and Druckman (2001), the one-to-one proportionality between the division of cabinet portfolios and the seat shares of the participating parties is 'one of the most impressive empirical findings in all of social science' (2001: 627).

Yet, the proportionality norm does not *fully* account for the allocation of government portfolios. Specifically, Browne and Franklin (1973) found that there was a slight bias in favour of small parties and that the party of the prime minister tended to be under-compensated (see also Bueno de Mesquita 1979: 71). Almost three decades later, and with a substantially different data-set, Warwick and Druckman (2005) reproduced a virtually identical result for the small-party bias. Warwick and Druckman (2001: 643) also showed that the undercompensation of formateurs is even substantially greater than in the Browne and Franklin results. Druckman and Roberts (2005) found that the West European pattern is largely reproduced in the more advanced East European countries. Even so, proportionality is by far the dominant regularity in portfolio allocation in parliamentary democracies.

The proportionality norm is first and foremost an *empirical* regularity. Its theoretical underpinnings have remained ambiguous. It is easy to see its *normative* foundation: fairness. Proportionality means that each coalition party is rewarded in proportion to its contribution to the parliamentary strength of the government, which corresponds to many people's ideas of fairness.[1] But there is little reason to think that party leaders are motivated by such abstract and altruistic ideas in their bargaining over cabinet portfolios. Thus, there are at least three reasons why we should expect real-world portfolio allocation to deviate from full proportionality: (*a*) Bargaining theory tells us that what should ultimately matter in coalition negotiations is bargaining power, and a party's bargaining power may be quite different from its size. (*b*) The proportionality norm treats all cabinet portfolios

---

[1] Fairness, of course, is a complex issue that cannot always be so easily resolved (see Brams 2006).

as equal and interchangeable, but in reality cabinet posts are quite different from one another. Moreover, different parties may vary substantially in their valuation of the same portfolio. (*c*) Proportionality may be difficult to attain simply because of the technical problems of dividing a small number of indivisible units among several, at times as many as five or seven, parties. Let us therefore consider each of these objections successively.

Bargaining power

There are thus powerful reasons that we should *not* expect a proportional division of cabinet portfolios. The most obvious one is that proportionality between seat shares and cabinet portfolios conflicts with the bargaining theories that have the strongest theoretical—game theoretical—foundations. As Ansolabehere et al. (2005: 551) stress, game theoretical models 'almost always express their predictions in terms of voting weight'. In their analysis, these authors show that seat shares and voting weights correlate positively, but that the association is not particularly strong. There are several nonlinearities, in particular moving from three-party parliaments (where all three parties can have equal weight) to four-party parliaments (where one party typically has greater weight). Overall, seat shares overstate the voting weight of larger parties (Ansolabehere et al. 2005: 555; Warwick and Druckman 2006: 652).

Attempts to explain portfolio allocation by means of bargaining power have a long history. Indeed, the first attempt to explain the patterns of portfolio allocation in coalition governments was game theoretical, more specifically based on the theory of constant-sum games in simple triads (Caplow 1956). This study introduced the concept of each player's *weight* resulting from its relevance for potential majority coalitions. The expected pay-offs for the players result from their weight. A minor player whose support is necessary for an attractive coalition to form can demand and expect a larger slice of the pay-offs than the share of parliamentary seats it contributes to the coalition. In applied coalition research, this perspective has informed the approaches based on such solution concepts as the *kernel* and the *bargaining set*. Of the two, the kernel is the more 'radical' solution concept (Schofield 1976). It derives the weight of parties from their game theoretical power and hence predicts for each party that is required for government formation the same pay-off. Overall, in empirical applications, it has failed to produce results that match the actual portfolio distribution better than the norm of proportionality, as it generally overestimates the pay-offs of small parties. Yet, the kernel concept has proved useful in indicating the *direction* of most deviations from proportionality (Schofield and Laver 1985: 149).

The bargaining set is a more realistic solution concept. It proceeds from a given coalition and compares the pay-offs each party receives against the office pay-offs it would get in a coalition with other partners. The portfolio allocation predicted is the one that reflects the bargaining power of each of the coalition parties, which means that small parties will often be overrepresented. While overall the proportionality norm outperforms the bargaining set in predicting portfolio allocations, this is not true for every country. According to Schofield and Laver (1985; see also Laver and Schofield 1990: 176), the proportionality norm is the better predictor of portfolio allocation for Luxembourg, Ireland, Austria, Germany, and Norway, while the bargaining set is the more successful solution concept for Iceland, Sweden, Denmark, Belgium, Finland, and Italy.

All these measures of bargaining power are institution free in the sense that they disregard any environmental rules or constraints that may favour some coalitions or parties over others. One attempt to understand the disproportionalities that such 'loaded dice' may introduce is the agenda-setting approach. Such theories assume the presence of a formateur, or first mover, whose bargaining power may be enhanced by this opportunity to make a first coalition offer. Baron and Ferejohn provide a theory applicable to all situations 'in which a fixed quantity of benefits is to be distributed once and for all' (1989: 1200), while Austen-Smith and Banks (1990) and Ansolabehere et al. (2005) have specifically focused on portfolio allocation. These theories predict that the formateur will tend to be overcompensated in portfolios. Yet, as important as it is to recognize the institutional environment, agenda-setting models may exaggerate the first-mover advantage. Several scholars have argued that the assumption that the formateur is in a particularly strong bargaining position is in many situations not realistic (Morelli 1999; Carmignani 2001: 317), and Warwick and Druckman (2006: 653–5) show that it does not hold empirically as formateur parties are not overcompensated in terms of cabinet offices.

Carroll and Cox (2007) argue that under pre-election alliances bargaining power may convert into a proportional allocation of cabinet portfolios. These authors identify three conditions that such pre-electoral alliances need to meet: (1) the parties must commit themselves to governing together provided they win a joint majority (and this majority is not controlled by a single party on its own); (2) they must refrain from campaigning against each other; and (3) they must agree on a proportional allocation of cabinet seats. According to Carroll and Cox (2007: 300–2) the logic of clause (1) is to make winning a public good for the allies, of clause (2) to discourage negative externalities from campaign activities, and of clause (3) to encourage activities that generate positive externalities. In their empirical tests (covering all parliamentary democracies from 1998 to 2003 and 14 Western European countries from 1945 to 2000), they find that coalitions based on pre-election alliances exhibit pure proportionality in portfolio allocation, whereas other coalitions feature some overcompensation of small parties. Hence, they find their theory confirmed. Yet, identifying pre-electoral alliances is often a tricky empirical issue that involves the danger of circular reasoning: there is a temptation to interpret the history of bargaining in the light of the coalitions that actually formed and thus to exaggerate the importance of prior commitments.

The striking proportionality of portfolio allocations might thus, at least in some circumstances, be a result of prior commitments that the coalition parties have made. Could it also reflect a commitment to the idea of proportionality on the part of politicians themselves? We should not expect politicians to subscribe to the norm of proportionality strictly for the sake of fairness, though we perhaps should not completely deny such motives. But politicians may also apply the norm of proportionality for several more instrumental reasons. First, political parties should not blatantly violate the voters' expectations about fair division. If party leaders look too greedy for government spoils, the voters may come to suspect the primary motivations of politicians. Yet, at the same time, party voters would expect their party not to give away strategic advantages too easily. Hence, we should perhaps expect party leaders to aim at a division of portfolios that is favourable to their own party (e.g. by claiming the most important portfolios), but which can still be defended with arguments of fairness (e.g. as conforming to the proportionality norm). Party leaders in an unfavourable bargaining situation may do themselves more harm by accepting a grossly unfair offer than by remaining out of government. On the other hand, one reason that politicians do not always fully exploit a favourable bargaining position is their desire to keep transaction costs low. Proceeding from the proportionality norm certainly makes coalition negotiations easier, as it removes one essential question ('How much shall they get?') from the agenda. Thus, transaction costs and their democratic accountability to their constituents may account for the fact that politicians often devise portfolio allocations that more closely resemble inter-party proportionality than their respective bargaining powers.

The quality of portfolios

The quality of portfolios seems a natural explanation for deviations from proportionality, as that regularity does not take into account the *quality* of cabinet portfolios. Quite simply, individual government portfolios are very different. Even without considering the Ministry of Silly Walks (© Monty Python) or the Ministry of Snow (© Michael Laver), it is clear that some portfolios (e.g. Finance or Foreign Affairs) have much greater weight than others (e.g. Foreign Aid or Tourism). Even though some otherwise minor departments can have great importance in particular countries, for example, Fisheries in Iceland, there are robust cross-national regularities in the valuations of different ministries. There is no doubt that all parties recognize that some portfolios are worth more than others, and we should not be surprised to see such valuations reflected in actual portfolio allocations. Instead, we would expect individual parties to maximize the aggregate value of the portfolios they receive, rather than their sheer numbers.

Thus, a deviation from full proportionality can mean very different things. It can reflect a situation in which some parties get more than their 'fair share' of the spoils and others less. Alternatively, it may simply be that the party that ends up with the best portfolios also has to settle for fewer of them, whereas the party that gets many posts also receives the less attractive ones. Perhaps the latter party would have even preferred to have fewer but more desirable portfolios. In order to make sense of such cases, we must therefore also probe into the qualitative dimension of portfolio allocation.

In order to demonstrate the impact of portfolio saliency in portfolio allocation, Warwick and Druckman (2001) conducted an interesting exercise. Working from the Laver and Hunt (1992) expert survey data, they converted the ordinal ranks given individual ministries by the country experts into weights and then examined the relationship between parliamentary representation and cabinet portfolio shares. Warwick and Druckman's weighting scheme (2001) gave the prime minister, their top portfolio, a weight that is on average almost 2.5 times the weight of the least valuable portfolio (2001: 644). The authors found that the weighted portfolio shares are almost perfectly correlated with the non-weighted ones ($r = .986$) (Warwick and Druckman 2001: 644). In order to produce a statistically significant overcompensation for the formateur party, the authors had to increase the weight of the prime ministership to an implausible value of 4.19 times that of a typical ministry. These results suggest that although ministries carry very different values, their allocation tends to take that qualitative dimension into account.

More recently, Druckman and Warwick (2005) have provided the most convincing measurement of portfolio salience so far for 14 Western European countries for the post-1945 period. It is based on an expert survey, involving between 3 and 17 respondents per country. The underlying assumption is that portfolios have an objective value, that is, are equally valued by all parties in the allocation game. Weighting portfolios by salience does not change the story: Warwick and Druckman (2006) show that proportionality in numbers is not undermined by great inequalities in portfolio quality. Indeed, the authors claim that taking into account the (objective) value of portfolios actually slightly reinforces the pay-off proportionality that they observe.

Yet, there is another way the quality of portfolios may affect the overall allocation of office pay-offs: the 'subjective' value of specific portfolios for particular parties. A patronage party may, for example, value departments that rank low with regard to policymaking capacity, but offer a great deal of patronage opportunities (e.g. the Ministry of Public Works). A policy-seeking party, on the other hand, may be much less interested in such departments than in other agencies that have fewer staff positions but more policy influence (e.g. the Ministry of Finance). Another important consideration is the match between the jurisdiction of the ministry and the core concerns and constituencies of particular parties.[2] Some studies have

---

[2] Take the Ministry of Defence in Austria. For the People's Party and the Freedom Party, which have held the post in various coalitions, this is a valuable department. Yet, for the Social Democrats it has always been a liability that is best avoided, given the party's ambivalent relationship to the army

begun to explore this issue empirically, identifying patterns of portfolio allocation by party family (Browne and Feste 1975; Budge and Keman 1990). In contrast, Laver and Shepsle (1990, 1996) build their theory of coalition *formation* on the idea that parties are driven by the desire to occupy specific ministries (which then give them control over their most treasured policy dimensions). Hence, within the same coalition of parties, some portfolio allocations may be viable and others not. Yet, it is very difficult to derive more general propositions concerning portfolio allocation from this model. Laver and Shepsle (1996) confine themselves to two policy dimensions and two corresponding portfolios. While the 'subjective' value of portfolios thus remains an important subject for future research, probing into it is beyond the ambitions of this chapter.

Technical problems of division

Finally, there are some technical issues that can explain deviations from the norm of proportionality. Portfolio allocation means that a limited number of government offices (in our data-set between 4 in the Jonsson I and II cabinets in Iceland in the late 1950s and 38 in the Messmer II cabinet in France in 1973) must be distributed among a relatively small number of parties (in our data ranging between 2 and 7, the latter being the D'Alema cabinet in Italy). In the latter situation, it is virtually impossible for each party to receive exactly the share of ministries that would correspond to the proportionality norm (Warwick and Druckman 2001: 638). Even in less complicated bargaining situations, it may not be feasible to divide up the portfolios in such a way that each party would get precisely its 'fair' share.[3]

HOW THE PIE IS DIVIDED

Measurement of disproportionality

We now examine the actual extent of proportionality in portfolio allocation in the coalitional systems in our sample. This section thus addresses the question whether cabinet positions are allocated according to the proportionality norm or whether differences in bargaining power lead to differences in portfolio allocation. We measure cabinet disproportionality by the following index D:

$$D = \sum |(m_i/tm) - (s_i/cs)|$$

(Müller 2008). Indeed, until 2007, the Social Democrats have held the Defence portfolio only in single-party cabinets (and resorted to appointing non-partisans about half of the time).

[3] Yet, Warwick and Druckman (2001) show that even when they control for this technical issue, portfolio allocation is not fully proportional.

Portfolio Allocation

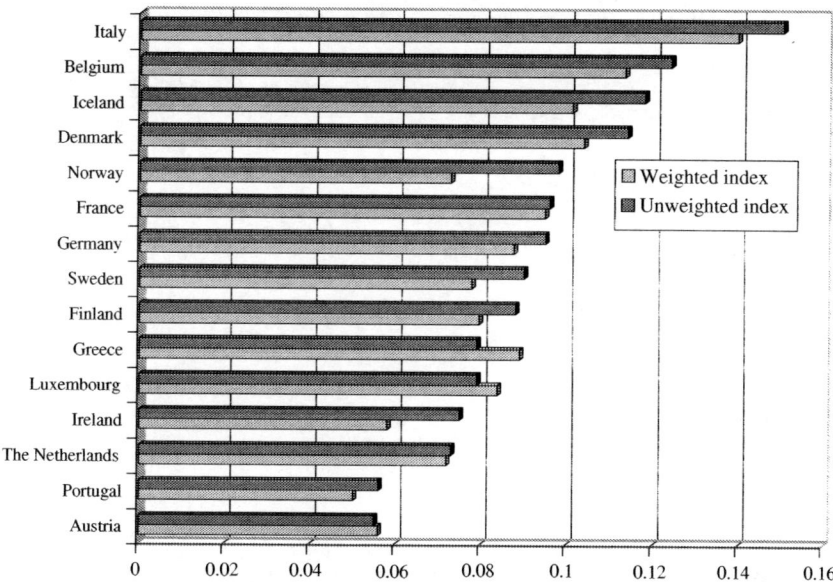

FIGURE 7.1. Disproportionality index of portfolio allocation by country

In this equation, m_i represents the number of ministry positions held by the ith party, tm represents the total number of such positions, s_i represents the number of parliamentary seats held by the ith party, and cs represents the number of parliamentary seats held by the entire cabinet. The index ranges from 0 (where ministerial allocations are perfectly proportional to seats held) to 1 (perfectly disproportional).

All non-partisan ministries are excluded from the total number of ministerial positions. If two parties share a single ministry (which is fairly common in Belgium, Finland, and Sweden), both parties are counted as having one ministerial position (not half of one).

Figure 7.1 shows the disproportionality of portfolio allocation in two versions. In the unweighted version, each cabinet office is treated equally. In the weighted version, the office of prime minister is counted as two other offices. This, of course, is an arbitrary decision [but a non-heroic one compared to that of Ansolabehere et al. (2005) to weight the prime minster's office as three portfolios or the 4.19 portfolio result of Warwick and Druckman (2001)]. Table 7.1 reports the disproportionality scores. It also contains the standard deviation of these measurements.

In both indices, four countries stand out with the highest degrees of disproportionality: Italy, Belgium, Denmark, and Iceland. On the other hand, Portugal, Austria, Ireland, and the Netherlands have had the lowest degrees of

TABLE 7.1. *Disproportionality index of portfolio allocation by country*

Country	Average weighted disproportionality	Standard deviation	Average unweighted disproportionality	Standard deviation	Number of coalition cabinets
Austria	0.056	0.048	0.055	0.045	16
Belgium	0.113	0.043	0.124	0.054	28
Denmark	0.104	0.046	0.114	0.050	17
Finland	0.079	0.043	0.088	0.048	33
France	0.095	0.082	0.096	0.083	17
Germany	0.088	0.054	0.095	0.059	22
Greece	0.089	0.010	0.079	0.012	2
Iceland	0.101	0.051	0.118	0.068	22
Ireland	0.058	0.036	0.075	0.019	10
Italy	0.146	0.057	0.150	0.059	34
Luxembourg	0.084	0.061	0.079	0.057	16
The Netherlands	0.072	0.063	0.073	0.055	22
Norway	0.073	0.040	0.098	0.039	8
Portugal	0.050	0.032	0.056	0.037	6
Sweden	0.078	0.073	0.090	0.055	7
Total	0.093	0.058	0.100	0.061	260

disproportionality. Higher standard deviations indicate a broader range of distributional formulas. This typically means that coalitions between a big and one or more small parties have alternated with more balanced coalitions. Given that the country rank orders are very similar and that the two indices are very highly intercorrelated (.92), we use the simpler, unweighted index in the remainder of this chapter.

Explaining disproportionality

We next use our clusters of explanatory variables to account for the variation in the proportionality of portfolio allocations. The cabinet is our unit of analysis. We thus seek to explain overall cabinet disproportionality, not the over- or under-compensation of individual parties. The literature review in the previous section suggests that though the differences between vote shares and seat shares are small, the bargaining power of the actors in the coalition game affects the allocation of cabinet seats. Given that neither the quality of portfolios nor technical problems in the division of spoils are crucial, this section will focus mainly on bargaining power. The greater the divergence of bargaining power from seat shares, the greater disproportionality we can expect. Bargaining power can be measured by indices such as the Banzhaf index (see Chapter 3). Although they constitute a natural starting point, bargaining power indices are mechanical measures. They cannot take into consideration the preferences of the actors or the context in which the bargaining takes place. The remainder of this section aims at doing that. Specifically, a number of variables in the regression (Table 7.2) will allow us to distinguish straightforward bargaining situations, which are well captured by the Banzhaf index, from more complex contexts.

Figure 7.1 and Table 7.1 suggest that disproportionality is the greatest in fragmented party systems and in systems with unstable governments. This is in line with Schofield and Laver's results (1985). The remainder of this section, using the unweighted disproportionality index, employs OLS regression analysis to explain differences in disproportionality (Table 7.2).

Table 7.2 tests the explanatory power of the blocks of variables that are employed throughout this volume. Together time and space contribute 20 per cent to the variance in disproportionality. This constitutes a baseline for the models employing the analytical variables. The final model, consisting exclusively of analytical variables, explains 23 per cent of the variance and thus outperforms the explanatory power of time and nationality. The final model contains all variables that were statistically significant in the full model or have been chosen because of theoretical expectations and proven to be robust. Two variables (number of cabinet parties and PM dissolution power), although statistically significant in the full model, were not included in the final model because they were not robust. A total of 11 variables are statistically significant and robust in the final model. Of the five clusters of analytical variables, structural attributes contribute the most. All other clusters taken by themselves contribute rather modestly to the explanation or, in the case of critical events, hardly at all. The remainder of this section first discusses the relevance of technical reasons for disproportional outcomes in portfolio allocation. It is followed by a discussion of bargaining power that is organized by cluster.

The analysis in Table 7.2 first shows that conditions that are likely to cause disproportionality for technical reasons work in the expected direction (see Warwick and Druckman 2001). Thus, disproportionality increases with the seat share of the largest party, whereas the allocation becomes more proportional when the cabinet is a surplus coalition and when the number of minister posts is large. A larger number of ministers clearly allow for a better matching of parliamentary and cabinet seat shares. Surplus parties, which are not necessary for a parliamentary majority, tend to be small and are likely to become overcompensated if only for technical reasons (no less than one cabinet seat can be handed out). Logically, this also means that the larger cabinet parties then cannot get their full share—hence the long-observed small party bias.

Substantively, the analysis suggests that the allocation of cabinet seats is proportional under conditions that do not give strategic advantages to one (or more) of the coalition parties. However, in situations that potentially privilege one (or more) of the government parties, portfolio allocation becomes more disproportional. This is born out most directly by the parliamentary bargaining power (as measured by the Banzhaf index) of the cabinet parties (cabinet fragmentation). When bargaining power is more fragmented, that is, when no cabinet party is

TABLE 7.2. *OLS regressions on unweighted portfolio disproportionality index*

Independent variables	Model 1	Model 2	Model 3	Model 4	Model 5	Model 6	Model 7	Model 8
Time								
1940s	0.03 (0.01)*						0.01 (0.02)	
1960s	−0.01 (0.01)							
1970s	0.02 (0.01)							
1980s	−0.01 (0.01)							
1990s	−0.02 (0.01)*						−0.01 (0.01)	
Austria	−0.04 (0.02)**							
Belgium	0.02 (0.02)							
Denmark	0.02 (0.02)							
Finland	−0.01 (0.02)							
France	−0.00 (0.02)							
Greece	−0.01 (0.04)							
Iceland	0.02 (0.02)							
Ireland	−0.02 (0.02)							
Italy	0.05 (0.02)**							
Luxembourg	−0.02 (0.02)							
The Netherlands	−0.03 (0.02)							
Norway	0.01 (0.02)							
Portugal	−0.04 (0.03)							
Sweden	−0.01 (0.02)							
Structure								
Post-election cabinet		−0.01 (0.01)*					0.00 (0.01)	
Absolute no. parl. parties		0.00 (0.02)						
Cabinet fragmentation		−0.02 (0.01)**					−0.01 (0.01)*	−0.02 (0.01)**
Largest party seat share		0.10 (0.06)					0.05 (0.07)	0.12 (0.06)**
Number of cabinet parties		0.03 (0.01)**					0.02 (0.01)**	
Majority cabinet		−0.03 (0.01)**					0.03 (0.01)**	0.03 (0.01)**
Surplus majority cabinet		−0.01 (0.01)					−0.03 (0.01)**	−0.04 (0.01)**
Number of cabinet ministers		−0.001 (0.0007)*					−0.00 (0.00)	−0.002 (0.001)**

	(1)	(2)	(3)	(4)	(5)	(6)	(7)	(8)
Preferences								
Polarization (BP weighted)			−0.00 (0.00)					
Issue dimensionality			−0.02 (0.02)					
No core party			−0.01 (0.01)					
Cabinet preference range			0.00 (0.00)					
Median party (1st dim.) in cab.			−0.02 (0.01)*				−0.02 (0.01)**	−0.03 (0.01)**
Median party (2nd dim.) in cab.			0.02 (0.01)**				0.02 (0.01)**	0.04 (0.01)**
Institutions								
Lower chamber only legislates				−0.02 (0.01)*			−0.001 (0.01)	−0.03 (0.01)**
Opposition influence				0.01 (0.003)**			0.005 (0.003)	
Constructive no-confidence				0.03 (0.02)			0.04 (0.02)**	0.04 (0.01)**
PM cabinet powers				−0.002 (0.003)			−0.004 (0.003)	
PM dissolution power				0.01 (0.01)			0.03 (0.01)**	
Semi-presidentialism				0.00 (0.01)				
Junior ministers exist				0.00 (0.01)				
Bargaining								
Prior cab.: conflict termination					0.01 (0.01)		0.02 (0.01)*	0.013 (0.007)*
Same parties in cabinet					−0.01 (0.01)		−0.00 (0.01)	
Cabinet bargaining duration					−0.00 (0.00)		−0.00 (0.00)	
Coalition agreement					−0.04 (0.01)		−0.01 (0.01)	
Policy agreement					−0.01 (0.01)			
Comprehensive policy agreement					0.01 (0.02)			
Coalition discipline (legislation)					0.01 (0.01)		0.01 (0.01)	0.02 (0.01)**
Critical events								
Terminal event lag (any)						0.02 (0.01)	0.004 (0.01)	
Electoral volatility						−0.000 (0.001)		
Inflation						0.000 (0.001)		
Unemployment						0.001 (0.001)	−0.000 (0.001)	
Growth						0.003 (0.001)*	−0.000 (0.001)	
Constant	0.10 (0.01)**	0.07 (0.04)*	0.15 (0.05)**	0.07 (0.02)**	0.12 (0.02)**	0.08 (0.02)**	0.06 (0.06)	0.05 (0.04)
Number of observations	260	260	257	260	260	216	224	255
Adjusted R^2	.20	.14	.04	.08	.06	.01	.23	.23

Notes: * $p < 0.10$; ** $p < 0.05$.

dominant, the outcomes are more proportional. Disproportionality increases with the largest party becoming bigger. As already noted, this is likely to indicate the overcompensation of small parties. Moreover, small parties may be pivotal and hence have a bargaining power exceeding their seat share. This is not the case in surplus cabinets and, indeed, here we find less disproportionality than in majority cabinets.

The presence of the median parties in the two most important policy dimensions in government underlines this reasoning. When only the median party in the first dimension is in the cabinet, the bargaining situation is probably less complex than in the cases when it is not in cabinet. When only the second dimension median party is in cabinet, it is likely to indicate a complex bargaining situation. The cabinet presence of the first dimension median party has a negative effect on disproportionality, while the presence of the second dimension median party has a positive one. When both median parties are in cabinet, the net effect in the regression is fairly close to zero.

Institutions also matter. When the lower chamber alone decides on legislation, we get a more proportional outcome compared to situations in which the lower chamber and other actors need to agree. This is the case when the second chamber or the president has decisive say in the enactment of new legislation. When such constraints on legislative decision-making exist, some government parties are likely to end up in a stronger and some in a weaker bargaining position than their seat shares in the first chamber suggest. Therefore, the portfolio allocation becomes more disproportional.

Disproportionality is also higher where the cabinet can be unseated only by a constructive vote of no-confidence. This rule reduces the walk-away values of those individual coalition parties that cannot credibly threaten to bring down the cabinet by becoming part of a new alternative majority. Hence, bargaining power is under this institution likely to be distributed more unequally than our measure would suggest. Finally, portfolio allocation is more disproportional when the coalition parties are tied to each other by a strong commitment to maintain coalition discipline in legislation. As coalition discipline rules are endogenous to coalition bargaining, it may mean that the same forces that lead to more disproportional portfolio allocations also underpin coalition decision-making rules. In sum, Table 7.2 suggests that coalition parties tend to respect the norm of proportionality when power relations are consistent with such norms. However, they diverge from it in situations that privilege some of them over others.

CHANGING THE SIZE OF THE PIE

Thus far the portfolio allocation literature has largely proceeded from the assumption that the number of portfolios is fixed (and hence portfolio allocation a fixed-sum game[4]). Yet, in the real world the number of ministries is typically not fixed but may change over time. Clearly, such changes occur for many reasons and lasting changes may reflect secular trends such as the growth of government or changes in the political agenda. New government departments are established in response to new policy demands, such as European integration or women's affairs. Conversely, agencies such as the department of post-war reconstruction or colonial affairs can become obsolete when realities change. In this section, however, we are interested in short-term changes in portfolio structure that are more likely to reflect bargaining considerations. Sometimes ministerial portfolios may be introduced, merged, or eliminated for purely strategic reasons that have much less to do with fundamental social change than with short-term partisan considerations. As Mershon (2002: 37) has argued with respect to post-war Italy, 'an increase in portfolios...can offset the office costs of building coalitions'. To the extent that the number of government posts is flexible, surplus coalitions 'need not exact sacrifices of office rewards' (Mershon 2002: 37).

Coalition negotiators may indeed find themselves in situations where they do not have enough offices to satisfy all relevant inter- and intra-party demands. Alternatively, they may find themselves in a situation in which they do not have enough *important* offices to be filled by the political heavyweights who should be included in the cabinet. Problems may also emerge from the mismatch between the existing ministerial structure and the 'legitimate' claims of coalition parties, when, for instance, one ministry would be considered insufficient, but two fully blown ministries would be considered too much. Provided that the number of ministries and their jurisdictions are at the discretion of the coalition parties, these problems can be solved. New ministries can be created, typically by splitting existing government departments. This not only increases the number of offices available but also reduces the value of the affected ministries. Conversely, in order to create offices that suit particularly important politicians, coalition architects may choose to merge existing ministries and thereby create super-ministries (e.g. a Ministry for Economy and Finance). Mergers of individual departments or more complex changes in the ministerial structure that reduce the number of positions may also result from the changes in the structure of 'legitimate' claims. Such changes may make it no longer necessary to maintain 'artificial' ministries, that is, those that were created not for policy-related reasons but in order to increase the number of available jobs.

When can we expect the number of ministers to go up or down? There is one straightforward expectation: the number of ministers is likely to increase with the number of parties represented in the cabinet. The more parties need to get a share, the fewer cabinet seats can be allocated among the leaders of each of

---

[4] Of course, portfolio allocation remains a fixed-sum game if we focus on cabinet seat *shares*. Yet, real-world politicians are often more interested in the absolute number of cabinet positions at their disposal.

them. Increasing the number of seats can be an easy way out. This is probably particularly likely when several parties come to the negotiation table with very different weights. While small parties need to get at least one or two cabinet seats, their larger partners will often prefer the tax payer to settle the bill by increasing the total number of cabinet seats.

In most countries, the government parties can indeed determine the size of the pie. Only in Ireland do they face a hard constraint, as the constitution stipulates: 'the government shall consist of not less than seven and not more than fifteen members' (Article 28).[5] In several countries (Austria, Belgium, Finland, Italy, Luxembourg, the Netherlands, and Norway), the number and structure of government departments are fixed by law. Hence, any change requires an act by parliament. While getting parliamentary approval is not difficult for majority governments, it may significantly constrain minority cabinets.[6]

Table 7.3 provides a first descriptive overview of ministerial offices in Western Europe. It contains information on both ministerial positions and ministries. The two need not be identical in number, as most countries know ministers without portfolio, and as government departments may not necessarily be headed by a single cabinet minister, and as one minister can be in charge of more than one ministry. Indeed, in nine countries the mean number of ministers is greater than the mean number of ministries. The opposite is the case in seven countries, whereas only Greece has the same values for both. The standard deviations of the number of ministers as well as the number of ministries suggest that short-time changes occur in most countries.

Table 7.3 shows that the countries differ considerably with regard to the overall number of ministers. While France, Italy, Greece, and the UK on average have more than 20 cabinet positions apiece, Austria, the Netherlands, and Ireland have fewer than 15 and Iceland and Luxembourg fewer than 10 (means). The differences between countries are larger than the differences over time. Clearly, the major countries tend to have larger cabinets than the smaller ones. Germany, which satisfies itself with 18 cabinet positions, is the exception among the major countries. On the opposite side, Greece and Belgium have allowed their political class to create a relatively large number of minister posts for themselves.

Table 7.4 provides a descriptive account of changes in the number of both ministers and ministries. Altogether in our sample of 405 post-war cabinets, we observe 270 changes in the number of ministers and 194 changes in the number of ministries. Thus, two-thirds of the cabinets assuming office had a different

---

[5] In several other countries, the constitution establishes a minimum number of cabinet seats either explicitly or by implication, for example, by listing a set of required cabinet offices. Yet, such constraints rarely bind, as we know of no coalition builders who have wanted to go below these limits.

[6] Indeed, in 1970 the Austrian minority government (the only one the country has had) did not succeed in winning a parliamentary majority for the creation of a ministry for health and environmental affairs. Moreover, creating a separate department for science and research required considerable time and parliamentary negotiations.

TABLE 7.3. *Number of ministers and ministries by country*

Country	Average no. of ministers	Min.	Max.	S.D.	Average no. of ministries	Min.	Max.	S.D.	N
Austria	13.8	11	17	1.8	12.7	10	15	1.8	22
Belgium	19.3	12	27	4.1	19.7	13	26	3.9	33
Denmark	17.8	12	24	3.1	18.7	12	24	3.1	31
Finland	15.7	13	18	1.4	11.6	11	13	0.7	44
France	26.7	16	38	6.4	21.2	14	34	5.8	23
Germany	18.0	5	25	3.8	17.3	14	22	2.1	26
Greece	21.1	18	27	2.8	21.1	19	25	1.7	10
Iceland	7.6	4	12	2.2	13.5	13	15	0.9	26
Ireland	14.1	11	15	1.2	14.4	12	16	1.2	22
Italy	24.2	16	33	4.3	19.6	14	26	2.2	51
Luxembourg	7.9	6	11	1.5	17.1	12	22	3.8	16
The Netherlands	14.3	10	16	1.3	13.9	13	15	0.8	23
Norway	16	13	19	2.0	15.5	11	20	2.0	26
Portugal	16.2	14	18	1.1	16.4	14	19	1.4	14
Spain	17.6	14	21	2.3	17.5	14	22	2.8	10
Sweden	18.4	15	22	2.4	13.1	11	15	1.3	26
United Kingdom	20.7	16	24	2.2	20.8	17	24	2.2	20
Total	17.5	4	38	5.7	16.5	10	34	4.0	423

number of ministers from their immediate predecessors, and half of the cabinets had a changed ministerial structure. Increases are more frequent than decreases. The number of ministers was particularly stable in Norway, Sweden, Ireland, Austria, and Luxembourg, where about half or more of the cabinets had the same number of ministers as the preceding cabinet. Conversely, France, Greece, and Spain witnessed change very frequently or even in every single case.

Table 7.5 is a simple cross-tabulation of the changes in the number of parties and the number of ministers. The table shows the expected relationship: an increase in the number of cabinet parties is likely to lead to an increase in the number of ministers. Conversely, a decrease in the number of cabinet parties is likely to lead to a decrease in the number of ministers. Stability in the number of parties typically goes together with stability in the number of ministers. This bivariate relationship is statistically highly significant.

It may be useful to provide a few more details on the occurrence of increases and decreases of ministerial positions (not represented in tabular form). In each decade from the 1940s to the 1980s, there were more increases in the number of ministers than decreases. The 1970s and 1980s stand out with 44 and 41 per cent, respectively, of the cabinets comprising more ministers than the preceding one, while only 30 and 25 per cent, respectively, had fewer members. This may reflect the new or intensified tasks governments have taken on, such as environmental protection and gender politics. In the 1990s the trend reversed itself, when for the first time more cabinets were shrunk compared with their immediate predecessors

TABLE 7.4. *Change in ministers and ministries by country*

Country	Ministers			Ministries			N
	Increasing cabinets	Decreasing cabinets	Cabinets with no change	Increasing cabinets	Decreasing cabinets	Cabinets with no change	
Austria	6	5	10	6	4	11	21
Belgium	11	14	7	10	11	11	32
Denmark	14	11	5	10	5	15	30
Finland	15	12	16	2	1	40	43
France	12	10	0	11	10	1	22
Germany	10	8	7	11	6	8	25
Greece	4	4	0	4	3	1	8
Iceland	9	6	10	5	2	18	25
Ireland	6	4	11	6	4	11	21
Italy	23	14	13	10	2	38	50
Luxembourg	5	3	7	7	4	4	15
The Netherlands	8	7	7	3	4	15	22
Norway	5	2	18	7	4	14	25
Portugal	4	4	5	5	5	3	13
Spain	5	3	1	5	3	1	9
Sweden	7	4	14	6	2	17	25
United Kingdom	9	6	4	9	7	3	19
Total	153	117	135	117	77	211	405

Portfolio Allocation

TABLE 7.5. *Cross-tabulation: change in no. of parties and no. of ministers*

	Decrease in no. of ministers	No change in no. of ministers	Increase in no. of ministers	Total
Decrease in no. of cab. parties	57 (56%)	28 (27%)	18 (17%)	103
No change in no. of cab. parties	47 (23%)	86 (42%)	73 (35%)	206
Increase in no. of cab. parties	13 (13%)	21 (22%)	62 (65%)	96
Total	117 (29%)	135 (33%)	153 (38%)	405

Note: Pearson's chi-squared tests: $\chi^2 = 74.52$, p value = 0.000.

than expanded (40% and 31%, respectively). Since decision-making bodies that are too large tend to degenerate to mere assemblies, cabinets cannot grow forever. If nothing more, the increased prominence of the idea of rolling back government has provided a suitable backdrop for efforts to maintain cabinets of a manageable size.

One might expect changes in the number of cabinet members to occur mainly in government formations that immediately follow elections. On the one hand, elections are more likely to bring not only government change but also policy change: winning parties or alliances may see the need to change the ministerial structure and possibly create new ministries in order to pursue their policy agendas. Moreover, cabinet turnover between elections may be caused by nothing more dramatic than the retirement of the prime minister and the succession of an heir from the same party, which we would not necessarily expect to imply significant policy changes. Yet, with regard to changes in the number of ministers, the difference between post-election and inter-election cabinets is minimal. In both cases, 29 per cent of the cabinet turnovers see a decrease in the number of ministers. Thirty-nine per cent of the post-election cabinets see an increase, while the respective figure for inter-election cabinets is 36 per cent, but the difference is hardly large or significant.

Explaining the number of ministers

In the remainder of this section we explain the number of cabinet ministers in both coalition and single-party systems with the help of OLS regression analysis (Table 7.6). Given the high correlation between the number of ministers and ministries, respectively, we shall in the remainder of this section concentrate on ministers only. This simplifies the presentation and minimizes measurement problems. The analysis proceeds blockwise. Each step tests for the explanatory power of a specific set of variables. Time and space together explain 77 per cent of the variance. This provides a trivial but challenging benchmark for the explanatory power of the analytical variables that make up the other blocks. Almost all the variables of the time and space block are statistically significant. On the one hand, this indicates the importance of country effects, on the other it highlights the secular trend noted above towards larger cabinets.

TABLE 7.6. *OLS regressions on the number of cabinet ministers*

Independent variables	Model 1	Model 2	Model 3	Model 4	Model 5	Model 6	Model 7	Model 8
Time								
1940s	−0.13 (0.55)							
1960s	2.23 (0.46)**							
1970s	2.57 (0.43)**							
1980s	3.88 (0.44)**							
1990s	3.49 (0.48)**							
Austria	−3.78 (0.80)**							
Belgium	1.73 (0.73)**							
Denmark	−0.01 (0.73)							
Finland	−1.53 (0.69)**							
France	8.24 (0.79)**							
Greece	1.92 (1.03)*							
Iceland	−9.85 (0.76)**							
Ireland	−3.71 (0.80)**							
Italy	6.56 (0.67)**							
Luxembourg	−9.15 (0.88)**							
The Netherlands	−3.29 (0.79)**							
Norway	−1.93 (0.76)**							
Portugal	−2.73 (0.92)**							
Spain	−1.27 (1.03)							
Sweden	0.69 (0.76)							
UK	3.23 (0.82)**							
Structure								
Post-election cabinet		−1.42 (0.50)**					−0.68 (0.43)	
Absolute no. parl. parties		0.73 (0.11)**					0.02 (0.12)	
Bargaining power fragmentation		1.14 (0.42)**					0.45 (0.34)	
Largest party seat share		39.9 (6.24)**					14.8 (5.47)**	9.61 (3.24)**
Coalition cabinet		−2.31 (0.84)**					−1.52 (0.71)**	−1.84 (0.64)**
Number of cabinet parties		1.23 (0.42)**					0.91 (0.33)**	1.05 (0.31)**
Surplus majority cabinet		1.93 (0.80)**					2.08 (0.62)**	1.98 (0.61)**

	M1	M2	M3	M4	M5	M6	M7	M8
Preferences								
Polarization (BP weighted)	−0.04(0.03)						0.10(0.03)**	0.11(0.02)**
Issue dimensionality	0.87(1.02)						−0.58(0.53)	
No core party	−4.09(0.56)**						−0.07(0.57)	
Cabinet preference range	0.02(0.01)							
Median party (1st dim.) in cab.	1.63(0.70)**							
Institutions								
Bicameralism			0.37(0.48)				−0.73(0.51)	
Positive parliamentarism			−0.30(0.45)				0.09(0.49)	
PM cabinet powers			−0.42(0.10)**				−0.36(0.14)**	−0.35(0.12)**
PM dissolution power			1.08(0.46)**				1.20(0.50)**	1.33(0.46)**
No. of seats in lower chamber			0.02(0.001)**				0.02(0.001)**	0.02(0.001)**
Bargaining								
Prior cab.: conflict termination				0.11(0.60)				
Same parties & PM in cabinet				−0.84(0.71)				
Cabinet bargaining duration				−0.02(0.01)**				
Coalition agreement				−3.88(0.67)**			0.58(0.53)	
							−0.15(0.58)	
Critical events								
Terminal event lag (any)					0.19(0.67)			
Electoral volatility					0.12(0.03)**		0.08(0.03)**	0.08(0.02)**
Inflation					−0.06(0.03)*		−0.03(0.02)	
Unemployment					0.24(0.07)**		0.13(0.06)**	0.12(0.05)**
Growth					−0.15(0.10)		−0.17(0.07)**	−0.17(0.07)**
Constant	15.6(0.62)**	−12.5(5.30)**	16.1(3.04)**	12.0(0.45)**	21.3(0.74)**	16.4(0.79)**	3.28(3.25)	5.04(1.77)**
Number of observations	423	406	402	414	392	353	347	347
Adjusted R^2	.77	.28	.15	.54	.09	.10	.61	.60

Notes: $^*p < 0.10$; $^{**}p < 0.05$.

Of the analytical variables those capturing institutions and structure stand out. By themselves institutional variables explain 54 per cent of the variance, while structural attributes account for 28 per cent. Variables measuring preferences alone explain 15 per cent of the variance, while the bargaining environment and critical event have a more modest impact. Altogether 11 variables are significant in the final model at the 5 per cent level. The final model accounts for about 60 per cent of the variance. Although this remains below the corresponding value for the atheoretical baseline model, the theoretically based model is more parsimonious in that it explains the bulk of the variance with a smaller set of predictors. The remainder of this section discusses the variables of the final model, proceeding blockwise.

Four structural attributes' variables are consistently statistically significant and robust in the final model. These are the largest party's seat share, the number of cabinet parties, coalition status, and the cabinet being a surplus majority cabinet. The coalition status, number of cabinet parties, and surplus majority cabinet variables should be interpreted jointly. All these variables suggest that cabinets tend to grow when this is convenient from an allocation perspective, particularly when there is a surplus coalition with a large number of parties. On the one hand, cabinets have more members when more demands (more cabinet parties) need to be satisfied and when the weights of the coalition partners are uneven. Thus, coalitions in which one party is particularly large, or which contain parties not necessary for a parliamentary majority, tend to have more cabinet members than coalitions lacking these attributes. This may be a direct effect of the small-party bias: if small parties get overcompensated (for technical reasons and/or because they have a strong bargaining position), their bigger partners are likely to push for a greater number of cabinet seats. When cabinets become larger, the undercompensation of larger parties may be avoided or, at least, rendered less painful.

Of the variables measuring preferences only the polarization of the parliamentary party system is statistically significant, though the effect is small. A more polarized party system seems to encourage government parties to increase their spoils. One possible interpretation is that in such situations fewer alternative coalitions are credible, so that the governing parties may feel more secure and therefore help themselves more generously to government resources. Polarization may also mean that party competition is primarily ideological and that voters care less about more symbolic issues such as the size of cabinet.

As already mentioned, institutions have a huge impact on the number of cabinet seats. Specifically, the single most powerful determinant in the model is the total number of seats in the lower house of parliament. This is mainly a control variable for country size, as small countries such as Luxembourg and Iceland have small parliaments (between 51 and 64 and 52 and 63 seats, respectively), while the bigger countries such as Germany and France have large parliaments with hundreds of members. Two additional institutional variables are significant, both having to do with the powers of the prime minister. When the prime minister has more extensive powers within the cabinet, there are fewer cabinet portfolios. However, when the prime minister has unconstrained dissolution powers, there are a greater number of cabinet portfolios.

Finally, three of the critical event variables are statistically significant and robust in the final model. Cabinets are likely to be bigger when electoral volatility and unemployment are high, whereas they tend to be smaller when economic growth is high. In other words, cabinets are smaller under favourable economic conditions than under unfavourable ones or in times of electoral uncertainty. While creating additional cabinet jobs will not be an effective measure against unemployment, such economic conditions may invite more government activism and thus lead to a greater number of cabinet ministers. A government presiding over economic prosperity may feel less need for such symbolic action.

In sum, country size is by far the most important determinant of cabinet size: bigger countries have larger cabinets. Within the range of our data-set, parliament size varies from fewer than 50 to more than 600. All else equal, the predicted difference between the smallest and largest parliament is about 10 cabinet seats. Clearly, the effects of country size are most decisive in driving these results. Yet coalitions are also likely to have larger cabinets when the weights of the coalition parties are very uneven and when they need to satisfy more demands (more cabinet parties).

WATCHDOG JUNIOR MINISTERS

Junior ministerships are executive appointments that do not carry full voting powers in the cabinet. Parliamentary democracies vary widely in the provisions for junior members. Some countries feature large numbers and often several categories of such appointments. In other countries, junior ministers simply do not exist. Where junior ministers do exist, they are typically among the minor spoils that can be given to cabinet parties. Junior minister posts, of course, are 'jobs for the boys', and as such may constitute a means to pacify specific intra-party groups that are not otherwise (sufficiently) represented in government. Having such positions available may also help political parties in their recruitment and training of key personnel, as party hopefuls can get experience in secondary government jobs. Having more politicians in a ministry may also help tighten up partisan control over the bureaucracy. All this may apply to any junior minister post, regardless of whether the respective ministry is held by the junior minister's party or not. Yet, there is another function junior ministers can fulfil: keeping tabs on and controlling the coalition partner. Junior ministers serving under a minister from a different party can be their respective party's 'watchdog'. Their presence can help reduce information asymmetries between the party in charge of the respective portfolio and the party nominating the junior minister. Although formally the subordinates of their respective senior ministers, in effect junior ministers, may be a check on them (see Müller and Strøm 2000; Thies 2001; Manow and Zorn 2004).

Yet, 'watchdog' junior ministers are only one mechanism by which coalition parties can keep their partners in check. Alternative vehicles are double ministerial appointments, partisan bureaucrats, and the use of other oversight arenas such as parliamentary committees. Appointing two full ministers to one ministry not only allows for some division of labour but also for mutual checks. Partisan bureaucrats are another possibility for intra-coalition control. If civil servants themselves are partisans, they may act as spies for their party when their ministry is headed by a minister from a different party (see Müller 2008). Finally, government policies that require legislation need to go through parliament. Martin and Vanberg (2004) show that the greater the ideological divergence between coalition partners in a specific policy area, the more parliamentary scrutiny the relevant bills receive. Hence, parliamentary committees under coalition government not only allow for the scrutiny of executive bills by the legislature, or of government bills by the opposition, but also provide opportunities for one government party to scrutinize another.

To be sure, each mechanism has its own advantages and disadvantages. On the whole, parliamentary committees have perhaps less specific knowledge than members of the executive, but they do have formal decision-making power. Indeed, ministers and parties need to win their approval in order to change the status quo. Partisan bureaucrats can only provide information (and silently try to promote their partisan goals) but have no formal powers. In contrast, cabinet ministers can issue a veto at the cabinet table. But a veto may make their own proposals vulnerable to being taken 'hostage'. Given that most ministers are primarily concerned about advancing their own departmental initiatives, dual ministerial appointments may not be the most effective mechanism of partisan control.

In contrast to bureaucrats, junior ministers can raise partisan issues with the minister and perhaps settle them. In contrast to full ministers, junior ministers are not constrained by the adversarial effects a conflict may have on their chances of advancing their own departmental policies. Because of the hierarchical nature of the formal relationship between ministers and junior ministers, it remains within the discretion of the former to determine whether it is possible to settle the issue at the departmental level. If this is not the case, 'watchdog' junior ministers can officially inform their party leaders and at the same time speak with greater knowledge than their co-partisans in cabinet-level negotiations.

Table 7.7 provides a descriptive account of the presence of 'watchdog' junior ministers. While every Italian cabinet has included such posts, France, Austria, the Netherlands, Belgium, and Germany have made frequent use of them. Sweden and Norway have employed some 'watchdogs', whereas Denmark, Finland, Greece,

TABLE 7.7. *Watchdog junior ministers by country (coalition cabinets only)*

Country	Watchdog junior ministers	Number of cabinets
Austria	15	17
Belgium	22	28
Denmark	0	17
Finland	0	33
France	15	17
Germany	10	22
Greece	0	2
Iceland	0	22
Ireland	9	10
Italy	36	36
Luxembourg	0	16
The Netherlands	21	23
Norway	3	8
Portugal	0	6
Sweden	3	7
Total	134	264

Note: Entries represent numbers of coalition cabinets that possess at least one junior minister from a party different than that of the minister.

Iceland, and Portugal have not had such ministry-internal checks at all. The three Nordic countries in the latter set simply have no institutional provision for junior ministers. For that reason the analysis in Table 7.8 excludes Denmark, Finland, and Iceland, but keeps those countries on board that could have had 'watchdog' junior ministers under existing institutions.

Under which conditions can we expect to see 'watchdog' junior ministers? Generally, the use of this type of junior ministers is more likely when the coalition parties do not trust each other very much. There are, of course, many reasons why coalition parties may not trust each other, leaving researchers with considerable measurement problems. Yet, we can identify some conditions that potentially make coalitions vulnerable, such as the potential threats of electoral volatility and a credible opposition.

Table 7.8 attempts to explain the presence of 'watchdog' junior ministers with the help of logit analysis. The first block of variables measures time effects. It functions again as a yardstick for the performance of the analytical variables that make up the other blocks. The results show a clear trend towards the greater use of 'watchdog' junior ministers over time (with an insignificant drop in the 1990s). Of the five clusters of analytical variables, institutions and structural attributes have the greatest explanatory power. By themselves, each of these clusters explains more than 20 per cent of the variance. Critical events, the bargaining environment, and policy preferences follow in that order and have more modest impact.

The final model brings together all variables that have been statistically significant or close to that mark in the full model, and whose effects are robust

TABLE 7.8. *Logistic regressions on watchdog junior ministers*

Independent variables	Model 1	Model 2	Model 3	Model 4	Model 5	Model 6	Model 7	Model 8	Impact[a]
Time									
1940s	−0.06 (0.58)								
1960s	0.39 (0.54)								
1970s	1.26 (0.58)**						2.44 (1.74)	1.84 (0.91)**	0.27 (0.11)
1980s	1.34 (0.56)**						2.72 (1.74)	2.48 (0.90)**	0.30 (0.11)
1990s	1.04 (0.59)*						−1.43 (1.60)		
Structure									
Post-election cabinet		−0.24 (0.52)							
Maximum cabinet duration		0.001 (0.001)					0.001 (0.001)		
Absolute no. parl. parties		0.44 (0.13)**					1.56 (0.55)**	0.73 (0.17)**	0.16 (0.04)
Bargaining power fragmentation		0.64 (0.34)*					−0.16 (0.56)		
Largest party seat share		4.39 (5.15)							
Number of cabinet parties		−0.52 (0.34)					0.82 (0.88)		
Surplus majority cabinet		1.42 (0.62)**					−1.37 (1.80)		
Preferences									
Polarization (BP weighted)			0.05 (0.03)*				0.20 (0.09)**	0.08 (0.04)*	0.15 (0.08)[a]
Issue dimensionality			0.46 (0.80)						
No core party			−0.68 (0.39)*				−0.85 (1.19)	−1.98 (0.69)**	−0.28 (0.10)
Cabinet preference range			0.004 (0.01)						
Median party (1st dim.) in cab.			1.44 (0.50)**				0.56 (1.28)		
Institutions									
Bicameralism				2.77 (0.55)**			7.86 (2.11)**	5.72 (1.05)**	0.65 (0.12)
Positive parliamentarism				−0.96 (0.61)			−2.43 (1.33)*	−2.28 (0.65)**	−0.29 (0.11)
PM cabinet powers				−0.27 (0.11)**			0.71 (0.48)		
PM dissolution power				−1.26 (0.61)**			−1.17 (1.70)		

	(1)	(2)	(3)	(4)	(5)	(6)	(7)	(8)
Bargaining								
Prior cab.: conflict termination								1.33 (0.95)
Same parties & PM in cabinet				1.10 (0.39)**				1.39 (1.38)
Cabinet bargaining duration				0.64 (0.51)				−0.001 (0.02)
Coalition agreement				0.02 (0.01)**				1.63 (1.34)
Polarization				−0.64 (0.39)			1.58 (0.70)**	0.37 (0.15)
Critical events								
Terminal event lag (any)						−0.72 (0.60)		−1.10 (1.18)
Electoral volatility						−0.02 (0.03)		
Inflation						0.11 (0.06)**		0.08 (0.05)*
Unemployment						0.26 (0.07)**		−0.10 (0.16)
Growth						0.04 (0.09)		
Constant	0.35 (0.38)	−5.00 (3.43)	−1.89 (2.44)	1.06 (0.57)*	0.35 (0.40)	−22.4 (6.38)**	−0.49 (0.66)	−7.85 (1.68)**
Number of observations	192	188	186	192	185	172	164	188
Pseudo-R^2	.05	.22	.08	.29	.11	.68	.15	.58
% Correctly predicted	.74	.76	.72	.80	.75	.94	.79	.92

Notes: *p < 0.10; **p < 0.05.

[a] Impact is the marginal effect of a unit change in the independent variable on the probability of the outcome occurring, calculated based on Model 8, with the following exception: the impact of Polarization (BP weighted) is for a 10 point change (1 standard deviation change).

across model specifications. This model accounts for almost 60 per cent of the variance and clearly outperforms the baseline estimates for the fixed effects of time and country. Substantively, several statistically significant variables capture situations in which coalition parties are likely to take a 'Leninist' approach ('Trust is good, control is better.'). When the number of parliamentary parties is high and hence many alternative coalitions can be formed, 'watchdog' junior ministers are more common. The two statistically significant institutional variables provide further support for this interpretation. Bicameralism increases the likelihood of 'watchdog' junior ministers. As single-chamber legislatures either do not have junior ministers at all (and therefore are excluded from the analysis) or do not practise 'watchdog' appointments, it is the bigger countries and some of the more complex coalition systems that feature such executive appointments. Positive parliamentarism, on the other hand, is negatively correlated with the use of 'watchdogs'. Since positive parliamentarism stabilizes incumbent governments, it may therefore reduce the need for 'watchdog' junior ministers.

Two preference variables are also associated with the incidence of 'watchdog' junior ministers. Parliamentary polarization increases the probability of such appointments, while the absence of a core party decreases it. Finally, the analysis in Table 7.8 suggests that path-dependency and transaction costs (and possibly political learning) affect the use of 'watchdog' junior ministers. The trend towards the use of 'watchdogs' (particularly in the 1970s and 1980s) coincides with a greater use of written coalition agreements. To the extent that coalition agreements contain policy commitments, they provide 'watchdog' junior ministers with a yardstick against which the acts of their ministers can be measured. These two mechanisms of inter-party oversight may thus mutually reinforce one another. The increasing recourse to formal coalition agreements may also indicate that coalition builders have felt that trust cannot serve as the only coalition cement.

Overall, bicameralism has the most dramatic impact on the likelihood of 'watchdog' junior ministers being appointed: coalition governments in bicameral systems are 68 percentage points more likely to appoint 'watchdog' junior ministers than those in unicameral systems, controlling for the impact of other variables. The presence of a coalition agreement also increases the likelihood of watchdog junior ministers by more than one-third. On the other hand, positive parliamentarism decreases the likelihood of watchdog junior ministers by nearly 30 percentage points.

CONCLUSION

This chapter has addressed three issues concerning the allocation of government positions: the disproportionality of ministerial appointments, the number of senior cabinet appointments, and the use of 'watchdog' junior ministers. In other words, it has addressed the division of the pie, its size, and the mutually checks on its consumption.

We have demonstrated once again that by and large cabinet portfolios are allocated proportionally among the cabinet parties. Although empirically powerful, the rule of proportionality conflicts with the most powerful theories of coalition bargaining. We have briefly reviewed the reasons why rational politicians may nevertheless agree to a largely proportional outcome and added some important considerations. Yet, our main contribution to this query is to demonstrate the impact of the context in which bargaining takes place. Substantively, our analysis shows that the allocation of cabinet seats is most proportional under conditions that do not strategically advantage one (or more) of the coalition parties. In contrast, in situations that potentially privilege one (or more) of the government parties, portfolio allocation is more disproportional. The analysis presented here in no way exhausts the research agenda in this field. Clearly, the empirical puzzle of proportional portfolio allocation remains a challenging task for further research.

The second issue addressed in this chapter is novel to the portfolio allocation literature. It proceeds from the idea that rather than fighting for shares of a given pie, coalition builders may agree to change (and perhaps most often increase) its size. We have therefore examined changes in the number of cabinet members appointed. While country size is by far the most important factor explaining cabinet size, cabinets have more members when more demands (more cabinet parties) need to be satisfied and when the weights of the coalition partners are very uneven.

Finally, this chapter has examined the conditions under which government coalitions feature the most important type of junior minister—the 'watchdog'. The appointment of such 'watchdogs' is one of the possible ways in which coalition parties can check the policy initiatives of their partners. Alternatives are dual ministerial appointments, partisan bureaucrats, and committee oversight. Compared to these alternatives, 'watchdog' junior ministers have some distinctive advantages. Theoretically, their appointment is to be expected when the partners to the coalition have reasons not to trust each other. This chapter has identified a set of objective situations that are likely to promote distrust between the coalition partners and that are empirically associated with the greater use of 'watchdog' junior ministers.

In sum, these analyses add considerably to our knowledge of the pay-offs of coalition politics, and especially those that consist of personal opportunities for policy influence and spoils. Much more needs to be known about the ways in which cabinet members and junior ministers relate to one another, to their cabinet colleagues, and to the civil servants under their authority. Our data suggest that political parties take such issues seriously. So should political scientists.

REFERENCES

Ansolabehere, Stephen, Snyder, James M., Jr., Strauss, Aarun B., and Ting, Michael M. (2005). 'Voting Weights and Formateur Advantages in the Formation of Coalition Governments', *American Journal of Political Science*, 49: 550–63.

Austen-Smith, David and Banks, Jeffrey (1990). 'Stable Governments and the Allocation of Policy Portfolio', *American Political Science Review*, 84: 891–906.

Baron, David P. and Ferejohn, John A. (1989). 'Bargaining in Legislatures', *American Political Science Review*, 83: 1181–206.

Brams, Steven J. (2006). 'Fair Division', in Barry R. Weingast and Donald Wittman (eds.), *Oxford Handbook of Political Economy*. Oxford: Oxford University Press.

Browne, Eric C. and Feste, Karen Ann (1975). 'Qualitative Dimensions of Coalition Payoffs: Evidences for European Party Government', *American Behavioural Scientist*, 18: 530–56.

—— and Franklin, Mark (1973). 'Aspects of Coalition Payoffs in European Parliamentary Democracies', *American Political Science Review*, 67: 453–69.

—— and Frendreis, John P. (1980). 'Allocating Coalition Payoffs by Conventional Norms: an Assessment of the Evidence for Cabinet Coalition Situation', *American Journal of Political Science*, 24: 753–68.

Budge, Ian and Keman, Hans (1990). *Parties and Democracy. Coalition Formation and Government Functioning in Twenty States*. Oxford: Oxford University Press.

—— and Laver, Michael (1986). 'Office Seeking and Policy Pursuit in Coalition Theory', *Legislative Studies Quarterly*, 11: 485–506.

Bueno de Mesquita, Bruce (1979). 'Coalition Payoffs and Electoral Performances in European Democracies', *Comparative Political Studies*, 12: 61–81.

Carmignani, Fabrizio (2001). 'Cabinet Formation in Coalition Systems', *Scottish Journal of Political Economy*, 48: 313–29.

Caplow, Theodore (1956). 'A Theory of Coalition in the Triad', *American Sociological Review*, 21: 489–93.

Carroll, Royce and Cox, Gary W. (2007). 'The Logic of Gamson's Law: Pre-election Coalitions and Portfolio Distributions', *American Journal of Political Science*, 51: 300–13.

De Winter, Lieven (2001). 'Parties and Government Formation, Portfolio Allocation, and Policy Definition', in Kurt Richard Luther and Ferdinand Müller-Rommel (eds.), *Political Parties in the New Europe*. Oxford: Oxford University Press.

Druckman, James N. and Roberts, Andrew (2005). 'Context and Coalition-Bargaining. Comparing Portfolio Allocation in Eastern and Western Europe', *Party Politics*, 11: 535–55.

—— and Warwick, Paul V. (2005). 'The Missing Piece: Measuring Portfolio Salience in Western European Parliamentary Democracies', *European Journal of Political Research*, 44: 17–42.

Gamson, William A. (1961). 'A Theory of Coalition Formation', *American Sociological Review*, 26: 373–82.

Laver, Michael and Hunt, W. Ben (1992). *Policy and Party Competition*. New York, NY: Routledge.

—— and Schofield, Norman (1990). *Multiparty Government. The Politics of Coalition in Europe*. Oxford: Oxford University Press.

—— and Shepsle, Kenneth A. (1990). 'Coalitions and Cabinet Government', *American Political Science Review*, 84: 843–90.

—— —— (1996). *Making and Breaking Governments*. Cambridge: Cambridge University Press.

Manow, Philip and Zorn, Hendrik (2004). 'Office versus Policy Motives in Portfolio Allocation', Max-Planck-Institut für Gesellschaftsforschung, MPIfG Discussion Paper 04/9.

Martin, Lanny W. and Vanberg, George (2004). 'Policing the Bargain: Coalition Government and Parliamentary Scrutiny', *American Journal of Political Science*, 48: 445–65.

Mershon, Carol (2002). *The Costs of Coalition*. Stanford, CA: Stanford University Press.

Morelli, Massimo (1999). 'Demand Competition and Policy Compromise in Legislative Bargaining', *American Political Science Review*, 93: 809–20.

Müller, Wolfgang C. (2007). 'The Changing Role of the Austrian Civil Service: the Impact of Politicisation, Public Sector Reform, and Europeanisation', in Edward Page and Vincent Wright (eds.), *From the Active to the Enabling State*. Houndmills, UK: Palgrave Macmillan.

—— (2008). 'Successful Failure: Ill-conceived Pre-commitments and Welcome Bargaining Failure Paving the Way to Minority Government in Austria', in Lieven De Winter, Rudy B. Andeweg, and Patrick Dumont (eds.), *Government Formation: Coalition Theory and Deviant Cases*. London: Routledge (forthcoming).

—— and Strøm, Kaare (eds.) (2000). *Coalition Governments in Western Europe*. Oxford: Oxford University Press.

Schofield, Norman (1976). 'The Kernel and Payoffs in European Government Coalitions', *Public Choice*, 26: 29–49.

—— and Laver, Michael (1985). 'Bargaining Theories and Portfolio Payoffs in European Coalition Governments, 1945–1983', *British Journal of Political Science,* 15: 143–64.

Thies, Michael F. (2001). 'Keeping Tabs on Partners: The Logic of Delegation in Coalition Governments', *American Journal of Political Science*, 45: 580–98.

Warwick, Paul V. and Druckman, James N. (2001). 'Portfolio Salience and the Proportionality of Payoffs in Coalition Governments', *British Journal of Political Science*, 31: 627–49.

—— —— (2006). 'The Portfolio Allocation Paradox: An Investigation into the Nature of a Very Strong but Puzzling Relationship', *European Journal of Political Research*, 45: 635–65.

8

Conflict Management in Coalition Government

Rudy B. Andeweg and Arco Timmermans

INTRODUCTION: 'BLONDEL'S PARADOX'

> 'If the principles of cabinet government were applied to the letter, the system would not merely be grossly inefficient, but truly not viable'
>
> (Blondel 1988: 4)

What Blondel refers to is the paradox that without conflicting views dividing the government, cabinet decision-making would be unnecessary, while at the same time cabinets must avoid conflicts in order to survive (also see Blondel and Müller-Rommel 1993). It stands to reason that Blondel's paradox will be most keenly felt in coalition cabinets in which the rivalry between the governing parties is a constant source of conflicts. Because of this permanent threat to the stability of the government, coalition governance is supposed to consist of conflict avoidance rather than of conflict management. In this light, the coalition agreement discussed in Chapter 5 is the most important mechanism for conflict avoidance: it identifies and defuses as many conflicts as possible before the government takes office. Unforeseen conflicts, which nevertheless arise during the coalition's incumbency, are postponed or hived off. In a way, Blondel legitimizes the older generations of coalition theory, which stopped when a coalition was formed, treating coalition governance as a static equilibrium between two coalition formations. Strange as it may sound, the first step in any study of coalition government is therefore to show that the internal dynamics of the government matter. This is what this chapter seeks to do.

Blondel's provocative paradox rests on implicit assumptions about coalition governance that can be questioned or qualified. It assumes that all conflicts threaten the life of the coalition, because (*a*) they always pit one governing party against another, (*b*) the only device for the resolution of conflicts is a majority decision in cabinet, and (*c*) those who have lost the conflict in this way will walk out and bring down the government. In this chapter, we argue that coalition governance implies conflict management (as well as conflict avoidance), that not all conflicts have the potential to bring down the government, that there are other decision rules for the resolution of such conflicts than declaring winners and losers; and above all, that coalition governments have developed alternative arenas to the cabinet's plenary session for the resolution of intra-coalition conflicts.

Our study probes into the governing coalition's internal dynamics, and as such it must be exploratory in nature. First, we are in uncharted waters when it comes to theory for precisely the reason mentioned above: that most existing theories of coalition governance focus on the government's formation and tend to ignore the government's functioning. Second, a large part of the government's internal dynamics remains hidden from public scrutiny. While it is no longer true that 'The most curious point about the Cabinet is that so little is known about it' (Bagehot 1965: 68), the information must be collected from memoirs, interviews, and expert judgements, rather than direct observation. To make up for this relative lack of testable theories and hard data, we shall illustrate our general argument with data based on the expert judgements that have been collected as part of this comparative study, and complement it with the analysis of four cases of management of different types of conflict in two different countries, the Irish Republic and the Netherlands.

ARENAS FOR CONFLICT MANAGEMENT

Any process of conflict management is structured by two decisions: who are recognized as participants in the resolution of the conflict, and what are the mechanisms by which the conflict should be resolved. In other words, the first decision involves the choice of an *arena* for conflict resolution; the second decision is the choice of procedures, of which the *decision rule* is the most important. Occasionally, the protagonists in a conflict may disagree on one or both of these choices, which transforms the original conflict over government policy into a meta-conflict over the proper arena and/or decision rule. Nedelmann describes such a transformation of an issue into a meta-conflict in Sweden, where some parties proposed to refer a conflict to the electoral arena, to be resolved by referendum. This led to a meta-conflict about the referendum (Nedelmann 1982: 177–84). Logically speaking, the choice of an arena and the choice of a decision rule are independent of each other, as a single arena may operate under different formal and informal decision rules [e.g. unanimity, qualified majority, simple majority, decision by interpretation (cf. Steiner and Dorff 1980)]. Empirically speaking, however, the two choices are often intertwined: in the Swedish example given by Nedelmann, the choice of the referendum not only recognizes the voters as participants in the resolution of the conflict but also implies a choice for 'decision by majority' as the decision rule. A particular arena tends to operate under a dominant decision rule, such as the informal decision-by-interpretation rule in most cabinet's plenary sessions. For that reason, we feel justified in this exploratory stage in concentrating on the choice of an **arena** for conflict management.

With regard to Blondel's paradox, it is relevant to ascertain whether conflicts are managed within the cabinet or not. Our central distinction is therefore between arenas that recognize only ministers as legitimate participants ('internal arenas'), and arenas that exclude ministers as legitimate participants ('external arenas'), with a number of arenas in between, in which both cabinet members and others participate ('mixed arenas'). On the basis of descriptive studies of particular countries' governments (collected in, for example, Laver and Shepsle 1994; Blondel and Müller-Rommel 1997; Müller and Strøm 2000), we selected two arenas in each of these three categories, for which we collected further information on their use from country experts:

— An *inner cabinet* (internal arena), that is, a group, which is not issue-specific, of the most senior cabinet ministers, typically including the prime minister and the deputy prime ministers. The members of the inner cabinet can each be responsible for a particular policy area or group of departments, such as Churchill's famous experiment with 'Overlords'. More often the composition of inner cabinets is of a political nature, bringing together the coalition parties' leading ministers. In some countries, such as Belgium, the deputy prime ministers even have a staff to assist them in the inner cabinet. Inner cabinets are sometimes an institutionalized feature of government, meeting regularly and known as such by the outside world, but more often they are little more than irregularly convened informal meetings (as in most German governments).

— A *cabinet committee* (internal arena), that is, a subset of ministers (cabinet ministers and/or junior ministers) that differs from an inner cabinet in that it is confined to a particular policy area and usually includes more ministers than just the coalition parties' leading ministers. In most countries, several cabinet committees exist that cover the main policy domains, but there is considerable variation in their significance (Mackie and Hogwood 1985; Andeweg 1997). In some countries, for example, they meet infrequently and can only prepare the discussion in the full cabinet, whereas in other countries their importance may override that of the cabinet itself, as in the Trudeau governments in Canada, in which cabinet committees were even given some autonomy over their own budgets. In a few countries, such as the Netherlands, cabinet committees may include civil servants or the president of the central bank; in that case, they were not included in our analysis (not being purely 'internal' arenas).

— A *coalition committee* (mixed arena) is a prominent feature of many coalition governments, but the label is used for a variety of arenas that bring together the leaders of the coalition. Here, we use the term restrictively to denote only one variety: a committee consisting of cabinet members (usually the parties' leading ministers) and party leaders outside the government, and not confined to a specific policy area. In Italy, for example, the 'majority summits' (*Vertici*) of the prime minister, sometimes other ministers, and party presidents meet to discuss the political agenda in general, or to deal with political crises. The fact that they are described both as an instrument to break deadlocks and as a threat to cabinet autonomy (Criscitiello 1993, 1996) testifies to their importance as an arena for managing conflicts.

— A *committee of ministers and parliamentary leaders* (mixed arena) differs from the coalition committee only in that the non-governmental politicians on the committee are members because of their leadership of the parliamentary party rather than of the party as such. Such formal or informal committees are quite common, because the constitutional relationship between government and parliament almost demands a mechanism for the coordination of government and parliamentary majority. In some governments, however, this committee also serves as an arena for the management of conflicts within the government. One of the most famous examples is the *Kressbronner Kreis* of Germany's 1966–9 grand coalition, which consisted of Chancellor Kiesinger (CDU), Deputy Chancellor Brandt (SPD), and the leaders of the parliamentary parties in the Bundestag, Barzel (CDU/CSU) and Schmidt (SPD) (Saalfeld 2000: 62). In the Netherlands, the 'turret consultation' (*torentjes-overleg)*, a weekly luncheon meeting of the prime minister, the deputy prime ministers, and the leaders of the coalition's parliamentary parties, has become institutionalized as the most important arena for the management of all potentially dangerous political conflicts (Timmermans and Andeweg 2000: 383–4).

— A *committee of parliamentary leaders* (external arena) has no ministers among its members. Such informal committees exist in many countries governed by coalitions, as the parliamentary parties in the majority are jointly responsible for shepherding the coalition's legislative proposals through parliament. Occasionally, such a committee becomes an arena for the management of conflicts within the government. When, for example, the FDP re-entered a coalition with the CDU/CSU in Germany in 1961, it demanded that a committee of leading members of the parliamentary parties be set up for that purpose (Saalfeld 2000: 61–2). Perhaps the FDP felt that this type of arena, being in parliament, would serve best to remind the much bigger Christian Democrats of the Liberals' much higher walk-away value. However, in this particular case, the lack of governmental representation created rather than resolved conflicts, and it was soon replaced by a mixed arena.

— A *party summit* (external arena) also does not include government ministers. It may or may not include parliamentary leaders, but not in that capacity: the party summit brings together the party leaders, most usually the party presidents. In Belgium, for example, the party presidents usually either stay out of the cabinet or give up the party presidency when they become ministers. In times of crisis (as during Tindemans IV concerning federalization), a meeting of the coalition parties' presidents is called upon to resolve the conflict (De Winter, Timmermans, and Dumont 2000: 328). The resulting compromises are often referred to as 'pacts' (and known by the name of the chateau where the party presidents met).

Of course, other arenas may exist and prove relevant (such as the electoral arena in the Swedish case cited above), but those listed here are the ones that have been most important for coalition politics in Western Europe in the post-war period. From this overview, it is clear that the most important variable distinguishing these arenas is the 'location' of the office that gives a politician entry to the arena (in cabinet, in parliament, and in the party organization). If the same politicians continue to constitute an arena for conflict management, despite having moved to a different office, this is treated as a different arena in this study. In Italy, for example, the most powerful politicians in the governing majority have been in the party organization during some governments, and in parliament, or in the cabinet in other governments. Accordingly, the summit meeting of the prime minister and the leaders of the coalition has been classified as a coalition committee, a committee of ministers and parliamentary leaders, or an inner cabinet. And in Belgium, the 1981-8 governments broke with the tradition of vesting the governing parties' leadership in the party presidents (with the party summit as crucial arena), when the parties appointed their true leaders as (deputy-) prime ministers (with the inner cabinet as dominant arena) 'in order to redefine the power relationship between cabinet and parties' (De Winter, Timmermans, and Dumont 2000: 328). It is precisely for this last reason that it is relevant to reflect such changes in different classifications, especially if such a shift is from an internal arena to an external (or mixed) arena or vice versa.

However, it is not always straightforward to apply the distinctions between the arenas when politicians combine a portfolio in government with a seat in parliament and a position in the party organization. In some countries, such as the Netherlands, the constitution and party bylaws preclude such a '*cumul des mandats*', but most countries have more permissive rules. In Austrian coalitions from 1953 to 1964, the coalition committee included the coalition parties' presidents, who 'leaving aside short periods of transition, also occupied the positions of Chancellor and Vice-Chancellor, respectively' (Müller 2000: 104). According to Blondel, this 'fusion' of party and governmental leadership is rarely complete, as there are rarely sufficient posts for the complete leadership of each coalition party organization and parliamentary party to join the government (Blondel 2000), but it can lead to problematic classifications nevertheless. We have reduced the problem in two ways. First, in cases of politicians combining several offices, we rely on the country experts to determine which office entitled them to participate in that particular arena. Second, in most of the analysis, we have combined the six arenas into three categories (internal, mixed, and external), which solves some ambiguous situations. In the Austrian example, the arena in question further consisted of

TABLE 8.1A. *Most commonly used arenas for cabinet conflict management by country*

Country	Internal		Mixed		External		N
	Inner cabinet	Cabinet committee	Coalition committee	Cab. + Parl. leaders	Parl. leaders	Party summit	
Austria		100					17
Belgium	57	43					28
Denmark		100					17
Finland	3	94		3			33
France		100					17
Germany			6	44	11	39	18
Greece	50				50		2
Iceland	100						22
Ireland			20			80	10
Italy			62			38	34
Luxembourg*			50				16
The Netherlands	61				39		23
Norway	57	43					7
Portugal		67	33				6
Sweden	43	57					7

Notes: Percentages of countries' cabinets 1945–99.
Countries with an asterisk (*) also relied on other arenas.

TABLE 8.1B. *Cabinet conflict management arenas used for most serious conflicts by country*

Country	Internal		Mixed		External		N
	Inner cabinet	Cabinet committee	Coalition committee	Cab. + Parl. leaders	Parl. leaders	Party summit	
Austria	53		47				17
Belgium	21	11				68	28
Denmark	100						17
Finland	6	52		42			33
France*			12			6	17
Germany				56	6	39	18
Greece					100		2
Iceland	100						22
Ireland					100		10
Italy			62			38	34
Luxembourg*			25			25	16
The Netherlands			48		52		23
Norway	86			14			7
Portugal						100	6
Sweden	100						7

Notes: Percentages of countries' cabinets 1945–99.
Countries with an asterisk (*) also relied on other arenas.

the leaders of the parliamentary groups and the central party secretaries, which led us to classify it as a mixed arena.

Table 8.1 shows the variation in the use that is made of these arenas for conflict management (both most commonly used and for the most serious conflicts) across countries. It should be emphasized that the real world of coalition politics is more varied than this picture since we include only the six arenas about which we questioned the country experts (although they had the option of mentioning 'other' arenas). Moreover, for each cabinet only one arena could be mentioned as most commonly used, and only one as used for the most serious conflicts. The fact that an arena is not mentioned for a particular cabinet therefore does not mean that this arena did not exist; only that it was not the arena that is most commonly used, nor the one used for the most serious conflicts. Incomplete as the picture presented in Table 8.1 may be, it does show that governments have set up a variety of arenas, other than the cabinet meeting itself, for the management of conflicts within government. Although we do not know how successful these arenas are in resolving conflicts, it is clear that conflict reduction prior to taking office and non–decision-making in office are not the only options in coalition governance. The next step is to further explore the pattern in Table 8.1: no arena is mentioned as the most common one, nor as the one used for the most serious conflicts, across all countries, but neither is any arena for these two purposes completely absent from all countries. This variation needs explanation.

CONFLICT CHARACTERISTICS AND TYPE OF ARENA

As we seek to explain the variation of arenas for conflict management, one hypothesis that suggests itself is that different conflicts are referred to different arenas. Conflicts can be classified in several ways. In one of the few (perhaps the only) comparative empirical studies of cabinet conflicts, Nousiainen (1993: 270) uses newspaper contents analysis to categorize cabinet conflicts according to policy domain. Most of the conflicts reported in the press during the 1970s and 1980s were about socio-economic issues, with some exceptions for countries in which cultural and ethno-linguistic problems were salient, as in Belgium, and some other exceptions that are less easily explained (Justice and General Administration in Finland and Germany). The patterns reported by Nousiainen show that conflict management varies somewhat between policy domains (most governments have more or less institutionalized procedures for resolving conflicts over the budget; EU institutions are more relevant to some policy areas than to others, and so on), but policy domain does not seem to be a major determining variable.

Conflicts can also be classified according to the seriousness of the threat they pose to the stability or even the survival of the cabinet. Such a classification goes to the heart of Blondel's paradox. When comparing the preferences of coalition partners, Luebbert (1986: 62–4) distinguishes between convergent, tangential, and divergent preferences. We can for present purposes ignore convergent preferences, as these do not involve any serious conflict. The difference between tangential and divergent preferences is really a matter of the relative salience of issues to parties as coalition members. In the case of tangential preferences, issues are of differing salience to different parties; one party may emphasize cultural issues but be relatively indifferent about economic issues, while a coalition partner may weight the issues in the opposite way. In such extreme cases, the bargaining sets of two (or more) parties are unrelated, unless the parties strategically conceal their preferences and systematically use less important issues to get concessions from other parties (since a party's actions will also become known to the voters, however, it seems to be a reasonable assumption that such disclosure forces them to behave sincerely most of the time). In such a situation of tangential preferences, 'logrolling' is a simple way to resolve their differences (except for conflicts about the government's priorities). This solution, however, is not practicable if parties have divergent preferences—hold conflicting views—about the contents of government policy. Typically, in this situation, parties give equal weights to the same issues but differ more or less fundamentally about goals and means. For this reason, divergent preferences are the ones that will involve the greatest threats to the government's survival.

A distinction that may reinforce the one just made is between constant-sum and variable-sum games. This distinction seems to be relevant both to cases of tangential preferences and to situations of divergent preferences. The nature of a negotiation game is in part a matter of perceptions, in which the resolution of divergent views often leads to a result in which the gains of one party are the losses of another. If parties have tangential preferences, they may easily agree to carry all of them out, but this is possible only on the condition of sufficient resources, particularly financial ones. In case the financial means for the implementation of any type of policy are scarce (which is the rule rather than the exception), and these means are necessary to realize substantive goals, negotiations involving 'selective emphases' may change from variable sum (realizing the cumulative list of preferences) into constant sum (the realization of goals that themselves are not in dispute requires a choice about the allocation of resources). Constant-sum games concern conflicts that are most threatening to cabinet survival. Once such high-risk conflicts have broken out, attempts to resolve them are likely to resemble crisis decision-making.

The type of conflict is defined not only by the pay-off structure but also by the characteristics of the players involved in the cabinet conflict, or more precisely by the types of institutional rules that structure the behaviour of ministers and other prominent party players. The cabinet—any cabinet—is, in Bagehot's famous words, 'a combining committee—a hyphen which joins, a buckle which fastens, the legislative part of the State to the executive part of the State' (Bagehot

1965: 68). Ministers are not only their party's agents within the government, but also a head of a government department, and as such they represent their portfolio. As a result, cabinet is not one single institution but contains (at least) two embedded institutions. It is both a coalition of political parties and a council of departmental chiefs. Political processes within these institutions resemble nested games (cf. Tsebelis 1990), and inter-party competition and interdepartmental rivalry constitute the centrifugal forces that may produce cabinet conflicts. The distinction between inter-party and interdepartmental conflicts is not exhaustive. As noted, in Belgium inter-cultural conflicts cannot be ignored. The Belgian constitution requires an equal number of Flemish-speaking and Francophone ministers (with the exception of the prime minister). Nevertheless, in most countries included in this study, inter-party and interdepartmental conflicts seem to be the two most clearly distinguishable types of cabinet conflict.

Of course, there is variation across political systems in this respect as well (Andeweg 1988). In governments composed of a single non-factionalized party, political conflicts are probably rare. Even in coalition governments where the party combinations are more or less permanent and do not span fundamental ideological cleavages (e.g. the French coalitions, or the coalitions of non-socialist parties in Norway and Sweden), political conflicts may not be frequent. Where ministers are not heads of executive agencies, as in Sweden, or where they are shielded from their department by a large *cabinet ministeriel*, as in Belgium, interdepartmental conflicts may not reach the cabinet agenda as often as in countries where ministers are deeply involved in the departments for which they are responsible.

As far as the scanty information about policy conflicts within cabinets allows us to do this, a comparison between interdepartmental and inter-party conflicts suggests that those of the interdepartmental type are most frequent. For Germany, Mayntz (1980: 156) observes: 'Conflicts which do become manifest in cabinet discussions are rarely of a purely partisan nature (for instance, FDP ministers against SPD ministers); more often they are structurally determined, reflecting the conflicting interests and orientations of the departments and their clientele.' In the Netherlands, a study of 96 cabinet conflicts reported by the press between 1973 and 1986 showed that 67 per cent of these conflicts were interdepartmental (Timmermans and Bakema 1990). Yet, while interdepartmental conflicts are more frequent, inter-party conflicts are more threatening to the survival of the government: a government department that loses in a conflict cannot leave the government, but a losing governing party can, and may bring down the government as a consequence.

In summary, we can conclude that the conflicts that are most threatening to the government's survival are those that involve divergent preferences, that are of a constant-sum character, and in which the protagonists are the political parties in the coalition. We can also conclude that there are other conflicts (tangential preferences, variable sum, and interdepartmental) that are less threatening to the

TABLE 8.2. *Conflict management arenas*

	Type of arena			No. of cabinets
	Internal	Mixed	External	
Most commonly used	67	17	16	249
Used for the most serious conflicts	38	30	32	235

Notes: Percentages of all cabinets reported.
Cabinets with other arenas (see Table 8.1) are excluded.

survival of the government and are also more frequent. Blondel's paradox implies that cabinets must avoid the management of conflicts in order to survive. The more threatening the conflicts are, the more plausible this hypothesis is. Our hypothesis is therefore that the most threatening conflicts will be hived off to arenas that are external to the cabinet, while the more frequent (and relatively innocuous) conflicts are more often resolved in arenas internal to the cabinet.

As a first test of this hypothesis, we can compare the answers by the country experts to the question about the most commonly used arena for conflict resolution with their answers to the question about the arena that is used for the most serious conflicts. The latter are defined as conflicts that according to the perceptions of the political actors have the potential to immediately threaten the survival of the cabinet. If we assume that the most commonly used arena deals with the type of conflict that occurs most frequently, and that the most frequent conflicts are also the least threatening ones, the pattern in Table 8.2 confirms our hypothesis: in 67 per cent of all coalition cabinets, internal arenas are the most commonly used for the management of conflicts, but in only 38 per cent of all coalition cabinets are the most serious conflicts referred to internal arenas. However, notwithstanding this clear and statistically significant association, it is not true that cabinets avoid having to resolve serious conflicts: only one-third of the most serious conflicts are completely exported from the cabinet to arenas within the coalition but outside the cabinet, and if we add 'internal' and 'mixed' arenas together, in 68 per cent of all cabinets, ministers are involved in the resolution of the most serious conflicts. In other words, the type of conflict is clearly an important factor, but it cannot explain all variation in the use of arenas for conflict management.

CABINET CHARACTERISTICS AND TYPE OF ARENA

As we have just argued, one crucial factor determining the arena is the nature of the conflict. Another important factor that will be our focus in this section is the cabinet itself and its suitability as an arena for conflict resolution. Our basic hypothesis is that coalition parties select the arena for conflict resolution on the basis of a cost–benefit calculation. All else equal, it is less costly to rely on pre-existing institutions, and particularly efficient ones such as the cabinet or subunits of the cabinet—in other words, internal arenas. Mixed or external arenas are more costly because they tend to be cumbersome and potentially more 'leaky'. But because they are more likely to be inclusive and operate by unanimity rules, they may be more likely to generate compromises that are acceptable to all parties. External arenas therefore tend to be chosen when the cabinet is weak, the bargaining situation complex, the opposition credible, or when the conflict is important and internal arenas are viewed as biased against the interests of some of the cabinet parties.

Let us now consider some of the concrete variables that might reflect these properties of the coalition and its environment and see what their expected effects might be. First, there are the *structural attributes* of the cabinet, as reflected in its composition. If the coalition is small (few parties, minimal winning, and small share of parliamentary seats), we expect relatively few serious political conflicts, enabling the cabinet to deal with the few conflicts that do arise internally. Fewer parties in the coalition also mean that a larger proportion of the leadership of these parties can join the government, facilitating internal management of the few political controversies that do arise. A coalition that is less tightly built will face a more complex bargaining situation with less room for all the parties' leaders in the government. This may lead to the more frequent use of arenas of a mixed or external character. Parties are also less likely to invest in costly (mixed or external) conflict management capacities when the government will be in office for only a short time (interim governments, caretaker governments, governments formed for the remainder of the parliamentary term after a crisis, and so on). Thus, we hypothesize governments that form immediately following elections, or other governments that can expect a long incumbency, to develop and use external arenas, whereas governments that can expect only a short tenure will use internal arenas.

A second aspect of the government's composition has to do with the *preferences* of the main players, that is, the political parties in the coalition. If a cabinet is homogeneous and compact in its policy preferences (ideologically connected, spanning a limited ideological range), we expect it to be better able to handle its conflicts internally. Another important question is whether the coalition contains a party that has viable alternatives to this particular coalition. Such a party may have little interest in keeping conflicts within cabinet. Like the German FDP in the 1961 case referred to above, it may prefer to remind its coalition partners of its high walk-away value by dealing with conflicts in arenas that include parliamentary leaders. We use the inclusion in the coalition of the party with the median legislator (on one or on two dimensions) and of the party with the highest score on the bargaining power index as (admittedly imperfect) indicators of this type of coalition composition. It should be associated with mixed or external arenas.

The *institutions* that provide opportunities for, or constrain, conflict management in government form the third cluster of independent variables. If, for example, the prime minister's institutional position is strong (e.g. with staff to monitor departments, and with the formal power to appoint and dismiss ministers, to determine the jurisdiction of ministries, to give instructions to ministers, and to control the agenda), then the prime minister has the facilities to adjudicate interdepartmental conflicts, and we expect routine conflict management to be contained largely in internal arenas. A weaker prime minister may need reinforcement by political leaders outside the cabinet, and we expect a more frequent use of mixed and external arenas. The situation is likely to be the reverse for the most serious conflicts: a prime minister can only be a member of one of the governing parties, and the more powers are vested in the premiership, the less likely the other parties in the coalition will be to accept decision-making in purely internal arenas where the prime minister dominates. A weaker prime minister will not arouse the same amount of party-political envy, and internal arenas may be used.

Yet another cluster of independent variables involves the *bargaining environment* of coalition governance. In part, this bargaining environment is reflected in the coalition agreement the parties may have set up before taking office. The negotiation of a comprehensive coalition agreement during government formation and the costs of setting up internal procedures and arenas for conflict management can be seen as investments that will pay off by reducing the transaction costs of conflict management during the government's tenure in office. If the coalition has invested in a coalition agreement, especially if it is a comprehensive one, this will reduce the number of serious conflicts and result in a less frequent use of mixed and external arenas. If the coalition always operates under a rule of coalition discipline when voting on the cabinet's legislative proposals, the cabinet can take its support in parliament for granted, and there is less need to involve parliamentary leaders in conflict management. In other words, internal arenas can be used with greater confidence.

Finally, we expect that when governments have to deal with policy conflicts, they are guided by events in their experiences and by their expectations of their electoral environment. Parties can therefore be expected to be more willing to pay the *ex ante* transaction costs of building external mechanisms of conflict management when they have experienced costly conflicts in the past or when the electorate is volatile and the results of future elections are therefore unpredictable.

To test these hypotheses, we use logit analysis.[1] The results are presented in Table 8.3 for the type of arena that is most commonly used for conflict management, and in Table 8.4 for the type of arena used for the management of the most serious conflicts. Each table contains eight models, employing specific variables from the blocks used throughout this book.

---

[1] In previous analyses we used multinomial logit analysis, using internal arenas as the baseline category. We measured the effect of each independent variable on the probability of mixed rather than internal arenas being used, and of external rather than internal arenas being used. These analyses yielded very similar but slightly weaker results. As the logit analysis is easier to interpret and less space consuming, we have eventually collapsed 'mixed' and 'external' arenas and used logit analysis.

Table 8.3 shows the results for the most common type of conflict management mechanism. Because the strong fixed effects of countries would otherwise tend to dwarf many of the other interesting effects, we have deleted them from the models in this table (interested readers can consult Table 8.1 for a country-by-country breakdown). Table 8.3 shows that preference-related and institutional variables are most helpful in explaining these mechanisms. Several features of the bargaining environment also have a systematic impact. On the other hand, there is no evidence of any temporal trend, and to the extent that critical events matter, their impact is weak and non-robust.

We find little overall effect of structural attributes. Several of these variables display a significant relationship in the initial partial estimation (model 2). However, none of these estimates survives the controls introduced in our full or final model. Our block of preference variables performs better than the structural attributes in the initial estimations, and several of these variables retain their impact in the more inclusive models. Thus, mixed or external arenas are more likely to be used when there are strong extremist parties, when the ideological range in parliament is narrow, when the number of issue dimensions is low, and when the cabinet is not ideologically connected. The last of these results is consistent with our expectations, whereas most of the others are not.

Institutional variables are among our strongest predictors of conflict resolution arenas. The two variables involved in our institutional cluster, positive parliamentarism and prime ministerial powers, by themselves explain more than one-third of the observed variance, according to our summary statistics. The use of mixed or external arenas increases with both of these variables (i.e. to say that such arenas are more common under positive parliamentarism and when the prime minister is strong). The former of these effects is as expected, whereas our hypothesis was that strong prime ministers would shift conflict resolution to external arenas (because the internal arena would be too biased in favour of the prime minister's party) only for the most serious issues. As it happens, the effect is actually most significant for the most common issues.

Finally, prior agreements between the coalition parties matter significantly. The mere existence of a coalition agreement considerably increases the probability that internal arenas are used. One would further expect that more comprehensive coalition agreements also preempt more, and more serious, conflicts, and that they would therefore enable the coalition to confine itself even more to arenas that are internal to the cabinet. As Table 8.3 demonstrates, this is indeed the case. Overall, our models suggest that positive parliamentarism and coalition agreements have the greatest impact on the most commonly used arenas. Positive parliamentarism increases the likelihood that the most commonly used arena is mixed or external by nearly 80 percentage points, while a coalition agreement increases the likelihood that the conflict management arena is internal by over 50 percentage points.

TABLE 8.3. *Logistic regressions on most common conflict management arena being mixed or external (not internal)*

Independent variables	Model 1	Model 2	Model 3	Model 4	Model 5	Model 6	Model 7	Model 8	Impact[a]
Time									
1940s	0.10 (0.55)								
1960s	−0.38 (0.48)								
1970s	−0.24 (0.45)								
1980s	−0.13 (0.43)								
1990s	0.10 (0.45)								
Structure									
Post-election cabinet		−0.45 (0.42)						2.18 (1.04)**	0.07 (0.07)
Max. possible cab. duration		−0.001 (.00)**						−0.002 (0.001)*	−0.04 (0.03)[a]
Bargaining power frag.		−0.63 (0.16)**					−0.11 (0.61)		
Cabinet seat share		−0.05 (0.02)**					0.01 (0.04)		
Number of cabinet parties		0.50 (0.23)**					0.08 (0.78)		
Max. barg. power pty. in cab.		1.92 (0.57)**					0.74 (1.59)		
Minimum-winning coalition		0.27 (0.49)							
Surplus-majority cabinet		0.38 (0.65)		−0.99 (1.04)					
Preferences									
Extremist party seat share			0.08 (0.02)**				0.30 (0.09)**	0.28 (0.08)**	0.02 (0.02)
Parliamentary preference range			−0.03 (0.01)**				−0.07 (0.04)**	−0.06 (0.02)**	−0.07 (0.04)[a]
Polarization (BP weighted)			−0.06 (0.03)**				0.03 (0.08)		
Issue dimensionality			−2.84 (0.78)**				−8.86 (2.55)**	−8.33 (2.34)**	−0.07 (0.04)[a]
No core party			−1.07 (0.43)**				0.57 (1.51)		
Cabinet preference range			0.01 (0.01)						

	M1	M2	M3	M4	M5	M6	M7	M8	Marginal effect
Median party (1st dim.) in cab.			−0.05 (0.49)						
Median party (2nd dim.) in cab.		0.93 (0.42)**					3.26 (1.17)**	2.94 (0.94)**	0.08 (0.07)
Connected cab.		−0.57 (0.40)					−1.05 (1.04)		
Institutions									
Positive parliamentarism				2.88 (0.36)**			4.01 (1.05)**	4.26 (0.96)**	0.78 (0.10)
Abs. majority no-confidence				−0.95 (0.57)*			−4.99 (1.81)**	−4.33 (1.42)**	−0.08 (0.07)
PM powers				0.40 (0.12)**			1.94 (0.51)**	1.49 (0.35)**	0.11 (0.09)
Bargaining									
Prior cab.: conflict termination					0.06 (0.32)				
Same PM & cabinet					−0.48 (0.47)		−0.23 (0.82)		
Cabinet bargaining duration					0.01 (0.00)*		0.02 (0.01)**	0.02 (0.01)**	0.08 (0.05)[a]
Inconclusive bargaining round					−0.58 (0.37)				
Coalition agreement					−1.45 (0.33)**		−3.31 (1.05)**	−2.83 (0.85)**	−0.53 (0.16)
Comprehensive policy agreement					−0.86 (0.36)**		−2.59 (1.14)**	−2.97 (0.97)**	−0.08 (0.07)
Critical events									
Terminal event lag (any)						−0.09 (0.40)			
Electoral volatility						0.00 (0.02)	−0.07 (0.05)	−0.08 (0.04)*	−0.04 (0.03)[a]
Constant	−0.59 (0.32)*	−0.14 (1.11)	9.37 (2.35)**	−3.27 (0.46)**	0.43 (0.33)	−0.75 (0.23)**	18.9 (7.6)**	19.3 (6.5)**	
Number of observations	249	247	244	249	243	231	231	231	
Pseudo-R^2	.00	.14	.30	.36	.18	.00	.77	.76	
% Correctly predicted	.67	.77	.77	.83	.77	.67	.94	.94	

Notes: *$p < 0.10$; **$p < 0.05$.

[a] Impact is the marginal effect of a unit change in the independent variable on the probability of the outcome occurring, calculated based on Model 8, with the following exceptions: Maximum possible cabinet duration is for a 500-day change, Parliamentary preference range is for a 25 point change, Issue dimensionality is for a 0.25 change, Cabinet bargaining duration is for a 30 day change, and Electoral volatility is for an 8 point change (1 standard deviation changes).

TABLE 8.4. *Logistic regressions on arena used for the most serious conflicts being mixed or external (not internal)*

Independent variables	Model 1	Model 2	Model 3	Model 4	Model 5	Model 6	Model 7	Model 8	Impact[a]
Time									
1940s	0.53 (0.55)								
1960s	0.17 (0.46)								
1970s	0.93 (0.46)**						1.89 (0.82)**	1.24 (0.60)**	0.28 (0.11)
1980s	0.82 (0.42)*						1.86 (0.75)**	1.01 (0.53)*	0.24 (0.11)
1990s	0.71 (0.45)						1.33 (0.91)		
Structure									
Post-election cabinet		−0.15 (0.41)					0.00 (0.00)		
Max. possible cab. duration		0.00 (0.00)					0.22 (0.30)		
Bargaining power frag.		−0.04 (0.16)							
Cabinet seat share		−0.01 (0.01)							
Number of cabinet parties		0.09 (0.23)					−0.19 (0.38)		
Max. barg. power pty. in cab.		1.58 (0.46)**					2.00 (0.73)**	2.06 (0.58)**	0.38 (0.11)
Minimum winning coalition		0.03 (0.46)							
Surplus majority cabinet		1.19 (0.65)*					1.77 (0.74)**	1.71 (0.53)**	0.35 (0.11)
Preferences									
Extremist party seat share			0.07 (0.02)**				0.04 (0.04)		
Parliamentary preference range			−0.02 (0.01)**				−0.01 (0.02)		
Polarization (BP weighted)			−0.11 (0.04)**				−0.12 (0.06)**	−0.14 (0.03)**	−0.03 (0.01)
Issue dimensionality			−1.90 (0.73)**				−1.85 (1.10)*	−1.79 (0.93)*	−0.11 (0.06)[a]
No core party			−0.43 (0.42)						
Cabinet preference range			0.02 (0.01)*						
Median party (1st dim.) in cab.			0.56 (0.46)						
Median party (2nd dim.) in cab.			0.34 (0.39)				−0.31 (0.52)		
Connected cab.			−1.09 (0.38)**				−0.23 (0.52)		

	1	2	3	4	5	6	7	8
Institutions								
Positive parliamentarism			2.54 (0.41)**			1.85 (0.57)**	2.23 (0.51)**	0.41 (0.10)
Abs. majority no-confidence			−0.50 (0.43)					
PM powers			0.05 (0.10)					
Bargaining								
Prior cab.: conflict termination					0.43 (0.31)	0.83 (0.52)	0.81 (0.46)*	0.19 (0.11)
Same PM & cabinet					−0.65 (0.43)	−0.38 (0.68)		
Cabinet bargaining duration					0.02 (0.01)**	0.01 (0.01)		
Inconclusive bargaining round					−0.65 (0.35)*	−0.75 (0.58)		
Coalition agreement					−0.88 (0.35)**	−1.09 (0.66)*		
Comprehensive policy agreement					−0.49 (0.31)	−1.63 (0.64)**	−1.14 (0.48)**	−0.25 (0.11)
Critical events								
Terminal event lag (any)				−0.33 (0.41)				
Electoral volatility				0.04 (0.02)*		0.07 (0.05)	0.08 (0.04)**	0.16 (0.08)[a]
Constant	−0.05 (0.31)	−1.59 (1.05)	8.48 (2.29)**	−0.34 (0.29)	0.95 (0.37)**	0.14 (0.26)	4.66 (3.48)	4.29 (2.84)
Number of observations	235	233	230	235	230	219	219	219
Pseudo-R^2	.02	.13	.27	.21	.11	.01	.51	.49
% Correctly predicted	.63	.67	.76	.71	.68	.62	.85	.84

Notes: * $p < 0.10$; ** $p < 0.05$.

[a] Impact is the marginal effect of a unit change in the independent variable on the probability of the outcome occurring, calculated based on Model 8, with the following exceptions: Issue dimensionality is for a 0.25 change, and Electoral volatility is for an 8 point change (1 standard deviation changes).

TABLE 8.5. *Cabinet conflict management arenas by written coalition agreements*

	Internal	Mixed	External	No. of cabinets
Type of arena most commonly used				
No written agreement	42	29	29	89
Written coalition agreement	80	11	9	160
Type of arena used for most serious conflicts				
No written agreement	21	41	38	80
Written coalition agreement	46	25	29	155

Note: Percentages reported.

The results for the most serious conflicts are displayed in Table 8.4. Here we find some fairly weak temporal effects, in that coalitions formed in the 1970s and 1980s are somewhat more likely to utilize external (or mixed) arenas, perhaps because of the more contentious politics of these decades, which would be consistent with our expectations. The effects of structural attributes are again fairly weak, but external arenas are more likely to be the choice of surplus-majority coalitions as well as of coalitions that include the party with the greatest bargaining power. Mixed or external arenas also correlate positively (but not robustly) with extremist party strength and negatively and more robustly with the parliamentary preference range and the effective number of issue dimensions. At least the latter two results are consistent with our expectations. A party system with a narrow preference range and a limited number of issue dimensions is one in which there is likely to be a credible opposition. The use of external arenas indicates that the governing parties are cognizant of the threat that this implies and are willing to invest in resilient mechanisms of conflict resolution.

Again, positive parliamentarism strongly correlates with the same institutional choice (and perhaps for similar reasons). A written coalition agreement, and more robustly a comprehensive one, once again correlates with the use of internal arenas, as we expected. Finally, electoral volatility, another indication of a challenging bargaining environment, is consistently and significantly associated with the use of mixed or external arenas of conflict resolution. As with the most common arena however, the two variables with the largest impact are positive parliamentarism and coalition agreements. However, unlike with the most commonly used arena, a number of other variables have quite sizeable effects: a one standard deviation increase in volatility increases the likelihood of reliance on mixed or external arenas by 16 percentage points, surplus-majority cabinets are 38 percentage points more likely to use mixed or external arenas than other cabinet types, and the presence of the largest parliamentary party in government has a similar impact.

One of our strongest results in Tables 8.3 and 8.4 is thus that coalition agreements are systematically related to the types of conflict management mechanisms that are used for the most common as well as for the most serious conflicts. In Table 8.5, we look more closely at the relationship between written coalition

TABLE 8.6. *Institutionalization of arenas for cabinet conflict management*

	Current: Internal	Current: Mixed	Current: External	No. of cabinets
Most commonly used arena				
Prior: Internal	99	1	0	156
Prior: Mixed	5	82	13	39
Prior: External	5	13	82	39
Used for most serious conflicts				
Prior: Internal	92	2	6	84
Prior: Mixed	3	89	8	65
Prior: External	6	10	84	70

Notes: Comparison to prior coalition cabinets.
Percentages reported.

agreements and the use of internal, mixed, or external arenas of conflict management. It is clear that the existence of a coalition agreement considerably increases the probability that internal arenas are used, both as the most common arena and as the arena for the most serious conflicts. The effect is most pronounced for the more frequent, less serious, conflicts, which rarely seem to be handled outside the cabinet when there is a written coalition agreement. In 80 per cent of these cases, an internal arena is in fact used, whereas the equivalent percentage is only 42 per cent for coalitions without a written agreement. This discrepancy reflects a divergence of paths in coalition governance: coalition parties may endeavour to resolve their differences either *ex ante* by investing in policy agreements or by resorting to more extensive institutions for *ex post* conflict management.

Our data also suggest a great deal of institutional consistency over time. In almost all cases, the type of arena most commonly used is the same as in the previous cabinet. The association is slightly less strong for the choice of arena for the most serious conflicts, especially when the previous cabinet relied on internal arenas (see Table 8.6). Altogether, though, the indications of path-dependency are so striking that one has to wonder whether we are not actually measuring country effects. Yet, the choice of a 'national' arena for conflict management is not so institutionalized that each country has its own specific set of arenas that remains constant across all its cabinets. The reader is referred back to Table 8.1: if each of our 15 countries had had one specific arena for the most common conflicts and one (potentially the same) specific arena for the most serious conflicts, and country thus fully determined the choice of arena, we would have had 30 cells in Table 8.1 each containing 100 per cent of the relevant observations. In fact, there are only 10 cells that contain 100 per cent of their respective national observations, and only in Denmark and Iceland is the choice of arena for both types of conflict fully institutionalized. In conjunction, Tables 8.1 and 8.6 point to partial institutionalization, which would be consistent with the existence of a trend. Institutions change, but this takes time.

TABLE 8.7. *Arenas for cabinet conflict management across time*

Decade	Internal arena	Mixed arena	External arena	Number of cabinets
Type of arena most commonly used				
1940s	59	23	18	22
1950s	64	21	14	42
1960s	73	20	8	40
1970s	71	22	7	45
1980s	67	5	28	58
1990s	62	19	19	42
Type of arena used for the most serious conflicts				
1940s	36	41	23	22
1950s	51	29	20	41
1960s	47	24	29	34
1970s	30	45	25	40
1980s	32	19	49	57
1990s	34	32	34	41

The specific patterns of change are interesting. Countries that have come to utilize an internal arena very rarely experience shifts to a mixed or external arena. This is particularly true if the internal arena is used for the most common conflicts. Countries that rely on mixed or external arenas, however, are somewhat more likely to change, though most of this change involves switches between these two types rather than the adoption of an internal arena.

One might wonder how much of this change may be due to secular changes in coalition governance. In Table 8.7 we have therefore broken down the type of conflict management arena by decade. The data show erratic fluctuations (e.g. a remarkable shift from mixed to external arenas in the 1980s), but no clear trend across all countries in our study. Internal arenas, for example, were particularly 'popular' in the 1950s and 1960s, but have since drifted back to the same incidence that they had at the beginning of the post-war period. If we check for trends within individual countries, there is not much evidence either: for the most serious conflicts internal arenas were increasingly used in Austria during the 1980s and 1990s, and for the same conflicts there seems to have been a shift towards mixed arenas in Finland and the Netherlands since the 1960s. But it is difficult to spot any broader trends.

The conclusion must be that the previous cabinet's choice of arena plays an important role, but that in most countries this choice is not completely fixed, and that changes over time rarely constitute a trend, but are explained by factors such as the inclusion of the party with the highest walk-away value in the coalition, and the existence of a coalition agreement. Together with the type of conflict, the choice of arena by the previous cabinet and characteristics of the cabinet or coalition seem to determine whether internal, mixed, or external arenas are used for conflict management.

ZOOMING IN: CONFLICT MANAGEMENT IN DUTCH AND IRISH COALITION CABINETS

So far, our discussion of arenas for the management of cabinet conflicts is confined to their overall importance. To illustrate how they may actually be employed and to provide a more dynamic view of conflict management in coalition governments, we now turn to two countries, Ireland and the Netherlands, and consider cases of coalition conflict management within these countries.

Patterns of conflict management in the Netherlands and Ireland

One of our findings in the cross-national analyses was that the presence of a written coalition agreement increases the likelihood that coalition parties use internal arenas to resolve their differences. We accounted for this pattern by arguing that coalition partners that have made *ex ante* investments to enhance policy homogeneity are better equipped to deal with problems 'in house' than if partners leave potential policy conflicts unattended. However, if serious conflicts do occur, even in coalitions with comprehensive agreements, mixed and external arenas become more important.

As we can see from Table 8.1, the Dutch case fits this general pattern. Cabinets with a coalition agreement deal with common matters largely internally, but switch to mixed arenas when serious conflicts surface and the stakes are high. While Dutch cabinets have always been coalitions, conflict management arenas have changed from largely external to mixed and internal arenas. Before the emergence of written and published coalition agreements in the mid-1960s, conflicts of all kinds were dealt with primarily by the parliamentary leaders and in most parties the party leader preferred to stay in parliament rather than enter the government (Dutch constitutional rules prevent a minister from being an MP at the same time). Since the 1960s, the practice of writing coalition agreements evolved, and with that change it also became usual for party leaders to accept a cabinet portfolio. As a consequence, day-to-day conflict management shifted to arenas within the cabinet, and escalated conflicts came under the informal jurisdiction of ministers and parliamentary leaders together. The rationale for the emergence of this mixed arena is easy to see: diverging interpretations of the deals included in a coalition agreement needed to be clarified or appeased by those who made these deals in the first place. Since the 1980s, the most important site is a weekly consultation meeting in the prime minister's office.

Things are different in Ireland, where internal cabinet arenas are hardly used for conflict management (see Table 8.1). External arenas stand out as the most important, and this is true in Ireland for all types of coalition cabinets—whether they operate with a coalition agreement or not, and whether they include the party with the highest walk-away value or not. Yet, the latter factor seems to be at the root of this Irish exception. In the elections of 1992, the Labour Party made substantial gains, and though it did not become the largest party, it became indispensable to the formation of a majority coalition because Fianna Fáil and Fine Gael excluded each other. Labour used its leverage to increase its influence and also the visibility of its influence over cabinet policy by demanding a number of institutional changes (Mitchell 2000: 135, 148–9). First, the role of its party leader within the cabinet was strengthened through the creation of an office of deputy prime minister, with civil servants attached and led by a junior minister. Second, ministerial cabinets were formed. Third, each cabinet minister was permitted to appoint a set of 'partnership programme managers'. These arrangements were meant to enhance ministerial control, so that the coalition parties could monitor the implementation of the coalition agreement and detect differences of interpretation at an early stage. Programme managers, members of the ministerial cabinets, and the party's most important junior minister together formed a coalition committee, which seems to have been institutionalized since then. Thus, the circumstances of the 1992–3 government formation have led to the creation of a new arena for conflict management, and path-dependency has ensured the continuation of this arena in later cabinets. The most serious conflicts continue to be dealt with by the party leaders making a temporary transfer away from the cabinet to an informal ad hoc party summit. It should be noted that the party leaders are also the prime minister and the deputy prime minister. As we noted before, such cases of 'fusion' make it difficult to determine whether we are dealing with an internal or external arena. However, the two politicians do act in their capacity of party leader in these circumstances. The fact that, during such conflict management in Ireland, cabinet meetings are sometimes even suspended until the matter is resolved (Mitchell 2000: 140) provides a further indication that conflict management is deliberately moved outside the official institutions.

Both electoral and intra-party reasons appear to account for this development. Electorally, Ireland has experienced negative incumbency effects that may particularly frighten smaller coalition parties (who typically suffer the most). Moreover, Labour Party leaders have often been under pressure from their own party activists, who demand a distinct socialist impact on government policy in return for providing a parliamentary majority. Yet, given a strong doctrine of collective cabinet responsibility combined with majority voting in cabinet the Labour Party is threatened by the prospects of 'loss of identity within a coalition' (Marsh and Mitchell 1999: 49). Conflict management institutions that involve party leaders from outside the cabinet may be a way to 'tie the party to the mast' and prevent costly concessions to the party's coalition partner(s).

How interdepartmental and inter-party conflicts are managed

These points may be illustrated with empirical cases of management of conflicts over government policy. We borrow from two studies of coalition policy conflicts, one on the life of the Irish FitzGerald II coalition government in office between 1982 and 1987 (Mitchell 1996), the other dealing with the Dutch Lubbers I coalition government between 1982 and 1986 (Timmermans 1998, 2003). We consider two cases for each cabinet, one on an interdepartmental policy conflict (the 'most common' conflict in our comparative analysis) and one on an interparty policy conflict (the 'most serious' conflict in the comparative analysis). The case analyses contain a brief presentation of the controversial issue and the political arrangement included in the coalition agreement, followed by a discussion of the implementation of this political arrangement and the way in which recurring conflicts were managed. Our choice of cases is selective: given the importance of the coalition agreement not only for conflict avoidance but also for later conflict management, we selected issues that were mentioned in some way in the coalition agreement, were placed on the cabinet agenda, and divided ministers or parties in office.

Policy controversy and temporary resolution: the coalition agreement

After the Irish general election in 1982, Fine Gael and Labour engaged in negotiations to build a coalition with a majority in the Dáil, the Irish Parliament. Both parties were condemned to form a coalition together, as Fianna Fáil then still refused to enter any coalition. It was Fianna Fáil, however, which controlled the median legislator, and the significant distance between the two prospective governing parties resulted in fierce policy conflict in all major fields, particularly with regard to economic issues and moral issues.

During the negotiations over what would become the FitzGerald II cabinet, the Labour Party (17 seats) was acutely aware of the need to remain visible in a coalition with the much larger Fine Gael (70 seats). This political need drove much of Labour's behaviour before and after it took office. One important issue was the budget deficit. The parties agreed to phase out the deficit in five years, but at Labour's insistence this reduction was made dependent on other macroeconomic goals such as economic growth and a reduction of unemployment. The compromise thus hardly reduced the risk of battles over cutbacks later on. With regard to moral issues, divorce featured prominently on the agenda of the negotiators. Labour pressed for legalisation of divorce, which required a change of the Constitution, a subject on which a referendum was to be held. Fine Gael, on the other hand, was deeply divided over this issue, which prompted party leader FitzGerald to aim for some form of procrastination. This was indeed the result of the negotiations: the coalition agreement contained a procedure stating that before the end of 1983, an Oireachtas committee (composed of MPs from both Houses of Parliament) would 'recommend on the problems of the protection of marriage under modern conditions and of marriage breakdown and on any legislative or constitutional action that may be required' (quoted in Mitchell 1996: 145). Delegation of the problem to a broad parliamentary committee was meant to contain the conflict for some time after the cabinet had formed.

In the Netherlands, the parliamentary election of 1982 was followed by a relatively quick government formation in which Christian Democrats (CDA) and Liberals (VVD) formed the Lubbers I government. This partnership was sealed by a much more detailed coalition agreement than ever before (and certainly more detailed than that of the FitzGerald II cabinet in Ireland), with a strong emphasis on economic and financial policy. Like the coalition parties in Ireland, the two Dutch parties agreed on a reduction of the budget deficit, but the Lubbers I coalition agreement contained far more explicit compromises over this and related issues—a set of clear commitments to cuts in all policy sectors to which the minister of finance could refer in his dealings with spending ministers. Moral issues also divided the parties in the Netherlands, but agreements in this area took the form of procedural or opaque and implicit compromises. The most controversial of these issues was euthanasia. Contrary to the CDA, the VVD advocated a more liberal policy in which euthanasia would remain unpunished under well-specified conditions. The Liberals anticipated parliamentary support on this particular issue from the Social Democrats (PvdA), the largest opposition party. The result of the negotiations was the following statement in the coalition agreement: 'The government will determine its policy after consulting a State Committee on Euthanasia. Until the government has defined its policy, the status quo will be maintained' (quoted in Timmermans 2003). This promise enabled the CDA to take the Liberals on board without alienating any of its internal party groups. It also illustrates the bargaining power of the CDA, even though on this policy dimension the VVD controlled the median legislator (Timmermans and Andeweg 2000: 360): at that time, VVD and PvdA still excluded each other as potential coalition partners.

During coalition formation, divorce in Ireland and euthanasia in the Netherlands were contained rather than substantively settled in large part because the bigger party's walk-away value was high enough to resist the other party's claims for concrete policy change. Since the change-oriented party in these cases—Labour in Ireland and the VVD in the Netherlands—had a high discount rate (was impatient), a vague or procedural agreement was better than a moratorium on the issue lasting four long years. The party's commitment to keep promises to its voters meant that it needed to reopen the battle during the coalition's lifetime.

Management of interdepartmental battles

Both in Ireland and the Netherlands, the budget deficit target was set as an interparty compromise during government formation, but once in office, ministers became primarily responsible for implementing them. During the initial coalition bargaining, the pain of the budget cutbacks is tempered because they are part of a larger package deal that contains benefits in other policy areas. However, such compensations offer little consolation to individual departmental ministers when they later face the task of cutting into their own budgetary flesh. As a consequence, in both countries ministers began to defend their departmental interests, engaging in interdepartmental conflicts over the interpretation of the commitments written down in the coalition agreement.

The FitzGerald II government and the Lubbers I government both prepared their first budget in early 1983. In both cases, the minister of finance showed himself a champion of austerity policy, opposed by the *big spenders* such as Social Affairs and Education and Health. However, in Ireland much was left open to be decided by the government, leading to recurring interministerial battles with a high risk of escalation. As on most policy conflicts beyond routine decision-making, the Irish cabinet appeared not to be the arena where such matters could be settled. Often conflicts were settled externally in meetings organized instantly between Prime Minister FitzGerald (Fine Gael), the minister of finance (also Fine Gael) and Labour Party leader Dick Spring (Mitchell 1996: 150). This informal arena was partly departmental (the presence of the minister of finance) but also party political (the presence of party leaders).

We already mentioned the Irish preference for external arenas as an expression of the electoral need of the much smaller coalition party to maintain its electoral profile, but this line of reasoning need not apply to interdepartmental (as opposed to partisan) conflicts such as the ones FitzGerald II frequently experienced. In this case, however, there was a clear risk that interdepartmental conflicts could transform into party-political conflicts because some of the biggest spending departments were in the hands of the Labour Party, whereas the minister of finance belonged to Fine Gael. This cabinet characteristic probably also induced the prime minister to oppose his own party's minister of finance during the struggle over the size of spending cuts in order to contain the conflict as much as possible.

The parties in the Lubbers I government had invested heavily in negotiating detailed agreements over economic and financial policy to reduce the transaction costs of such policy decisions once in office, but this did not entirely prevent such conflicts from arising. There was less risk, however, of the recurring conflicts in this field changing from interdepartmental to inter-party, and the arena in which these common conflicts were managed was the inner cabinet, an internal arena. This conforms to the general pattern found for most governments in the countries included in this study. The degree of ministerial compliance with the economic paragraphs in the coalition agreement was high—in the view of many surprisingly so for a piece of paper carried along during four years of international economic uncertainty. The usual procedure in the informal meetings of the inner cabinet and of the 'Pentagon'—an informal cabinet committee containing the prime minister and the four key ministers in this field—was that the minister of finance referred to the relevant language in the agreement. If this was not sufficiently persuasive, Prime Minister Lubbers engaged in creative interpretation whenever possible and forced decisions unilaterally or took his ministers apart to get them to abide with the targets set in the coalition agreement. Ministerial interaction and prime ministerial activism within the Pentagon thus effectively prevented the escalation of budgetary battles. A favourable condition was that the spending ministers had been directly involved in the negotiations over the coalition agreement. In this sense, the arena for decisions about the implementation of the compromises resembled the government formation arena where they were made in the first place.

Management of inter-party conflicts

Divorce and euthanasia were clearly inter-party conflicts during the government formations, and they remained of this type throughout the coalitions' lives. In Ireland, the divorce issue was quasi-depoliticized by placing it under the scrutiny of an Oireachtas (Full Parliamentary) committee—containing all parliamentary parties—on Marriage Breakdown. Fianna Fáil, the main opposition party, used a strategy of issue expansion by linking it to abortion on which a 'moral civil war' was going on (Mitchell 1996: 244). The coalition parties reached intra-cabinet peace on this issue by delegating the issue to the committee even beyond the initial deadline of 1983 mentioned in the coalition agreement. The committee did not in fact present its report until April 1985. The main recommendation was that the constitutional ban on divorce be removed, but the committee was too divided itself to propose any further legislative action on divorce. As a consequence, the issue boomeranged back to FitzGerald's two-party coalition, where the controversy centred on a referendum on the constitutional amendment that was to be organized by the government before the next parliamentary elections. This is an example of a meta-conflict over the choice of a conflict management arena and implicitly also about the appropriate decision rule. As Mitchell (2000: 140) observes about this period, cabinet meetings were regularly suspended—at Labour's request—to allow the two party leaders to meet in informal inter-party summits, the typical form of arena used for the most serious conflicts in Ireland.

In early 1986, a new explicit agreement was reached: a referendum would indeed be held before the next general elections. In addition, a bill would be proposed, allowing courts to grant a restricted form of divorce under 'certain circumstances'. FitzGerald realized that these concessions to Labour were necessary to keep the party within the coalition. Labour's perceived lack of pay-offs from coalition policy increased its discount rate (impatience) and the party credibly committed itself to leaving the cabinet in the event that no referendum would be held. FitzGerald could not afford too much patience because his own party was internally divided and had bad electoral prospects if early elections were held. For this reason, new inter-party summits were organized. For his own party, FitzGerald suggested a free vote on divorce legislation, and by agreeing to hold a referendum the party leaders delegated decision power to the electorate. Despite his formal powers, Prime Minister FitzGerald was in an awkward position, and this induced him to declare that the cabinet would take a neutral position in the referendum. These procedures were used to manage a conflict over an issue that had grown beyond the coalition's policymaking capacity (Mitchell 1996: 252–3).

The referendum was held in June 1986 and resulted in a massive defeat of the proposed constitutional amendment. The consequence of the defeat was that once again the issue boomeranged back into the coalition. This time, however, anticipation of general elections deterred both parties from dealing with the issue.

In the Netherlands, the Lubbers I coalition agreement mentioned that on euthanasia a State Committee would be consulted—an attempt to depoliticize the matter. More than in the Irish case, the issue was transferred (be it temporarily) to experts outside the political arenas. The State Committee reported in August 1985, just 10 months before the next scheduled parliamentary elections. The CDA found this late enough to try to defer the matter, but for the VVD it was still not too late to press for policy change. The State Committee recommended that under certain conditions euthanasia should no longer be punishable. One reason why the VVD persisted was that in 1984, a private member's bill on euthanasia had been introduced by an MP from D66, an opposition party close to the VVD in this field of policy. This put the VVD in an awkward position. On the one hand, a legislative majority in favour of liberalizing euthanasia, consisting of VVD, D66, and PvdA, was now within reach. On the other hand, the VVD was bound by rules of coalition loyalty and discipline, unless the issue had been explicitly exempted, which was not the case. The significance of these rules for coalition continuation was stressed by the Christian Democrats.

The VVD chose a strategy in which support for the parliamentary initiative was made dependent on an attempt to draft a bill on euthanasia by the cabinet itself. This reduced the likelihood of a legislative amourette with opposition parties, but it also brought the conflict into the cabinet, with the two ministers most directly involved belonging to different parties. Other than in the field of socio-economic policy, these ministers had not negotiated the relevant paragraph in the coalition agreement themselves. For these reasons, the Dutch remedy of transferring highly controversial matters from the broad and public external arenas of parliament to internal and informal arenas within the cabinet was less likely to be effective. The government draft that emerged eventually was more restrictive (and closer to the status quo) than the private member's bill. The VVD did not want to commit itself to this draft and advocated a continuation of parliamentary discussions of the private member's bill. The party also refused to enforce intra-party or coalition discipline on this issue, which irritated the CDA's parliamentary leadership:

The VVD seems to participate in two coalitions. One is the formal coalition with the CDA, in which the country's economic and financial problems are dealt with. The other is an informal coalition with the PvdA and D66 to strike deals on non-materialist issues over the CDA's head. Euthanasia is just one example.... In the next coalition agreement, firm commitments must be made, for otherwise we do not know where we stand with the VVD (quoted in Timmermans 2003).

While the CDA kept trying to shelve the issue or at least to keep discussions limited to informal mixed arenas containing ministers and prominent MPs, the parliamentary group of the VVD had ideological and electoral reasons to prefer the more public parliamentary arena. However, the party's walk-away value was reduced by its realization that its prospects of prolongation in office after the next parliamentary elections were dependent on continued good relations with the CDA, while the latter party could alternatively govern with the PvdA. A few months before the 1986 elections, Prime Minister Lubbers stated that his party's ministers would not sign any legislation before the elections, which was taken as a threat to resign if the VVD persisted with its intention to legislate. After Lubbers had met informally with the two parliamentary leaders, the VVD gave way and proposed that both bills be reviewed by the Council of State, the government's highest constitutional advisory body. The effect of this manoeuvre was that no political decision could be taken before the elections, and that after the elections the issue would be transferred to the government formation arena. As in Ireland, this inter-party conflict could only be contained, not resolved.

CONCLUSION

In this chapter, we have analysed the mechanisms that coalition parties devise for conflict management and resolution. We classified these devices as falling into three different institutional arenas: those internal to the cabinet, external ones, and mixed types and surveyed the use of such arenas for two classes of intra-coalition conflicts: those that are most common, and those that are most difficult to resolve. We argued that the construction and use of external or mixed arenas imply additional costs to the parties relative to internal arenas, and that, all else equal, parties tend to prefer internal decision-making arenas. They will resort to external institutions when the coalition is fragile or the bargaining environment complex, when they have no definitive prior policy agreement to fall back on, or when the internal environment is likely to be biased in favour of one of the parties (e.g. because the prime minister has extensive institutional powers).

These expectations were in large part confirmed in our analysis. The large-n cross-national analysis shows that internal arenas are most likely to be used when there exists a comprehensive coalition agreement, when the party system is fragmented and ideologically polarized (which we interpret as an environment in which the opposition is unlikely to be credible), and when the constitution is one of negative, rather than positive, parliamentarism. Historically, positive parliamentarism has often arisen as a way to protect the executive in otherwise fragile polities. Therefore, we expect that societies with positive parliamentarism might also have systematically more fragile coalitions (at least in the minds of party leaders), and the correlation between this institutional feature and external arenas for conflict resolution therefore makes sense. We also found that countries tend to cluster in their choice of conflict management arenas, but that few countries are entirely uniform over their post-1945 histories. We found no significant evidence of systematic trends in conflict resolution over time.

After our consideration of the aggregate cross-national evidence, we moved on to a focused comparison of four cases of conflict management in two countries—Ireland and the Netherlands. Inevitably, a comparative case study cannot deal with all factors that were found relevant in the comparative analysis. Precisely by keeping many variables constant (time period, existence of a coalition agreement, and similar policy domains) the comparison gains strength, but loses variety. Nevertheless, the case studies confirm and help clarify the major findings of the comparative analysis.

Most of all, they underline the importance of the nature of the conflict that confronts the cabinet. The interdepartmental budgetary conflicts proved easiest to resolve, especially in the Netherlands, where they were managed in internal arenas. Although the Dutch prime minister occupies a relatively weak position, or precisely because the junior coalition party did not have to fear his dominance within the cabinet, he was able to play a substantial role in these internal arenas. In this case, it may also be relevant that this particular prime minister was widely regarded as a strong personality, despite his lack of formal powers.

In Ireland, similar budget conflicts proved more difficult to resolve, and were eventually settled in external arenas. This difference of degree with the Dutch case can be explained by the fact that, due to the particular distribution of portfolios in the Irish cabinet, these interdepartmental conflicts could easily be transformed into an inter-party conflict. Our two partisan conflicts show how hard it is for coalition cabinets to manage such conflicts. The fact that both cabinets first sought to depoliticize them, and the fact that both cases ended in non–decision-making, provides some support for Blondel's scepticism about the very possibility of cabinet decision-making. However, it should be noted that divorce in Ireland and euthanasia in the Netherlands are exceptionally difficult cases: they involved divergent preferences that were deeply rooted in the respective parties' ideologies, and were of a constant-sum character.

The case studies also enrich our understanding of the impact of some of the factors in our comparative analysis. In that analysis, we found evidence that a party's walk-away value (operationalized as the inclusion of the party with the highest bargaining power in the cabinet) is an important predictor of the use of external arenas. This played an important role in both cabinets in our case studies: in Ireland the fact that the parties had equal walk-away values resulted in a compromise on divorce (a referendum amending the constitution to satisfy Labour, and only modest changes in material divorce law planned after the expected support for the constitutional amendment to satisfy the conservative wing of Fine Gael); in the Netherlands the fact that the VVD and the PvdA excluded each other as coalition partners at the time provided the CDA with the much higher walk-away value that it used to prevent a liberalization of euthanasia. What is not captured in the comparative analysis is that, regardless of its walk-away value, the junior partner in a coalition has a strong incentive to prefer mixed or external arenas, as these are usually (although not always) more public than inner cabinets or cabinet committees, and the prime minister is less dominant in these arenas. This can be seen in the strategies of both the Dutch VVD and the Irish Labour Party, and especially in the behaviour of the latter party as it was so much smaller. The search for visibility to maintain an electoral profile by smaller governing parties is likely to have an impact on conflict management in other countries' governments as well.

The impact of the coalition agreement also becomes more evident from the case studies. Apparently, coalition agreements are no prophylactics against conflicts during the cabinet's incumbency. The comparative analysis shows that coalition agreements do increase a cabinet's capacity to manage conflicts internally, but somewhat surprisingly it makes little difference whether the agreement is comprehensive or not. The case studies suggest two lines of inquiry to solve this puzzle. First, an agreement may be comprehensive, but if it contains many vague compromises that require substantial decision-making later on (such as making budget cutbacks contingent on economic growth and unemployment in the Irish case, compared to mentioning specific targets in the Dutch case), it does not really reduce the risk of conflicts during the life of the cabinet. Second, if further decision-making is required to implement an agreement, but this involves ministers in their capacity of heads of departments rather than in their role as their party's bridgehead in the cabinet, the resulting conflicts will be primarily interdepartmental and hence easier to handle in internal arenas (as in the case of the budget cutbacks in the Dutch cabinet).

The case studies also shed more light on the relationship between having a coalition agreement and the use of internal arenas. To the extent that conflicts over interpretation of the agreement are about implementation, the conflicts will be primarily interdepartmental and handled internally. If, however, the conflicts over the interpretation are about the policy direction itself, they can only be settled by the most authoritative exegetes, namely, those who wrote the agreement. The more party prominents who were involved directly in the negotiations over the government formation also participate in the cabinet, the more internal (or at most mixed) arenas will be used even for managing the most divisive political issues. The Dutch case shows that the rise of coalition agreements coincided with an increase of party prominents in the cabinet. Had this latter shift in recruitment not taken place, we are likely to have seen a heavier reliance on external arenas, despite the existence of coalition agreements. That such use of arenas is highly path-dependent, is shown by the Irish case, in which changes brought about at Labour's insistence, quickly institutionalized.

Our study of conflict management in coalition cabinets is clearly an exploratory one. We began this chapter by referring to the null hypothesis that cabinets cannot manage conflicts because they are too threatening to their survival. Both the comparative analysis and the case studies show that, yes, there is life after a government's formation. Some conflicts are indeed too hot to handle by ministers only, and such conflicts may even go unresolved, but cabinets have developed arenas other than its plenary session in which conflicts are managed, and the use of these arenas can be explained by characteristics of both the conflict and the cabinet.

REFERENCES

Andeweg, Rudy B. (1988). 'Centrifugal Forces and Collective Decision-Making; The Case of the Dutch Cabinet', *European Journal of Political Research*, 16: 125–51.

—— (1997). 'Collegiality and Collectivity: Cabinets, Cabinet Committees, and Cabinet Ministers', in Patrick Weller, Herman Bakvis, and R. A. W. Rhodes (eds.), *The Hollow Crown: Countervailing Trends in Core Executives*. London: Macmillan.

Bagehot, Walter (1965 [first published 1867]). *The English Constitution*. London: Fontana.

Blondel, Jean (1988). 'Decision-Making Processes, Conflicts and Cabinet Government', EUI Working Papers 88/327.

—— (2000). 'A Framework for the Empirical Analysis of Government-Supporting Party Relationships', in Jean Blondel and Maurizio Cotta (eds.), *The Nature of Party Government*. Houndmills, UK: Palgrave.

—— and Müller-Rommel, Ferdianand (1993). 'Introduction', in Jean Blondel and Ferdinand Müller-Rommel (eds.), *Governing Together: The Extent and Limits of Joint Decision-making in Western-European Cabinets*. London: Macmillan.

—— —— (eds.) (1997). *Cabinets in Western Europe*. London: Macmillan.

Criscitiello, Anarita (1993). 'Majority Summits: Decision-Making Inside the Cabinet and Out: Italy 1970–1990', *West European Politics*, 16, No. 4: 581–94.

—— (1996). 'Alla ricerca della collegialita di governo: I vertici di maggioranza dalla 1970 al 1994', *Rivista Italiana di Scienza Politica*, 26: 365–89.

De Winter, Lieven, Timmermans, Arco, and Dumont, Patrick (2000). 'Belgium: On Government Agreements, Evangelists, Followers, and Heretics', in Wolfgang C. Müller and Kaare Strøm (eds.), *Coalition Governments in Western Europe*. Oxford: Oxford University Press.

Laver, Michael and Shepsle, Kenneth A. (eds.) (1994). *Cabinet Ministers and Parliamentary Government*. Cambridge: Cambridge University Press.

Luebbert, Gregory M. (1986). *Comparative Democracy: Policymaking and Governing Coalitions in Europe and Israel*. New York, NY: Columbia University Press.

Mackie, Thomas T. and Hogwood, Brian W. (1985). 'Formal Committee Structures', in Thomas T. Mackie and Brian W. Hogwood (eds.), *Unlocking the Cabinet: Cabinet Structures in Comparative Perspective*. London: Sage.

Marsh, Michael and Mitchell, Paul (1999). 'Office, Votes, and Then Policy: Hard Choices for Political Parties in the Republic of Ireland, 1981–1992', in Wolfgang C. Müller and Kaare Strøm (eds.), *Policy, Office, or Votes?* Cambridge: Cambridge University Press.

Mayntz, Renate (1980). 'Executive Leadership in Germany: Dispersion of Power or Kanzlerdemokratie?', in Richard Rose and Ezra N.Suleiman (eds.), *Presidents and Prime Ministers*. Washington, DC: American Enterprise Institute.

Mitchell, Paul (1996). 'The Life and Times of Coalition Governments: Coalition Maintenance by Event Management', Ph.D. dissertation, Florence: European University Institute.

—— (2000). 'Ireland: From Single-Party to Coalition Rule', in Wolfgang C. Müller and Kaare Strøm (eds.), *Coalition Governments in Western Europe*. Oxford: Oxford University Press.

Müller, Wolfgang C. (2000). 'Austria: Tight Coalitions and Stable Government', in Wolfgang C. Müller and Kaare Strøm (eds.), *Coalition Governments in Western Europe*. Oxford: Oxford University Press.

—— and Strøm, Kaare (eds.) (2000). *Coalition Governments in Western Europe*. Oxford: Oxford University Press.

Nedelmann, Birgitta (1982). *Rentenpolitik in Schweden; ein Beitrag zur Dynamisierung soziologischer Konfliktanalyse*. Frankfurt am Main: Campus.

Nousiainen, Jaakko (1993). 'Decision-Making, Policy Content and Conflict Resolution in Western European Cabinets', in Jean Blondel and Ferdinand Müller-Rommel (eds.), *Governing Together: The Extent and Limits of Joint Decision-making in Western-European Cabinets*. London: Macmillan.

Saalfeld, Thomas (2000). 'Germany: Stable Parties, Chancellor Democracy, and the Art of Informal Settlement', in Wolfgang C. Müller and Kaare Strøm (eds.), *Coalition Governments in Western Europe*. Oxford: Oxford University Press.

Steiner, Jürg and Dorff, Robert H. (1980). *A Theory of Political Decision Modes*. Chapel Hill, NC: University of North Carolina Press.

Timmermans, Arco (1998). 'Policy Conflicts, Agreements, and Coalition Governance', *Acta Politica*, 33: 409–32.

—— (2003). *High Politics in The Low Countries*. Aldershot, UK: Ashgate.

—— and Andeweg, Rudy B. (2000). 'The Netherlands: Still the Politics of Accommodation?', in Wolfgang C. Müller and Kaare Strøm (eds.), *Coalition Governments in Western Europe*. Oxford: Oxford University Press.

—— and Bakema, Wilma E. (1990). 'Conflicten in Nederlandse Kabinetten', in Rudy B. Andeweg (ed.), *Ministers en Ministerraad*. The Hague: SDU.

Tsebelis, George (1990). *Nested Games. Rational Choice in Comparative Politics*. Berkeley, CA: University of California Press.

9

Cabinet Termination

Erik Damgaard

INTRODUCTION

This chapter investigates the causes of cabinet termination in Western Europe since the Second World War. This is a topic that has hitherto received little scholarly attention. Until recently, political science research has primarily focused on the size, party composition, portfolio allocation, and duration of cabinets. Within the past decade or so, attention has increasingly turned to the termination of cabinets. Yet, this emerging literature has primarily been interested in the consequences of termination for cabinet duration, rather than in the behavioural forms that cabinet resignation takes, or the conditions and motivations that drive it.

This chapter differs from the mainstream of studies in the coalition politics literature. The focus here will be on the forms that cabinet termination takes and on the factors that help us explain the variation in their respective end games. We shall not be concerned with the implications of different forms of termination for cabinet duration—that will be the subject of Chapter 10. And while one of the forms of termination we shall examine is general elections, we shall not be concerned about who gains or loses in such elections or why. Those will instead be topics explored in Chapter 11. Here we shall simply investigate the differing ways in which parliamentary governments come to their 'demise' and the causes of these various fates.

Why is such a study important? The first and most obvious reason is simply that we know so little about these questions. And if government formation is crucial in parliamentary democracies—which virtually all authors in the coalition politics literature either explicitly declare (notably Laver and Schofield 1990) or tacitly assume—then the termination of the very same cabinets must be equally important. It is indeed remarkable that so little attention has been given to this topic. Second, empirical observations show that the formation of one cabinet is often highly contingent upon the demise of its predecessor. On the whole, therefore, formation and termination of cabinets delineate political processes that we cannot and should not study in mutual isolation.

Existing studies are in fact concerned with the important link between formation and termination, as they often use the same independent variables to explain cabinet formation, durability, and termination. There are three main approaches in studies of cabinet formation, duration, and termination (cf. Browne, Frendreis, and Gleiber 1986; Budge and Keman 1990; von Beyme 2000). In Lupia and Strøm's terms (1995), the traditionally dominant literatures may be called the 'structural attributes' (of the cabinet itself or its political environment) and the 'critical events' (resulting from exogenous destabilizing effects) perspectives, respectively. These labels correspond to the most important explanatory variables highlighted by each approach. Attempts to synthesize these perspectives can be found in King et al. (1990) and Alt and King (1994). A third approach is that of 'strategic interaction' (between and possibly within political parties) (see Lupia and Strøm 1995). All three approaches may help us to understand cabinet termination as well as formation.

The 'strategic interaction' approach is possibly the most powerful of the three, and it is the one that has most strongly motivated this book and this chapter. At the same time, this approach also requires a much more detailed knowledge of inter- and intra-party affairs than is usually found among scholars doing large-scale comparative research. Although a large part of the purpose of this chapter is to explore new ground in coalition studies, it is also based on an unprecedented data-set which allows us to answer questions on which we have until now had little solid information. We shall therefore have a unique opportunity to understand the causes of cabinet termination in the parliamentary systems of Western Europe (and by implication, beyond). As in the other chapters in this volume, our explanatory variables include fixed effects of country and time, structural attributes, party preferences, institutional rules, the bargaining environment, and critical events.

What is a cabinet termination?

There is hardly anything that fascinates political observers more than transitions from one executive to the next. But at the same time, defining precisely when such transitions take place in parliamentary democracies is not an altogether straightforward task. Is it whenever the prime minister changes? Is it when any member of the cabinet leaves? Is it when the party composition of the cabinet changes? Is there necessarily a change whenever there is a general election?

While there are several broadly adopted answers to these questions, there is no universally accepted standard. All studies of cabinet formation, durability, and termination are bound to face difficult questions of this kind, and all existing definitions have their shortcomings. Damgaard (1994, 2000*b*), for example, sympathizes with Dodd (1976), Lijphart (1984, 1999), and Lewin (1998) in disagreeing with the prevailing academic convention that a general election by definition ends the tenure of the incumbent government. In many cases, elections bring little or no change in the occupants of high office. And while in some countries there are institutional rules and norms that require at least a formal recognition that the voice of the people has been heard (e.g. through a requirement that the prime minister tender his or her resignation), there are many in which no such regularity exists and the incumbent government can instead proceed as if nothing had happened unless called upon to do otherwise (the so-called 'continuation rule'). The point is not that there is an objectively better way to define the beginning or end of a cabinet, but rather that all such definitions are by their nature arbitrary and that any definition of a cabinet has implications for our measures of duration and for our possible explanations of termination. We should therefore select our definitions carefully and in the best possible knowledge of their implications.

This chapter adopts the cabinet definition proposed by the Comparative Parliamentary Democracies project (Müller and Strøm 2000). We record a change of cabinet whenever there is a change in the set of parties holding cabinet membership, a change of prime minister, or a general election (whether regularly scheduled or following an early dissolution). Clearly, many cabinets that are terminated by this standard do in fact live on according to other criteria. We shall return to this issue later in this chapter. Yet, the advantage of counting new cabinets as rigorously as we do is that we capture most of the circumstances that accompany substantial changes in the parliamentary bargaining environment. Specifically, however small the changes may be, every general election generates a new distribution of parliamentary seats and bargaining power. And if we believe that these are important parameters in coalition bargaining, as we do, then it is necessary to take account of these changes by recognizing the situation as a new bargaining environment. By keeping close track of changes in the relevant parameters, we can also more easily examine the consequences of counting cabinets differently from our standard procedure.

Technical and discretionary terminations

It is clear from the discussion above that we may want to distinguish between several different types of cabinet terminations. For the remainder of this chapter, our most important distinction will be between technical and discretionary cabinet terminations. **Technical** terminations are all those that occur for reasons that are beyond the control of the players in the coalitions game, the leaders of the different political parties. These include regular elections as prescribed in the constitution, other constitutional circumstances (e.g. the election of a new president) that require the cabinet to resign, or such events as the death or sudden ill health of the prime minister (which we generously assume is not directly caused by the acts of other party leaders). We also count a technical termination when a prime minister resigns for other non-political reasons (e.g. old age or a family emergency). Parliamentary actors cannot normally control such circumstances, which is the main reason we wish to distinguish them from the other main category of terminations. These technical terminations are also mutually exclusive, at least in the sense that any one would be sufficient and that they are unlikely to coincide by chance.

We distinguish technical terminations from **discretionary** terminations, which are deliberately brought about by the actors involved, even if these actors may feel that they have no other options. Discretionary cabinet terminations therefore involve strategic actions decided upon by party leaders calculating what their best choice might be, given their goals and the options available in a given parliamentary situation (cf. Laver and Schofield 1990; Strøm 1990; Müller and Strøm 1999 on party goals and trade-offs among them). Discretionary types of termination include general elections called before the end of the regular term, voluntary enlargements of the cabinet to include previously unrepresented parties, prime ministerial resignations caused by votes of no confidence in parliament, voluntary resignations by the prime minister for other political reasons, cabinet resignations due to defeats imposed by opposition parties in parliament, resignations caused by conflicts *within* cabinet parties, and terminations caused by conflict *between* coalition parties for policy and/or personal reasons. Such forms of termination are not mutually exclusive, as more than one type may be involved simultaneously. In sum, a **discretionary** cabinet termination results from acts that are both political and discretionary, and any particular case of cabinet turnover may in fact be due to several such acts or circumstances.

The existing literature recognizes the variety of circumstances that may be associated with cabinet termination, but there is no standard way of dealing with it analytically. While the specific technical terminations can, in principle, be identified unequivocally, discretionary terminations cannot be mapped in such categorical terms. As Budge and Keman (1990: 187) rightly remark, breakdown and termination are perhaps the most difficult aspects of government behaviour to analyse because of 'difficulties in pinning down and putting into focus such diffuse phenomena'. Budge and Keman (1990) note the fact that a discretionary change of government may have more than one cause. The authors nevertheless report only on what they consider to be the most important cause or 'circumstance' of a cabinet dissolution. They therefore define their types of termination as mutually exclusive. Browne, Frendreis, and Gleiber (1986), on the other hand, report all possible causes or circumstances of critical events leading to a cabinet termination. The present project strikes a middle course between these two alternatives. We identify a limited number of types of discretionary termination, as just listed above, but do not insist in our coding that these be mutually exclusive. Whether more than one type is involved in the demise of a given cabinet can only be determined empirically.

Yet, it is important through all of this to recall that discretionary and technical terminations are mutually exclusive. The section below first reports on the occurrence of various forms of 'technical' and 'discretionary' cabinet termination, including cross-national and over-time variation in both respects. It also looks into the interesting question of whether cabinets, terminated for whatever reasons, in some important sense get a new lease on life after their demise. If that is indeed the case, it may suggest that the termination of one cabinet may actually serve to secure the survival of the very same administration more broadly defined. In the next main section, we describe the termination of the cabinets in our sample and break these data down by country, decade, and cabinet type. We then explore the question whether these cabinet terminations, as we record them, really constitute fundamental turnovers in the politics of their respective countries. Finally, we examine, through multinomial logit models, the causes of different modes of cabinet termination.

CABINET TERMINATION

Technical Termination

As can be seen in Table 9.1, which includes the full set of cabinets, almost 40 per cent of all cabinets in Western Europe terminate for technical reasons. There is, however, noticeable variation across countries. Thus, in Luxembourg, Norway, and Sweden technical terminations account for more than one-half of all cabinets, whereas discretionary causes account for the majority of terminations in the remaining countries under study, with the Netherlands as a borderline case at 50 per cent each. Technical terminations are particularly rare in Italy and Ireland (about 10%), although for different reasons. In Italy, the high rate of discretionary terminations is due to the high incidence of inter-party and intra-party conflict, whereas in Ireland the discretionary terminations overwhelmingly take the form of early elections.

Most of the technical terminations (70%) are clearly due to regular elections, while quite a few (25%) are due to other constitutional requirements, and a few (5%) to the death of the prime minister. These findings generally agree with results reported in earlier studies (e.g. Budge and Keman 1990; Woldendorp, Keman, and Budge 1993; von Beyme 2000) that have adopted very similar operational definitions of cabinet change and termination. Regular elections account for about one-half or more of the technical cabinet terminations in Luxembourg, the Netherlands, Norway, and Sweden, whereas they account for only a small share of all terminations in Denmark, Ireland, and Spain.

Apart from regular elections and the quite irregular death of prime ministers (which has occurred disproportionately in Scandinavia for some peculiar, but probably quite incidental reason) there are further national variations, however. They mainly concern Finland, where presidential elections until recently required at least the formal resignation of cabinets (Nousiainen 2000), and France (since

TABLE 9.1. *Types of termination by country*

Country	No. of Cabinets	**Technical termination**	Regular elections	Other constitutional reason	Death of PM	**Discretionary termination**	Early election	Voluntary cabinet enlargement	Cabinet defeat	Intra-party conflict	Inter-party policy conflict	Inter-party personal conflict
Austria	21	**9**	7	2	0	**12**	9	0	0	3	6	1
Belgium	32	**6**	5	1	0	**26**	11	2	1	3	16	1
Denmark	30	**7**	1	3	3	**23**	20	1	10	1	2	0
Finland	43	**17**	10	7	0	**26**	4	6	3	1	14	0
France	22	**9**	4	5	0	**13**	5	0	1	6	2	0
Germany	25	**11**	11	0	0	**14**	2	3	2	8	5	2
Greece	10	**4**	1	3	0	**6**	6	0	0	1	1	0
Iceland	25	**13**	10	2	1	**12**	7	1	1	1	7	1
Ireland	21	**2**	0	2	0	**19**	16	0	3	7	3	3
Italy	50	**4**	4	0	0	**46**	7	2	13	19	15	12
Luxembourg	15	**11**	9	1	1	**4**	2	0	0	1	3	1
The Netherlands	22	**11**	10	1	0	**11**	5	0	1	2	6	0
Norway	25	**17**	13	4	0	**8**	0	1	3	2	2	0
Portugal	13	**5**	3	1	1	**8**	4	0	4	0	2	3
Spain	7	**1**	1	0	0	**6**	6	0	0	3	0	0
Sweden	25	**20**	16	2	2	**5**	1	1	0	0	3	0
UK	19	**8**	4	4	0	**11**	10	0	1	1	0	0
Total	405	**155**	109	38	8	**250**	115	17	43	59	87	24
% of total	100	**38.3**	26.9	9.4	2.0	**61.7**	28.4	4.2	10.6	14.6	21.5	5.9

1958) where presidential powers are strong (Thiébault 2000). In addition to semi-presidentialism, still other constitutional reasons, such as a prime minister's voluntary retirement from political life, have played a role in countries such as Norway, the UK, and Ireland. However, 'voluntary' retirements sometimes appear to be at least partially politically motivated, especially in Ireland (Mitchell 2000), and should therefore not necessarily in all cases be considered purely technical resignations. Two special cases of 'other constitutional' terminations occurred in Denmark in 1953, as a process of constitutional amendment required two general elections to be held in rapid succession (Damgaard 2000*b*). Two Danish cabinets therefore had to die for technical reasons within a few months' time of one another.

Discretionary termination

Most of the discretionary termination types listed in Table 9.1 have a distinct flavour of conflict or competition between, or within, political parties in parliament and government. Yet one type, voluntary cabinet enlargements, tastes more of cooperation than of conflict. We have indeed defined such terminations restrictively, so as to exclude any termination that was accompanied by a general election, intra-coalition conflict, or a parliamentary defeat. Hence, this type of cabinet change, presumably often from minority to majority status, might in some cases be regarded as a strengthening of existing cabinets rather than as their replacement by new ones. Although enlargement termination has never, or only rarely, occurred in most of the countries included in the analysis, it certainly has in Finland—which alone accounts for 6 of 17 cases. Yet, the total number of such termination cases amounts to only about 7 per cent of all discretionary cabinet terminations. Since this type of discretionary termination is so rare and atypical, we shall in a later section of this chapter analyse it separately.

A second distinct type of discretionary termination is early elections. Early elections account for a far greater number of discretionary terminations (114 in total, or 44%), and are particularly frequent in Austria, Denmark, Greece, Iceland, Ireland, Spain, and the UK. Cabinet defeats (43 cases) have been relatively common in Denmark, Italy, Portugal, Norway, and Ireland. Intra-party conflicts, found in 59 cases, occur relatively often in Italy, Germany, France, Ireland, and Spain. Such terminations seem to be particularly common in countries that feature factionalized parties (see Druckman 1996), and it may be that the personalistic electoral systems of Italy (until the early 1990s) and Ireland have contributed to the relatively high incidence in these countries. Inter-party conflicts in coalition cabinets account for a substantial number of terminations in Belgium, Austria, Finland, Germany, Iceland, Italy, and the Netherlands, but of course not in Greece, Spain, and the UK, which have rarely or never had coalition cabinets.

TABLE 9.2. *Types of termination by cabinet type*

Termination type	Coalition cabinets	Single-party cabinets	All cabinets
Technical	37.1	41.8	38.3
Discretionary	62.9	58.2	61.7
($N = 100\%$)	(248)	(141)	(405)
Technical			
Regular election	75.0	62.7	70.3
Other constitutional	19.6	32.2	24.5
Death of PM	5.4	5.1	5.2
($N = 100\%$)	(92)	(59)	(155)
Discretionary			
Early election	35.3	59.8	44.0
Voluntary enlargement	3.9	11.0	6.8
Cabinet defeat	12.2	25.6	17.1
Intra-party conflict	24.4	23.2	23.6
Inter-party policy conflict	55.8	na	34.8
Inter-party personal conflict	15.4	na	9.6
($N = 100\%$)	(156)	(82)	(250)

Notes: Percentages reported.

Number of cases in parantheses.

Single-party and coalition cabinets

This latter point invites a closer inspection of the differences in termination between single-party and coalition cabinets. Table 9.2 provides a simple breakdown of terminations by these cabinet types. Keep in mind that within each category, we could make finer distinctions, such as between minority and majority cabinets. Nevertheless, Table 9.2 shows that technical terminations are somewhat more frequent for single-party cabinets than for coalitions, and that the opposite is then necessarily the case for discretionary terminations.

More interesting, perhaps, is the variation displayed among the different forms of discretionary termination. There are three clear patterns in the data reported in Table 9.2. First, single-party cabinets tend to end more frequently than do coalition cabinets because of early elections, voluntary enlargements, and defeats in parliament. Second, controversies between cabinet parties are the most common mode of termination among coalition cabinets, representing 55 per cent of the observations in that category. (Of course, by definition this type of conflict cannot occur in single-party cabinets.) Third, there is no real difference between single-party and coalition cabinets in the incidence of termination caused by intra-party conflict.

These are interesting results. The high incidence of serious inter-party conflict in coalition cabinets suggests that such cabinets may have a generic weakness compared to single-party administrations. Yet, we should be careful not to jump to such a conclusion. If single-party cabinets compensated for their lack of inter-party conflict by a higher rate of intra-party conflict, the only meaningful difference might be that broad parties brought the forces of division within their respective tents. But the virtually identical rates of intra-party conflict terminations suggest that this is not the case and that single-party cabinets may be systematically less susceptible than coalitions to internal conflict. The 'glue' that binds individual parties together may simply be stronger than the adhesive that can be applied to coalition governments (see Chapter 5). Perhaps this is because electoral incentives much more commonly converge within political parties than between them.

Temporal developments

Thus far, we have described cabinet terminations without looking for patterns of change over time. But considering what we know about electoral volatility and party system change in the second half of the twentieth century, and particularly since the 1970s, one could expect that patterns of cabinet termination may have changed considerably. Table 9.3 therefore breaks our data on cabinet termination down by decade. (Note that the overall number of cabinets is somewhat larger in the 1970s and 1980s than in the two preceding decades, caused to some extent by the inclusion of Greece, Portugal, and Spain from the 1970s on.) Table 9.3 demonstrates that there were relatively fewer technical, and therefore more discretionary, terminations in the 1970s and 1980s compared to the 1950s and 1960s (and apparently to the 1990s). This difference is primarily due to larger proportions of early elections and inter-party conflict terminations in the 1970s and 1980s. This development may reflect greater party-system volatility and more institutional turbulence in the two latter decades compared to the first decades in our sample (cf. Damgaard, Gerlich, and Richardson 1989; Mair and Smith 1990; Damgaard 1992).

Termination or survival?

Do cabinet terminations, such as we have defined them above, actually matter? Do they imply meaningful changes in the executive branch, or do the cabinets that we have coded as terminated in fact get a new lease on life after their death? The literature (cf. Strøm 1990; Müller and Strøm 2000; Narud and Valen, Chapter 11) informs us that, on average, incumbent cabinets and parties tend to lose votes in elections, which of course may, but need not, affect their prospects of participating in the next cabinet. Budge and Keman (1990: 182–7) entertained this hypothesis as they explored not only the electoral fate of cabinet parties but also the effects of inclusion in one cabinet upon participation in the next. They did not find much support for their expectations, however. Thus, inter-party conflicts between cabinet parties leading to a premature termination, for example, did not appear to make cabinet parties less likely to cooperate again in a successor cabinet. These results correspond well with existing accounts of cabinet formation

TABLE 9.3. *Types of termination by decade*

Decade	No. of cabinets	N (%)		Early election	Cabinet defeat	Intra-party conflict	Inter-party (policy/personal) conflict
		Technical termination	Discretionary termination				
1945–49	26	12 (46.2)	14 (53.8)	5	2	5	9
1950–59	79	29 (36.7)	50 (63.3)	21	9	14	22
1960–69	68	30 (44.1)	38 (55.9)	15	8	11	11
1970–79	85	23 (27.1)	62 (72.9)	28	9	11	23
1980–89	85	30 (35.3)	55 (64.7)	31	12	11	22
1990–99	62	31 (50.0)	31 (50.0)	15	3	7	14
N (%)	405	155 (38.3)	250 (61.7)	115	43	59	101

Cabinet Termination

TABLE 9.4. *Cabinet composition and predecessors by country*

Country	Same party composition	Same PM	Same party and PM	(N = 100%)
Austria	76.2	61.9	47.6	21
Belgium	28.1	37.5	6.3	32
Denmark	40.0	56.7	26.7	30
Finland	7.0	27.9	0.0	43
France	50.0	31.8	18.2	22
Germany	36.0	76.0	28.0	25
Greece	40.0	20.0	20.0	10
Iceland	32.0	28.0	20.0	25
Ireland	33.3	23.8	14.3	21
Italy	20.0	32.0	0.0	50
Luxembourg	46.7	53.3	26.7	15
The Netherlands	22.7	40.9	18.2	22
Norway	52.0	36.0	32.0	25
Portugal	53.8	38.4	30.8	13
Spain	66.7	55.6	44.4	9
Sweden	64.0	60.0	48.0	25
UK	68.4	42.1	42.1	19
Total	38.3	41.5	20.9	407

in the Netherlands and Belgium (De Winter, Timmermans, and Dumont 2000; Timmermans and Andeweg 2000).

The simple question to be asked is whether a cabinet that has terminated, for whatever technical or discretionary reason, is likely to be reborn as the successor cabinet—thus in some sense replacing itself. Table 9.4 shows for all 17 countries the extent to which terminated cabinets (as defined above) have had immediate successors with the same party composition, the same PM, or both of these characteristics.

According to Table 9.4, more than 40 per cent of all 'new' cabinets have had the same PM as the 'old' one, indicating a considerable degree of leadership continuity. In 6 of our 17 countries, the PM has in a majority of cases stayed on in the next cabinet. Only in Finland, France, Greece, Iceland, and Ireland have fewer than about one-third of all outgoing prime ministers managed to hang on in the new cabinet. For no country is the continuation rate less than 20 per cent.

Table 9.4 further shows that almost 40 per cent of the successor cabinets have had the same party composition as the ones that they replaced. This proportion ranges all the way from only 7 per cent in Finland to 76 per cent in Austria. Finally, Table 9.4 shows that more than 20 per cent of all new cabinets have had both the same PM and the same party composition as the ones that they replaced. The proportions here range from zero in Finland and Italy to close to 50 per cent in Austria and Sweden. Thus, in many countries, and particularly such as Austria and Sweden, a considerable proportion of new cabinets are actually outgoing

TABLE 9.5. *Cabinet composition and predecessors by decade*

Decade	Same party composition	Same PM	Same party and PM	($N = 100\%$)
1945–49	30.8	42.3	19.2	26
1950–59	40.5	43.0	20.3	79
1960–69	47.1	42.7	23.5	68
1970–79	31.4	34.9	15.1	86
1980–89	36.1	45.4	24.4	86
1990–99	41.9	41.9	22.6	62
Total	38.3	41.5	20.9	407

cabinets that have managed to survive elections. Overall, one out of five cabinets is not really a new one, but rather an old one continuing in office or immediately re-constituted upon some kind of formal resignation. A further breakdown (not reported here) reveals that a majority of survivor cabinets have straddled regular elections.

This finding is of considerable theoretical interest. It means, for example, that many cabinets are more durable than indicated by standard measures, and that an expectation of survival in office may actually explain the termination of a given cabinet. One obvious example of the latter is a cabinet calling early elections in the hope of prolonging its term in office. On the other hand, the majority of cabinets (as defined by the identity of the PM and party composition) cannot expect to be reborn with the same PM or partisan composition.

In Table 9.5, the relevant data are broken down by decade. The most conspicuous finding is that the 1970s (and less so the 1980s), once again, represent a deviant pattern. During that decade, relatively few prime ministers and parties, and therefore also cabinets, were able to survive beyond general elections or in other ways be reconstituted. The 1970s are indeed the period with the highest level of cabinet volatility since the Second World War.

EXPLAINING DISCRETIONARY TERMINATION

As already revealed in Table 9.1, the majority of cabinet terminations in most countries are discretionary. The simple but indeed difficult question is what institutional, structural, and situational conditions account for this variation in termination. All authors that have contributed to our existing scholarship in this field acknowledge the difficulties in providing a simple and adequate answer to this question. Cabinet terminations are complex phenomena, which are frequently 'overdetermined' and where many of the participants have strategic reasons to conceal the real forces at work.

In the final section of this chapter, we shall examine the effects of the usual sets of variables, including decade and country, structural attributes, party preferences, institutions, bargaining environment, and critical events, on cabinet termination. To simplify the analysis, we have reduced the set of termination types to three. The first type is simply any technical termination. The second type is discretionary termination due to any type of conflict or defeat. It excludes only two subtypes of discretionary terminations: voluntary enlargements and early elections *not* associated with any reported conflict. This second category therefore includes termination caused by parliamentary defeat, inter-party policy or personal conflict, and intra-party controversies. Finally, our third category encompasses only early elections *not* combined with any form of parliamentary defeat, inter-party disagreements, or intra-party conflict. The remaining observations, the 17 cases of voluntary enlargement, will be kept out of the analysis at this stage because of the paucity of such observations. We shall return to them later in this chapter.

The three main types of termination represent quite different circumstances. Technical terminations are by definition beyond the control of the parties in the coalition game. When they occur, it is often because the incumbent parties have survived the competing risks associated with the parliamentary game. It is therefore often appropriate to think of technical terminations as a default category that captures cabinets that survive other 'risks' or 'temptations' to which they are exposed. This interpretation is not always appropriate. Some technical terminations may be caused by politically random events, such as the death of the prime minister or the head of state, which should not be interpreted within this framework. Yet, as Table 9.1 shows, more than two-thirds of all technical terminations are due to regularly scheduled elections. Most cabinet parties would presumably interpret such terminations precisely as we have suggested above: as the reflection of a successful survival strategy.

Defeats or conflicts are by their nature undesirable circumstances that we assume that most parties will wish to avoid. Again, this may not be universally true. There may be some governing parties that expect to benefit from such endings. And *ex post*, there will certainly be some incumbents that end up on the winning side of subsequent elections or parliamentary negotiations. Yet, on the whole we see conflictual terminations as signs of weakness on the part of the government, and we assume that most governing parties would prefer to avoid this type of closing.

Finally, early elections in the absence of any conflict or parliamentary defeat are a sign of constructive action on the part of the government. Elections may be called before the end of a constitutional term for several reasons. But if we focus on only those early elections that are not associated with any discernible conflict within or between parties, it follows that we are talking about the strategic use of dissolution powers (Strøm and Swindle 2002). It is a matter of timing elections optimally. Informed by public opinion polls and its private information about the upcoming political agenda and its ramifications, the government may decide to pick a convenient time to confront the electorate, rather than wait until it is forced to do so. Cabinet parties will have to calculate their expected costs and benefits resulting from an early election. The relevant currencies usually involve at least policy, office, and votes (Müller and Strøm 1999). One may conjecture that votes and office, in particular, loom large in considerations of calling early elections. They indicate that the governing party or parties expect to do well, or at least better than would be the case if they chose to wait until the end of the regular parliamentary term.

According to this line of reasoning, we should expect cabinets to be tempted to dissolve parliament at the most opportune time during the parliamentary term. This expectation, of course, presupposes that dissolution is constitutionally possible, which is not the case in Norway, and that the constitutional rules are not otherwise highly restrictive, as in Sweden, where a prematurely elected Riksdag can only function for the remainder of the original term (thus buying no additional tenure for the incumbents). Apart from that, the expectation should apply no matter how the cabinets emerged from the bargaining processes, what the specific rules of dissolution are, and how the economy is performing. There is a twist to this story, however, as Alastair Smith (2004) has elegantly pointed out. At least in majoritarian systems, early elections may take place when the incumbents have private information that suggests a likely downturn in their fortunes in the future. Nonetheless, we shall assume that early elections without conflict constitute a more desirable form of exit than does termination caused by conflict or defeat.

Explanatory variables

The independent variables in the following analyses relate to the general explanations of coalition politics (or null hypotheses) discussed by Lupia and Strøm in Chapter 2. The first explanation is that country-specific or temporal factors ultimately explain coalition politics, leaving very little room for more general and theoretical causal relationships: all the important determinants of coalition politics are unique to, and embedded in, the particular political system or the specific period in which they operate.

The second possible explanation finds explanations in the structural attributes of cabinets and parliaments. Some cabinets, for example single-party governments or minimal-winning coalitions, are simply better equipped than others to avoid conflicts and survive. Thus it is to be expected that minority cabinets are more likely to end because of a parliamentary defeat than are majority cabinets. In contrast to minority cabinets, majority cabinets cannot lose a vote in parliament as long as their own MPs stand united against the opposition. Structural attributes might also plausibly be linked to terminations through early elections. Presumably, single-party cabinets can more easily agree on an early election date than can coalition cabinets with several parties, as the electoral prospects of these parties are likely to differ. In fact, Budge and Keman (1990: 167) find that single-party cabinets were more likely to call early elections ('anticipated elections' in their terms) than were (majority or minority) coalition cabinets. Strøm and Swindle (2002) hypothesize that minority governments may often have much to gain and little to lose through election and find that they actually use dissolution powers more frequently than do majority governments. One might also argue that minority cabinets, unlike majority cabinets, cannot be held fully responsible by the voters for a given state of affairs precisely because they do not command a majority of their own. In this respect, minority cabinets may posses a relative electoral advantage compared to majority cabinets.

The third hypothesis is that actor preferences are decisive: preferences alone, and specifically those that have to do with policy choices, explain cabinet terminations. The greater the policy range of the incumbent government, for example, the worse its prospects for a comfortable end. As argued by Bortne (1998), inter-party policy conflicts leading to termination are expected to be most likely in broad coalitions. Another type of inter-party conflict is personal antagonism or competition, which does not readily lend itself to theorizing. Yet, we know from our data that such conflicts are much more prominent in some countries than in others. In the Italian case, for example, personal conflicts are often associated with policy conflicts (Verzichelli and Cotta 2000), whereas in the Danish case no personal conflicts were reported (Damgaard 2000*b*). Finally, all types of cabinet may break down due to intra-party conflicts. Some parties are not coherent units but rather 'coalitions of factions' (Laver and Schofield 1990: 19–22), and intra-party revolt in such parties is an ever-present possibility (Mitchell 1999). Thus, on the one hand, broad multiparty governments multiply the potential sources of intra-party risk, while on the other hand a cabinet consisting of a single large party may be more likely to face ideological factions.

Yet another possibility is that the best explanation of cabinet termination lies in particular political institutions, rules, or procedures. Some institutions, for example, make early elections easy to call, whereas others, such as the constructive vote of no confidence, make incumbents hard to defeat. A fifth possibility is the terminations are driven by features of their bargaining environment, such as whether the incumbent parties have crafted a comprehensive and committal coalition agreement. A long period of bargaining and numerous rounds of inconclusive cabinet formation bargaining might indicate problems that render a cabinet more susceptible to subsequent crises. Yet, we expect that the immediate effects of the initial bargaining process are most acutely felt during early stages of the cabinet's life and that these effects will typically be reduced by the time the cabinet reaches the end of its life. Finally, it may be that cabinet terminations are driven mainly by critical events. Cabinets may find a beautiful death if the economy performs well and no nasty scandals befall them; otherwise, they may come to a painful demise. Although these various explanations do not automatically translate into a distinct set of variables that can be used in empirical analysis of cabinet termination, they do nevertheless help to organize the analyses that follow, and Table 9.6 is indeed organized around them.

Model estimation and results

Since our dependent variable (terminations) will thus take three values that are not easily ranked in any ordinal sense, we shall employ a multinomial logistic regression design. The first part of the multivariate analysis (Table 9.6a) compares the conditions under which conflict terminations (category 2) occur with the conditions that produce technical terminations (category 1). The second part of the analysis (Table 9.6b) compares early elections (without any associated defeat or conflict) (category 3) with technical resignations (category 1), which is thus the baseline against which the coefficients in both parts of the table should be interpreted. In the following, we shall compare the effects of different clusters of explanations across these two parts of the overall model. For a further discussion of methods and estimation procedures, the reader should consult Chapter 3.

Note first that the explanatory power of national and temporal fixed effects is limited. There is a weak tendency for technical resignations to be more common in the 1990s than in earlier decades. This effect extends to conflict terminations as well as to the early elections. In other words, all else equal, each of these alternative terminations was less likely in the 1990s than at earlier times. Note, however, that these effects are not entirely robust across the different model specifications.

We focus next on the structural attributes of cabinets. We distinguish between various types of cabinets (single-party minority, minority coalition, minimal winning coalition, and surplus coalition, see also Chapter 6) because they are expected to effect termination differently in one or more ways. It is commonly observed that on average, majority cabinets stay in office longer than do minority cabinets (see also Chapter 10), and that they do not resign as often as do minority governments because of parliamentary defeats (Damgaard 2000*a*). Minimum winning cabinets may be particularly favoured (Dodd 1976). We would expect these and similar effects to show up in Table 9.6. Yet, even though the initial block estimates are in most cases consistent with these patterns, the results are not very strong or robust in the more comprehensive models. Recall that our baseline cabinet type is a minority, single-party cabinet. Interestingly, there are no robust effects of minority coalition or minimum winning status. The number of cabinet parties increases the risk of a conflict termination, but this effect is not statistically significant across our model specifications. Yet several structural attributes do affect the likelihood of conflict terminations vis-à-vis alternative fates. When we control for other relevant factors, conflictual terminations are more likely when bargaining power is dispersed, and when the party with the greatest bargaining power is not represented in the cabinet. The same conditions promote voluntary early elections (again, as compared to technical terminations).

TABLE 9.6. *Multinomial logistic regressions of government termination type*

Independent variables	Model 1	Model 2	Model 3	Model 4	Model 5	Model 6	Model 7	Model 8	Impact[a]
				a. Conflict vs. Technical					
Time									
1940s	0.03 (0.42)								
1960s	−0.33 (0.38)								
1970s	0.29 (0.35)								
1980s	0.13 (0.35)								
1990s	−0.82 (0.43)*						−0.24 (0.47)	−0.76 (0.51)	−0.08 (0.08)
Structure									
Post-election cabinet		0.19 (0.25)					−0.36 (0.54)		
Bargaining power fragmentation		−0.01 (0.11)					−1.16 (0.69)*		
Number of cabinet parties		0.48 (0.21)**					0.06 (0.17)	0.26 (0.14)*	−0.003 (0.03)
Max. bargaining power pty. in cab.		−0.21 (0.43)					0.40 (0.29)		
Minority coalition		0.34 (0.53)					−0.95 (0.63)	−0.90 (0.50)*	−0.05 (0.09)
Minimum winning coalition		−0.31 (0.40)					0.30 (0.87)		
Surplus majority cabinet		0.26 (0.61)					0.51 (0.79)		
Preferences							0.65 (1.01)		
Extremist party seat share			0.05 (0.01)**				0.04 (0.02)*	0.04 (0.02)**	0.01 (0.003)
Parliamentary preference range			−0.02 (0.01)**				−0.01 (0.01)	−0.02 (0.01)**	−0.06 (0.02)[a]
Polarization (BP weighted)			0.02 (0.02)						
Issue dimensionality			0.31 (0.49)						
Cabinet preference range			0.02 (0.01)**				0.01 (0.01)	0.03 (0.01)**	0.18 (0.05)[a]
Median party (1st dim.) in cab.			0.16 (0.33)						
Institutions									
List PR				−0.61 (0.39)*			−1.10 (0.66)*	−1.15 (0.48)**	0.04 (0.08)
Bicameralism				0.47 (0.30)					
Positive parliamentarism				1.18 (0.32)**			1.36 (0.38)**	1.34 (0.35)**	0.24 (0.07)
Abs. majority no-confidence				−0.11 (0.37)			−0.82 (0.52)	−0.90 (0.36)**	−0.10 (0.05)
Cabinet rule: PM consensus				−0.45 (0.46)			−0.06 (0.41)		
PM powers				−0.16 (0.09)*			0.02 (0.14)		
PM dissolution powers				0.05 (0.55)					

(*cont.*)

TABLE 9.6. (*Continued*)

Independent variables	Model 1	Model 2	Model 3	Model 4	Model 5	Model 6	Model 7	Model 8	Impact[a]
Bargaining									
Cabinet bargaining duration					0.01 (0.005)**		0.01 (0.01)		
Inconclusive bargaining round					−0.11 (0.29)				
Coalition agreement					−0.06 (0.33)				
Comprehensive policy agreement					−0.78 (0.30)**		−0.18 (0.44)		
Coalition discipline dummy					−0.07 (0.27)		1.27 (0.55)**	0.78 (0.39)**	0.07 (0.06)
Critical events									
Terminal event lag (any)						−0.19 (0.33)	0.03 (0.41)		
Electoral volatility						−0.01 (0.02)			
Unemployment (end)						0.13 (0.03)**	0.11 (0.05)**	0.10 (0.04)**	0.007 (0.007)
Inflation (end)						0.06 (0.02)**	0.09 (0.03)**	0.08 (0.03)**	0.008 (0.004)
Constant	0.09 (0.24)	−0.96 (0.57)	−0.88 (1.49)	0.53 (0.50)	0.25 (0.27)	−0.90 (0.30)**	−1.77 (1.24)	−0.63 (0.90)	

b. Voluntary early election vs. Technical

Independent variables	Model 1	Model 2	Model 3	Model 4	Model 5	Model 6	Model 7	Model 8	Impact[a]
Time									
1940s	−0.51 (0.73)								
1960s	0.40 (0.49)								
1970s	0.85 (0.47)*								
1980s	0.83 (0.47)*								
1990s	0.03 (0.54)								
Structure									
Post-election cabinet		−0.21 (0.31)					−0.33 (0.58)		
Bargaining power fragmentation		0.29 (0.13)**					0.11 (0.66)		
Number of cabinet parties		0.39 (0.28)					−1.16 (0.80)		
Max. bargaining power pty. in cab.		−0.99 (0.45)**					0.82 (0.22)**	0.75 (0.19)**	0.13 (0.04)
Minority coalition		−1.20 (0.69)*					0.62 (0.42)		
Minimum winning coalition		−2.44 (0.63)**					−0.74 (0.77)	−1.23 (0.59)**	−0.16 (0.07)
Surplus majority cabinet		−2.81 (0.98)**					−0.80 (1.00)		
							−1.64 (1.07)		
							−2.50 (1.44)*		

	(1)	(2)	(3)	(4)	(5)	(6)	(7)	(8)
Preferences								
Extremist party seat share	−0.01(0.02)					0.02(0.03)	0.01(0.02)	−0.002(0.004)
Parliamentary preference range	−0.01(0.01)					0.00(0.01)	−0.01(0.01)	−0.01(0.06)[a]
Polarization (BP weighted)	0.03(0.02)							
Issue dimensionality	1.12(0.57)*							
Cabinet preference range	−0.03(0.01)**					−0.02(0.02)	−0.01(0.01)	−0.11(0.07)[a]
Median party (1st dim.) in cab.	−0.23(0.37)							
Institutions								
List PR		−0.82(0.46)*				−1.23(0.75)	−2.17(0.53)**	−0.37(0.10)
Bicameralism		0.05(0.39)						
Positive parliamentarism		0.50(0.40)				0.77(0.54)	0.64(0.47)	−0.01(0.08)
Abs. majority no-confidence		−0.85(0.45)*				−1.59(0.68)**	−1.14(0.48)**	−0.14(0.06)
Cabinet rule: PM consensus		0.62(0.55)				0.30(0.55)		
PM powers		0.21(0.11)**				0.36(0.19)*		
PM dissolution powers		−0.05(0.63)						
Bargaining								
Cabinet bargaining duration			−0.01(0.01)			−0.01(0.01)		
Inconclusive bargaining round			0.28(0.37)					
Coalition agreement			−0.52(0.46)					
Comprehensive policy agreement			0.19(0.44)			−1.17(0.69)*		
Coalition discipline dummy			1.33(0.40)**			2.10(0.82)**	2.49(0.57)**	0.23(0.06)
Critical events								
Terminal event lag (any)				0.56(0.36)		0.14(0.46)		
Electoral volatility				−0.00(0.02)				
Unemployment (end)				0.17(0.04)**		0.12(0.06)*	0.17(0.05)**	0.03(0.01)
Inflation (end)				0.08(0.02)**		0.13(0.03)**	0.11(0.03)**	0.01(0.005)
Constant	−1.16(0.36)**	−0.36(0.66)	−3.34(1.74)*	−1.11(0.66)	−1.426(0.43)	−2.32(0.39)**	−4.90(1.76)**	−2.79(1.14)
Number of Observations	388	381	370	388	375	328	331	339
Pseudo-R^2	0.02	0.12	0.10	0.09	0.08	0.06	0.30	0.26
% Correctly predicted	0.46	0.56	0.54	0.52	0.50	0.49	0.67	0.62

Notes: * $p < 0.10$; ** $p < 0.05$.

[a] Impact is the marginal effect of a unit change in the independent variable on the probability of the outcome occurring, calculated based on Model 8, with the following exceptions: Parliamentary preference range and Cabinet preference range are for 25 point changes (1 standard deviation changes).

These results suggest that cabinets live more dangerously when there is a credible opposition and/or when the bargaining environment is complex. Note also that there is a robust and statistically significant tendency for surplus majority cabinets to avoid early elections, which likely reflects the conflicting electoral prospects typically found in such cabinets.

Our next cluster of predictors is a set of preference-related variables. It includes the preference range within the cabinet and the parliament, respectively, the number of issue dimensions, polarization, extremist party seats shares, and a dummy variable for whether the first-dimension median party is represented in the cabinet. We expect conflictual terminations to be more likely, and early elections perhaps less so, when the incumbent parties are heterogeneous in their preferences, as well as when the opposition is homogeneous (not dispersed). The results give some support to these expectations. The greater the preference range of the governing parties, and the smaller the range of parliament as a whole, the more likely we are to see conflictual terminations. These results are very consistent and robust across different model specifications. The preference variable cluster is much less effective in identifying early elections. There is some evidence in the initial block that a policy-heterogeneous cabinet is less likely to call early elections, but this result loses its statistical significance when we control for other blocks of variables. All in all, the results in this block suggest that although early elections may more significantly be driven by other factors, preference profiles help us understand which cabinets are most susceptible to conflict-driven terminations. But, importantly, what matters in such circumstances is not just the preference profile of the cabinet itself, but also that of the opposition.

Our third block of explanatory variables comprises a set of institutional rules described in previous chapters. The collective explanatory power of this block of variables is on a par with those of the two previous blocks (structural attributes and policy preferences). Surprisingly, the most consistently significant variable is list PR, which enhances the prospects of technical terminations over either conflict or early elections. A constructive vote of no confidence similarly (though less robustly) increases the chances of a technical termination, while it reduces the incidence of either of the other types of termination. In this sense, our results suggest that the constructive vote of no confidence has precisely the effects that it was designed to have: it stabilizes incumbent governments and makes them less likely to topple. Positive parliamentarism has the opposite effect: it reduces the incidence of technical terminations and boosts the likelihood of alternative exits and especially conflictual terminations. Strong prime ministerial powers (excluding dissolution powers) enhance the likelihood of early elections, but it is interesting to note that prime ministerial dissolution powers by themselves have no significant effect on this outcome.

Our measures of the bargaining environment turn out to have less significant effects on cabinet termination. The variables included are the duration of the cabinet formation process, whether or not there was at least one inconclusive round of bargaining prior to cabinet formation, the level of coalition discipline, whether or not the cabinet was based on a coalition agreement, and if so, whether this agreement was comprehensive in policy terms. The variables capturing the bargaining process prior to the cabinet's formation turn out to have no significant effects in our full or final models. This is not surprising, since we would expect the effects of such pre-formation events to be stronger at earlier stages of the cabinet's life and attenuate as we get closer to its point of termination. What is significant is the level of discipline expected of representatives of the governing parties. Where norms of coalition discipline are strong, cabinets are much less likely to be terminated under conflictual circumstances. Norms of coalition discipline also strongly depress the incidence of early elections and thus enhance the prospects of a technical termination. There is much less of an effect of having a written coalition agreement, or a comprehensive one. In the initial block estimates, a comprehensive coalition agreement significantly reduces the incidence of conflictual terminations. This effect, however, turns out not to be robust to more inclusive model specifications.

The final block of explanatory variables is designed to capture the effects of critical events. This block includes two economic indicators that might possibly influence the likelihood of premature or conflictual cabinet termination, namely, the rates of joblessness and inflation (consumer price index), both measured during the last year of the cabinet's tenure. 'Good' economic indicators (high employment and low inflation) should stabilize a government but might also encourage it to call early elections in the hope of electoral reward. 'Poor' economic indicators, on the other hand, should make a cabinet vulnerable in the parliament as well as in the electoral arena. In that situation, the cabinet may not want early elections, but it could nevertheless be forced to resign. Our critical events block also contains two non-economic predictors: a lagged variable for terminal events associated with the previous cabinet and our measure of electoral volatility. Neither of these two variables turns out to be significantly related to termination in any of our specifications. This should probably not surprise us greatly, since again the effects of variables associated with the previous cabinet or election will likely have been weakened by the time we reach this point in the parliamentary 'life cycle'.

It is more plausible to think that contemporaneous rates of inflation or unemployment might matter. And indeed they do. Both unemployment and inflation are strongly and robustly associated with cabinet termination, and their main effects are precisely the ones that we would expect. The higher the level of unemployment or inflation, the less likely the cabinet is to experience a technical termination. The most immediately intuitive part of this story is that both types of economic hardship strongly increase the risk of a conflictual termination. Moreover, the effects of the two variables are amazingly similar in size and significance levels. One extra percentage point of unemployment hurts the incumbents just slightly more than one additional percentage point of inflation. The less obvious part of the story is that both variables also increase the likelihood of a voluntary early election, again by strikingly similar magnitudes. Following Smith (2004), these may reflect the fact that incumbents call elections when they have reason to believe that the economy is about to get worse.

Overall, our models suggest that the impact of a number of our independent variables on the cause of government termination is quite substantial. As expected, increasing the cabinet preference range by one standard deviation (25 points) increases the probability of a termination due to conflict by 18 percentage points. Perhaps more surprisingly, positive parliamentarism increases the likelihood of a termination due to conflict by 24 percentage points. List PR decreases the likelihood of an early election by 37 points, while strong coalition discipline increases the likelihood of an early election by 23 percentage points.

Recall from earlier sections of this chapter that the preceding analysis has dealt with all the possible modes of termination, except one: voluntary enlargement of the coalition not associated with any conflict. We have identified all such observations in our data, and there are 17 in all. The paucity of such cases makes it appropriate to deal with them separately in rare events logistic regression analysis. We have estimated a set of eight such models, with specifications that mirror those reported in Table 9.6. For economy of presentation, we do not report the full analysis here. The results are, however, easy to report.

In our full and final models, there are only three analytical variables that significantly contribute to our explanation of non-conflictual voluntary enlargements. The first of these is bargaining power fragmentation. Cabinets that exist in dispersed bargaining environments are significantly more likely than others to experience voluntary enlargement of the coalition of governing parties. The reason may be that it is precisely in environments of fragmented bargaining power that the incremental party can add strength to the government. Second, the policy range covered by the cabinet matters. The broader this preference range, the less likely the cabinet is to be expanded by one or more additional parties. Finally, we find that unemployment has a significant and robust effect. The higher the level of joblessness, the less likely it is that new parties will enter the existing government. In the latter case, it is presumably the lack of pull factors that accounts for this result. Opposition parties are likely to think twice before boarding a ship that is already sinking.

CONCLUSION

This chapter is a search for explanations of different forms of cabinet termination. The existing literature on coalition politics has paid very little attention to such questions, focusing instead on cabinet membership and duration. Recent scholarship on cabinet duration, however, suggests that parliamentary governments during their tenure face competing risks from their environments. In this chapter, we move closer to an understanding of such risks by examining the circumstances under which different cabinets come to their demise. We distinguish most basically between technical (whose circumstances are normally beyond the control of the actors involved) and discretionary terminations, with a range of subcategories within each of these main types.

Our analysis highlights the importance of counting rules for our understanding of cabinet change. Turnover in the executive branch is rarely an all-or-nothing proposition. Depending on our counting rules, we always run the risk of recording change where others see continuity, or conversely observing continuity where others see turnover. By the definitions adopted in this project, we have shown that 20 per cent of the cabinet terminations under study constitute only minimal turnovers, in which the new cabinet represents the same parties and the same PM as its predecessor and the only change is typically that a general election has taken place. The percentage of such survivors varies dramatically across countries, from 0 per cent in Finland and Italy to 48 per cent in Austria and Sweden (Tables 9.4 and 9.5). These findings suggest that for many purposes it may be important to consider alternative specifications in future analyses of cabinet duration and termination. Yet, for our purposes it is important to record all significant changes in the bargaining environment, and general elections almost inevitably give rise to such changes.

By our definitions, it turns out that more than 60 per cent of all cabinet terminations are discretionary while almost 40 per cent are technical. However, there is considerable variation in the distribution of the two termination types across countries and some over time. In the 1970s and 1980s, for example, discretionary terminations were more frequent than in the preceding and following decades (Table 9.3). There is also systematic variation across cabinet type. Discretionary termination is more frequent for coalition cabinets than for single-party cabinets. Among discretionary terminations, most coalition cabinets end because of controversies between cabinet parties, but many cabinets also 'die' because of intra-party conflict or due to defeats or crises in the parliamentary arena (Table 9.2).

We have employed a multinomial logit model to identify the causes of three different forms of cabinet termination: technical terminations, early elections not precipitated by any cabinet defeat or crisis, and finally all terminations associated with partisan or parliamentary defeats, conflicts, or crises. As in other chapters in this volume, we have considered six blocks of explanatory variables, as well as a full and a final comprehensive model. All these blocks have some explanatory power, and none clearly dominates the others. Structural attributes matter in the sense that the more fragmented the opposition is compared to the governing parties, the greater the likelihood of avoiding conflictual terminations. And surplus majority coalitions appear particularly vulnerable to conflict or defeat. More surprisingly, however, minimal winning coalitions are not particularly favoured nor minority governments especially exposed. Preferences also make a difference, as cabinets with heterogeneous policy preferences are more likely to suffer conflictual terminations. Institutions and rules clearly matter, as a constructive vote of no confidence clearly protects incumbent parties against conflictual terminations, whereas positive parliamentarism seems to be a difficult environment in which to navigate. Strong prime ministerial powers render cabinets more likely to end in conflict or early elections, whereas surprisingly strong dissolution powers have no robust effect on the likelihood of early elections. Finally, high unemployment and/or inflation strongly and robustly predispose the cabinet towards either early elections or a conflictual termination.

All in all, these results suggest that all facets of the parliamentary bargaining environment must be taken into account if we are to understand the ways in which parliamentary governments are ended. Many of these variables work in ways that are consistent with our theoretical expectations or simple intuitions, but some of the results that we have found clearly call for us to reconsider our ideas about this phase of the life cycle of democratic politics. This is an aspect of coalition politics that has been seriously neglected, and it does not deserve to be. Indeed, if we continue to do so, we shall be ill placed to understand the competing risks and rewards of coalition politics. There is therefore every reason to hope that more research will be done on the complexities of cabinet termination politics.

REFERENCES

Alt, James and King, Gary (1994). 'Transfer of Governmental Power', *Comparative Political Studies*, 27: 190–210.

Bortne, Øystein (1998). *Coalition Termination in Post-1973 Western Europe*. Bergen: Department of Comparative Politics.

——Frendreis, John, and Gleiber, Dennis W. (1986). 'Dissolution of Governments in Scandinavia: A Critical Events Perspective', *Scandinavian Political Studies*, 9: 93–110.

Budge, Ian and Keman, Hans (1990). *Parties and Democracy. Coalition Formation and Government Functioning in Twenty States*. Oxford: Oxford University Press.

Damgaard, Erik (ed.) (1992). *Parliamentary Change in the Nordic Countries*. Oslo: Scandinavian University Press.

——(1994). 'Termination of Danish Government Coalitions: Theoretical and Empirical Aspects', *Scandinavian Political Studies*, 17: 193–212.

——(2000*a*). 'Minority Governments', in Lauri Karvonen and Krister Ståhlberg, (eds.), *Festschrift for Dag Anckar*. Åbo: Åbo Akademi University Press.

——(2000*b*). 'Denmark: The Life and Death of Government Coalitions', in Wolfgang C. Müller and Kaare Strøm (eds.), *Coalition Governments in Western Europe*. Oxford: Oxford University Press.

——Gerlich, Peter, and Richardson, J. J. (eds.) (1989). *The Politics of Economic Crisis*. Aldershot, UK: Avebury.

De Winter, Lieven,. Timmermans, Arco, and Dumont, Patrick (2000). 'Belgium: On Government Agreements, Evangelists, Followers, and Heretics', in Wolfgang C. Müller and Kaare Strøm (eds.), *Coalition Governments in Western Europe*. Oxford: Oxford University Press.

Dodd, Lawrence C. (1976). *Coalitions in Parliamentary Government*. Princeton, NJ: Princeton University Press.

Druckman, James N. (1996). 'Party Factionalism and Cabinet Durability', *Party Politics*, 2: 397–407.

King, Gary, Alt, James, Burns, Nancy, and Laver, Michael (1990). 'A Unified Model of Cabinet Dissolution in Parliamentary Democracies', *American Journal of Political Science*, 34: 846–71.

Laver, Michael and Schofield, Norman (1990). *Multiparty Government. The Politics of Coalition in Europe*. Oxford: Oxford University Press.

Lewin, Leif (1998). 'Majoritarian and Consensus Democracy: The Swedish Experience', *Scandinavian Political Studies*, 21: 195–206.

Lijphart, Arend (1984). *Democracies. Patterns of Majoritarian and Consensus Government in Twenty-One Countries*. New Haven, CT: Yale University Press.

—— (1999). *Patterns of Democracy*. New Haven, CT: Yale University Press.

Lupia, Arthur and Strøm, Kaare (1995). 'Coalition Termination and the Strategic Timing of Parliamentary Elections', *American Political Science Review*, 89: 648–65.

Mair, Peter and Smith, Gordon (eds.) (1990). *Understanding Party System Change in Western Europe*. London: Frank Cass.

Mitchell, Paul (1999). 'Coalition Discipline, Enforcement Mechanisms, and Intraparty Politics', in Shoun Bowler, David M. Farrell, and Richard S. Katz (eds.), *Party Discipline and Parliamentary Government*. Columbus, OH: Ohio State University Press.

—— (2000). 'From Single-Party to Coalition Rule', in Wolfgang C. Müller and Kaare Strøm (eds.), *Coalition Governments in Western Europe*. Oxford: Oxford University Press.

Müller, Wolfgang C. and Strøm, Kaare (eds.) (1999). *Policy, Office, or Votes?* Cambridge: Cambridge University Press.

—— —— (eds.) (2000). *Coalition Governments in Western Europe*. Oxford: Oxford University Press.

Nousiainen, Jaakko (2000). 'Finland: The Consolidation of Parliamentary Governance', in Wolfgang C. Müller and Kaare Strøm (eds.), *Coalition Governments in Western Europe*. Oxford: Oxford University Press.

Smith, Alastair (2004). *Election Timing*. Cambridge: Cambridge University Press.

Strøm, Kaare (1990). *Minority Government and Majority Rule*. Cambridge: Cambridge University Press.

—— and Swindle, Stephen M. (2002). 'The Strategic Use of Parliamentary Dissolution Powers', *American Political Science Review*, 96: 565–98.

Timmermans, Arco and Andeweg, Rudy B. (2000). 'The Netherlands: Still the Politics of Accomodation?', in Wolfgang C. Müller and Kaare Strøm (eds.), *Coalition Governments in Western Europe*. Oxford: Oxford University Press.

Thiébault, Jean-Louis (2000). 'France: Forming and Maintaining Government Coalitions in the Fifth Republic', in Wolfgang C. Müller and Kaare Strøm (eds.), *Coalition Governments in Western Europe*. Oxford: Oxford University Press.

Verzichelli, Luca and Cotta, Maurizio (2000). 'Italy: From "Constrained" Coalitions to Alternating Governments?', in Wolfgang C. Müller and Kaare Strøm (eds.), *Coalition Governments in Western Europe*. Oxford: Oxford University Press.

von Beyme, Klaus (2000). *Parliamentary Democracy*. Houndmills, UK: Palgrave.

Woldendorp, Jaap, Keman, Hans, and Budge, Ian (1993). 'Special Issue: Political Data 1945–1990. Party Government in 20 Democracies', *European Journal of Political Research*, 24 (1).

10

Institutions, Chance, and Choices: The Dynamics of Cabinet Survival

Thomas Saalfeld

INTRODUCTION

'Chance ends some governments.... The electoral calendar terminates other executives.... Still other governments collapse as a result of deliberate party choice' (Mershon 2002: 143). Understanding the sources of cabinet durability[1] and the dynamics of cabinet termination in parliamentary systems of government is 'a very important substantive concern for political science' (Laver 2003: 23). After all, low levels of cabinet duration may have implications for the extent to which executives are able to dominate legislatures (Lijphart 1999: 129); for ministerial efficiency vis-à-vis the bureaucracy (Huber and Lupia 2000); for a political system's and government's policy performance (Huber 1998); and for democratic regime legitimacy (Linz 1978: 66–9; Warwick 1994: 5). In post-war Western Europe, cabinet durations have varied considerably within and across countries (see Table 10.1). There is a prolific tradition of empirical and theoretical work in comparative political science seeking to explain such variations (see the survey in Laver 2003). Nevertheless, progress has been hampered, firstly, by a lack of integration of theoretical and empirical work (Mershon 2002: 187; Laver 2003: 38–9). Secondly, despite the theoretical improvements resulting from the rise of institutionalism and the use of non-cooperative game theory in modelling coalition bargaining (e.g. through Lupia and Strøm 1995),[2] there has been a lack of empirical data describing the institutional

---

[1] In this chapter, the terms 'duration', 'survival', and 'stability' will be used synonymously to describe the empirically observable time elapsed between a cabinet's formation and its termination. The term 'durability', by contrast, will be used when the focus is on (statistical or theoretical) models predicting the potential duration (see Laver 2003: 24).

[2] The most influential non-cooperative bargaining models have focused on cabinet formation. See, e.g. Baron and Ferejohn (1989); Merlo (1997); Morelli (1999); and Diermeier and Merlo (2000). Lupia and Strøm (1995) focus on coalition terminations.

TABLE 10.1. *Median cabinet duration by country*[a]

Country	Period	CIEP[b] (years)	Median duration 1945–99	N	Median duration 1945–69	N	Median duration 1970–99	N
Austria	1945–97	4	700	21	689	11	1,202.5	10
Belgium	1946–95	4	297.5	32	511	15	288	17
Denmark	1945–98	4	629	30	735	14	524	16
Finland	1945–95	3/4[c]	264	43	287.5	24	254	19
France	1959–97	5	577.5	22	461	7	583	15
Germany	1949–98	4	652	25	505	14	898	11
Greece	1977–96	4	677	10	—	—	677	10
Iceland	1944–99	4	864	25	864	13	838	12
Ireland	1944–97	5	892	21	1,024	10	815	11
Italy	1945–98	5	233	50	212	24	248.5	26
Luxembourg	1945–95	6/5[d]	1,369	15	979.5	10	1,795	5
The Netherlands	1945–98	4	762.5	22	659.5	12	1,202.5	10
Norway	1945–97	4	715	25	747	11	600	14
Portugal	1976–95	4	272	13	—	—	272	13
Spain	1977–96	4	997	7	—	—	997	7
Sweden	1945–98	4/3/4[e]	728	25	570.5	12	913	13
United Kingdom	1945–97	5	1,124	19	792.5	10	1,260	9
Median/total			568	405	582	187	534	218

[a] The observation window in each country starts with the first election after the end of the Second World War or the first democratic election for countries that were not liberal democracies in 1945. It ends with the last cabinet terminated before 1 January 2000. Cabinets that were still in office on 1 January 2000 were excluded from the calculations in this table.

[b] CIEP: Constitutional inter-election period (maximum time between elections). Data taken from Bergman et al. (2003: 131–3).

[c] Three years until 1954.

[d] 1945–54: Six years with half of the Chamber renewed every three years.

[e] The duration of the CIEP was four years 1920–69, three years 1970–94 and four years since.

parameters constraining coalition bargaining. Thirdly, there have been doubts whether traditional research designs are well suited to model the effects institutions have on cabinet durability where these institutions could be endogenous to the model (see Mershon 2002: 24–5; Diermeier 2006: 175). Fourthly, the transaction costs of bargaining have been neglected in most models of coalition bargaining.

The present chapter does not purport to resolve all of these issues. It is part of a collective endeavour to narrow the gap between theoretical and empirical traditions with a focus on actor-centred institutional analysis (Scharpf 1997) and the transaction costs actors face, and seek to contain, when bargaining in parliamentary systems of government; to provide first analyses of a new data-set collected especially for this volume (including data on institutions of coalition governance, which are an important addition to the literature in conceptual and empirical terms); and to provide an interpretation of the results based on the bargaining-theoretic framework set out in the second chapter. The present work seeks to provide an account of the dynamics of cabinet (and, in particular, coalition) governance and durability in the interval between formation and termination. Because it focuses largely on the effects structural factors and institutions have on the costs and benefits of governing, a comparative rather than an ideographic approach is appropriate. The chapter tests predictions about the covariation between relevant actors' resources, their policy preferences, the institutional constraints they face, and the risks posed by random events, on the one hand, and cabinet duration (the dependent variable), on the other. A number of predictions will be derived from the bargaining-theoretic framework outlined in the second chapter of this volume. The use of event-history analysis as a statistical method ensures that the dynamics of cabinet survival, modelled as an underlying bargaining process, can be observed and examined in a longitudinal design that is more appropriate than traditional cross-sectional regression techniques.

CABINET DURATION IN WESTERN EUROPE: VARIATIONS ACROSS SPACE AND TIME

Defining the beginning and end of cabinets and measuring cabinet duration is far from trivial in a comparative context (cf. Lijphart 1984; Laver and Schofield 1990: 145; Warwick 1994: 26–8; Huber 1998: 577–81; Laver 2003: 25–7). Different national constitutions, conventions, and actor perceptions often make it difficult to determine the beginning and end of cabinets across a large number of political systems. This is compounded by disagreement amongst researchers leading to considerable variations in measurement (cf. Mershon 2002: 27).[3] The data-set in this volume follows a widely accepted definition according to which cabinets begin when they are appointed by a head of state. A cabinet is considered to be terminated with any change in the set of parties holding cabinet membership,[4] any change in the identity of the head of government, and any general election, whether mandated by the end of the constitutional inter-election party (CIEP) or

---

[3] Mershon (2002: 27) provides a few examples:

For instance, German government duration from 1949 to 1987 averaged 37 months according Laver and Schofield ... and only 20 months according to Woldendorp, Keman, and Budge ... In the data set compiled by Strøm ..., Italian governments lasted 10 months on average between 1946 and 1987, whereas Laver and Schofield ... measure average government duration in Italy as 13 months over the same span.

[4] We count as members of the cabinet those and only those parties that have designated representatives with cabinet voting rights. Hence parties supporting the cabinet in parliament without holding cabinet portfolios are not included.

precipitated by a premature dissolution of parliament (Müller and Strøm 2000: 12).[5]

For descriptive purposes, the dependent variable—the time elapsed between a cabinet's appointment and termination—can be measured in two ways: (*a*) the actual duration in days and (*b*) the 'relative duration' as a percentage of its maximum feasible duration (Müller and Strøm 2000: 16–17). Table 10.1 (see p 328) presents information about the median cabinets' durations in days for all 17 West European parliamentary democracies in our sample during the entire window of observation between 1945 (or the respective establishment of a liberal democracy) and the end of the year 1999, breaking the period down into two sub-episodes, 1945–69 and 1970–99. The table reveals considerable cross-national and diachronic differences. Overall, Luxembourg, the United Kingdom, and Spain had the most long-lived cabinets; Italy, Finland, and Portugal experienced the lowest values for the respective median cabinet (1945–99). Comparing the median values in the two sub-episodes mentioned above (by country), the steepest increases occurred in Luxembourg (+815.5 days), the Netherlands (+543), and Austria (+513.5), and the largest decreases were witnessed in Belgium (−223), Denmark (−211), and Ireland (−209).

Even a brief glance at Table 10.1 reveals that the two countries with the highest median cabinet durations between 1945 and 1999 (Luxembourg and the United Kingdom) had CIEPs of at least five years. Given the fact that regular elections at the end of the CIEP are defined as terminal events, cabinets in such countries obviously have the potential for longer durations than countries with shorter CIEPs for largely technical reasons. A further source of distortion in the analysis of median values in days is that cabinets formed immediately after elections have by definition higher 'life expectancies' than cabinets formed at a later point during the CIEP. In order to correct for such bias, Table 10.2 provides data on the median cabinets' 'relative' durations by country expressed as percentage of the remainder of the CIEP (the maximum possible duration). If we rank the countries according to their median cabinet's *relative* duration, the median cabinets in the Netherlands, Norway, and Sweden had the most long-lived median cabinets surviving for the entire remainder of the CIEP (1.0). The median cabinets in Italy (0.23), Portugal (0.29), and Belgium (0.33) experienced relatively low relative durations between approximately one-quarter and one-third of their maximum possible duration. If we compare the sub-episodes 1945–69 and 1970–99 again, Germany (+0.36), Finland (+0.30), and Iceland (+0.25) had the largest increases in relative duration, whereas Ireland (−0.19), Italy (−0.13), and Belgium (−0.11) had the most marked decreases.

Sceptical readers might suspect that most cabinet terminations could be 'technical' artefacts of our definitions rather than reflecting 'real' differences in cabinet

---

[5] Nevertheless, the research design of this chapter is based on a very clear distinction between regular and early elections.

Institutions, Chance, and Choices

TABLE 10.2. *Median relative cabinet duration by country*

Country	Period	Median relative duration 1945–99	Total N 1945–99	Median relative duration 1945–69	N	Median relative duration 1970–99	N
Austria	1945–97	0.75	20	0.73	10	0.82	10
Belgium	1946–95	0.29	32	0.35	15	0.24	17
Denmark	1945–98	0.50	30	0.52	14	0.49	16
Finland	1945–95	0.58	43	0.50	24	0.80	19
France	1959–97	0.61	22	0.62	7	0.60	15
Germany	1949–98	0.68	25	0.56	14	0.92	11
Greece	1977–96	0.93	10	—	—	0.93	10
Iceland	1944–99	0.77	25	0.67	13	0.92	12
Ireland	1944–97	0.59	21	0.68	10	0.49	11
Italy	1945–98	0.23	48	0.27	22	0.18	26
Luxembourg	1945–95	0.98	15	0.86	10	1.00	5
The Netherlands	1945–98	1.00	22	1.00	12	1.00	10
Norway	1945–97	1.00	25	1.00	11	0.91	14
Portugal	1976–95	0.33	13	—	—	0.33	13
Spain	1977–96	0.83	6	—	—	0.83	6
Sweden	1945–98	1.00	25	1.00	12	1.00	13
United Kingdom	1945–97	0.78	19	0.74	10	0.78	9
Median/total		0.62	401	0.64	184	0.60	217

stability. At first glance at least, *technical terminations* such as *regular* elections or the death of the head of government (events triggered by events ending the life of a cabinet due to the definitions we chose for the purposes of this study rather than choices made by the actors[6]) are less interesting for behavioural analysis than *discretionary terminations*. The latter typically take two principal forms: early elections and cabinet replacements. Yet, the sceptic's suspicion is not supported by our data: Between 1945 and 1999, 238 of 390 cabinets (61%) with valid observations were terminated before the expiry of the CIEP as a result of actors' choices (see also the similar findings of Mershon 2002: 144–5). More importantly, even decisions *not* to terminate a cabinet before the expiry of the CIEP are, of course, *also* choices made by the actors worthy of explanation.

Table 10.3 demonstrates that the median duration of cabinets covaries with certain structural features of the cabinet: Majority status, for example, is clearly associated with cabinet longevity. Compared to majority status, the question whether a cabinet consists of one or more parties seems less important. Minimal-winning status, too, is strongly associated with cabinet longevity. These cross-national

---

[6] For example, the Danish Prime Minister Hans Hedtoft died in office in January 1955 and was succeeded by Hans Christian Hansen, who in turn died in office in February 1960. These are clearly two cabinets ended by 'random effects' in rapid succession (see Mershon 2002: 143).

TABLE 10.3. *Median cabinet duration by cabinet type*

Cabinet type	Median duration in days	Median relative duration
Majority cabinet	685.5	0.73
Minority situation	522.5	0.57
Non partisan cabinet	105	0.40
Single-party cabinet	614	0.60
Single-party majority cabinet	981	0.80
Single-party minority cabinet	533	0.47
Coalition cabinet	569.5	0.64
Majority coalition	613	0.70
Minority coalition	351	0.43
Minimal-winning cabinet	868	0.77
Surplus majority cabinet	445	0.46
Minimal connected cabinet	704	0.74
All cabinets	568	0.62

comparisons and comparisons across types of cabinets confirm that cabinet terminations are an important field for political analysis as they are, on the whole, influenced but not determined by institutional constraints or chance. Political and strategic factors are clearly crucial in understanding the conditions of cabinet durability.

EXPLAINING CABINET DURABILITY: THE STORY SO FAR

The first attempts at explaining variations in cabinet durations—whether in the 'European politics tradition' (Laver and Schofield 1990: 7–11) or the tradition of cooperative game theory—focused on the effects of so-called *structural attributes* of the relevant political systems, party systems, and cabinets (see the sections on 'structures' and 'institutions' below; for a summary of the most important findings see Laver and Schofield 1990: 147–55; Warwick 1994: 1–14; Grofman and van Roozendaal 1997; Laver 2003). Despite the discovery of a number of empirical regularities, the work in the structural-attributes tradition has been criticized for the static nature of its explanations. Although at least the game-theoretic work in the structural-attributes tradition specified causal mechanisms, it did so in a peculiar way: Cabinet terminations were effectively seen as the theoretical 'flip side' of cabinet formation: the same causal variables favouring the formation of certain types of equilibrium cabinets (e.g. minimal-winning coalitions) were also taken to be responsible for such cabinets' longevity. The main empirical problem is that such explanations typically 'reference government or parliamentary attributes whose values are fixed or set at the time a government takes office;

none takes account of the (subsequent) events that actually bring governments down' (Warwick 1994: 8). At a theoretical level, some cabinet-specific structural attributes may not be as exogenous to the explanatory model as they seem at first glance. For example, Diermeier and Merlo (2000: 63) argue that minimal-winning coalitions may be chosen during coalition bargaining, *because* they promise to be more durable.

Advocates of the *critical-events* perspective did not offer any answers to these theoretical issues (see Grofman and van Roozendaal 1994). They attacked the very causal determinism of the structural-attributes approach arguing that the vast majority of cabinets were terminated in response to unpredictable events such as deaths or ill-health of prime ministers, scandals, dramatic downturns in the economy, sudden shifts in public opinion and the like (Frendreis, Gleiber, and Browne 1986: 621, 623). The randomness of such events (from a political scientist's perspective) implies that the conditional probability of discretionary cabinet terminations is predicted to be constant over time.[7] Strøm challenged the non-strategic nature of random-effects models from a *theoretical* vantage point taking issue with the assumption that the events causing cabinets to fall are exogenous and random. 'In reality', he asserts, 'such events...are frequently engineered, or at least affected, by players in the game (i.e. parties inside or outside the government)' (Strøm 1988: 929). The most powerful *empirical* critique follows from Warwick's work (1994) who found for a sample of West European cabinets that the hazard rate of discretionary cabinet terminations is not constant at all, but tends to rise with cabinet age (see also Warwick and Easton 1992). Nevertheless, works in the random-events tradition made one lasting contribution to the debate about cabinet durability: They replaced the traditional cross-sectional regression-analytic approach with the longitudinal approach of event-history analysis, which is a more appropriate statistical technique to model the processes between cabinet formation and termination.

This methodological lead was taken up by the authors of a number of *unified models* combining the causal reasoning of the structural-attributes approach with the sort of stochastic environment suggested by random-events theorists. King et al. (1990) presented a stochastic process model, which—unlike the early work of Browne and his associates—make the hazard rate of cabinet survival a function of a range of covariates. Whilst this unified perspective represented a major improvement in the statistical theory and methods used to analyse cabinet durability, it still did not go much beyond existing models in specifying the causal mechanisms that were thought to drive the dynamics of cabinet survival in the interval between cabinet formation and termination. Subsequently, however, Lupia and Strøm (1995) developed a testable, dynamic game-theoretic model of discretionary coalition dissolutions accounting for the rising hazard rates for cabinet terminations towards the end of the CIEP and emphasizing the importance

---

[7] For example, the risk a discretionary cabinet termination should not be increased in the early days or later on in the 'life' of a cabinet.

of transaction costs in explaining these dynamics (see also the second chapter of this volume). This model is capable of integrating structural and other variables (see below) and combining them with a dynamic perspective including the possibility of random shocks subsequent to cabinet formation. Diermeier and his collaborators (Diermeier and Stevenson 1999, 2000; Diermeier and Merlo 2000) later built on this model. Key elements of the Lupia and Strøm framework will drive the empirical analyses carried out in the present chapter.

SOURCES OF CABINET DURABILITY

All decisions about cabinet continuation or termination can be modelled as being the result of more or less complex bargaining. Bargaining in coalitions resembles the type of 'two-level game' suggested by Putnam (1988) in his analysis of international negotiations: the *first level* represents the bargaining between party leaders over the formation and maintenance of a coalition, whereas the *second level* represents (usually) simultaneous intra-party bargaining between party leaders and backbenchers (for a game-theoretic model see Laver 1999). Since governments in parliamentary systems of government need the support of a majority in the chamber, the ability of party leaders to commit to inter-party deals closed in coalition negotiations or in cabinet depends crucially on sufficient support for the bargaining result from their own backbenchers. The intra-party dimension of bargaining also applies to single-party majority cabinets, which do not have to rely on inter-party bargaining to survive in office (although they may still need to negotiate to get their legislation passed, if there are strong institutional veto players in the system). Nevertheless there is conclusive evidence that even the leaders of single-party majority cabinets have to rely at least on some intra-party bargaining to ensure backbench support not only for the cabinet's decisions but ultimately also for their survival in office (e.g. Cowley 2002). In the present study, the intra-party dimension cannot be explicitly assessed due to a lack of data. Like all other studies in the field, I will largely treat intra-party bargaining as a black box (Laver and Schofield 1990: 15), although some institutions such as the prime minister's dissolution powers are likely to have a bearing on such processes (for related models on the impact of the confidence vote see Huber 1996; Diermeier and Feddersen 1998*a*, 1998*b*). The collection of more detailed data on intra-party conflict remains an important desideratum of research.

The theoretical framework employed here explicitly recognizes the importance of transaction costs arising from such commitment problems and other uncertainties in political bargaining, a very real problem which is often not accounted for in conventional accounts of cabinet durability. Like in all bargaining situations, coalition parties have a common interest to cooperate, but have conflicting interests over the distribution of benefits arising from the cooperation. In coalition politics, parties typically face (*a*) *search costs* including the effort spent in locating information about opportunities for exchange with potential coalition partners as well as information about their credibility and ability to commit to a deal; (*b*) *negotiation costs* resulting from difficulties in negotiating the distribution of policy and office benefits; (*c*) *enforcement costs* arising from the incomplete nature of coalition contracts (see second chapter), uncertainty in the political environment and time-dependence of the value of benefits from a cooperation (see second chapter). Uncertainty about the credibility and opportunism of (potential) coalition partners are particular problems in coalition bargaining processes, especially as parliamentary parties are at least in partial competition with each other and because party leaders need to win the support of their backbenchers for inter-party agreements at leadership level. Governance structures such as coalition agreements and coalition governance institutions may contain commitment problems to an extent. If the coalition parties care about a longer-term collaboration with each other and/or about their own reputation as credible coalition partners, there may be intrinsic incentives reducing the risk of opportunism and coalition break-up. High search costs or high levels of asset specificity (where at least one party makes an irreversible political investment in the coalition and reduces its own walk-away value) may also stabilize coalitions (for a general survey of transaction-cost politics see Dixit 1998: 37–102; for a definition of search, negotiation, and enforcement costs see North and Thomas 1973: 93). The impact of cabinet-specific governance structures on cabinet durability has never been assessed in a quantitative comparative design and will be one main focus of the present study.

One of the key characteristics of the framework set out in the second chapter is the way in which structural attributes, preferences, institutions, and critical events are modelled to affect termination decisions and, hence, cabinet durability: Firstly, the cabinet parties' resources and policy positions as well as institutions and external events (such as bad news from opinion polls) influence their bargaining power by affecting their respective walk-away values.[8] However, we do not expect a straightforward 'one-to-one' relationship between walk-away values and discretionary cabinet terminations (e.g. high walk-away values, high cabinet instability), because secondly, coalition bargaining always involves transaction costs. Parties care about the distributional effects of bargaining *and* its efficiency. A party with a high walk-away value may consider seeking a better offer from alternative coalition partners, but it may also eschew the possible transaction costs involved in negotiations with an 'out party' and convert its credible threat of

---

[8] This extends to intra-party bargaining. There are examples where party leaders have walked away from their parties and founded new parties or joined others. Examples include the British Prime Ministers David Lloyd George and Ramsay Macdonald in the inter-war years. More recently (2005), Israeli Prime Minister Ariel Sharon left Likud, the party he led, and set up the Kadima party.

walking away into policy and office benefits by *renegotiating the existing coalition agreement*.

In Chapter 2 of this volume Lupia and Strøm outline their model of coalition bargaining and cabinet termination in terms of the costs and benefits faced by the actors. The arguments need not be repeated here. In the following sections, theoretical expectations derived from this framework and the conventional literature will be tested using the data collected for this volume. This new dataset covers a larger number of countries and cabinets than previous studies and includes—unlike previous studies—information on governance structures that are likely to have a strong bearing on the transaction costs of coalition bargaining. The dependent variable is the conditional probability for a discretionary cabinet termination to occur at any particular point in time, given that the cabinet has survived up to that point ('hazard rate'). Changes in hazard rates are taken to indicate that causal effects are at work. For example, an increasing hazard rate of early elections after a certain number of cabinet-days is taken to indicate a change in the relevant actors' incentives at (or prior to) that point in time. The hazard-rate models presented in this chapter are specified as Cox proportional hazard models assuming the existence of a baseline hazard rate [$h_0(t)$], which indicates the underlying probability of cabinet termination over time when the vector of all covariates is zero. However, no assumptions are made about the distribution of probabilities of the occurrence of such 'failures' over time.[9] The covariates may lead to shifts in the hazard rate from this baseline, assuming that the impact of the covariates is the same across the entire life-course of a cabinet (proportionality assumption).[10] This statistical model is appropriate to test Lupia and Strøm's dynamic framework, because it allows estimating the effects of time-constant as well as time-varying covariates.[11] Because the time-varying covariates (independent variables) used here are measured on an annual basis, a record is created for each cabinet-year indicating the occurrence (or non-occurrence) and exact day of cabinet 'failure', along with values for a number of time-constant and time-varying covariates.

A key issue in event-history models is the 'censoring' of certain records. While event-history models have always used censoring to deal with incomplete information about the start and/or end dates of records in a data-set, theoretical

---

[9] Hazards could be rising or falling following various mathematical functions—or they could remain constant over time.

[10] The extent to which this assumption is violated by a number of covariates needs to be investigated systematically in future studies. The tests carried out for the present study do not suggest serious distortions.

[11] The Cox proportional hazards model used here measures duration from a cabinet's inauguration. Diermeier and Stevenson (2000) argue that measurement from the end of the CIEP would be a more appropriate approach to testing the Lupia and Strøm framework. For the purposes of this chapter, I have used the conventional method, but intend to re-estimate some of the models following the Diermeier and Stevenson design in a follow-up study.

censoring has played an important role in the study of cabinet survival: King et al. (1990) as well as Warwick (1994), for example, censor all cabinet records within 12 months of the end of the CIEP. Such censored records remain in the analysis and are essentially treated as cases for which the actual failure time is unknown. The main argument for this censoring regime is that many cabinets are terminated in the year preceding regular elections, and that such failures (so-called 'CIEP failures') should be treated differently from 'real' discretionary terminations. Diermeier and Stevenson (1999), by contrast, do not censor CIEP failures, arguing that the latter capture an important strategic element in cabinet behaviour relating to the electoral cycle. They find that the rising hazard rate of early elections contrasts in interesting ways with the almost constant hazard rate discovered for cabinet replacements. Therefore they maintain that theory-based censoring of CIEP failures essentially corresponds to analysing only one specific subset of hazards, namely replacement hazards (Diermeier and Stevenson 1999: 1067). In order to uncover potential differences in the dynamics of different termination types, I employ Diermeier and Stevenson's censoring regime (1999) in a competing-risk design: (*a*) When estimating the *general risk of discretionary cabinet terminations (pooled hazards)*, the records of all cabinets terminated due to technical reasons (e.g. termination by regular election or death of a Prime Minister) and all cabinets that were still in office on 31 December 1999 (the endpoint of or 'window of observation') were 'right-censored';[12] (*b*) for the estimation of the *risk of cabinet replacement (replacement hazards)*, the records of cabinets that failed due to technical terminations, all cabinets that were still in office on 31 December 1999 and those terminated by early elections were right-censored; and (*c*) in order to estimate the *risk of early elections (early election hazards)*, I censored the records of cabinets terminated due to technical reasons, all cabinets that were still in office on 31 December 1999 and those terminated by a reshuffle, involving a change in the person of the prime minister or a cabinet's party-political composition.

As already suggested, the use of event-history analysis reflects an approach to the study of cabinet terminations that differs fundamentally from the traditional cross-sectional comparisons on which the descriptive evidence in the second section of this chapter is based. Tables 10.1–10.3 report the median durations of cabinets across countries and certain types of cabinets. Figure 10.1 has two main purposes: Firstly, it illustrates the different approach of event-history analysis. Based on the duration of all 422 cabinets in our data-set, it plots the predicted (conditional) probabilities of discretionary cabinet terminations (pooled hazards, replacement hazards, and early election hazards) for each cabinet-day. Secondly,

---

[12] Right-censoring means effectively that the appropriate cabinets are treated as if the time of their failure was unknown. For a brief discussion of censoring in event-history analysis see Box-Steffensmeier and Jones (2004: 16–19). For a discussion of censoring in the event-history analysis of cabinet terminations see King et al. (1990: 852–5), or van Roozendaal (1997: 81), Laver (2003: 31). It has to be emphasized, however, that I am not using King et al.'s specific censoring regime.

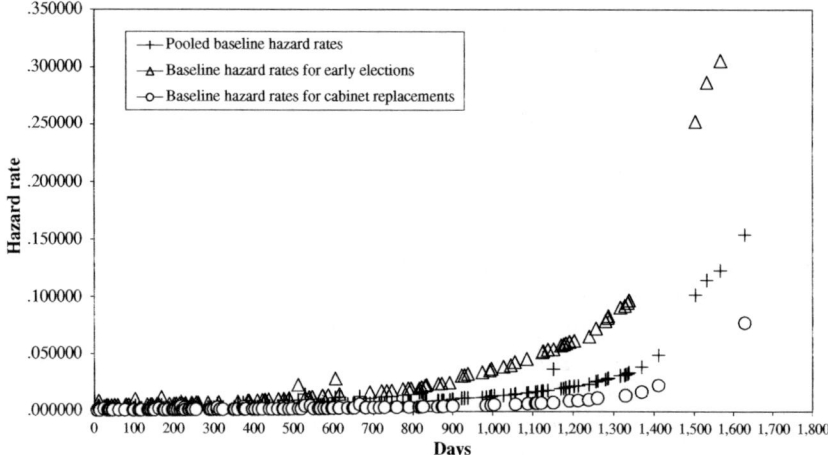

FIGURE 10.1. Competing risks of discretionary cabinet terminations: early election hazards, replacement hazards, and pooled hazards

the figure provides strong confirmation of Warwick's finding (1994) of rising rather than constant hazard rates (as predicted by advocates of the random-events approach). More specifically, Figure 10.1 confirms Diermeier and Stevenson's result (1999) that the hazard rate of early elections rises sharply after approximately 1,000 days in office, whereas the hazard rate for cabinet replacements remains virtually unchanged. The latter hazard rate corresponds more closely to predictions based on the random-events perspective.[13] These findings provide strong support for Lupia and Strøm's bargaining model, where pay-offs and costs are strongly driven by the stage of electoral cycle.

In the following analyses, the covariates will be organized in six theoretically guided 'blocks' estimating a spatial-temporal, structural, preference-based, institutional, bargaining-environment and critical-events based model. The final model at the bottom of Table 10.4 presents an encompassing Cox proportional hazards model built from all covariates that are significant at least at the 10 per cent level.[14] This allows us to establish the best-fitting model for all three competing

---

[13] A log-rank test for the equality of survivor functions was performed for discretionary and technical terminations. With a χ^2 of 361.84 (one degree of freedom), the null hypothesis of equal survivor functions could be rejected at the 1% level of significance. Subsequently, a stratified log-rank test was performed for termination through early elections controlling for discretionary terminations versus technical terminations. The null hypothesis of equality of survivor functions could be rejected at the 1% level of significance with a χ^2 of 14.74 (one degree of freedom).

[14] Technically, the variables were identified by a stepwise backward elimination procedure. This approach seemed appropriate given the fact that in this chapter there are practically three dependent variables and that there would be different best-fitting models for different risks of cabinet termination. I first entered the full set of all covariates used in this chapter. This set of covariates is based on the theoretical framework set out in the second chapter. In a backward elimination procedure, covariates

risks and provides some statistical controls for the variables entered as part of theoretically guided blocks.[15]

Spatial-temporal factors

Although this chapter is mainly concerned with the way termination decisions are affected by institutions, random events, and the actors' strategic responses to such constraints in parliamentary bargaining, factors peculiar to particular countries (such as unobserved historical and cultural factors) or periods are often believed to influence the duration of cabinets. The block of spatial-temporal covariates in Table 10.4 reports the hazard ratios and standard errors of three Cox proportional hazards models with the three types of risks of discretionary cabinet terminations as dependent variables and dummy variables for country identities (not reported in Table 10.4) and the decade of cabinet termination (beginning with the 1940s) as covariates. In order to allow an intuitive interpretation, I am reporting the exponents of the estimated hazard rates ('hazard ratios') here and throughout the chapter. The hazard ratio for each covariate is the factor by which we multiply the baseline hazard to get the hazard rate, resulting from a unit change in the independent variable in question and controlling for the other covariates. Put simply, ratios equal to one indicate that as a covariate's value changes by one unit, the marginal change in the hazard is zero. Ratios greater than one imply an increasing and accelerating risk of cabinet failure as the value of the covariate increases by one unit. Ratios less than one imply this risk is decreasing and decelerating as the value of the covariate increases by one unit (Box-Steffensmeier and Jones 1997: 1450). For each model, I will report three separate estimates: (*a*) one estimate for the *general risk of discretionary terminations* (the most encompassing operationalization), (*b*) one for *cabinet replacements* during the CIEP, and (*c*) one for *early elections*. The country identities were coded as dummy variables with the Federal Republic of Germany as the reference category. The decades of cabinet termination were also coded as a series of dummy variables with the 1950s as the reference category. In other words, the hazard ratios indicate the extent to which the risk of discretionary cabinet terminations differs from cases where all dummy variables are zero: German cabinets terminated during the 1950s.

are considered for removal from an initial model containing all the explanatory variables. At each stage, the variable chosen for exclusion is the one leading to the smallest reduction in the fit of the model. Only covariates that are statistically significant at least at the 10% level remain in the model. The dummy variable for coalition cabinets was 'locked' irrespective of its significance or contribution to the model in order to provide the necessary control (or stratification) variable for covariates that pertain to coalition cabinets only.

[15] The presentation of results differs slightly from the other chapters in this volume, because I wish to use the competing risks perspective to compare the effects of the chosen independent variables on what are effectively three dependent variables.

TABLE 10.4. *Cox proportional hazards models: competing risks analysis of durability*

Bloc	Independent variables	Type of termination risk		
		General risk	Replacement	Early election
Decade	1940s	1.49 (0.45)	1.57 (0.61)	1.35 (0.68)
	1960s	0.71 (0.16)	0.69 (0.19)	0.80 (0.28)
	1970s	1.27 (0.24)	1.34 (0.39)	1.14 (0.34)
	1980s	0.91 (0.19)	0.76 (0.21)	1.13 (0.35)
	1990s	0.57 (0.13)**	0.51 (0.16)**	0.66 (0.23)
	Log-likelihood	−1,420	−773	−599
	LR χ^2	168.43	181.25	84.51
	N failing due to risk	244	137	107
Structure	Majority cabinet	0.43 (0.10)***	0.40 (0.13)***	0.39 (0.13)***
	Cabinet seat share	1.00 (0.01)	0.99 (0.01)	1.01 (0.01)
	Number of cabinet parties	1.28 (0.16)*	1.55 (0.25)***	0.81 (0.18)
	Minimal-winning status	0.57 (0.13)**	0.39 (0.12)***	1.01 (0.37)
	Max. bargaining power party in cab.	0.81 (0.19)	1.72 (0.57)	0.27 (0.10)***
	Coalition cabinet	1.33 (0.39)	2.04 (0.78)*	0.95 (0.45)
	Max. possible cabinet duration	0.99 (0.00)***	0.99 (0.00)**	0.99 (0.00)***
	Effective number of parl. parties	0.99 (0.09)	0.96 (0.10)	1.07 (0.15)
	Log-likelihood	−1350	−770	−548
	LR χ^2	156.78	104.02	115.38
	N failing due to risk	233	131	102
Preferences	Cabinet preference range	0.99 (0.01)***	1.00 (0.00)	0.98 (0.01)***
	Minimal connected cabinet	0.73 (0.13)*	0.64 (0.17)*	0.90 (0.24)
	Median party (1st dim.) in cabinet	0.72 (0.13)*	1.10 (0.30)	0.48 (0.11)***
	Conservative cabinet	0.67 (0.13)**	0.64 (0.18)	0.74 (0.20)
	Socialist cabinet	0.71 (0.12)**	0.57 (0.14)**	0.87 (0.21)
	Parliamentary preference range	1.00 (0.00)	1.00 (0.01)	1.00 (0.01)
	Polarization (BP weighted)	1.03 (0.01)**	1.02 (0.01)	1.04 (0.02)***
	Effective number of issue dimensions	1.68 (0.42)**	1.13 (0.37)	3.43 (1.29)***
	Extremist party seat share	1.06 (0.01)***	1.07 (0.01)***	1.02 (0.01)
	Log-likelihood	−1,415	−786	−608
	LR χ^2	112.43	113.74	40.20
	N failing due to risk	239	134	105
Institutions	Length of CIEP	1.01 (0.00)***	1.01 (0.00)***	0.57 (0.12)***
	Positive parliamentarism	1.71 (0.28)***	2.58 (0.61)***	1.37 (0.31)
	Opposition influence	1.36 (0.08)***	1.48 (0.14)***	1.33 (0.12)***
	Cabinet rule: Unanimity	1.43 (0.31)	1.13 (0.40)	1.44 (0.43)
	PM powers (1–7)	0.95 (0.03)	0.84 (0.04)***	1.15 (0.07)**
	PM dissolution powers	1.48 (0.28)**	1.19 (0.35)	1.83 (0.46)**
	Bicameralism	1.83 (0.32)***	2.46 (0.65)***	1.67 (0.43)**
	Semi-presidentialism	3.87 (0.80)***	6.78 (1.89)***	2.17 (0.80)**
	Log-likelihood	−1,445	−793	−626
	LR χ^2	108.40	139.91	18.22
	N failing due to risk	243	137	106
Bargaining	Existence of coalition agreement	0.52 (0.10)***	0.52 (0.13)***	0.54 (0.16)**
	Comprehensive policy agreement	0.90 (0.17)	0.77 (0.18)	1.24 (0.38)
	Coalition discipline in legislation	1.14 (0.18)	1.88 (0.33)***	0.44 (0.11)***
	Same PM and cabinet	0.69 (0.13)**	0.86 (0.22)	0.54 (0.15)**
	Cabinet bargaining duration	1.00 (0.00)	1.01 (0.01)*	1.00 (0.00)

(*cont.*)

TABLE 10.4. (Continued)

Bloc	Independent variables	Type of termination risk		
		General risk	Replacement	Early election
	Coalition cabinet	1.02 (0.23)	1.07 (0.34)	1.27 (0.40)
	Majority cabinet	0.28 (0.05)***	0.24 (0.06)***	0.32 (0.08)***
	Max. Possible cabinet duration	0.99 (0.00)***	0.99 (0.00)**	0.99 (0.00)***
	Log-likelihood	−1,354	−780	−548
	LR χ^2	148.21	85.26	116.49
	N failing due to risk	233	131	102
Critical Events	Electoral volatility (previous election)	1.01 (0.01)	1.01 (0.01)	1.00 (0.01)
	Inflation (time varying)	1.03 (0.00)***	1.03 (0.01)***	1.03 (0.01)***
	Unemployment (time varying)	1.06 (0.02)***	1.03 (0.02)	1.08 (0.02)***
	Interaction Conservative cab. X inflation	0.96 (0.02)**	0.95 (0.03)**	0.98 (0.02)
	Interaction Socialist cab. X unemployment	0.96 (0.02)**	0.92 (0.03)***	0.99 (0.02)
	Log-likelihood	−1,319	−748	−567
	LR χ^2	37.29	21.47	24.73
	N failing due to risk	220	122	98
Best fit	Majority cabinet	0.44 (0.09)***	0.55 (0.16)**	0.23 (0.07)***
	Minimal-winning status	0.36 (0.10)***	0.23 (0.09)***	—
	Max. bargaining power party in cabinet	0.32 (0.08)***	0.57 (0.18)*	0.31 (0.11)***
	Coalition cabinet	0.99 (0.21)	1.24 (0.36)	0.54 (0.18)*
	Max. possible cabinet duration	0.99 (0.00)***	—	0.99 (0.00)***
	Effective number of parl. parties	1.29 (0.09)***	1.48 (0.13)***	1.75 (0.23)***
	Minimal connected cabinet	3.51 (1.06)***	3.76 (1.59)***	3.84 (1.40)***
	Median party (1st dim.) in cabinet	—	—	0.34 (0.09)***
	Conservative cabinet	0.58 (0.14)**	—	0.51 (0.18)*
	Effective number of issue dimensions	1.78 (0.41)**	—	3.45 (1.41)***
	Extremist party seat share	—	—	0.95 (0.02)**
	Length of CIEP	—	0.41 (0.13)***	1.82 (0.52)**
	Positive parliamentarism	2.13 (0.38)***	5.51 (1.62)***	1.70 (0.50)*
	Opposition influence	1.16 (0.08)**	1.62 (0.14)***	—
	Cabinet rule: Unanimity	1.76 (0.44)**	—	5.81 (2.26)***
	PM powers (1–7)	—	—	1.29 (0.10)***
	PM dissolution powers	1.58 (0.33)**	—	2.55 (0.70)***
	Bicameralism	2.86 (0.63)***	5.32 (1.70)***	2.33 (0.72)***
	Semi-presidentialism	2.70 (0.74)***	7.84 (2.92)***	—
	Cabinet bargaining duration	—	—	0.99 (0.01)*
	Inflation (time varying)	1.04 (0.01)***	1.04 (0.01)***	1.07 (0.01)***
	Unemployment (time varying)	—	0.95 (0.03)**	—
	Log-likelihood	−1,141	−641	−433
	LR χ^2	272.08	179.52	228.16
	N failing due to risk	211	118	93

Notes: The results are reported with a precision of two digits after the decimal point. This led to a number of cases where the rounded hazard ratio was 1.00. In order to indicate the causal direction of significant effects, the value was rounded down to 0.99 (if less than 1) or up to 1.01 (if greater than 1), where it attained a level of significance at least at the 10% level. All χ^2 tests are significant at least at the 5% level of significance.

* $p < 0.10$; ** $p < 0.05$; *** $p < 0.01$.

Is there evidence of significant variations in cabinet durability for specific historical periods operationalized as decade of cabinet termination? The hazard ratios estimated in the block of spatial-temporal correlates suggest that the answer is generally 'no'. Compared to the reference category, the only decade with a significantly different risk of discretionary cabinet terminations are the 1990s when the risk for a West European cabinet to be terminated before the end of the CIEP as the result of (strategic) choices made by relevant political actors was reduced to almost half of the risk of discretionary cabinet terminations for the reference category (0.57). This reduction in the general risk is largely due to a statistically significant reduction of the hazard ratio for cabinet replacements, whereas the reduction in the risk of early elections is statistically insignificant.

What of the peculiarities of particular countries? These effects are not reported in Table 10.4, but can be summarized as follows: The general risk of discretionary terminations is significantly below the reference category in Luxembourg, Sweden, and the UK, whereas Denmark's, Finland's, and Italy's risks are significantly higher. This largely corresponds to the first impressions gained in Tables 10.1 and 10.2. A comparison of the competing risks demonstrates that Italy is the only country where the risk of discretionary cabinet terminations is higher than the reference category across all three risks. Austria, Iceland, Ireland, Luxembourg, the Netherlands, Sweden, and the United Kingdom experienced a significantly lower risk of *cabinet replacements* than the reference category, whereas the risk of early elections was significantly higher in Belgium, Denmark, Greece, Iceland, Ireland, Italy, Portugal, and Spain.[16]

Table 10.4 also reports the log-likelihoods of the models with decades of cabinet formation and country identities as covariates as well as the absolute difference between the log-likelihoods of the models with and without these covariates multiplied by a factor of two. A value of twice the difference between the log-likelihoods follows a χ^2 distribution. All χ^2 tests reported here suggest that the differences between the models with and without covariates are significant at least at the 1 per cent level. This suggests, firstly, that the addition of variables capturing unobserved peculiarities of time and space significantly improve the fit of the overall model and, secondly, that the occurrence of discretionary cabinet terminations is unlikely to be random: Especially the existence of a number of significant country-specific parameter estimates and the overall improvement of the log-likelihoods suggest that there are some systematic effects at work. It will be the task of the analyses below to uncover, as far as possible, the underlying structural, preference-based, institutional and strategic factors that are—at least in part—reflected in the significant effects of some of the country identities.

---

[16] The hazard ratio for early elections in Norway is zero and statistically insignificant. This reflects the fact that the Norwegian constitution rules out early elections.

Structural attributes of the cabinet

The second block of event-history models reported in Table 10.4 covers many of the structural attributes discussed in the extant literature, including characteristics of the parties in cabinet and the party system in general. The variables measuring structural attributes of the cabinet largely reflect the government parties' parliamentary resources. General party-system attributes provide some information about the attractiveness of potential alternative coalition partners outside the cabinet (reflecting the potential costs of cabinet replacements). A number of such structural characteristics have repeatedly been found to influence the risk of discretionary cabinet terminations in previous investigations: majority status, the number of parties in cabinet, and the question whether a cabinet has minimal-winning status, although most theoretical accounts are unspecific about the particular risk (early elections or cabinet replacement) to which these variables contribute. It is beyond the scope of this chapter to probe further the possibility that some of the cabinet-specific covariates are endogenous to the bargaining model (see above). This will have to be left to further analyses of the data.

Irrespective of the particular type of termination risk (cabinet replacement or early election), cabinets commanding a *parliamentary majority* can be expected to have better survival chances than minority cabinets, because they are less vulnerable to parliamentary defeat and normally do not face any transaction costs of bargaining with external support parties. Defeats may trigger either elections or the formation of an alternative cabinet (see, e.g., King et al. 1990: 363 or Warwick 1994: 36). High transaction costs of bargaining with external support parties may induce government party leaders to replace a minority cabinet with a majority coalition. Like in most previous empirical studies, majority status is coded here as a dichotomous variable registering whether the government commands an overall parliamentary majority at the time of its formation.

While majority status can be expected to reduce the risk of both cabinet replacements and early elections, previous studies have used the *size of the government's majority* as a proxy measure for the value government parties attach to the possession of office. Building on Lupia and Strøm's model (1995), Smith (2004: 87) argues—for single-party cabinets in the UK—'the decision to call an early election depends on the value of another period in office to the value of a new term in office' and predicts the following: 'when the government has a large majority it is less likely to go to the polls early. In contrast, a minority government, or one with only a slim majority, has a greater incentive to seek a working majority' through early elections (Smith 2004: 88). In order to establish whether Smith's argument for single-party cabinets can be generalized to apply to all cabinets, the structural block in Table 10.4 will include a variable measuring the cabinet's seat share in parliament. All other variables being equal, therefore, the *risk of early elections should decrease* with increasing parliamentary majorities.

A further variable that can be expected to influence the conditional probability of early elections is *single-party status* (as opposed to a multiparty cabinet). Except when the head of state has unilateral dissolution power, single-party cabinets can be expected to be more likely to be terminated by early elections than other types of cabinet, because the leaders of single-party cabinets are less constrained in their decision to call such elections (and have more scope for the manipulation of the timing of elections) than the leaders of coalition cabinets (Strøm and Swindle 2002: 581–2). In the case of single-party majority cabinets, early elections either will be decided unilaterally by the Prime Minister or may have to be negotiated within one government party only. In the present study, this proposition will be tested in a competing-risk design using a dummy variable for coalition cabinets, which takes the value of zero for single-party cabinets and the value of one for coalition cabinets.

The number of parties in the cabinet also has a plausible link with cabinet survival: The larger the number of parties in cabinet, the more scope for inter-party disagreement and the higher the potential transaction costs of managing conflict, especially when there are strongly diverging preferences concerning policy or the distribution of offices. Coalition cabinets with large numbers of parties are therefore likely to be more sensitive to even relatively small perturbations of the initial equilibrium on which the cabinet's formation was based and may suffer from more complex internal bargaining problems.

Cabinet *minimal-winning status* is a further structural variable pertaining to the cabinet itself that has traditionally been influential in game-theoretic models of coalition formation and durability (Dodd 1976). It is based on the assumption that political parties primarily care about the spoils of office (which, unlike policy benefits, are private goods). Minority governments are likely to be defeated by the opposition parties seeking to capture government office themselves. Surplus majorities will be vulnerable, because all parties can improve their share of portfolios and other positions by losing one or more parties without jeopardizing the cabinet's overall parliamentary majority (Laver and Schofield 1990: 150–1). In addition, Diermeier and Merlo (2000: 63) argue that minimal-winning coalitions are characterized by lower levels of transaction costs than all its alternatives. Minority cabinets need constantly to negotiate with outside parties that are willing to support the government and surplus-majority cabinets are likely to involve high costs of renegotiations, especially if some coalition partners are large relative to the formateur party.

Given the bargaining-theoretic framework on which this volume is based, it is essential to capture structural properties of the cabinet parties that impact on their relative *bargaining power* (expressed in their walk-away values). Van Roozendaal (1997: 77–8) argues that the inclusion of what he calls the 'dominant party' with credible exit options is likely to have a stabilizing effect: The fact that dominant parties have the 'possibility to sanction other parties' behaviour in the coalition by credibly threatening to exit' gives such parties a strong bargaining position. More to the point:

The possibility of using credible exit threats can be seen as a mechanism to induce cooperative behaviour between the parties in governments. It can be safely assumed that cooperation between government parties is more likely to be stabilizing than destabilizing for the government. Therefore we can expect that governments in which cooperation is induced via credible exit threats will be more stable, hence more durable, than governments in which this is not the case.

The effect of the inclusion of the party with the highest bargaining power in the cabinet will be tested below using a dichotomous covariate with a value of one for cabinets that include the party with the highest Banzhaf (1965) bargaining power index value and zero for all other cabinets.

Lupia and Strøm argue in the second chapter of this volume that *the value government parties attach to the share of seats and other resources they currently control* is not time-constant: The opportunity costs of early elections decrease as the CIEP approaches (see also Lupia and Strøm 1995). The closer the formation of a cabinet to the end of the CIEP, the lower the value government parties attach to the present parliamentary seat share as a resource to influence policy, the more likely are early elections. The *maximum duration of a cabinet* at the point of its formation will therefore have to be controlled in the analyses of variables in the block of structural attributes.[17]

In addition to party-political properties of the cabinet, there has been some evidence that the structure of the party system as a whole constitutes part of the *bargaining environment* cabinets operate in and may influence their longevity. A number of traditional studies operationalizing the complexity of the cabinet's bargaining environment through fractionalization or effective party-system size indices found confirmation for the importance of the complexity of the bargaining environment: The more fractionalized a parliament, the lower the durability of cabinets emanating from this parliament (e.g. Taylor and Herman 1971; Sanders and Herman 1977; Powell 1982; Grofman 1989; King et al. 1990).[18] Others, however, have challenged the relevance of the bargaining environment as an explanation of cabinet duration on theoretical (Tsebelis 2002: 212–14) and empirical (Warwick 1994: 63–7) grounds. For the purposes of this study we are using the effective number of parliamentary parties (Laakso and Taagepera 1979) as an indicator of the overall complexity of a cabinet's bargaining environment in Laver and Schofield's sense (1990) and—in line with the bargaining-theoretic

---

[17] This measure is similar to, but more accurate than, the traditional measure of 'post-election status' in many standard models of cabinet durability such as the one presented by King et al. (1990).

[18] Warwick (1994: 72) finds in his analyses that the statistical significance of the fractionalization index disappears, once the effective number of parties in the *cabinet* is controlled for. This will be checked with the new data-set in our own analyses.

framework employed here—as a proxy measure for number of potential opposition parties that could be candidates for inclusion in the cabinet (leading to a cabinet replacement). The policy costs of the inclusion of an opposition party are, of course, strongly influenced by their policy preferences, which will be covered in the preference-based block below and the best-fitting model.

Like for the temporal-spatial covariates, the 'structural' block in Table 10.4 summarizes the results of three Cox proportional hazard models for the general risk of discretionary cabinet terminations, cabinet replacements, and early elections. Despite the observation that—under certain conditions—minority cabinets can be surprisingly long-lived (Strøm 1990b; 1994), cabinets with an overall *parliamentary majority* are less likely to fail due to a discretionary termination than minority cabinets. The effect of the covariate 'majority status' is strong and statistically significant across all three risks—the general risk of discretionary terminations, the risk of cabinet replacements and the risk of early elections—and irrespective of the question whether or not variables from other blocks are held constant (Table 10.4). This confirms the findings in standard accounts of cabinet durability (see, e.g., King et al. 1990; Warwick 1994). The *cabinet's seat share*, by contrast, makes no statistically significant difference, again, irrespective of the model specification. This suggests that Smith's findings (see above) (2004) cannot easily be generalized beyond the specific British context of single-party cabinets.

If the *number of cabinet parties* is accepted as a proxy measure for the transaction costs of inter-party bargaining, the risk of discretionary cabinet terminations could have been expected to increase with the number of parties in the cabinet. At first glance, the results for the structural block in Table 10.4 seem to confirm this expectation—at least for the general risk of discretionary terminations and the risk of cabinet replacements. However, the effect of this covariate is rendered statistically insignificant in the best-fitting model including variables from other blocks. As expected, *minimal-winning status* reduces the general risk of discretionary terminations, and the analyses in the structural block in Table 10.4 demonstrate that this is largely due to the strong and significant increase in replacement hazards. This effect remains significant; indeed it becomes stronger, when covariates from other blocks are held constant in the best-fitting model. The effect of minimal-winning status on replacement hazards is consistent with the interpretation that minimal-winning coalitions are more durable than other cabinet types, because *ceteris paribus* they tend to involve relatively low transaction costs.

In the structural block, the *inclusion of the party with the largest parliamentary bargaining power* in the cabinet reduces the risk of early elections significantly. When factors from other blocks are controlled for, the covariate's effect becomes stronger and more robust: It has the expected risk-reducing and -delaying effect on all three hazards, and the effects are statistically highly significant. Given that the best-fitting model includes statistical controls for single-party/coalition government, this finding suggests, as Lupia and Strøm (1995) claim, that the strongest party is likely to be in a good position to renegotiate the terms of the coalition agreement and extract so many advantages in this process that cabinet replacements as well as early elections become unattractive alternatives, even when covariates such as preference diversity are held constant. Conversely, this finding suggests that the cabinet may be vulnerable to outside offers, if the party with the strongest bargaining power is excluded.

The general risk of *coalition cabinets* to be terminated prematurely is not significantly higher than for single-party cabinets. However, this conceals interesting and diverging dynamics for the different sub-risks, and these findings are largely in line with our theoretical expectations. In the structural block, coalition cabinets are significantly more likely to be replaced by alternative cabinets than single-party cabinets—but they are less likely to be terminated by early elections, although the latter effect is not statistically significant in the purely structural model. In the best-fitting model at the bottom of Table 10.4, coalition cabinets reduce the risk of early elections significantly, whereas this covariate's effect on cabinet replacements is in the expected causal direction but statistically insignificant. These significance tests suggest that the estimates are not entirely robust; nevertheless, they are consistently in the causal direction predicted on the basis of Lupia and Strøm's framework (1995).

The *maximum possible cabinet duration* at the time of a cabinet's formation was entered into the structural block to account for the theoretical expectation that the retention value of the current seat share and government position is likely to decline as the end of the CIEP approaches. This expectation is fully confirmed. Given that one single day constitutes a one unit change, this covariate has (expectedly) a small but statistically highly significant risk-increasing and accelerating effect on all three hazards in the structural block. Interestingly, the effect on *cabinet replacements* is statistically insignificant in the best-fitting model controlling for other variables. This is not surprising as the baseline hazard rate of cabinet replacements is relatively flat (Figure 10.1).

The only structural variable measuring the complexity of the cabinet's bargaining environment in this block is the *effective number of parliamentary parties*. The theoretical expectation that an increase in the effective number of parties would tend to increase the risk of discretionary terminations is not confirmed in the purely structural model. However, when variables from other blocks (including the ideological diversity of the cabinet and parliament) are held constant, the effective number of parliamentary parties does have the expected destructive effect: increases in the number add to, and accelerate, all three risks studied here. The effects are substantial and highly significant. This finding suggests that the structural complexity of a cabinet's party-political bargaining environment does matter, despite the doubts raised by Tsebelis (2002: 212–14) and Warwick (1994: 63–7) who advocate a concentration on the cabinet's ideological preference range.[19] It is also more in line with our bargaining-theoretic perspective, which

---

[19] Further tests will be necessary using all of Warwick's various operationalizations (1994).

suggests that a larger number of parties in the parliament is likely to produce a larger number of potential outside offers and higher transaction costs due to increased commitment problems for cabinet parties.

Policy preferences

Recent spatial models of cabinet durability have placed considerable emphasis on the relevant actors' policy preferences as predictors of cabinet durability—in conjunction with certain features of the party system and the constitution [e.g. the politics of cabinet government and portfolio allocation in Laver and Shepsle's work (1996, 1998) or veto players in Tsebelis's work (2002: 215–18)]. In addition to such theoretical models more valid measurements of appropriate indicators have been developed (e.g. Laver and Hunt 1992; Budge et al. 2001; Benoit and Laver 2006). This policy-focused and institutional perspective has enriched the literature on cabinet durability and provided significant improvements over earlier 'policy-blind' and 'institution-free' game-theoretic models, which tended to assume that office-seeking or electoral motivations dominate policy motivations—and that, hence, policies and institutions were purely instrumental and endogenous. Nevertheless, our theoretical framework suggests that such factors as such are unlikely to dominate the explanation of cabinet durability in Western Europe as actors can be expected to care about the transaction costs of bargaining as well as policy-related costs.

In many empirical analyses, variables capturing ideological properties of the *party system as a whole* have been shown to have a statistically significant impact on the durability of cabinets. In particular, the number of cleavages structuring the party system, the ideological range of the party system, and the share of seats controlled by extremist parties (or parties considered to be illegitimate by other actors in the system) were shown to reduce the durability of cabinets. Nevertheless, there have been very different interpretations of these findings: Laver and Schofield (1990: 157), for example, advanced the view that party-system polarization measured a crucial dimension of the cabinet parties' 'bargaining environment' and had a direct causal effect on cabinet durability: A complex bargaining environment is likely to generate a 'distribution of bargaining power that is far more susceptible to slight perturbations' contributing to coalitions that are less stable than those in less fractionalized and polarized party systems (Laver and Schofield 1990: 157). Warwick (1994: 53), by contrast, claims that the inverse empirical relationship between various party-system polarization measures and cabinet duration was due to an *indirect causal relationship*, namely the effect that polarization and extremist party seat share tend to have on the ideological range of the cabinet itself: In the presence of strong extremist parties, he argues, 'coalitions must form around the political center, uniting often amorphous and diverse collections of parties and ideologies to amass majority support' (see Warwick 1994: 65–7 for empirical evidence).

The theoretical framework employed here is capable of integrating both dimensions—cabinet characteristics and bargaining environment—in a logically consistent way: The differences between the parties' policy preferences are treated as part of the policy costs and benefits faced by parties inside and outside the cabinet. The larger the ideological range within the cabinet, the more costly policy compromises are likely to be for one or more participants. In addition, the transaction costs of 'policing' coalition bargains may increase as the incentives for opportunistic behaviour may be considerable where the cabinet parties' preferences are not well aligned (see Martin and Vanberg 2004). Properties of the party system as a whole have a bearing on the availability of outside options for the cabinet parties and their strategic environment. In a party system with a small or moderate ideological range overall, some 'out parties' are likely to be ideologically close to one or more of the government parties. If it is true that the policy costs of forming alternative coalitions are relatively low in such situations, government parties may have incentives to contemplate the replacement of the current cabinet with an alternative one—provided that the value of the incumbent cabinet is comparatively low, the transaction costs of a cabinet replacement are low, and walk-away values cannot be turned into favourable renegotiations within the existing cabinet. Conversely, strong extremist parties or parties that are seen to be illegitimate by cabinet participants may reduce the range of feasible coalition options to a small set of parties, which may—as Warwick suggests—be ideologically very diverse thus increasing the policy costs of collaboration. A strong presence of extremist parties may also influence the information uncertainties (and, hence, transaction costs) of coalition bargaining as the electoral and strategic environment becomes more uncertain for the coalition parties—especially in situations described as 'polarized pluralism' (Sartori 1976: 131–45) and/or 'multipolar' party systems (Laver and Schofield 1990: 157–8).

A large number of indicators have been developed to measure the *ideological diversity within cabinets*.[20] For the purposes of the current analysis, data of the Manifesto Research Group were used to calculate the ideological range within each cabinet (without weighting it by the size of the parties; for a description and discussion of this variable please refer to the third chapter of this volume). If Warwick (1994) is right, this measure of ideological cabinet range should be inversely related to cabinet duration (see, e.g., Laver 1974; Warwick 1979, 1992, 1994; Browne, Gleiber, and Mashoba 1984*a*). One of the variables used by Axelrod (1970) to add an ideological dimension to the policy-blind minimal-winning theorem was the identification of minimal-winning coalitions consisting of ideologically 'connected' parties, that is, parties that are adjacent to each other on a single left-right continuum. In a number of studies, the minimal-connected-winning criterion performed relatively well in

---

[20] It has to be emphasized, however, that all these measures neglect the question of intra-party cohesion and focus on the extent of inter-party agreement practically treating cabinet parties as unitary actors.

predicting the nature of cabinets formed (for example, Bäck 2003). A dummy variable for 'minimal-connected-winning coalition' will be used to test whether 'connected' cabinets are also less vulnerable to the risk of early discretionary termination than 'unconnected' cabinets (see also Warwick 1994: 67–8). Finally, the overall ideological positioning of the cabinet was taken into account in the form of two dummy variables for conservative-dominated or socialist-dominated cabinets. There is nothing in the Lupia and Strøm model to predict a significant effect of these variables per se, but they will become theoretically more relevant when the policy-related costs of maintaining the existing cabinet in the face of certain types of external shocks will be added as variables at a later stage (below).

Finally, the bargaining power of a party may depend on its location in the ideological space as well as its size (in parliamentary seats). In the previous section, bargaining power was measured on the basis of seat shares only. The median-voter theorem captures seat distribution as well as ideological centrality in relation to other parties in the system (see also van Roozendaal 1992). According to Laver and Schofield's summary (1990: 111), the theorem 'predicts a more or less dictatorial role for the party that controls the median legislator' in the policy space. In a coalition situation, this party would seem to have a particularly high walk-away value, because the policy costs for other parties to form a cabinet without it would always be higher than the policy costs of forming a cabinet including the median. Nevertheless, this advantage enjoyed by the party controlling the median legislator need not necessarily lead to increased cabinet instability as it could be used by that pivotal party to renegotiate the existing coalition agreement in its own favour, especially if the transaction costs involved in the formation of alternative cabinets are perceived to be high. The importance of the median legislator for cabinet durability resonates with Laver and Shepsle's portfolio-allocation model (1996, 1998), where cabinets are assumed to be in equilibrium—and therefore likely to remain stable—'if the government portfolio with jurisdiction over each relevant policy dimension is allocated to the party with the median legislator on that dimension' (Laver and Shepsle 1996: 66). It is beyond the scope of the present chapter to test Laver and Shepsle's framework. Nevertheless it has been possible for each cabinet to identify the party controlling the median legislator for the most important policy dimension and test for the effect the inclusion of this party has on cabinet duration. Cabinet membership of the party controlling the parliamentary median legislator on the most important dimension is coded as a dummy variable.

As suggested earlier, the *ideological properties of the party system as a whole* (including any 'out parties') may influence cabinet durability in addition to the ideological diversity of the cabinet itself. Such ideological properties of the party system can be said to constitute part of the *bargaining environment* surrounding the cabinet (Laver and Schofield 1990: 155). The risk of discretionary cabinet terminations is believed to increase with increasing parliamentary preference diversity. I am using the unweighted *parliamentary preference range* (in points of the party manifesto data-set), the *parliamentary preference range weighted* by the parties' bargaining power *(Banzhaf index)*, the *effective number of issue dimensions* structuring the parliamentary party system and the *seat share of extremist parties* as operationalization of the complexity and diversity of the cabinet's bargaining environment. As always, all variables are described in the third chapter.

The results of the tests of the preference-based predictions are reported in Table 10.4. Against our theoretical expectations, the general risk of discretionary cabinet terminations is very slightly, but significantly, *reduced* as the *cabinet's preference range* increases. A comparison of the disaggregated risks (replacement and early election hazards) suggests that this is due to a reduction in the risk of early elections. When other background variables are controlled for in the best-fitting model (bottom of Table 10.4), the effect of cabinet preference range is no longer statistically significant, however. Superficially, this finding is at variance with Warwick's results (1994). However, Warwick's claim mainly refers to majority cabinets. The ideological range of minority cabinets would not necessarily be expected to have a significant effect, because such cabinets have to rely on outside support—and the ideological preferences of support parties are not accounted for in the data-set we use. If we re-estimate the best-fitting model for majority cabinets only (not reported in the tables), the effect of the cabinet's ideological range is indeed in the expected causal direction and statistically significant at the 5 per cent level: The larger the preference range, the higher the hazard ratio of *cabinet replacements*.

The status as *minimal-connected-winning coalition* and the presence of the party controlling the *median legislator* on the most important policy dimension have the expected risk-reducing effect and are statistically significant, if only ideological and preference-related variables are included in the model (as in the block 'Preferences' in Table 10.4). A look at the disaggregated hazards reveals that the risk-reducing effect of minimal-connected-winning status is largely due to this covariate's delaying effect on replacement hazards (ideologically compact minimal-winning cabinets—including single-party cabinets—are less likely to be replaced during the CIEP than other cabinets), whereas the risk-reducing effect of the *inclusion of the median legislator* on the most important policy dimension is largely due to the delaying effect this covariate has on early election hazards. The strong risk-reducing effect of the inclusion of the median legislator on the risk of early elections remains stable, even if variables from other blocks are controlled for in the best-fitting model. The effect of the status *as minimal-connected-winning cabinet* is puzzling, however. If covariates from other blocks are held constant in the best-fitting model, the delaying effect the covariate had on discretionary cabinet terminations in the preference-based block (Table 10.4) turns into a strong and statistically highly significant accelerating effect for all three risks: the pooled hazard as well as the replacement and early election hazards. This surprising result needs further and more detailed investigation, although there are some suggestions in the literature that ideologically connected parties may be fierce competitors for very similar voters (see, e.g., Katz 1980: 52–3).[21]

From the perspective of the bargaining- and transaction-cost theoretic framework applied here, the risk-reducing effects of the dummy variables *socialist* and *conservative* cabinet are difficult to interpret without further analyses. These effects are significant for the general risk of discretionary terminations and, in the case of socialist cabinets, for the risk of cabinet replacements. If further covariates from other blocks are controlled for in the best-fitting model, there remains a significant delaying effect of the status as conservative cabinet on the general risk and the risk of early elections, whereas the effect of the covariate 'socialist cabinet' is reduced to statistical insignificance. This is likely to be due to the fact that nearly two-thirds of all cabinets classified as 'socialists' were single-party cabinets. As soon as coalition and majority status are controlled in the best-fitting model at the bottom of Table 10.4, the effect of this covariate is reduced to statistical insignificance.

With the exception of the parliamentary preference range (which makes no statistically significant difference for the general risk of discretionary terminations), the variables measuring various ideological dimensions of the cabinets' *bargaining environment* all have the expected significant accelerating effect: The more *polarized* (index weighted by the relevant party's bargaining power) a parliament is, the larger the *effective number of issue dimensions* and the larger the *share of seats held by extremist parties*, the higher the risk of discretionary terminations. If only variables from the preference-based block are considered, the risk-increasing effects of polarization and the effective number of issue dimensions seem to be largely due to the accelerating effect these covariates have on the risk of early elections. The share of seats controlled by extremist parties, by contrast, primarily accelerates the risk of cabinet replacements, which is in line with Mershon's (2002) and Warwick's analyses (1994). When significant effects from other blocks are added to the model (best-fitting model, bottom of Table 10.4), however, only the effective number of issue dimensions continues significantly to increase and accelerate the risk of discretionary cabinet terminations in general (but has no significant effect on the sub-risks of cabinet replacements and early elections). In contrast to the results of the preference-based block, the share of seats controlled by extremist parties now reduces and delays the risk of early elections significantly, but has no significant effect on cabinet replacements and the general risk of discretionary terminations. In the light of our transaction-cost framework, this would seem to suggest that the strength of extremist parties may contribute to electoral uncertainty and increase the election-related risks expected by parliamentary majorities.

---

[21] The effect is robust, even if separate analyses are carried out for single-party and coalition cabinets as well as for majority and minority cabinets.

Institutions

In the theoretical framework on which this chapter is based, institutions are expected to influence—but not determine—the actors' decisions about cabinet continuation or termination in a number of ways: Institutions constrain the temporal parameters (e.g. length of the CIEP remainder), expected discount rates, and transaction costs of cabinet bargaining; influence the mechanisms of coalition formation (e.g. through explicit investiture requirements or rules determining a formateur) and determine the actors that are involved in formation and termination decisions (e.g. political parties and heads of states); influence the transaction costs of decision-making during the lifetime of a cabinet and the majorities needed by that cabinet (e.g. in the case of bicameralism with incongruent majorities in both chambers); may privilege certain actors within a cabinet (e.g. the prime minister), protect smaller or less resourceful coalition partners (e.g. through decision-making rules stipulating unanimous decision-making in cabinet); and influence the costs of losing government office (e.g. in the extent to which a move to the opposition benches excludes parties from policy influence).

Looked at superficially, the *length of the CIEP* could be expected to have an obvious—prolonging—influence on the life expectancy of a cabinet. Strøm and Swindle (2002: 587), however, demonstrate that the risk of early elections *increases* with the length of the CIEP. The reason is the actors' assumed comparison of the continuation value of the current parliament, on the one hand, and the expected benefits from an early election, on the other: Following Lupia and Strøm's reasoning (1995), they expect the relative continuation value of the current parliament to decline over the course of a parliamentary term and therefore predict a risk-increasing impact of this covariate, especially during the later stages of the CIEP (Strøm and Swindle 2002: 584).

A parliamentary investiture requirement leads to the early 'death' of those proposed cabinets failing this constitutional hurdle. This tends to express itself in increased hazard ratios overall and has been treated as a standard explanatory variable since King et al. (1990: 863) (see also Warwick 1994; Diermeier and Stevenson 1999). In this volume, we do not use the mere presence of an investiture requirement but apply a stricter definition in generating our dummy variable *positive parliamentarism* where the cabinet actually needs the support of an overall parliamentary majority to be elected (see Chapter 3 of this volume). Nevertheless, the presence of positive parliamentarism, operationalized as a dummy variable, can also be expected to increase the risk of discretionary cabinet terminations.[22]

If *opposition parties* have possibilities to influence policy (provided they care about policy rather than having an exclusive office orientation), being in opposition does not necessarily mean exclusion from the policy process.[23] In such cases,

---

[22] The effect of this covariate is not proportional over the life-course of a cabinet. It will be a task for further investigation and statistical analysis to test for the impact of non-proportionality.

[23] This effect is particularly strong in the case of minority cabinets.

moving from government to opposition does not involve a complete loss of policy influence, but may avoid voter blame for policy failure, which tends to be pinned on governments. Strong opposition influence on policy, therefore, should increase the risk of early cabinet replacements, whereas our theoretical framework would not suggest an obvious link of this covariate with the risk of early elections.

If a prime minister has the power to unilaterally dissolve parliament and call a general election, the risk of early elections is likely to increase, because heads of government may use their dissolution powers for political gain either by cutting their expected electoral losses or by 'political surfing' when favourable external circumstances prevail (see also Strøm and Swindle 2002; Kayser 2005). We also know that prime-ministerial powers to combine the vote on a policy proposal with a vote on the future of the government as a whole (confidence vote)—a strongly related source of power for the head of government—reduce the risk of commitment problems in inter-party and intra-party bargaining (Huber 1996; Diermeier and Feddersen 1998). Intuitively, therefore, the risk of cabinet replacements should be reduced if prime ministers enjoy such far-reaching powers. If the *prime minister has wide-ranging agenda-setting powers in the cabinet*, he or she has a significant amount of 'residual rights of control' in the event of intra-cabinet disagreement or unanticipated contingencies (Strøm and Müller 1999*a*: 273). This could prolong the survivability of cabinets as it strengthens the bargaining power of the prime minister. If the prime minister is more constrained, for example by a unanimity rule in cabinet, the opposite could be the case, because each party has a veto and may be tempted to engage in relatively aggressive hardball tactics potentially increasing the transaction costs of coalition bargaining.

Finally, in *semi-presidentialism* and *bicameral systems* the party or parties in the cabinet may be faced with additional 'institutional veto players'. In his work on veto players Tsebelis (2002) suggests that an increase in the number of veto players will tend to reduce the size of the winset of the status quo in the policy-outcome space and hence reduce the scope for policy change. This is likely to lead to policy *immobilisme* and to increase the probability of discretionary cabinet terminations, unless the status quo is unattractive for all veto players (Tsebelis 2002: 207, 215–18). Tsebelis's argument is largely based on the preferences of those actors identified as veto players, but it is not incompatible with the bargaining- and transaction-cost theoretic framework on which the present analysis is based. If a second chamber or a president are veto players and if their policy preferences differ from the ones held by the cabinet parties, bargaining is likely to become more complex and the costs of decision-making are likely to increase, creating incentives for the actors to resolve any impasse arising from this situation either by forming an alternative cabinet more in line with the President's or the second chamber's preferences, or by going back to the electorate.

The hazard-rate model reported in the 'institutional' block of Table 10.4 demonstrates that the *general* risk of discretionary cabinet terminations is increased and accelerated slightly but significantly with the *length of the CIEP*.

This finding is in line with our theoretical expectations. However, the prediction that longer CIEPs are likely to lead to a higher risk of early elections only holds in the best-fitting model with statistical controls for the significant effects of covariates from other blocks. It is interesting that the best-fitting model also suggests a significant reduction in the risk of cabinet replacements as the length of the CIEP increases. In general, therefore, long CIEPs seem to provide a stable framework for inter-party cooperation and sequential bargaining between the coalition partners. The longer the horizon of a coalition, the more coalition parties are likely to care about the future costs of defection for short-term benefits (Dixit 1998: 71). At the same time, long CIEPs tend to increase the incentives for the manipulation of the election date, especially at the later stages, as the tests for the maximum potential duration of cabinets suggest (see above).

The existence of *positive parliamentarism* increases—as expected—the general risk of discretionary terminations and the risk of cabinet replacements, while it does not have a significant effect on the risk of early elections in the institutional block. If covariates from other blocks are controlled for, the risk-increasing and risk-accelerating effect of the existence of positive parliamentarism is strong and significant for all three risks considered here. This is in line with standard accounts of cabinet survival (King et al. 1990; Warwick 1994).

If we look at institutional covariates only, high levels of *opposition influence* significantly increase the risk of all three types of cabinet termination: the pooled hazard, the hazard of cabinet replacements, and the hazard of early elections. If statistically significant covariates from other blocks are held constant, only the general and replacement hazards are statistically significant—and their effect is in the expected causal direction: The risk of cabinet replacements increases, if a change from the government onto the opposition benches does not involve a complete loss of policy influence. Again, this is very much in line with the framework employed for the purposes of this study, in which the expected costs of governing and losing government power are important parameters of the dynamics of coalition bargaining.

As predicted, the existence of a *unanimity rule in cabinet* decision-making (protecting smaller coalition parties from domination through a larger coalition partner) generally seems to increase the three risks of cabinet termination, if only institutional variables are accounted for. If variables from other blocks are controlled in the best-fitting model at the bottom of Table 10.4, the existence of a unanimity rule seems to increase the general risk of discretionary terminations, and this effect is largely due to its strong and highly significant impact on the early election hazards. In other words, a unanimity rule seems to increase the transaction costs of decision-making within the cabinet to such an extent that parliamentary majorities often resort to early elections in order to reduce the costs of coalition.

In the purely institutional model estimated in Table 10.4, the parameter estimates for the degree of *prime-ministerial powers in cabinet* corroborate the predictions that extensive powers reduce the risk of cabinet replacements and increase the risk of early elections. If the head of government dominates in the cabinet, he holds 'residual rights of control' identifying him or her as the one who has the right to make final decisions on matters not specified in the coalition agreement. If covariates from other models are taken into account, however, only the statistically significant accelerating effect on early election hazards survives. This finding is echoed in the parameter estimates for the covariate *prime-ministerial dissolution powers*, which clearly suggests a significant increase in the risk of early elections both in the institutional block of Table 10.4 and the best-fitting model at the bottom of the same table. The most plausible interpretation of these findings is that strong and independent prime ministers make use of their constitutional rights to determine the most favourable election date where the bargaining costs associated with early elections are low (see also Smith 2004; Strøm and Swindle 2002) and heads of government benefit from the credible threat of a dissolution in containing commitment problems arising from intra-party bargaining.

The predictions about the effect of semi-presidentialism and bicameralism are strongly supported by the Cox proportional hazards models presented here—even without any information about the policy preferences of the second-chamber median and/or the president in a semi-presidential system. *Bicameralism* increases all three discretionary termination risks in both the institutional block and the best-fitting model controlling for other covariates. *Semi-presidentialism* increases the risk of early elections significantly in the institutional block, which may be a reflection of some presidents' dissolution powers. This is confirmed in the best-fitting model which suggests that the general risk and the risk of early elections increase significantly and strongly, if a political system is semi-presidential. The fact that these effects are so robust and consistent even without any information about all veto players' preferences seems to suggest that there are likely to be factors other than ideology—such as the transaction costs of decision-making—that influence discretionary cabinet terminations.

Bargaining environment

One of the key contributions this chapter seeks to make to the existing literature on cabinet durability is a stronger focus on the role of cabinet-specific institutions that shape the bargaining between coalition parties in the under-researched interval between the formation and termination of a cabinet. Coalition parties in Western Europe often use more or less formalized coalition agreements and conflict-management devices to deal with disagreements emerging after coalition negotiations have been concluded. Such institutions of coalition governance impose various degrees of coalition discipline in voting and other parliamentary activities; coalition partners pre-commit themselves in such agreements; they 'provide information to coalition partners, ease communication between them and contain conflict or facilitate its resolution' (Strøm and Müller 1999: 258). The present study is the first one to assess the impact of such institutions on coalition durability drawing on new data specifically collected for the purposes of this volume. One of the methodological problems encountered in the attempt to estimate the effects of institutions of coalition governance is the risk of endogeneity since these institutions are frequently modified and manipulated as coalitions evolve. As a result, it is often not clear whether the use of a particular conflict-management device in a coalition is a correlate or cause of a coalition crisis. For the purposes of this chapter, I seek to reduce this risk by focusing on institutions that are either rooted firmly in the country's constitution (such as rules of cabinet government and prime-ministerial powers) or are in place before the coalition is inaugurated (such as coalition agreements).

The existence of formal *ex ante coalition agreements* on policies, portfolio allocation, and mechanisms of conflict management in the event of unexpected changes in the policy environment can be predicted to stabilize coalition cabinets for at least four reasons: Firstly, coalition agreements—'the most binding, written statements to which the parties of a coalition commit themselves' (Strøm and Müller 1999a: 264–5)—are often public documents in which the coalition parties pre-commit themselves to particular policies. Although these documents are not legally binding, they may be costly to renege on: If a party or individual minister fails to adhere to the policies defined in the coalition agreement, other parties inside or, indeed, outside the government may exploit the defector's loss of credibility. A reputation for honesty is a valuable bargaining resource in the longer term, especially in environments characterized by information uncertainty (Dixit 1998: 72). After all, parties do care about the longer-term costs of bargaining. Secondly, the mere existence of an extensive coalition agreement indicates that the parties concerned have already explored the various zones of mutual agreement, exchanged a significant amount of information about each other's preferences and reservation values, and formalized the result of the negotiations in a public document. Thirdly, comprehensive policy documents emerging from coalition negotiations will often be ratified by some wider party body. A formal ratification process within the coalition parties is likely to reduce the risk of cabinet terminations due to intra-party dissent. Finally, coalition agreements that include mutually agreed provisions about structured mechanisms for conflict management with regard to unanticipated events in the lifetime of the emergent coalition could be hypothesized to have better survival chances than coalitions where agreement on such institutions does not exist.[24] For the purposes of the present study, these expectations will be tested through the use of two dummy variables, the first of which registers the presence or absence of a *formal coalition agreement* and

---

[24] It has to be emphasized, however, that there may be generally accepted rules of conflict resolution, which do not have to be written down in a coalition agreement. There is also some evidence (e.g. Germany) that the institutions defined in a coalition agreement often fail to work in practice and will be replaced during the lifetime of a coalition.

the second indicates whether the coalition agreement included a *comprehensive agreement on public policy*.[25]

Given the inevitably high level of information uncertainty about unpredictable events that may occur during the lifetime of a cabinet, even comprehensive policy agreements can never be complete contracts. Therefore, many coalition agreements include *procedural rules* prescribing how the coalition partners will deal with disagreement in the face of unexpected events—and any other policy disagreements not covered in the coalition agreement. These institutional arrangements of coalition governance typically include a certain amount of *coalition discipline* especially in legislation. In other words, there is often a rule that coalition parties will not vote against each other on legislative proposals, if there is disagreement. This practically introduces a unanimity principle to coalition politics and avoids trust-undermining opportunistic alliances across the government-opposition divide. In the statistical analyses, a dummy variable was used to register the existence of such a rule.

Beyond voluntary coalition agreements, a country's constitution and statutes may provide further conflict-management mechanisms or at least mechanisms that specify and assign 'residual rights of control' to particular actors 'by identifying the party that has the right to make final decisions on matters not specified in the contingencies of the contract' (Strøm and Müller 1999*a*: 273). In a recent paper, Heller (2001) emphasized the importance of 'last offer' amendments in protecting the government from opportunistic alliances between government and opposition parties to pass—or bring down—a bill against the government's wishes. The prime minister's powers to combine a particular policy decision with a vote of confidence is a further institutional device, although it is often a last resort for a head of government struggling to maintain party and coalition discipline (Huber 1996; Diermeier and Feddersen 1998). In the present context, I will examine the impact of two constitutional mechanisms: the head of government's power to (*a*) *control the cabinet agenda* and (*b*) use his or her parliamentary *dissolution powers* as a means of disciplining not only his or her own party's backbenchers but also the coalition parties. Both of these variables are covered in the block on bargaining in Table 10.4 and have been commented on above.

The bargaining between parties and the extent to which they need to rely on formal agreements will also be influenced by the experience coalition partners have had with one another before the cabinet's inauguration. If, for example, a coalition cabinet formed after a regular election is the *continuation of a successful cooperation between the government parties* before the election, a certain amount of mutual trust and high levels of information about the coalition partner(s) are likely to have been built up already. In this case, a previous coalition has practically served as screening device reducing information uncertainty and

---

[25] In order to keep single-party governments in the analysis, they were treated as if they were coalitions with a formal agreement. Simultaneously a control variable was introduced registering whether or not a cabinet was a coalition cabinet.

perceived commitment problems. A track record of successful cooperation between certain parties may also create some form of 'asset specificity' (see above) increasing the transaction costs of deals with alternative coalition partners. Both factors should provide better conditions for cabinet longevity than cases where a political partnership is still untested.

The *length of coalition bargaining* prior to the formation of a cabinet would suggest either a high level of attention to detail in the negotiations or a high level of bargaining complexity. The former can be expected to reduce the risk of discretionary cabinet terminations; in the latter case, we would expect an increased risk. King et al. (1990: 858–9) seem to favour the latter perspective, Warwick (1994: 37), by contrast, favours the former. The theoretical framework outlined in the second chapter argues that no such inferences can be drawn. Yet, there have been theoretical arguments suggesting that long bargaining duration indicates a sequence of offers and counter-offers, which tends credibly to reveal a great deal of privately held information to uniformed parties in the bargaining process, including preferences, reservation values, and walk-away values. This may in fact help to avoid problems of 'adverse selection'. Moreover, long bargaining durations could indicate that parties have held out 'for the best political-economic circumstances associated with a higher expected government duration' (Diermeier 2006: 171).

In addition to the bargaining variables above, at least three general background variables will have to be controlled for in the block on bargaining and coalition governance (Table 10.4): Firstly, it is obvious that the analysis of the effect of inter-party conflict-management devices obviously makes only sense for multiparty cabinets. Yet, in order to avoid the loss of single-party cabinets for the entire analysis, the following adjustments were made: Rather than coding single-party cabinets as missing observations, the values for cabinet bargaining duration, existence of a formal coalition agreement, and existence of a comprehensive policy agreement, and existence of coalition discipline in legislation were all set to a value of one. In other words, single-party cabinets were treated like highly formalized and cohesive multiparty cabinets. In addition, a dummy variable for coalition versus single-party cabinets was introduced in order to control statistically for the effect of this manipulation. Secondly, I controlled for the majority status of cabinets. Minority cabinets may reduce the scope for inter-party conflict within the cabinet, but may have to rely on fairly extensive bargaining with outside support parties. Any conflict-management devices used by minority governments with supporting parties are not covered in this analysis. Finally, the cabinet's maximum life expectancy to the end of the CIEP shapes the actors' time horizons as well as their discount rates for sequential deals. Therefore, the maximum possible cabinet duration will also be controlled for in the models of coalition bargaining.

An analysis of the data demonstrates that the *existence of a coalition agreement* does reduce all three risks of discretionary cabinet terminations by approximately one-half, if only the variables in the 'bargaining block' are entered into the model.

However, the effects of this covariate are rendered statistically insignificant when variables from other blocks are controlled for in the best-fitting model. Similarly, the effects of the covariates *same Prime Minister and cabinet* and *coalition discipline in legislation* do not show up as statistically significant effects in the best-fitting model at the bottom of Table 10.4. The only covariates from this block that do 'survive' after statistical controls for covariates from other blocks are the cabinet bargaining duration and the maximum possible cabinet duration: The longer the coalition negotiations lasted before the cabinet was formed, the lower the risk of early elections. The shorter the cabinet's maximum possible duration at the time of its formation, the higher the risk of discretionary terminations through early elections. The effects of prime-ministerial powers and cabinet decision-making have been commented on in the section on institutions.

The findings presented above suggest that—when other variables are held constant—the most important institutions shaping the longevity of cabinets are not those based on the voluntary institutions set up by the coalition cabinets themselves (which may not be as durable as features of the constitution) but by constitutional provision (e.g. prime-ministerial powers) and the way time (especially the electoral cycle) shapes the actors' expectations of the costs and benefits of breaking the government. This may be a result of the risk of endogeneity of cabinet-specific covariates pertaining to coalition governance.

Critical events

In their attack on the structural-attributes approach, critical-events theorists argued that cabinets were largely terminated in response to 'random events' outside the scope of political-science theories rather than structural attributes (Browne, Gleiber, and Mashoba 1984*a*; Browne, Frendreis, and Gleiber 1984*b*, 1986; Cioffi-Revilla 1984; Frendreis, Gleiber, and Browne 1986). The analysis of pooled, replacement, and early election hazards above renders key assumptions of the critical-events perspective implausible and underscores the need to focus on the actors' strategic calculus in response to such external shocks and institutional constraints. Nevertheless, the present study will seek to estimate—and control for—the impact of certain developments outside the parliamentary arena that may, in some cases, amount to external shocks of the type described by the advocates of the random-events perspective, because (European) voters hold governments accountable for their consequences (Listhaug 2005).

In the work of most critical-events theorists, such 'random shocks' are not actually measured, but inferred from a probability distribution. Warwick (1994: 75–83), by contrast, used the magnitude in the year-on-year changes of economic indicators such as inflation and unemployment as covariates and found significant effects (see also Robertson 1983*a*; 1986*a*). Yet he also found (*a*) that the impact of a deterioration of the macroeconomic situation on cabinet survival is highly dependent on the electoral cycle (with cabinets more likely to be terminated in response to poor economic performance in the later stages of their incumbency), (*b*) that cabinets including socialist parties are more likely to fall as a result of high levels of inflation, whereas (*c*) non-socialist cabinets are more vulnerable to high levels of unemployment. In the critical-events block of Table 10.4, I will retest the impact of changes in the rate of inflation compared to the previous year, changes in the rate of unemployment as well as the interaction effects with the political persuasion of the relevant cabinet first identified by Warwick (1994). In addition, I will test for the experience of high levels of electoral volatility in the election preceding the cabinet's formation. Unlike the macroeconomic situation expressed in changes in the rate of inflation or unemployment, electoral volatility in the previous election is a time-constant covariate, which captures the extent to which the parties collectively experienced a recent electoral shock. It could also be seen as a proxy measure for the extent to which they perceive to be in a situation of strategic uncertainty and to which they are likely to be concerned over further dramatic shifts in electoral support.

The parameter estimates for the covariates capturing the impact of external economic and electoral developments demonstrate that the general risk of discretionary terminations as well as the risk of cabinet replacements and early elections is indeed increased, if the rates of inflation and unemployment rose in the preceding year (although the effect is not statistically significant for the risk of cabinet replacements in response to changes in the rate of unemployment). This would be in line with the critical-events perspective. However, like Warwick I find significant interaction effects between the party-political composition of a cabinet and the vulnerability to macroeconomic developments. This confirms Warwick's interpretation (1994: 92) that 'socialist governments do not terminate when their unemployment records fall behind the norm for governments of that type—presumably because of the favourable reputation they share on the issue— but they are at greater risk if their inflation performance is off the mark. For nonsocialist governments, the immunity pertains to inflation and the vulnerability to unemployment.' The parameter estimates are statistically significant for the general risk of cabinet terminations and the risk of cabinet replacements. However, if covariates from other blocks are controlled for (best-fitting model at the bottom of Table 10.4), only the risk-increasing effect of inflation remains statistically significant across the board. Unemployment now reduces the risk of cabinet replacements moderately but statistically significantly, but has no significant effect on the general risk or the risk of early elections.[26] The interaction effects lose their significance in the best-fitting model. Thus, the evidence suggests that economic 'shocks' affect termination decisions, but they do not dominate them. Structural and institutional factors seem to be more important 'shock absorbers' than the government parties' ideological position.

---

[26] This may be due to the fact that unemployment is considered to be a 'lagging indicator' in business cycles.

The covariate measuring electoral volatility in the previous election does not have a statistically significant effect in any of the models estimated. This may be due to the fact that parties update their information on likely voter responses throughout the lifetime of a parliament. Therefore, data on electoral volatility in the previous elections are likely to lose their importance as the parliamentary term progresses. This measurement problem could only be remedied through the use of time-varying survey data on government popularity. Unfortunately, however, such data are not available for all countries and the entire window of observation.

CONCLUSIONS

Asked about the powers of politicians and financial elites in the United Kingdom, a former British Chancellor of the Exchequer replied: 'All these people are actually at the mercy of events.... It's a bit like sitting ... in a ... sailing ship and the wind's coming at you: Sometimes there are gales, sometimes there's not. Really these people have to be judged by how they tack in the wind.'[27] This view strongly echoes the main tenets of the random-events perspective in the study of cabinet durability: The fate of politicians in office is ultimately determined by (*a*) the nature and severity of unforeseen exogenous events and (*b*) their individual skills in surfing the 'waves' in unpredictable 'weather conditions'. The results of this chapter demonstrate that this analogy is inappropriate. Unquestionably, there *are* storms powerful enough to sweep away a cabinet: Some cabinets get terminated due to the death of a prime minister in office; others are ended by international crises, economic recessions or scandals. All cabinets in our sample of 17 West European countries face certain 'death' at the end of the respective CIEP. Yet, although the maximum life expectancy of a cabinet tends to be fixed exogenously, even the fact that a cabinet stayed in office until the last day of the CIEP is the result of relevant actors' choices. A considerable proportion of cabinets get terminated well before the end of the CIEP as the result of discretionary decisions made by the relevant actors. The evidence presented in this chapter also suggests that cabinet durability is not merely a function of the actors' (policy) preferences. A large number of findings point to the importance of constitutional and structural factors, which constrain the actors' strategies, expectations, and cost-benefit analyses.

The empirical analyses in the present chapter are guided by Lupia and Strøm's framework for the analysis of coalition bargaining and their theory of strategic cabinet dissolutions. This framework has at least three attractions for the purposes of the present study: Firstly, it produces testable propositions about the link

---

[27] Kenneth Clarke on the BBC Radio 4's *Today Programme* on 'Who runs Britain', 12 December 2005, 8:45 a.m. (author's own transcript). The former Chancellor of the Exchequer referred to top politicians and bankers.

Institutions, Chance, and Choices

between constitutional and other structural variables, on the one hand, and cabinet durability, on the other, in a dynamic rather than static framework. Secondly, it is sufficiently general to integrate a large number of structural, institutional, and time-varying independent variables into a coherent game-theoretic argument modelling the micro-mechanisms driving relevant actors' termination decisions (without resorting to ad hoc explanations); the focus of their causal argument is on the impact of constitutions and structures on walk-away values and transaction costs. Thirdly, the framework is based on relatively realistic assumptions including an explicit recognition of transaction costs in politics.

The chapter uses a new data-set specifically collected for the purposes of this volume and tests a variety of propositions on institutions of cabinet governance ranging from constitutional provisions (such as the length of the CIEP) to cabinet-specific institutions (such as the existence and nature of coalition agreements)— controlling for a large number of structural variables, relevant parties' policy preferences and exogenous events (such as changes in the economic situation). The tests take up the methodological impetus provided by advocates of various unified approaches to the study of cabinet durability (King et al. 1990; Warwick 1994) in recognizing that constitutional constraints, structural attributes of cabinets, and game-theoretic equilibria at the time of a cabinet's formation matter, but that the effect of these factors is subject to time-varying processes during the entire 'life' of a cabinet. This chapter goes beyond these works by adding a focus on structures and institutions of coalition governance, which only become relevant after cabinet formation thus beginning to unlock the impact of institutions shaping the processes of coalition governance. This chapter identifies a number of methodological issues concerning the endogeneity of cabinet-specific properties of coalition governance, which need further investigation with suitable techniques (see Diermeier 2006).

The empirical tests carried out in this chapter confirm a number of accepted predictions in standard accounts of cabinet durability (e.g. King et al. 1990; Warwick 1994): For example, the analyses presented here confirm once again that cabinets have better survival chances, if they control a parliamentary majority, if they have minimal-winning status, if they do not have to survive an investiture vote (in our operationalization 'positive parliamentarism'), and if they do not have to operate in a fractionalized party-political bargaining environment. Even where the results merely seem to confirm conventional wisdom, the competing-risks design allows *more precise conclusions* about the nature of the termination risk caused by certain covariates and more meaningful tests of relevant hypotheses. In the best-fitting model in Table 10.4 minimal-winning status, for instance, reduces and positive parliamentarism increases the risk of cabinet replacements, whereas they do not (and are not theoretically expected to) affect the risk of early elections significantly.[28]

---

[28] If only pooled hazards are estimated, the two risks are conflated and predictions on the basis of these hazards may be misleading.

What of the dynamic processes between cabinet formation and termination—and the institutions influencing cabinet durability in this interval? The analyses presented here confirm Diermeier and Stevenson's finding (1999) of rising early election hazards and nearly constant replacement hazards. In other words, the electoral cycle is very likely to affect the parties' costs of governing, even when many constitutional and other structural features remain constant. Accounting for these dynamics, the competing-risk analyses suggest that the covariates capturing the existence and nature of conflict-management and transaction-cost reducing devices of coalition governance (e.g. coalition agreements or coalition discipline) generally do not attain statistical significance in the best-fitting model in Table 10.4. The most plausible explanation for the lack of impact in multivariate analyses is that the cabinet-specific mechanisms of coalition governance are likely to be constantly changed and adapted as a cabinet 'matures' (e.g. Saalfeld 2000: 60–3). Thus the researcher is faced with problems of endogeneity. By contrast, many of the 'harder' constitutional constraints impacting on parliamentary bargaining in the interval between cabinet formation and termination do display the expected effects on the hazard rates of discretionary cabinet termination (including the length of the CIEP, the maximum possible duration of a cabinet, decision rules in cabinet, prime-ministerial powers, or the number of partisan and institutional veto players). These institutions seem to have a powerful and enduring impact on the transaction costs of decision-making. With regard to these covariates, the findings presented in this chapter strongly support the theoretical framework on which this chapter is based and an actor-centred, institutional perspective.

REFERENCES

Axelrod, Robert (1970). *Conflict of Interest: A Theory of Divergent Goals with Applications to Politics*. Chicago IL: Markham.

Banzhaf, John F. (1965). 'Weighted Voting Doesn't Work: A Mathematical Analysis', *Rutgers Law Review*, 19: 317–43.

Bäck, Hanna (2003). *Explaining Coalitions: Evidence and Lessons From Studying Coalition Formation in Swedish Local Government*. Uppsala: Uppsala Universitet.

Baron, David P. and Ferejohn, John (1989). 'Bargaining in Legislatures', *American Political Science Review*, 83: 1181–206.

Benoit, Kenneth and Laver, Michael (2006). *Party Policy in Modern Democracies*. London: Routledge.

Bergman, Torbjörn, Müller, Wolfgang C., Strøm, Kaare, and Blomgren, Magnus (2003). 'Democratic Delegation and Accountability: Cross-National Patterns', in Kaare Strøm, Wolfgang C. Müller, and Torbjörn Bergman (eds.), *Delegation and Accountability in Parliamentary Democracies*. Oxford: Oxford University Press.

Box-Steffensmeier, Janet M. and Jones, Bradford S. (1997). 'Time Is of the Essence: Event History Models in Political Science', *American Journal of Political Science*, 41: 1414–61.

Browne, Eric C., Gleiber, Dennis W., and Mashoba, Carolyn (1984*a*). 'Evaluating Conflict of Interest Theory: Western European Cabinet Coalitions, 1945–80', *British Journal of Political Science*, 14: 1–32.

——Frendreis, John P., and Gleiber, Dennis W. (1984*b*). 'An "Events" Approach to the Problem of Cabinet Stability', *Comparative Political Studies*, 17: 167–97.

————(1986). 'The Process of Cabinet Dissolution: An Exponential Model of Duration and Stability in Western Democracies', *American Journal of Political Science*, 30: 628–50.

Budge, Ian, et al. (2001). *Mapping Policy Preferences: Estimates for Parties, Electors, and Governments 1945–1998*. Oxford: Oxford University Press.

Cioffi-Revilla, Claudio (1984). 'The Political Reliability of Italian Governments: An Exponential Survival Model', *American Political Science Review*, 78: 318–37.

Cowley, Philip (2002). *Revolts and Rebellions: Parliamentary Voting Under Blair*. London: Politico's.

Diermeier, Daniel (2006). 'Coalition Government', in Barry R. Weingast and Donald A. Wittman (eds.), *The Oxford Handbook of Political Economy*. Oxford: Oxford University Press.

——and Feddersen, Timothy J. (1998). 'Cohesion in Legislatures and the Vote of Confidence Procedure', *American Political Science Review*, 92: 611–21.

——and Merlo, Antonio (2000). 'Government Turnover in Parliamentary Democracies', *Journal of Economic Theory*, 94: 46–79.

——and Stevenson, Randolph T. (1999). 'Cabinet Survival and Competing Risks', *American Journal of Political Science*, 43: 1051–68.

————(2000). 'Cabinet Terminations and Critical Events', *American Political Science Review*, 94: 627–40.

Dixit, Avinash K. (1998). *The Making of Economic Policy: A Transaction-Cost Politics Perspective*. Cambridge, MA: MIT Press.

Dodd, Lawrence C. (1976). *Coalitions in Parliamentary Government*. Princeton, NJ: Princeton University Press.

Frendreis, John P., Gleiber, Dennis W., and Browne, Eric C. (1986). 'The Study of Cabinet Dissolutions in Parliamentary Democracies', *Legislative Studies Quarterly*, 11: 619–28.

Grofman, Bernard (1989). 'The Comparative Analysis of Coalition Formation and Duration: Distinguishing Between-Country and Within-Country Effects', *British Journal of Political Science*, 19: 291–302.

——and van Roozendaal, Peter (1994). 'Toward a Theoretical Explanation of Premature Cabinet Termination with Application to Post-War Cabinets in the Netherlands', *European Journal of Political Research*, 26: 155–70.

————(1997). 'Review Article: Modelling Cabinet Durability and Termination', *British Journal of Political Science*, 27: 419–51.

Heller, William B. (2001). 'Making Policy Stick: Why the Government Gets What It Wants in Multiparty Parliaments', *American Journal of Political Science*, 45: 780–98.

Huber, John D. (1996). 'The Vote of Confidence in Parliamentary Democracies', *American Political Science Review*, 90: 296–82.

Huber, John D. (1998). 'How Does Cabinet Instability Affect Political Performance? Portfolio Volatility and Health Care Cost Containment in Parliamentary Democracies', *American Political Science Review*, 92: 577–91.

Huber, John D. and Lupia, Arthur (2000). 'Cabinet Instability and Delegation in Parliamentary Democracies', *American Journal of Political Science*, 45: 18–33.

Katz, Richard S. (1980). *A Theory of Parties and Electoral Systems*. Baltimore, MD: Johns Hopkins University Press.

Kayser, Mark A. (2005). 'Who Surfs, Who Manipulates? The Determinants of Opportunistic Election Timing and Electorally Motivated Economic Intervention', *American Political Science Review*, 99: 17–28.

King, Gary, Alt, James E., Burns, Nancy Elizabeth, and Laver, Michael (1990). 'A Unified Model of Cabinet Dissolution in Parliamentary Democracies', *American Journal of Political Science*, 34: 846–71.

Laakso, Markku and Taagepera, Rein (1979). 'Effective Number of Parties: A Measure with Applications to Western Europe', *Comparative Political Studies*, 12: 3–27.

Laver, Michael (1974). 'Dynamic Factors in Government Coalition Formation', *European Journal of Political Research*, 2: 259–70.

—— (1999). 'Divided Parties, Divided Government', *Legislative Studies Quarterly* 24(1): 5–29.

—— (2003). 'Government Termination', *Annual Review of Political Science*, 6: 23–40.

—— and Hunt, W. Ben (1992). *Policy and Party Competition*. New York, NY: Routledge.

—— and Schofield, Norman (1990). *Multiparty Government: The Politics of Coalition in Europe*. Oxford: Oxford University Press.

—— and Shepsle, Kenneth A. (1996). *Making and Breaking Governments: Cabinets and Legislatures in Parliamentary Democracies*. Cambridge: Cambridge University Press.

———— (1998). 'Events, Equilibria, and Government Survival', *American Journal of Political Science*, 42: 28–54.

Lijphart, Arend (1984). 'Measures of Cabinet Durability: A Conceptual and Empirical Evaluation', *Comparative Political Studies*, 17: 265–79.

—— (1999). *Patterns of Democracy: Government Forms and Performance in Thirty-Six Countries*. New Haven, CT: Yale University Press.

Linz, Juan J. (1978). *The Breakdown of Democratic Regimes: Crisis, Breakdown, and Reequilibration*. Baltimore, MD: Johns Hopkins University Press.

Listhaug, Ola (2005). 'Retrospective Voting', in Jacques Thomassen (ed.), *The European Voter: A Comparative Study of Modern Democracies*. Oxford: Oxford University Press.

Lupia, Arthur and Strøm, Kaare (1995). 'Coalition Termination and the Strategic Timing of Parliamentary Elections', *American Political Science Review*, 89: 648–65.

Martin, Lanny and Vanberg, Georg (2004). 'Policing the Bargain: Coalition Government and Parliamentary Scrutiny', *American Journal of Political Science*, 48: 13–27.

Merlo, Antonio (1997). 'Bargaining over Governments in a Stochastic Environment', *Journal of Political Economy*, 105: 101–31.

Mershon, Carol (2002). *The Costs of Coalition*. Stanford CA: Stanford University Press.

Morelli, Massimo (1999). 'Demand Competition and Policy Compromise in Legislative Bargaining', *American Political Science Review*, 93: 809–20.

Müller, Wolfgang C. and Strøm, Kaare (eds.) 'Coalition Governance in Western Europe: An Introduction', in Wolfgang C. Müller and Kaare Strøm (eds.), *Coalition Government in Western Europe*. Oxford: Oxford University Press.

North, Douglass C. and Thomas, Robert P. (1973). *The Rise of the Western World: A New Economic History*. Cambridge: Cambridge University Press.

Powell, G. Bingham (1982). *Contemporary Democracies*. Cambridge, MA: Harvard University Press.

Putnam, Robert D. (1988). 'Diplomacy and Domestic Politics: The Logic of Two-Level Games', *International Organization*, 42: 427–60.

Robertson, John D. (1983a). 'The Political Economy and the Durability of European Coalition Cabinets: New Variations on a Game-Theoretic Perspective', *Journal of Politics*, 45: 932–57.

—— (1983b). 'Toward a Political-Economic Accounting of the Endurance of Cabinet Administrations: An Empirical Assessment of Eight European Administrations', *American Journal of Political Science*, 28: 693–709.

Saalfeld, Thomas (2000). 'Germany: Stable Parties, Chancellor Democracy, and the Art of Informal Settlement', in Wolfgang C. Müller and Kaare Strøm (eds.), *Coalition Governments in Western Europe*. Oxford: Oxford University Press.

Sanders, David and Herman, Valentine (1977). 'The Stability and Survival of Governments in Western Democracies', *Acta Politica*, 12: 346–77.

Sartori, Giovanni (1976). *Parties and Party Systems: A Framework for Aanlysis*. Cambridge: Cambridge University Press.

Scharpf, Fritz W. (1997). *Games Real Actors Play: Actor-Centered Institutionalism in Policy Research*. Boulder, CO: Westview.

Smith, Alastair (2004). *Election Timing*. Cambridge: Cambridge University Press.

Strøm, Kaare (1988). 'Contribution to "Contending Models of Cabinet Stability"', *American Political Science Review*, 82: 923–30.

—— (1990a). 'A Behavioral Theory of Competitive Political Parties', *American Journal of Political Science*, 34: 565–98.

—— (1990b). *Minority Government and Majority Rule*. Cambridge: Cambridge University Press.

—— (1994). 'The Presthus Debacle: Intraparty Politics and Bargaining Failure in Norway', *American Political Science Review*, 88: 112–27.

—— and Müller, Wolfgang C. (1999). 'The Keys to Togetherness: Coalition Agreements in Parliamentary Democracies', *Journal of Legislative Studies*, 5: 255–82.

—— and Swindle, Stephen M. (2002). 'Strategic Parliamentary Dissolution', *American Political Science Review*, 96: 575–91.

Taylor, Michael and Herman, Valentine (1971). 'Party Systems and Government Stability', *American Political Science Review*, 65: 28–37.

Tsebelis, George (2002). *Veto Players: How Political Institutions Work*. New York, NY: Russell Sage Foundation and Princeton, NJ: Princeton University Press.

van Roozendaal, Peter (1992). 'The Effect of Dominant and Central Parties on Cabinet Composition and Durability', *Legislative Studies Quarterly*, 17: 5–36.

van Roozendaal, Peter (1997). 'Government Survival in Western Multi-Party Democracies: The Effect of Credible Exit Threats via Dominance', *European Journal of Political Research*, 32: 71–92.

Warwick, Paul V. (1979). 'The Durability of Coalition Governments in Parliamentary Democracies', *Comparative Political Studies*, 11: 465–98.
——(1992). 'Ideological Diversity and Government Survival in West European Parliamentary Democracies', *Comparative Political Studies*, 25: 332–61.
——(1994). *Government Survival in Parliamentary Democracies*. Cambridge: Cambridge University Press.
——and Easton, Stephen (1992). 'The Cabinet Stability Controversy: New Perspectives on a Classic Problem', *American Journal of Political Science*, 36: 857–76.

11

Coalition Membership and Electoral Performance

Hanne Marthe Narud and Henry Valen

INTRODUCTION

Democracy means that all political bargaining takes place in the shadow of future elections. The previous chapters have shown that in parliamentary democracies some governments engineer elections, that many governments experience them, and that all governments are affected by them. This chapter sets out to analyse the electoral rewards and punishments experienced by parties participating in parliamentary governments. In so doing, we will combine theories of coalition governance with theories of electoral choice. The core of the so-called trade-off model as formulated by Strøm (1990a; see also Müller and Strøm 1999) is the conflict that parties commonly face between vote seeking, on the one hand, and policy and office seeking on the other. The model is based upon the notion that voters judge governing parties retrospectively upon their performance (Fiorina 1981; 1997). Governing parties may be held to more severe standards than opposition parties, particularly concerning consistency between promise and performance. In terms of vote seeking it may therefore be a disadvantage to hold office—this may lead to a negative 'incumbency effect' (see, e.g., Rose and Mackie 1983).[1]

Strøm's model seeks to define the institutional conditions under which voters constitute a constraint on parties in government. Which circumstances make it more likely that voters will turn against the incumbent government for its performance in office? This question forms the point of departure for the present chapter, in which we will focus upon various sets of independent variables that we expect to have an impact upon the electoral fortunes of incumbents. In addition to the conventional economic variables, such as rates of inflation and unemployment, we include system-specific variables, such as election formula and government

[1] Note that the assumptions generated here run contrary to the hypothesized effect of incumbency in the USA. In the latter case incumbency is considered to be an asset for vote seeking. Presidents have substantial resources at their disposal to help secure their re-election, and Congressmen and Senators have even greater certainty of re-election (see, e.g., Cronin 1980: 43–6; Polsby and Wildavsky 1980: 65–7).

type. In addition, we incorporate variables that capture the ideological position of parties as well as changes in the political environment. Concerning the latter, the most interesting factors are the use of parliamentary dismissal and dissolution powers, and the possible effect of early termination on the electoral fortunes of incumbent parties. In the subsequent analysis our model specifications include two types of dependent variables: (*a*) aggregate support for the total of incumbent parties and (*b*) support for individual parties in the incumbent coalition government. This approach implies that we take into consideration the specific problems facing parties in multiparty systems, where coalition governments are more often the norm than the exception.

This chapter is organized in three main parts. First, we review the relevant literature on the field and discuss the theoretical framework in more detail. In so doing, we present eight substantive hypotheses about the electoral fate of incumbents. These concern the impact of system-specific variables, the effect of economic performance variables, and the impact of government duration on the electoral performance of cabinets. In the second part of the chapter, we test these hypotheses empirically by examining the electoral fate of cabinets and incumbent parties in 17 West European countries based on their aggregate election results in the post-war period. Note that the data collected give us a unique opportunity to do a comprehensive test of the impact of the structural as well as the political variables we believe matter to the electoral fate of governments. The third— and final—part of the chapter discusses the results in light of the theoretical framework.

INCUMBENCY AND ELECTORAL PERFORMANCE

The main question this chapter raises is what explains the performance of incumbent parties at the polls. Rose and Mackie (1983) have previously addressed the electoral effects of incumbency. They do not begin with a specific hypothesis as to the direction of such effects, but specify three possible outcomes—winning votes, losing votes, or staying about the same. They then seek to identify and explain these results for incumbent parties. The model in which parties are in almost perfect competition is called the 'equilibrium model'. This model predicts no change in the vote for the governing party. The second model, which probably applies particularly to the US case, is that of 'exploiting office'. It predicts that the vote will rise as a result of a party being in office (see, e.g., Cronin 1980; Polsby and Wildavsky 1980). The 'pendulum swing' model, on the other hand, is closely related to the 'negative incumbency hypothesis' (Strøm 1990*a*), and predicts that participation in office will cost votes. We may think of these liabilities as transaction costs resulting from government responsibility. The important question then is under which circumstances we should expect incumbents to suffer electoral liabilities, and how they can minimize these costs.

Clarity of responsibility and electoral performance

Several authors have suggested that government accountability is related to party-system properties. Defenders of two-party systems, for instance, argue that two parties simplify the alternatives, thereby making voter choice easier (Schattschneider 1942; Dahl 1966; Epstein 1967). Hence, since party-system type is highly correlated with the electoral system, we would expect a difference between incumbents in list proportional representation (PR) systems, on the one hand, and majority-plural systems, on the other. According to the logic of retrospective voting, with only two parties competing, voters can more easily assign blame and punish the government for poor performance by voting against it. Voters in multiparty systems, on the other hand, are less likely to employ such retrospective penalties. With a coalition government, there is no indication as to which incumbent the voters should hold accountable—or as to which alternative party they should turn to (Rosenstone 1995).[2] The basic argument in the literature on democratic choice has been that coalition government obscures accountability, thereby reducing the ability of the electorate to assign blame (Austen-Smith and Banks 1988; Laver and Shepsle 1990; Strøm 1990*b*; Rosenstone 1995; Narud 1996*b*). To a certain extent, the same logic applies to minority governments. Since these governments must rely on the support of opposition parties to enact legislation, they can always attempt to shift the blame for policy failures to other parties (Strøm 1990*b*; Powell and Whitten 1993). Hence, we should expect the electoral fate of incumbents to vary with government type. Responsibility is clearest with single-party majority governments, it is least clear with coalition governments, whereas minority governments lie somewhere in between. The key argument is that electoral performance is strongly related to the visibility of responsibility, hence:

H1. We expect weak governments, which can deflect accountability, to do better at the polls than strong governments.

It follows that incumbent governments in list PR systems should do better than governments in majority-plural systems, that voters should be less likely to turn against minority governments than majority governments, and that they should be least likely to punish coalition governments.[3]

---

[2] This argument is valid also in prospective terms. The proposition then would be that the effect of incumbency is related to the voters' perception of the parties' future achievements, and that they vote for those parties they believe would be best qualified for dealing with certain policies.

[3] See however Strøm (1985), for a different argument. Linking the analysis of government performance to the objective of parties, Strøm argues that minority governments are rational cabinet

These structural cabinet attributes thus help voters make sense out of their voting decisions retrospectively, as they will be more likely to assign responsibility to some governments than to others. But if voters are sophisticated in their retrospection, they may also consider the feasible alternatives to the incumbents. The less attractive these alternatives, the less harsh the voters' judgement may be. Hence, the characteristics of a cabinet itself are only one of the factors that help voters assign responsibility for political outcomes. Structural attributes of the entire party system or parliament may also affect such judgements, to the extent that they structure the way that voters think of alternatives to the incumbent parties. Thus, the more fractionalized and polarized the party system, and the greater the strength of extremist parties, the less credible any opposition is likely to be. Consequently, the less likely the voters may be to turn against the incumbent parties.

H2. We expect government electoral performance to correlate positively with party-system fragmentation, polarization, and extremism.

Economic conditions, critical events, and electoral performance

The above reasoning implies that the effect of incumbency is conditioned by the clarity of responsibility of the actors involved. But clarity in relation to what? One of the most widely recognized assumptions has been that the electoral fate of governments is linked to the country's economic performance (Fiorina 1981; Lewis-Beck 1988, 1991; Lewis-Beck and Paldam 2000; Dorussen and Taylor 2002). Voters will reward the government when economic conditions are good, but they will punish the incumbent when economic conditions are poor. Hence, clarity of responsibility refers to the government's control, or rather, the electorate's perceptions of the government's control, over economic development in a given country. By considering the national economic performance in the period before an election, voters assign blame or credit to the incumbent government, and the vote is shifted accordingly.[4]

Considerable research efforts have gone into specifying precisely how the economy influences elections. The general conclusion resulting from these efforts, as reported by, for example Paldam (1981) and Schneider (1984), seems to be that economic variables normally explain between 20 and 40 per cent of the variation

---

solutions without significant performance liabilities. He finds that minority governments generally perform as well as their natural competitors, that is, majority coalitions (Strøm 1985: 738–9).

[4] In general, the various models of economic voting have received little empirical support (for an overview see Lewin 1991). Lewis-Beck (1986), for instance, found very limited evidence that personal retrospective economic considerations, whether simple or mediated, had any effect on the vote. However, when related to mediated retrospective evaluations of the *national* (as opposed to the personal) situation, economic factors have been found to correlate clearly with voting behaviour (see, e.g., Butler and Stokes 1969; Miller and Listhaug, 1985; Aardal and Listhaug 1986).

in government popularity (as measured in regular opinion polls). Moreover, the relative importance of economic factors varies between countries and over time. Anderson (1995a), for instance, demonstrates that the effect of economic conditions on cabinet support varies with party-system change (measured in terms of the effective number of parties). Contextual factors that help clarify the responsibility for economic management, like governing party target size or the availability of alternatives, contribute to the understanding of differences in economic effects across countries (Anderson 2000; Bengtsson 2004). Unemployment, real disposable income, and inflation are the most consistent influences, whereas a country's balance of trade is generally not significant (Harrop and Miller 1987: 218). We are in no position to review all the literature of relevance here. Nor will we recapitulate the methodological discussion in connection with the application of aggregate data versus survey data, or whether various social groups differ in their demands of and response to the economy. It suffices to note that the main criticism raised against macro-level studies has to do with their lack of sensitivity to shifts in social and political forces (see, e.g., Lewis-Beck 1986). The micro-level data, on the other hand, are more sensitive to 'small-nation' problems, resulting for example from the influence of the international environment.

For the present purpose we will simply use the three macroeconomic indicators that we expect to have an impact upon the electoral performance of incumbent governments: rates of unemployment, inflation rates, and economic growth [in terms of the annual percentage change in gross domestic product (GDP)]. We operationalize economic growth as low levels of inflation and unemployment and high GDP growth, and recession as high levels of inflation and unemployment and low GDP growth.[5]

H3. We expect the incumbent government to do worse when the economy is poor, that is, in times of economic recession, than when the economy is good. And consequently, incumbents will do better in times of economic growth.

Yet, economic events are only one type of critical event that might affect the electoral performance of incumbents. Others exogenous shocks may be reflected in the circumstances surrounding the cabinet's termination. These may be popular opinion developments or national security events (e.g. threats of war or civil war), or even personal events (e.g. some sort of scandals). The more troubled these events, the less well we expect the government to do. Our country specialists have indicated the various types of exogenous events associated with the cabinet's termination (see Müller and Strøm 2000), and our expectation is that such events

---

[5] The data were made available by Paul V. Warwick, who collected information on the economic indicators from among others the International Monetary Fund (IMF), and the Organization for Economic Cooperation and Development (OECD). See Warwick (1994: 76–83) for a more thorough description of these data.

generally indicate dissent, which we expect to be a liability at election time. Hence,

H4. The existence of terminal events should negatively influence the incumbent parties' electoral performance.

COALITION GOVERNMENTS AND ELECTORAL PERFORMANCE

So far, we have treated the incumbent parties as one entity. In a coalition government, however, it is not clear which ones of the incumbent parties are to be held responsible for economic difficulties. In this context Eulau and Lewis-Beck (1985) suggest that party policy rather than incumbency per se condition economic voting. Hence, in a multiparty coalition system, we should expect the electoral fate of individual parties to vary according to the control they exercise over certain policy areas, and the extent to which voters relate economic performance to the programmatic commitment of certain parties.

Economic conditions and government portfolios

For the present purpose, we define 'control' over certain policy areas as the specific types of portfolios a party possesses in the government. If coalition policy is implemented through ministerial departments for which ministers are responsible, as indeed Laver and Shepsle (1990, 1996) claim, and if individual parties seek to maximize own policy through their position in government, we should expect the electoral fate of parties to vary according to the control they have over the most important government portfolios (in terms of the economy), the Prime Ministry or the Ministry of Finance. We assume then that the party supplying the Prime Minister and/or Minister of Finance will be seen as responsible for government policies in general, and for economic conditions in particular. Hence, to examine the relation between government portfolios and electoral performance, information on the parties of the PM and Minister of Finance will be included as control variables in the analysis. In this context, we will examine the possibility that the parties holding the Prime Ministry and/or Ministry of Finance will fare worse in the subsequent election than other incumbent parties in times of poor economic conditions, and, conversely, do better when the economy is good.

Economic conditions and ideological leaning

The above arguments imply that the allocation of ministerial portfolios matters for the electoral performance of incumbents. Another factor to be considered is the ideological leaning of the government, and the perceived role of individual parties in the management of the economy. Powell and Whitten (1993) suggest that voters' assignment of blame or credit is linked to the ideological leaning of the cabinet and the saliency of certain policies to distinctive subgroups of the electorate. Left-wing governments have been inclined to strengthen the role of the state and the public sector, drawing their electorates basically from working-class and lower-middle-class constituencies. Right-wing governments, on the other hand, have been more concerned with the role of private enterprise in stimulating the economy, and have attracted middle- and upper-middle-class voters. Hence, from differences in the policy packages of governments, evidence suggests that the effects of economic performance vary for governments of different ideological persuasions (Powell and Whitten 1993).[6]

Combined with the theories of 'issue voting', some interesting perspectives may be drawn from the above arguments. The party in government has captured office under a party label, and in order to satisfy its own supporters it must seek to maximize the policy pay-offs reflected in the party's political orientations. According to the 'saliency theory' of party competition (Budge and Farlie 1983), parties build their electoral support on issue types which they have made their 'own', for example welfare, agriculture, public spending—and on these areas of policy they enjoy a relative advantage (see also Laver and Budge, 1992).[7] Hence, voters will reward those parties they perceive to have promoted their own policies, and they will punish those incumbents that have failed to do so. In this context, Anderson (1995b) suggests that voters structure credit and blame according to the parties' issue competencies and priorities.[8] Social democrat/socialist governments have most commonly been regarded as having a better grip on the unemployment problem, whereas conservative parties are more successful in keeping the inflation down (see, e.g., Hibbs 1977). Hence, we will examine whether governments dominated by social democrats and/or socialist and communist parties

---

[6] In this context Pacek and Radcliff (1999) argue that in highly developed welfare states, such as, for example, the Scandinavian ones, left-of-centre parties, rather than the actual incumbent governments, may be the recipients of blame or credit for the state of the economy. In large measure, this is attributed to the predominant role such parties have played in the development and maintenance of the institutionalized welfare systems.

[7] A related perspective is to be found in the 'issue-ownership' hypothesis developed by Petrocik (1996), which claims that, during the electoral campaign, candidates (or parties) are likely to gain the most by advertising on those issues over which they can claim 'ownership'. The psychological premises for this hypothesis are that voters associate certain views with particular parties, and are therefore more receptive to messages that confirm rather than disconfirm existing stereotypes. Therefore they find some sources more credible than others concerning particular policy areas. For this reason, candidates' advertisements will be more powerful when they address issues on which they enjoy a relative advantage.

[8] Christopher Anderson (1995b) examines the impact of economic conditions on public support for coalition governments in two smaller European countries, Denmark and the Netherlands. Contrary to the present analysis, Anderson applies monthly opinion surveys to examine changes in support for the governing parties.

will do worse than other incumbents in times of high unemployment, and if governments dominated by conservative and/or liberal parties will do worse than other incumbents in times of high inflation.[9]

Median position

If the ideological leaning of the government is significant, we also expect the strategic position of individual parties to matter. Here, the concept of 'centre parties' or parties occupying the median position has been important in theories of coalition building as well as in election theories.[10] The 'median voter theorem' derives from Duncan Black's original work (1958) and became famous from Anthony Downs' *An Economic Theory of Democracy* (1957). Downs assumes that the policy space has one dominant ideological dimension, a left-right continuum, on which parties manoeuver for support.[11] By shifting their support from one party or coalition of parties to another, voters can then determine the composition of governments. The 'guidance' for parties in the two-party Downsian model is to take a position in the policy space as close as possible to the median voter.[12] The

---

[9] Anderson (1995*b*: 353) argues exactly the opposite: Since left or centre-left parties seek to avoid high unemployment and right or centre-right parties attempt to avert high inflation, it would be irrational for voters to punish leftist governments when unemployment rises and to blame conservative governments when inflation is high.

[10] Note, that the 'centre concept' has also been much debated in the party-system literature. See, e.g., Duverger (1954); Sartori (1976); Daalder (1984).

[11] The Downsian approach has frequently been criticized for its unidimensionality, and for its narrowly economic conception of policy space. Such assumptions may be too stylized for some competitive multiparty systems, in which parties and voters articulate a variety of issue positions. 'Neoclassical' proximity theorists therefore have transformed these models significantly. Enelow and Hinich (1984), for instance, include non-economic issues in a multidimensional policy space. In their view, and contrary to Downs (1957), political pay-offs are not restricted to purely economic self-interest: they may also relate to moral or philosophical questions. The crucial factor is the extent to which these issues are important enough to affect voting choice (Enelow and Hinich 1984: 2–3). The proximity logic, however, is the same as for Downs: voters choose parties on the basis of ideological proximity and cast their vote for parties that are closest to them in policy space.

[12] The 'proximity logic' of the Downsian model has been challenged by the so-called 'directional model' of issue voting, which argues that voters prefer parties to take strong stands and to mark the ideological direction (Rabinowitz and Macdonald 1989; Listhaug et al. 1990; Macdonald et al. 1991; 1998). In directional theory the centre is 'empty': a neutral zone of indifference irrelevant for voters' evaluation of parties. The two models differ most fundamentally in how they conceptualize political issues. In proximity theory, voters are supposed to have specific policy preferences on issues, in directional theory, they are supposed to have only diffuse preferences for one side or the other of an issue debate. In proximity theory the parties adjust to the preferences of the voters, in directional theory they shape the public opinion. While the perspective of proximity theory is one in which the major parties tend to converge towards the centre position in order to grab the in-between voters, the perspective of directional theory is one in which the large parties tend to move away from one another so as to present idealized and coherent pictures of the voters' positions. Obviously, the prospects for the centrist catch-all party are very different in the two perspectives. Interesting in its own right, it is not clear, however, what is the implication of this debate for the electoral performance of coalition parties.

party holding the median legislator on this dimension also has a large advantage in coalition bargaining, in that it cannot be dislodged by any contiguous bloc of opposition parties either on its left or on its right.

Although the party holding the median legislator will tend to be located towards the middle of the voter distribution, it need not be precisely centrist by all definitions. In coalition theory, the term 'centre' has been given different meanings. It has been used to denote either the party holding the median legislator, which is a 'pivotal party' in common game-theoretic terms (Hazan 1996, 1997), or a party located halfway between the extremes on the dominant policy dimension, or perhaps a moderate party without a very precise location on the most important dimension (e.g. a Christian Democratic Party). Even though the term centre has not been defined uniformly, in coalition theory a centrist position has been regarded as a great bargaining advantage. Indeed, many theories see the median party as indispensable for the formation and survival of a coalition. The median party has a strategic asset over the other parties, since its position enables it to play off the parties to its left and its right against each other, thereby carrying the advantage of its pivotal position into the government coalition itself (de Swaan 1982; Laver and Schofield 1990). Hence, the centre is the vote getting as well as the policy-getting place. Consequently, it should be less of a liability in terms of electoral performance.

H5. The median party or the party holding a centrist position within the cabinet will perform better electorally than the other parties in the coalition.

Consequently, as a corollary we may in infer that:

H6. Cabinets that include the median party or that have a centrist policy position will perform better electorally than those that do not.

BARGAINING, INSTITUTIONS, AND TRANSACTION COSTS

The trade-off between vote seeking, office seeking, and policy-influence occurs in any type of democratic political system. In multiparty systems, however, the tactical considerations involved in deciding which compromises can be accepted become especially complicated. Here, the decision to join a coalition is not the only moment at which trade-offs must be considered. Not all coalitions manage to survive the maximum period of office, but fall, either because of internal difficulties among the coalition partners or by loss of support in parliament. Moreover, in response to events and ongoing competition among the coalition partners (or legislative support parties), governing parties constantly renegotiate the initial policy 'deal'. This means that the consideration of whether to participate in a coalition is an ongoing decision, in which the *transaction costs* for governing must be reconsidered at each moment in which new events are emerging or tensions between the coalition partners occur (Lupia and Strøm 1995). Hence, the electoral performance of parties ought to be examined in this strategic context.

The power to dismiss or to dissolve parliament and call early elections are key institutional features of parliamentary regimes, and may be considered as two of the most important agenda powers given to the political players (Strøm and Swindle 2002). It provides them with an institutional device that may be used strategically for partisan and electoral purposes, as well as for a more general democratic objective.

H7. Incumbents that benefit from permissive dissolution powers, or from other strong executive powers, should perform better electorally than those that do not.

We would, of course, expect incumbent parties to exercise such powers particularly when they stand to gain. This opportunistic use of their institutional powers should in turn be reflected in their electoral fates. In their model of the strategic use of dissolution powers, Lupia and Strøm (1995) hypothesize that dissolution is most likely when parties expect large benefits from an election, when they face small election costs, when they face large costs for negotiating non-electoral transfers of power, or when they derive little value from the seats they currently control or from the other coalitions they could enter. In addition, their model assumes that dissolution becomes more likely at the end of the constitutional terms (Lupia and Strøm 1995: 656). If there is a 'wear and tear' on parties in government, which the negative incumbency hypothesis indeed states, then we should generally expect a tendency for parties to suffer more electorally the longer they control government. From this assumption we may infer that:

H8. In electoral terms, incumbents will benefit from early elections when they call them. The longer the duration of a cabinet, the larger the loss of votes.

EMPIRICAL ANALYSIS

We will now examine these propositions empirically by looking at the impact of government terminations on the electoral fortunes of incumbent parties. In the previous discussion we have generated several theoretical arguments about the electoral costs of incumbent parties. We expect the electoral performance of incumbents to vary with system-specific variables, such as different types of governments and the number of parties in the system. In addition, we assume that it will vary with cabinet attributes, with institutional differences, with the bargaining environment and with events in the recent past, with government portfolio allocation, as well as with the parties' policy positions. Finally, we expect the parties' electoral performance to vary with the control and timing of elections.

TABLE 11.1. *Electoral performance of cabinets by country*

	Mean % loss/gain	Std. deviation	N
Austria	−1.87	5.51	19
Belgium	−3.82	4.84	32
Denmark	−0.79	4.95	30
Finland	−2.77	3.73	36
France	−2.32	14.04	22
Germany	−0.72	4.57	25
Greece	−4.53	2.62	9
Iceland	−2.72	5.76	25
Ireland	−4.47	4.04	21
Italy	−2.47	8.34	46
Luxembourg	−3.76	4.87	14
The Netherlands	−2.82	5.62	21
Norway	−1.08	4.49	25
Portugal	−4.15	12.48	9
Spain	−9.49	13.65	7
Sweden	−2.14	3.40	25
United Kingdom	−1.82	4.02	19
Total	−2.59	6.57	385

Note: Average percentage of gain or loss of votes, 1945–99.

Consistently with previous work in this field, we measure the electoral performance of incumbents by examining the share of the aggregate vote received by the governing party or coalition of parties (see, e.g., Powell 1981; Rose and Mackie 1983; Strøm 1990*b*; Powell and Whitten 1993; Narud 1996*a*). Before turning to the multivariate analysis, we will report some results between electoral performance and some of the independent variables. Let us start out by simply looking at the electoral fate of governments in 17 West European parliamentary regimes in the post-war period. Here, the unit of analysis is the set of governing parties collectively for each election in each country.

Table 11.1 clearly demonstrates that in all countries there is an 'adverse incumbency effect'. On average, incumbent parties have in the postwar period lost 2.59 per cent of the total national vote. Enormous variations exist, however, among individual countries in the magnitude of the electoral losses. On average, incumbency costs have been greatest in Spain, where the incumbents have lost a staggering 9.49 per cent of the votes. But even in Ireland, Greece, and Belgium, incumbent cabinets have suffered substantial losses. Incumbency costs have been smallest in Germany and Denmark. Furthermore, the large standard deviations for some of the countries indicate great variations in the electoral gains and losses for incumbents from one election to the next. This tendency is most pronounced in France, Portugal, and Spain and least pronounced in Greece, Sweden, and Finland (though note the low number of elections in Spain, Greece, and Portugal).

Our data cover a period of more than 50 years. One may wonder whether the incumbency losses reflected in Table 11.1 have held throughout that entire period.

TABLE 11.2. *Electoral performance of cabinets by decade*

Decades	Mean loss/gains of incumbents	Std. deviation	N	Number of winning cabinets	Number of losing cabinets
1940s	−0.10	5.76	22	9	13
1950s	−1.08	4.18	76	35	37
1960s	−1.43	6.46	67	20	47
1970s	−2.10	5.98	78	31	46
1980s	−3.44	6.76	84	16	66
1990s	−6.28	8.39	58	11	46

Note: The data show average percentage of loss or gain of votes for 17 West European democracies. 1945–99 broken down by the termination date of the cabinets (i.e. by decades of cabinet termination).

Alternatively, does the electoral fate of incumbents differ over time? Table 11.2 and Figure 11.1 present the mean of these results by decade for all 17 countries jointly.

The trend in these data is obvious and powerful: the average incumbency loss has increased monotonically over time. These losses were fairly low in the 1940s and the 1950s, then began increasing significantly in the 1970s, accelerated in the 1980s, and almost doubled again in the 1990s. Fairly large standard deviations indicate that even so, the electoral fate of incumbent parties has varied a great deal within each decade. Nonetheless, the number of 'losing' cabinets in any decade is consistently higher than the number of 'gainers', though this discrepancy only becomes striking from the 1960s on.

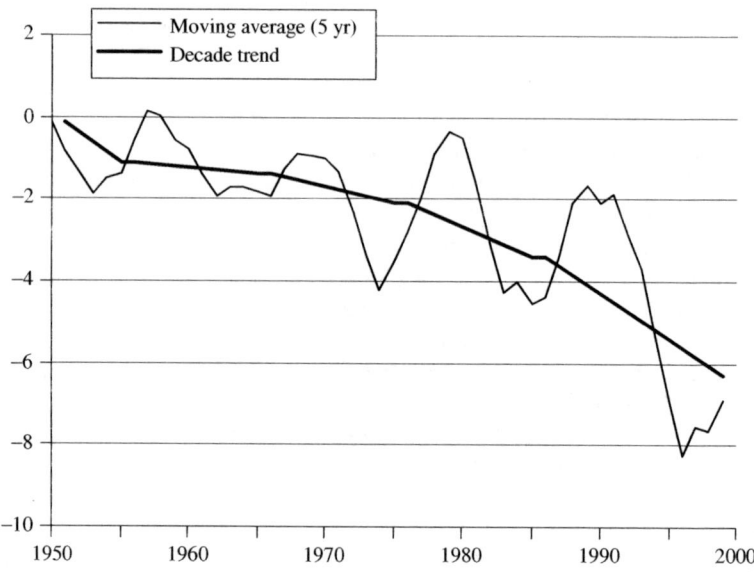

FIGURE 11.1. Cabinet electoral performance

The trend reflected in Figure 11.1 is consistent with the general tendency over the last few decades towards increasing electoral volatility (Pedersen 1983; Dalton, Flanagan, and Beck 1984; Crewe and Denver 1985; Irwin and van Holsteyn 1989; Aardal and Valen 1997; Dalton and Wattenberg 2000). The fact that electoral results have been particularly volatile in the 'new' democracies, Spain, Portugal, and Greece (cf. Table 11.1) might suggest that the increase in incumbency losses since the 1970s have been greatly impacted by the inclusion of these countries. Yet, in reality the adverse incumbency effect went well beyond these particular countries. In the 1990s incumbency losses were very high even in well-established democracies such as Austria, Great Britain, Italy, and the Netherlands.

Individual parties

Before focusing on the various sets of independent variables that we assume have an impact upon the electoral performance of incumbents; let us map the electoral fate of individual parties. Are certain parties affected more than others as a result of government responsibility? Previous studies have demonstrated that it is in fact rare for all coalition partners to suffer the same electoral fate, and that coalition partners usually see their votes move in opposite directions (Rose and Mackie 1983; Narud 1996a). Thus, vote exchange among coalition partners may result in only minor aggregate change for the coalition as a whole. It is reasonable to ask then which parties in the coalition tend to lose votes. In a coalition government, it is quite possible that specific parties will be identified more directly with government policies and thus be held more 'responsible' than others are. Table 11.3 gives an overview of the electoral fate of individual parties based on their ideological position within the coalition as well as their control of certain government portfolios (the Prime Ministry and the Ministry of Finance).

All types of incumbent parties lose votes. On the average, the PM's party manages best, while parties holding a median position within the cabinet tend to suffer the greatest losses, which runs contrary to our hypothesis (H5). Observe that the categories listed in Table 11.3 are not mutually exclusive. The PM and the Minister of Finance, for example, may happen to come from the same party. However, in the subsequent multivariate analyses they are treated separately.

TABLE 11.3. *Average vote change by incumbent parties and cabinets*

	Average loss/gain	Std. deviation	N
All incumbents (all parties, all cabinets)	−1.07	4.51	544
PM's party	−0.84	4.72	163
Finance Minister's party[a]	−1.05	4.51	196
Median legislative party[b]	−1.35	4.80	125

[a] If more than one finance minister in a particular cabinet, both are counted.

[b] If median legislative party is in the cabinet.

TABLE 11.4. *Electoral performance by cabinet type*

Cabinet type	Mean % loss/gain	Std. deviation	% loss/share of seats[a]	N
Single-party government	−2.40	6.25	−0.041	141
Cabinet majority, minimal winning, MWC (50% + 1)	−2.95	7.85	−0.049	114
Cabinet majority, minimal connected winning coalitions, MCWC	−2.42	6.87	−0.036	75
Minority government	−1.48	6.21	−0.025	135
Cabinet surplus majority	−3.48	6.02	−0.050	85

Note: Average percentage of votes lost or gained.

[a] The cabinet's percentage loss divided by the cabinet share of seats in parliament.

Types of governments and electoral performance

The next question is the impact of government-specific factors on the electoral performance of incumbents. Are minority governments less vulnerable than majority governments? And are coalition governments less likely to be punished by the electorate than single-party governments? Table 11.4 gives an overview of the mean gains and losses for the various types of governments.

We immediately see that all cabinet types share the liability of incumbency. However, minority governments perform better in subsequent elections than all the other types of cabinets listed in the table. This is consistent with the results reported by Strøm (1984, 1990b), who found that the average majority coalition lost more than three times as much as substantive minority cabinets.[13] The main message of the table is that the loss of votes increases with the size of the cabinet. Broadly based coalition governments (oversized coalitions) have the poorest electoral results. Naturally, this tendency may be related to the size itself: oversized majority governments obviously have more to lose than simple majority governments and especially minority governments. However, even when controlling for the relative size of the cabinet—its overall share of the parliamentary seats (the second column from the right), the tendencies run in the same direction. Thus, the simple proposition that voters are more likely to punish single-party governments than coalition governments does not receive any support. In addition, when we control for electoral system, there is no tendency for governments in list PR systems to do better than governments in majority systems (table not reported here). Temporally, we again find that the 1990s have been particularly turbulent years. The average losses are much higher in the 1990s than in the preceding five decades. Only surplus coalition governments deviate from this tendency, as

---

[13] Strøm distinguishes between 'substantive' and 'formal' minority governments, the latter being: 'governments whose legislative support is negotiated prior to government formation through explicit, comprehensive, and more than short term contracts' (Strøm 1990b: 62). We have not made this distinction in the present data.

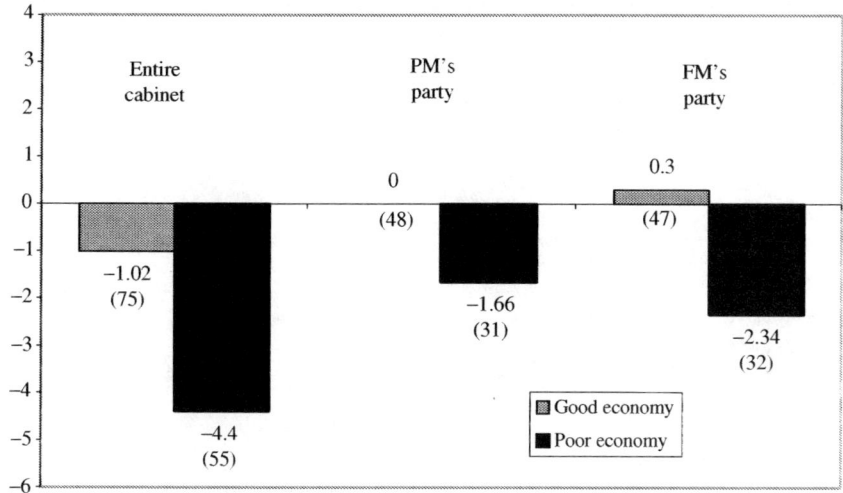

FIGURE 11.2. Electoral performance by economic conditions. Average percentage of votes lost or gained in 17 West European democracies, 1945–99. No. of cases in parentheses

these types of governments lost more on average in the 1980s than in the 1990s. Hence, in a long-term perspective, the heightened electoral volatility in recent years coincides with an increased tendency towards punishing incumbent parties. Apparently, this trend occurs regardless of cabinet type.

Economic conditions and electoral performance

In order to examine the impact of economic conditions on the electoral performance of incumbent parties, we have made a distinction between particularly 'good' economic conditions and particularly 'bad' economic conditions. 'Good' economic conditions are defined as times of low inflation, low unemployment rate, and high GDP growth.[14] 'Bad' economic conditions are defined as times of low GDP growth.[15] Our hypothesis is that voters are less likely to turn against governments when the economic conditions are 'good', and, consequently, the incumbent parties will lose fewer votes in prosperous times than in economic turbulent times. Moreover, we expect the party of the PM and/or the party of the Minister of Finance to be more severely affected by the economic conditions than all the governing parties taken together. Figure 11.2 presents cabinet performance by different economic conditions. Observe that the number of cases included in the analysis has dropped as a result of our categorization.

[14] GDP growth is higher than 3.5% and jobless rate and inflation are lower than 6%.
[15] GDP growth is lower than 1%. We did not factor in consumer prices and unemployment into bad economic conditions because the number of cases drops to just a handful.

TABLE 11.5. *OLS regressions on cabinet electoral performance (government ideology and economic performance)*

'Rightist' governments[a]	3.057*	'Leftist' governments[b]	0.203
Annual consumer price inflation rate[c]	−0.005	Jobless rate[d]	−0.280**
The interaction between 'rightist' profile and inflation rate	−0.261*	The interaction between 'leftist' profile and jobless rate	0.053
R^2	0.020		0.029
N	383		353

Note: Figures are unstandardized regression coefficients.

[a] Majority of cabinet seats are held by conservative or liberal parties.

[b] Majority of cabinet seats are held by social democrat, left socialist, or communist parties.

[c] Consumer price index in the year in which the cabinet end.

[d] Jobless rate in the year in which the cabinet end.

** $p < .01$; * $p < .05$.

Figure 11.2 clearly gives support to our hypothesis: in times of economic growth and prosperity, the governing parties do much better at the polls than in times of economic recession. This tendency is clearer for the PM's party—and even more so for the party of the Minister of Finance. However, contrary to what we should expect, there is no clear reward when economic conditions are 'good'. The government as a whole loses votes irrespective of the states of the economy, and only for the party of the Minister of Finance is there a slight reward for good economic performance.

We now turn to the relationship between the economic indicators and the ideological leaning of the government. Initially, we have hypothesized that there will be a negative relationship between 'rightist' governments (conservative/liberal party dominance) and a high rate of inflation, and that 'leftist' governments (communist/left socialist/social democratic party dominance) are negatively affected by a high rate of unemployment. Table 11.5 reports the relationship between these two types of governments, economic conditions and electoral performance. Included are also two interactive variables, in which the ideological leaning of the government is taken together with the relevant economic variables. That is, 'leftist' governments are interacted with rates of unemployment, whereas 'rightist' governments are interacted with rates of inflation. In this table our dependent variable is the change of votes for all cabinets jointly.

By first looking at the simple connection between electoral performance and ideological leaning, Table 11.5 suggests no significant relationship between the 'leftist' leaning of the cabinets and electoral performance. There is, on the other hand, a significant—and positive—relationship between rightist governments and their performance at the polls. In addition, we observe a negative and significant relationship between 'rightist' governments and inflation, indicating that coalitions with conservative or liberal party dominance do not travel well with a high rate of inflation. Inflation alone, however, does not have any significant effect on the electoral performance of cabinets. The opposite tendency is evident for jobless rate. Table 11.5 indicates that unemployment has a strong and negative impact on the electoral fortunes of cabinets, but, surprisingly, this tendency does not seem to hit cabinets with a 'leftist' ideology relative to others. Overall, the explained variance is low for both models, but it is somewhat higher for the one examining the relationship between leftist governments and unemployment.

Table 11.5 is based on the results for the entire post-war period. One possibility, however, is that variation exists between different decades regarding the effect of the economic indicators. Unemployment was marginal in many Western democracies for the first two or three decades after the Second World War, but it increased towards the end of the 1970s and thereafter. The magnitude of inflation, on the other hand, was greater and fairly stable before 1970 than it was in the subsequent three decades when greater fluctuations occurred.[16] Indeed, before 1970 the positive relationship between a 'rightist' profile and electoral performance is even stronger than observed in Table 11.5 (significant at .01 level). Inflation, on the other hand, does not have any significant effect. In the period after 1970 neither the 'rightist' leaning of the government nor the inflation rate has any significant effects on electoral performance. By contrast, unemployment has a significant and negative effect on the cabinets' electoral result after 1970, whereas this indicator is not significant in the period before 1970. However, there is still no indication that 'leftist' governments have suffered relative to others as a result of unemployment in any of the periods mentioned.

Cabinet termination and electoral performance

The simple formulation of the incumbency liability hypothesis is that parties lose votes as a result of government responsibility. We have just seen that this hypothesis holds true for all types of governments as well as for the various types of incumbent parties. Moreover, we have argued that this 'wear and tear' on parties in government would lead us to expect a tendency for parties to suffer more substantial losses the longer they sit in government. Forcing an early election may cause a sizeable reallocation of legislative power to the benefit of the governing parties resulting in greater bargaining power (Lupia and Strøm 1995).

Investigating this possibility empirically suggests that there is a *strong and negative* correlation between electoral performance and cabinet duration (significant at .000 level).[17] The longer the life of a cabinet, the larger the loss of votes. This would in fact indicate that in certain situations it might be an advantage for the incumbent parties to terminate a cabinet prematurely. By remaining in office they may have to accept further policy concessions and a possible decrease in popular support. By using a competitive strategy, on the other hand, the party clarifies its ideological position and may thereby gain votes. This is not without risks, of

---

[16] According to OECD statistics, average inflation for the OECD countries in the period 1960–7 was 2.7%; 1967–73, 5.1%; and 1974–80, 10.2%. *Historical Statistics, 1960–1980*. Paris: OECD 1982.

[17] The T-value of the bivariate regression is –7.680 and the explained variance is .13.

TABLE 11.6. *Vote change by cabinet termination*

	All cabinets			Coalition cabinets only		
	Mean	Std. deviation	N	Mean	Std. deviation	N
Regular elections	−3.33	6.93	106	−3.39	7.47	69
Other technical terminations	−2.99	6.20	43	−2.14	8.03	21
Early elections, no conflict	−1.04	6.68	67	−3.14	7.82	26
Early elections, conflict	−3.17	6.24	41	−2.16	4.75	32
Cabinet replacement/enlargement	−2.24	5.87	131	−2.32	6.19	99
Non-personal terminal events	−2.97	7.66	60	−3.88	8.39	34

course. Should the parties be unable to convince the voters that the break was for good reason, terminating a government may lead to electoral loss (Narud and Irwin 1994). As a next step, therefore, let us have a look at how the electoral fate of governments relates to different causes of termination.

In Table 11.6 we distinguish between cabinets that are terminated after regular elections and those that are terminated prematurely. Cabinets forced to leave office for 'other technical reasons' (second row) are cabinets that were terminated for reasons beyond the control of the relevant parties, for example the death of a Prime Minister, or simply other constitutional provisions that require the cabinet's resignation (e.g. at the time of the accession of a new head of state). In addition, we have defined some of the circumstances that may provoke early elections, such as parliamentary defeat at the hands of the opposition, conflicts between coalition parties, or conflicts within any of the coalition parties. In order to see the impact of these situations *without* an early election, we have defined the category: 'other discretionary reasons'.[18] Terminations caused by 'critical events' refer to those associated with popular opinion shocks, international and national security events (e.g. threats of war or civil war), or economic events (recessions, unfavourable shocks, etc.). Observe that these columns are not mutually exclusive, since several different kinds of events can be involved in the resignation of the same cabinet. The table reports the results for all cabinets jointly, as well as for coalition cabinets only.

Table 11.6 reports some interesting results. First of all, when we look at all the cabinets jointly, those that are terminated after regular elections suffer greater electoral damage than cabinets that are terminated due to early elections. Of course, the former category is highly correlated with the 'duration' variable discussed initially, since it includes those governments that have served the maximum parliamentary term. Hence, the electoral advantage of dissolving parliament would be a strong motivating factor for the strategic timing of elections.

The patterns for coalition governments are different. They lose almost as much in early elections as they do in regular ones. However, the *causes* of early elections

---

[18] This indicator also involves voluntary enlargement of the coalitions (when there has been no early election).

seem to matter in non-obvious ways. When early elections are due to conflicts between the parties or parliamentary defeats, the incumbent parties in coalition governments lose much *less* on average than they do at regular elections or when early elections are called in situations of no conflict. The reason for this non-obvious result may be that when coalition governments call elections in a situation of conflict, the voters may reward one of the incumbent parties (rather than the opposition) while punishing others. One example can be found in John A. Costello's first cabinet in Ireland (1948–51), which broke down when the Prime Minister distanced himself from a controversial post-natal care measure proposed by his own Minister of Health. The voters imposed a devastating loss on the latter minister's party (Clann na Poblachta), whereas Costello's Fine Gael was able to register the largest gain of any party. Coalition cabinets suffer the heaviest losses of all when they are terminated because of critical events, that is as a result of popular opinion shocks, some sort of security events, or economic events. However, the observations in this category are relatively few, and the large standard deviations indicate an enormous dispersion in votes gained or lost among the coalition cabinets.

Summary

The analysis so far suggests only partial support for our hypotheses. The data do not lend support to our system-specific hypothesis. There is no tendency for coalition governments to do better than single-party governments, or for incumbent parties in majority systems to fare worse than those in multiparty PR systems. Rather, the loss of votes seems to correlate with size itself; the larger the government, the larger the loss of votes. Our economic indicators do better. Consistent with our expectations, economic conditions seem to have a substantial impact upon the electoral fate of incumbent governments. The relationship between the ideological leaning of the cabinet and its electoral fate under specific economic conditions is less clear. There is a clear negative effect of a high jobless rate on the incumbent's vote, but it is not significantly related to the government's 'leftist' profile. On the other hand, high inflation is significantly related to the electoral fate of cabinets dominated by 'rightist' parties. Finally, for all cabinets jointly electoral change correlates with the relative duration of cabinets as well as the timing of elections.

COMPREHENSIVE ANALYSIS

We now set out to test our hypotheses more broadly, including all the relevant variables discussed initially. The final three tables present a series of blockwise OLS regressions presenting the various clusters of explanatory variables identified earlier in this book. In the first series (Table 11.7), the dependent variable is the aggregate electoral performance of all cabinet parties. In the second series (Table 11.8), the dependent variable is the electoral performance of the PM's party, whereas the third series (Table 11.9) examines the electoral performance of the Finance Minister's party.[19]

Table 11.7 thus reports the results for all cabinets jointly. The first block reinforces our previous results and shows that incumbency losses have increased monotonically, even when we control for country effects. First of all, Table 11.7 indicates that the national context is significantly related to our dependent variable. Consequently, the inclusion of the nations contributes to the explained variance of the model, but only relatively modestly. The decade of cabinet termination has a negative significant effect on electoral performance, confirming our previous results. The strong coefficients for the 1980s and 1990s indicate that the electoral losses of European cabinets have been particularly severe during these decades.

The second block shows that several structural factors are systematically related to electoral performance. More surprisingly, however, electoral fortunes decline with the number of parliamentary parties, whereas other structural cabinet attributes have no significant effects. The results confirm that the larger the cabinet's share of parliamentary seats, the larger the losses tend to be, and that electoral results tend to improve with the bargaining fragmentation of the party system (and thus with the absence of credible alternatives). All of these effects hold up in the final model specification, when we control for any significant factors. They indicate that the likelihood of losing votes increases with the size of the cabinet, whereas it decreases with more parties in the legislature. A likely explanation is that political liabilities tend to be atomized with an increasing number of parties, and, consequently, the incumbent cabinet is not challenged by credible government alternatives.

Three of the preference variables introduced in block three turn out to be significantly related to the proportion of votes gained or lost: extremist party seat share (positive), polarization (positive), and cabinet preference range (negative), but none of these retains its significance in the final, comprehensive model. Thus, there is little support for hypotheses 5 and 6. On the other hand, when controls are introduced, we find an interesting tendency for cabinets with a 'rightist' majority to do better than others.

Institutions show no significant effects, contrary to hypothesis 7. But we do find a positive effect of early elections, when these are not called in a crisis situation. This result is consistent with hypothesis 8 and holds up in the final model. We also find support for the related proposition that electoral performance declines with cabinet duration, but this effect is not statistically significant. Most of the critical

---

[19] If there is more than one Finance Minister's party, we average the electoral performance of these parties.

TABLE 11.7. *OLS regressions on cabinet electoral performance*

Independent variables	Model 1	Model 2	Model 3	Model 4	Model 5	Model 6	Model 7	Model 8
Time and space								
1940s	1.34 (1.55)							
1960s	−0.81 (1.08)							
1970s	−1.13 (1.03)							
1980s	−2.27 (1.05)**						−1.51 (1.02)	−1.97 (0.81)**
1990s	−5.36 (1.14)**						−4.83 (1.27)**	−4.88 (0.95)**
Austria	−1.43 (1.94)							
Belgium	−3.63 (1.71)**							
Denmark	−0.16 (1.72)							
Finland	−2.63 (1.67)							
France	−1.03 (1.86)							
Greece	−1.91 (2.51)							
Iceland	−2.48 (1.81)							
Ireland	−3.68 (1.88)*							
Italy	−2.14 (1.59)							
Luxembourg	−4.00 (2.14)*							
The Netherlands	−2.49 (1.88)							
Norway	−0.37 (1.80)							
Portugal	−2.34 (2.51)							
Spain	−7.52 (2.74)**							
Sweden	−1.60 (1.80)							
UK	−1.33 (1.94)							
Structure								
Absolute no. parl. parties		−0.35 (0.15)**					−0.26 (0.17)	−0.26 (0.14)*
Bargaining power fragmentation		0.80 (0.33)**					0.82 (0.35)**	0.72 (0.25)**
Cabinet seat share		−0.07 (0.03)**					−0.05 (0.04)	−0.07 (0.02)**
Number of cabinet parties		0.18 (0.50)						
Minimum winning coalition		−1.16 (1.10)						
Surplus majority cabinet		−0.92 (1.52)					−0.51 (1.17)	
Preferences								
Extremist party seat share			0.08 (0.03)**				0.06 (0.04)	0.05 (0.03)
Polarization (BP weighted)			0.09 (0.04)**				0.06 (0.05)	

(*cont.*)

TABLE 11.7. (*Continued*)

Independent variables	Model 1	Model 2	Model 3	Model 4	Model 5	Model 6	Model 7	Model 8
Preferences (*cont.*)								
Cabinet preference range			−0.03 (0.02)*				−0.04 (0.02)	
Median Party (1st dim.) in cab.			−0.44 (0.88)				4.61 (1.43)**	3.62 (1.17)**
Conservative cab.			1.47 (0.92)				0.42 (1.36)	
Socialist cab.			0.76 (0.81)					
Institutions								
Bicameralism				−0.54 (0.75)				
PM powers				−0.16 (0.19)				
PM dissolution powers				−0.51 (0.81)				
Semi-presidentialism				−0.77 (0.99)				
Bargaining								
Comprehensive policy agreement					−1.27 (0.81)		−1.32 (0.94)	
Coalition Discipline in Legislation					−0.52 (0.57)			
Relative cab. duration					−1.54 (1.00)		−0.44 (1.16)	
Early election (no conflict)					1.62 (0.90)*		1.42 (0.97)	1.54 (0.87)*
Critical events								
Unemployment (end)						−0.27 (0.10)**	−0.12 (0.13)	
Inflation (end)						−0.05 (0.04)	−0.01 (0.04)	−0.01 (0.03)
Growth (end)						0.16 (0.13)	0.14 (0.14)	
Conservative cab. × inflation						−0.09 (0.08)	−0.33 (0.12)**	−0.28 (0.10)**
Socialist cab. × unemployment						0.07 (0.11)	0.18 (0.17)	
Terminal events: Opinion shock						−2.19 (2.02)	−2.04 (1.97)	−3.04 (1.83)*
Terminal events: Security						1.61 (1.85)	−2.25 (1.42)	
Terminal events: Economic						−0.42 (1.41)		
Constant	1.02 (1.46)	1.05 (2.04)	−4.05 (1.07)**	−0.78 (1.61)	−0.20 (1.38)	−1.31 (0.88)	0.54 (2.79)	1.18 (1.62)
Number of observations	385	385	381	385	384	348	344	383
Adjusted R^2	.07	.04	.02	.00	.02	.03	.15	.14

Note: Figures are unstandardized regression coefficients.

[a] Germany has been used as the reference category, and Greece has been taken out of the analysis, since we lack the economic indicators for this country.
[b] Conservative and liberal parties hold a majority of the cabinet seats.
[c] Communist, left socialist, and social democratic parties hold a majority of the cabinet seats.

* $p < 0.10$; ** $p < 0.05$.

events variables turn out to be insignificant, but we do find that conservative cabinets suffer under high inflation, and that terminal events associated with public opinion shocks depresses the electoral success of governing parties. (Note that these terminal events are identified independently of the electoral results, so that this finding is less obvious than it might seem.)

All in all, we find that no single block explains a very large share of the variance in electoral performance, but that our final, comprehensive models have decent explanatory power, given the variety of factors that may affect electoral performance (adjusted R^2 of .14–.15). These models certainly do much better than the control models in block one, which capture only spatio-temporal effects. Thus, our theoretically defined models add considerably to our understanding of variations in the electoral fate of European cabinets.

The next question is how much our approach contributes to the understanding of the electoral results of individual parties. Table 11.8 presents the results for the Prime Minister's party. The first block reports trends that are very consistent with those for the cabinet as a whole: electoral losses have on average tended to rise from decade to decade over the whole post-war period. Of the structural attributes in block 2, our findings suggest that only surplus majority status has a significant and negative effect on the electoral fortunes of the PM's party. It maintains its effect throughout the relevant specifications. Minimum winning cabinets also tend to do worse than minority cabinets, though not significantly so. Among the preference variables, polarization stands out as consistently positive and significant, which again is consistent with hypothesis 2. The variables capturing the bargaining environment do not in themselves have any effect on electoral change, and the explained variance of this model is zero. Among the institutional variables, semi-presidentialism is the only one that makes it into the final specification. PM parties in semi-presidential systems seem to do considerably worse than others.

The critical events variables form a much more powerful block. The explained variance of this block alone is a respectable .14. Only one of the economic indicators has any significant impact by itself, namely the Gross Domestic Product (GDP), which has a positive effect on the electoral result of the PM's party. In addition, the interaction between conservative governments and inflation is consistently significant and in the expected direction. When conservative parties hold the premiership and encounter inflation, they stand to lose substantially. The estimated effect of critical events indicates that the PM's party suffers from cabinet terminations that are caused by economic events or, more strongly so, popular opinion shocks.

In sum, the results for the PM's party are stronger than those for the cabinet as a whole, with an adjusted explained variance of .27. This may suggest that the party holding the flagship position is singled out for particular accountability by the voters. The previous tables also confirm the results from the previous analyses; the economic variables are important for the electoral results of incumbent cabinets.

TABLE 11.8. *OLS regressions on PM party's electoral performance*

Independent variables	Model 1	Model 2	Model 3	Model 4	Model 5	Model 6	Model 7	Model 8
Time								
1940s	0.51(1.37)							
1960s	−1.12(1.02)							
1970s	−1.10(0.96)							
1980s	−2.25(0.95)**							
1990s	−2.96(1.02)**						−0.63(0.87)	
Austria	−2.01(1.56)						−1.41(1.05)	−1.76(0.80)**
Belgium	−2.47(1.33)*							
Denmark	0.28(1.50)							
Finland	−2.30(1.29)*							
France	−3.67(1.64)**							
Greece	2.17(4.64)							
Iceland	0.16(1.40)							
Ireland	−2.44(1.81)							
Italy	−1.79(1.29)							
Luxembourg	−3.93(1.57)**							
The Netherlands	−0.99(1.39)							
Norway	−1.66(1.97)							
Portugal	−11.91(3.36)**							
Sweden	−2.26(1.98)							
Structure								
Absolute no. parl. parties		0.12(0.15)					0.17(0.12)	0.21(0.11)*
Bargaining power fragmentation		0.20(0.32)						
Cabinet seat share		0.02(0.03)						
Number of cabinet parties		0.48(0.49)						
Minimum winning coalition		−0.96(0.99)						
Surplus majority cabinet		−2.71(1.25)**					−1.55(0.81)*	−1.49(0.73)**
Preferences								
Extremist party seat share			−0.02(0.03)					
Polarization (BP weighted)			0.10(0.04)**				0.12(0.04)**	0.12(0.04)**
Cabinet preference range			−0.02(0.02)				0.00(0.02)	

	(1)	(2)	(3)	(4)	(5)	(6)	(7)	(8)
Median Party (1st dim.) in cab.		0.68 (0.89)				0.64 (1.16)		0.86 (1.02)
Conservative cab.		−0.69 (0.88)						
Socialist cab.		−0.21 (0.85)						
Institutions								
List PR			−0.32 (1.10)			0.21 (1.38)		
Bicameralism			−1.43 (0.67)**			−0.43 (0.88)		
PM powers			−0.15 (0.17)					
PM dissolution powers			−1.08 (0.76)					
Semi-presidentialism			−2.25 (0.91)**			−1.63 (1.04)		−1.56 (0.79)**
Bargaining								
Comprehensive policy agreement				−0.76 (0.65)		−0.59 (0.70)		
Coalition discipline in legislation				−0.47 (0.55)				
Relative cab. duration				0.06 (0.94)				
Early election (no conflict)				1.32 (1.04)		0.97 (0.96)		
Critical events								
Unemployment (end)					−0.08 (0.08)	−0.05 (0.10)		
Inflation (end)					0.04 (0.03)	0.09 (0.03)**	0.04 (0.03)	
Growth (end)					0.17 (0.10)*	0.21 (0.11)*	0.21 (0.09)**	
Conservative cab. × inflation					−0.22 (0.08)**	−0.35 (0.10)**	−0.29 (0.10)**	
Socialist cab. × unemployment					0.11 (0.13)			
Terminal events: Opinion shock					−9.15 (2.26)**	−9.35 (2.17)**	−10.37 (2.16)**	
Terminal events: Security					1.93 (1.76)	−1.54 (1.29)		
Terminal events: Economic					−2.78 (1.31)**			
Constant	1.97 (1.17)*	−3.76 (2.03)*	−2.42 (1.07)**	1.22 (1.51)	0.10 (1.26)	−1.32 (0.74)*	−3.36 (2.26)	−4.33 (1.08)**
Number of observations	234	234	231	234	234	204	202	204
Adjusted R^2	.08	.02	.01	.02	.00	.14	.27	.21

Note: Figures are unstandardized regression coefficients.

[a] Germany has been used as the reference category, and Greece has been taken out of the analysis, since we lack the economic indicators for this country.

[b] Conservative and liberal parties hold a majority of the cabinet seats.

[c] Communist, left socialist, and social democratic parties hold a majority of the cabinet seats.

* $p < 0.10$; ** $p < 0.05$.

TABLE 11.9. *OLS regressions on finance minister's party's electoral performance*

Independent variables	Model 1	Model 2	Model 3	Model 4	Model 5	Model 6	Model 7	Model 8
Time								
1940s	1.52 (1.44)							
1960s	−1.21 (1.02)							
1970s	−0.88 (0.97)							
1980s	−2.02 (0.95)**						−0.77 (0.90)	
1990s	−2.38 (1.03)**						−1.36 (1.12)	
Austria	0.26 (1.66)							
Belgium	−2.04 (1.32)							
Denmark	0.16 (1.48)							
Finland	−1.00 (1.27)							
France	−0.22 (1.52)							
Greece	1.49 (3.32)							
Iceland	−0.81 (1.39)							
Ireland	−3.08 (1.80)*							
Italy	−1.09 (1.34)							
Luxembourg	−3.33 (1.56)**							
The Netherlands	0.09 (1.38)							
Norway	−3.24 (1.95)*							
Portugal	−7.56 (4.61)							
Sweden	−1.54 (1.96)							
Structure								
Absolute no. parl. parties		0.18 (0.15)						
Bargaining power fragmentation		−0.10 (0.32)						
Cabinet seat share		0.03 (0.03)					0.14 (0.12)	
Number of cabinet parties		0.11 (0.48)						
Minimum winning coalition		−0.88 (0.97)						
Surplus majority cabinet		−1.34 (1.25)					−0.94 (0.74)	
Preferences								
Extremist party seat share			0.03 (0.03)					
Polarization (BP weighted)			0.04 (0.04)					
Cabinet preference range			−0.01 (0.02)					

Variable	(1)	(2)	(3)	(4)	(5)	(6)	(7)	(8)
Median Party (1st dim.) in cab.		0.76 (0.85)					2.54 (1.11)**	1.35 (0.98)
Conservative cab.		−0.07 (0.82)					0.88 (1.44)	
Socialist cab.		0.62 (0.83)						
Institutions								
List PR			0.05 (1.08)					
Bicameralism			−0.17 (0.66)					
PM powers			−0.08 (0.17)					
PM dissolution powers			−0.88 (0.75)					
Semi-presidentialism			−0.04 (0.87)					
Bargaining								
Comprehensive policy agreement					−1.42 (0.63)**		−1.17 (0.70)*	−1.35 (0.60)**
Coalition discipline in legislation					−0.55 (0.51)			
Relative cab. duration					0.57 (0.91)		0.59 (0.99)	
Early election (no conflict)					−0.53 (0.97)			
Critical events								
Unemployment (end)						−0.02 (0.08)	0.02 (0.11)	
Inflation (end)						0.05 (0.03)	0.07 (0.03)**	0.06 (0.03)*
Growth (end)						0.25 (0.11)**	0.15 (0.12)	
Conservative cab. × inflation						−0.22 (0.08)**	−0.34 (0.10)**	−0.28 (0.09)**
Socialist cab. × unemployment						0.07 (0.12)	0.06 (0.24)	
Terminal events: Opinion shock						−10.39 (2.53)**	−10.16 (2.53)**	−10.61 (2.48)**
Terminal events: Security						1.55 (1.82)	−3.66 (1.43)**	−1.96 (1.24)
Terminal events: Economic						−3.11 (1.36)**	−2.14 (1.50)	
Constant	0.91 (0.17)	−3.22 (2.00)	−2.59 (1.03)**	−0.71 (1.51)	0.40 (1.20)	−1.75 (0.79)**	−2.14 (1.50)	−0.44 (0.56)
Number of observations	229	229	228	229	229	197	197	217
Adjusted R^2	.03	−.01	−.01	−.01	.01	.14	.17	.12

Note: Figures are unstandardized regression coefficients.

[a] Germany has been used as the reference category, and Greece has been taken out of the analysis, since we lack the economic indicators for this country.

[b] Conservative and liberal parties hold a majority of the cabinet seats.

[c] Communist, left socialist, and social democratic parties hold a majority of the cabinet seats.

* $p < 0.10$; ** $p < 0.05$.

Finally, then, we examine the electoral fortune of the Finance Minister's party. Can we trace a particularly significant effect of the economic indicators on the party in charge of the economy? Table 11.9 presents the electoral results for the party of the Minister of Finance. In short, the results for this party are considerably weaker. Apart from the critical events block, we find no consistently significant results, except that comprehensive policy agreements curiously seem to hurt the Finance Minister's party. Not even the fixed effects for decades hold up in this case. Only the macroeconomic and critical events variables are important for the electoral fate of this party. In the initial block estimates, the Finance Minister's party is slightly rewarded for economic (GDP) growth, but this effect is not robust to specifications. Consistently with the previous models, high inflation rates are associated with poor electoral performance for the party responsible for the economy, but only when the government has a 'rightist' majority. In addition, terminal events generally depress the electoral fortunes of the Finance Minister's party. Yet, the explained variance does not go beyond .17 in any of the specifications, and it is almost entirely due to the critical events variables.

CONCLUDING DISCUSSION

Votes, office, and policy influences are goals that most parties seek to achieve. At first, we would think of such goals as complementary and reinforcing: winning enough votes enables a party to gain office and the opportunity to implement good policies which, in turn, may lead to even more votes. In practice, however, it appears that these goals are almost independent and sometimes conflicting: winning office may force a party to make unpopular decisions, which may in turn decrease its vote share. In this chapter, and consistent with results from previous research, we have seen that cabinets indeed have good reason to fear such incumbency costs. Our main concern has been to define under which circumstances the price for governing is particularly high.

Initially, we specified several hypotheses for defining such circumstances, which are all related to the clarity of responsibility of the incumbents. We expected governments consisting of several parties to do better than single-party governments. We also anticipated that other structural attributes and institutions might play a role. We anticipated that the electoral fate of incumbents would be systematically related to macroeconomic conditions. Here, we expected the incumbent governments to do worse when the economy is poor, and to do better when it is good. And we expected the 'wear and tear' on parties in office to be negatively correlated with cabinet duration; hence, the longer the duration of the cabinet, the more likely it is that it will lose votes. In terms of electoral performance, therefore, incumbents will benefit from early elections. How much support have we received for our hypotheses? Let us sum up the most important results before discussing their implications. We will start with the results for all cabinets jointly.

- We find no direct support for the hypothesis that cabinets consisting of several parties will do better than single-party governments. Rather, the negative effect of an increasing share of seats indicates a 'mechanic' effect of size itself: the more you have—the more there is to lose.
- Voters tend to be less hard on incumbents when there are no good alternatives. The greater the fragmentation of the bargaining environment, the better the performance of the incumbents.
- As expected, the economic variables are clearly related to gains and losses of incumbent parties. Cabinets lose much more in poor economic times than they do when the economy is good. But not all cabinet parties suffer alike. Our results consistently show that conservative parties are much more susceptible to inflation than leftist parties are to unemployment.
- Our hypothesis that incumbents will benefit from early elections is partly supported by the data. The results indicate that incumbent vulnerability increases with time, and that cabinets benefit from early elections.

The described tendencies concern all incumbent parties. The results for the Prime Minister's party and the party of the Minister of Finance add some more information to the picture.

- The party of the PM is clearly affected by the structural variables, primarily by the polarization of the parties in parliament and structural cabinet characteristics. Parties holding the prime ministership in oversized coalitions also do particularly poorly.
- The impact of the structural variables is less pronounced for the party of the Minister of Finance. Only the effective number of parties has a positive effect.
- As expected, the party of the Minister of Finance is affected most severely by the macroeconomic variables, particularly inflation, but also the ideological composition of the government is of relevance. The combination of a rightist profile and inflation has a significant and negative impact upon the electoral result of the party of the Minister of Finance.
- Neither the duration of the cabinet nor early elections are significantly related to the electoral performance of the PM's party or the party of the Minister of Finance. Only critical events affect these parties in a negative direction.

The analyses reveal that we are faced with some very complex relationships. In general, these results suggest that the strongest effects are found in the most proximate circumstances surrounding the election, that is, in terminal events and macroeconomic conditions. Institutions and structural attributes generally matter less. These results may not tell the whole story, but we end our discussion on three observations.

The first has to do with the impact of the economy. The ancient Norse sagas tell us that the Vikings killed their king in times of poor harvest. When times were prosperous, however, they would reward him. The data presented here suggest a similar tendency, although 'punishments' and 'rewards' are of a much less dramatic nature. The fact that the party holding the portfolio of the Minister of Finance is most severely affected by the economic conditions indicates that voters are likely to hold this party accountable for the economic performance of the cabinet. This portfolio includes economic priorities, and thus renders it particularly vulnerable to economic fluctuations. This finding is consistent with the grievance-asymmetry hypothesis (or a negative bias in the electorate), stating that voters are particularly alert to economic troubles (see, e.g., Dorussen and Palmer 2002: 10).

It is somewhat surprising that the incumbent parties do not fare better in times of economic growth and prosperity. One reason could be the saliency of other types of issues in the election. In 'good' times voters may take the economy for granted, and this makes way for non-economic issues on the political agenda. In addition, there is the possibility that good economic development over a longer period creates expectations among the voters that are almost impossible to meet. By most objective economic measures, affluence has increased in the Western world over the last few decades and the standard of living has improved (Dalton 2004). It could be that the policy performance of the government is falling short of voters' expectations, simply because they expect governments to 'deliver' even more than they already do in terms of welfare, education, and other types of benefits when the economy is good, whereas these types of expectations are not salient in times of economic recession. We are not in a position to elaborate on these matters in the present chapter, but they are worthwhile pursuing in future research.

Our second observation concerns the electoral advantages of early elections. The benefit of early elections is not a general phenomenon, but restricted to situations in which there are conflicts between parties or defeats in parliament. This tendency suggests that the strategic timing of elections is important, and that incumbent parties would sometimes benefit from a competitive strategy rather than further compromising when conflicts arise.

Finally, we have seen that governing parties considered collectively tend to lose votes, and that their average losses have become progressively larger over the last few decades. The fact that electoral losses have increased so significantly over the years adds a new dimension to the analyses of voter volatility. It indicates that voters have become more prone to let frustrations over public policy hit the government per se, irrespective of party affiliations. This, in turn, means that incumbency liabilities are a more crucial aspect in the trade-off considerations that the parties must make between office, policy, and votes.

The analysis presented in this chapter concerns a topic that has been debated ever since the introduction of popular elections. Public support is the 'currency' of political parties, and is one of the most important factors determining their strength and credibility at the bargaining table. Coalition decisions are often constrained by the electoral considerations of individual parties. The electoral result of incumbents is normally interpreted as the electorate's reactions to government performance. In a two-party system the question of 'credit' and 'blame' for policy performance is fairly easy and straightforward. In a multiparty coalition system, however, it is much more complex. Even so, this chapter has shown some systematic ways in which voters respond to parliamentary governments and the parties that control them. Once the results are in, the politicians update their beliefs and expectations, go back to the bargaining table, and the life cycle of democratic politics begins anew.

REFERENCES

Aardal, Bernt and Listhaug, Ola (1986). *Economic Factors and Voting Behavior in Norway 1965–1985*, Working Paper no. 4. Oslo: Institute for Social Research.
—— and Valen, Henry (1997). 'The Storting Election of 1989 and 1993: Norwegian Politics in Perspective', in Kaare Strøm and Lars Svåsand (eds.), *Challenges to Political Parties*. Ann Arbor, MI: Michigan University Press.
Anderson, Christopher (1995a). 'Party Systems and the Dynamics of Government Support', *European Journal of Political Research*, 27: 93–118.
—— (1995b). 'The Dynamics of Public Support for Coalition Governments', *Comparative Political Studies*, 28: 350–83.
—— (2000). 'Economic Voting and Political Context: A Comparative Perspective', *Electoral Studies*, 19: 151–70.
Austen-Smith, David and Banks, Jeffrey S. (1988). 'Elections, Coalitions and Legislative Outcomes', *American Political Science Review*, 82: 405–22.
Bengtsson, Åsa (2004). 'Economic Voting: The Effect of Political Context, Volatility, and Turnout on Voters' Assignment of Responsibility', *European Journal of Political Research*, 43: 749–67.
Black, Duncan (1958). *The Theory of Committees and Elections*. Cambridge: Cambridge University Press.
Budge, Ian and Farlie, Dennis (1983). *Voting and Party Competition*. London: Wiley.
Butler, David and Stokes, Donald (1969). *Political Change in Britain: The Evolution of Electoral Choice*. London: Macmillan.
—— (1974). *Political Change in Britain: The Evolution of Electoral Choice*, Second edn. London: Macmillan.
Crewe, Ivor and Denver, David (1985). 'Conclusion', in Ivor Crewe and David Denver (eds.), *Electoral Change in Western Democracies. Patterns and Sources of Electoral Volatility*. London: Croom Helm.
Cronin, Thomas E. (1980). *The State of the Presidency*. Boston, MA: Little, Brown.
Daalder, Hans (1984). 'In Search for the Center of European Party Systems', *American Political Science Review*, 78: 92–109.

Dahl, Robert (ed.) (1966). *Political Opposition in Western Democracies*. New Haven, CT: Yale University Press.

Dalton, Russell J. (2004). *Democratic Challenges. Democratic Choices*. Oxford: Oxford University Press.

——and Wattenberg, Martin P. (eds.) (2000). *Parties without Partisans*. Oxford: Oxford University Press.

——Flanagan, Scott C., and Beck, Paul A. (eds.) (1984). *Electoral Change in Advanced Industrial Democracies. Realignment or Dealignment?* Princeton, NJ: Princeton University Press.

De Swaan, Abram (1982). 'The Netherlands: Coalitions in a Segmented Polity', in Eric C. Browne and John Drejmanis (eds.), *Government Coalitions in Western Democracies*. New York, NY: Longman.

Dorussen, Han and Palmer, Harvey D. (2002). 'The Context of Economic Voting: An Introduction', in Han Dorussen and Michaell Taylor (eds.), *Economic Voting*. London: Routledge.

——and Taylor, Michaell (eds.) (2002). *Economic Voting*. London: Routledge.

Downs, Anthony (1957). *An Economic Theory of Democracy*. New York, NY: Harper & Brothers.

Duverger, Maurice (1954). *Political Parties: Their Organization and Activity in the Modern State*. London: Methuen.

Enelow, James and Hinich, Melvin J. (1984). *The Spatial Theory of Voting. An Introduction*. Cambridge: Cambridge University Press.

Eulau, Heinz and Lewis-Beck, Michael (1985). *Economic Conditions and Electoral Outcomes in the United States and Western Europe*. New York, NY: Agathon.

Epstein, Leon D. (1967). *Political Parties in Western Democracies*. New York, NY: Praeger.

Fiorina, Morris P. (1981). *Retrospective Voting in American National Elections*. New Haven, CT: Yale University Press.

——(1997). 'Voting Behavior', in Dennis C. Mueller (ed.), *Perspectives on Public Choice: A Handbook*. Cambridge: Cambridge University Press.

Harrop, Martin and Miller, William L. (1987). *Elections and Voters*. London: Macmillan.

Hazan, Reuven Y. (1996). 'Does the Center Equal Middle?' *Party Politics*, 2: 209–28.

——(1997). *Centre Parties. Polarization and Competition in European Parliamentary Democracies*. London: Pinter.

Hibbs, Douglas A. (1977). 'Political Parties and Macroeconomic Policy', *American Political Science Review*, 71: 1467–87.

Irwin, Galen and van Holsteyn, Joop (1989). 'Towards a More Open Model of Competition', *West European Politics*, 12: 112–38.

Laver, Michael and Budge, Ian (eds.) (1992). *Party Policy and Government Coalitions*. New York, NY: St. Martin's Press.

——and Schofield, Norman (1990). *Multiparty Government*. Oxford: Oxford University Press.

——and Shepsle, Kenneth (1990). 'Coalitions and Cabinet Government', *American Political Science Review*, 84: 873–90.

————(1996). *Making and Breaking Governments: Cabinets and Legislatures in Parliamentary Democracies*. New York: Cambridge University Press.

Lewin, Leif (1991). *Self-Interest and Public Interest in Western Politics*. New York, NY: Oxford University Press.
Lewis-Beck, Michael (1986). 'Comparative Economic Voting: Britain, France, Germany, Italy', *American Journal of Political Science*, 30: 315–46.
—— (1988). *Economics and Elections: The Major Western Democracies*. Ann Arbor, MI: University of Michigan Press.
—— (1991). 'Introduction', in Helmut Norpoth, Michael Lewis-Beck, and Jean-Dominique Lafay (eds.), *Economics and Politics: The Calculus of Support*. Ann Arbor: University of Michigan Press.
—— and Paldam, Martin (2000). 'Economic Voting: An Introduction'. *Electoral Studies* 19: 113–21.
Listhaug, Ola, Macdonald, Stuart E., and Rabinowitz, George (1990). 'A Comparative Spatial Analysis of European Party Systems', *Scandinavian Political Studies*, 13: 227–54.
Lupia, Arthur and Strøm, Kaare (1995). 'Coalition Termination and the Strategic Timing of Elections', *American Political Science Review*, 89: 648–65.
Macdonald, Stuart E., Listhaug, Ola, and Rabinowitz, George (1991). 'Issues and Party Support in Multiparty Systems', *American Political Science Review*, 85: 1108–31.
—— Rabinowitz, George, and Listhaug, Ola (1998). 'On Attempting to Rehabilitate the Proximity Model: Sometimes the Patient Just Can't Be Helped', *Journal of Politics*, 60: 653–90.
Miller, Arthur and Listhaug, Ola (1985). 'Economic Effects on the Vote in Norway', in Heinz Eulau and Michael Lewis-Beck (eds.), *Economic Conditions and Electoral Outcomes*. New York, NY: Agathon Press.
Müller, Wolfgang C. and Strøm, Kaare (eds.) (1999). *Policy, Office or Votes?* Cambridge: Cambridge University Press.
———— (eds.) (2000). *Coalition Governments in Western Europe*. Oxford: Oxford University Press.
Narud, Hanne Marthe (1996a). 'Party Policies and Government Accountability: A Comparison between the Netherlands and Norway', *Party Politics*, 2: 479–507.
—— (1996b). 'Electoral Competition and Coalition Bargaining in Multi-Party Systems', *Journal of Theoretical Politics*, 8: 499–525.
—— and Irwin, Galen A. (1994). 'Must the Breaker Pay? Cabinet Crises and Electoral Trade-offs', *Acta Politica*, 29: 265–84.
Pacek, Alexander C. and Radcliff, Benjamin (1999). 'Economics and the Left Party Vote in Scandinavia: A Cross-National Analysis'. *Scandinavian Political Studies*, 22: 295–306.
Paldam, Martin (1981). 'A Preliminary Survey of the Theories and Findings on Vote and Popularity Functions', *European Journal of Political Research*, 9: 181–200.
Pedersen, Mogens (1983). 'Changing Patterns of Electoral Volatility in European Party Systems; 1948–1977', in Hans Daalder and Peter Mair (eds.), *Western European Party Systems: Continuity and Change*. London: Sage.
Petrocik, John R. (1996). 'Issue Ownership in Presidential Elections, with a 1980 Case Study', *American Journal of Political Science*, 40: 825–50.
Polsby, Nelson and Wildavsky, Aron (1980). *Presidential Elections*. New York, NY: Charles Scribner's Sons.

Powell, G. Bingham (1981). 'Party Systems as Systems of Representation and Accountability', Paper prepared for presentation at the Annual Meeting of the American Political Science Association, New York, 3–6 September.

—— and Whitten, Guy D. (1993). 'A Cross National Analysis of Economic Voting: Taking Account of the Political Context', *American Journal of Political Science*, 37: 391–414.

Rabinowitz, George and Macdonald, Stuart E. (1989). 'A Directional Theory of Issue Voting', *American Political Science Review*, 83: 93–121.

Rose, Richard and Mackie, Thomas (1983). 'Incumbency in Government: Asset or Liability', in Hans Daalder and Peter Mair (eds.), *Western European Party Systems: Continuity and Change*. London: Sage.

Rosenstone, Steven (1995). 'Electoral Institutions and Democratic Choice', Paper presented at the workshop on 'The Impact of Institutional Arrangements on Electoral Behaviour', ECPR Joint Sessions of Workshops, Bordeaux, April 27–May 2.

Sartori, Giovanni (1976). *Parties and Party Systems: A Framework for Analysis*. Cambridge: Cambridge University Press.

Schattschneider, E. E. (1942). *Party Government*. New York, NY: Farrar and Rinehart.

Schneider, F. (1984). 'Public Attitudes towards Economic Conditions and Their Impact on Government Behavior', *Political Behavior*, 6: 211–27.

Strøm, Kaare (1984). 'Minority Governments in Parliamentary Democracies', *Comparative Political Studies*, 17: 199–227.

—— (1985). 'Party Goals and Government Performance in Parliamentary Democracies'. *American Political Science Review*, 79: 738–54.

—— (1990*a*). 'A Behavioral Theory of Competitive Political Parties', *American Journal of Political Science*, 34: 565–98.

—— (1990*b*). *Minority Government and Majority Rule*. Cambridge: Cambridge University Press.

—— and Swindle, Stephen M. (2002). 'Strategic Parliamentary Dissolution', *American Political Science Review*, 96: 575–91.

Warwick, Paul (1994). *Government Survival in Parliamentary Democracies*. Cambridge: Cambridge University Press.

12

Conclusion: Cabinet Governance in Parliamentary Democracies

Kaare Strøm, Torbjörn Bergman, Wolfgang C. Müller, and Benjamin Nyblade

INTRODUCTION

The previous eight chapters have provided an analysis of the various phases of what we have called the life cycle of cabinet-level politics in Western European parliamentary democracies. This is a subject of no mean importance, since parliamentary government is the most common form of democratic governance and indeed the type of regime under which approximately one-third of the world's population lives. No other type of political regime, presidential, military, communist, or whatever, shapes the daily lives of similar numbers of human beings.

There are many important and distinctive aspects of parliamentary governance, but cabinet governance is surely at the heart of policymaking in parliamentary democracies. This is because parliamentary systems rely so heavily on delegation of authority to elected representatives of the people, and because the typical chain of delegation in parliamentary democracies is so singular, with the preponderance of formal decision-making power vested in the members of the national parliament. Moreover, the most distinctive feature of parliamentary democracy is that this national parliament directly controls who holds the chief executive offices: the prime ministership and the rest of the cabinet portfolios.

While parliamentary democracy is found in many parts of Asia as well as in some African nations and in Commonwealth countries across the world, Western Europe is still its heartland. As noted in Chapter 1, parliamentary democracy comes in a majoritarian as well as a proportional version. In Western Europe, the proportional type has become by far the dominant form. Because proportional systems rarely reward any party with a parliamentary majority, this form of government depends on and is conducive to inter-party bargaining over high stakes. The most critical contestation is for control of the executive branch of government, represented at its apex by the cabinet. It is therefore no surprise that this topic has become a significant concern among students of politics.

This book is a contribution to the study of government coalition bargaining in parliamentary democracies, and it is a contribution in which we present a particular framework within which many different aspects of cabinet and coalition politics can be understood: a cyclical process defined by the accountability of politicians to their democratic principal, the citizens. Since the 1970s coalition research has been criticized as treating all of the different episodes of coalition formation (to which most studies confined themselves) as isolated, mutually independent events, rather than viewing them within the context of previous coalition formations and the satisfaction the parties derived from these experiences. In Michael Laver's words (1974: 259), '(i)t is not true...that the slate is wiped clean after every election, with parties searching for coalition partners as if the political world had just been created.' Yet, not much research has followed from this observation (see, however, Franklin and Mackie 1983).

In this volume, we have given expression to this insight through a conception of coalition politics as a sequence of mutually interdependent stages of bargaining and decision-making. This is what we call the coalition cycle or, more generally, the democratic life cycle, as illustrated in Chapter 1. In this coalition cycle, each stage is influenced by the preceding ones and, in turn, each stage affects all future ones.

The life cycle of coalition politics begins and ends with popular elections. It does so in the literal sense that these are the decisive events around which parliamentary political life is centred, and it does so in the more figurative sense that elections tend to shape the behaviour of politicians in all their various political games and activities. But the parliamentary life cycle also implies that the different phases of parliamentary politics are interdependent, so that no part of the political process can be understood except in recognition of the events that have gone before it as well as those that are expected to follow. And finally, the parliamentary life cycle means that politics is cyclical, that there are events that typically and regularly repeat themselves, never exactly or in the form of predestination, but nevertheless in recognizable and predictable ways.

As Chapter 1 points out, our ambition in this volume has been to enhance our knowledge through better theory, better data, and better methods. Our theoretical agenda is anchored in our conception of the life cycle of parliamentary politics. Through this simple lens, we can more easily appreciate the roles of the shadow of the past, as well as the promise of the future, in coalition politics. This approach also helps us understand why coalition bargaining in parliamentary democracies is both critical and difficult, and why our conception of that bargaining must recognize that politicians necessarily face substantial uncertainties, risks, constraints, and transaction costs. As the various chapters have shown, these complexities systematically affect coalition bargaining and parliamentary decision-making in a variety of ways.

We have contributed to the development of better data in several different ways. One problem with cross-national studies of coalition politics is that they have tended to recycle the same data on post-Second World War parliamentary democracies. We have sought to go beyond this sample in several ways, for example, by including coalitional systems (such as Iceland and Portugal) that are often not included in such projects. More importantly perhaps, we have added to our sample more majoritarian parliamentary democracies (such as Greece, Spain, and the United Kingdom) in which cabinet coalitions are not common. This broader sample has helped give us a broader comparison set and to avoid certain kinds of selection bias in the study of parliamentary cabinets. We have also improved on existing studies by adding a broad range of institutional and historical variables. In particular we have been able to draw on new data that fill the gap between coalition formation and coalition termination and detail the constitutional and societal context of this bargaining (Müller and Strøm 2000; Strøm, Müller, and Bergman 2003).

We believe that our data are not only more comprehensive but also better and more reliable than in most previous studies of this kind. In our analysis, we have employed a variety of data-sets that have become standard sources in the field. But to a large extent, the data presented and analysed here have been collected and generated by our own contributors. As we pointed out in Chapter 1, we have gone through much painstaking work in order to ensure that these data both reflect the insights of the country specialists and are truly comparable. Our contributors are not just 'country experts', but also specialists in coalition studies. They have published most of the data employed here under their own names (see chapters in Müller and Strøm 2000; Strøm, Müller, and Bergman 2003; Indridason 2005) and hence have tied their professional reputations to the quality of the data.

While this is not a project that has sought to push the frontiers of social science methods, we have deliberately aimed to avail ourselves of the rich tool kit of statistical methods that has become available to students of parliamentary politics. This has allowed us to examine a variety of data with methods that are appropriate for their particular purposes. Our methods include qualitative historical case studies such as in Chapter 8, since we believe that they can serve important purposes in coalition research, particularly in fields in which our knowledge is still preliminary and incomplete, and where precise data may be hard to find.

Yet, most analyses in this book have employed a more extensive design and quantitative methods. Our specific methodological approach—cross-sectional analysis of pooled data covering the various stages of the democratic life cycle in both coalition and single-party government systems—is not the only possible choice. We do hope that the theoretical ideas and empirical results of the present volume will encourage both case study research and rigorous game-theoretical modelling. For example, two of our most interesting findings, the strategic importance of prime ministerial powers and the fact that variables derived from constitutional design (institutions) are more important during coalition governance than at the formation and termination stages of coalition bargaining, are precisely the sorts of results that lend themselves to such further research.

DYNAMIC COALITION RESEARCH: RESULTS

We will return to these broader questions in the concluding sections of this chapter. Before that, however, we shall summarize the rich empirical results that this study has generated. While each chapter summarizes its own results, it is worth taking some time here to briefly consider their respective conclusions. Since our idea of a life cycle of democratic politics suggests that the different phases of coalition politics should be systematically interrelated, it is also worth dwelling on how our results compare across chapters. Moreover, it behooves us to compare the contributions of each of the blocks of independent variables on which we have relied in our analysis. Table 12.1 provides a summary of the results from the final statistical models from every full set of analyses. Rather than list every coefficient considered or even every variable found to be significant, the table instead simply reports whether in the final model particular types of variables significantly contribute to the explanation of each of the various stages of the life cycle of cabinet governance.

A quick glance at Table 12.1 suggests several noteworthy findings that hold up across the various analyses in this volume. First, it is clear that, consistently with the expectations discussed in Chapter 2, none of the outcomes in which we are interested can be explained solely by a single cluster of explanatory factors, or even by a combination of two such clusters. It is simply not the case that preferences, structural factors, or institutions alone can explain cabinet governance. In order to explain any one of the various phases of coalition politics, it is quite clearly necessary to consider variables such as preferences, structural factors, or institutions in conjunction with relevant endogenous and exogenous factors, such as prior bargaining outcomes and critical events in the cabinet's political environment, that also influence the bargaining environment.

To scholars in the field it may come as no surprise that as we look across the cabinet life cycle, attributes such as the size and seat share of parties, the preferences of those parties, and the institutional rules of the game consistently help explain the variation in cabinet governance in Western Europe. It may be more surprising, however, that the vast bulk of our analyses also find that prior cabinet features and/or prior bargaining outcomes have a robust impact on cabinet governance, suggesting that the shadow of the past affects a wide range of governance decisions in parliamentary democracies. But such political decisions are not simply coloured by past experiences, they are also conditioned by exogenous forces in the political environment. Thus, our results show that various exogenous factors such as critical events, electoral volatility, and economic performance influence not only cabinet durability, but most other stages of cabinet governance as well.

TABLE 12.1. *Core results*

Type of variable	4.5	4.6	5.11	6.4	6.5	7.2	7.6	7.8	8.3	8.4	9.6	10.4	11.7	11.8	11.9
Timing of cabinet formation	x								x						
Parliamentary party structure	x	x	x	x	x	x	x					x	x	x	
Cabinet structural features					x	x	x			x	x	x	x	x	
Parliamentary party preferences	x	x	x	x	x	x		x	x	x	x	x		x	
Cabinet preferences						x	x		x		x	x	x		
Legislative institutions		x	x	x	x	x	x	x			x	x			
Legislative–executive institutions		x	x	x	x	x	x	x	x	x	x				
Executive institutions	x		x	x	x		x		x			x		x	
Prior cabinet features	x			x	x	x									
Prior bargaining outcomes				x	x			x	x	x	x	x	x		
Terminal events	x			x						x					
Electoral volatility												x	x	x	x
Economic factors				x			x					x	x	x	x

Notes: Variables are grouped by block and type of variable within block. Numbers refer to the table which reports the statistical results for that independent variable. An x marks when at least one variable of a type is significant in the final model. *Legislative* institutions include Bicameralism, Opposition Influence, and List PR. *Legislative–executive* institutions include Positive Parliamentarism and an Absolute majority requirement for no confidence votes. *Executive* institutions include PM cabinet power, PM dissolution power, and Semi-presidentialism.

Dependent Variables
4.5 Inconclusive bargaining round
4.6 Cabinet formation duration
5.11 Written coalition agreement
6.4 Coalition formation
6.5 Type of government
7.2 Cabinet disproportionality index
7.6 Number of cabinet ministers
7.8 Watchdog junior ministers
8.3 Most commonly used conflict management arena
8.4 Arena for most serious conflicts
9.6 Type of government termination
10.4 Cabinet durability
11.7 Cabinet electoral performance
11.8 PM party's electoral performance
11.9 Finance minister's party's electoral performance

Coalition bargaining and formation

Let us now briefly discuss the major findings of each chapter in turn. In Chapter 4, the first empirical chapter, De Winter and Dumont examine the process that leads up to the formation of a new cabinet. Specifically, they look for determinants of two important aspects of this process: the duration of the cabinet formation process and the incidence of 'hiccups', more precisely inconclusive bargaining rounds. Empirically, their results underscore the importance of political institutions that have not been properly appreciated in the previous literature. De Winter and Dumont highlight the importance of such institutional factors as prime ministerial power. Where the prime minister has the institutional power to control the cabinet's agenda and offer binding guidelines for the line ministers, there are few bargaining rounds. The same is true for semi-presidential systems in which the president can insert himself into the cabinet formation process. Where such conditions exist, there are also fewer bargaining rounds.

But institutions are not all that matters. Consistent with the existing literature on the topic, De Winter and Dumont find that cabinets that are formed immediately after an election are more likely to be preceded by inconclusive bargaining rounds than are those that are formed later in the parliamentary term. Inconclusive bargaining rounds are also more frequent when the parliamentary party system is more fragmented and when party competition takes place across cross-cutting dimensions of conflict. Finally, the critical events literature is corroborated at least in the sense that exogenous events sometimes complicate coalition bargaining. Specifically, when events associated with national security concerns impinge, it makes the bargaining process more likely to go awry, at least to the extent that it results in incomplete bargaining rounds.

The causes of a long formation period are similar. Interestingly, both the number of bargaining rounds and its duration have declined over time. The difference between the first post-war decades and the 1990s is particularly notable. In general, bargaining over government formation is also more protracted immediately after an election and when the parties can look forward to a significant period in office. A higher number of parties, party system fragmentation, and preference polarization (in the absence of a core party) have the same effect of prolonging the bargaining process. In contrast, when political competition occurs primarily along one dimension, when the PM can unilaterally call new elections, or when an elected president can intervene in the process, the formation period is shorter.

In sum, the success and speed of bargaining over cabinet formation are determined by a large number of factors, related both to actors' bargaining strength, to their preferences, and also to the bargaining environment. Yet, De Winter and Dumont find two explanatory clusters particularly powerful: preferences and structural attributes. They also conclude that in initial coalition bargaining, the complexity of the process seems to matter more than the uncertainty inherent in it.

Conclusion: Cabinet Governance in Parliamentary Democracies

Coalition agreements

Coalition parties sometimes forge specific and comprehensive governance agreements before they take office together. But while some coalitions of parties conclude such written agreements, others do not. Even when they do exist, coalition agreements vary greatly in their contents and comprehensiveness. In Chapter 5, Müller and Strøm analyse the causes of this variation.

Müller and Strøm argue that preference diversity, uncertainty, and the potential for opportunism create incentives for coalition partners to come to agreement on ground rules for governance before they go into coalition with one another. Uncertainty about the future and about what the other coalition partners will do once in office might linger even after the parties have agreed that they will try to form a new government. Such uncertainty is particularly troubling when the coalition members differ greatly in their preferences and when they have reason to fear opportunistic behaviour. Politicians know that governments make thousands of decisions and that monitoring in a coalition government can be a costly enterprise. On the other hand, transaction costs and audience costs may make it unattractive to invest in a formal agreement, and parties may be particularly unlikely to do so when the perceived value of the coalition is low.

The descriptive account shows a significant trend in coalition agreements over time, which is corroborated in the multivariate analysis. In recent decades, more cabinet coalitions have had an explicit and written initial coalition agreement. Müller and Strøm see such explicit agreements as a manifestation of coalition governance through *ex ante* means, which they contrast with an *ex post* control pattern typified by checks and balances such as 'watchdog' junior ministers. In this area, they detect a north–south pattern, in which a written agreement (*ex ante* control) is more prevalent in Northern Europe. In the south, parties are more inclined to rely on *ex post* control mechanisms. Both these findings are consistent with a path-dependency argument. National solutions, once adopted (and presumably found effective), have a tendency to be chosen over and over again. Specifically, where parties have come to rely on written coalition agreements, they tend to continue to produce such mechanisms of joint governance. Path dependence may in fact be driven by transaction costs and very likely is in this context. It is less costly to rely on mechanisms that have proven to work than to create new ones from scratch.

Yet the use of written coalition agreements is not simply explained by regional clusterings and temporal trends. When the number of parliamentary parties is large, when one party is close to the majority threshold, or when extremist parties are strong, the coalition partners are less likely to write a coalition agreement. More generally, when one party is in a dominant bargaining position, a written coalition agreement is less likely. This may be because the asymmetry of power is so great that weaker coalition partners are in no position to constrain the dominant party.

On the other hand, coalition contracts are particularly common when the median party on the left–right dimension is in the coalition and when there is no core party. Where several dimensions of political competition exist, parties that are in a favourable bargaining position along one but not all of these may use coalition agreements to try to neutralize issues that fall along dimensions on which their bargaining position is less advantageous. One common thread throughout these results is thus that coalition partners often commit to an agreement on policies and procedures for reasons of mutual insurance.

Cabinet type

In Chapter 6, Mitchell and Nyblade re-examine the questions of when coalitions form in the first place and specifically when minimal winning coalitions are likely to occur. In their pursuit of these theoretical questions, the authors go back to Riker's classic size principle (1962), on which they expand. The size principle predicts that under a specified set of assumptions, parties will form only minimal winning coalitions. In their set of corollaries, Mitchell and Nyblade build on this theory so as to predict that the more the bargaining situation differs from the assumptions of Riker's theory, the greater the likelihood that the cabinet will deviate from minimal winning size. Thus, the more restrictive the decision rule, the larger the coalition, the greater the information uncertainty, the more likely a surplus majority coalition, and the lower the value of being in government, the greater the probability of a minority government.

The second major theoretical concern guiding Mitchell and Nyblade's analysis has to do with the distribution of bargaining power among the parliamentary parties. The more dispersed this bargaining power, the more likely it is that a coalition (rather than a single-party government) will form, and the larger this coalition will tend to be.

Mitchell and Nyblade examine two cabinet outcomes: (*a*) whether or not a coalition is formed and (*b*) the type or numerical status of the cabinet (minority, MWC, or surplus majority). They find both of their major theoretical propositions corroborated. That is to say, the more the bargaining situation resembles the simplicities assumed in Riker's model, the more common minimal winning coalitions tend to be. And the greater the share of bargaining power that a single party possesses, the less likely we are to see cabinet coalitions.

As simple and gratifying as these results may sound, they do in fact imply that a wide range of variables affect the type of cabinet that is formed in parliamentary democracies. Thus, Mitchell and Nyblade find that variables from every one of our explanatory clusters have significant effects on the type of cabinet that forms. Consistent with prior scholarship, they report that party policy preferences and the distribution of seats in parliament matter, with coalitions being more likely

Conclusion: Cabinet Governance in Parliamentary Democracies 411

to form when the bargaining powers of the largest party and the median party are weak. Positive parliamentarianism (the requirement that an incoming cabinet must first win a majority vote in parliament) and semi-presidentialism both increase the likelihood of coalition formation, as each of these institutions provides incentives for coalitions, in the one case by raising the bar for a successful cabinet and in the other by allowing for presidential intervention. Other factors affect the likelihood of coalition formation by influencing the value of being a junior coalition partner relative to being in opposition. Coalitions are less likely to form when the prime minister is particularly powerful, when a critical event terminated the previous government, and when electoral volatility is high. Each of these conditions is likely to diminish the value of being a junior partner in government.

What explains the *type of government* (minority, MWC, or surplus coalition) formed? Again, Mitchell and Nyblade find that a wide range of variables that relate to bargaining strength help explain cabinet type. The greater the bargaining powers of the largest and median parties, the more likely a minority government will form. In the absence of a party at the dimension-by-dimension median, a minimal winning coalition is more likely. And the more the preferences of parliamentary parties are polarized, the less likely a surplus government. But not only the traditional structural and preference variables are significant explanatory factors. Prime ministerial cabinet powers, opposition influence, positive parliamentarism, and semi-presidentialism all influence the type of cabinet formed, as does the electoral environment and the circumstances of the previous government's termination. In sum, Mitchell and Nyblade's analysis shows that even when the larger causal story can be encapsulated in intriguingly simple and parsimonious theoretical terms, a large number of diverse features of the bargaining situation help us understand this basic puzzle of coalition politics.

Portfolio allocation

In Chapter 7, Verzichelli moves on to investigate the distribution of portfolios among the partners once a coalition cabinet has formed. This chapter utilizes our new data to examine a well-established finding: the proportionality norm, which implies that coalition parties obtain a share of the cabinet portfolios that is in strict proportion to the share of the parliamentary votes they bring to the coalition. Yet the chapter also expands on previous scholarship both by examining the number of portfolios created and by providing a look at how cabinet parties try to control ministerial 'dictators' by using 'watchdog' junior minsters from other coalition parties to monitor the senior ministers.

Verzichelli seeks first to identify and explain deviations from the proportionality norm. His multivariate analysis shows a tendency towards disproportionality in portfolio allocation when (*a*) one party is numerically dominant and/or (*b*) the median party is present in the cabinet. Political parties are much more likely to sustain the proportionality norm under a fragmented party system and when there is no median party on multiple dimensions. These results reinforce one of the main empirical lessons of this volume: the importance of strategic advantage (a high walk-away value). But these are not the only variables that promote disproportionality. Disproportionality is also associated with positive parliamentarism and with systems in which one parliamentary chamber is solely responsible for national legislation. Finally, disproportionality may emerge (or be exacerbated) when the coalition partners can count on disciplined and cohesive behaviour from their respective parliamentarians. All in all, structural attributes are the most potent cluster explaining disproportionality in portfolio allocation, whereas critical events seem to be of little discernible consequence.

In the long run, the number of ministerial portfolios is of course endogenous to the bargaining that goes on among the coalition parties, and Chapter 7 provides a novel analysis of the number of cabinet portfolios. Verzichelli's analysis suggests that when economic conditions (such as unemployment) are unfavourable, the coalition parties increase the number of portfolios to provide additional incentives for government participation. Economic growth, on the other hand, tends to decrease the number of portfolios. In a similar vein, electoral volatility also correlates positively with the number of cabinet ministers, as additional posts may be created to compensate for the risk of a serious downturn in popular approval.

Otherwise, the number of cabinet ministers has to do with institutional designs that do not change much over time. A larger number of seats in the parliament, which is strongly correlated with country size, can also lead to institutional pressures to provide more cabinet posts. The PM's powers over cabinet governance and parliamentary dissolution both matter, albeit in different ways. While centralized cabinet decision-making tends to lead to fewer ministers, the prime minister's power to dissolve parliament correlates positively with the number of cabinet ministers. One of the more significant findings, both statistically and substantively, is that the number of ministers also increases with the number of cabinet parties.

The third major theme in Verzichelli's analysis is the allocation of junior ministerships. As noted elsewhere in this volume, it is commonly argued that political parties use junior appointments to monitor ministries headed by their respective coalition partners. Our data show that such 'watchdog' ministers are used when the coalition parties expect to govern together for an extended period, when they decide that a written contract is needed, when there are significant policy differences between the parties with the most bargaining power (polarization), and when bicameralism adds a degree of complexity to the decision-making process. The practice tends to be less common under positive parliamentarism or when there is no party at the median of all relevant conflict dimensions. Thus, critical portfolio allocation decisions depend on a variety of parameters, but again

Conclusion: Cabinet Governance in Parliamentary Democracies 413

structural attributes and political institutions are the most powerful explanatory clusters.

Cabinet conflict management

Coalition agreements, careful portfolio allocation, and the use of watchdog ministers may help coalition parties coordinate their policy decisions, but these devices cannot solve all the conflicts that may arise from coalition governance. In Chapter 8, Andeweg and Timmermans analyse the mechanisms that political parties set up to manage conflicts that arise while they govern together. While this is a topic of obvious importance, it has been almost completely unexplored, so that there is precious little literature to build upon. The discussion in this chapter is therefore more qualitative and case-oriented than are the other chapters in this volume, as it opens up a novel avenue of political research. Yet, the authors also report interesting statistical results on the use of different kinds of conflict resolution arenas.

The chapter focuses on the distinction between on the one hand conflict management arenas that are internal to the cabinet as an institution and on the other hand those that are external or mixed, such as meetings of party leaders, party conferences, and the like. Andeweg and Timmermans find that coalition governments use internal mechanisms, such as coalition committees, to keep transaction and audience costs low. As the authors point out, the use of external or mixed arenas implies additional costs to the parties relative to internal arenas, and all else equal, parties tend to prefer internal decision-making arenas. They will resort to external institutions when the coalition is fragile or the bargaining environment complex, when they have no definitive prior policy agreement to fall back on, or when the internal environment is likely to be biased in favour of one of the parties (e. g. because the prime minister has extensive institutional powers). Chapter 8 suggests that when bargaining and conflict resolution is more complex, external and mixed conflict management arenas are used more often, although the results are not quite so simple.

There are very important country differences and significant evidence of path dependency. This is illustrated by the case study of Ireland, where internal cabinet arenas are hardly ever used for conflict management. But the general pattern suggests that significant differences in walk-away values (operationalized as the inclusion of the party with the highest bargaining power in the cabinet) is an important predictor of the use of external arenas for serious conflicts. It seems that junior coalition partners have a strong incentive to favour mixed or external arenas, as these are usually more public than inner cabinets or cabinet committees, and as the prime minister is less dominant in the latter arenas. Thus, having an institutionally strong PM, or for that matter, a system of positive parliamentarism, can make it difficult to keep and manage conflicts within the cabinet.

Cabinet termination

The best-laid plans and the most elaborate mechanisms cannot always help coalition parties solve their differences, and sometimes these conflicts lead to the cabinet's termination. In Chapter 9, Erik Damgaard examines the conditions under which cabinets terminate. While the existing literature has paid much attention to cabinet duration (which we examine in Chapter 10), very little has been said about the actual causes of cabinet termination. These clearly fall into several distinct categories. Most commonly, cabinets serve the bulk of their constitutionally mandated period, terminating for what we refer to as 'technical' reasons, with the holding of regular elections. In some cases governments voluntarily choose to call early elections, while in others cabinets fall due to conflict between or within the parties that participate in them. But what are the conditions and the strategic calculations behind this variation?

The general answer is that governments tend to terminate for technical reasons, rather than due to conflict, when they face simpler and less challenging times. When economic conditions are difficult (such as when unemployment or inflation is high), conflictual terminations are more likely to occur. The same is true when the bargaining situation is complex. Particular institutions affect the likelihood of governments terminating earlier than their mandated term. Thus, governments are less likely to fall due to conflict or early parliamentary elections in PR systems, but more likely to fall under positive parliamentarism, which may have a tendency to make for uncomfortable coalitional 'marriages'. Similarly, enforced coalition discipline in parliamentary voting increases the likelihood of conflictual terminations, perhaps because it does not permit the various coalition partners to express disagreements over policy.

Cabinet duration

The determinants of cabinet duration have received a great deal of attention in the field of coalition studies, and the literature has recently come to adopt increasingly advanced statistical techniques. In order to speak to this literature, our chapter that addresses this topic is structured somewhat differently from the other empirical chapters, but the main conclusions suggest the value of our theoretical approach and comport with the empirical findings of the other chapters.

In Chapter 10, Thomas Saalfeld confirms earlier results that parliamentary cabinets face rising early-election hazard rates and nearly constant replacement hazard rates. That is to say, the risk of a cabinet being replaced by another cabinet without an election occurring is roughly the same on its first day of office as it is one, two, or three years into its term, whereas the risk of a cabinet terminating due to an early election rises with its time in office. However, many factors influence cabinet durability beyond this baseline hazard rate. In fact, variables from all of

Conclusion: Cabinet Governance in Parliamentary Democracies   415

our explanatory blocks are significant predictors of cabinet duration in the models Saalfeld presents.

Based on the final specification of Saalfeld's model, it turns out that those who value durable cabinets should wish for a minimal winning majority and politically conservative cabinet that includes the party with the largest bargaining power and which is formed well before the next scheduled election! Others, if they hope to see the cabinet fall quickly, should look for a minority or surplus majority cabinet in a party system characterized by a number of cross-cutting conflict dimensions and with high levels of inflation. Add positive parliamentarism, high opposition influence, unanimity cabinet decision rules, a PM with dissolution powers, or semi-presidentialism, and the result is likely to be a short-lived cabinet.

Electoral performance

Throughout the coalition cycle, party politicians are always concerned with the next upcoming election. The election date is when old sins are accounted for and a new mandate given. In our final empirical chapter (Chapter 11), Hanne Marthe Narud and Henry Valen analyse the electoral rewards and punishments experienced by parties participating in parliamentary governments. Their results show that voters in the most recent decades analysed (the 1980s and 1990s) have become much more inclined to punish their governments than previous generations were. This trend is remarkably strong and robust. While these results might in part be a consequence of the inclusion of Greece, Portugal, and especially Spain in the data-set from the 1970s, robustness checks suggest that it is a broader trend. The analyses also suggest that incumbents are better off at election time if they have formed minimal winning coalitions and particularly if they have avoided surplus coalitions. In the aggregate, the more parties the ruling coalition includes and the more seats that it controls, the more severe are its losses.

The tendency for incumbents to lose votes can be counteracted. When the party system is fragmented, incumbents do better. And cabinets that go into elections early (perhaps because they have indeed chosen their timing) are more likely to win votes than are cabinets that sit out the regular parliamentary term. Conservative cabinets (as opposed to mixed or socialist ones) do better than others. On the other hand, conservative cabinets seem to be particularly punished for high levels of inflation, and not surprisingly, all cabinets that experience a critical event related to public opinion (be it due to scandals, policy failure, or other causes) also tend to lose votes to the opposition.

One innovation in Narud and Valen's analysis is their separate consideration of the determinants of the electoral fortunes of the PM's and the finance minister's parties. Their intriguing results suggest that voters in the aggregate are surprisingly discriminating in their judgements. Whereas the party of the PM and in particular the party of the finance minister receive extra credit (votes) for a growing economy, in particular conservative finance minister's parties get punished for high levels of inflation. Furthermore, the party of the finance minister does not do as well in the presence of a comprehensive policy agreement, perhaps because it is not able to take sole credit for financial policies and outcomes. On the other hand, voters tend to reward the PM's party when the government is confronted by a large number of highly polarized parliamentary parties. However, PM's parties rarely get rewarded as much in semi-presidential systems (perhaps because the president takes credit for any successes), and seem to be punished when they preside over surplus majority cabinets.

CLUSTERING THE EXPLANATORY VARIABLES

The first two chapters of this volume have suggested that the variation in cabinet governance cannot be fully explained by any single factor or type of variable. Instead, we must analyse cabinet governance as a process of ongoing bargaining that is influenced by a wide range of factors inside and outside the parliamentary arena. The results from each of our empirical chapters have corroborated this argument. Having identified six sets of variables that we consider important to coalition bargaining, we can confidently say that our results confirm that each of these clusters has an important role to play in explaining cabinet governance and coalition politics. We now consider the relevance of each of these various clusters of independent variables in turn.

Time and space

The first cluster of variables that our contributors have considered is time and space, which we have captured as the fixed effects of decades and particular countries. The coalitions literature contains ample evidence of country effects, and indeed some analysts have argued that apart from such national differences, there are few systematic determinants of coalition politics. And it is indeed apparent that there are important governance differences among our countries. The first multivariate empirical tests of coalition theory found that between-country differences drove much of the observed variation in cabinet types (see Chapter 1). Such effects hold up in many of the analyses in this volume as well, but we believe it is valuable to push the analysis a bit further. Country effects are not equally important at all stages of the life cycle. From our dynamic perspective, we find 'country' to be a particularly strong determinant of the observed pattern at two of the life cycle stages: One is at the time of the formation process, when national peculiarities drive much of the variance in bargaining rounds and formation duration. The other phase in which national effects are particularly prominent is coalition governance (specifically meaning the use of coalition agreements and different conflict management arenas). Even at these stages, however, our more theoretically driven variables generally explain the cross-national variation quite well.

The existing literature has shown much less interest in effects of time, but our analysis shows some dramatic temporal trends as well. This is perhaps most dramatically true with respect to the formation process and electoral performance. Over time there has been a decline in the number of inconclusive bargaining rounds prior to cabinet formation, with a dramatic drop-off in the 1990s. The formation duration process has seen a more curvilinear pattern, with governments in the 1970s taking longer to form than governments before or since that time. At the other end of the life-cycle, voters have become much more inclined to punish incumbent governments. Politicians now find it harder to use government positions to maximize votes. If maximizing votes were all that mattered to European politicians, parties would currently be better off staying in opposition!

Yet, with regard to coalition governance—the period between formation and termination—there are fewer temporal trends. True, we have seen an increase in the frequency of coalition agreements, in the use of 'watchdog' junior ministers, and in reliance on mixed or external arenas for managing serious conflicts among coalition parties. However, there appear to be no strong trend in the type of cabinet formed, in portfolio disproportionality, in cabinet duration, or in the conditions under which cabinets terminate. Although cabinets were more durable in the 1990s than previously, it may be premature to tell whether this is the beginning of a trend or an aberration.

Structural attributes

Our analysis of the impact of structural attributes has focused on three types of variables: those related to timing (relative to the electoral calendar and the constitutional inter-election period), those related to the attributes of parliamentary parties, and those having to do with the attributes of cabinets and cabinet parties. Not surprisingly, perhaps, structural attributes related to timing had the least consistent impact across the cycle of cabinet governance. They play an important role in explaining the cabinet formation process, as coalition formation immediately following elections is more likely to result in inconclusive bargaining rounds and long periods of negotiation. However, the only other consistent result we find is that the greater the possible cabinet duration of the cabinet, the higher the likelihood of termination due to an early election. Other aspects of cabinet governance seem less directly influenced by the timing of cabinet formation.

On the other hand, almost all of our analyses find that structural attributes related to the number and size of parliamentary parties play an important role in explaining cabinet governance—the only exception being that these variables do not seem to have a robust impact on the arena used for coalitional conflict management. Yet, we should keep in mind that such conflict management is already conditional on the existence of a coalition government, which as Chapter 6 shows is strongly related to certain structural attributes. Fragmentation of the parliamentary party system (operationalized in various ways across the different chapters: greater absolute or effective number of parties, lower seat share or bargaining power of the largest party, etc.) increases the probability of an inclusive bargaining round, the duration of coalition bargaining, and the incidence of cabinet coalitions. Fragmentation also increases the likelihood that the coalition will be based on a written agreement, that portfolio allocation will be disproportional, that the number of cabinet ministers will be increased, and that watchdog junior ministers will be installed.

Not surprisingly, cabinets' structural attributes also have a substantial impact on most aspects of cabinet governance. Cabinet type (minority vs. majority, single-party, minimal winning, or surplus coalition) has a robust impact on the proportionality of portfolio allocation, on the number of cabinet ministers, but not on the likelihood of watchdog junior ministers. Although cabinet type does have the expected effects on cabinet durability, the type of termination (technical, voluntary early election, or conflictual) cabinets experience depends more critically on whether or not the cabinet includes the most powerful party.

Preferences

Although in its parsimony Riker's original contribution (1962) to the field stripped away all consideration of policy preferences, the next two decades of coalition research were dominated by 'policy-based' theories. And according to almost all empirical coalition research over the past 30 years, policy preferences do matter in coalition politics. Unsurprisingly, our findings concur with that claim. Perhaps a more interesting finding is that in most of our analyses, the distribution of policy preferences among all parliamentary parties has a more substantial impact on the various stages of cabinet governance than the policy range within the cabinet itself.

In our analysis, we have focused on the dispersion of party policy preferences, on the dimensionality of the policy space, on the interaction between policy preferences and bargaining power, and specifically on the bargaining power of the median (in two-dimensional space: core) party. Our results show that polarization in parliamentary preferences and complexity in the distribution of policy preferences are positively associated with the duration of initial coalition bargaining and with the likelihood of a formal coalition agreement. The same conditions decrease the likelihood of surplus coalitions. The greater the bargaining power of the median party, the less likely a coalition government, and particularly a surplus coalition. Ideological polarization increases the number of cabinet ministers and the likelihood that watchdog junior ministers will be appointed. And with higher issue dimensionality we are more likely to see low cabinet duration and conflict management arenas internal to the cabinet.

Conclusion: Cabinet Governance in Parliamentary Democracies   419

Institutions

Much of the interest in institutions in the coalition literature originated with attempts to explain cabinet type. We too find evidence of the importance of institutions at the stage of initial coalition bargaining. However, our results indicate that the importance of institutions is perhaps even greater further along the life cycle of cabinet governance. We also find that the influence of the institutional variables we have considered in this volume ends at the stage of cabinet termination; they do not have a robust effect on how incumbents do in the next election.

In our analysis, we have considered a broad range of institutional variables having to do with fundamental constitutional properties as well as with parliamentary and cabinet procedures. Several institutional variables stand out as having significant explanatory power across the various stages of cabinet governance. Positive parliamentarism increases the likelihood of coalition formation, decreases the incidence of watchdog junior ministers, and increases the probability that coalition governments will choose mixed or external conflict management arenas, while also decreasing government duration and increasing the likelihood of early cabinet termination. Semi-presidentialism prolongs the time to cabinet formation and increases the likelihood of a coalition (particularly a surplus coalition) and also the probability of a coalition agreement. The same constitutional feature also depresses cabinet duration.

Perhaps the most intriguing institutional effect is the robust impact of prime ministerial powers at a variety of stages of the parliamentary life cycle. It has long been suggested that unilateral dissolution powers vested in the PM will affect cabinet duration, a claim corroborated in Chapter 10. But we also find that such dissolution powers influence the likelihood of watchdog junior ministers and increase the duration of coalition bargaining. Moreover, the PM's cabinet powers (over the agenda, in regards to the selection and removal of other ministers, etc.) also influence many stages of cabinet governance. Where the PM is vested with strong institutional powers, there are fewer inconclusive bargaining rounds over government membership, and coalitions (particularly surplus ones) are less likely to form. Strong PM powers are likewise associated with a smaller set of cabinet members and a lower probability that arenas internal to the cabinet will be used to resolve major conflicts. Furthermore, cabinet duration is affected not only by the PM's dissolution powers but by his cabinet powers as well.

Bargaining environment and critical events

Since at least the 1980s, the coalitions literature has increasingly recognized that parliamentary politics is influenced by endogenous and exogenous factors in the broader bargaining environment. Our bargaining environment variables attempt in part to capture how the behaviour of parties and political actors at one stage of the parliamentary life cycle might influence other stages. Other variables in this explanatory cluster are designed to capture conditions in the bargaining situation (such as international conflicts or economic recessions) that politicians are less able to control, but that nevertheless may significantly impinge on their coalitional choices and strategies.

If we are simply to count variables that are robust and significant in our final models, the overall effects of the bargaining environment and of critical events would be somewhat smaller than those of our other blocks. Nevertheless, these variables can at times have substantial and very important effects. As expected, we do find that decisions at most stages of the parliamentary life cycle are influenced by what transpired at previous stages. Thus, the likelihood of inconclusive bargaining rounds is influenced by the causes of the termination of the prior cabinet. And inconclusive bargaining rounds in turn increase the likelihood of single-party and/or minority cabinets. The existence of a comprehensive coalition agreement and insistence on coalition discipline in legislative matters both increase the likelihood that conflict among coalition partners will be managed through internal cabinet arenas. Moreover, a lengthy initial bargaining process enhances the durability of the cabinet that ultimately forms.

Exogenous critical events may also influence many aspects of cabinet governance, particularly at the later stages of the parliamentary life cycle. Certain critical events have an impact on the earlier stages as well: the occurrence of a critical event decreases the likelihood of a coalition, as does electoral volatility in the prior election. Electoral volatility is also associated with an increase in the number of cabinet portfolios, whereas it decreases the likelihood that coalition cabinets will choose internal cabinet arenas for their most serious conflicts.

Economic hardships, specifically inflation and unemployment, diminish cabinet duration as they raise the risk of cabinet termination due to conflict within or between the government parties. Inflation also has a negative effect on the government's electoral performance, particularly when the government is politically conservative. The effect of unemployment on cabinet electoral performance is less robust, whereas economic growth improves the electoral fortunes of the prime minister's party in particular.

Summing up the results by explanatory clusters

In sum, all of our explanatory clusters capture factors that make a difference in parliamentary politics, even though some variables are more equal than others. Time and space are sometimes very important parameters, particularly for the formation process and for some aspects of the governance mechanisms that coalition parties choose. Structural attributes tend to be important throughout the entire life cycle of parliamentary politics, except that they seem to have little discernible

Conclusion: Cabinet Governance in Parliamentary Democracies

impact on how cabinets terminate. Similarly, preferences are of great consequence throughout the parliamentary life cycle, except that they do not seem to have any robust effect on the choice of conflict resolution mechanisms. These instead tend largely to be consequences of political institutions and previous choices.

Institutions also almost always matter, though least impressively at election time. Thus, although most of the institutional variables we have considered are of little consequence for electoral performance, they do have dramatic effects on cabinet type, governance mechanisms, and cabinet duration. Institutions that give a particular actor a strategic advantage are particularly important in the formation process. Prime ministerial powers over parliamentary dissolution and cabinet decision-making are also important at almost every stage of coalition politics.

The bargaining environment, on the other hand, is especially critical for the later stages of the parliamentary life cycle. Even more so, critical events tend to be important only after the cabinet partners may have lost some of the initial pleasure of being in government: they are increasingly important towards the end of the parliamentary life cycle as we have conceived it.

In our analyses we have explored the effects of a wide range of new variables that have not been considered in previous studies, and many of our analyses also focus on dependent variables that hitherto have been underexplored. Such a design obviously enables us to report a large number of new results, which is naturally gratifying. However, as we look at our results throughout, one general finding stands out. While the explanatory power of our respective clusters varies across the different stages of the cabinet life cycle, in none of our analyses does any single cluster of variables explain a very large share of the variance in which we are interested. In every set of analyses, it is a combination of three or more clusters that best explain our data. To us, it is this finding that most strongly justifies our theoretical approach. The puzzling and intriguing facets of coalition politics rarely have only one, single explanation. Instead, the events and patterns that matter so much in parliamentary politics reflect a complex combination of opportunities, events, constraints, rules, designs, and expectations.

PERSPECTIVES ON FUTURE RESEARCH

There is unlikely to be a last word on parliamentary governance. Even if there is, we are under no illusion that this volume has provided it. We began our research project by recognizing that empirical research has not kept pace with theoretical developments in coalition research. One of our ambitions has been to shrink this gap. Whatever success we have had, there are many issues that remain, and we shall in this section try to identify some of the most important ones.

Extensions to new democracies and non-parliamentary systems

For most of its history, coalition research has confined itself to Western Europe. Only occasionally have interesting cases from other parts of the world, in particular Commonwealth countries and Israel, been added. This has not only been parochial, but it also raises questions about the validity and generality of much of our existing knowledge. The good news from this perspective is that the Third Wave of democratization has generated many new democracies with multi-party systems. In particular, parliamentary democracies have been established in Central and Eastern Europe that institutionally belong to the same family as the Western European systems that have constituted the bedrock of coalition research. Many of these systems are now stable democracies, as testified by the accession of ten of them to the European Union, and clearly they should be included in all future coalition research. Some early such steps have been undertaken (Druckman and Roberts 2005; Amorim Neto and Strøm 2006), and more needs to be done. Efforts have recently also been undertaken more systematically to include parliamentary systems outside Europe (e.g. Carroll and Cox 2007). The parties and party systems in such countries may be more fluid than in the West (see e.g. Toole 2000), to the point that it makes the life of parliamentary researchers more difficult (see Zielinski, Slomczynski, and Shabad 2005), but the great advantage is that these cases may also introduce institutional and behavioural variance beyond what is found in Western Europe and permit more 'out-of-sample' testing of key theoretical propositions.

Coalition research does not need to be confined even to parliamentary democracies. All multiparty systems that do not vest all power in the hands of one (cohesive) political party require the formation and often maintenance of coalitions of some sort (see Chapter 2). Although presidential systems have a distinct institutional setup, the basic logic of bargaining should be the same. It would therefore be a worthwhile attempt to formulate coalition theories that cover both parliamentary and presidential systems (Amorim Neto 2006).

Data needs

Even though the coalitions literature has become much better endowed with data than it was even recently, there remains a large agenda of data generation and collection. One of these challenges lies in measurement, and perhaps particularly in the measurement of preferences. Preferences are a key concept for most brands of coalition theory. Consequently, coalition research will benefit from all improvements in their measurement. This volume has drawn on such sources as party preference data from the Comparative Manifesto Project (CMP) (Budge et al. 2001) and an expert survey conducted in 1989 (Laver and Hunt 1992). The Manifesto Research Group (MRG) has regularly updated its research and widened its geographic scope (Klingemann et al. 2006), thus providing a great service to

Conclusion: Cabinet Governance in Parliamentary Democracies

the discipline. Yet, the underlying coding scheme goes back to the late 1970s (Budge, Robertson, and Hearl 1987: xv) and consequently reflects the political agenda of that time. Both the coding scheme and the saliency theory underlying the CMP approach have been subject to at times heated debate (for recent and more nuanced accounts, see the contributions in Laver 2001 and Marks 2007).

The expert survey tradition in coalition research has been invigorated by the recent works by Benoit and Laver (2006), Marks et al. (2006), and Warwick (2006). Notwithstanding the considerable merits of these works, the fact remains that good expert surveys are demanding tools that cannot be carried out often enough to catch the dynamics of party strategy. This is due to resource constraints, perhaps more so on the side of the surveyed experts (who are drawn from a small and in some countries indeed tiny pool) than on the side of the researchers.

Notwithstanding the merits of both strands of research, the very nature of the scientific enterprise suggests that no specific method or theory will remain the state of the art forever. And currently computer-aided content analysis of political documents seems to be an attractive alternative (Pennings and Keman 2002) that recognizes the importance of official party documents but is less time bound and labour-intensive than the CMP approach. The most prominent representative of this approach is the Words Score method developed by Michael Laver and associates (Laver and Garry 2000; Laver 2001; Laver, Benoit, and Garry 2003). At any rate, we are optimistic that the measurement of party positions can be greatly enhanced by refining and applying these tools. Yet, expert analysis of party documents will need to be continued, since future coalition research will likely ask questions of high specificity that can be addressed only by expert coders.

Another focus of future research should be institutions. The present volume is the most comprehensive attempt to date to employ institutional data in coalition research. Yet, we see several ways to go beyond what we have achieved here. One relates to public, i.e. constitutional and other legal constraints on coalition politics. With regard to formal (legal) institutions, we have identified quite a comprehensive range of the rules that impinge on the classic issues of coalition studies: coalition formation and termination. Yet, the impact of formal institutions on coalition *governance* is a much larger conceptual territory, and the consequences of specific rules are not always obvious. We can imagine, for instance, that different rules of parliamentary scrutiny and third-party auditing of ministries and government agencies impact on coalition behaviour (see Martin and Vanberg 2005). So may the specific provisions of freedom of information acts, or the institutions regulating the mass media, for example. The second way in which institutional analysis should be extended relates to the private institutions of coalition governance: coalition contracts, decision-making rules, and coalition governance institutions that are strictly private agreements between the coalition parties.

Preferences and institutions help explain coalition behaviour. Yet, before behaviour can be explained it needs to be defined and measured. For most of its history, coalition studies have lived on a diet that has been largely devoid of actual behavioural data save on cabinet formation and termination. Even these crucial moments in the life of coalitions have mostly been treated as (final) outcomes rather than as processes. Thus, analysts have left aside most parameters of the formation or termination process and largely failed to investigate the internal dynamics of bargaining. Cabinet reshuffles constitute an exception to this rule (Huber 1998; Huber and Lupia 2001; Huber and Martinez-Gallardo 2004; Kam and Indridason 2005), but even this most easily observable aspect of the life of governments has not seen much attention. However, most action in coalition politics does not consist in the appointment or dismissal or reshuffle of ministers, and our empirical studies should reflect that fact.

Finally, coalition research can benefit from a more systematic use of public opinion data. Much of coalition theory is concerned with the impact of voter preferences on the duration of coalitions and the power distribution within them (e.g. Lupia and Strøm 1995; Laver and Shepsle 1998). Yet, little has been done to document and track such effects. One problem has been that in most countries public opinion data is available only for a fraction of the time frame that typically is adopted in coalition studies. Yet, by now the era of systematic mass surveys in most countries dates back several decades. Nonetheless, large cross-national projects using survey data would face many practical problems given the differences in data availability and quality. Thus, small-N studies might be the logical way to proceed in the short run.

Methods

The community of coalition researchers has always recognized the merits of very different methodological approaches. While individual researchers may be committed to a specific mode of research—game theoretical modelling, cross-national statistical analysis, configurative research on individual countries, or case studies of coalition politics—many have employed more than one approach. Even more so, most researchers recognize the distinctive contributions to the common enterprise that result from research in other traditions. This is a distinctive strength of the coalition studies field, which should by all means be maintained.

Yet, diversity and mutual toleration should sometimes give way to more ambitious integration of different approaches. Coalition research should make greater efforts to integrate different methods under a single overarching research design. In our larger project, we have combined configurative country studies with large-N cross-national analysis of pooled data. And although the present volume champions the latter approach we have also made use of case studies (in Chapter 8). Yet, in principle coalition studies are well suited for 'nested analysis'—which implies moving back and forth between statistical analyses and case study research (see Lieberman 2005; Bäck and Dumont 2007).

PARLIAMENTARY DEMOCRACY: PROMISES AND COSTS

As we have noted above, parliamentary democracy is but one way to organize the policy process in a democratic polity. Different democratic regimes represent competing designs that aim to meet two fundamental challenges: on the one hand to sustain popular sovereignty and on the other to produce a desirable package of public goods and other policy outputs. To put it mildly, both of these goals are more easily said than done. There are many challenges and many ways in which the pursuit of one of these objectives may jeopardize the other. In this section, we shall focus on one set of such challenges, which we identify with two sets of costs. Before we proceed, however, we should note that these are by no means the only, or even the most fundamental, challenges facing parliamentary democracies. Among the problems we shall thus not mention are the fundamental problems associated with any form of popular sovereignty, such as the fact that there may not be any unique or definitive way to establish a collective preference ordering over public policy, or that even if such collective preferences could be identified, they might be fickle or malevolent.

Without in any way downplaying the problems associated with human frailty or the inherent complications of group decision-making, we shall in our closing observations concentrate on two other problems, namely, those of agency costs and transaction costs. Agency costs refer to the vertical relationship between politicians and the citizens from whom their power derives. Transaction costs may also relate to the relationship between citizens and politicians, but is primarily a feature of the relationships between politicians in the process of policymaking.

The presence of agency costs and transaction costs means that communities may not get the policies they want, and that whatever policies they do get may not be provided in an efficient or timely manner or implemented and enforced with any success. These challenges face the citizens of any polity based on the idea of popular sovereignty. And although democracy, at least in reasonably wealthy societies, has proven quite robust, there is no reason to believe that it can anywhere be impervious to such challenges in the long run. In other words, transaction costs as well as agency costs can pose grave threats to any society that aspires to be democratic.

Parliamentary democracies are no exception. Even though one-third of the world's population now lives under parliamentary democracies, and even though most of these states are stable, wealthy, and peaceful, there is no guarantee that they will always be so. Parliamentary democracy failed in Germany in the 1930s, in France in the 1950s, in Nigeria and Greece in the 1960s, and arguably in Italy in the 1980s. In each of these cases, agency and/or transaction problems were among the causes of their demise.

This volume has examined the ways in which Western European democracies under parliamentary rule cope with the issues of making timely and effective decisions that their citizens will accept. While it has not been our primary objective to identify and measure transaction and agency costs in parliamentary politics, we have argued that transactions between politicians, as well as their interactions with the citizens, are beset by such problems. Moreover, they drive many of the specific institutions and strategies of parliamentary politics. Agency problems may arise at any stage of the parliamentary chain of delegation, but in our context the most important loci are in the delegation from voters to parliamentarians and in the delegation from parliament to the cabinet.

It is plausible to think that there may often be a trade-off between agency costs and transaction costs, and that different types of democracies represent different preferences over these evils. Thus, communities can sometimes lower agency costs by increasing transaction costs and vice versa. And whereas a majoritarian parliamentary system seems to represent a greater tolerance for agency costs relative to transaction costs, a Madisonian checks-and-balances polity would seem to embody the reverse preference order. By implication, one might also expect proportional parliamentary systems to exhibit lower agency costs and higher transaction costs relative to their majoritarian counterparts.

Agency costs are driven in large part by the preferences of these different political actors, and since these preferences are unobservable, we cannot directly measure the degree of agency loss in the different political systems in our sample. What we can observe are the occasions when agency problems come to the surface in the form of a revocation of existing agency relationships. In other words, when voters 'terminate' their parliamentarians, or parliamentarians their cabinet members, we can reasonably infer that something has gone awry.

In Chapter 11, we have seen remarkable evidence concerning agency problems between voters and parliamentarians. From decade to decade, the electoral fortunes of incumbent parties have been getting progressively worse. Voters have become increasingly restive, fickle, and punitive. This temporal trend is remarkably strong and monotonic, and it is quite robust across the range of Western European countries. There is no country in which the average incumbent does not suffer a setback, and in almost all countries the expected losses have been growing over time.

Is there a general institutional solution to such democratic agency problems? Our analysis suggests a dose of scepticism on this count. As noted, there is no country in which incumbents have systematically fared well. Denmark and Norway come closest, but more careful scrutiny reveals that much of this performance is due to the stability of electoral results in the early post-war period.

Conclusion: Cabinet Governance in Parliamentary Democracies 427

In more recent years, Norway certainly has not been a paragon of voter contentment. One might at first glance also surmise that the relatively favourable performance of the Scandinavian countries reflects a more general advantage for proportional over majoritarian polities. After all, PR systems are designed to give more faithful expression to popular preferences, and one might well suppose that majoritarian systems would foster greater agency problems simply by virtue of their electoral rules. Moreover, in the present sample these expectations would seem borne out by the extremely large average incumbency losses in Spain, a relatively majoritarian system. Yet, on closer inspection, there seems to be little support for these expectations. Very proportional systems such as Belgium and Luxembourg have some of the highest average incumbency losses in our sample, whereas majoritarian systems such as France and the UK score much lower. And the regression results show that the number of cabinet parties, as well as the number of parties in parliament, is negatively related to electoral success.

Thus, there is little evidence that proportionalism can prevent agency losses between voters and parliamentarians. Nor do our data suggest that such institutions commend themselves with respect to the delegation relationship between the parliament and the cabinet. Again, our best data in this respect are those that relate to the circumstances in which parliament terminates its relationship with a particular cabinet. In Chapter 9, Damgaard analyses the circumstances under which cabinets terminate under conditions of conflict, rather than for technical reasons. His results show that the likelihood of such conflictual terminations increases with the policy range of the cabinet parties, as well as the strength of extremist parties in parliament. Strong extremist parties and ideologically heterogeneous cabinets are of course much more likely to be found in proportional than in majoritarian systems. On the other hand, List Proportional Representation has the unexpected effect of depressing the likelihood of a conflictual termination. The evidence on agency problems is thus mixed; it is difficult to identify a set of countries or institutions that are uniquely favoured on this score.

Transaction costs are a somewhat different story. Transaction costs of course beset a whole host of different facets of coalition politics, but in this study we have specifically examined one prominent manifestation of such costs: the initial bargaining process leading up to the formation of a new cabinet. Time and energy spent on this process are by implication resources that cannot be applied to other political endeavours. Our very first empirical chapter examined the determinants of bargaining duration and inconclusive bargaining rounds. As De Winter and Dumont show, four countries stand out with respect to inconclusive bargaining rounds: Belgium, the Netherlands, Finland, and Iceland. The same countries are among those that have the longest bargaining periods, though on this score the Netherlands stands out from all the rest, whereas Austria joins the league of the countries with lengthy bargaining periods. Clearly, these are all polities that fall towards the proportional rather than the majoritarian pole among

European parliamentary democracies. This association between proportionalism and transaction costs is corroborated in the multivariate analysis.

In the real world of coalition politics, transaction costs are hardly manifested only in the initial bargaining process. Indeed, coalition agreements and conflict management mechanisms are institutions that owe their very existence to the fact that transaction costs remain a concern throughout any period of coalition governance. These institutions are in themselves, of course, strongly associated with proportional, rather than majoritarian, polities, thus seemingly confirming the link between proportionalism and transaction costs. Yet, this correlation between proportionalism and transaction costs may be less solid than it appears. Transaction costs may and do arise in majoritarian systems as well, but in those settings such costs may attach to intra-party rather than inter-party politics. The fact that the research design in this study allows us to capture the latter more easily than the former may well account for some of the apparent advantage of majoritarian polities with respect to transaction costs.

Thus, the issues of agency and transaction costs run deeply through the entire life cycle of parliamentary governance, and our analysis here has only begun to scratch their surface. On the other hand, while agency problems as well as transaction problems permeate so many aspects of coalition politics, we should resist the temptation to view these phenomena strictly through this lens. Thus, we have argued above that electoral results may reflect agency problems between voters and their representatives in parliament. Yet, it would be seriously incomplete to consider elections only as a manifestation of agency problems.

We have argued that there is a life cycle to the politics of parliamentary countries. While it is in the very nature of this cycle that it recurs and recurs, it nevertheless has a stage that all politicians and citizens recognize as focal: popular elections. Elections are the most effective ways in which politicians can be brought into line with their constituents, and they are a powerful way in which gridlock can be broken. Voting does not ensure that such problems will be solved—indeed most of the contemporary world's worst tyrants can claim an electoral mandate, and some might even have been elected without rigging the polls. But even though they are not sufficient, competitive elections are a necessary condition for effective democracy.

In this book, we have shown how the shadow of elections past and future shapes the interaction between politicians at every stage of their parliamentary bargaining. As noted above, one of our most striking results is the growing competitiveness of parliamentary elections across Western Europe. With growing frequency, voters across Western Europe have withdrawn the mandates that they have given to their respective politicians. As we have suggested, this is certainly a troubling indication of agency problems. At the same time, however, volatile elections are a sign that voters expect politicians to deliver, and they are an indication that those voters have the confidence to hold their leaders to account and the means to do so. Ultimately, this is just what democracy requires.

REFERENCES

Amorim Neto, Octavio (2006). 'The Presidential Calculus: Executive Policy Making and Cabinet Formation in the Americas', *Comparative Political Studies*, 39: 415–40.

—— and Strøm, Kaare (2006). 'Breaking the Parliamentary Chain of Delegation: Presidents and Non-partisan Cabinet Members in European Democracies', *British Journal of Political Science*, 36: 619–43.

Bäck, Hanna and Dumont, Patrick (2007). 'Combining Large-n and Small-n Strategies: The Way Forward in Coalition Research', *West European Politics*, 30: 467–501.

Benoit, Kenneth and Laver, Michael (2006). *Party Policy in Modern Democracies*. London: Routledge.

Budge, Ian, Robertson, David, and Hearl, Derek (eds.) (1987). *Ideology, Strategy and Party Change: Spatial Analyses of Post-war Election Programmes in 19 Democracies*. Cambridge: Cambridge University Press.

—— Klingemann, Hans-Dieter, Volkens, Andrea, Bara, Judith, and Tannenbaum, Eric (2001). *Mapping Policy Preferences. Estimates for Parties, Electors, and Governments 1945–1998*. Oxford: Oxford University Press.

Carroll, Royce and Cox, Gary W. (2007). 'The Logic of Gamson's Law: Pre-election Coalitions and Portfolio Allocations', *American Journal of Political Science*, 51: 300–13.

Druckman, James N. and Roberts, Andrew (2005). 'Context and Coalition-Bargaining. Comparing Portfolio Allocation in Eastern and Western Europe', *Party Politics*, 11: 535–55.

Franklin, Mark N. and Mackie, Thomas T. (1983). 'Familiarity and Inertia in the Formation of Governing Coalitions in Parliamentary Democracies', *British Journal of Political Science*, 13: 275–98.

Huber, John D. (1998). 'How does Cabinet Instability affect Political Performance: Credible Commitment, Information, and Health Care Cost Containment in Parliamentary Politics', *American Political Science Review*, 92: 577–92.

—— and Lupia, Arthur (2001). 'Cabinet Instability and Delegation in Parliamentary Democracies', *American Journal of Political Science*, 45: 18–33.

—— and Martinez-Gallardo, Cecilia (2004). 'Cabinet Instability and the Accumulation of Experience: The French Fourth and Fifth Republics in Comparative Perspective', *British Journal of Political Science*, 34: 27–48

Indridason, Indridi H. (2005). 'A Theory of Coalitions and Clientilism: Coalition Politics in Iceland 1945–2000', *European Journal of Political Research*, 44: 439–64.

Kam, Christopher and Indridason, Indridi H. (2005). 'The Timing of Cabinet Reshuffles in Five Westminster Parliamentary Systems', *Legislative Studies Quarterly*, 30: 327–63.

Klingemann, Hans-Dieter, Volkens, Andrea, Bara, Judith, Budge, Ian, McDonald, Michael D. (2006). *Mapping Policy Preferences II*. Oxford: Oxford University Press.

Laver, Michael (1974). 'Dynamic Factors in Government Coalition Formation', *European Journal of Political Research*, 2: 259–70.

—— (ed.) (2001). *Estimating the Policy Position of Political Actors*. New York, NY: Routledge.

—— and Garry, John (2000). 'Estimating Policy Positions from Political Texts', *American Journal of Political Science*, 44: 619–34.

—— and Hunt, W. Ben (1992). *Policy and Party Competition*. New York, NY: Routledge.

Laver, Michael, Benoit, Kenneth, and Garry, John (2003). 'Extracting Policy Positions from Political Texts Using Words as Data', *American Political Science Review*, 97: 311–31.

Laver, Michael J. and Shepsle, Kenneth A. (1998). 'Events, Equilibria, and Government Survival', *American Journal of Political Science*, 42: 28–54.

Lieberman, Evan S. (2005). 'Nested Analysis as a Mixed-Method Strategy for Comparative Research', *American Political Science Review*, 99: 435–52.

Lupia, Arthur and Strøm, Kaare (1995). 'Coalition Termination and the Strategic Timing of Parliamentary Elections', *American Political Science Review*, 89: 648–65.

Marks, Gary, Hooghe, Liesbeth, Nelson, Moira, and Edwards, Erica (2006). 'Party Competition and European Integration in the East and West', *Comparative Political Studies*, 39: 155–75.

—— (ed.) (2007). 'Special Symposium: Comparing Measures of Party Positioning: Expert, Manifesto, and Survey Data', *Electoral Studies*, 26 (1).

Martin, Lanny W., and Vanberg, Georg (2005). Coalition Policymaking and Legislative Review, *American Political Science Review*, 99: 93–106.

Müller, Wolfgang C. and Strøm, Kaare (eds.) (2000). *Coalition Governments in Western Europe*. Oxford: Oxford University Press.

Pennings, Paul and Keman, Hans (2002). 'Towards a New Methodology of Estimating Party Policy Positions', *Quality & Quantity*, 36: 55–79.

Riker, William H. (1962). *The Theory of Political Coalitions*. New Haven, CT: Yale University Press.

Strøm, Kaare, Müller, Wolfgang C., and Bergman, Torbjörn (eds.) (2003). *Delegation and Accountability in Parliamentary Democracies*. Oxford: Oxford University Press.

Toole, James (2000). 'Government Formation and Party System Stabilization in East-Central Europe', *Party Politics*, 6: 441–61.

Warwick, Paul V. (2006). *Policy Horizons and Parliamentary Government*. Houndmills, UK: Palgrave Macmillan.

Zielinski, Jakub, Slomczynski, Kazimir M., and Shabad, Goldie (2005). 'Electoral Control in New Democracies', *World Politics*, 57: 365–95.

Index

Aardal, Bernt 372 n., 381
accountability 242, 371, 391
 electoral 125, 242, 404
 mechanisms 4, 161
 structures 2, 101
Adrian, Charles R. 26
agency costs 3, 161–2, 425–8
agency problems, *see* agency costs
agenda control 10, 17, 161, 162, 241, 280, 354, 358, 378, 408, 419
agenda setting, *see* agenda control
Aghion, Phillippe 180, 181
Aldrich, John H. 2, 119 n. 16
Allison, Paul D. 121 n.
Alt, James E. 29, 302
Amorim Neto, Octavio 77, 422
Andeweg, Rudy B. 27, 34, 41, 88, 91, 154, 186 n., 271, 272, 277, 292, 311, 413
Anderson, Christopher 373, 375, 376 n. 9
Ansolabehere, Stephen 141 n. 13, 240, 241, 245
Arkins, Audrey 68
asset specificity 70, 71 n., 335, 359
audience costs 165, 169, 409, 413
Austen-Smith, David 25, 36, 75, 141 n. 13, 241, 371
Austria 10, 13, 18, 27, 33 n., 131, 139 n. 10, 148, 151, 162–3, 170, 171, 172, 174, 176, 177, 185, 195, 208, 241, 243 n., 245, 252, 253, 260, 273, 288, 307, 311, 323, 330, 342, 381, 427
 Austrian People's Party (ÖVP) 10, 27, 139 n., 243 n.
 Christian Socials 18
 Freedom Party 13–14, 27, 243 n.
 Social Democrats 10–11, 13–14, 18, 27, 243 n. 2
Axelrod, Robert 22, 30, 166, 202, 203, 204, 216, 217, 349

Bäck, Hanna 35, 56, 88, 124, 141 n. 13, 152 n., 205, 425
Bagehot, Walter 270
Bakema, Wilma E. 277
Bale, Tim 6 n. 5,
Bandyopadhyay, Siddhartha 18 n.
Banfield, Edward C. 54
Banks, Jeffrey S. 25, 36, 75, 141 n. 13, 241, 371
Banzhaf index 63 n., 96, 191 n., 231, 246–7, 345, 351
Banzhaf, John F., III, 63 n., 345
bargaining:
 advantage 191
 definition 59
 inter-party 14, 53, 123, 125, 143, 160, 334–5, 346, 354, 355, 403
 intra-party 14, 73, 123, 201 n. 2, 259, 334, 335 n., 354, 356
 post-election 12, 138, 145
 requirements 57–8
 situation 66, 134–5, 136–7, 138, 141 n. 14, 153, 187, 202, 211, 231, 244, 247, 250, 279, 410, 411, 414; *see also* bargaining environment
bargaining complexity 21, 58, 70, 101, 123–4, 125, 133–4, 135–7, 138–9, 140–2, 145, 151, 153, 172, 190, 246, 250, 280, 286, 296, 320, 334, 344, 345, 347, 348, 349, 351, 354, 359, 404, 408, 413, 414; *see also* bargaining environment
bargaining costs, *see* agency costs; audience costs; transaction costs
bargaining duration, *see* cabinet formation, duration
bargaining environment 15, 19, 20–1, 25–8, 75, 78, 91, 92, 93, 101–2, 137, 148, 172, 190, 193, 202, 219–20, 229–30, 258, 261, 279, 281, 286, 296, 303, 315, 320, 322, 323, 324, 345, 347, 348–9, 350–1, 352, 356–60, 363, 378, 391, 397, 406, 408, 413, 419–20, 421

bargaining power 9, 10, 24, 29, 62–7, 78, 80, 91, 95–7, 99, 125, 128, 139, 142, 153, 163, 191–2, 202, 213–15, 202, 213–4, 216, 218, 220, 222, 228–9, 230–2, 233, 239, 240–2, 244, 246, 247, 250, 286, 298, 303, 335, 344–5, 346–7, 348, 350, 351, 352, 386, 410–11, 413, 415, 418
  asymmetry 191–2, 202, 250, 409
  fragmentation 95–96, 141, 145, 148, 202, 229, 247, 316, 322, 388, 397, 410, 418
  see also walk-away value
bargaining rounds 28, 29, 40, 41, 67–8, 79, 124, 125, 128–33, 135, 136, 137, 138, 139, 143, 151–2, 153–4, 408, 416
  inconclusive 90, 102, 129–3, 139, 141, 143, 144–5, 148, 153–4, 193, 201, 220, 229, 231, 233, 315, 320–1, 408, 417–18, 419, 420, 427
bargaining uncertainty 13–14, 18, 66–7, 69–71, 78, 79, 91, 102, 124, 133–5, 137–8, 139, 140, 153, 160, 167–8, 186, 190, 193–4, 212, 213, 215, 216, 220, 232, 259, 335, 349, 352, 357, 358–9, 408–9, 410
  definition 13
  see also discount rate; information; opportunism
Baron, David P. 25, 36, 75, 126, 129, 141 n. 13, 241, 327 n. 2
Bastow, Simon 161 n.
Bates, Robert H. 34
Beck, Paul A. 381
Belgium 7 n. 6, 28, 65, 96 n. 5, 101, 130, 131, 142 n. 13, 143, 144, 148, 160, 171, 172, 176, 177, 185, 195, 209, 217, 241, 245, 252, 260, 271, 272, 273, 275, 277, 307, 311, 330, 342, 379, 427
  Rassemblement Walloon 217
  Tindemans IV Cabinet (1977) 272–3
  Volksunie (VU) 217
Bengtsson, Åsa 373
Benelux, see Belgium; the Netherlands; Luxembourg
Benoit, Kenneth 37, 39 n. 27, 348, 423
Bergman, Torbjörn 1, 2, 4, 6 n. 5, 12 n., 16, 24, 40, 41, 52, 87, 96, 100, 101, 109, 142, 142 n. 14, 151 n. 18, 219, 328, 405
Bernhard, William 28
Beyme, Klaus von 19, 302, 305
bicameralism 4, 7, 24, 96 n. 5, 98, 100–1, 142, 143, 152, 192, 211, 218–19, 250, 264, 353, 354, 356, 412
Black, Duncan 376
Blais, André 5
Blomgren, Magnus 109
Blondel, Jean 16, 31, 32, 35 n., 269, 271, 273, 276, 278, 297
Blossfeld, Hans-Peter 122
Bogdanor, Vernon 6 n. 5, 34
Bortne, Øystein 315
Box-Steffensmeier, Janet M. 122, 337 n. 12, 339
Brams, Steven J. 126, 134 n., 239 n.
Britain, see United Kingdom
Browne, Eric C. 19, 20, 28, 34, 57, 75, 204, 238, 239, 244, 302, 304, 333, 349, 360
Brundtland, Gro Harlem 68
Budge, Ian 20, 23, 23 n. 14, 24, 34, 38, 39, 56, 65, 89, 98, 99, 141, 205, 215 n. 9, 218, 237, 239, 244, 302, 304, 305, 309, 315, 329 n. 3, 348, 375, 422, 423
Bueno de Mesquita, Bruce 239
Butler, David 372 n.

cabinet (government):
  definition 6
  as unit of analysis 88–9
  see also coalition
cabinet appointment 72, 100, 101, 168, 185, 237, 259–60, 264–5, 330, 413, 424; see also portfolio; portfolio allocation
cabinet authority 162–3, 180–2, 182–3
cabinet committee 271, 293, 298
cabinet continuation 142, 151, 295, 303, 311, 334, 353
cabinet dissolution 12, 24, 29, 71–2, 74–5, 76, 77, 100, 154, 247, 259, 303, 313–14, 315, 320, 324, 330, 344, 354, 356, 358, 370, 378, 412, 413, 419, 421; see also elections, early
cabinet durability 327–9, 332, 334–5, 342, 345, 346, 348, 350, 356–7, 362–4, 406, 414, 418, 420

cabinet duration 21, 31, 92, 121, 151, 190, 216, 277, 327, 329, 330, 331, 333, 337, 345, 347, 360, 385, 414–15, 418, 419, 420, 421
cabinet formation 30, 90, 123–6, 153, 201, 332, 408, 411, 419, 421, 427
  definition 124
  duration (bargaining duration) 131, 137, 138, 148–54, 193, 220, 229–30, 232, 233, 320, 359, 360, 408, 416, 417, 418, 427
cabinet governance 90, 101–2, 162, 329, 335, 417, 419
  inner 271, 273
  membership 30, 329
  size determinants 202–4, 205, 212, 213
cabinet stability 75, 121, 162; *see also* cabinet duration
cabinet survival, *see* cabinet duration
cabinet tenure, *see* cabinet duration
cabinet termination 92, 301–24, 329–31, 337, 343, 378, 414, 418, 419
  conflictual *see* cabinet termination, discretionary
  definition 302–3
  discretionary 128, 131, 303, 304, 305, 307, 309, 312–13, 320–2, 323, 331, 333, 335, 336–9, 342, 343, 346, 347, 350–2, 353–6, 359–60, 362–3, 386, 414, 420, 427
  technical 126, 128, 148, 303–4, 305, 307, 309, 313, 316, 320–2, 323, 331, 337–8, 386, 414, 427
  see also cabinet replacement; elections, early; coalition enlargement, voluntary
cabinet transition 126, 302
cabinet turnover 53–4, 55, 124, 255, 304, 305, 323; *see also* cabinet termination
cabinet type 21, 30, 201, 204, 208, 221, 230, 308, 316, 323, 331, 346, 382, 410–11, 416, 418, 421
  caretaker 66, 186, 196, 221 n. 17, 279
  coalition 6, 7, 202, 206, 308, 309, 314, 323, 344, 347, 371, 382–3, 386–7, 410
  majority 7, 91, 139, 206–9, 214, 314–15, 320, 331, 334, 343, 344, 359, 371, 382, 391, 410, 415, 416
  minimal-connected winning (MCWC) 203–4, 217, 349–50, 351

  minimal or minimum winning (MWC) 21, 190, 202–3, 204, 205–8, 211–13, 215, 217, 218, 221, 228, 229, 231, 232, 316, 323, 332, 333, 344, 346, 349–50, 391, 410–11, 415
  minority 7, 91, 202, 204, 206, 208–9, 213, 215, 228, 229, 230, 232, 314–15, 316, 343, 346, 359, 371, 382, 391, 410–11, 415, 420
  multiparty 91, 126, 160, 165, 170, 344, 359, 374, 397
  non-partisan 7, 8, 109, 141 n. 12, 221 n. 17
  replacement 331, 337–9, 342–3, 346–7, 349, 351–2, 354–6, 361, 363–4
  single-party 7, 91, 124, 139, 165, 202, 206, 207–8, 214, 308, 309, 314–15, 316, 323, 334, 344, 347, 359, 371, 382, 397, 410, 420
  successor 123, 124, 309, 311–12, 323
  surplus (oversized) 142, 163, 190, 202, 204, 206, 207–9, 212, 213–15, 217, 219, 221, 228, 229–30, 231, 232, 247, 258, 320, 323, 344, 382–3, 391, 397, 410–11, 415–16, 418, 419
  survivor *see* successor
  undersized 201, 212
Canada 90, 271
  Trudeau Cabinets 271
Caplow, Theodore 240
Carmignani, Fabrizio 241
Carroll, Royce 241, 422
Carrubba, Clifford J. 35, 212, 214, 222
Caulier, Jean-François 96, 97
Chatterjee, Kalyan 18 n.
Chen, Yongmin 181
Chertkoff, Jerome M. 126
Churchill, Winston 271
Cioffi-Revilla, Claudio 75, 360
Clarke, Kenneth 362
coalition agreements 14–17, 18, 90–1, 159–60, 164–5, 169–74, 187, 191, 194, 195, 264, 269, 273, 280, 281, 286, 289, 291, 292, 298, 315, 321, 336, 356, 357, 359, 409–10, 413, 416, 417, 418, 419, 420, 428
  formal 165, 166, 167, 168, 169, 186, 194, 357–8, 418
coalition alternatives 76, 137, 141, 191, 279
coalition committee 271–2, 273, 413

coalition, definition 6, 52
coalition discipline 16, 102, 160, 164, 165, 174, 176–9, 195, 250, 280, 295, 321–2, 356, 358, 359, 360, 364, 412, 414, 418
coalition enlargement, voluntary 92, 128, 133, 304, 307, 308, 313, 322, 386 n.
coalition formation 9, 211, 220–1, 221, 230, 231, 404, 411, 417, 422, 423
  coalescence 15, 51–2, 59–62, 64, 66, 69–70, 72 n., 75, 141, 214, 215 n. 9
coalition governance 9, 31–3, 53, 79, 160, 165, 184–5, 195, 269, 336, 356, 403, 413, 417, 423, 428; *see also* conflict
  ex ante mechanisms 182, 183 195, 357, 409
  ex post mechanisms 182–3, 185, 196, 409
coalition life cycle 9, 10, 17, 52, 58, 59, 79, 86, 123, 126, 403–4, 406, 428
  phases 9, 85, 90
coalition membership 9, 22, 30–1, 66–7, 143, 163, 369; *see also* incumbency
coalition type
  convex 140
  grand 11, 139 n., 177, 205, 220–1, 272
  pre-election 125, 170, 171 n. 3, 241
  proto-coalition 30, 96
  purple 56
  rainbow 56
commitment 61, 168
  credible 67, 212–13, 232
  mechanisms 212, 220
  problems 93, 101, 334–5, 348, 356, 359
  see also credibility; opportunism; bargaining uncertainty
Comparative Manifesto Project (CMP) 422, 423
Comparative Parliamentary Democracy Data Archive 109, 303
conflict:
  avoidance 169
  characteristics 52, 275–8
  inter-departmental 277, 290, 292–4, 297, 298
  inter-party 165, 277, 290, 294–6, 297, 305, 307, 308, 309, 315, 359
  intra-coalition 160, 270, 296, 305, 307, 308, 309,
  intra-party 11, 308–9, 315, 308, 309, 313, 315, 323

  management mechanisms 91, 269–70, 278, 281 286, 289–90, 297, 356–7, 413, 417, 428
  resolution arena 270, 271–3, 275, 278–81, 286–8, 289–90, 296–9, 413, 418–19, 420
  resolution procedure 270, 292, 421; *see also* decision rules
  see also cabinet termination, discretionary
continuation rule 142, 151, 303
constitutional inter-election period (CIEP) 28, 74, 89n., 121, 190, 215, 329, 330, 331, 333, 336 n. 11, 337, 339, 342, 345, 347, 351, 353, 354–5, 359, 362, 364, 417
contracts 60, 159, 174, 180, 185, 410
  complete 63, 175, 182, 358
  incomplete 14, 175, 181, 335
  restrictive 69–70, 177, 190, 192, 193, 194
  see also coalition agreements
cooperation:
  electoral 17
  inter-party 5, 6, 160, 166–7, 345, 355, 358–9
Cotta, Maurizio 315
country-specific determinants, *see* spatio-temporal determinants
Cox proportional hazard models 121, 139, 336, 338, 339, 346, 356
Cowley, Philip 334
Cox, Gary W. 2, 17, 24, 62, 241, 422
credibility 57 n., 61–2, 63, 67, 79, 213, 335, 345, 399; *see also* commitment; walk-away value
Crewe, Ivor 381
Criscitiello, Anarita 272
Crombez, Christophe 30, 120, 204, 214, 216, 218, 221, 232
Cronin, Thomas E. 369 n., 370
cumul des mandats 273

Daalder, Hans 376 n. 10
Dahl, Robert A. 1, 2, 371
Dalton, Russell J. 381
Damgaard, Erik 6, 41, 92, 302, 307, 309, 315, 316, 414, 427
Davidsson, Lars 142
De Ridder, Martine M. 175

de Swaan, Abram 22, 30, 34, 39, 55, 202, 203, 204, 216, 377
De Vries, Miranda 140
De Winter, Lieven 18, 34, 41, 88, 90, 124, 134, 154, 159, 201, 233, 239, 273, 311, 408, 427
decision-making mechanisms, *see* decision rules
decision rules 16, 24, 211, 213, 219, 270, 294, 410
　collective 16, 162
　decision-by-interpretation 270–1
　decision-by-majority 270
　formal 270
　informal 125, 270
　majority 64, 65
　qualified majority 24, 51, 151, 270
　quantitative, *see* investiture; bicameralism
　simple majority 23 n. 15, 51, 211, 270
　special majority 142–3
　supermajority 142, 151, 154, 211, 214
　unanimity 16, 162, 270, 279, 354, 355, 358, 415
Deemen, A. M. A. van 31
delegation 1–2, 4, 29, 51–2, 62, 77, 102, 161–2, 167, 181, 291–2, 294, 403, 426, 427
　problems 93, 101
democracy 1, 2, 3, 56, 123, 205, 215 n. 9, 330, 369, 425, 428
　consociational 177, 196
　parliamentary, *see* parliamentarism
　representative 1–2, 9, 51
democratic deficit 51
Denmark 98, 131, 142, 171, 172, 174, 176, 177, 180–1, 183, 185, 195, 205, 208, 209, 241, 245, 260, 262, 287, 305, 307, 315, 330, 331 n., 342, 375 n. 8, 379, 426
　Centre Democrats 209
　Radical Liberals (RL) 209
Denver, David 381
departmentalism 161–3
Dewatripont, Mathias 181
Diermeier, Daniel 21, 25, 29 n., 31, 36, 36 n. 23, 36 n. 24, 75, 78, 79, 85, 126, 134, 137, 138, 139, 140, 141, 141 n. 13, 142, 145, 148, 151 n., 193, 327 n. 2, 328, 333, 334, 336 n. 11, 337, 338, 344, 353, 354, 358, 359, 363, 364
discount rate 66–8, 76, 79, 153, 294, 353, 359; *see also* bargaining uncertainty
Dittrich, Karl 27
Dixit, Avinash K. 335, 355, 357
Dodd, Lawrence C. 6 n. 3, 21, 34, 39, 99 n., 302, 316, 344
Dorff, Robert H. 270
Dorussen, Han 372, 398
Downs, Anthony 376
Downs, William M. 35, 56, 166
Dreijmanis, John 20, 34
Druckman, James N. 24, 37, 101, 143, 219, 239, 240, 241, 243, 244, 245, 247, 307, 422
Dumont, Patrick 34, 41, 88, 90, 96, 97, 124, 134, 141 n. 13, 152 n., 154, 159, 201, 206, 233, 273, 311, 408, 425, 427
Dunleavy, Patrick 161 n.
Duverger, Maurice 376 n. 10

Easton, Stephen T. 75,
elections:
　alliances 17, 24, 96 n. 5, 125, 170, 241; *see also* coalition type, pre-election
　decisive 5, 209, 404
　early 12, 17, 74, 75, 89 n., 92, 122, 128, 131–3, 152, 305, 307–8, 309, 313–16, 320–2, 323–4, 330 n., 331, 336–9, 342–7, 351–6, 360–1, 363–4, 378, 385–7, 388, 396–7, 398, 414, 415, 417, 418
　electoral advantage 166, 315, 398
　electoral connection 9, 62, 79
　electoral expectations 11, 73, 76, 92, 209, 280
　performance 12, 85, 92, 103, 103 n., 133, 213, 369–75, 376 n. 12, 377, 378–9, 381–2, 383–5, 388, 391, 396–7, 415–16, 417, 420, 421
　strategic timing 12, 386, 398
electoral systems 4–5, 24–5, 100, 371
　proportional representation (PR) 2, 4, 5, 7, 61, 100, 123, 320, 322, 371, 382, 403, 414, 427, 428
Elgie, Robert 7 n. 7
Elklit, Jørgen 2
Elster, Jon 165
employment, *see* unemployment

Enelow, James 376 n. 11
enforcement mechanisms 169, 174–5,
    180–1, 186–7, 195, 260, 335
  ex ante 91, 182–3, 192, 194, 195, 409
    see also identifiability
  ex post 25, 91, 182–3, 185, 196, 409 *see
    also* accountability, verification
Epstein, David 69
Epstein, Leon D. 371
Eraslan, Hulya 36
event history analysis 90, 92, 105,
    121–2, 139, 329, 333, 336–7,
    343
events, critical 28–9, 31, 56–7, 76–7,
    102–3, 143, 148n., 152, 154, 193–4,
    220–1, 230, 247, 258, 259, 261, 281,
    302, 316, 321, 333, 360–2, 372–4,
    386–7, 391, 396, 397, 406, 408, 412,
    419–20, 421 *see* inflation;
    unemployment; volatility, electoral
events, random 29, 104, 313, 329, 333–4,
    338, 339, 360, 362
exogenous events, *see* critical events

Farlie, Dennis 375
Feddersen, Timothy J. 334, 354, 358
Ferejohn, John A. 241, 327 n. 2
Feste, Karen Ann 244
Finland 8, 28, 56, 101, 130, 131, 144, 151,
    164, 170, 171, 172, 177, 180–1, 185,
    193, 195, 208, 209, 217, 221 n. 17,
    241, 245, 252, 260, 261, 275, 288,
    305, 307, 311, 323, 330, 342, 379,
    427
  popular front (1966) 164
  Centre Party 164
  Social Democrats 164
  Communists 164
  Greens (GR) 217
  Christian League (CHR) 217
FitzGerald, Garret 291–2, 293, 294
Fiorina, Morris P. 369, 372
Flanagan, Scott C. 381
Forestiere, Carolyn 219
formateur 65, 126, 128, 137, 139, 141
    n. 13, 143, 239, 241, 243, 344,
    353
France 7, 8, 24, 98, 101, 109, 118, 130,
    131, 139 n., 142, 148, 151, 170, 171,
    172, 176, 185, 193, 196, 244, 252,
    253, 258, 260, 277, 305, 307, 311,
    379, 426, 427

Chaban Delmas Cabinet (1969) 139 n.
Communist Party 139 n.
Couve de Murville Cabinet (1968) 139 n.
Fifth Republic 7, 109, 118
Gaullist Coalitions 139 n.
Mauroy II Cabinet (1981) 139 n.
Messmer I Cabinet (1972) 139 n.
Messmer II Cabinet (1973) 244
Socialist Coalition 139 n.
Frank, Robert H. 166
Franklin, Mark N. 20, 26, 89, 94, 126, 204,
    205, 238, 239, 404
Frendreis, John P. 28, 28 n., 57, 75, 239,
    302, 304, 333, 360
Frognier, André 32
Fudenberg, Drew 66, 69

Gabel, Matthew J. 99
Gamson, William A. 21, 32, 91, 203 n. 4,
    238
Gamson's Law; *see* portfolio allocation,
    proportionality norm
Garry, John 39 n. 26, 39 n. 27, 423
George, David Lloyd 335 n.
Gerlich, Peter 162, 309
Germany 11, 12 n., 13, 18, 25, 33 n.,
    65, 70, 94, 96 n. 5, 130, 131,
    139 n., 142 n. 13, 148, 167, 170,
    171, 172, 177, 185, 208, 241, 252,
    258, 260, 271, 272, 275, 277, 279,
    307, 329 n. 3, 330, 339, 357 n., 379,
    426
  Adenauer II–V Cabinets (1953–60)
    139 n.
  Bundestag 18, 272
  Christian Democrats (CDU/CSU) 11,
    18, 65, 139 n., 272
  Free Democrats (FDP) 11, 18, 65, 70,
    139 n., 272
  Greens 13, 167
  Red-Green Coalition 13
  Social Democrats 65, 167
Gleiber, Dennis W. 19, 28, 28 n., 57, 75,
    302, 304, 333, 349, 360
Goldberg, Arthur S. 13
Golder, Sona N. 125, 137, 138, 139, 142,
    142 n. 14, 151 n.
Gordon, Sanford C. 75
government, *see* cabinet
Greece 37, 89, 90, 98 n. 7, 109, 118,
    128 n., 129 n. 5, 130, 131, 142, 144,
    171, 177, 183, 252, 253, 260, 307,

309, 311, 342, 379, 381, 405, 415, 426
gridlock 52, 354, 428
Groennings, Sven 34
Grofman, Bernard 18 n., 21, 29, 30, 74, 94, 123, 136, 140, 332, 345
Gross Domestic Product (GDP) 118, 373, 383, 391, 396

Haider, Jörg 14
Hansen, Hans Christian 331 n.
Harrop, Martin 373
Haughey, Charles 68
Hazan, Reuven Y. 377
hazard rate 31, 75, 92, 121, 333, 336–9, 346, 347, 354, 355, 364, 414
hazard ratio 121, 339, 342, 351, 353
Headey, Bruce 31
Hearl, Derek 423
Hedtoft, Hans 331 n.
Heller, William B. 24, 358
Herman, Valentine 21, 23 n. 14, 204, 345
Hibbs, Douglas A. 375
Hinich, Melvin J. 376
Hogwood, Brian W. 271
Holsteyn, Joop van 381
Huber, John D. 24, 39 n. 27, 62, 65, 99, 172, 327, 329, 334, 354, 358, 424
Hunt, W. Ben 37, 39 n. 25, 98, 219, 243, 348, 422

Iceland 37, 89, 90, 98 n. 7, 109, 130, 131, 142, 144 n., 170, 171, 176, 185, 208, 209, 219, 241, 242, 244, 245, 252, 258, 261, 287, 307, 311, 330, 342, 405, 427
   Jonsson I–II Cabinets (1958–59) 244
identifiability 137, 141
ideology, *see* preferences
immobilisme, *see* gridlock
incumbency 370–99, 415, 417, 419
   advantage 151
   costs 209, 290, 369, 370, 371 n. 2, 372, 378, 379–81, 382, 385, 388, 398, 426–7
Indridason, Indridi H. 40, 143, 405, 424
inflation 118, 122, 148 n., 321, 324, 360–1, 369, 373, 375–6, 383–5, 387, 391, 396, 397, 414, 415–16, 420
information 13, 213
   asymmetry 137, 161, 180–2, 259–60, 313–14

complete 36, 129, 167, 202, 211–12, 231
costs 25, 26, 133, 175, 335
incomplete 36, 66–7, 134–5, 137, 138, 167, 204, 214
see also bargaining uncertainty
institutions (as determinants of coalition bargaining) 23–5, 56, 58, 65–6, 77, 79, 100–1, 126, 139, 141–3, 145, 151–2, 154, 162, 167, 180, 192–3, 195, 211, 218–19, 229, 250, 258–9, 264, 277, 279–80, 281, 315, 320, 324, 334, 353–6, 357, 360, 361, 364, 378, 388, 391, 405, 406, 408, 411, 419, 421, 423
   electoral, *see* electoral system
   procedural rules, *see* continuation rule; formateur
   see also bicameralism; decision rules; investiture; prime minister powers
International Monetary Fund (IMF) 118, 373 n.
investiture requirement 65, 89 n., 100–1, 142, 219, 229, 232, 353, 363; *see also* positive parliamentarism
Ireland 67, 68, 142, 170, 171, 174, 176, 177, 185, 208, 209–10, 212, 241, 245, 252, 253, 270, 289–90, 291–2, 293, 294, 297, 298, 305, 307, 311, 330, 342, 379, 387, 413
   Costello I Cabinet (1948) 387
   Labour Party 67, 212, 290–4, 297, 298
   Fianna Fáil 68, 210 n., 290, 291, 294
   Fine Gael 67, 210 n., 290, 291, 293, 297, 387
   FitzGerald II Cabinet (1982) 291–4
   Killarney Compromise 67
   Progressive Democrats (PD) 68
Irwin, Galen 381, 386,
Israel 28, 64, 65, 90, 166 n., 422
   Labour Party 64, 65
   Likud Party 64, 65, 335 n.
   Kadima Party 335 n.
issue dimensionality, *see* policy dimensions
Italy 7 n. 6, 8, 28, 53, 54, 55, 56 96 n. 5, 101, 131, 140 n. 10, 143, 170, 174, 183, 195, 196, 205, 208, 228, 241, 245, 251, 252, 260, 272, 273, 305, 307, 311, 315, 323, 329 n. 3, 330, 342, 381, 426

Italy (*cont.*)
  Christian Democrats (CD) 53, 54, 55
  Communists 55, 98 n. 6
  D'Alema Cabinet (1998) 244
  De Gasperi V–VII Cabinets (1948–51) 140 n. 10
  Italian Social Movement (MSI) 55–56
  Republican Party (PRI) 55, 140 n. 10

Jones, Bradford S. 122, 337 n., 339
Jun, Uwe 166
Jungar, Ann-Cathrine 34
junior ministers 91, 105, 161–2, 181–2, 183, 185, 196, 238, 259–61, 264, 265, 290, 409, 411–12, 417, 418–19

Kaashoek, Remco 75
Kalandrakis, Tasos 205, 215, 221 n. 16, 222
Kam, Christopher 424
Katz, Richard S. 352
Kayser, Mark A. 354
Kelley, E. W. 34
Keman, Hans 89, 153, 205, 215 n. 9, 239, 244, 302, 304, 305, 309, 315, 329 n. 3, 423
Keohane, Robert O. 88
Kim, Dong-Hun 181
King, Gary 29, 74, 88, 89 n., 123, 135, 302, 333, 337, 337 n., 343, 345, 346, 353, 355, 359, 363
Klingemann, Hans-Dieter 25, 39, 422
Kosovo 13, 167
Krehbiel, Keith 167
Kreps, David M. 26, 60, 67, 166
Kropp, Sabine 34

Laakso, Markku 96, 164, 345
Laffont, Jean-Jacques 67, 175
Larsson, Torbjörn 162
Latvia 166 n.
Laver, Michael J. 14, 18 n., 20, 21, 22, 23, 24, 25, 27, 29, 30, 31, 32, 33, 34, 35, 36, 37, 38, 39 n., 53 n., 56, 65, 68, 76, 77, 85, 98, 99, 123, 126, 126 n. 3, 135, 136, 140, 141, 161, 162, 163, 180, 182, 191, 201, 203, 204, 205, 207, 209, 214, 214 n., 215, 216, 218, 219, 232, 237, 239, 240, 241, 242, 243, 244, 247, 271, 301, 304, 315, 327, 327 n. 1, 329, 329 n. 3, 332, 334, 337 n., 344, 345, 348, 349, 350, 371, 374, 404, 422, 423, 424
Leblang, David 28
legislators
  backbenchers 334–5, 358
  median 140, 151, 164, 191, 209–10, 279, 291, 292, 350–1, 377; *see also* party, median
logrolling 214, 276
Leipart, Jørn Y. 125
Leiserson, Michael 22, 30, 34, 36 n. 23, 136, 203 n. 4
Levine, David K. 69
Lewin, Leif 128, 302, 372 n.
Lewis-Beck, Michael 372, 373, 374
Lieberman, Evan S. 425
Lijphart, Arend 2, 5, 34, 56, 86, 140, 143, 302, 327, 329
Linz, Juan J. 327
Listhaug, Ola 360, 372 n.
Loewenberg, Gerhard 181
Luebbert, Gregory M. 22, 56, 68, 123, 276
Lupia, Arthur W. 12, 21, 23, 29, 31, 36, 41, 62, 65, 67, 71, 74, 76, 77, 78, 136, 211, 215 n. 9, 302, 314, 327, 333, 334, 336, 338, 343, 345, 346, 347, 350, 353, 362, 378, 385, 424
Luxembourg 8, 90, 95, 142, 170, 171, 176, 177, 183, 185, 206, 208, 241, 252, 253, 258, 305, 330, 342, 427

McCarty, Nolan 24, 65
McCubbins, Mathew D. 62, 67
Macdonald, Ramsay 335 n.
Macdonald, Stuart E. 376 n. 12
Mackie, Thomas T. 20, 26, 89, 94, 126, 166, 204, 205, 220, 271, 369, 370, 379, 381
McMillan, John 63
Mair, Peter 86, 87, 309
majority situation 139–140, 213, 221 n. 16, 221 n. 17
  definition 139
  manufactured 5, 201
  threshold 409
  see also cabinet type
Manow, Philip 180, 260
Marks, Gary 423
Marsh, Michael 67, 68, 290
Marshall, William 168

Martin, Lanny W. 31, 33, 34, 89, 120 n. 19, 138, 139, 145, 181, 204, 205, 260, 349
Martinez-Gallardo, Cecilia 424
Mashoba, Carolyn 19, 28, 349, 360
Mattila, Mikko 11 n. 8, 220
Mayntz, Renate 141, 277
Mellors, Colin 35
Merlo, Antonio 25, 36, 78, 79, 327 n. 2, 333, 334, 344
Mershon, Carol 6 n. 3, 251, 327
Miliband, Ralph 55
Mill, John Stuart 86
Miller, William L. 373
Milnor, A. J. 5
ministers, committee of 271–3, 293
ministers, number of 91, 95, 247, 251–3, 255, 259, 265, 412, 418; *see also* portfolio; portfolio allocation
ministries, *see* portfolio; portfolio allocation
minority situation 5, 61, 140, 144, 206, 222; *see also* cabinet type
Mitchell, Brian R. 118
Mitchell, Paul L. 41, 67, 68, 91, 95, 290, 291, 293, 294, 295, 307, 315, 410, 411
monitoring, *see* verification
motivation, *see* party motivation
Morgenstern, Oskar 21
Morelli, Massimo 241, 327 n. 2
Mueller, Dennis C. 11 n. 9, 18 n.
Müller, Wolfgang C. 1, 2, 4, 6, 7, 12 n., 16, 17, 18, 18 n., 23, 24, 30, 32, 33, 33 n., 34, 36 n. 24, 37, 40, 41, 52, 53, 87, 89, 89 n., 91, 96, 98 n. 7, 100, 102, 109, 134, 135, 136, 160, 162, 164, 166, 168, 177 n., 180, 213, 219, 238, 244 n. 2, 260, 271, 273, 303, 304, 309, 314, 330, 354, 356, 357, 358, 369, 373, 405, 409
Müller-Rommel, Ferdinand 16, 31, 32, 35 n., 269, 271

Narud, Hanne Marthe 41, 92, 136, 187, 209, 220, 309, 371, 379, 381, 386, 415
NATO 13, 167
Nedelmann, Birgitta 270
negotiation costs, *see* transaction costs
Nelson, Forrest D. 119 n. 16

the Netherlands 54, 56, 66, 95, 118, 126 n. 2, 130, 131, 142, 144, 148, 152–3, 160, 171, 172, 176, 177, 185, 186, 206, 217, 245, 252, 260, 270, 271, 272, 273, 277, 288, 289, 291–7, 298, 305, 307, 311, 330, 342, 381, 427
van Agt III Cabinet (1982) 186
Biesheuvel II Cabinet (1972) 186
Christian Democrats (CDA) 54, 153, 292, 295–6, 298
Democrats '66 (D'66) 126 n. 2, 217, 295
Liberals (VVD) 292, 295–6, 297–8
Lubbers I Cabinet (1982) 291–6
Social Democrats (PvdA) 292, 295–6, 297
turret consultation 272
Zijlstra Cabinet (1966) 186
Neumann, John von 21
Nigeria 426
Nordhaus, William A. 11
North, Douglass C. 167, 335
Norway 5, 11, 12, 68, 77, 95, 130, 131, 142, 148, 170, 171, 172, 174, 177, 185, 208, 209, 212, 222, 241, 252, 253, 260, 277, 305, 307, 314, 330, 342 n., 426–7
Christian People's Party (KRF) 209, 212
Conservative Party 68, 209
Labour Party 11, 68, 209
Nousiainen, Jaakko 24, 275, 305
Noviello, Nicholas 30
Nyblade, Benjamin 41, 91, 95, 99, 218, 232, 410, 411

office benefits 32, 57, 67, 91, 163, 166, 168, 237, 241, 335
expected 26, 353
incumbent 378, 396, 397, 398
individual 59–60, 64–5
party 64–5, 69, 72–5, 169, 349, 378, 385
policy advantage 57, 74, 166
short-term 355
spoils 23, 159, 166, 174, 242, 246, 258, 259, 265, 344
see also portfolio; portfolio allocation
O'Halloran, Sharyn 69
opportunism 69–71, 79, 91, 160, 168–9, 174, 182, 186, 187, 190–2, 193–4, 195, 210, 335, 349, 358, 378, 409

opportunity costs 27, 73, 345
Organization for Economic Cooperation and Development (OECD) 118, 373 n., 385 n. 16

pacts, *see* coalition agreements
Pajala, Antti 96 n. 5, 140
Paldam, Martin 372
Palmer, Harvey D. 398
Pappi, Franz Urban 25
parliamentarism (parliamentary democracy) 2, 4–5, 9, 61, 66, 71, 74, 77, 79, 80, 161, 162, 179, 182, 195–6, 201, 212, 231–2, 237, 239, 259, 301, 369, 403–5, 406, 410, 422, 425–8
parliamentarism, negative 24
parliamentarism, positive 101, 142, 151, 192, 194, 219, 229, 231, 264, 281, 286, 296, 320, 322, 324, 353, 355, 363, 411, 412, 413, 414, 415, 419; *see also* investiture
parliament, majority, *see* party, seat share
party:
  anti-system 23 n. 14, 141, 192, 218, 228
  coalitionable 139, 140, 141
  core 99, 151, 191, 218, 228–9, 230, 264, 408
  effective number of 95–7, 137, 141, 216 n. 11, 217, 345, 347–8, 373, 397, 418
  extremist 99–100, 151, 191–2, 281, 286, 320, 348–9, 351, 352, 372, 388, 409, 418, 427
  incumbent 383, 387, 391, 397; *see also* incumbency
  median 22, 97–8, 100 n., 140, 191, 194, 204, 209–10, 217–18, 228, 230–1, 232, 250, 279, 320, 350, 376–7, 381, 410–11, 412, 418; *see also* legislator, median
  number of (absolute) 95–7, 136, 138, 141, 145, 151, 190, 205, 215–16, 22, 228, 247, 251, 253, 258, 264, 344, 346, 388, 408, 409, 417–18, 427; *see also* party, effective number of
  pivotal 70, 99, 137, 163, 190, 250, 350, 377; *see also* party, median
  seat share 96, 99–100, 190–1, 214–16, 222, 228, 239, 246–7, 250, 258, 343, 345, 350, 406, 418
  summit 272–3, 290, 294

Party Manifesto Research Group (MRG) 39 n. 26, 98, 99, 141, 349, 422
party motivation:
  office-seeking 22, 23, 204, 208–9, 212–13, 237, 348, 369, 396
  policy-seeking 22, 23, 32, 209, 238, 243–4, 348, 369, 396
  vote-seeking 135, 209, 348, 369, 396
party system 17, 21, 145, 191, 286, 314, 345, 348–9, 370, 371, 377, 399, 415, 422
  complexity 21, 145, 217
  fragmentation 95, 101, 137, 141, 148, 217, 247, 296, 323, 372, 388, 408, 412, 415, 418
  see also structural determinants
path dependency 54–5, 153, 184–6, 196, 264, 287, 290, 298, 409, 413, 421
Pedersen, Mogens 381
Pelizzo, Ricardo 99
Pennings, Paul 423
Persson, Torsten 175
Peters, B. Guy 40 n.
Peterson, Robert L. 175
Petrocik, John R. 375 n. 7
Pfahler, Madelaine 172
Philipp, Wilfried 162
Pijnenburg, Bert 35
Pinto-Dushinsky, Michael 123
Poguntke, Thomas 70
polarization, *see* preferences
policy dimensions 39, 97–9, 140–1, 145, 148, 151, 191, 194, 203–4, 209–10, 217–18, 228, 230, 244, 250, 279, 286, 292, 320, 348–52, 376–7, 408, 410, 411, 412, 415, 418
Polsby, Nelson W. 369 n., 370
portfolio:
  saliency 243, *see also* portfolio allocation, qualitative
  structure 250–3, 255, 265
  valuation 240, 242
portfolio allocation 14, 15–16, 29, 91, 161–2, 174, 204, 237–65, 350, 357, 374–5, 381, 398, 411–13, 418
  disproportionality 244–7, 250, 264, 412, 417
  proportionality norm 91, 238–40, 241–4, 265, 411–12, 417
  qualitative 238, 242–4

Index

quantitative, *see* portfolio allocation, proportionality norm
Portugal 37, 90, 96 n. 5, 100, 109, 129 n. 5, 130, 131, 170, 171, 172, 174, 176, 183, 185, 193, 245, 261, 307, 309, 330, 342, 379, 381, 405, 415
Powell, G. Bingham 2, 56, 345, 371, 375, 379
preferences (as determinants of coalition bargaining) 21–3, 39, 55–6, 66, 72, 76, 87, 97–100, 134–5, 145, 148, 152, 153, 191–2, 195, 202–5, 210, 213, 216–18, 228–9, 230, 231, 258, 261, 264, 276, 277, 279, 281, 286, 315, 320, 322, 324, 346, 348–53, 354, 375, 388, 391, 406, 408, 411, 418, 421, 422, 426
   cohesion 97, 140–1
   connected 98, 140, 191, 203–4, 217, 279, 281, 349–50, 351
   distribution of 210, 218, 418
   divergent 10, 99, 126, 139, 141, 145, 148, 151, 165–7, 174, 181, 186–7, 195, 260, 276, 277, 297, 344, 409
   diversity 22, 56, 99, 138, 141, 151, 160, 167, 191, 203, 218, 228, 347, 348–51, 409
   polarization 99, 138, 141, 191, 218, 230, 258, 264, 296, 320, 348–9, 352, 372, 388, 391, 408, 411, 412, 416, 418
   tangential 276
presidentialism 2, 4, 211, 422
Press, Charles 26
Presthus, Rolf 68
Pridham, Geoffrey 34
prime minister powers (PM powers) 12, 24, 101, 143, 145, 148, 151, 154, 192–3, 219, 229 n., 258–9, 280, 281, 294, 296, 297, 320, 324, 353, 354, 355–6, 358, 364, 405, 408, 411, 412, 413, 415, 419, 421; *see also* agenda control; cabinet dissolution; vote, confidence
proportionality norm *see* portfolio allocation
Przeworski, Adam 86
Putnam, Robert D. 334

Rabinowitz, George 376 n. 12
Ragin, Charles C. 19 n.

Raunio, Tapio 11 n. 8, 220
reservation value 63, 166, 357, 359; *see also* walk-away value
responsibility 26 n., 182, 290, 370–3, 381, 385, 396
Rey, Patrick 181
Reynolds, Andrew 2
Richardson, J. J. 309
Riker, William H. 21, 22, 30, 32, 55, 202, 203, 203 n. 4, 204, 205, 206, 208, 211, 212, 213, 214, 215, 215 n. 9, 410, 418
risk, definition 13–14; *see also* opportunism; bargaining uncertainty
Roberts, Andrew 239, 422
Robertson, David 205, 423
Rohwer, Götz 122
Rokkan, Stein 55
Roland, Gerard 175
Roozendaal, Peter van 18 n. 11, 21, 22, 29, 30, 31, 36 n., 74, 123, 134, 136, 136 n., 137, 138, 139, 140, 141, 141 n. 13, 142, 145, 148, 151 n., 191, 193, 332, 337 n., 344
Rose, Richard 166, 220, 369, 370, 379, 381
Rosenstone, Steven 371
Rudzio, Wolfgang 33 n.

Saalfeld, Thomas 5 n., 18, 41, 92, 272, 364, 414, 415
Salanié, Bernard 175
Sanders, David 21, 345
Sartori, Giovanni 1, 2, 6 n. 4, 86, 96, 214, 349, 376 n. 10
Scharpf, Fritz W. 141, 328
Schattschneider, E. E. 2, 371
Schneider, Friedrich 372
Schofield, Norman 20, 21, 22, 23, 24, 25, 29, 30, 53 n., 56, 85, 123, 126 n. 3, 135, 136, 140, 141 n. 13, 191, 201, 203, 203 n. 5, 204, 207, 209, 237, 239, 240, 241, 247, 301, 304, 315, 329, 329 n. 3, 332, 334, 344, 345, 348, 349, 350
Schröder, Gerhard 13
Schumpeter, Joseph A. 2
Schüttemeyer, Suzanne S. 34
screening procedures 100, 126, 151–2, 192, 194, 358

semi-presidentialism 101, 151, 154, 179, 192–3, 195, 211, 219, 229, 231, 232, 307, 354, 356, 391, 408, 411, 415, 416, 419
Sened, Itai 30, 204
Shabad, Goldie 422
shadow of the future 10, 14, 15, 17, 58, 63, 71, 79–80, 166, 369, 428
shadow of the past 15, 17, 36, 85, 193, 404, 406, 428
Shapley, Lloyd S. 64 n., 96
Shapley-Shubik index 63 n., 96
Sharon, Ariel 335 n.
Shepsle, Kenneth A. 14, 29, 31, 32, 33, 34, 36, 76, 77, 99, 161, 162, 163, 166, 180, 182, 204, 205, 214, 214 n., 215, 217, 218, 218 n., 232, 237, 244, 271, 348, 350, 371, 374, 424
Shipan, Charles R. 172
Shively, W. Phillips 104
shocks, *see* critical events
Shubik, Martin 63 n., 96
Shugart, Matthew S. 5, 140
Siaroff, Alan 5
size principle 203, 211, 212, 213, 410
Sjöblom, Gunnar 35
Slomczynski, Kazimierz M. 422
Smith Alastair 12, 314, 322, 343, 346, 356
Smith, Gordon 309
Spain 7, 37, 89, 90, 95, 98 n. 7, 109, 118, 129 n. 5, 130, 131, 170, 206, 208, 222, 231, 253, 305, 307, 309, 330, 342, 379, 381, 405, 415, 427
spatio-temporal determinants 19–20, 55, 66, 76, 94–5, 128 n., 131, 145, 152, 153, 177, 204, 222, 247, 255, 261, 281, 286, 309, 314, 316, 336, 339, 342, 382, 388, 391, 409, 416–17, 420, 426
specialization, *see* asset specificity
Spring, Dick 293
Steiner, Jürg 270
Steinmo, Sven 54
Stevenson, Randolph T. 21, 29 n., 31, 34, 75, 89, 120 n. 19, 204, 205, 334, 336 n. 11, 336, 338, 353, 364
Stiglitz, Joseph E. 166, 175 n., 181
Stokes, Donald E. 373 n. 4
Straffin, Philip 30
Strøm, Kaare 1, 2, 4, 6, 6 n. 3, 7, 12, 12 n., 16, 21, 23, 24, 28, 29, 30, 31, 32, 33,
34, 36, 36 n. 2, 37, 40, 41, 52, 53, 53 n., 56, 61, 65, 68, 71, 74, 76, 77, 78, 87, 89, 89 n., 91, 96, 98 n. 7, 100, 102, 109, 123, 125, 134, 135, 136, 137, 141, 142, 151, 151 n., 160, 161, 161 n., 162, 163, 164, 166, 180, 204, 205, 207, 209, 211, 213, 215 n. 9, 218, 219, 221, 232, 238, 260, 271, 302, 303, 304, 309, 313, 314, 315, 327, 329 n. 3, 330, 333, 334, 336, 338, 343, 344, 345, 346, 347, 350, 353, 354, 356, 357, 358, 362, 369, 370, 371, 371 n. 3, 373, 378, 379, 382, 385, 405, 409, 422, 424
structural determinants 20–1, 95–7, 99, 139, 148, 152, 190–1, 214–16, 222, 228, 230–1, 247, 258, 261, 279, 281, 286, 314–15, 316, 323, 332–4, 343–8, 360, 361, 372, 388, 391, 396, 397, 406, 408, 412, 413, 417–18, 420; *see also* cabinet type; party; party system; preferences, polarization
Sturm, Roland 34
Sweden 5, 7 n. 6, 12 n., 54, 89 n., 95, 98 n. 6, 100, 128 n., 131, 142, 148, 170, 171, 172, 177, 180–1, 185, 208, 212, 219 n., 222, 241, 245, 253, 260, 270, 273, 277, 305, 311, 314, 323, 331, 332, 342, 379
  Agrarian Party 212
  Christian Democrats 54
Swindle, Stephen M. 12, 12 n., 24, 77, 151, 313, 315, 344, 353, 354, 356, 378
Switzerland 54

Taagepera, Rein 5, 96, 140, 345
Tabellini, Guido 175
van der Tak, Theo 27
Taylor, Alan D. 134 n.
Taylor, Michael 21, 34, 203, 204, 345
Taylor, Michaell 372
Teune, Henry 86
Thelen, Kathleen 54
Thiébault, Jean-Louis 25, 307
Thies, Michael F. 24, 33, 34, 101, 143, 181, 238, 260
Thomas, Robert P. 335
Thurner, Paul W. 25
time determinants, *see* spatio-temporal determinants

Index

Timmermans, Arco 33, 34, 41, 88, 91, 159, 160, 186 n., 272, 273, 277, 291, 292, 295, 311, 413
Tirole, Jean 66, 67, 163, 180
Toole, James 422
transaction costs 25–8, 60–1, 63 n., 66, 69–79, 91, 92, 125, 135, 169, 185, 186–7, 190, 195, 196, 242, 264, 380, 334–5, 343, 344, 346, 347–9, 350, 352, 354, 355, 377–8, 409, 425–6, 427–8
  definition 60
  see also opportunism; specialization
Tsebelis, George 16, 163, 180, 277, 345, 347, 348, 355

unemployment 148 n., 259, 321, 322, 324, 360–1, 373, 375–6, 383–5, 397, 412, 414, 420
unicameralism 250, 264
United Kingdom (UK) 5 n., 7, 31, 37, 89, 90, 95, 98 n. 7, 99, 109, 131, 142, 144, 148, 170, 206, 222, 252, 307, 330, 335 n., 342, 343, 346, 362, 381, 405, 427
  Labour Party 5 n.

Valen, Henry 41, 92, 136, 187, 209, 220, 309, 381, 415
Vanberg, Georg 31, 33, 138, 139, 145, 181, 260, 349
Verba, Sidney 88
verification mechanisms 168, 175, 181, 290, 409, 411, 412
Verzichelli, Luca 41, 91, 180, 185, 315, 411, 412
veto 16, 161, 163–5, 180, 183, 260, 334, 354, 356, 364
volatility, electoral 13, 102, 135, 140, 143, 194, 220–1, 230, 232, 259, 286, 309, 321, 361, 362, 381, 383, 398, 406, 411, 412, 420
Volden, Craig 30, 35, 212, 214, 222
vote, confidence 4, 13, 24, 73, 100, 219, 304, 334, 354, 358
  constructive 4, 56, 219, 250, 315, 320, 324

walk-away value 63–6, 67–8, 70, 75, 78–9, 91, 136, 140, 153, 213, 216, 218, 250, 269, 272, 279, 288, 289, 292, 296, 297–8, 335–6, 344–5, 349, 350, 412, 413 *see also* credibility
Ware, Alan 2
Warwick, Paul V. 21, 22, 34, 37, 55, 75, 89, 99 n., 118, 122, 123, 125, 126, 134 n., 135, 136, 137, 141, 161 n., 204, 205, 216, 218, 232, 239, 240, 241, 243, 244, 245, 247, 327, 329, 332, 333, 337, 338, 343, 345, 345 n. 18, 346, 347, 348, 349, 350, 351, 352, 353, 355, 359, 360, 361, 363, 373 n., 423
watchdog ministers 412–13; *see also* junior ministers
Wattenberg, Martin P. 381
Weingast, Barry R. 168
Wessels, Bernhard 25
Westminster system 123
Whitten, Guy D. 371, 375, 379
Wildavsky, Aaron 369 n., 370
Willemé, Peter 125, 126
Williamson, Oliver E. 26, 69, 79
Woldendorp, Jaap 305, 329 n. 3
Wright, John R. 13

Zielinski, Jakub 422
Zorn, Hendrik 180, 260